The Cambridge Companion to the Symphony

Few genres of the last 250 years have proved so crucial to the course of music history, or so vital to public musical experience, as the symphony. This *Companion* offers an accessible guide to the historical, analytical and interpretative issues surrounding this major genre of Western music, discussing an extensive variety of works from the eighteenth century to the present day. The book complements a detailed review of the symphony's history with focussed analytical essays from leading scholars on the symphonic music both of mainstream composers, including Haydn, Mozart and Beethoven, and of recent figures, such as Carter and Berio. With chapters on a comprehensive range of topics, from the symphony's origins to the politics of its reception in the twentieth century, this is an invaluable resource for anyone with an interest in the history, analysis and performance of the symphonic repertoire.

JULIAN HORTON is Associate Professor and Head of the School of Music at University College Dublin. His research focusses on nineteenth-century instrumental music, with special interests in the symphonies of Anton Bruckner and the analysis of sonata forms. His publications include *Bruckner's Symphonies: Analysis, Reception and Cultural Politics* (2004) and chapters and articles in *The Cambridge Companion to Bruckner* (2004), *Music Analysis*, *Music and Letters* and *Musical Quarterly*.

The Cambridge Companion to

THE
SYMPHONY

EDITED BY

Julian Horton

University College Dublin

CAMBRIDGE
UNIVERSITY PRESS

CAMBRIDGE
UNIVERSITY PRESS

University Printing House, Cambridge CB2 8BS, United Kingdom

Cambridge University Press is part of the University of Cambridge.

It furthers the University's mission by disseminating knowledge in the pursuit of education, learning and research at the highest international levels of excellence.

www.cambridge.org
Information on this title: www.cambridge.org/9780521884983

© Cambridge University Press 2013

First published 2013
Reprinted 2014

Printed in the United Kingdom by TJ International Ltd, Padstow, Cornwall

A catalogue record for this publication is available from the British Library

Library of Congress Cataloguing in Publication data
The Cambridge companion to the symphony / edited by Julian Horton.
pages   cm. – (Cambridge companions to music)
Includes bibliographical references and index.
ISBN 978-0-521-88498-3 (hardback) – ISBN 978-0-521-71195-1
(paperback)   1. Symphony.   I. Horton, Julian, editor.   II. Series: Cambridge companions to music.
ML1255.C26   2012
784.2′184–dc23

2012022008

ISBN 978-0-521-88498-3 Hardback
ISBN 978-0-521-71195-1 Paperback

Contents

Tables and figures

Tables

Figures

Musical examples

Contributors

Mark Anson-Cartwright is Assistant Professor of Music Theory at Queens College and The Graduate Center, City University of New York. His articles on the music of Bach, Haydn, Mozart, Beethoven, Wagner and Wolf have appeared in various journals, including *Music Analysis*, *Music Theory Spectrum*, *Journal of Music Theory* and *Dutch Journal of Music Theory*. He is currently doing analytical research on the vocal music of Bach.

Mark Evan Bonds is the Cary C. Boshamer Distinguished Professor of Music at the University of North Carolina at Chapel Hill, where he has taught since 1992. He holds degrees from Duke University (BA), Christian-Albrechts-Universität Kiel (MA) and Harvard University (Ph.D.). His books include *Wordless Rhetoric: Musical Form and the Metaphor of the Oration* (1991), *After Beethoven: Imperatives of Symphonic Originality* (1996) and *Music as Thought: Listening to the Symphony in the Age of Beethoven* (2006). He has published essays on the music of Haydn and Mozart and is currently working on a history of the idea of absolute music.

David Brodbeck is Professor and the Robert and Marjorie Rawlins Chair of Music at the University of California, Irvine. He has published on a wide range of topics related to Brahms and other nineteenth-century German composers. His current research focusses on the intersection of music, politics and constructions of social identity in the reception of new music in late Hapsburg Vienna. Recent publications include 'Dvořák's Reception in Liberal Vienna: Language Ordinances, National Property, and the Rhetoric of *Deutschtum*' (*Journal of the American Musicological Society*), 'Hanslick's Smetana and Hanslick's Prague' (*Journal of the Royal Musical Association*) and '"Ausgleichs-Abende": The First Viennese Performances of Smetana's *Bartered Bride*' (in a special volume of *Austrian Studies* entitled *Word and Music*).

Pauline Fairclough is Senior Lecturer in Music at the University of Bristol. She has published widely on Shostakovich and Soviet culture and is currently engaged on a study of Soviet concert repertoire. Books include *The Cambridge Companion to Shostakovich* (with David Fanning), *Shostakovich Studies II* and *A Soviet Credo: Shostakovich's Fourth Symphony* (2006).

David Fanning is Professor of Music at the University of Manchester and has a varied career as scholar, pianist and critic. Author and editor of books on Nielsen and Shostakovich, his ongoing research projects include a historical survey of the symphony in the Soviet Union and (with Michelle Assay) a completion of the late Per Skans's life-and-works study of the Shostakovich disciple, Mieczysław Weinberg, his 2010 book *Mieczysław Weinberg: In Search of Freedom* being a concise 'advance' version of the Weinberg study. He is also active as critic for *The Gramophone* and the *Daily Telegraph*, and as a BBC broadcaster and public speaker. As a pianist he was for twenty-five years chamber-music partner of The Lindsays, the University of

Manchester's quartet-in-residence, a role he has since continued with the Brussels-based Quatuor Danel.

Alain Frogley is Professor of Music History at the University of Connecticut; he has also taught at Oxford, Lancaster and Yale, and in 2005–6 was a Fellow of the American Council of Learned Societies. He has written on Beethoven sketches and performance history, and published extensively on the music of the late nineteenth and twentieth centuries, including two books on Vaughan Williams; he has also contributed entries to the revised *New Grove* dictionary. His most recent work includes research into the reception of British music in Nazi Germany, racial Anglo-Saxonism in music, and post-colonial studies in musicology. He is currently working on a book about music and the modern metropolis, centred on Vaughan Williams's *A London Symphony*. He has written and presented programmes for BBC radio and lectured at Carnegie Hall and the Kennedy Center.

Daniel M. Grimley is a University Lecturer in Music at Oxford University and Tutorial Fellow in Music at Merton College, having taught previously at the Universities of Nottingham and Surrey. He has published widely on Scandinavian music, Finnish music, the work of Elgar and Vaughan Williams, and music and landscape. His books include *Grieg: Music, Landscape and Norwegian Identity* (2006), and *Carl Nielsen and the Idea of Modernism* (2010), and he edited the *Cambridge Companion to Sibelius* (2004). In 2011, he was the Scholar-in-Residence at the Bard Festival, for which he edited the volume *Jean Sibelius and his World* (2012). Future projects include books on Delius and on music and landscape in Nordic music, 1890–1930.

Julian Horton is Associate Professor and Head of the School of Music at University College Dublin. He is author of *Bruckner's Symphonies: Analysis, Reception and Cultural Politics* (Cambridge, 2004) and a contributor to *The Cambridge Companion to Bruckner* (2004). He has published articles on issues in the analysis of nineteenth-century music in *Music Analysis, Musical Quarterly, Music and Letters* and *Dutch Journal of Music Theory*, and is currently completing a monograph on Brahms's Piano Concerto No. 2.

John Irving is Professor of Music History and Performance Practice at Canterbury Christ Church University. He was previously Director of The Institute of Musical Research, School of Advanced Study, University of London, and has held Chairs at The University of London and The University of Bristol. He has published five books on the music of Mozart, principally on his instrumental and chamber works, and has a particular interest in performance practice. He is also a performer on the fortepiano, clavichord and harpsichord, with several CD recordings to his credit.

Simon P. Keefe is James Rossiter Hoyle Chair of Music and Head of Department at the University of Sheffield. He is the author of more than forty journal articles and book chapters, mostly on Mozart and late eighteenth-century music, and author or editor of eight books, including most recently *The Cambridge History of Eighteenth-Century Music* (2009) and the monograph *Mozart's Requiem: Reception, Work, Completion* (2012), both for Cambridge University Press. Professor Keefe was elected to life membership of the Academy for Mozart Research at the International Mozart

Foundation in Salzburg in 2005 and is general editor of the Royal Musical Association monographs series.

Steven Vande Moortele is Assistant Professor of Music Theory at the University of Toronto. His research concentrates on theories of musical form, the analysis of instrumental music from the late eighteenth to the early twentieth century, and the music of Arnold Schoenberg. He is the author of *Two-Dimensional Sonata Form: Form and Cycle in Single-Movement Instrumental Works by Liszt, Strauss, Schoenberg, and Zemlinsky* (2009).

Mary Sue Morrow is Professor of Musicology at the University of Cincinnati. Her publications include *Concert Life in Haydn's Vienna: Aspects of a Developing Musical and Social Institution* (1989), *German Music Criticism in the Late Eighteenth Century: Aesthetic Issues in Instrumental Music* (1997) and (as co-editor with Bathia Churgin) *The Symphonic Repertoire*, vol. I: *The Eighteenth-Century Symphony* (2012).

Michael Spitzer is Professor of Music at the University of Liverpool. A theorist and musicologist, he has written widely on classical and early Romantic music, and is author of *Metaphor and Musical Thought* and *Music as Philosophy: Adorno and Beethoven's Late Style*. He is presently writing a book on the history of musical emotion.

Alan Street teaches at the University of Kansas. Formerly Editor of the journal *Music Analysis* (2005–11), his research interests include various aspects of the relationship between music theory and critical theory.

Richard Will is Associate Professor of Music at the University of Virginia. He is author of *The Characteristic Symphony in the Age of Haydn and Beethoven* (Cambridge, 2002), co-editor of *Engaging Haydn: Culture, Context, and Criticism* (Cambridge, 2012), and a contributor to *C. P. E. Bach Studies* (Cambridge, 2006), *The Cambridge History of Eighteenth-Century Music* (2009) and other essay collections and journals.

John Williamson is Emeritus Professor and former Head of Music at the University of Liverpool. He has published extensively on Mahler and such contemporaries as Busoni, Zemlinsky, d'Albert and Schoenberg in symposia and journals; is the author of books on Pfitzner and Strauss; and editor of volumes on Bruckner and on words and music.

Acknowledgements

I would like to thank Vicki Cooper and all the editorial and production team at Cambridge University Press for their most generous help, support and patience. Profound thanks are also due to my colleagues at University College Dublin for their support during the preparation of this volume: Ciarán Crilly, Melissa Devereux, Desmond Earley, Orla Flanagan, Jaime Jones, Frank Lawrence, Wolfgang Marx, Thérèse Smith and Harry White.

1 Introduction: understanding the symphony

JULIAN HORTON

Contexts

Writing in 1849, Richard Wagner famously announced the symphony's death at Beethoven's hands and its transformation into music drama. Chiding contemporaries for misunderstanding Beethoven's symphonic achievement, Wagner dismissed subsequent efforts as mere form and style without historical significance:

> The forms in which the Master [Beethoven] brought to light his world-historical wrestling after Art, remained but *forms* in the eyes of contemporaneous and succeeding music-makers, and passed through Mannerism across to Mode; and despite the fact that no other instrumental composer could, even within these forms, divulge the smallest shred of original inventiveness, yet none lost courage to write symphonies . . . without for a moment happening on the thought that the *last* symphony [Beethoven's Ninth] had *already been written*.[1]

A century later, Theodor Adorno compounded such qualms with anxiety over the death of the symphonic listening experience.[2] Adorno fretted that the necessary conditions for absorbing the Beethovenian symphony were being undermined by the practice of radio broadcasts, which for him destroyed the genre's social identity by reducing it to the condition of domestic music; in effect, the symphony ceased to be a public experience and instead became 'a piece of furniture'.[3] The initiation of a symphonic argument moreover relied for its perception on a 'dynamic intensity', which for Adorno could only be realised in live performance, through the establishment of a species of symphonic 'time-consciousness'. Denuded of this possibility, the music is 'on the verge of relapsing into time', that is, into an atomised succession of musical events.[4] The symphony thus becomes trivialised as an object of mass consumption, thereby assisting the commodification of art music and concomitantly accelerating the 'regression of listening'.[5]

Wagner's and Adorno's remarks furnish a useful starting point from which to introduce the formidable historical, philosophical and analytical challenges that the symphony poses. On the one hand, reports of the genre's

[1]

demise have been regular, and usually involve complaints of anachronism, cultural redundancy or incompatibility with modern musical systems or expressive needs. Thus Wagner's comments reflected concerns for the symphony's health tracking back into the 1830s; a comparable crisis developed in the Austro-German context in the wake of Mahler's achievement; and the attitude of the avant-garde after 1945 represented an even more virulent assault on the symphony's technical, cultural and political *raison d'être*. On the other hand, such reports are invariably greatly exaggerated. Wagner's prognosis, like those before and after, proved premature: the symphony did not wither away or become subsumed into an all-encompassing music drama, but reinvented itself in a bewildering variety of guises, folding into its remit influences from the chamber-musical to the operatic, addressing audiences from the whole of humanity to an elite minority and serving ideological masters as disparate as socialist realism and radical individualism.

Similarly, although opportunities to take the symphony out of the concert hall have since proliferated to an extent that Adorno could scarcely have imagined in 1941, the genre's position in the orchestral repertoire remains firm, and the persistence of the kind of time consciousness that Adorno considered endangered is instantiated in diverse trends in reception history since his death, most obviously the surge of interest in Mahler and Bruckner in the English-speaking world, which has played a key role in refreshing public symphonic appetites (the issues surrounding this persistence are finessed by Alan Street in Chapter 18). Moreover, as both David Fanning and Daniel Grimley observe below, twentieth-century symphonists also embraced alternative modes of temporal understanding: the genre survives in the age of musical mass media because composers are able to make the fractured sense of narrative it engenders an object of symphonic discourse.

To understand the symphony is therefore in an important sense to understand its capacity for renewal. This is, in part, the product of an inherent flexibility, born of the fact that the aesthetic and technical connotations of the term 'symphonic' have, for much of the genre's history, run considerably ahead of any constraints placed on them by the title 'symphony'. Over time, this has enabled a remarkable generic elasticity, which has allowed composers to shift continuously the symphony's terms of reference. Thus the genre's relative clarity at the turn of the nineteenth century was rapidly obscured by post-Beethovenian incorporations of dramatic, literary and poetic aspirations. Such suppleness is boldly announced by Berlioz's *Roméo et Juliette* of 1839. Classical genre markers are present in the orchestral first movement (the 'Introduction'), slow movement (the 'Scène d'amour'), Scherzo ('La Reine Mab') and multi-part choral Finale, but they are woven together with a succession of operatic scenes, which bring the symphony into direct confrontation with its theatrical counterpart. A comparable situation prevails in Mendelssohn's Symphony No. 2 of 1840, except that Mendelssohn questions the distinction between symphony and oratorio: the first three movements, which proceed along normal generic lines, emerge at the start of the Finale as the 'Sinfonia' of a sacred oratorio, the nine numbers of which parody Handelian and Bachian practice. Both Berlioz and Mendelssohn respond directly to Beethoven's 'Choral' Symphony, emphasising in turn its theatrical and liturgical implications. By the end of the nineteenth century, Mahler could comfortably apply similar thinking in a broad range of generic conflations: symphony and orchestral lied (Second, Third and Fourth symphonies); symphony and cantata (Second Symphony); symphony and oratorio (Eighth Symphony).

This diversification accelerated in the early twentieth century, as already precarious generic distinctions collapsed along with the very notion of a common practice. These circumstances applied not only to classical paradigms, but also to typical nineteenth-century distinctions. Liszt, for instance, clearly distinguished between his *Eine Faust-Symphonie*, which is a multi-movement programme symphony, and his single-movement symphonic poems. Yet by the First World War, this separation had lost much of its meaning. On the one hand, Schoenberg deployed a conflation of movement cycle and sonata form in his Chamber Symphony Op. 9 and the symphonic poem *Pelleas und Melisande*. On the other hand, as Steven Vande Moortele investigates in Chapter 11, Strauss enlarged Liszt's single-movement prototype to the point where the symphonic poem mutated back into the symphony, most obviously in the *Sinfonia domestica*, in which the programmatic narrative follows a linked succession of symphonic movement types.

No less remarkable is the symphony's adaptability to diverse systemic contexts. The classical symphony is a cycle of tonal forms, which articulate the basic relationships of diatonic tonality. The same forms, however, persist in changed systemic circumstances: nineteenth-century symphonists introduced tonal relationships, chiefly cycles of thirds and semitonal pairings, which classical composers scarcely employed; and classical forms continued to exert an influence even in a post-tonal context. This is possible because the symphony's formal parameters are separable: the tonal properties of sonata form can be modified or abandoned, but a recognisable genre marker will remain in place so long as sonata-type thematic or textural procedures are deployed. Similarly, a symphonic movement may be loosely rhapsodic or densely motivic; yet if it applies generic concepts of material, textural or tonal contrast, then the resulting structures will be recognisably symphonic.

The technical challenges that such adaptations engender have contributed in no small measure to a further sustaining characteristic, which is the genre's aesthetic prestige: the symphony continues to attract composers even as the idioms and musical systems from which it arose slip from universal usage, because symphonic mastery still confers technical legitimacy. Practitioners dismissive of the symphony's relevance or confident in their ability to subsume it and move on betray more than a hint of excessive protestation in so doing. Wagner's polemics for instance conceal uncertainty at the prospect of composing symponic structures without a dramatic, theatrical scaffold;[6] and even the most acerbic post-war modernists have smuggled symphonic ambitions, if not symphonic forms, into their music. Stockhausen's *Gruppen*, for example, simulates a kind of panoptically Mahlerian symphonic experience, despite its integral–serial mode of expression and lack of any discernible symphonic genre markers. When the epithet 'symphony' fails as a generic category, the cachet of symphonic competence nevertheless persists.

Case study: symphonic idealism as history, form and politics

Many of the issues broached here will be addressed in detail in the following chapters. The durability they help to explain can be illustrated *in nuce* by scrutinising one historical thread: what might be termed the 'idealist' symphony, that is, the symphony as a vehicle for utopian aspiration. Like all subsequent aspects of the genre's extra-musical complexion, symphonic idealism has its roots in the fact that the first fifty years or so of the symphony's history straddle the Enlightenment. This means that, in addition to exemplifying the emergence of *galant* styles out of the high Baroque, it also reflects a progression from the aristocratic and monarchic structures of early modern Europe to the industrialised, democratic, secular and market-driven economies that prefigure our own time. Developing out of early eighteenth-century baroque courtly and theatrical genres, the symphony had by the century's end become enmeshed in a mode of mercantile reception and consumption, which furnished the grounds for the genre's reinvention as the quintessential musical narrative of emancipation.

By the 1830s, contact with idealist philosophy and the sheer force of Beethoven's symphonic achievement had transformed the genre into a paradigm of artistic autonomy and utopian ambition.[7] Comparisons of Beethoven's musical achievement with Hegel's philosophy, which are numerous and persistent, exemplify this with special clarity; Wagner's identification of the world-historical aspect of Beethoven's symphonies foregrounds precisely this association.[8] In a crucial sense, the post-Beethovenian symphony is therefore a vehicle of bourgeois idealism, which in socio-political terms is manifest in the notion of aesthetic community, given literary voice in the 'Pedagogical Province' described in Book II of Goethe's *Wilhelm Meisters Wanderjahre*, and most pragmatically embodied in the numerous music festivals that sprang up in the German lands in the early nineteenth century, which invariably made Beethoven's symphonies their core repertoire.[9] In aesthetic terms, idealism takes the form of an ambition to embody literary, poetic or philosophical ideals in formal and material narratives, formatively expressed in the so-called struggle–victory plot archetype of Beethoven's Fifth Symphony, as well as in the natural pictorialism of his Sixth.[10] Although challenged by the claims of Wagnerian music drama, the ambition to curate progression towards an imagined better world remained potent up to the threshold of the First World War, being variously evident in (for example) Brahms's First Symphony, Tchaikovsky's Fifth, Mahler's Eighth and Elgar's First.

A crucial structural feature of such aspirations resides in the shift from classical 'concentric' planning, which located much of a work's weight in its first movement and conceived of the finale as a region of security and consolidation, to nineteenth-century goal-directedness or 'teleology', which gave new emphasis to the finale and the processes of which it is a culmination.[11] This innovation, normally traced to Beethoven's Fifth and Ninth symphonies, exploited deferral of cadential, modal and expressive resolution as the technical means of the nineteenth century's new idealism; the struggle–victory narrative is facilitated by a reorientation of classical form.

The effects of this shift can be clarified through comparison of three C minor symphonies composed within a hundred-year period: Haydn's Symphony No. 95 of 1791; Beethoven's Symphony No. 5 of 1808; and the 1890 revision of Bruckner's Symphony No. 8. Haydn places his Symphony's pivotal turn from C minor to C major in the transition from first to second theme in the first movement's recapitulation. This is achieved with considerable nonchalance: the exposition's nineteen-bar transition is replaced by a three-bar extension of the first theme, which slides sequentially into the C major reprise of the second theme at bar 129, in which key the movement remains until its conclusion. This mode switch allows Haydn to recapitulate his expository major-key second theme in the tonic without changing its modality (III becomes I). The result is that the 'hankering of C minor for its parallel major', which Joseph Kerman identifies as a basic trait in Beethoven's C minor works, is fulfilled two thirds of the way through the first movement, leaving the Finale simply to reinforce a resolution that has already been attained.[12] And this is precisely what happens: aside from the sixteen-bar minor-mode interjection beginning at bar 152, Haydn's Finale makes scant attempt to revisit the tonic minor, maintaining C major in a sonata form without development.

Beethoven's first movement, in contrast, makes a dramatic point of failing to sustain C major. Haydn's mode switch is initially imitated; but the major-mode recapitulation of the second theme and closing section is undone by the coda, which categorically enforces C minor. As the Symphony unfolds, Beethoven makes this negation do markedly unclassical aesthetic labour, turning C major's deferral into an agent of teleology. The first movement's modal uncertainty is swept away by the famous elision of Scherzo and Finale, which imposes forcefully the latter's triumphant C major march. This initiates a movement which in the scale of its design, orchestration and gesture dwarfs its predecessors, culminating in the coda's unprecedented post-cadential excess. Beethoven not only relocates the mode switch to the start of the Finale, but dramatises it in a way that is alien to Haydn's musical sensibility.

Bruckner takes Beethoven's idea considerably further, making structural and expressive capital not only out of sustaining C minor beyond the first movement, but of questioning its very identity as a global tonic. In the first movement's main theme, C minor is presented as one possible tonic, which is denied cadential confirmation for the entirety of the movement, thanks to the persistent intrusions of D-flat major and B-flat minor.[13] As the Symphony progresses, this condition worsens: the Scherzo contains one tonic perfect cadence, which is located in the middle of its development section (bars 91–5); the Adagio tonicises D♭; and it is left to the Finale's coda (beginning at bar 647 in Leopold Nowak's edition) both to stabilise C minor and convert it into C major.

The differences between classical 'concentric' planning and nineteenth-century teleology are starkly exposed here: Haydn achieves C major in bar 129 of his first movement, Beethoven in bar 1 of his Finale, and Bruckner only 23 bars before the end of his Symphony. Not only tonal strategy, but also a host of material processes reinforce these different orientations. Haydn, for instance, has little use for overt cross-movement thematic references; Beethoven relates his movements through loose recall of his first movement's main theme; Bruckner deploys inter-movement relationships extensively, celebrating the attainment of C major at the end with a grand conflation of the primary themes of his Symphony's four movements.

With the approach of the Great War, such lofty ambitions collapsed into their opposite, at least within the Austro-German sphere. In response to Mahler's world-encompassing aims, Schoenberg composed chamber symphonies, thereby transmuting the genre into a private, domestic medium and undermining decisively a distinction that was basic to his Beethovenian antecedents' social character. Simultaneously, the genre was adopted as one of the principal vehicles of musical nationalism, becoming essential to the construction of nationally defined traditions in Britain, France, Scandinavia, Russia, the Czech lands and the USA. The manufacture of cultural identity, which accompanied symphonic idealism within the German lands in the early decades of the nineteenth century, was consequently repeated at a distance in other contexts, from *ars gallica* in France after the Franco-Prussian War of 1871 to Scandinavia, the English musical renaissance and Russia, where the symphony's importance persisted from Balakirev to Shostakovich unimpeded by the sense of cultural crisis gripping *fin-de-siècle* Vienna. By the 1930s, however, even these idealist strains proved hard to sustain. Sibelius turned towards an increasingly abstract mode of thought, culminating in the dense single-movement design of his Seventh Symphony (1924); Stravinsky objectified rather than extended Beethovenian paradigms in his Symphony in C (1938–40); Vaughan Williams replaced the post-Elgarian sweep of his *Sea* and *London* symphonies with the more economical and ideologically critical expressive stance of the *Pastoral Symphony* and the trilogy of symphonies flanking the Second World War; and in Soviet Russia, nineteenth-century utopianism persisted as an officially sanctioned public veneer, which masked the terrifying realities of Stalinism.

The dissolution of goal-orientated idealism in this time is particularly acute in works that seem transparently indebted to it. Vaughan Williams's Symphony No. 4, completed in 1934, is notable for its extensive reliance on nineteenth-century precedents, primarily Beethoven's Fifth.[14] This is most blatant in its elision of Scherzo and Finale, which draws on Beethoven's example to an extent that borders on literal quotation. Beyond this, Vaughan Williams makes considerable use of thematic cross-referencing, founding all four movements on a common pool of ideas, which are drawn together in the Finale's fugal coda.

The crucial difference between Vaughan Williams's Symphony and its nineteenth-century forebears resides not only in its obviously post-tonal idiom, which exploits modal dualism to generate a strikingly dissonant harmonic palette, but also in the fact that its aping of the struggle–victory narrative and strenuous efforts at cyclical integration ultimately count for nothing. At the Symphony's end, its opening returns, and with it the grating semitonal conflict characterising that material in the first movement. The final bars starkly reiterate this opposition without mediation or resolution, piling G-flat minor onto F minor, before closing with a single, brutal assertion of the open fifth F–C. Whereas Beethoven achieves his moment of overcoming at the Finale's opening, and Bruckner at its end,

Vaughan Williams's exhaustive contrapuntal synthesis effectively leads nowhere: the whole edifice of formal-thematic integration culminates in a restatement of the Symphony's generative problem, negating the teleological process with startling pessimism.

If symphonic idealism can be problematised compositionally by short-circuiting its well-worn narrative trajectories, it can also be interrogated critically by exposing cultural-political subtexts. Prominent in this respect is Susan McClary's interpretation of the recapitulation in the first movement of Beethoven's Ninth as an allegory of sexual brutality: the point of reprise for her embodies a 'juxtaposition of desire and unspeakable violence', engendering 'an unparalleled fusion of murderous rage and yet a kind of pleasure in its fulfilment of formal demands'; Robert Fink has more recently carried this reading into the Finale, pointing out that crucial voice-leading characteristics enabling McClary's interpretation resurface as cyclical devices.[15] As a homosexual counterpart to her reading, McClary has posited a threefold dialogue in the first movement of Tchaikovsky's Fourth Symphony between a militaristically construed 'fate' (the introductory theme), an effeminate masculine first theme and a sexually threatening feminine second theme.[16] Altogether, for McClary, Beethoven and Tchaikovsky reveal two contrasting facets of masculine symphonic sexual politics, the former masking impotence with patriarchal violence, the latter portraying femininity as sexually alien.

No less problematic is the tendency to channel post-Beethovenian utopianism into twentieth-century extremism, in which respect Bruckner's case is especially revealing. The so-called 'war of the Romantics', which in late nineteenth-century Vienna pitted Brahmsian conservatism against Lisztian programme music and post-Wagnerian (that is to say, Brucknerian) symphonism, became an aesthetic variant of the dispute between the liberal centre and the nationalist, pan-German right.[17] For the liberals, Brahms's rationalism, embodied in the motivic logic of his symphonies, guaranteed their aesthetic credibility, and as such stood against Bruckner's apparently formless Wagnerism. For Bruckner's supporters, Brahms confused public and domestic modes of musical thought (symphonic monumentality and chamber-musical rationalism), thus reducing the symphony's status in the name of an arid academicism. Both positions were foils for political opinion: the Brahmsians associated with an increasingly embattled and characteristically Semitic liberalism, which had held sway in the 1860s and 70s; Bruckner's most extreme apologists were also staunchly anti-Semitic proponents of the new right, which secured political ascendancy with the appointment of Karl Lueger as Mayor of Vienna in 1897.[18]

Whilst Brahms's superficially conservative technique became paradigmatic for second-Viennese modernism, post-Wagnerian commentators in

Germany and Austria stressed Bruckner's conservatism with mounting stridency, culminating in the cultural politics of the Third Reich. The Nazi view of Bruckner is encapsulated in Joseph Goebbels's speech to the International Bruckner Society, given at the Regensburg Bruckner Festival of 1937, at which Hitler received the Society's honorary medal.[19] Goebbels elevated Bruckner's music as a purely German expression of 'blood and soil', praising its emotional stance as a triumph of true feeling over shallow (by which Goebbels meant Jewish) intellectualism, and in so doing annexing the composer as a precursive standard-bearer for National Socialism. The *Zeitschrift für Musik* reported the Festival with appropriate solemnity; its account is accompanied by photographs, one of which shows Hitler standing reverently before the bust of Bruckner in the Regensburg Valhalla.[20] The catastrophic Central-European endgame of post-Beethovenian symphonic idealism is captured in a single image: a profoundly Catholic Austrian composer, whose vision of symphonic utopia was characteristically Christian, is transformed into an icon of German fascism, before whom the architect of European war and genocide stands humbled.

The legacy of the Second World War posed fresh dilemmas for composers with a lingering interest in the nineteenth-century model. Yet the international avant-garde's forceful rejection of past modes of expression in the 1950s, which seemingly ruled out of court anything as bourgeois or traditional as the symphony, led in time to a new diversity of symphonic practice, which scrutinised the idealist lineage through a self-consciously deconstructive lens (Berio), or absorbed recognisably its formal preoccupations into a late-modernist idiom (Lutosławski; Carter; Maxwell Davies; Henze). At the same time, the lasting popularity of the nineteenth-century symphonic repertoire attests to a taste for idealism, which persists in the concert hall and the recording studio, even if it endures only as a more-or-less covert trace in contemporary composition. In a sense, we still aspire to the better worlds expressed by this music.

Objectives

The Cambridge Companion to the Symphony offers scholarly yet accessible essays on these and a wide range of other symphonic subjects. It is not a chronological survey of works or composers, although sensitivity to chronology is built into its design. Such accounts are readily available: prominent English-language examples include the volumes edited by Robert Simpson, D. Kern Holoman, Robert Layton and Michael Steinberg, as well as the monumental review of the genre initiated by the late A. Peter Brown, which remains ongoing.[21] Neither does it advance a comprehensive or unified appraisal: the volume's coverage is wide, but lacunae inevitably occur; and no attempt has been made to resolve divergences of opinion where they arise.

Rather, the *Companion* furnishes diverse perspectives on the symphonic repertoire, in three broad methodological categories – history, analysis, and genre, reception and performance – which define the book's parts. Part I comprises four essays, which together appraise the genre's history from its origins to the present: John Irving and Mary Sue Morrow focus on the eighteenth century, dealing respectively with Vienna and other national contexts; David Brodbeck addresses the symphony's development from the immediate reception of Beethoven and Schubert to the Vienna of Mahler and Schoenberg; and David Fanning takes up the narrative in the early twentieth century, pursuing the diverse consequences of the Mahlerian legacy and the dual achievements of Sibelius and Nielsen up to the present time.

Part II follows the same chronological path, but mines into the repertoire's analytical detail. In Chapter 6, Michael Spitzer offers an account of formal strategies in the early symphony, paying close attention to Sammartini, Stamitz, Kraus, C. P. E. Bach, J. C. Bach and Boccherini. Simon Keefe and Mark Anson-Cartwright respond in chapters 7 and 8 with studies of Haydn, Mozart and Beethoven, exploring a range of factors articulating form, from theme to timbre. My own twin contributions in chapters 9 and 10 complement David Brodbeck's essay, considering in turn cyclical thematic transformation and tonal strategy as structural features of the nineteenth-century symphony. Steven Vande Moortele's chapter then investigates what he terms 'two-dimensional form', that is, the practice, evolving from Liszt to Sibelius and Samuel Barber, of conflating sonata form and the traditional symphonic movement cycle in a single-movement design. Lastly, in Chapter 12, Daniel Grimley introduces core analytical problems raised in dealing with the twentieth-century symphony, instantiated in five representative works: Sibelius's Fourth Symphony; Stravinsky's *Symphony of Psalms*; Berio's *Sinfonia*; Carter's *Symphony of Three Orchestras*; and Pelle Gudmundsen-Holmgreen's *Symphony, Antiphony*.

The essays collected in Part III turn to broader contextual questions. In Chapter 13, Richard Will offers an account of the relationship between the symphony and the development of the orchestra in the eighteenth century; this is balanced by Alan Street's assessment of the symphony in the modern performing canon in Chapter 18. Between these poles, chapters 14 to 17 focus on questions of reception and generic identity: Mark Evan Bonds looks at the nineteenth-century reception of Beethoven; John Williamson investigates the range of works and ideas emerging under the rubric of the programme symphony; Pauline Fairclough examines the Austro-German legacy in Soviet Russia; and Alain Frogley explores the symphony's twentieth-century British evolution, furnishing a case study of the internationalism that David Fanning charts in Chapter 5.

Notes

1 'The Artwork of the Future', in *Richard Wagner's Prose Works, vol. I: The Art-work of the Future*, trans. William Ashton Ellis (London, 1892), 69–213, this quotation 127.
2 Theodor W. Adorno, 'The Radio Symphony: An Experiment in Theory', in *Essays on Music*, ed. Richard Leppert, trans. Susan H. Gillespie (Berkeley, 2002), 251–70.
3 Ibid., 257.
4 Ibid., 259.
5 On this subject, see for example 'On the Fetish Character of Music and the Regression of Listening', in ibid., 288–317.
6 The notion of Wagner as a frustrated symphonist has been expressed by commentators from Nietzsche to Egon Voss: see Friedrich Nietzsche, *The Birth of Tragedy and the Case of Wagner*, trans. Walter Kaufmann (New York, 1967) and Egon Voss, *Richard Wagner und die Instrumentalmusik: Wagners symphonische Ehrgeiz* (Wilhelmshaven, 1977). For a contrasted view, see John Deathridge, *Wagner beyond Good and Evil* (Berkeley, 2008), 190–3.
7 The seminal statements of this aesthetic in relation to Beethoven are of course E. T. A. Hoffmann, Review of Beethoven's Fifth Symphony, *Allgemeine musikalische Zeitung*, 12 (4 and 11 July 1810), 630–42 and 652–9 and 'Beethovens Intrumentalmusik', in *Sämtliche Werke* vol. II/1 (1856), 55–8, 60–1 and 62–4.
8 Well-known examples include Theodor W. Adorno, *Hegel: Three Studies* trans. Shierry Weber Nicholson (Cambridge, Mass., 1993), Carl Dahlhaus, *Ludwig van Beethoven: Approaches to His Music* trans. Mary Whittall (Oxford, 1991), Janet Schmalfeldt, 'Form as the Process of Becoming: The Hegelian Tradition and the "Tempest" Sonata', *Beethoven Forum*, 4 (1995), 37–71 and also *In the Process of Becoming: Analytic and Philosophical Perspectives on Form in Early Nineteenth-Century Music* (New York and Oxford, 2011), and Michael Spitzer, *Music as Philosophy: Adorno and Beethoven's Late Style* (Bloomington, 2006).
9 See Johann Wolfgang Goethe, *Wilhelm Meisters Wanderjahre*, Book II, in *Sämtliche Werke*, vol. XVII, ed. Karl Richer (Munich, 1985–98) and Mark Evan Bonds, *Music as Thought: Listening to the Symphony in the Age of Beethoven* (Princeton, 2006), 75–8.

10 On this subject, see for instance Anthony Newcomb, 'Once More between Absolute and Program Music: Schumann's Second Symphony', *19th-Century Music*, 7/3 (1984), 233–50. On the aesthetic dimension of the Fifth Symphony's narrative trajectory as it relates to E. T. A. Hoffmann's famous reading of the work, see Bonds, *Music as Thought*, 44–62.
11 On the notion of the 'summative' finale, see Michael Talbot, *The Finale in Western Instrumental Music* (New York and Oxford, 2001), 81–105.
12 Joseph Kerman, 'Beethoven's Minority', in *Write All These Down: Essays on Music* (Berkeley, 1994), 217–37. On the special issues surrounding classical minor-mode sonata forms, see also James Hepokoski and Warren Darcy, *Elements of Sonata Theory: Norms, Types, and Deformations in the Late-Eighteenth-Century Sonata* (New York and Oxford, 2006), 306–17.
13 On the structural implications of this theme's harmony, see for example Julian Horton, *Bruckner's Symphonies: Analysis, Reception and Cultural Politics* (Cambridge, 2004), 135–42, Benjamin Korstvedt, *Bruckner: Symphony No. 8* (Cambridge, 2000), 28–30, and William Benjamin, 'Tonal Dualism in Bruckner's Eighth Symphony', in William Kinderman and Harald Krebs, eds., *The Second Practice of Nineteenth-Century Tonality* (Lincoln, 1996), 237–58.
14 For a recent analysis of this work, see J. P. E. Harper-Scott, 'Vaughan Williams's "Antic" Symphony', in Matthew Riley, ed., *British Music and Modernism* (Aldershot, 2010), 175–96.
15 See Susan McClary, *Feminine Endings: Music, Gender, and Sexuality* (Minneapolis, 1991), 128–30 and Robert Fink, 'Beethoven Antihero: Sex, Violence and the Aesthetics of Failure, Or Listening to the Ninth Symphony as Postmodern Sublime', in Andrew Dell'Antonio, ed., *Beyond Structural Listening: Postmodern Modes of Hearing* (Berkeley, 2004), 109–53.
16 See McClary, *Feminine Endings*, 67–79.
17 On these matters, see for example Margaret Notley, 'Brahms as Liberal: Genre, Style, and Politics in Late Nineteenth-Century Vienna', *19th-Century Music*, 17 (1993), 107–23,

'Bruckner and Viennese Wagnerism', in Paul Hawkshaw and Timothy L. Jackson, eds., *Bruckner Studies* (Cambridge, 1997), 54–71, and *Lateness and Brahms: Music and Culture in the Twilight of Viennese Liberalism* (New York and Oxford, 2007).

18 Perhaps the most well-known account of the cultural politics of *fin-de-siècle* Vienna appears in Carl Schorske, Fin-de-siècle *Vienna* (New York, 1980).

19 On the Nazi reception of Bruckner, see Bryan Gilliam, 'The Annexation of Anton Bruckner: Nazi Revisionism and the Politics of Appropriation', in Hawkshaw and Jackson, eds., *Bruckner Studies* (Cambridge, 1997), 72–90, Benjamin Korstvedt, 'Anton Bruckner in the Third Reich and After: An Essay on Ideology and Bruckner Reception', *Musical Quarterly*, 80 (1996), 132–60, and Morten Solvik, 'The International Bruckner Society and the NSDAP: A Case Study of Robert Haas and the Critical Edition', *Musical Quarterly*, 83 (1998), 362–82.

20 See Paul Ehlers, 'Das Regensburger Bruckner Erlebnis', *Zeitschrift für Musik*, 104 (1937), 745–8.

21 Robert Simpson, ed., *The Symphony*, 2 vols. (London, 1966 and 1967); D. Kern Holoman, *The Nineteenth-Century Symphony* (New York, 1997); Robert Layton, *A Guide to the Symphony* (New York and Oxford, 1995); Michael Steinberg, *The Symphony: A Listener's Guide* (New York and Oxford, 1995); A. Peter Brown, *The Symphonic Repertoire*, vol. II: *The First Golden Age of the Viennese Symphony: Haydn, Mozart, Beethoven, and Schubert* (Bloomington, 2002), *The Symphonic Repertoire*, vol. III, Part A: *The European Symphony ca. 1800–ca. 1930: Germany and the Nordic Countries* (Bloomington, 2007), and *The Symphonic Repertoire*, vol. IV: *The Second Golden Age of the Viennese Symphony: Brahms, Bruckner, Dvořák and Selected Contemporaries* (Bloomington, 2003); A. Peter Brown and Brian Hart, *The Symphonic Repertoire*, vol. III, Part B: *The European Symphony ca. 1800–ca. 1930: Great Britain, Russia, and France* (Bloomington, 2008); Mary Sue Morrow and Bathia Churgin, eds., *The Symphonic Repertoire*, vol. I: *The Eighteenth Century Symphony* (Bloomington, 2012).

PART I

Historical overview of the genre

2 The Viennese symphony 1750 to 1827

JOHN IRVING

Mozart, recently dismissed from the service of the Archbishop of Salzburg, wrote optimistically to his father on 4 April 1781, claiming that Vienna was the best place in the world for someone of his profession.[1] It is understandable that he should have formed this impression of the Austrian capital. It had an abundant infrastructure for musical production and consumption. In the main, this was a result of both the Hapsburg dynasty, for whom Vienna already had been the principal residency for over a century, and of the Holy Roman Empire.[2] Together, the monarchy (Maria Theresa from 1740 to 1780; Joseph II from 1780 to 1790, Leopold II from 1790 to 1792 and Francis II from 1792 to 1835), and the Holy Roman Emperors (successively Francis I, Maria Theresa's husband until 1765, thereafter Joseph II, Leopold II and Francis II, until the Empire's abolition in 1806) brought in train a bureaucracy numbering, by Mozart's time, at least 10,000. Vienna was a hive of political and cultural activity and acted as a magnet for many thousands of affluent nobles resident in the city or else more-or-less loosely inhabiting its peripheries. One such was Prince Joseph Friedrich von Sachsen-Hildburghausen, whose musical establishment was among the finest in Vienna, in which the twelve-year-old Carl Ditters (later, 1773, von Dittersdorf) received his musical instruction and a first taste of orchestral playing. Diversity of opportunity acted as a powerful generator for the city's rich and varied musical life. It is against this background that the hundreds of musicians employed in court establishments such as the Hofkapelle worked. Successive Kapellmeisters Georg von Reutter (1751–72), Florian Leopold Gassmann (1772–4), Giuseppe Bonno (1774–88) and Antonio Salieri (1788–1825) were, in effect, civil servants whose positions were assured for life. Others enjoyed a more precarious living as singers, players and teachers.

While Vienna's public concert life does not look so active as, say, London's at the same time,[3] that impression hides the fact that 'public' does not necessarily mean an event in a dedicated concert hall with tickets on sale to the 'public-at-large'. True, in Mozart's Vienna, there was a dearth of what might pass for 'concert halls', but he managed to give, as a soloist and part-promoter, over seventy concerts there in the first five years following his arrival in 1781. Concert series were supported by the

[15]

Vienna Tonkünstlersocietät from 1772, and subsequently by the Gesellschaft der Musikfreunde (from 1814). Venues for concerts were diverse, and included theatres such as the Kärntnertortheater (originally built in 1709, burned down and rebuilt in 1761 from which point it was managed by the court as a centre for German-language comedies), and the Burgtheater (where Gluck's *Orfeo ed Euridice* had received its premiere in 1762 and later established as a National Theatre by the future Joseph II in 1776), the Augarten (a royal park, opened to the public by Joseph), the Mehlgrube dance hall, Jahn's restaurant, the Trattnerhof, masonic lodges (especially during the early 1780s), and in the palaces of the aristocracy (Prince Auersperg's, for instance) as well as in the homes of, for instance, Baron Gottfried van Swieten, Joseph II's education minister. Many concerts are known to have taken place in the homes of Vienna's nobility. Not all these locations supported symphonic repertoire, though Beethoven's *Eroica* Symphony received its first performance in the palace of Prince Lobkowitz in 1804 (it was rehearsed by the Prince's own orchestra).

Increasingly at the turn of the century the royal and imperial court was overtaken as a source of patronage by the nobility, most especially in the field of instrumental music. Beethoven, who made Vienna his home from 1792, was supported almost wholly by the aristocracy, to whom he dedicated many works and who seem to have perceived in his instrumental output an expressive voice whose originality and universality of appeal sat uncomfortably with past arenas of patronage in which a musician was a mere servant. To a degree his output, including his symphonic output, shaped the taste of the high aristocracy, rather than vice versa. Allied to the aristocratic engagement with a developing aesthetic of instrumental music and its possible meanings was an emerging civic musical scene in which a freshly liberated genre such as the symphony might find a stage for its representation to an inquisitive public. While it is undoubtedly true that the political repression of the Metternich era restricted the growth of public musical concerts in Vienna (from 1815 large public gatherings were systematically forbidden within what was effectively a police state), music itself was not a focus of censorship. Starting in 1819, Franz Xavier Gebauer and Eduard von Lannoy promoted the Viennese 'concerts spirituels' – public events given by an amateur orchestra, and featuring symphonies by Haydn (who, from 1790 until his death had been resident in Vienna, though his later symphonies were written for London's, not Vienna's concert life), Mozart and Beethoven. Professional performances of instrumental repertoire, however, tended on the whole to take place in aristocratic and affluent bourgeois homes in the Viennese suburbs, rather than in large public spaces. Nevertheless, these gatherings were a species of what we would call concerts and provided a space in which the symphony might enter into a dialogue with its listeners; this would affect its generic boundaries while simultaneously catalysing the musical appreciation of those listeners. Presentation of a symphony in the context of a concert affected the composer's organisation of his material. Since the audience was there on purpose, and actually *listening to the music*, it was essential that the musical material displayed some degree of logic in its construction; that it engaged the senses and perhaps also the minds of those listeners; that it emphasised points of departure and arrival, as well as contrasts of theme, key and texture; that it deployed the orchestral forces in an exciting way. In a direct sense the concert context dictated the manner in which the symphony proclaimed itself to the audience. That relationship between the symphony and the audience manifested itself in various ways, for instance in terms of continuity: a symphony was performed as a whole in such settings – albeit with applause, or even other compositions in other genres as quasi-entr'actes between movements – which inevitably focussed attention on the relative qualities, scorings, lengths, *affekt* or thematic interrelations between movements, including overtly cyclic ones as in Beethoven's Fifth Symphony. This situation defines the symphony generically as something existing in relation to a perceiver who is challenged in a particular representation to form an impression of it on, for example, an emotional level, or in constructional terms, and perhaps in relation to other, similar works. In other words, its generic identity emerges through its particular usage, and a concert representation was in contrast to the usage sometimes made of individual symphonic movements in the mid eighteenth century at the Gradual or Offertory in celebrations of Mass, either within large Viennese churches or in nearby monasteries. The diary of Beda Hübner, Librarian at St Peter's Benedictine Monastery in Salzburg, records that on 8 December in Salzburg Cathedral one of the infant Mozart's symphonies was performed at Mass to the great delight of all the assembled musicians. Likewise, some symphonies by Karl von Ordonez (1734–86) were evidently intended for such situations; manuscript copies are found in the monastery of Göttweig (copies of Haydn's symphonies are likewise preserved in monastery libraries).

Public representation of a symphony to a paying audience from different social classes, which has come together for a concert representation of orchestral music at a particular time and place, is a different matter to its representation by liveried musician-servants with polished shoe-buckles before an Empress and her retinue in between the courses of a banquet. Even when such performances were notionally 'concerts', they were primarily social occasions at which there was also music (to judge from the diaries of aristocrats such as Count Karl Zinzendorf). The arena in which the symphonies of Beethoven were presented to the Viennese of the early nineteenth century and that in which the symphonies of Georg Christoph Wagenseil (1715–77; Wagenseil was Maria Theresa's music teacher) were produced are different creatures indeed, and mark out the approximate boundaries of the journey of the Viennese symphony to be explored below.

Beginnings

The influence of the Hapsburgs stretched far and wide, geographically as well as culturally. Vienna was a cultural crossroads and acted as a magnet for composers from parts of Germany, the Czech lands, present-day Slovenia and northern Italy. In the eighteenth century the region of Lombardy was a Hapsburg dominion and this goes some way towards explaining the early stylistic development of the symphony in Vienna, which owes much to the three-movement operatic overture of the type found in the work of Leo, Sammartini, Jommelli and Galuppi (this repertoire is considered in more detail in chapters 3 and 6). Their overtures during the 1740s and 1750s typically feature in their opening movements a clearly coordinated approach to thematic and tonal statement, contrast and return in which uniformity of baroque rhythmic patterning has been sacrificed for an overall symmetry of four- and eight-bar phrase and cadence schemes delineated by relatively slow and regular harmonic rhythms and an almost stereotypical functional hierarchy within the orchestration (leading melodies stated by the upper strings, perhaps reinforced by a pair of oboes, to which an energetic bass line of lower strings – perhaps with bassoon, though not necessarily a sixteen-foot string bass – acted as a counter-pole with a harmonic filler often supplied by long notes in the horns, doubled, with a dash of rhythmic activity, by the violas). While binary designs in the first movements of Italian opera overtures are still numerically in the minority (behind ritornello forms) by mid-century, such traits made no small impact on contemporary Viennese symphonists.

Contrast between two principal themes is particularly common in the work of the Italian-trained Georg Christoph Wagenseil, whose early career in Vienna was substantially as an operatic composer.[4] Almost all of Wagenseil's symphonies are in three movements, and the fact that many were published widely (both in France and England) shows that their appeal transcended the local circumstances of their production for the court of Maria Theresa. Among such works are his *Six Simphonies a Quatre Parties Avec les Cors de Chasses Ad libitum ... Oeuvre III ...* (Paris, *c.* 1760). At the foot of the title page is the comment 'On vend les Cors de Chasses séparément' – a token of the relative hierarchy within the orchestral texture that was to remain fundamental to the conception of the Viennese symphony for some years to come. Perhaps their popularity rested partly on their relatively slight, yet convincingly proportioned dimensions, especially in respect of thematic recapitulation, partly on the catchy and unpretentious minuet finales with which many conclude.

Wagenseil, court composer from 1739 until his death, was a crucial figure in the development of the symphony.[5] He composed over seventy such works, the majority of which are in three movements: fast–slow–fast (typically a 3/8 time or 3/4 time minuet). In terms of formal organisation, he favoured full, rather than curtailed, recapitulations, allowing space for thematic and tonal contrast sometimes featuring subdominant recapitulations and digressions to the minor mode. That suggests a forward-looking mindset (along with his adoption of a *galant* idiom, especially within the central slow movements), which had consigned the undifferentiated surface and harmonic rhythms of baroque ritornello practice to the past. Ultimately, Wagenseil achieved a convincing level of segmentation within his movement forms that was to bear further fruit in the symphonies of later Viennese generations.

Wagenseil's Viennese contemporary Georg Matthias Monn (1717–50) was perhaps less influential, both internationally and locally.[6] None of his symphonies was published during his lifetime, though that is not a reflection of their general quality, which is comparable with Wagenseil, especially in the design of first movements, which frequently have two clearly defined and contrasting themes, a clear sense of periodic phrasing and tonal logic (including, as in Wagenseil, excursions to the minor mode) and full recapitulations. Monn's first-movement forms arguably feature a more strongly defined developmental purpose to the material immediately following the central dominant or equivalent cadence than those of his contemporary. Monn is credited with composing the earliest-known four-movement symphony (in which the minuet comes in third place). This work in D major, dating from 1740, is however the only four-movement symphony in Monn's surviving output of sixteen and although it survives in autograph, the designation 'sinfonia' is in a later hand. It must therefore be regarded as atypical, and while many of the emergent features of what may loosely be termed the 'Viennese classical style' are to be found in the symphonies of Monn and Wagenseil, the four-movement model apparently arose in Mannheim, where it was gradually established in the

symphonies of Johann Stamitz between 1740 and 1750,[7] works widely
circulated in print across musical Europe and ultimately influential on
Viennese composers too.

Developments

So far the contribution of what may be termed the 'first-generation' Viennese
symphonists has been investigated through an assessment of constructional
features, especially first movements, the organisation of which may be read in
part as a record of advancing coordination in the handling of internal
elements, and in part as a record of transmission of material between different
genres (opera overture, but equally church sonata and partita, to symphony).
That complex generic trace reflects something of the relationship of the
composer with his material, either on a point-to-point scale or on a broader
sweep of (usually three) successive movements. But whether constructional
features such as the separation of thematic presentation into two contrasting
aspects, or the coordination of thematic return with tonal return were
dictated in any sense by the circumstances of their presentation in court,
chamber or church we may doubt. At this stage in its development, performance settings for the Viennese symphony did not determine it compositionally to a strong degree. That is to say, for the earliest Viennese
symphonists, no stable tradition of listening determined in advance their
manipulation of musical materials as a response. By contrast, effects such as
Haydn's use of high horns in his Symphony No. 60, the shocking *fortissimo*
chords in the Andante of the 'Surprise' Symphony, No. 94, Mozart's theatrical
late recapitulation of the opening theme (*premier coup d'archet*) in the first
movement of the 'Paris' Symphony, K 297, Beethoven's exhilarating recapitulation of the main theme over a dominant pedal in the first movement of
the Symphony No. 7 – all of these are *rhetorical* elements of classical
symphonic language and derive from usage in a concert situation in which
rhetoric was expected by attentive listeners. In 1760 that was still not really
the case. On the title page of Wagenseil's Op. 3 symphonies of *c.* 1760 referred
to above, the four (string) parts are sufficient on their own without the two
horns, whose parts could be purchased separately and therefore optionally.
Clearly in such a context the contribution of the horns is not so essential to
the effect as it was some forty years later in the first-movement recapitulation
of Beethoven's *Eroica* Symphony. Wagenseil's musical materials do not exist
in an essential relation with their *representation in sound*; in Beethoven's they
most assuredly do. That observation is an interesting marker of generic
difference (and distance travelled).

What we may establish as generic *traits* of the symphony in Vienna by *c.* 1760 include:

1. A tendency to derive first-movement structures from binary form models, rather than ritornellos, usually involving at least two contrasting themes, both of which are recapitulated, and negligible 'development' of material immediately after the central double-bar.
2. An emerging recognition of the importance of key contrast and the vital role of cadential punctuation in achieving this; clear separation between different kinds of thematic functionality, contained within a steadily moving harmonic rhythm; symmetry and proportion as regulative elements of the structure, which operates in an interconnected way on the levels of local phrase, sentence and paragraph. Contrast, rather than uniformity, became a key element of coherence.
3. A succession of three (fast–slow–fast) rather than four movements, the third (final) movement often resembling a minuet: short, unpretentious and generally in binary form.
4. A presumed hierarchy of orchestral functions, in which winds are secondary to strings, and in which horn parts are often dispensable. At this stage, details that were soon to become relatively standard, such as the four-part string basis (the bass part comprising cello, string bass and potentially a bassoon), supplemented by a pair of oboes (or flutes), and a pair of horns, were still in flux; Wagenseil's published symphonies include his Op. 2 (1756) entitled 'trios en symphonie' (i.e. trio-symphonies for two violins and bass).

At this point in its development, the Viennese symphony as a genre exists somewhere between internally conceived constructional boundaries on the one hand and a plethora of contrasting performance contexts on the other. The former are emerging into quite clear patterns. By contrast, the latter must surely have detracted from the establishment of a clear generic focus. There was, as yet, no single institutional context for its presentation, and what we may call the 'practice of public reception' counts for a lot in this regard. While the expressive rhetoric of the later Viennese symphony was significantly shaped in the concert hall, presentations of the works of Monn or Wagenseil and their contemporaries within courtly, and primarily social, contexts tended to diminish recognition of an independent generic value. For instance, in a performance of a symphony as a kind of background music at a Viennese banquet, any guests who were paying careful attention, however fleetingly, to the symphony would probably have related what they heard to their existing social experience of music, and the likeliest connection would have been with the opera overture. Thus, their reception perspective is not likely to have exerted any strong generic impetus upon symphonic development. Likewise, the performance of symphonies – for example, the four extant *Sinfonie Pastorale*

of Leopold Hofmann (1738–93), or his small-scale B-flat symphony of
c. 1763 (Badley B♭1)[8] – within Catholic liturgical contexts (in which the
focus is on the celebration of the Eucharist, to which, momentarily, the
music is a background) will not have assisted the symphony's generic
separation from the church sonata, from which, in formal terms, Viennese
symphonies trace some of their material ingredients. Moreover, performance practice impinges strongly on reception: surviving (usually single)
sets of manuscript playing parts, for instance in monastery libraries,
repeatedly hint that the numbers of strings involved in performances of
symphonies in such contexts were small (sometimes even one to a part),
suggesting that there was no strong distinction to be made between a
symphony and other genres of predominantly string chamber music. For
example, when he first joined the musical establishment at Esterhaza
(1761), Haydn's orchestral complement amounted to a total of thirteen
to fifteen players: six violins, one viola, one cello, one bass, two oboes, two
horns and a bassoon (some flexibility existed within this scheme, since
most of the players could offer more than one instrument: a flute,
for instance is employed in Symphony No. 6, *Le Matin*). Subsequently,
during the 1770s, the size of the Esterhaza band increased, and there
are documented performances of symphonies in Vienna by the
Tonkünstlersocietät (founded 1771) with sizeable numbers of performers.
But the link between the symphony genre and chamber music persisted
remarkably long. At the end of the century, Haydn's 'London' symphonies
were subsequently issued in various chamber-music arrangements by
Johann Peter Salomon (most popularly for flute, string quartet and
piano *ad libitum*). The difference between this situation (in which
Haydn's symphonies could still be a chamber-music experience) and the
looser generic situation of the 1750s was that these were clearly *adaptations for domestic purposes* of something originally experienced in a public
concert setting and whose expressive parameters were decisively dictated
by that original setting. In the case of the early Viennese symphony it is
not so clear from the music that there was any or much difference between
a domestic and any other imaginable forum of presentation in the first
place.

All of this prompts the realisation that we must look elsewhere for
reception stimuli impinging upon the development of the Viennese symphonic genre. Arguably, this is to be found in an examination of influence.
The institutional framework for musical instruction in eighteenth-century
Vienna revolved around the choir schools (for instance, at St Stephen's
Cathedral, or the Michaelerkirche) and, ultimately, it was centred on the
personnel of the Hofkapelle. Among the more important connections are
these: Fux (1660–1741) was Wagenseil's teacher; in turn Wagenseil taught

at least one member of a later generation of Viennese symphonists, Leopold Hofmann; Dittersdorf's (1739–99) teacher was the Imperial Kapellmeister, Giuseppe Bonno (1711–88); Dittersdorf is said to have contributed to Johann Vaňhal's (1739–1813) musical training after the latter had moved to Vienna in 1760–1; Josef Leopold Eybler (1765–1846) trained initially at St Stephen's, and subsequently with Johann Georg Albrechtsberger (1736–1809), who had received his training in the choir school of the Augustinian monastery at Klosterneuburg and subsequently as a pupil of Monn; Albrechtsberger (revered by Mozart as an organist) became a colleague of Hofmann, succeeding him as Kapellmeister at St Stephen's in 1793; his most famous pupil was Beethoven (from 1794, his previous teacher, Haydn, having left Vienna temporarily for his second London visit). In such a close-knit environment, it is understandable that the generic hallmarks of the Viennese symphony might to a large extent have been determined internally, in a progressive, influential dialogue between professionals working with the materials of their symphonic craft and defining the genre constructionally from within. That ongoing dialogue bore fruit in the increasing sophistication with which segmented formal functions within movements (especially first movements) are handled in the work of, for instance, Hofmann, Ordonez, Vaňhal and Dittersdorf. This ultimately led to a less casual relation between the different movements, in particular to a balanced conception in which the finale was regarded as providing a firm sense of closure to the three- (or four-) movement work, a kind of counterpole to the opening move-ment. As a result, the finale was now far less frequently in binary form, longer, and tending towards rondo structure, or, from the 1770s, sonata-rondo (in which sonata form maps onto the tonal logic of the refrains and episodes), and occasionally fugal types or even themes and variations.

Understanding this journey is not without its frustrations, principally because the surviving sources do not allow us to piece together a reliable chronology. Almost half of Leopold Hofmann's fifty symphonies – a significant number of which may have been primarily intended for litur-gical use, to judge from the quantity of sources surviving in monasteries such as Göttweig – have four (not three) movements; he was among the earliest of Viennese composers to adopt this expanded outline (though we should remember that some of these are in a slow–fast–slow–fast sequence and that others are effectively three-movement works with slow introduc-tions).[9] More contemporary sources survive for Hofmann's symphonies than for any other composer of the era save Haydn and Pleyel (like those of his teacher, Wagenseil, Hofmann's symphonies appeared in print in Paris; four were published there by Sieber in 1760, for example). But a chronol-ogy for his symphonies is not easy to establish with certainty, and it is not safe to assume that, for instance, his three-movement works were super-seded by four-movement ones. Perhaps the innovatory aspect of a four-movement plan contributed to their popularity, but it is perhaps their sure command of texture and form that guaranteed their wide appeal. Concertante elements are occasionally found, for example in the F major symphony of *c.* 1760 (Badley F2), a three-movement work whose second-placed minuet features a central trio specifically for solo viola, cello and bass, contrasting with surrounding tuttis (strings and oboes). Similar concertante elements are found elsewhere within the emergent Viennese symphonic tradition, notably in Haydn's slightly later programmatic set, *Le Matin*, *Le Midi* and *Le Soir* (*c.* 1761–2) and subsequently in such works as the Larghetto of Dittersdorf's four-movement A minor Symphony (Grave a1, *c.* 1770–5),[10] which features prominent cello solos along with punctuating interjections for a pair of horns, and the Adagio molto of Vaňhal's D major Symphony (Bryan D17)[11] of 1779 (in three, not four, movements), which may as well be the slow movement of an oboe con-certo. Hofmann also preceded Haydn in the employment of a slow introduction to first movements, for example in the D major symphony of *c.* 1762 (Badley D4), in which the relatively lightweight and pithy character of the extremely economical Allegro molto is contextualised by a preceding Adagio of considerable *gravitas*. The main Allegro molto discriminates effectively between its primary, secondary, connective and cadential materials. Interestingly, there are quite clear resemblances between the second-movement Andante and the opening Adagio intro-duction. Interrelations between thematic elements is likewise a character-istic of the symphonies of Florian Leopold Gassmann (whose position as Imperial Kapellmeister Hofmann failed to secure on Gassmann's death in 1774),[12] though here the references are typically between the successive themes within an exposition in a quasi-organic succession as the tonal narrative away from the opening tonic unfolds.

For the Viennese symphony emergent between *c.* 1760 and 1780 (the period spanned by the production of symphonies by Dittersdorf and his contemporary, Vaňhal), growing confidence in the coordination and proportioning of theme, rhythm, harmony, tonality and texture contri-butes substantially to the impression of an overall trend towards a narra-tive whose unfolding features emerge as a logical succession of elements specifically designed to be noticed by listeners: Vaňhal's C major *Sinfonia Comista* (Bryan C11, *c.* 1775–8) affords a clear example. In the concertante Larghetto of Dittersdorf's A minor Symphony, mentioned above, repeat-ing cadential refrains supplied by the two horns are not simply an attrac-tive colouristic device, contrasting with the solo cello's episodes, but are precisely coordinated with the arrival of moments of tonal articulation upon which the overall form depends. Both sound and structure are surely meant to be recognised by a listener; an element of meaning derives from dialogue between the abstract musical conception and a listener paying attention to it in real time. That listener would also have noted the currency of Dittersdorf's opening Vivace (which employs three horns), which is firmly in the tempestuous *Sturm-und-Drang* idiom that was sweeping Viennese music in the early 1770s. *Sturm und Drang* is a feature too of some symphonies by Vaňhal from this period. His G minor Symphony (Bryan g1), published in Paris in 1773–4, but perhaps dating from the late 1760s, is a case in point. It makes prominent use of tone colour (notably two pairs of horns tuned in G and high B flat, and concertante parts for violin and viola in the second of its four movements, Andante cantabile) in addition to the expressive harmonic colours obtainable from the minor mode, its driving syncopations and sudden dramatic contrasts of dynamic, register, texture and accentuation, reminiscent in character of more famous symphonies in G minor by Haydn (Hob. I:39) and Mozart (K 183). Moreover, Vaňhal's orchestration is pioneering. In a D minor Symphony (Bryan d2), one of five symphonies of his advertised for sale by Breitkopf in Supplement XII (1778) of their Thematic Catalogue, he uses no fewer than five horns (in two pairs, crooked in F and D, with an additional one in A), giving him a wide range of notes and once again allowing the horns' full participation in the exploitation of expressive harmonic potential. And several symphonies (among them Bryan D17 and C11, mentioned above, and C3, D2 and A9) use pairs of clarino trumpets.

Conclusions

Vaňhal's output marks an important point of arrival in the development of the Viennese symphony. His are works of considerable individuality, technically assured, inventive, substantial in length and also in intellectual concentration, requiring, indeed, a certain degree of concentration on the part of the listener if they are to be satisfactorily realised. His symphony Bryan D2 (*c.* 1763–5) has, in its first movement, a genuine development section, which introduces a new theme during its course. Symphony A9, of uncertain date, is a single-movement symphony in three sections (fast–slow–fast), though its dimensions and expressive range far exceed those of the Italian opera overtures that were once a prototype for the earlier Viennese symphony; its opening and closing sections include unmistakable cross-references, the Finale's closing material returning to the opening bars of the work. The majority are in four movements, a scheme within which there is purposeful regard for the overall proportions, the finales sometimes being considerably extended and typically in rondo, sonata-rondo or sonata form. They may well have been known to Haydn (ten of Vaňhal's symphonies are preserved in the Esterházy archives) and also to Mozart (who played chamber music with Vaňhal); certainly the 62-bar slow introduction (in the minor mode) to Vaňhal's D major symphony (Bryan D17) has strong similarities both to the introduction of the 'Linz' Symphony, K 425 and to that of the 'Prague' Symphony, K 504.

While the symphonies of Vaňhal may, in sum, be claimed to represent a maturity in the development of the Viennese classical symphony that served as a platform from which were launched the final achievements of the genre's four greatest exponents, Haydn, Mozart, Beethoven and Schubert, that claim requires substantial qualification. First, Vaňhal's symphonies are exemplary of an achievement stemming from an environment of fairly loose, intertextual progress among Viennese composers generally towards mastery of technique allied to form, rather than the product of a single, paradigm-shifting individual. Secondly, an agenda of progress towards Haydn and Mozart, followed by Beethoven and Schubert and their lesser adjuncts, Czerny, Ries, Spohr, Cherubini, Gyrowetz, et al., is one whose motives (originating perhaps in a conflation of nineteenth-century political, aesthetic and especially nationalist debates) are highly questionable. Such debates redefined the symphonic genre in an act of retrospective *Rezeptionsgeschichte* that was bound up with the invention of a Viennese classical canon supported by institutions such as the professional concert, the complete edition, the founding of conservatoires, the discipline of musical *Formenlehre* and the rapid rise of serious musical criticism. As a consequence, the Viennese symphony at the turn of the nineteenth century assumed what would remain its destiny as the most prestigious among instrumental genres. Within this species of *Rezeptionsgeschichte*, the symphony was expected to be individual, to possess inherently dramatic qualities, to encapsulate in addition to mere technical control of its materials an aesthetic of progress beyond 'absolute music'. In Beethoven's symphonies, which played a pivotal role in launching the Viennese symphony into this exciting uncharted territory, the genre is once more redefined as a public demonstration – celebration, even – of topics such as the sublime (for example, the first movement of the *Eroica*, which at nearly 700 bars, is the longest symphonic movement Beethoven ever composed); of overarching unity in diversity, expressed cyclically in the Fifth Symphony through thematic transformation of theme, through the linking of different movements and, indeed, through the dissolution of boundaries separating movements, as the Scherzo gives way to the culminating finale; of 'fate' and 'strife-to-victory' (exemplified in some readings of the same symphony); of the naturalistic as a retreat from the dehumanising perspectives of war and industrialisation in the 'Pastoral' Symphony; and, in the Ninth's Finale, the transformation of the genre through the medium of the human voice singing of an imagined redemption attainable only beyond the material realm.[13] Poetic ideas, to be sure; and such was now expected of the symphony. Crucially, the baritone addresses the audience as 'Friends', directly inviting their involvement, for it is within that shared framework of endeavour that Beethoven's Ninth Symphony must have its meaning if all men are to be brothers, rejecting past agendas (as Beethoven, metaphorically, has just rejected his previous themes in turn) and striding confidently forth into joy. This moment is a turning point in the symphonic genre; the symphony as civic agency has remained a powerful reception metaphor ever since (this event is considered below in chapters 8 and 9).

One casualty of this historiographical agenda was Schubert, whose symphonies were eclipsed throughout the nineteenth century and beyond by the mighty achievement of his idol, Beethoven. Like Beethoven's nine symphonies, Schubert's eight travel a path away from late eighteenth-century classical purity, symmetry and elegance towards the frontier of transcendence articulated in the writings of the German Romantics, Wackenroder, Tieck, E. T. A. Hoffmann and the Schlegels. But Schubert's 'Beyond' arguably lay deep within himself. His 'Unfinished' and 'Great' C major symphonies conform uneasily to early nineteenth-century expectations of the symphonic genre, and this may be a contributory cause to their painfully slow acceptance into the canon (they were only even premiered in 1839 and 1865 respectively), for they trace a path not towards the attainment of a public and civic spiritual brotherhood of all mankind, but a private and interior world of half-lights and self-doubts whose technical musical language is often not far removed from the lied. While there are no voices in Schubert's symphonies, the vocality of his personal symphonic genre is unmistakable. In his hands, as in Beethoven's, the Viennese symphony had travelled far.

Notes

1 For Mozart's letter, see Emily Anderson, ed., *The Letters of Mozart and His Family*, 3rd rev. edn, ed. Stanley Sadie and Fiona Smart (London and Basingstoke, 1985), no. 396. See also Otto Eric Deutsch, *Mozart: A Documentary Biography*, trans. Eric Blom, Peter Branscombe and Jeremy Noble (London, 1990), H. C. Robbins Landon, *Mozart: the Golden Years* (London, 1989) and Elaine Sisman, *Mozart: The 'Jupiter' Symphony* (Cambridge, 1993).

2 For an overview of life and society in Hapsburg Vienna, seen against the backdrop of the Enlightenment, see Derek Beales, *Enlightenment and Reform in Eighteenth-Century Europe* (London and New York, 2005). The musical picture is painted in Daniel Heartz, *Haydn, Mozart and the Viennese School 1740–1780* (New York and London, 1995).

3 See, for instance, Susan Wollenberg and Simon McVeigh, eds., *Concert Life in Eighteenth-Century*

Britain (Aldershot, 2004) and Mary Sue Morrow, *Concert Life in Haydn's Vienna: Aspects of a Developing Musical and Social Tradition* (Stuyvesant, 1989).

4 Eighteenth-century sources of Wagenseil's symphonies survive in numerous locations, among them the Bibliothèque du Conservatoire, Brussels, the Národní Muzeum, Prague, the Gesellschaft der Musikfreunde and Nationalbibliothek, Vienna and the Library of Congress, Washington DC.

5 See John Kucaba, 'The Symphonies of Georg Christoph Wagenseil' (Ph.D. diss., University of Boston, 1967). Subsequent references to Wagenseil's symphonies draw on the editions ed. John Kucaba in Barry S. Brook, gen. ed., *The Symphony, 1720–1840*, Series B, vol. III: *Georg Christoph Wagenseil: Fifteen Symphonies, D1, D9, C8, C3, C4, G1, Eb2, C7, F1, Bb2, D2, G2, G3, E3, Bb4* (New York and London, 1981).

6 See Kenneth E. Rudolf, 'The Symphonies of Georg Mathias Monn (1715–1750)' (Ph.D. diss., University of Washington, 1982). Works consulted can be found in Barry S. Brook, gen. ed., *The Symphony, 1720–1840*, Series B, vol. I: *Georg Matthias Monn: Five Symphonies, Thematic Index D-5, Eb-1, A-2, Bb-1, Bb-2* (New York and London, 1985).

7 Eugene K. Wolf, *The Symphonies of Johann Stamitz: A Study in the Formation of the Classic Style* (Utrecht, 1981).

8 Numbers for Hofmann's symphonies throughout refer to Artaria Editions AE022, 24 and 26, ed. Alan Badley (Wellington, 1995). On Hofmann's symphonies, see G. C. Kimball, 'The Symphonies of Leopold Hofmann (1738–1793)' (Ph.D. diss., Columbia University, 1985).

9 A handful of the seventy symphonies of Karl von Ordonez (1734–86) are in four movements, and very occasionally there are slow introductions; see D. Young, 'The Symphonies of Karl von Ordonez (1734–1786)' (Ph.D. diss., University of Liverpool, 1980). For editions of Ordonez's

symphonies, see Barry S. Brook, gen. ed., *The Symphony, 1720–1840*, Series B, vol. IV: *Carlos d'Ordoñez: Seven Symphonies, C1, F11, A8, C9, C14 minor, G1, Bb 4*, ed. A. Peter Brown with the assistance of Peter M. Alexander (New York and London, 1979).

10 Editions of Dittersdorf's symphonies consulted are Dittersdorf a1 (k95), ed. V. Luithlen, *Denkmäler der Tonkunst in Österreich*, lxxxi, Jg.xliii/2 (Vienna, 1936) and also Barry S. Brook, gen. ed., *The Symphony, 1720–1840*, Series B, vol. I: *Carl Ditters von Dittersdorf: Six Symphonies, Thematic Index e1, Eb3, E2, A10, D9, C14*, ed. Eva Badura-Skoda, thematic index by Margaret H. Grave (New York and London, 1985). On Dittersdorf's symphonies, see also Margaret H. Grave, 'Dittersdorf's First-Movement Form as a Measure of his Symphonic Development' (Ph.D. diss., New York University, 1977).

11 Editions of Vaňhal's symphonies consulted are: Vaňhal g1, ed. H. C. Robbins Landon, *Diletto musicale* 38 (Vienna and Munich, 1965); Vaňhal C11, ed. Alan Badley (Wellington, 1996); Vaňhal d2, ed. Alan Badley (Wellington, 1996); Vaňhal C3, ed. Alan Badley (Wellington, 1997); Vaňhal A9, ed. Alan Badley (Wellington, 1997); Vaňhal D2, ed. Alan Badley (Wellington, 1998). On Vaňhal's symphonies, see Paul R. Bryan, *Johann Wanhal, Viennese Symphonist: His Life, and His Musical Environment* (Stuyvesant, 1997).

12 See George R. Hill, 'The Concert Symphonies of Florian Leopold Gassmann (1729–1774)' (Ph.D. diss., New York University, 1975). Editions of Gassmann's symphonies can be found in Brook, gen. ed., *The Symphony, 1720–1840*, Series B, vol. X: *Florian Leopold Gassman: Seven Symphonies: 23, 26, 62, 64, 85, 86, 120*, ed. George R. Hill (New York and London, 1981).

13 See, in this respect, Nicholas Cook, *Beethoven: Symphony No. 9* (Cambridge, 1993).

3 Other classical repertories

MARY SUE MORROW

It is symptomatic of our perception of the eighteenth-century symphony that this part of the volume has been divided into 'The Viennese Symphony 1750 to 1827' and 'Other Classical Repertories', a division that reflects our preoccupation with the path the eighteenth-century symphony took *en route* to Haydn, Mozart and Beethoven. Although no one will quarrel with the Viennese trinity's pre-eminence as symphony composers, the focus on their roots and influences has done scant justice to the symphonic cornucopia that the century produced.[1] Estimates of the number of symphonies composed during the century range up to 20,000, and even a brief sampling reveals an almost bewildering variety of formats (from one up to seven or more movements), textures (ranging from fugal to completely homophonic), orchestration (from three-part strings on up) and formal procedures. Moreover, we have mostly paid attention to the 'concert symphony', a designation not used until the late eighteenth century, and have tended to define the 'real' or 'mature' symphony as a serious, four-movement work for an orchestra of strings and winds, a definition that excludes or marginalises much of the repertoire. This repertoire reflects the eighteenth century's conception of the symphony as an instrumental work that could be used in the theatre (to precede an opera), in church (as Gradual music in the Catholic mass, for example), or in the chamber, where it generally served to open a concert. Although certain characteristics were typically associated with particular functions (i.e. *forte*, tutti openings for opera *sinfonie*), the fact remains that opera *sinfonie* frequently appeared in concerts, and 'chamber' symphonies (or movements of them) often served as Gradual music. For the eighteenth century, a *sinfonia* was a *sinfonia*, so if we wish to explore the genre fully, we would do well to consider all of its manifestations.[2]

What follows might be described as a 'socialist' history of the symphony. It identifies no 'major figures'; it does not trace influence or connections; it does not chronicle innovations or attempt to identify who did what first. Instead, it views symphonic composition as a collective enterprise in which thousands of composers participated; by taking this approach, I hope to expand the slender standard narrative thread into a complex tapestry of colours and patterns. Because of space limitations I have narrowed my focus and have concentrated on form, structure and expression, and the ways they interact with texture and orchestration.[3] I do not claim that my narrative is better than the standard one; merely that it shows us different things and perhaps makes us ask different questions.

Regions of composition

The symphony was found all over Europe as well as in lands where European culture was imported, and the composers themselves were a peripatetic lot. Italians and Bohemians, and to a lesser extent musicians from the German states, could be found everywhere (see Table 3.1). Luigi Boccherini (1742–1805) and Gaetano Brunetti (1744–98) both abandoned their native Italy for service in Spain; the Bohemian Josef Mysliveček (1737–81) spent much of his career in Italy; and his compatriot Johann Stamitz (1717–57) established his reputation in the palatinate of Mannheim, in southern Germany. The Mannheim-born Franz Beck (1734–1809) was active in France; the Swedish-born Johan Agrell (1701–65) in Kassel and Nuremberg; and the Scotsman Alexander Reinagle (1756–1809), of Austrian descent, immigrated to Philadelphia, in the newly formed United States. Such travels make a narrowly focussed study of ethnic or regional characteristics in symphonic composition tricky and perhaps of questionable value, although some differences in regional preferences and patterns of cultivation can be identified.

It is useful to distinguish between the *composition* and the *cultivation* of the symphony. For most of the century, composition was done by resident composers at courts or aristocratic households and thus occurred in relatively few places. These composers wrote for a specific orchestra and often for a specific occasion, even though their symphonies might later travel to other places in manuscript copies or in prints (often pirated). *Cultivation* was done by the thousands of institutions (including courts with resident composers) who purchased or otherwise acquired symphonies for performance at their concerts or celebrations or theatres or church services. These places created the demand that sparked the century's symphonic fecundity. In the early part of the century, most symphonies were distributed in manuscript parts, often acquired during the course of travel. After the middle of the century, distribution channels increasingly ran through music publishers and music sellers, most of whom offered

Table 3.1 *Selected immigrant composers of symphonies*

Name	Dates	Symphonies (parentheses indicate lost work)	Region of birth	Main region of activity
Ignaz Holzbauer	1711–83	*c.* 60	Austria	Germany
Johann Michael Haydn	1737–1806	44	Austria	Salzburg
Jan Zach	1699–1773	28	Bohemia	Germany
Jan Křtitel Jiří Neruda	1706–*c.* 1776	13 (18)	Bohemia	Germany
Wenceslaus Wodiczka	1712–74	24 (24)	Bohemia	Germany
Johann Stamitz	1717–57	58	Bohemia	Germany
Johann Georg Lang	1722–98	38	Bohemia	Germany
Florian Leopold Gassmann	1729–74	32 (12)	Bohemia	Vienna
Franz Xaver Pokorny	1729–94	*c.* 145	Bohemia	Germany
Josef Mysliveček	1737–81	*c.* 45 (5)	Bohemia	Italy
Wenzel Pichl	1745–1805	36	Bohemia	Austria, Italy
Georg Druschetzky	1745–1819	27	Bohemia	Austria, Hungary
Josef Bárta	1746–87	13	Bohemia	Vienna
Amadeus Ivančič	*fl. c.* 1750	21	Bohemia?	Austria
Antonio Rosetti	1750–*c.* 1792	43	Bohemia	Germany
Adalbert Gyrowetz	1763–1850	*c.* 32	Bohemia	Vienna
Joseph Touchemoulin	1727–1801	18	France	Germany
Johann Ernst Eberlin	1702–62	26 (10)*	Germany	Salzburg
Johann Adolph Scheibe	1708–76	7 (*c.* 60)	Germany	Denmark
Johan Daniel Berlin	1714–87	3	Germany	Norway
Leopold Mozart	1719–87	*c.* 70	Germany	Salzburg
Carl Friedrich Abel	1723–87	46	Germany	England
Franz Ignaz Beck	1734–1809	34 (1)	Germany	France
J. C. Bach	1735–82	*c.* 85	Germany	England
Carl Stamitz	1745–1804	51	Germany	Various regions
Franz Anton Hoffmeister	1754–1812	31 (13)	Germany	Vienna
Joseph Martin Kraus	1756–92	14	Germany	Sweden
Luigi Boccherini	1743–1805	27	Italy	Spain
Gaetano Brunetti	1744–98	37	Italy	Spain
Franz Xaver Richter	1709–89	83	Moravia	Germany
Paul Wranitzky	1756–1808	51	Moravia	Austria
Anton Wranitzky	1761–1820	15	Moravia	Austria
Simoni dal Croubelis	*c.* 1727–*c.* 1790	12	Netherlands?	Denmark
François-Joseph Gossec	1734–1829	46 (3)	Netherlands	France
Johan Agrell	1701–65	28	Sweden	Germany

both manuscript and printed parts and were eager to sell works that would have a wide market, a point to which I shall return later.

In Italy, the opera *sinfonia* – generally in three movements until the one-movement form emerged in the late 1770s – remained a major outlet for Italian symphonic creativity for most of the century. Opera *sinfonie* by composers like Niccolò Jommelli (1714–74) can be found in eighteenth-century symphony collections throughout the continent. The three-movement form, well established by the 1730s, favoured first movements with a noisy primary theme using tutti strings and winds leading to transitions with tremolos and crescendos, quieter contrasting second themes and bustling closing sections. The melody-based slow movements, often in the parallel minor, gave way to quick and lively finales, frequently in triple meter. The ceremonial function of the opera *sinfonia* meant that it was not – and indeed should not – be tied to the operatic subject (something never understood or acknowledged by eighteenth-century German writers), an approach that meant it could easily be transferred to the chamber, or even to the church. Early Italian *sinfonie* originally intended for chamber or church settings tended to call for three- or four-part strings and boasted a more flexible texture and structure than the opera *sinfonia*. During the 1740s and 1750s, wind parts became more common in chamber symphonies: nearly one third of Giovanni Battista Sammartini's (1700/01–75) sixty-eight symphonies, many from before 1760, add two horns or trumpets to the string choir.[4] Although Italian composers wrote for larger ensembles as the century progressed, wind instruments do not appear to have played as significant a role in Italy as they did in Northern Europe, perhaps because the instruments themselves were harder to find.[5] The imaginative use of the winds by the Italian emigrants Gaetano Brunetti and Luigi Boccherini clearly demonstrates that with the proper resources, Italians could easily hold their own in the area of orchestration.

The impact of Italian symphonies was widely felt, particularly in the first half of the century. In the lands of the Hapsburg monarchy, the impact was both direct – with the presence in Vienna of figures like Bartolomeo Conti (1682–1732), Antonio Caldara (*c.* 1670–1736) and later Antonio Salieri (1750–1825) – and indirect (with the importation of Sammartini's symphonies by the Count Harrach and the acquisition of Italian symphonies by the Esterházy family, documented in the Esterházy catalogues from 1740 and 1759–62).[6] Outside of Vienna, the symphony was composed and cultivated not only in cities like Pressburg and Prague, but also on the private estates of the nobility and in the numerous monasteries and convents. During the first half of the century, a strong fugal tradition threaded through Austrian symphonic composition and the liking for counterpoint never completely died out, although increasingly it was incorporated into a more homophonic style. As early as the 1760s, Austrian composers chose three- and four-movement formats with about the same frequency, but later turned to the four-movement F–S–M/T–F format with a sustained intensity not found in other regions of Europe. Perhaps because of the strong Bohemian wind tradition, works for strings alone were in the minority – even in the early part of the century – and disappeared almost entirely from the 1760s.

Much of the symphonic composition in southern Germany stemmed from its courts – the efforts of Johan Agrell in the free city of Nuremberg notwithstanding – particularly those in Mannheim, Wallerstein, Munich, Mainz, Trier and Cologne. Their musical establishments not only employed local composers, but also absorbed a whole flotilla of Bohemians, including Johann Stamitz (1717–57) and Antonio Rosetti (*c.* 1750–92), both known for their imaginative and varied use of the wind instruments. Stamitz and his colleagues in Mannheim made effective use of Italian techniques – including string tremolos and crescendos – using winds both for sonic and harmonic reinforcement and for melody. Rosetti had a particular knack for orchestration, often enriching the string texture by dividing the violas and using the winds with delicacy and finesse. Both composers had access to excellent orchestras (at the courts in Mannheim and Wallerstein, respectively), a fact that no doubt helped to stimulate their orchestral imaginations. (As Niccolò Jommelli observed, if you have a good orchestra, you must keep them busy or they will start to give you trouble.) The later Mannheim composers, for example Christian Cannabich (1731–98), Carl Joseph Toeschi (1731–88) and Franz Fränzl (1736–1811), have sometimes been accused of merely dabbling in colourful orchestral effects, but such comments belie the importance of such effects. In fact, particularly with composers like Rosetti, the skilful use of the orchestra to delineate structural function and create tension often goes hand in hand with the simple delight in the play of sonorities.

In northern Germany, the courts and aristocratic patrons sponsored most symphonic composition, although free cities like Hamburg and Leipzig certainly contributed to publication and performance. The Italian opera *sinfonia* had its effect here as well, but the north-German repertoire, particularly in the first two thirds of the century, showed great diversity in terms of movement structure. In the 1730s and 1740s Johann Gottlob Harrer (1703–55) composed a number of three-movement quasi-programmatic symphonies (some with large wind sections) intended for specific occasions, weaving hunting calls and well-known dance tunes into a mostly homophonic compositional fabric. At the court of Hessen-Darmstadt, Johann Christoph Graupner (1683–1760) and Johann Samuel Endler (1694–1762) showed a preference for symphonies with four or more movements (such large-scale works make up nearly half of Graupner's 113 symphonies), often with very large ensembles sometimes requiring three trumpets.[7] Much of the symphonic activity here appears to have taken place in the first part of the century, with the rate of production dropping sharply after around 1770.

France and Britain had more in common with each other than with the rest of Europe in terms of the cultivation of the symphony. For both, the centre of symphony composition, performance and publication was in their capital cities, though their smaller cities could also boast of musical societies that required symphonies for concerts. In the first two thirds of the century, the sheer number of music publishers in Paris and London completely dwarfed that of all competing cities except, perhaps, for Amsterdam. Paris and London also had a flourishing concert life – both public and private – and eagerly welcomed musical immigrants into their midst. Native composers like Simon Le Duc (1742–77) and the French-speaking immigrant from the Netherlands François-Joseph Gossec (1734–1829) grafted the metric patterns of the French language onto the Italian opera *sinfonia* style to create symphonic 'Frenchness'. In the later part of the century, French composers showed a definite preference for the grand and brilliant, particularly with regard to orchestration.[8] British taste favoured tuneful, diatonic melodies with lively dance-like rhythms,[9] but audiences were also not unmindful of the charms of well-placed counter-point, preferences that help to explain the popularity of the immigrant J. C. Bach (1735–82) and the adulation that greeted the symphonies of Joseph Haydn.

Areas on the geographical periphery of Europe and those on other continents participated in both the composition and the cultivation of symphonies, though the latter was more frequent than the former. Even if immigrant composers dominated the compositional scene (as did Luigi Boccherini and Gaetano Brunetti in Spain), native-born talents also participated (as with the group of Catelonian composers active around Barcelona after about 1770).[10] Lands with music-loving monarchs and established musical institutions, such as Sweden, produced their own local symphony composers even early in the century – for example Johan Helmich Roman (1694–1758) and Johan Agrell – but other places, parti-cularly in the colonial world, did so only towards the century's close. Immigrant composers completely dominated the musical world of the North-American colonies and the young United States; in South America, the only known symphony by a native-born Brazilian, for example, was written by José Maurício Nunes Garcia (1767–1830) in 1790.[11]

Symphonic style and form

Any attempt to describe general (as opposed to composer-specific) pat-terns and trends in eighteenth-century symphonic composition is in some ways a foolhardy undertaking, given the number of works involved and the fact that so many of them have never been studied. What follows can thus not be considered definitive, but is offered as a possible narrative framework for understanding and interpreting the symphonic data that we do have. Briefly stated, the first half of the century witnessed a variety of approaches – on every level of composition – to works labelled 'symphony'. Although a few patterns can be identified, particularly locally, the differences in everything from number of movements to texture to formal procedures were considerable. By the end of the 1750s, recognisable patterns and conventions common across all the regions of composition had begun to coalesce, giving the genre a more definite shape. These conventions proved advantageous both to composers and listeners; the best composers were those who could exploit them by playing on the expectations they created. Whereas we have tended to view conventional patterns as straight-jackets for the imagination (a sign of our continuing attachment to nineteenth-century aesthetic values), for eighteenth-century composers they appear to have functioned as a stimulus, providing a basic framework upon which they could construct endless delightful and subtle variations.

Early eighteenth-century approaches

From the beginning, most composers chose the three-movement, F–S–F format commonly found in the Italian opera *sinfonia* for the overwhelming majority of their works, although one- and two-movement works remained a strong second choice. (It should be noted that many of the latter had two-tempo movements, so that they could also be heard as having three or four connected movements.) Four-movement symphonies were less common before the 1750s and can be found in a variety of patterns (not just F–S–M/T–F), as seen in the sampling given in Table 3.2.

North-German composers, as indicated above, had a particular fondness for works in four or more movements, sometimes with programmatic titles. Graupner's Symphony in E flat (Nagel 64 from *c*. 1747–50) features five quick movements: Vivace, Poco Allegro, Allegro, Poco Allegro, Tempo di Gavotte. Endler's Symphony in E flat (E♭4 from 1757) has both dance and programmatic components: Allegro molto; Menuet I and II, Marche, Contentement, Bourrée I and II, Le bon vivant I and II. For interior slow movements, composers seem to have preferred the tonic or relative minor – a choice that maintained tonal unity and was potentially less jarring to the sensibilities when the movements were very brief – but occasionally chose the subdominant or dominant.

During this period, strings in an *a 3* (two violins and basso) or *a 4* (two violins, viola and basso) configuration formed the core of performance forces, although *a 3* works became rarer by the 1740s. When available, wind instruments (most commonly horns, oboes or trumpets) could join this core string group, particularly in Italian opera *sinfonie* and for

Table 3.2 *Examples of four-movement plans before 1760*

Composer	Work	Date	Movement 1	Movement 2	Movement 3	Movement 4
Joseph Camerloher	Symphony in E flat (C 26)	*c.* 1730–43	Largo staccato	Allegro	Andante cantabile	Allegro
Giovanni Alberto Ristori	Symphony in F major	1736	Allegro assai (F)	Andante (modulating)	Allegro (d)	Vivace assai (F)
Johann Helmich Roman	Symphony in G minor (BeRi 30)	1737–52	Con spirito (g)	Andante (D)	Vivace (g)	Andante (G)
Francesco Barsanti	Overture in B minor, Op. 4/5	1742	Andantino e staccato	Allegro	Andantino e staccato	Forte-Menuet
Johann Samuel Endler	Symphony in D (D1)	*c.* 1750	Allegro assai	Menuet I and II	Andante	Les Postillons
Johann Samuel Endler	Symphony in E flat (E♭ 2)	*c.* 1750	Allegro	Allegro moderato	Vivace	Menuet I and II
Johan Agrell	Symphony in D (D:557111)	*c.* 1750	Allegro (D)	Andantino (d)	Allegro assai (D)	[Minuet & Trio] (D)
Louis Aubert	Symphony in D, Op. 2/5	before *c.* 1755	Ouverture: Vivement et marquée	Lent	Menuet	Contredanse
Louis Aubert	Symphony in D, Op. 2/6	before *c.* 1755	Vivement	Lentement	Pantomime: Modérément	Gai sans vitesse
Karl von Ordonez	Symphony in c (C14)	before *c.* 1755	Allegro	Andante	Menuetto/ Trio	Allegro con spirito
Karl von Ordonez	Symphony in C (C1)	before 1756	Adagio	Allegro di molto	Andante	Finale: Tempo di menuet
Wenzel Birck	*Sinfonia* in G (IV/13)	*c.* 1750s	Allegro molto	Fuga ma non troppo presto	Menuet/Trio	Fantasia: Presto assai
Wenzel Birck	*Sinfonia* in G minor	*c.* 1750s	Non troppo presto	Fuga allegro	Menuet	La Risposta: Non troppo presto

ceremonial occasions at court or in church. For example, the Symphony in C by Georg Reutter the Younger (1708–72) calls for *a 4* strings, organ and two brass choirs, each with two clarini, two trombe and timpani.[12] Endler's Symphony in D (D4), written for a New Year's Day celebration in 1750, requires *a 3* strings, oboe, two horns, three clarini and timpani. The use of winds in more ordinary circumstances increased gradually throughout the period, although instrumentation often remained flexible: the title page of Jean-Férry Rebel's 1737 Symphony, *Les eléments*, announces that 'This symphony is engraved in such a way that it can be played in concert by two violins, two flutes, and one bass', adding that a harpsichord could also play it alone. Moreover, the score itself indicates a number of places where other instruments – specifically two violas, basso continuo, piccolos (petites flutes), oboes, horns and bassoons – could be added.[13] Although Rebel's work is unusual in the extent of its suggested alternatives, flexibility with regard to wind parts was widespread. Published works often had *ad libitum* wind parts to make them more marketable and – conversely – trumpet or horn parts could be added to make a work more festive or to cater for a patron's wishes.[14]

Although wind instruments in this repertoire tend to play either *colla parte* with the strings or to reinforce the harmony, we should not discount the effect that they had on the listener's sonic experience. Moreover, composers often highlighted the wind instruments or used them in a more subtle interplay. In Johann David Heinichen's (1683–1729) Symphony in D (written after 1717), pairs of flutes and oboes play *colla parte* with the strings, but the two horns have occasional solos. Agrell's woodwinds usually play *colla parte* with the strings, but in his Symphony in C major (from the early 1740s), he makes sophisticated use of their penetrating sonority, with the oboes reinforcing the syncopated harmonic shifts made by the strings and the horns entering in alternation with punctuation that drives to the downbeat (Example 3.1). Rightly known for his imaginative orchestral effects, Johann Stamitz frequently used winds as solo instruments in secondary themes, temporarily relegating the normally dominant strings to an accompaniment role. During this period, wind instruments often dropped out for middle slow movements, thus creating a sonic contrast with the surrounding *tutti* fast ones, although sometimes, as in Giovanni Battista Lampugnani's (*c.* 1708–*c.* 1788) Symphony in D (D6, *c.* 1750) and some of Graupner's early works, the horns continue the harmonic supporting role evident in the outer movements.

Early symphonies exploited a wide variety of textures, from strictly fugal to essentially contrapuntal to purely homophonic. The preference for fugues in instrumental composition has been associated with Vienna; however the technique can be found across the continent. The Swedish composer Ferdinand Zellbell, Jr (1719–80) opened his D minor Symphony with a first movement slow introduction leading to a fugue followed by a sarabande and gigue, and several composers in England – Francesco Barsanti (1690–1772), Thomas Arne (1710–88), Maurice Green (1696–1755) – incorporated fugal movements in their symphonies from the 1740s and 1750s. (Interestingly, Padre Giovanni Battista Martini (1706–84), famous all over Europe for his counterpoint treatise, did not include any fugal movements in his twenty-four symphonies.) Although arrangements like Zellbell's follow the pattern of the French overture and suite, with slow dotted openings leading to fugues followed by dance movements, not all fugal movements fall into that category: Wenzel Birck's (1718–63) *Sinfonia* No. 9 has a 107-bar Presto before its fugue,[15] and most of Franz Xaver Richter's (1709–89) symphonic fugues appear in finales.[16]

Example 3.1 Johan Agrell, Symphony in C major, I, bars 15–23.

Even in the early part of the century, fugues and fugal textures appear in only a tiny fraction of all symphony movements; I have considered them at some length here because their persistent presence in the repertoire helps to explain the continuing importance of counterpoint in later eighteenth-century works.

The predominant symphonic texture was of course homophony, both in the unison/massed sound and the melody-with-accompaniment varieties. Throughout the first half of the century, however, composers consistently mixed a soupçon of counterpoint into their symphonies, often to articulate structural functions. Antonio Brioschi (*fl. c.* 1725–*c.* 1750) commonly turned contrapuntal in his development sections, while Sammartini often used contrapuntal transitions that contrast with the unison or homophonic primary and closing sections. By way of contrast, Agrell often distinguished his secondary themes by introducing counterpoint, along with reduced orchestration and dynamics. These examples show that fugal and contrapuntal techniques were quickly absorbed into the newer formal procedures that began to dot the symphonic landscape.

In terms of formal structure, most early first movements fell somewhere along the continuum of binary to sonata forms (mostly the latter), but some are ritornello-based and others blend aspects of ritornello and sonata construction. Slow movements and other fast movements rarely made use of ritornello techniques and mostly fall towards the binary end of the continuum. Conventions for delineating the sections of sonata movements were just beginning to emerge, but the first three basic sonata types described by James Hepokoski and Warren Darcy for the later eighteenth century can easily be identified in this repertoire as well.[17] In general, composers of this period were establishing the rules of the game (*à la* Leonard Meyer) with great vitality and spirit, exploring possibilities for generating tension and excitement (tremolos, crescendos, rising lines, etc.) and for expressivity.[18] Often, the expressive centre of the work was in the (frequently) minor-mode slow movement, which habitually featured nuanced dynamic contrast, sighing appoggiaturas and cantabile melodies. Georg Benda (1722–95) makes the most of the sonic possibilities of the strings in the slow movement his *Sinfonia* I in F major by juxtaposing pizzicato and arco motives, ending with a delightfully quizzical pizzicato weak-beat afterthought (Example 3.2).[19]

Expressive choices, however, were not limited to the slow movement. Opening major-mode movements often featured diversions to the minor dominant in S (the subordinate theme), a tactic particularly popular in Italian opera *sinfonie* of the 1730s as seen in Leonardo Leo's *Amor vuol sofferenza* from 1736 (Example 3.3a and b). Similar techniques are employed by such diverse composers as Agrell, Harrer, Leopold Mozart (1719–87) and Georg Wagenseil (1715–77). The long primary section of Sammartini's Symphony No. 10 in F major even encompasses a plaintive contrasting section in the tonic minor. Development sections frequently traverse minor-mode areas, often with a strong cadence to the relative minor just before the recapitulation. In many cases, this expressivity relies on local-level contrast, nowhere more strongly than in the symphonies of C. P. E. Bach (1714–88). In his Symphony in F of 1755 (Wq 175) rests, chromatic excursions and

Example 3.2 Georg Benda, *Sinfonia* No. 1 in F major, I, bars 12–15; 24–6.

dynamic contrasts enhanced by changes of orchestration all combine to create local-level drama and structural-level tension. The *piano* trills in bar 7 give way in the next measure to a minor-mode variant of bar 6, which is followed by a *forte* outburst on V^7/V to begin the transition. Its path to V, however, is continually derailed by further chromatic diversions and *piano* interpolations, delaying the cadence in the dominant until bar 32 (Example 3.4).

Bach's symphonies, like many others from the first part of the century, derive their energy from such local-level contrasts, together with lively and

Example 3.3a Leonardo Leo, Overture to *Amor vuol sofferenza*, I, bars 1–5.

engaging motives, a consistent quaver pulse and a forward trajectory that minimises sectional and functional delineation. Such techniques, particularly when used skilfully, work very well in shorter movements; for more extended compositions, other organisational strategies needed to be devised. Many of the formal conventions we associate with sonata form emerged as composers began to incorporate these local contrasts into a larger compositional trajectory in which the various sections of the movement assumed particular functional responsibilities. The trajectory was

Example 3.3b Leonardo Leo, Overture to *Amor vuol sofferenza*, I, bars 12–17.

created in large part by the creation of expectations, which could then be fulfilled, deflected, or even subverted. This approach became the defining feature of late eighteenth-century symphonic style.

Late eighteenth-century conventions

By the 1760s, conventional practices in all elements of symphonic composition had coalesced into patterns discernible throughout the European continent. The three-movement F–S–F pattern continued as the most common movement format, with the four-movement scheme (mostly, though not always, F–S–M/T–F) the strong second choice. Only at the very end of the century did the F–S–M/T–F format start to dominate, and even then some composers who had flirted with the four-movement pattern early in their careers chose the three-movement variety in their later works, among them Cannabich, Toeschi and Ignaz Pleyel

Example 3.4 C. P. E. Bach, Symphony in F major, Wq 175, I, bars 1–36.

Example 3.4 (cont.)

(1757–1831). Rather than seeing their choice as a 'reversion' to an outdated practice (as has generally been the case), we might more profitably ask what advantages or disadvantages the two options might have had. Composers like Joseph Haydn took advantage of the minuet's compact and absolutely predictable form to stretch and play with musical parameters like rhythm and texture. For others, the inclusion of the minuet might simply have expanded the symphony beyond a usable length, especially given the increasing length

Example 3.4 (cont.)

and complexity of the other movements (something that probably explains the nearly complete disappearance of symphonies in more than four movements). One- and two-movement symphonies still maintained a presence in the repertoire in France, the Austrian lands and especially in Italy, where they continued to be of importance in church settings. For example, twenty-four of the Franciscan priest Stanislao Mattei's (1750–1825) twenty-seven symphonies are single-movement works intended for church performances in Bologna.[20]

In the area of orchestration, the *a 8* configuration (*a 4* strings plus two oboes and two horns) emerged as the overwhelming favourite. This particular convention may well have been driven by market forces: music publishers and dealers clearly preferred symphonies with instrumental requirements that most ensembles could cover. Although strings-only symphonies continued to appear well into the second half of the century, by the 1790s the theorist Heinrich Christoph Koch could state that audiences generally expected to hear winds in symphonies.[21] Works requiring large wind ensembles still tended to come from courts with substantial orchestras (e.g. Mannheim and Wallerstein), and some evidence suggests that such large-scale pieces were much less likely to see publication. The Cannabich symphonies published by Götz in the 1770s call for the standard *a 8* orchestra, but those written just for the Mannheim court often add two clarinets, and the unpublished No. 44 is for a double orchestra.[22] Nonetheless, a number of Cannabich's unpublished symphonies require only the *a 8* ensemble, perhaps because of its practicality or because it was the most effective choice for relatively small spaces. Separate parts for flutes, bassoons and cellos became increasingly common (clarinet parts remained rare), and trumpets and timpani still seem to have been reserved for works intended to convey ceremony and splendour. In fact, although instrumental requirements grew steadily, a 'full' wind complement of pairs of flutes, oboes, clarinets, bassoons, horns and trumpets did not become a standard choice until the early nineteenth century.

The variety of formal approaches found in the early part of the century had by now coalesced into the sonata types described by Hepokoski and Darcy, particularly for opening fast movements. Sonata forms also predominate in slow movements and finales, though rondos or other part forms, and occasionally simple binaries, can be found as well. Although the Type 3 sonata (having a recapitulation beginning with P in the tonic) seems to have been increasingly preferred, the Type 2 (in which the return to the tonic coincides with post-P materials) was also very common. It would be anachronistic to assume (as has often been done) that the Type 2 was 'more primitive' than the 'full' Type 3, since a single symphony could easily have both, and neither individually nor collectively did composers 'progress' from Type 2s to Type 3s. One suspects, in fact, that the choice of a Type 2 might have been practical as well as aesthetic, keeping the performance time manageable as movement length increased.

Sonata form proved to be the ideal solution to the organisational challenge of longer movements, providing both the framework and flexibility for creating works that were both immediately understandable as types yet distinctly different as pieces. In the exposition, for example, the two main patterns (two-part and continuous) described by Hepokoski and Darcy are ubiquitous. Many composers, like J. C. Bach, preferred the two-part approach with its clearly delineated secondary theme articulated by a strong medial caesura, dynamic and textural changes (often to *piano* and reduced orchestra) and sometimes contrasting material. This pattern (which incorporated the local contrasts described above into a larger structure) provided aural guidance to listeners but nonetheless allowed for the small yet piquant variations so essential to the style. The C minor slow movement of Bach's Op. 6, No. 5 reaches a v:HC medial caesura in bar 14, but instead of a second theme in v, we hear one in III.[23] The frequency with which transition material led to a medial caesura made it possible for composers (particularly Joseph Haydn) to subvert this expected pattern with a continuous exposition that avoided a secondary theme entirely. These continuous expositions typically have a very different sound and trajectory from the continuity described above in the C. P. E. Bach symphony because their transitions, which continue past the temporal point where a secondary theme would normally have appeared, have a relentlessness that creates an ever greater need for the tonal closure the exposition requires. Here too, the techniques for creating this tension (crescendos, addition of instruments, motivic shortening, sequences, deceptive cadences, etc.) could be combined in an infinite variety of ways, so that each work could provide a new listening experience. All parts of the sonata structure could be manipulated in this fashion: 'development' sections could present new material; 'recapitulations' could undertake further development. Procedures found in Gossec's recapitulations, for example, range from more-or-less exact repetitions to those that reorder the exposition themes, or incorporate new material that had been introduced in the development, or involve considerable recomposition.[24] In creating these variations on the sonata theme, individual composers differed widely both in degree and techniques, but all except the worst usually managed to devise an unexpected twist or an artfully different sound to delight both the ear and the mind.

Orchestration often played a significant role in this manipulation of conventions and in the overall success of the work. Many first-movement primary themes are noisy, exciting, triadic affairs played by the full ensemble, but the first movement of Cannabich's Symphony No. 57 in E flat opens with violins and clarinets sustaining an E♭ over the moving bass line; by bar 7, the clarinet has taken over the melody, while the violins and *basso* line punctuate with turn figures. At any point in the movement, this configuration would be arresting, but it is particularly so for an opening. Like Cannabich, Rosetti had a knack for configuring the orchestra in unexpected ways and using the winds at exactly the right moment. His D major Symphony from *c.* 1788 opens with a single noise-killing chord before the violas, cellos, basses and bassoons enter with the theme, punctuated by the violins and upper winds. The third movements of Brunetti's four-movement symphonies – all dances but not all minuets – use a wind quintet for the A section and strings for the second, an inversion of the often-used procedure of featuring winds in the B section (or trio) of the minuet. In the Symphony No. 9 in D, the Allegro Minuetto first section, scored for two oboes, two horns and bassoon, leads to a B section for strings and timpani.

In the late eighteenth century, texture was closely related to orchestration and wind usage, because subtle use of instrumentation could create variety in an essentially homophonic texture. Purely fugal movements are relatively rare and tend to call attention to themselves. Luigi Borghi's rondo Finale to his Op. 6, No. 6, published in 1787, dissolves into a fugue, as if to defy conventional expectations.[25] Joseph Martin Kraus's 1789 one-movement *Sinfonia per la chiesa*, written for the blessing of the parliament in Sweden, opens with a slow introduction followed by a fugue, albeit one in two sections (the first repeated!), ending with a substantial section presenting the fugue theme homophonically. More commonly, composers wove counterpoint and a variety of textures into the fabric of formal procedures, using the differences and shadings to delineate formal areas (just as earlier composers had done), but also to complicate them. In the first movement of his F major Symphony (Mennicke 97 from before 1762), Johann Gottlieb Graun (1702/3–71) introduces a brief contrapuntal interchange just at the point when a secondary theme seems to be emerging (bar 30) to convert from a two-part to a continuous exposition (Example 3.5). The transition in the first movement of Cannabich's Symphony No. 73 in C moves noisily and homophonically towards V as expected, but at the moment when V/V arrives and S should appear, he switches to the minor mode and reduces the texture to *piano* contrapuntal lines, in effect derailing the transitional train and stretching the tension over another 20 bars (Example 3.6). The contrapuntal minuets that turn up in the symphonies of Joseph Haydn, W. A. Mozart, Wenzel Pichl (1741–1805), Gossec and Brunetti count as sly tweaks to convention in their conflation of the most learned of musical styles with the most courtly and *galant* of dances.

The increasing length of individual movements and the variety of textures and styles they incorporated meant that composers needed to develop new strategies for creating unity even beyond the trajectory provided by sonata form. Perhaps the most common technique was the derivation of transition and closing materials from the opening primary material, a practice so ubiquitous it is found even in melody-rich compositions like those of W. A. Mozart. Composers as disparate as Karl

Example 3.5 Johann Gottlieb Graun, Symphony in F major (Mennicke 97), I, bars 24–42.

Example 3.5 (cont.)

V: PAC

d'Ordonez (1734–86) and Gossec were fond of constructing intricate motivic connections among seemingly contrasting themes. Although Pichl's slow introduction to the first movement of his Op. 1, No. 5 has no motivic connection to the material that begins in bar 67, the slow, regular quaver motion, the restricted range, the legato markings and *piano* dynamic level call up the aural memory from earlier in an even more compelling way than a motivic recurrence could have done (Example 3.7a and b). Sometimes such techniques connected movements as well. Nearly all of Michael Haydn's (1737–1806) late symphonies share motives among all the movements, a procedure also found in the works of Pichl and Adalbert Gyrowetz (1763–1850) among others. Although sometimes the shared motives can seem too generic to be convincing as cyclic links, when used in combination with parallels of texture and articulation, they signal a clear connective intention on the part of the composer.[26] Beginning as early as 1771, Boccherini explored even more extreme manifestations of unity, sometimes reprising large sections of earlier movements in the later ones. The Finale of his Symphony No. 21 (G. 496) comprises a complete repetition of the first movement's recapitulation.[27] These instances should put the often cited cyclic aspects of some of Haydn's and Beethoven's symphonies in perspective. Such techniques were part of a new set of symphonic conventions just beginning to emerge at the end of the century.

Expressive choices during the later part of the century also broadened and deepened the paths laid out by earlier composers. In addition to the minor mode, composers increasingly made use of distantly related tonalities, particularly third-related or Neapolitan keys, both for brief chromatic digressions and for longer excursions away from the tonic. For example, the C major Symphony (from the 1770s or 1780s) of the Norwegian composer Johan Heinrich Berlin (1741–1807) reaches B major as the point of furthest remove

Example 3.6 Christian Cannabich, Symphony No. 73 in C major, I, bars 31–66.

Example 3.6 (cont.)

Example 3.6 (cont.)

Example 3.7a Wenzel Pichl, Symphony in F major, Op. 1/5, I, bars 1–8.

in the development section of the first movement. Often these keys were introduced as a way of subverting convention, an act which itself became an expressive choice. If you expect the development section to begin with some form of P in V, then it will come as quite a shock when a three-bar unison *fortissimo* string semibreve on ♭VII/V follows directly on the close of the exposition. This technique can be found in the first movement of one of Rosetti's most popular works, the Symphony in F major (F1), from *c.* 1776 (Example 3.8).[28] Of course, Rosetti had a fondness for this type of disruption (it is also found in the first movement of his B♭1), and once the listener begins to *expect* disruption, then its expressive value can begin to fade. But for eighteenth-century symphony

Example 3.7b Wenzel Pichl, Symphony in F major, Op. 1/5, I, bars 67–79.

composers, the trick to continuing effectiveness, whether in the use or the disruption of convention, was not in *that* you did it but in *how*. For example, Pasquale Anfossi's (1727–97) *Sinfonia* in B flat (B♭5) from 1776 has an ingenious disruption of expectations in the middle of the first movement's secondary theme. S begins quite properly in V (F major) in bar 25 with a two-bar motive repeated exactly to create a four-bar phrase ending with a V:IAC. After a crotchet rest, however, comes a jarring unison *forte* C♯ and a two-bar diversion to D minor that loses its punch and returns to a relentlessly regular eight-bar consequent in F major (Example 3.9).

The piquancy of the brief moment, however, disappears when the whole section is repeated exactly, thus regularising the disruption and robbing it of its power. On the other hand, in the first movement of J. C. Bach's Symphony in E flat, Op. 6, No. 5, the sudden appearance of D♭ unison *fortissimo* tremolos at the beginning of the development after the

Example 3.8 Antonio Rosetti, Symphony in F major (F1), I, bars 64–71.

conclusion of the exposition in B-flat major gains in effectiveness because the movement is a non-repeating sonata form. Thus, although the subsequent music absorbs it into a relatively normal progression, its initially shocking quality remains, undiminished by repetition.

Example 3.9 Pasquale Anfossi, *Sinfonia* in B flat (B♭5), I, bars 25–49.

Example 3.9 (cont.)

Conclusion

In 1713, Johann Mattheson defined a symphony as an instrumental piece without restrictions, and though he went on to describe a typical Italian opera sinfonia as having a brilliant opening movement and a dance-like finale, he made it clear that composers were entirely free to follow their own inspiration as long as the music did not thereby become chaotic.[29] As indicated above, composers did just that in the early decades of the century; for them the possibilities were – if not limitless – then excitingly vast, even if tidy modern historians might see the situation as chaotic. The extensive circulation of manuscript parts throughout Europe, however, meant that most composers were not working in isolation; as a result, by the middle of the century the symphony had begun to coalesce into a recognisable genre, with conventions governing everything from the number of movements to orchestration to formal procedures. Yet even if later eighteenth-century composers perhaps had less freedom to do what they wanted in a symphony, they gained the power that such conventions provide: a basic structure that did not have to be invented anew with each composition. With this structure ensuring intelligibility, composers could then concentrate on subtlety and nuance, delighting their listeners with small changes and surprises in each new piece. For it should be emphasised that the symphony in the eighteenth century was meant to be comprehended on the very first listening.[30] That was its true function, whether in the church, theatre or chamber, and that was what made it so successful. It requires a certain retraining of our post-Mahlerian ears to appreciate fully the artistry and feel the excitement that so enchanted eighteenth-century audiences, but once you've managed that, you may find yourself thinking, as I have over the past few years: 'so many symphonies, so little time'.

Notes

1 A sampling can be found in Barry S. Brook and Barbara Heyman, eds., *The Symphony, 1720–1840: A Comprehensive Collection of Scores in Sixty Volumes*, 60 vols. (New York, 1979–86). This collection, which is organised by geographical region, includes full scores of previously unpublished symphonies, as well as brief biographical and analytical essays on the composers included.

2 During the second half of the century, particularly in the English-speaking world, the terms 'overture' and 'symphony' were virtually interchangeable. In continental usage, the word overture tended to be reserved for works that follow the movement pattern we associate with the French overture, but it was not used in the modern sense to refer to the instrumental work preceding an opera.

3 I have also, for the moment, sidestepped the issue of redefining what constitutes historical significance, which until now has mostly been determined by a composer's 'innovations' (e.g. the first four-movement symphony) or his relationship to Haydn, Mozart and Beethoven. I address this question in the final chapter of Mary Sue Morrow and Bathia Churgin, eds., *The Symphonic Repertoire*, vol. I: *The Eighteenth-Century Symphony*, currently in preparation, to be published by Indiana University Press.

4 See Newell Jenkins and Bathia Churgin, *Thematic Catalogue of the Works of Giovanni Battista Sammartini* (Cambridge, Mass., 1976).

5 Although Italy had a long tradition of brass and violin manufacturing, it lagged far behind Northern Europe in the production of other wind instruments. See John Spitzer and Neal Zaslaw, *The Birth of the Orchestra: History of an Institution, 1650–1815* (New York and Oxford, 2004), 172–3.

6 Bathia Churgin, 'Giovanni Battista Sammartini', in *New Grove Online*, available at www.oxfordmusiconline.com, accessed 20 November 2008; Ulrich Tank, *Studien zur Esterházyschen Hofmusik von etwa 1620 bis 1790* (Regensburg, 1981), 67. In his biography of Haydn, Giuseppi Carpani asserts that Nicholas Esterházy had a standing order for new music by Sammartini. See *The Lives of Haydn and Mozart*, trans. L. A. C. Bombet, 2nd edn (London, 1818), 107–8.

7 These have sometimes been designated as 'suite symphonies'. The Italian composer Fortunato Chelleri wrote three of these, but they do not appear to have been common in Italy. See Bathia Churgin, 'Fortunato Chelleri', in Brook and Heyman, eds., *The Symphony, 1720–1840*, vol. A3, xxvii.

8 See Robert Gjerdingen, 'The Symphony in France', in Morrow and Churgin, eds., *The Eighteenth-Century Symphony*, 551–70.

9 See Simon McVeigh, 'The Symphony in Britain', in Morrow and Churgin, eds., *The Eighteenth-Century Symphony*, 629–61.

10 Josep M. Vilar i Torrens, 'The Symphony in Catalonia, *c.* 1760–1808', in Malcolm Boyd and Juan José Carreras, eds., *Music in Spain during the Eighteenth Century* (Cambridge, 1998), 157–71.

11 Bertil van Boer, 'The Symphony on the Periphery', in Morrow and Churgin, eds., *The Eighteenth-Century Symphony*, 726, citing Cleofe Person de Mattos's introductory essay for José Mauricio Nunes Garcia, *Aberturas* (Rio de Janeiro, 1982), 9–12. The work is a one-movement *Sinfonia funebre* in E-flat major.

12 Judging from the performance parts preserved in the Gesellschaft der Musikfreunde in Vienna, the strong brass presence was supported by a relatively large string ensemble with as many as twelve violins. This symphony can be found under the call number GDMF XIII 8577 and has performance dates in the 1740s and early 1750s.

13 *The Symphony, 1720–1840*, vol. D1, 1.

14 Either Johann Christoph Graupner or Johann Samuel Endler appears to have added brass parts to the strings-only symphonies of Joseph Camerloher for performance at the court in Darmstadt. See Suzanne Forsberg, 'Joseph and Placidus von Camerloher', in Morrow and Churgin, eds., *The Eighteenth-Century Symphony*, 341.

15 Sinfonia // a 4tro // Violino Primo // Violino Secondo // viola, e Basso // Del Sig. Wenceslao Reimondo Birck, ÖNB MS 3610.

16 Richter has seven fugal finales (three dating from *c.* 1760 to 1765, the others earlier), one fugue in an opening movement and one in a second, as well as a one-movement adagio-fuga 'Sinfonia da chiesa'. See Bertil van Boer, 'Franz Xaver Richter', in Brook and Heyman, eds., *The Symphony, 1729–1840*, vol. C14, xxvii–xxxviii. Although an unusually high number for the middle of the century, it is not an overwhelming one considering that he wrote eighty-three symphonies.

17 James Hepokoski and Warren Darcy, *Elements of Sonata Theory: Norms, Types, and Deformations in the Late-Eighteenth-Century Sonata* (New York and Oxford, 2006). Though the various default levels they identify do not – as should be expected – always hold for works before the middle of the century, their system can be adapted to this repertoire quite profitably.

18 See Leonard B. Meyer, *Style and Music: Theory, History, and Ideology* (Chicago, 1989), and 'Innovation, Choice, and the History of Music', *Critical Inquiry*, 3 (1983), 517–44.

19 This symphony, composed between 1750 and 1765, is for *a 4* strings and two horns, with the horns tacet in this movement (a typical procedure for the mid century).

20 Rey M. Longyear, 'Stanislao Mattei', in Brook and Heyman, eds., *The Symphony, 1720–1840*, vol. A8, x. Mattei lived from 1750 to 1825, but all his symphonies were written before 1804.

21 Heinrich Christoph Koch, *Musikalisches Lexikon* (Frankfurt, 1802, repr. Hildesheim, 1964), 1385–8.

22 J. C. Bach and Stanislao Mattei also wrote works for double orchestra.

23 Adena Portowitz, 'J. C. Bach', in Morrow and Churgin, eds., *The Eighteenth-Century Symphony*, 662–83.

24 Judith K. Schwartz, 'François-Joseph Gossec', in Morrow and Churgin, eds., *The Eighteenth-Century Symphony*, 585–626.

25 Simon McVeigh, 'The Symphony in Britain', in *The Eighteenth-Century Symphony*, 432.

26 Richard Agee notes the striking similarity of the second theme groups in Pichl's *Il marte*. See his 'Wenzel Pichl', in Brook and Heyman, eds., *The Symphony, 1720–1840*, vol. B7, liii.

27 Joseph Haydn also experimented with this type of recall in his Symphony No. 48.

28 Sterling Murray, 'Antonio Rosetti', in Brook and Heyman, eds., *The Symphony, 1720–1840*, vol. C6, xxxv. Boyer in Paris published the Symphony in 1779.

29 Johann Mattheson, *Das neu-eröffnete Orchestre* (Hamburg, 1713; repr. Laaber, 2004), 171–2.

30 Mark Evan Bonds makes this point in his *Wordless Rhetoric: Musical Form and the Metaphor of the Oration* (Cambridge, Mass., 1991).

4 The symphony after Beethoven after Dahlhaus

DAVID BRODBECK

Over the ten years or so before his death in 1989, Carl Dahlhaus returned time and again to the nineteenth-century symphony. Typifying his thinking is the following passage, which illustrates the 'quasi-narrative, "grand project"' approach that characterised Dahlhaus's historiographic style as a whole:

> The history of the symphony seems to be a history of the consequences that could be drawn from the models of the symphonic shaped by Beethoven (from the Third and Seventh symphonies, in the case of Berlioz; the Sixth, in the case of Mendelssohn; and the Ninth, in the case of Bruckner). Yet the historical development exhibits a breaking off at mid-century. Between the symphony's immediate afterlife [*Nachleben der Symphonie*] 'in the shadow of Beethoven', a circumstance of symphonic history in which extremes such as Berlioz and Mendelssohn could exist next to one another in a rare historical configuration, and a 'second age of the symphony', which ran from the 1870s to the beginning of the twentieth century, is a chasm of a quarter century that is only poorly filled by Gade, Raff, and Rubinstein. And in [this] 'dead era' of the symphony, the 'symphonic poem', which was developed by Liszt from the concert overture, emerges as the epoch-making genre of orchestral music in the grand style. Still, the break in continuity shows that in the history of the symphony ... the aesthetic presence of an overpowering tradition in the concert repertoire not only could lay the foundation for, but also take the place of, the compositional development of the genre. The former happened at the end of the century; the latter, at the middle.[1]

Dahlhaus situates Beethoven in the centre of a 'circumpolar' history of the genre. Here is no development whereby 'each step is a result of a previous one and a prerequisite of a later one'; instead, all 'significant works' are understood to stand in a direct relation to one or another of Beethoven's symphonies and to reveal little more than 'fleeting connections' with any intervening works.[2] In other words, for Dahlhaus virtually every symphony *after* Beethoven – at least every one of any historical importance – was best understood primarily *in relation to* Beethoven.

This comprehensive narrative, told with the help of a relatively small number of carefully selected works, has not gone without critical comment by Anglophone scholars.[3] But there has been nothing in Britain or the United States like the widespread critique of Dahlhaus's work that has characterised much German scholarship on the symphony during the last twenty-five years. Thanks to this body of work – and to a rash of recordings of symphonies by many of the century's lesser-known figures – we now have a much better sense of the symphonic landscape than we did before.[4] It lies well beyond the limits of the present essay to survey this vast expanse, and what I offer instead will to a large degree be a 'tale of two cities', Leipzig and Vienna. Inevitably my emphasis will fall on symphonies by German composers; still, the symphonic programmes that characterised both locales invite some consideration of symphonies by non-German composers as well. Limiting the geographical scope in this way also gives focus to questions pertaining to historical, social and political context, questions of a kind that famously find no place in Dahlhaus's *Problemgeschichte*. Yet they are well worth asking and will, in turn, raise certain doubts about his tale of the genre's slow decline, death and resurrection.[5]

After Beethoven

The late A. Peter Brown described Leipzig as the 'epicentre of symphonic compositions' in the period from the 1830s to the 1870s.[6] The presence in the city of several music publishers and important music journals, as well as one of Europe's leading conservatories, contributed to its preeminence, but pride of place in this account must fall to the Gewandhaus Orchestra. This venerable institution (founded in 1781) occupied the leading edge of a gradual trend away from the miscellaneous concert programming of the past, with its preference for 'entertaining' admixtures of instrumental and vocal pieces, concerted and solo numbers, not always played in their entirety, towards the new, more 'serious' approach that eventually came to define the modern symphony concert, with an overture and a concerto in the first half, followed, in the second, by a symphony (which gained in prominence by coming last and standing alone).[7] By the 1820s subscribers could look forward to hearing complete performances of all nine Beethoven symphonies on a regular basis; selected symphonies by Haydn and Mozart were heard frequently as well. Nevertheless, room was still found for three or four new symphonies every season.

'German music blooms so finely here', wrote Robert Schumann in his *Neue Zeitschrift für Musik*, 'that, without ignorance, our city may venture to compare its productions to those of the richest fruit and flower gardens of other cities'. He continued:

> Our concert music stands at the most brilliant summit of all. It is well known that a worthy home for German music has been secured in the now fifty-years-old Gewandhaus concerts, and that this institution accomplishes more at present than it ever did before. With a famous composer at its head, the orchestra has brought its virtuosity to still greater perfection during the last few years. It has probably no German equal in its performance of symphonies.[8]

The unnamed famous composer was Felix Mendelssohn, who conducted the orchestra from 1835 until his death in 1847. Although Mendelssohn's programmes were dominated by the music of the Viennese classical composers, he also instituted a series of 'historical concerts' (each devoted to a grouping of composers from the more distant past) and made certain to perform several contemporary works each year.[9] Within the subscription concerts, for example, Mendelssohn introduced no fewer than forty-five new symphonies, including three each by Louis Spohr (nos. 5–7), Johann Wenzel Kalliwoda (nos. 5–7) and Franz Lachner (nos. 5–7), two each by Niels Gade (nos. 1–2), Julius Rietz (nos. 1–2) and Robert Schumann (nos. 1–2), Franz Schubert's 'Great' C major Symphony and his own Symphony No. 3 ('Scottish').[10] Various benefit and extraordinary concerts provided the opportunity for introducing still other new works, including Mendelssohn's Symphony No. 2 (*Lobgesang*), Schumann's Symphony No. 4 (in its original orchestral dress from 1841), together with his *Overture, Scherzo and Finale* and, from France, Hector Berlioz's *Symphonie fantastique* and Félicien David's *Le Désert* (each conducted by its composer). Newly introduced works often were repeated in subsequent programmes; Schubert's 'Great' C major, for example, was heard twelve times during the Mendelssohn era.

In principle, the concerts of the Gewandhaus Orchestra encouraged the silent aesthetic contemplation of music, the 'selfless immersion into a music that manifested "another world"', and so performed an educative and edifying function (*Bildungsfunktion*): in such a context, as Dahlhaus notes, music was intended to be 'understood' and not merely to be 'enjoyed'.[11] Yet there was more to this than 'vintage German transcendentalism', inasmuch as the symphony was constituted 'not only aesthetically but also as a relation of nations'.[12] This distinction comes through clearly in August Kahlert's review of Mendelssohn's Symphony No. 3, introduced at the Gewandhaus on 3 March 1842 and published a year later:

> For a long time the symphonic field has indisputably belonged to the Germans . . . France and Italy, for all the trouble they take with it, do not

> understand this dream world of tones which the German has created, where
> no words are required which guide the listener's fantasy to a definite
> thought, but rather where the free forms of the tonal structures make
> themselves the law-givers.[13]

Seen in this way, then, the *Bildungsfunktion* of the symphony concert
assumes not only an aesthetic, but also a national dimension that
Dahlhaus, with his aversion to political interpretation, seems loath to
acknowledge.

Complicating this picture, however, was the *Symphonie fantastique.*
Introduced at the Gewandhaus on 4 February 1843 (and thus undoubtedly
on Kahlert's mind as he penned his review of the 'Scottish' Symphony), this
work had in fact already been the subject of considerable interest in 1835,
following the publication of Schumann's lengthy and extravagant review of
the work when it appeared in Franz Liszt's piano reduction.[14] Here (and not
for the last time) Schumann offers his take on the recent historical development of the genre: 'After *Beethoven*'s Ninth Symphony, greatest of all
instrumental works in external proportions, form and intention seemed to
have been exhausted . . . Later symphonic composers sensed this, and some
of them even took refuge in the comfortable forms of Haydn and Mozart'.[15]
Schumann goes on to list a number of more recent composers, regretting
that 'none . . . had ventured to make any significant modifications to the old
forms – if we leave aside isolated attempts such as the most recent symphony
of Spohr'.[16] He finds more to praise in Mendelssohn's development of
the concert overture as an alternative to the symphony – Schumann appears
to be unaware of the 'Italian' Symphony, performed by the London
Philharmonic Society in March 1833 and immediately withdrawn by the
composer – and then acknowledges that he had begun to doubt whether the
symphony had any future at all.

With all this as background, Schumann turns to the form of Berlioz's
first movement, so strange on the surface. 'Yet we ought always to look
at a thing on its own terms', he cautions. 'The stranger and more
ingenious a thing outwardly appears, the more carefully we ought to
judge it.' Reminding his readers that the outlines of Beethoven's music,
too, had once seemed unintelligible, he contrasts Berlioz's unorthodox
form with that of 'the earlier norm'. He provides diagrams of both, finds
nothing preferable about the latter in either variety or uniformity, and
adds, 'We only wish we possessed a truly colossal imagination and could
then pursue it wherever it goes.' Here – for all his doubts about programme music – Schumann seems to have discovered the step forward
from Beethoven that he found lacking in so much contemporary symphonic fare.[17]

Having nothing to do with this idea, by contrast, was Gottfried Wilhelm
Fink, editor of Leipzig's *Allgemeine musikalische Zeitung*. Schumann's nomi-
nation of a potential French successor to Beethoven in the realm of the
symphony was by itself an affront; even worse, the *Neue Zeitschrift für
Musik* had recently published without comment a translation of an article
from a recent French journal that made the claim that François-Joseph
Gossec had 'founded the true character of the symphony' and that Haydn
had merely been his 'successor'.[18] To this Fink responded indignantly:

> The old is vanished, and everything has begun anew. The essence, therefore
> also the concept, of the symphony has completely changed, has become
> grand; one should therefore distinguish it from the old with the name 'grand
> symphony' [*große Symphonie*]. That is its name, and the honour of having
> created it belongs exclusively to the Germans, and this honour will not be
> taken from us.[19]

Schumann probably would not have disagreed with this sentiment, the gist
of which had already appeared in E. T. A. Hoffmann's famous review of
Beethoven's Symphony No. 5 (July 1810), with its claims that the German
composer 'unveils before us the realm of the mighty and the immeasur-
able'.[20] But the two critics part company over the question of whether any
real progress in the genre might be possible beyond that achieved by
Haydn, Mozart and Beethoven (those 'three heroes of our music', as
Fink described them).[21] Again relying heavily on Hoffmann's aesthetics
of 'pure' instrumental music, the conservative Fink takes qualities such as
large dimensions, expanded forms, richness of medium and elevated ideas
that Hoffmann had extolled in Beethoven's Fifth and subsumes them all
under his notion of the grand symphony, presumably attempting to
establish in this way standards for the genre that he knew the Romantics
would find impossible to meet.[22]

A prize symphony

This critical colloquy between the editors of Leipzig's two music period-
icals provides the best context in which to examine one of the most talked-
about symphonies of the 1830s, Franz Lachner's Symphony No. 5 in C
minor (*Sinfonia passionata*), widely known as the 'Prize Symphony' by
virtue of its having won a competition for new symphonies sponsored by
the 'concerts spirituels' in Vienna in 1835.[23] Following its performance at
the Gewandhaus on 27 October 1836, both Schumann and Fink weighed
in with memorable reviews that tell us a good deal about the contemporary
state of symphonic politics.

Schumann came first and took the unusual step of pitching his remarks as a response to a story told tongue-in-cheek by his friend Wilhelm Florentin von Zuccamaglio, published under the pseudonym Gottschalk Wedel as a kind of preface to Schumann's review.[24] Here the protagonist dreams that he has written a symphony for the competition in the style of the *Symphonie fantastique*, certain that the judges would favour this 'new artistic fashion', only to awaken in a cold sweat to learn with relief that the prize had already gone instead to a proper German composer, Franz Lachner of Munich. 'Our gentle Gottschalk Wedel has worked himself into quite a rage over the Frenchman Berlioz!' begins Schumann's anonymous review.[25] He continues in jest for a few lines, but when he moves on to the music at hand, he turns serious – and unusually merciless. '[Lachner's] symphony is lacking in style', he writes, 'a mixture of German, Italian and French, comparable to Romansh.' The best comparison Schumann could find was Meyerbeer's operas, but these works – which, for Schumann, epitomised the worst of Philistine culture – certainly offered no suitable model for the elevated genre of the German symphony. The critic could forgive neither the 'sprawling breadth' (the work runs about an hour), nor the overly obvious (and overused) allusion in the first two movements to the famous rhythmic motive of Beethoven's Fifth and the associated lack of any real thematic substance. Even still, the first movement at least shows 'a kind of passion, if perhaps not the most poetical source'. Not so the Adagio, 'which ends on every page and never stops!' And with that comes the *coup de grâce*: 'Were there but uncouth blunders, formal weaknesses, excesses, then there would be something to talk about and improve, and some reason for encouragement. Here, though, one can only say things like "it is tedious", or "it will pass", or sigh, or think about something else.'

Fink took a very different stance. He begins by making a careful analysis of each movement, and though he shares some of Schumann's reservations, he nevertheless concludes, 'without fearing the slightest contradiction from connoisseurs I must therefore pronounce this symphony of Lachner's a thoroughly capable and skilful work ... The flow of ideas is natural, straightforward [*unverschnörkelt*], never tied together in confusion.'[26] Fink notes with approval that Lachner's 'inner essence of musical poetry is more like that of Haydn and Mozart than of Beethoven', and then explains the difference:

> The newer style of poetry is freer, more unbound, more passionate, fuller of movement, more colourful, more developing, in the way of a novella, in unrelated and unmotivated plot situations; at the same time the diabolical force of claws piercing into what wounded or feverishly moved humanity

has restlessly grasped, violently pushing forward toward either terrible pain or externally rushing lust. By contrast, the old style of poetry is more ordered, more honouring of [deep] thought, more internal, more reflected, more motivated, more true, giving oneself more to the deep world of emotion than to staged acts, and loving and creating at the same time joyful, human encouragement, refreshment, and uplift.[27]

Fink explicitly associates the older (one might say, classical) style with the 'Prize Symphony': '[Lachner's] passion', he writes, 'is not the so-called Romantic [passion]'. And while Fink ties the newer style to no musical work in particular, it is easy enough to associate it in a negative way with the programme of the *Symphonie fantastique* ('terrible pain', 'externally rushing lust') and the unusual music to which it gave rise. It thus seems clear enough whom the critic had in mind when he castigates those composers who falsely claim to be Beethoven's disciples and who become 'drunk on [Beethoven's] wine [only to] sing, not in exaltation but in inebriation'.[28] Who else apart from Berlioz might have inspired such imagery?

A 'new norm'

Two years later, in a review from July 1839 of recently published symphonies by Gottfried Preyer, Karl Gottlieb Reißiger and, again, Lachner (this time, the Sixth, in D major), Schumann trained his focus on a more sober group of Beethoven's disciples. He begins by placing Beethoven's symphonies at the very centre of German national identity:

> When a German speaks of symphonies he speaks of Beethoven: he considers
> the two words as one and indivisible; they are his pride and joy. Just as the
> Italian has Naples, the Frenchman has the Revolution, and the Englishman
> his merchant marine, so the German has his Beethoven symphonies.
> Because of Beethoven he forgets that he cannot boast of a great school of
> painters, and he wins in spirit the many battles forfeited to Napoleon.
> He may even dare to place Beethoven on the same plane as Shakespeare.[29]

As the critic continues, he implicitly takes note of the extent to which Beethoven's symphonies had come to dominate the public concert and so, in effect, the self-understanding of the German bourgeoisie. Yet, in what seems a clear reference to his earlier criticism of the 'Prize Symphony', he laments the failure of any living German composer to come to terms with this patrimony and to build on it meaningfully in his own music:

> We do find reminiscences – particularly, though, only of the earlier
> symphonies of Beethoven, as if each one needed a certain period before it
> could be understood – reminiscences too frequent and too strong; only

rarely do we find continuation or command of this magnificent form, where
measure after measure the ideas appear to change but are connected by an
inner spiritual bond.

After briefly mentioning Berlioz (a 'phenomenon' known more in
Germany by hearsay than by his music itself) and Schubert ('whose
accomplishments in the area of the symphony [had] not yet become
public'), Schumann turns to the works at hand. While he is fairly merciless
with Preyer and Reißiger, he treats Lachner more kindly than before. Once
again, however, Schumann chides the composer for his long-windedness,
urging him not to milk each of 'his beautiful ideas' dry, but rather to mix
them in with other 'new, ever more beautiful ones'. He concludes: 'everything as in Beethoven. And so we always come back to this godly [com-
poser] and would add nothing further today than to hope that Lachner
might move forward on the path towards the ideal of a modern symphony,
which after Beethoven's passing it is granted to us to arrange in a new
norm. Long live the German symphony, and may it blossom and thrive
anew!' The contradiction lying at the heart of this admonition is evident.
Mark Evan Bonds has suggested that for Schumann the new norm could
only be measured against the standard set by Beethoven. Yet, as Siegfried
Oechsle has noted, what the critic calls for here – beauty and diversity of
thematic-motivic invention – is not exactly what one takes to be the
defining properties of Beethoven's symphonies.[30] At all events,
Schumann had already found something close to what he was looking
for in Schubert's 'Great' C major Symphony (1825–8), which he had
'discovered' in a visit during the previous winter to the Vienna home of
Schubert's brother Ferdinand.[31] This work 'matched Beethoven's symphonies in length, drive, weight, and freshness of form but ... with
[Schubert's] special brand of expansiveness, leisureliness, lyricism, instrumental colour, and harmonic finesse'.[32] Whereas in 1835, in his review of
the *Symphonie fantastique*, Schumann could only hope that 'after
Beethoven's nine muses [Schubert] might have borne us a tenth', five
years later, in an equally remarkable review of the 'Great' C major,
Schumann could write Berlioz out of the history of the German symphony
once and for all as merely 'an interesting foreigner and madman'.[33] Here,
too, was everything that the 'Prize Symphony' had not been: in contrast to
Lachner's 'never-ending' essay, with its feeble imitations of Beethoven's
manner, stands Schubert's work, with its 'heavenly length, like a novel in
four volumes by Jean Paul', and its 'complete independence' from
Beethoven's symphonies.[34]

   The 'Great' C major led directly to Schumann's own breakthrough as a
symphonist.[35] Drafted in a scant four days in January 1841 and introduced

at the Gewandhaus to great acclaim two months later, Schumann's Symphony No. 1 ('Spring') shows a host of Schubertian influences, extending from its prominent use of a melodically similar introductory horn call to matters of tonal planning and musical rhetoric. Schumann was not alone in being swept up in the moment. Mendelssohn's 'Scottish' Symphony (many of whose themes can be described as 'songs without words') and Gade's Symphony No. 1 (largely based on the Danish composer's song 'Paa Sjølunds fagre sletter'), both of which date from the following year, likewise respond in their own way to the Schubertian model.[36]

By contrast, Dahlhaus discusses the 'Scottish' and 'Spring' symphonies – he leaves Gade's enormously popular 'Nordic' work unmentioned – entirely in terms of Beethoven, and by that measure each inevitably falls short.[37] A brief digression will help to explain why. Dahlhaus argues for a close connection between the idea of aesthetic autonomy (Hoffmann's 'pure' instrumental music) and the nineteenth century's striving to *Bildung*, that quintessentially German ideal of education leading to character formation, which 'fulfils no tangible function in everyday life', but rather, by presuming an inner detachment from the 'realm of necessity', offers a 'counter-instance' to the alienating 'functionalization of humankind'.[38] Herder's concept of *Bildung zur Menschheit*, in turn, helps to explain why Dahlhaus claims the symphony as the illustrative model of aesthetic autonomy. *Menschheit* (humanity) carries a double meaning; it refers not only to the totality of humankind, which commentators from the early nineteenth century on maintained was the symphony's rightful intended audience, but also to the humanity of the individual. With their will towards monumentality (characterised by easily grasped thematic ideas that are intimately bound to the orchestral medium and are easy to follow in their subsequent development) and dramatic teleological form – the exoteric and esoteric sides of the 'symphonic style' – Beethoven's symphonies seemed to encompass both sides of the humanity idea.[39] The composer's chamber music likewise dealt in *thematische Arbeit*, but it was only his symphonies, because of their monumentality and association with the institution of the public concert (as opposed to private musical culture), that became the musical representative of bourgeois humanitarian ideas in the sense outlined above.

But here is where, for Dahlhaus, the Romantic composers come up short. To be sure, he praises Mendelssohn's ability in the 'Scottish' Symphony to shape a successful symphonic movement through the use of lyrical themes, but these cannot give rise to an appropriately monumental edifice. By the same token, Dahlhaus draws a pointed contrast between the 'sublime uniformity' of Beethoven's Fifth and Seventh symphonies, whose ostinato themes are the vehicle for real melodic development, and the rather different uniformity that characterises Schumann's Symphony No. 1, which, because its main theme couples a motoric ostinato rhythm to a largely unchanged sequence of pitches, 'falls short of its vindicating sublimity'.[40] As Scott Burnham has noted, Schumann is faulted in this case 'for trying to be Beethovenian without fully understanding the nature of Beethoven's music'.[41]

Things look very different, however, when we let go of Dahlhaus's idea that these works constitute the dying breath of an implied 'first age of the symphony' dominated by Beethoven and the idea of the sublime, and follow Oechsle in positing Schubert's 'Great' C major Symphony and the idea of humanity (in the sense of the individual and not of the masses) as having sparked the beginning of a new era of the Romantic symphony.[42] By 1839, Oechsle argues, during a period marked by social processes of liberalisation and equalisation in which the independence of the individual was more strongly accented than before, the genre was 'ripe . . . for the reception of the revolutionary attempt to produce grand symphonic form on the basis of an "individual" that was initially absolutely unthematic and in and of itself not suited to represent the symphonic "masses"'.[43]

Dahlhaus argues that the essence of a successful symphonic movement resides in the critical 'double function of a symphonic main theme, which Beethoven elevated to the status of a rule': it was to be broken down into its constituent parts in the development only to return intact at the beginning of the recapitulation as the 'triumphant goal and result' of what had come before it.[44] But none of the works under consideration follows this 'rule'. Each begins with important cantabile material that is introduced 'outside the form' (that is, in a slow introduction) – the horn call, in the case of Schubert and Schumann; the song or song-like themes, in the case of Mendelssohn and Gade.[45] And in all four works, this material eventually recurs in the main body and even determines its form. This results in a distinctly non-Beethovenian 'epic-lyrical monumentality', whereby the symphonic structure is created, not through the dramatic working out of a main thematic idea, but rather, as Oechsle puts it, 'as a process of integration of an originally extraterritorial, individual, "capricious" subject-matter that seems strictly limited in its [symphonic] working potential'.[46]

Seen in this way, the 'Great' C major Symphony stands as the central work in a *Problemgeschichte* that is very different from Dahlhaus's conception. With the discovery of Schubert's Symphony and its 'new norm', a dike was opened through which a stream of new symphonies now might flow freely. (This is a very different metaphor, of course, from that having to do with Beethoven's shadow.) Indeed, for all its reputation as a work in which the composer 'overcomes difficulty' in the manner of the heroic Beethoven, Schumann's Symphony No. 2 in C (1846) is unthinkable in the absence of Schubert's symphony in the same key, and the same thing can be said for Gade's Second and Third symphonies (1843 and 1847).[47]

The 'dead era'

Yet Dahlhaus argues that the symphony fell into a 'crisis' around mid-century, in that some twenty years would pass following the appearance of Schumann's Symphony No. 3 (1850) before there would come another orchestral 'work of distinction that represented absolute rather than program music'.[48] With the deaths, not only of Mendelssohn and Schumann, but also, in Wagner's provocative formulation in *Opera and Drama* (1851), of the genre itself, historical development in the orchestral realm now seemed to shift to the symphonic poem, established by Liszt and marked by features such as *Mehrsätzigkeit in der Einsätzigkeit* and thematic transformation.[49] This allows Dahlhaus to dispense with the ensuing 'dead era' in the history of the older genre simply by invoking the names of the popular Gade (eight symphonies altogether), Anton Rubinstein (six) and Joachim Raff (no fewer than eleven), while leaving their music and the broader context in which it was heard entirely unexamined.[50] To do otherwise, he explains, would be to give undue weight to 'mere statistics' at the expense of 'music-historical facts' based on 'aesthetic judgments'.[51]

There is something to be gained, however, by not passing too quickly over this period. 'Serious' programming of the type that had characterised the concerts of the Gewandhaus Orchestra during the Mendelssohn era gradually took hold elsewhere.[52] Moreover, subscription concerts on the Leipzig model were established, not only in major urban centres such as Vienna, Berlin and Dresden, but in smaller towns as well. While the balance between living and dead composers in concert programmes continued to shift in favour of the latter – the music of Schubert, Schumann and Mendelssohn, after all, had now joined that of Haydn, Mozart and Beethoven in the corpus of available repertoire from the past – works by contemporary composers still held a respectable share in concert programmes, in the order of 20 to 30 per cent, depending on the locale and decade.[53]

Fearing that concerts might become too hidebound, critics used their pens to urge the inclusion of new works.[54] As a result, there was no dearth of orchestral *Novitäten* in the third quarter of the nineteenth century, which witnessed the composition, premiere or publication of approximately 500 new orchestral compositions.[55] This list includes a range of programmatic types, including such once-popular works as Johann Joseph Abert's 'Columbus' Symphony (1864), Joseph Rheinberger's four-movement 'symphonic tone painting' *Wallenstein* (1866) and Heinrich Hofmann's *Fritjof* Symphony (1874), but the lion's share consists of more-or-less traditional multi-movement symphonies. And though fully half of these works were what Grotjahn calls 'nine-day wonders' (*Eintagsfliegen*), no small number achieved status as 'short-term hits' (*kurzfristige Spitzenreitern*) and some were heard often enough over a long enough period of time to warrant her characterisation of them as 'living classics' (*lebende Classikern*).

Among the works in this last-named category are several that attest to a continuing 'Mendelssohn cult'. Heading this group is Gade's Symphony No. 4 (1850), with ninety-one performances by 1875; the composer's earlier First and Third symphonies retained their popularity as well, with fifty-five and thirty performances respectively. At eighty-nine performances during the same period, Anton Rubinstein's 'Ocean' Symphony (1851, rev. 1863, 1880), a 'characteristic' work that shows clear affinities with Mendelssohn's *Hebrides* and *Meeresstille und glückliche Fahrt* overtures, was as familiar a presence in concert programmes as Gade's Fourth.[56] Other popular works in the Mendelssohn style include Ferdinand Hiller's Symphony in E Minor (1849), inscribed with a motto from Emanuel Geibel (*Es muß doch Frühling werden*) and Julius Rietz's Symphony No. 3 in E flat (1855).

Works that date from the 1860s, of course, had a more difficult furrow to plough: they had to compete, not only with the symphonies of the Viennese Classical composers and the first generation of Romantics but also, almost as soon as they appeared, with those that came during Dahlhaus's 'second age of the symphony'. Yet even among this group, too, are several that could be heard with some frequency over the next several decades, including the Symphony No. 1 in D minor by Robert Volkmann (1863), a handful of works by Joachim Raff, as well as Max Bruch's Symphony No. 1 (1868) and Albert Dietrich's Symphony in D minor (1870), exemplifying the Mendelssohn and Schumann traditions respectively.[57]

Conspicuous by his absence here was Brahms, but this composer carried unique burdens dating back to Schumann's encomium 'Neue Bahnen' (1853), with its foretelling of a grand symphony to come from the then-unknown composer. Matters were only made worse in 1860, when, with no such work to show, Brahms instigated a public 'Manifesto' against the historical claims made on behalf of Liszt and the symphonic poem in the pages of the *Neue Zeitschrift für Musik*, which, under the editorship of Franz Brendel, beginning in 1845, had coupled a progressive, anti-Romantic stance with a denial of the continued historical viability of traditional genres such as the symphony.[58] Relatively few critics took such an extreme position, however, and there is no reason to believe that most critics – despite the occasional reproach that the main theme of this symphony or that was not 'truly symphonic' (*echt symphonisch*) – were determined to find fault with composers for failing to meet a set of standards derived from middle-period Beethoven or as codified by the likes of Fink.[59]

Indeed, the aesthetic demands of the symphony after 1850 seem on balance to have been reduced well beyond even the 'new [non-Beethovenian] norm' for which Schumann had once called. Writing about Woldemar Bargiel's Symphony in C (1860), for example, one critic noted, with no particular regret, that 'It is no "grand" work in the eminent sense that we have before us, since the "grand" in this sense, which is sometimes called the "monumental", may in our times be hard to find in the realm of art.'[60] What often comes across instead is a concept of the genre as *mittlere Musik* (music of an intermediary *niveau*), which allowed one to assume the proper attitude of a *Bildungshörer* without having to forgo simpler pleasures: one did not have to choose between art and entertainment.[61] In such an environment, composers could respond to growing market demands for new music while knowing that they were not charged to seek a place in the canon. (That Brahms carried higher ambitions – and composed accordingly – helps to explain the lukewarm reception that often greeted his challenging symphonies.)[62] Even *mittlere* works should demonstrate technical solidity, but they should steer clear of becoming overburdened with too much 'art'. Terms frequently appearing in reviews that may now seem patronising – 'pretty', 'fresh', 'interesting' – were in fact in step with listeners' expectations, while those that may now seem more favourable – 'grand', 'deep', 'monumental', 'significant' – were seldom used and then mostly as a way of negatively characterising works for their excesses in either length or instrumental forces.[63]

By the same token, originality was not essential. When one critic wrote of Hiller's *Es muß doch Frühling werden* Symphony that it was made up of motives taken from Mendelssohn, Schumann and others, this was not necessarily seen as a fault, since the work sprang from a 'refined artistic spirit' and showed 'nothing of that morbidity that attaches to almost our entire modern literature and from which the productions of even our most highly honoured younger powers cannot completely be freed'.[64] 'At all events', as Grotjahn notes, 'a workmanlike, cleanly executed "beautiful" symphony is preferred to works that expect their listeners to deal with complex contents and unusual musical effects.'[65] Many of these themes are neatly summed up in Eduard Hanslick's report on the first Viennese performance of the period's most often played work of all:

> Gade's Fourth Symphony in B flat made the most agreeable impression . . . Neither grand [*groß*] nor thrilling [*hinreißend*], but rather quite 'charming' – that's how one must call a work from which a pure spirit, a warm temperament speaks to us in moderate, exquisite locution. The limitation that the composer imposed on the themes and the extent of the movements stands the work in good stead . . . We prefer to praise works of the genuine, modest aura of the B-flat Symphony too much rather than too little in a time when hardly anyone writes an orchestral piece without the firm intent of unconditionally outdoing Beethoven.[66]

Another prize symphony

If Gade's eight symphonies extend from the age of Mendelssohn and Schumann clear through the 1860s, the eleven symphonies of Joachim Raff appeared, one every year or two, from the mid-1860s through the first decade of the genre's 'second age'. This composer claimed to follow a 'middle way' between the New German (Berlioz–Liszt) and conservative (Mendelssohn–Schumann) factions in the musical politics of the day. As Louis Köhler put it, 'he is a New German (*vulgo* "Musician of the Future") in classical guise'.[67] Thus while nine of Raff's symphonies carry a descriptive title, only the Fifth (*Lenore*), based on the famous *Sturm-und-Drang* ballad by Gottfried August Bürger, follows Liszt in having a programmatic basis in literature (*Eine Faust-Symphonie*, *Dante* Symphony, the symphonic poems). For the most part, as in the Symphony No. 3 (*Im Walde*), with its colourful delineation of the German forest, the composer aimed to realise traditional symphonic forms with the help of a scrupulous use of tone painting, an attempt 'to write programme music that shall at the same time be absolute music' that Hugo Riemann later contemptuously dismissed as 'an aesthetic lie'.[68]

Although the Symphony No. 1 (*An das Vaterland*) fell by the wayside long before either the *Im Walde* or *Lenore* symphonies, this earlier work warrants some further attention here. Evidently composed between 1859 and 1861, it was selected as the first-place winner in a competition for new symphonies announced by Vienna's Gesellschaft der Musikfreunde in April 1861. Reviewing the first performance, which took place in Vienna on 26 February 1863, Hanslick acknowledges that *An das Vaterland* contains 'ingenious and absorbing features, poetic moments and original technical experiments', but its 'affectedness, bizarrerie and floridness' made it impossible for the critic to want to hear any of its parts again.[69] He continues:

> A fiery, brilliant, very self-conscious yet sparsely productive nature works here with great exertion to get beyond Beethoven. If never-ending volubility is a character trait of the Germans, then in this respect Raff has aptly portrayed his fellow-countrymen. But the German people, who like to recognize themselves in the ideal mirror of Beethoven's symphonies, will find it difficult to feel flattered in Raff's first movement.[70]

Hanslick's comment about Raff's portrayal of the Germans was prompted by the work's programme, which the critic reproduces in full.[71] The first three movements are poetic in nature, depicting, in turn, the 'German character', 'the German forest' and the 'homely hearth'. The fourth and fifth movements, by contrast, are explicitly political: the fourth concerns the 'failed attempt to found the unity of the fatherland', symbolised by quotation of Gustav Reichardt's well-known setting of Ernst Moritz Arndt's patriotic poem 'Was ist des Deutschen Vaterland?' ('What is the German's Fatherland?'); the Finale begins with a 'lamentation' on this defeat followed, at last, by a 'renewed upswing' in the ensuing *Allegro trionfale*, symbolised by a peroration on the borrowed patriotic hymn.

In view of Hanslick's reputation as an opponent of programme music, what he makes of all this is naturally of some interest. In a review written only one month earlier, the critic had noted with approval that Rubinstein's 'Ocean' Symphony 'carries no poetic guide apart from the inscription "Ocean". The composer is liberal enough to allow our fantasy full freedom.'[72] It was precisely a lack of such freedom for the listener that irritated in the case at hand. 'It requires a fair amount of self-control', Hanslick begins, 'not to be prejudiced against [Raff's] music from the start on account of this poetic-political user's manual [*Gebrauchsanweisung*].' He continues:

> Nowadays one is no longer so Philistine as to resent the composer for every poetic stimulus or hint; but one is already, thank God, over and above a musical hair-splitting [*Musikdeutelei*] of such exactness. For whom the motto ('An das Vaterland') or the simple inscription 'Germany' is not sufficient, to him it will also be of no avail if Herr Raff has distributed the complete *Allgemeine Zeitung* from the year 1848 'for a better understanding'. In the entire symphony, a direct connection to the political program is presented only by the melody of the 'German's Fatherland', whose appearance, rising, suppression, and extinguishing moreover contain a palpable symbolism.[73]

Raff was not thinking solely about the failed revolution of 1848 and the dashed hopes of German national unity, however, but was also looking ahead. In the foreword to the first edition of the score, he reports that he had set to work on the Symphony under the first impression of the Armistice of Villafranca (1859), which ended active hostilities between the combined Franco-Italian forces of the Second Empire and the Kingdom of Piedmont–Sardinia and those of Francis Josef's Austrian Empire. As a result, Austria lost most of her Italian holdings and impetus was given to the movement towards Italian unification. These developments were not without ramifications elsewhere, and in the same year leading German liberal nationalists met in Frankfurt to form the *Deutsche Nationalverein* with the goal of unifying the German states in the *kleindeutsch* solution under Prussian leadership. Meanwhile, traditional Austrian hopes for hegemony in Germany under a *großdeutsch* solution were beginning to fade, and this may explain why Hanslick made no mention of the peroration of 'Was ist des Deutschen Vaterland' coming at the end (the symbolism in that omission is palpable). However that may be, Wolfram Steinbeck seems on the right track when he posits *An das Vaterland* as one of the first truly national symphonies: 'That it is a German work, what is more, that is locked into a concrete (and at that time moving) historical situation is remarkable. The universal claim of the symphony is destroyed through the particularly national subject matter.'[74] But while Europeans had long identified and accepted the symphony as being a German art – the enormous prestige of Beethoven had seen to that – Raff's Symphony No. 1 was more than simply a national work; it was a self-consciously nationalist one.

The national symphony outside the German cultural sphere

The rise of important national schools, both to the east in Russia and to the west in France, is a defining feature of music history in the later decades of the century. (The situation in Bohemia stands somewhat apart on account of its close historical–cultural relations with Austria and *Mitteleuropa* more generally.) In Russia, the first symphonies by Mily Balakirev, Aleksandr Porfirevich Borodin and Nikolai Rimsky-Korsakov date from the 1860s. There was a certain paradox in the timing of this development, coming as it did in the wake of the 'death of the symphony' and the transferral of the symphonic style into a new genre, the symphonic poem, that was seemingly more amenable to nationalist musical discourse. As Andreas Wehrmeyer has noted:

> While, on the one hand, the 'Balakirev Circle' felt itself bound to the New German School, to its progressive harmonic thinking, its inclination to

profile the national and the exotic, it wanted, on the other hand, to reconstruct its turning to the symphonic poem, to the programmatic, to the opening up of formal principles – in fact there was a belief in the sublimity and along with that in the future of the traditional symphony, which it was valid for Russia to develop according to national inflections.[75]

Among the members of the 'Mighty Handful' (*moguchaya kuchka*), Beethoven exercised a strong hold and provided a powerful model for cultural accreditation.

What for these composers was not valid, however, were the earlier accomplishments in the genre by their fellow Russian Anton Rubinstein, whose affinities with Mendelssohn in his early symphonies, among other works, made him unacceptably 'German'. (That Rubinstein was born a Jew probably should not be overlooked either in explaining the antipathy towards him.) Reviewing a St Petersburg performance of the 'Ocean' Symphony in 1869, for example, Borodin claimed: 'Here, as in most other works by Rubinstein, is shown this same repetition of banalities of a routine à la Mendelssohn. One finds in the ideas the same paltriness and shortness of breath, the same lack of colour in the instrumentation, the same conventional symmetry in the formal construction.'[76]

Tchaikovsky, by contrast, was an admirer of the 'Ocean' Symphony and, more fundamentally, shared Rubinstein's openness to Western principles of form. His Fourth, Fifth and Sixth symphonies, of course, are staples of the standard repertory. The Fourth (1878) provides Dahlhaus with an example of how, in the 'second age of the symphony', a composer who employed un-Beethovenian materials could nevertheless create a large-scale symphonic form by adopting techniques from the symphonic poem. (This work and Dahlhaus's assessment of it are considered again in Chapter 9.) The 'fate motive' played by the horn and trumpet at the outset appears at first to function as an introduction. By using the same theme to initiate the recapitulation, Dahlhaus argues, the composer contravenes Beethovenian norms by transferring it from an introductory to a formally constitutive role, thereby creating a 'monumentality that remains a decorative façade unsupported by the internal form of the movement'.[77] Yet Schumann's Symphony No. 1 (a work that Tchaikovsky was known to have admired) likewise opens, as we have seen, with a somewhat similar horn call that is originally presented 'outside the movement' and eventually becomes integrated into the form as a whole. Seen in this way, Tchaikovsky's work provides another example of the 'epic–lyrical monumentality' that characterised an important group of symphonic works from the 1840s and so suggests a continuous historical development that is at odds with Dahlhaus's dialectical model.[78]

A handful of major French composers likewise took up the genre during these years (two examples each by Charles Gounod, Georges Bizet and Camille Saint-Saëns, with numerous echoes of Beethoven, Mendelssohn and Schumann), but operatic hegemony in France made this something of a thankless task, as did the overwhelming preference for older, mostly German repertoire in the programmes of the Société des Concerts du Conservatoire, Société de Sainte-Cécile and Jules Pasdeloup's Concerts Populaires de Musique Classique. Moreover, although the composition of a 'school symphony' (*symphonie d'école*) formed a student's capstone requirement at the Conservatoire, the genre itself was held in no special high regard.[79]

It took military humiliation at German hands in the Franco-Prussian War (1870–1) to begin to turn matters around. The Société Nationale de Musique was founded on 25 February 1871 by Saint-Saëns and a number of other composers with the patriotic 'intention to let French instrumental music speak for itself in a language of its own'.[80] Yet under its motto *ars gallica*, the Society in fact 'fostered the most thoroughgoing Germanification (or "New-Germanification") French music ever endured', as Richard Taruskin has wryly put it, whose 'chief concern was to prove that the Germans, with their absolute music, had no lock on "lofty musical aims"'. The task, then, was nothing less than to produce a body of non-programmatic orchestral and chamber music designed 'to rival the German and even surpass it in its demonstrative profundity of content'.[81]

In the event, however, it was the music of Berlioz and Wagner, respectively, that was more likely to be included in the orchestral programmes of the newly founded Concerts Colonne (1873) and Concerts Lamoureux (1881). Not until the later 1880s did the 'New-Germanified' French symphony really come into its own. Saint-Saëns's 'Organ' Symphony (1886), Vincent d'Indy's *Symphonie sur un chant montagnard français* (1886), César Franck's Symphony in D minor (1886–8) and Ernest Chausson's Symphony in B flat (1889–90) – these works share a number of features, none more prominent (nor more important in the effort to establish 'lofty aims' along New German lines) than cyclic form, characterised by the dramatic return of material from one movement to another, thematic transformation and a variety of other formal experiments.

Symphonic politics in Vienna

These same years saw Vienna reclaim the status it had ceded to Leipzig in the 1830s as the most important centre of symphonic activity in the

German cultural sphere. In 1860 the Wiener Philharmoniker formally established a regular subscription series and elected Otto Dessoff as their conductor. Dessoff was followed, in 1875, by Hans Richter, who conducted the group over the last quarter of the century, during what one commentator has called its 'golden era'.[82] Most programmes contained at least one newer work, and nearly every season offered at least one premiere, most notably Johannes Brahms's Second and Third symphonies (1877 and 1883, respectively) and Anton Bruckner's Symphony No. 8 (1892). The opening of a new home for the Gesellschaft der Musikfreunde in 1870 further shaped the city's musical life; in its magnificent Großer Musikvereinssaal were given not only the Philharmonic's concerts, but also those of the Society's own series of choral and orchestral programmes, which included the first Viennese performances of Brahms's Symphony No. 1 (1876) and Bruckner's Second and Third symphonies (1876 and 1877, respectively).

The familiar Brahms–Bruckner polemics of the day not only reflected a fundamental aesthetic disagreement – over the relative merits of 'rational elaboration' (Brahms) versus 'inspired invention' (Bruckner) – but also fell out along a growing political fault line within Vienna's bourgeoisie.[83] Brahms's tradition-orientated style suited the taste of Vienna's older *Bildungsbürgertum*; indeed, as Margaret Notley has suggested, it seemed actually to project the typically middle-class values of logical thinking, self-restraint and accomplishment earned through hard work. Significantly, the cultural outlook of these 'commercial, industrial, academic, professional meritocrats', as Ernst Gellner put it, still reflected much of the liberal nationalist ideology of 1848.[84] For this social stratum, which included a disproportionate number of Jews, Germanness was not a birthright, but something that could theoretically be acquired by any ambitious *Bürger* through a conscious embracing of liberal cultural values such as education and property ownership. If this side of the cultural divide could make little sense of Bruckner's sprawling symphonies, which seemed to be more a matter of emotional outpouring than of intellectual control, it was precisely that aspect of the music (along with Bruckner's avowed worship of Wagner) which appealed to those musicians and music critics who reflected the more ethnically delineated German nationalist sentiment that began to form among younger segments of the bourgeoisie in the 1880s. Along with this form of German nationalism came a new *völkisch* cultural critique, whereby essentialist 'German' and 'non-German' traits were opposed in a set of binary oppositions that always privileged the former against an (implied liberal and Jewish) 'other': idealism as opposed to materialism; inwardness as opposed to superficiality; morality as opposed to intellect; rural as opposed to urban; and so on.[85] From this time forward, German identity became a matter of contention in the reception of new symphonies (that most German of genres).

Brahms's long-awaited emergence as a symphonist – and with a work that invited comparison with Beethoven's Ninth and was even dubbed 'The Tenth Symphony' – drew from Wagner a predictably vitriolic response, expressed in a series of essays published in the *Bayreuther Blätter*.[86] Of particular interest are Wagner's biting comments in the essay 'On the Application of Music to Drama' regarding the 'symphony compositions' of Brahms and other composers of the 'Romantic-Classical school'. No composer other than Beethoven is mentioned by name but the inferences are clear. All but Brahms were Jews and none was shown in a favourable light. After dismissive allusions to Anton Rubinstein's 'programmatic oceanic birds' ('Ocean' Symphony), Joseph Joachim's 'Hungarian' Concerto and Felix Mendelssohn's 'Scottish' Symphony, Wagner comes at last to the 'sterling symphonist disguised in a *Numero Zehn*' and with that to a less opaque style, so as not to be misunderstood:

> We cannot believe that instrumental music has been assured of a thriving future by the creations of its latest masters . . . [Instead of] unthinkingly assigning these works to the Beethovenian legacy . . . we should come to realize the completely un-Beethovenian things about them. And that ought not to be too difficult, considering how unlike Beethoven they are in spirit.

And this was especially true, Wagner held, in the case of the absolute symphony, which took on a 'clammy cast of melody' that had been inappropriately transplanted from the chamber into the concert hall: 'What had been fixed up as quintets and the like was now served up as symphonies. Paltry "melody-chaff", comparable to a mixture of hay and old tea . . . '

These essays gave intellectual 'cover' to a future strand of anti-Semitic musical discourse (while setting a precedent for lumping Brahms in with the Jews).[87] At the same time, they gave new life to old notions of the *große Symphonie* and sowed doubts about the generic propriety of the Romantic symphony, above all in terms of its themes, which were seen to fall short of the 'truly symphonic'.[88] Although, as suggested earlier, it is easy to overstate the importance of this kind of essentialist thinking in the reception of new works introduced in the years following Wagner's mid-century pronouncement of the death of the symphony, it seemed to take an especially strong hold in the 1880s and 1890s among Vienna's Wagnerian critics.[89] Brahms had more powerful champions in the liberal press, especially Hanslick, but even in this quarter certain doubts about his symphonic style occasionally came to the surface.[90]

Still, it is important to stress that the symphony was not inevitably a high-stakes affair. Consider the case of Robert Fuchs, a genuinely popular composer with Viennese audiences who, with two symphonies, several orchestral serenades and a piano concerto under his belt by the end of the 1880s, was heard as often in the Philharmonic's subscription concerts as any other living composer apart from Brahms himself. Fuchs's breakthrough as a symphonist came in November 1884 with the premiere of the Symphony No. 1, Op. 37. To be sure, for the critic Theodor Helm (a recent convert to Bruckner's cause and clearly reflecting the Wagnerian line described above), this was little more than a 'very pretty, charming work'; its main theme, he acknowledged, was 'truly symphonically conceived', but overall the composition left him with 'the feeling that Fuchs's creative power [was] insufficient for the wide scope of a grand symphony'.[91] Yet Hanslick (echoing the sentiments expressed a quarter of a century earlier in his review of Gade's Fourth) offers a considerably different take:

> New forms, unimagined revelations are not to be expected – 'Nature would burst', says Schumann, if she wanted to produce nothing but Beethovens. Fuchs deserves praise for demanding none of this straining from [his symphony] and ventures none of that vigorous storming of the heavens from which most young composers come home with bloody heads. He proceeds with sureness and grace within the boundaries of his amiable talent and writes in a naturally flowing way, with an uncorrupted sense of the beauty of the form and of the sound.[92]

What evidently mattered to this important critic – and, no doubt, to the majority of the orchestra's well-heeled subscribers – was that the composer had set his sights on expressing the beautiful, not the sublime. As for Brahms, he described the Symphony as Fuchs's 'best larger work, and far better, more buoyant, and polished than I ever expected . . . He carries on in such a cosy, intimate way.'[93]

Cosiness and intimacy is not what one associates with Bruckner's symphonies, of course. Owing to Hanslick's opposition, these were largely kept off the Philharmonic's subscription programmes throughout the 1880s, and it fell to the Vienna Academic Wagner Society to keep Bruckner the symphonist in the public eye.[94] It was, after all, easy enough to associate Bruckner with the deceased 'Master' (despite the latter's limited interest in the former). In part, this had to do with certain musical similarities involving outward features such as size and scope, instrumentation and harmonic language. But, as Thomas Leibnitz has argued, Bruckner's devotees seem to have recognised a certain spiritual kinship between the music of the two, in that both 'demanded total devotion from the listener', although not of the critical, rational sort required fully to apprehend the work of Brahms.[95] On the contrary, Bruckner's symphonies, in the Wagnerian manner, 'aroused a state of overwhelming feeling that brought listening into the vicinity of a mystical and cultic experience' – a far cry indeed from the bourgeois sensibilities of the Philharmonic's patrons.[96]

Not until 21 March 1886, with the Symphony No. 7, did the Philharmonic's subscribers have the opportunity to hear a Bruckner symphony in its entirety. (No doubt the orchestra was responding here at least in part to the recent breakthrough performances of this work in Leipzig and Munich.) The Vienna Academic Wagner Society afterwards presented Bruckner with a laurel wreath inscribed 'To the German symphonist, Master Anton Bruckner, in faith and veneration'.[97] In an earlier time, of course, the expression 'German symphonist' would have amounted to a tautology, but in the politicised environment of the moment, it carried pointed meaning among the Viennese Wagnerians, as suggested above. Yet the liberal critics Hanslick (who likened the work to a 'symphonic boa-constrictor'), Gustav Dömpke (who asserted that 'Bruckner composes like a drunkard') and Max Kalbeck (who described the work as 'no more than an impromptu comedy') found less flattering ways to characterise the composer and his music, and Bruckner disappeared once more from the subscription concerts.[98] Dahlhaus termed this period 'one of the sorriest chapters in the history of music criticism', although he might have noted that Bruckner could at least count on the strong support of Helm, critic for the German-nationalist *Deutsche Zeitung*.[99] Moreover, by 1890, when the composer's symphonies finally began to appear regularly in the Philharmonic's programmes, Helm had been joined by a new, younger breed of national–liberal (and anti-Semitic) critics who published in the newly established *Deutsches Volksblatt* (1889) and *Ostdeutsche Rundschau* (1890), for whom Bruckner represented nothing less than the Aryan ideal of a symphonic composer.[100]

Was ist deutsch?

Far removed from this Aryan ideal, but enjoying a place at the very centre of late Hapsburg musical culture, was Carl Goldmark, best known for *The Queen of Sheba*, which opened at the Vienna Court Opera on 10 March 1875. Goldmark's debut as a symphonist came one year later, on 5 March 1876, when the Philharmonic players introduced *Ländliche Hochzeit* (*Rustic Wedding*), a colourful symphony in five suite-like movements that likewise was highly popular in its day.[101] Our concern here, however, is with the composer's less well-known Symphony No. 2, heard in the Philharmonic concerts on 26 February 1888, during a period when Viennese anti-Semitism, in a new racialist manifestation, was beginning to gather some political force, and in particular with the work's reception by the critic Ludwig Speidel, who, along with Hanslick, was the most influential of Vienna's liberal critics.

'With Goldmark', notes Speidel, 'the East is doubly present: by birth and heritage; he is Hebrew and Hungarian, Jew and gypsy'. He continues:

> Apart from his *Queen of Sheba*, where Judaism is local colour, in his earlier instrumental works there welled up from time to time quite melancholic, anxious, strangely crimped melodies, which stemmed from the synagogue or his own strained disposition. In . . . his symphony, this inclination toward the Orient is set aside; not even so much as a trace of dialect is left over.[102]

For Speidel, the supposed lingering influence in the opera of Goldmark's traditional Jewish upbringing was unseemly, too redolent of the ghetto, and the critic is only too happy to note how, in the new symphony, no trace of this aspect of the composer's heritage can be detected.[103]

There could be no denying, by contrast, that the second movement, marked by two outbursts in the *verbunkos* style, looks towards the other side of Goldmark's Eastern heritage. Yet this was a matter of no special dismay; after all, as Speidel notes, Haydn, Beethoven and Schubert had long ago incorporated gypsy music 'as an interesting province into the empire of German music'. (The implication, of course, is that a musical style that might somehow reflect *Ostjudentum*, with its assumed religious obscurantism, was fundamentally incompatible with that empire.) And with that, the critic turns happily from the subject of Goldmark's Eastern heritage to his firm embrace of liberal German culture:

> [The symphony] is German in its invention and certainly German in its aesthetic rendering. The first movement is in both respects the most outstanding, with a peacefully and nobly performed main idea, in which the capacity for development and advancement is distinctly marked. Only with the development, however, is it shown what a devil of a theme this had been in the first place. The composer reduces it with passionate energy into its constituents, and as if from a witch's cauldron it rises again to its initial beauty.

The end of this passage almost reads like an account of a Beethovenian sonata form, and it clearly recalls Dahlhaus's notion of a Beethovenian 'rule' regarding the 'double function' of a symphonic main theme as something to be broken down in the development and then triumphantly recombined at the outset of the recapitulation. Thus, striking as Speidel's comments about oriental inclinations and musical imperialism may be, what seems really at stake for him is to establish Goldmark's *German* credentials. The Jew has been assimilated; the gypsy, colonised; the German, celebrated. And we have no reason to think that Goldmark – who utterly embraced a German cultural identity – would have objected.[104]

Antonín Dvořák, by contrast, would never have counted himself among the Germans, but that did not stop Hanslick, the Czech composer's greatest Viennese champion, from writing about his music as though he did.[105] Hanslick's determination to treat Dvořák as an acculturated German betrays, of course, his continuing commitment to traditional liberal nationalist ideology. The younger Helm, by contrast, who came of age in the 1860s, after the Czech national movement had begun to threaten traditional German prerogatives in Bohemia, tended to see dif-ference based in ethnicity where Hanslick did not.[106] And among those still-younger critics of the *Deutsches Volksblatt* and *Ostdeutsche Rundschau* who evince the radical ideology of pan-Germanism in their work, we see the tendency to denigrate both the Jews and the Czechs, treated more or less interchangeably as aliens within the German nation and enjoying undue favourable treatment under the Hapsburg state.

The critical response to Dvořák's Symphony No. 8, heard in the Philharmonic series on 3 January 1891, illustrates every aspect of this complex picture. Whereas Hanslick writes favourably about the work, Helm looks disparagingly at Dvořák's 'addiction to Slavic national com-position'.[107] This last remark pales, however, in comparison to the over-the-top rhetoric employed by Camillo Horn (a German Bohemian) in his review for the *Ostdeutsche Rundschau*.[108] Much of this scathing account consists of a gloss on Hanslick's review, in which the *deutschnational* critic interweaves passages adapted from that account with his own caustic commentary. Horn then takes wider aim at the liberal critic as a 'foreign' representative of the despised supranational monarchy:

> As in everything else so also unfortunately in the essence of art do we see the striving of the state and of the Germans, or, to put it better, of those who want to be numbered among them, to rear the Slavs and Jews to the detriment of their own people. Thus . . . Dvořák received a state stipend long before Bruckner; but what is Dvořák next to a Bruckner?

Here Horn treats Hanslick (whose mother was a baptised Jew) not as a fellow German but as one 'who wanted to be numbered among them'. And this 'imposter' had not only sat on the state commission that awarded the Slavic composer several stipends in the 1870s, but was also largely respon-sible for impeding Bruckner's fortunes in the Imperial capital. To a pan-Germanist like Horn, then, the critic of the *Neue freie Presse* was an almost irresistible target – as both a Jew (however Hanslick might have thought of himself) and a powerful representative of the hated liberal nationalist elite, and as both an opponent of an unjustly neglected *echt* German composer and a champion of an unworthy Slavic one. Just how unworthy becomes clear, finally, in the essay's concluding lines, wherein, by likening Dvořák to Meyerbeer, Horn in effect condemns him as a Jew:

> Dvořák, who ... might appropriately be called the Bohemian Meyerbeer, is only original where he is Slavic; but where he is Slavic he is for the most part vulgar ... [If only] our artists were national, then that and much else would be better. Will this ever happen? We can only hope!

Although coarse rhetoric of this kind is scarcely representative of Viennese society as a whole, much less of the elite that retained its hold over the institutions of culture, it cannot escape notice that the 1890s, which saw Karl Lueger's Christian Social Party rise to municipal power on an openly anti-Semitic appeal, marked the securing at last of a firm place in the Philharmonic's repertoire for Bruckner, capped by the triumphant premiere of the Symphony No. 8 on 18 December 1892. Subscribers trickled out of the hall after each of the movements (Hanslick himself before the Finale), but this evidence of discomfort on the part of the city's 'meritocrats' only encouraged the large crowd of some 300 Bruckner partisans, including many students with pan-German sympathies who gathered in the standing room and gallery of the Großer Musikvereinssaal. Writing this time in the *Deutsches Volksblatt*, Horn praised the 'German feeling and thinking, which endowed the second movement that the composer himself had christened "the German Michael", with eloquent expression', while the composer's triumph stimulated an anonymous writer for the *Ostdeutsche Rundschau* to enthuse in a manner worthy of Wagner himself: 'What makes Bruckner so valuable a musician is his unconscious recognition of the true mission of music, namely the direct illustration of the primordial shaping, destroying, conflicting world-feeling-elements.'[109] An account less apt to describe the music of Brahms, not to speak of Fuchs, Goldmark or Dvořák, is difficult to imagine.

Epilogue

In September 1898, Hans Richter abruptly resigned the position he had held for more than twenty years as director of the concerts of the Vienna Philharmonic and was replaced by Gustav Mahler, then entering his second season as director of the Imperial Court Opera.[110] The presence in Lueger's Vienna of a thriving anti-Semitic press meant that Mahler's status as a Jew (despite the baptism he had recently undergone in order to work at the court) would not go unmentioned in discussions of his work in these two key appointments. The *Deutsche Zeitung* pulled no punches: 'In our view, in a German city only a *German* appears qualified to interpret German music, [and this is] a condition that Mahler is just not able to fulfill'.[111] Nevertheless, in an era in which Jews dominated Vienna's public life more than ever, the power and influence that Mahler exercised as head of both the Court Opera and the Philharmonic concerts was beyond question, and despite all the controversy he engendered (much of it having little to do with anti-Semitism), Mahler was undoubtedly 'one of the city's few authentic celebrities, with many more admirers than detractors'.[112]

In one sense, Mahler's association with the Wiener Philharmoniker reminds us of our starting point. As had been the case sixty years earlier with Mendelssohn and the Gewandhaus Orchestra, once again we find a composer of the first rank in a position of leadership of a pre-eminent orchestral series. Like those of Mendelssohn, Mahler's programmes were dominated by the music of Beethoven but also included selected symphonies by Haydn and Mozart as well as works by Schubert, Schumann and Mendelssohn himself. To this established canon was added music by the recently deceased Brahms (including the Second and Third symphonies) and Bruckner (abridged versions of the Fourth, Fifth and Sixth symphonies). On the other hand, the once-popular Fuchs now lost his place entirely in the orchestra's repertoire, while Goldmark and Dvořák, the other two living favourites of the Richter era, were represented only by shorter, non-symphonic works (mostly concert overtures and other programmatic compositions). To be sure, Mahler widened the orchestra's repertoire by conducting its first performances of a number of other compositions from the preceding half-century, including Liszt's *Festklänge*, Hermann Goetz's Symphony in F, César Franck's *Variations symphoniques*, as well as pieces by Bizet, Tchaikovsky and Smetana. But apart from Richard Strauss's *Aus Italien*, the only 'modernist' works that were heard during Mahler's time at the orchestra's helm were two symphonies of his own, the Second, in the annual Nicolai benefit concert, in April 1899, and the First, in a subscription concert in November 1900.

In April 1901 Mahler resigned his position as director of the Philharmonic concerts after only three turbulent seasons.[113] Although his symphonies remained a notable presence on Viennese concert bills for several years thereafter – each of the first seven was heard at least once in the Imperial city between 1902 and 1909; the Ninth received its première there posthumously in 1912 – it cannot be said that any of these works went down especially well with the largely conservative

Viennese audiences, nor with many of the city's music critics.[114] By the turn of the century, Vienna was gripped by the same 'suspicion of new music', as William Weber has put it, that now characterised public concert life more generally. Unfamiliar works of any kind – still more those of the 'modernist' stripe – were anathema to audiences, and most critics were quick to denounce new music 'in and of itself'.[115] To be sure, Mahler could always count on support from a vocal minority of mostly younger listeners. Moreover, certain liberal critics such as Richard Heuberger, Max Kalbeck and Julius Korngold, Hanslick's successor at the *Neue freie Presse*, consistently accorded the composer a measure of guarded respect, despite their aesthetic misgivings.[116] After all, if the aesthetic core of the earlier Bruckner–Brahms debate had had to do with the relative merits of 'inspired invention' as opposed to 'logical elaboration', then it is easy enough to see how Mahler's characteristic (and virtuosic) technique of breaking down his tunes into their constituent motives and then recombining them in ever new melodic and contrapuntal patterns would now have its appeal for the same critics who had always supported Brahms at Bruckner's expense.[117] Yet at a time when even Brahms's works were only now becoming an 'easier sell' in Vienna, we can scarcely wonder at the puzzlement caused by Mahler's symphonies, with their unheard-of dimensions, idiosyncratic formal designs and many stylistic discontinuities (which the composer made all the more puzzling by resolutely refusing to 'explain' them by means of a programme).

Hanslick was in attendance at the Philharmonic's performance of the Symphony No. 1 in 1900. Like Kalbeck and the other younger liberal critics mentioned above, he seems to have *wanted* to give the composer's work its due, yet he scarcely knew how to go about it. (For once, he regretted the absence of a programme that might show the way.) In conveying this state of affairs, the aging critic began with a brief anecdote and ended with a frank acknowledgment of his own limitations:

> 'One of us must be crazy and it is not I!' This is how two stubborn scholars ended a long argument. It probably is I, I thought with genuine modesty, after recovering from the horrific Finale of Mahler's D major Symphony. As a sincere admirer of the conductor Mahler, to whom the Opera and the Philharmonic Orchestra are so deeply indebted, I do not want to be hasty in my judgement of his strange symphony. On the other hand I owe sincerity to my readers and thus must sadly admit that the new symphony is the kind of music which for me is not music .... At a future performance of the symphony, I hope to be able to expand this brief review, which here is more confession than judgement. At present I lack a full appreciation of what at times this most intelligent composer also lacks: 'the grace of God'.[118]

Several years later Mahler would find himself in a somewhat similar situation after hearing the first performance of Arnold Schoenberg's taut, one-movement Chamber Symphony, Op. 9, given at the Musikverein on 8 February 1907. In a public display of his own guarded respect for the younger composer, Mahler came to Schoenberg's defence as the expected hue and cry broke out in the hall, just as he had done three days earlier when a similar scene erupted during the premiere of Schoenberg's First String Quartet.[119] But, like Hanslick, he could only go so far in his own appreciation. 'I don't understand his music', Mahler confessed afterwards to his wife, Alma, 'but he's young and perhaps he's right. I am old and I dare say my ear is not sensitive enough.'[120]

The very notion of a 'chamber symphony', something that Brahms but certainly not Wagner might have imagined (although Schoenberg's work was indebted to both), is clearly at odds with concepts such as the symphonic style and monumentality. At the same time, it is emblematic of what Dahlhaus characterises as 'a shift in accent in the system of musical genres' that took place in the early twentieth century in the transition from musical modernism to the New Music: in a 'tricky dialectics' (*vertrackte Dialektik*), chamber music – that erstwhile 'reserve of conservatives who clung to the old because they were baffled by the new' – now displaced the Lisztian symphonic poem and Wagnerian music drama as the principal means of 'progressive' musical expression.[121] But when Dahlhaus goes on to argue that the symphony as represented by Bruckner and Mahler had formed a 'quasi-neutral' genre in the party polemics at the turn of the century we have reason once again to take pause.[122] In Vienna, at any rate, the highly charged question of who counted as German was never far from the surface in any critical account of that most 'German' of genres.

Notes

1 Carl Dahlhaus, *Die Musik des 19. Jahrhunderts* (Laaber, 1980), 65. I take my characterisation of Dahlhaus's historiographic method from James Hepokoski, 'The Dahlhaus Project and Its Extra-Musicological Sources', *19th-Century Music*, 14/3 (1991), 238–9, n. 3. Hepokoski was prompted in part by the recent publication of *Die Musik des 19. Jahrhunderts* in an English translation: *Nineteenth-Century Music*, trans. J. Bradford Robinson (Berkeley and Los Angeles, 1989). Unless otherwise indicated, however, I provide my own translations. I am grateful to Professor Hepokoski, as well as to Walter Frisch and Sanna Pederson, for their comments on earlier versions of this essay.

2 Dahlhaus, *Die Musik des 19. Jahrhunderts*, 125.

3 See, for example, Sanna Pederson, 'On the Task of the Music Historian: The Myth of the Symphony after Beethoven', *Repercussions*, 2 (1993), 5–30.

4 Enormously helpful, too, are the three instalments in A. Peter Brown's *Symphonic Repertoire* series devoted to the nineteenth and early twentieth centuries (excluding Beethoven and Schubert), which together run to nearly 3,000 pages. See A. Peter Brown, *The Symphonic Repertoire*, vol. III, Part A: *The European Symphony ca. 1800–ca. 1930: Germany and the Nordic Countries* (Bloomington, 2007); A. Peter Brown and

Brian Hart, *The Symphonic Repertoire*, vol. III, Part B: *The European Symphony ca. 1800–ca. 1930: Great Britain, Russia, and France* (Bloomington, 2008); and A. Peter Brown, *The Symphonic Repertoire*, vol. IV: *The Second Golden Age of the Viennese Symphony: Brahms, Bruckner, Dvořák and Selected Contemporaries* (Bloomington, 2003).

5 For a thoughtful overview that is focussed more than I am here on matters of musical style, see James Hepokoski, 'Beethoven Reception: The Symphonic Tradition', in *The Cambridge History of Nineteenth-Century Music*, ed. Jim Samson (Cambridge, 2001), 424–59. As implied by its title, this article is largely accepting of Dahlhaus's model, but this is developed in quite a nuanced reading.

6 Brown, *The European Symphony from ca. 1800 to ca. 1930: Germany and the Nordic Countries*, 28.

7 For a thorough and most useful study of changing concert-programming practices in this regard, see William Weber, *The Great Transformation of Musical Taste: Concert Programming from Haydn to Brahms* (Cambridge, 2008), esp. 169–207. See also Rebecca Grotjahn, *Die Sinfonie im deutschen Kulturgebiet 1850 bis 1875: Ein Beitrag zur Gattungs- und Institutionengeschichte* (Sinzig, 1998), 102–7 and Antje Pieper, *Music and the Making of Middle-Class Culture: A Comparative History of Nineteenth-Century Leipzig and Birmingham* (Basingstoke, 2008), 105–10.

8 Robert Schumann, 'Musikleben in Leipzig während des Winters 1839–40', *Neue Zeitschrift für Musik*, 12 (1840), 139, trans. in Brown, *The European Symphony from ca. 1800 to ca. 1930: Germany and the Nordic Countries*, 4–5.

9 The standard reference is Alfred Dörffel, *Geschichte der Gewandhausconcerte zu Leipzig*, 2 vols. (Leipzig, 1884).

10 For a complete listing of new repertoire from 1801 to 1881, see Brown, *The European Symphony from ca. 1800 to ca. 1930: Germany and the Nordic Countries*, 9–23 (Tables I/4–I/9).

11 Dahlhaus, *Die Musik des 19. Jahrhunderts*, 41.

12 The first quotation is taken from Pieper, *Music and the Making of Middle-Class Culture*, 63; the second, from Sanna Pederson, 'A. B. Marx, Berlin Concert Life, and German National Identity', *19th-Century Music*, 18/2 (1993), 89. For discussion of the symphony as a 'German' genre, see Mark Evan Bonds, *Music as Thought: Listening to the Symphony in the Age of Beethoven* (Princeton and Oxford, 2006), 88–91.

13 A[ugust] K[ahlert], *Allgemeine musikalische Zeitung*, 45 (1843), col. 341.

14 Robert Schumann, Review of Berlioz, *Symphonie fantastique*, *Neue Zeitschrift für Musik*, 3 (1835), 1–2, 33–5, 37–8, 41–4 and 49–51, trans. Ian Bent as 'R. Schumann: "[Review of Berlioz: *Fantastic* Symphony]" (1835)', in *Music Analysis in the Nineteenth Century*, 2 vols., ed. Ian Bent (Cambridge, 1994), vol. II, 161–94 (hereafter: Schumann–Bent). On Schumann's conflicted attitude towards Berlioz, see Leon Plantinga, *Schumann as Critic* (New Haven and London, 1967), 235–50.

15 The quotations from Schumann's review in this and the following paragraph are taken from Schumann–Bent, 171–5.

16 Here Schumann is referring to Louis Spohr's once wildly popular programmatic Symphony No. 4 (*Die Weihe der Töne*), composed in 1832 and given no fewer than seventeen performances at the Gewandhaus between 1834 and 1869, more than half of which took place during the Mendelssohn era. For Schumann's devastating review of the Gewandhaus performance of 5 February 1835, see *Neue Zeitschrift für Musik*, 11 (1835), 65–6, trans. in Brown, *The European Symphony from ca. 1800 to ca. 1930: Germany and the Nordic Countries*, 95.

17 Both Dahlhaus (*Nineteenth-Century Music*, 154–6) and Jon Finson (*Robert Schumann and the Study of Orchestral Composition: The Genesis of the First Symphony Op. 38* [Oxford, 1989], 20–2) suggest that Schumann is attempting to reassure his readers that Berlioz's design can be derived from standard practice and therefore need not be so forbidding. Yet, as Fred Everett Maus has argued, Schumann's concluding remark seems to privilege originality, not dependence on tradition. See Fred Everett Maus, 'Intersubjectivity and Analysis: Schumann's Essay on the *Fantastic* Symphony', in *Music Theory in the Age of Romanticism*, ed. Ian Bent (Cambridge, 1996), 125–37.

18 M[arie] Miel, 'Über Sinfonie, über die Sinfonien Beethovens, und über ihre Aufführung in Paris', *Neue Zeitschrift für Musik*, 1 (1834), 101.

19 G. W. Fink, 'Ueber die Symphonie, als Beitrag zur Geschichte und Aesthetik derselben', *Allgemeine musikalische Zeitung*, 37 (1835), cols. 505–11, 521–4, 557–63 (at col. 511).

20 E. T. A. Hoffmann, unsigned review of Beethoven's Fifth Symphony, *Allgemeine musikalische Zeitung*, 12 (1809/10), cols. 630–42, 652–69; trans. Martin Clarke, with David Charlton and Ian Bent, in Bent, ed.,

Music Analysis in the Nineteenth Century, vol. II, 146.

21 Fink, 'Ueber die Symphonie', col. 523. For discussion of the long-running tension between the two critics, which involved both mutual disgust at the other's editorial policies and plain personal animosity and was often played out in print, see Plantinga, *Schumann as Critic*, 23–39 (esp. 30–9).

22 Fink, 'Ueber die Symphonie', col. 523. A few years later, Fink described the attributes of the grand symphony at greater length in his article 'Symphonie oder Sinfonie', in *Encyklopädie der gesammten musikalischen Wissenschaften: oder Universal-Lexicon der Tonkunst*, ed. Gustav Schilling, 6 vols. (Stuttgart, 1838; repr., Hildesheim and New York, 1974), vol. VI, 541–51. For discussion, see Siegfried Oechsle, *Symphonik nach Beethoven: Studien zu Schubert, Schumann, Mendelssohn und Gade* (Kassel, 1992), 24–31, and Walter Frisch, '"Echt symphonisch": On the Historical Context of Brahms's Symphonies', in *Brahms Studies*, vol. II, ed. David Brodbeck (Lincoln and London, 1998), 114–16.

23 Ulrich Konrad, 'Der Wiener Kompositionswettbewerb 1835 und Franz Lachners *Sinfonia passionata*: Ein Beitrag zur Geschichte der Sinfonie nach Beethoven', in *Augsburger Jahrbuch für Musikwissenschaft 1986*, ed. Franz Krautwurst (Tutzing, 1986), 209–39. See also Wolfram Steinbeck, 'Franz Lachner und die Symphonie', *Franz Lachner und seine Brüder: Hofkapellmeister zwischen Schubert und Wagner* (Tutzing, 2006), 133–43.

24 *Neue Zeitschrift für Musik*, 5 (1836), 147–8.

25 This and the next several quotations are from *Neue Zeitschrift für Musik*, 5 (1836), 151–2. My translations in this paragraph are adapted from Plantinga, *Schumann as Critic*, 191–2.

26 G. W. Fink, 'Preissinfonie', *Allgemeine musikalische Zeitung*, 39 (1837), cols. 201–9, 217–22 (the analysis in cols. 201–9; the quotation at col. 217).

27 Ibid., cols. 218–19. I am grateful to Annegret Fauser for her assistance in translating this colourful passage.

28 Ibid., col. 220.

29 Robert Schumann, 'Neue Symphonien für Orchester', *Neue Zeitschrift für Musik*, 11 (1839), 1–3 and 17–18 (at 1); translation here and below adapted from Finson, *Robert Schumann and the Study of Orchestral Composition*, 19; and Frisch, '"Echt symphonisch": On the Historical Context of Brahms' Symphonies', 117.

30 Mark Evan Bonds, *After Beethoven: Imperatives of Originality in the Symphony* (Cambridge, Mass. and London, 1996),

111–17; Oechsle, *Symphonik nach Beethoven*, 374–5.

31 Schumann arranged to have the score sent to Mendelssohn, who conducted the work in its premiere at the Gewandhaus on 21 March 1839, but he remained in Vienna at the time of that performance and so had not yet heard the symphony at the time of this review.

32 L. Michael Griffel, 'Schubert's Orchestral Music: "Strivings after the Highest in Art"', in Christopher H. Gibbs, ed., *The Cambridge Companion to Schubert* (Cambridge, 1997), 203.

33 Schumann–Bent, 171; Robert Schumann, 'Die 7te Symphonie von Franz Schubert', *Neue Zeitschrift für Musik*, 12 (10 March 1840), 81–3 (here at 82).

34 Schumann, 'Die 7te Symphonie von Franz Schubert', 82–3.

35 See, for example, Schumann's letter of 11 December 1839 to his friend Ernst A. Becker, quoted in Bonds, *After Beethoven*, 110–11.

36 On the 'Great' C major in this context, see Siegfried Oechsle, 'Schubert, Schumann und die Symphonie nach Beethoven', in *Probleme der symphonischen Tradition im 19. Jahrhundert*, ed. Siegfried Kross and Marie Luise Maintz (Tutzing, 1990), 284–92, Marie Luise Maintz, '"... In neuverschlungener Weise" – Schuberts Einfluß auf die Symphonien Schumann', in ibid., 117–18, and Finson, *Schumann and the Study of Orchestral Composition*, 36–8, 44–5 and 56. On the symphonies by Mendelssohn and Gade, see Oechsle, *Symphonik nach Beethoven*, 376–84. Hereafter, unless otherwise indicated, all descriptive or analytical references to individual symphonies will be to their first movements.

37 In 1842 Gade's symphony was turned down for performance by the Copenhagen Music Society for being too 'Germanic', but it delighted the Leipzig audience on account of its exotic 'national tone' when Mendelssohn introduced it there instead on 2 March 1843. See Anna Harwell Celenza, *The Early Works of Niels W. Gade: In Search of the Poetic* (Ashgate, 2001), 169–76.

38 Carl Dahlhaus, 'Symphonie und symphonischer Stil um 1850', in *Jahrbuch des Staatlichen Instituts für Musikforschung Preußischer Kulturbesitz 1983/84*, ed. Dagmar Droysen-Reber and Günther Wagner (Kassel, 1987), 43–4.

39 Ibid., 45–6. For a convenient summary, see Carl Dahlhaus, 'Wagners Stellung in der Musikgeschichte', in *Richard-Wagner-Handbuch*, ed. Ulrich Müller and Peter Wapnewski (Stuttgart, 1986), 73, trans. by Alfred Clayton as 'Wagner's Place in the

History of Music', in *Wagner Handbook*, ed.
Ulrich Müller and Peter Wapnewski, trans.
and ed. John Deathridge (Cambridge, Mass.
and London, 1992), 102. A more detailed
account is provided in Carl Dahlhaus, *Ludwig
van Beethoven: Approaches to his Music*
(Oxford, 1991), 67–90.
40 Dahlhaus, *Nineteenth-Century Music*,
156–60.
41 Scott Burnham, 'Novel Symphonies and
Dramatic Overtures', in Beate Perrey, ed., *The
Cambridge Companion to Schumann*
(Cambridge, 2007), 154. Ironically,
Schumann's own instinct, in his reviews of the
Symphonie fantastique and 'Great' C major
Symphony, was to praise each work precisely
in terms of what he claimed they were *not*,
namely, imitations of Beethoven; see Bonds,
After Beethoven, 116.
42 Siegfried Oechsle, 'Die
problemgeschichtliche Vitalität der
Symphonie im 19. Jahrhundert', in *Aspekte
historischer und systematischer
Musikforschung: Zur Symphonie im 19.
Jahrhundert, zu Fragen der Musiktheorie, der
Wahrnehmung von Musik und Anderes*, ed.
Christoph-Hellmut Mahling and Kristina
Pfarr (Mainz, 2002), 19–27.
43 Oechsle, *Symphonik nach Beethoven*, 376.
44 Dahlhaus, *Die Musik im 19. Jahrhundert*, 221.
45 Oechsle, *Symphonik nach Beethoven*, 377.
46 Ibid., 376, 383.
47 Burnham ('Novel Symphonies and
Dramatic Overtures', 154–7) shares an
insightful observation about the uniformity of
the opening Allegro of Schumann's Second by
way of contrasting the music with Beethoven's
Seventh. On the Schubertian resonances in
Schumann's Second, see Brown, *The European
Symphony from ca. 1800 to ca. 1930: Germany
and the Nordic Countries*, 262–77, and John
Daverio, *Robert Schumann: Herald of a 'New
Poetic Age'* (New York and Oxford, 1997),
315–22. On Gade, see Brown, *The European
Symphony from ca. 1800 to ca. 1930: Germany
and the Nordic Countries*, 431–52.
48 Dahlhaus, *Die Musik des 19. Jahrhunderts*,
220. Schumann's Fourth Symphony (1851)
dates from 1841 but was withdrawn following
its first performance and issued to the public
only after undergoing a thorough
reorchestration ten years later.
49 What Wagner had in mind, of course, was
the claim that the Beethovenian symphonic
style had been subsumed within the music
drama, and Dahlhaus follows this line of
thinking in suggesting a similar
transformation, not only of the concert
overture (Liszt's symphonic poems), but also

of the solo concerto (Henry Litolff's *concert
symphonique*) and mass (Liszt's *Graner
Messe*). See Dahlhaus, 'Symphonie und
symphonischer Stil um 1850', 39–41, and
Dahlhaus, 'Liszts Idee des Symphonischen', in
his *Klassische und romantische Musikästhetik*
(Laaber, 1988), 392–3.
50 See Dahlhaus, *Die Musik des 19.
Jahrhunderts*, 65 and 197; Dahlhaus, 'Symphonie
und symphonischer Stil um 1850', 38, and
Dahlhaus, 'Liszts Idee des Symphonischen', 392
(Rubinstein only).
51 Dahlhaus, *Die Musik des 19. Jahrhunderts*,
197. For a thoughtful critique of this position,
see Wolfram Steinbeck, *Romantische und
nationale Symphonik*, part I of *Die Symphonie
im 19. and 20. Jahrhundert*, by Wolfram
Steinbeck and Christoph von Blumröder
(Laaber, 2002), 156–60. See also Siegfried
Kross, 'Das "Zweite Zeitalter der Symphonie" –
Ideologie und Realität', in *Probleme der
symphonischen Tradition im 19. Jahrhundert*,
16, and compare Frisch, '"Echt symphonisch":
On the Historical Context of Brahms's
Symphonies', 122–4.
52 See Rebecca Grotjahn, 'Zur Bedeutung der
Sinfonie im Musikleben 1850 bis 1875', in
Mahling and Pfarr, eds., *Aspekte historischer
und systematischer Musikforschung* (Mainz,
2002), 49–57, on which I base much of the
following discussion.
53 Grotjahn, *Die Sinfonie im deutschen
Kulturgebiet*, 154–202.
54 In his review of the Vienna Philharmonic's
concert of 8 March 1863, for example, Eduard
Hanslick wrote, 'By featuring two new works
[Brahms's Second Serenade (1859) and the
Symphony in C minor (1863) by Moriz
Käsmayer] . . . the Philharmonic players
fought with praiseworthy decisiveness against
the often made complaint – including in these
pages – of an exclusivity in its programs
that borders on rigidity.' See Ed[uard]
H[anslick], 'Musik', *Die Presse* (13 March
1863).
55 For an alphabetical listing by composer, see
Grotjahn, *Die Sinfonie im deutschen
Kulturgebiet*, 323–64. Somewhat less complete
(but still useful) counts are provided in
Walter Frisch, *Brahms: The Four Symphonies*
(New Haven and London, 2003), 7–10, and
F. E. Kirby, 'The Germanic Symphony of the
Nineteeth Century: Genre, Form,
Instrumentation, Expression', *Journal of
Musicological Research*, 14 (1995), 193–221.
56 See Steinbeck, *Romantische und nationale
Symphonik*, 170–2, and Andreas Wehrmeyer,
'Zur historischen Stellung der Symphonien
Anton Rubinsteins', in Mahling and Pfarr, eds.,

Aspekte historischer und systematischer Musikforschung, 209–11.

57 See Matthias Wiegandt, *Vergessene Symphonik? Studien zu Joachim Raff, Carl Reinecke und zum Problem der Epigonalität in der Musik* (Sinzig, 1997), 105–314, Falke, *Die Symphonie zwischen Schumann und Brahms*, 19–52 and 157–283, Steinbeck, *Romantische und nationale Symphonik*, 167–70, 173–5, and Frisch, '"Echt symphonisch": On the Historical Context of Brahms's Symphonies', 124–30.

58 On the Manifesto, see David Brodbeck, 'Brahms, the Third Symphony, and the New German School', in Walter Frisch and Kevin Karnes, eds., *Brahms and His World*, rev. edn (Princeton, 2009), 103–7. It is worth noting that, among Liszt's twelve symphonic poems, only *Les Préludes* (1848) and *Tasso* (1849) attained status as 'living classics' during the period under question.

59 This helps to explain the paradox that Frisch observes in the case of Friedrich Chrysander's review of Max Bruch's First Symphony (*Allgemeine musikalische Zeitung*, 4 [1869], 67) of a favourable account that contains sharp criticism of the suitability of the main theme for symphonic treatment. Emanuel Klitzsch's review of the same work (*Neue Zeitschrift für Musik*, 66 [1870], 282) calls the main theme 'truly symphonic' but finds fault in what Bruch does with it. See Frisch, '"Echt symphonisch"', 124–30.

60 *Leipziger Allgemeine musikalische Zeitung*, 1 (1866), col. 103.

61 Grotjahn, *Die Sinfonie im deutschen Kulturgebiet*, 278.

62 In this way, as J. Peter Burkholder has argued, Brahms established the very model of the modern composer by explicitly writing works for the 'concert hall as museum'; see J. Peter Burkholder, 'Brahms and Twentieth-Century Music', *19th-Century Music*, 8 (1984/5), 75–83.

63 Grotjahn, *Die Sinfonie im deutschen Kulturgebiet*, 264–6.

64 *Allgemeine musikalische Zeitung, Neue Folge*, 3 (1865), col. 521.

65 Grotjahn, 'Zur Bedeutung der Sinfonie im Musikleben 1850 bis 1875', 56.

66 Ed[uard] H[anslick], 'Concerte', *Die Presse* (22 November 1860); repr. in Eduard Hanslick, *Aus dem Concertsaal* (Vienna, 1870), 208.

67 Louis Köhler, *Neue Zeitschrift für Musik*, 62 (1866), 26.

68 Hugo Riemann, *Geschichte der Musik seit Beethoven* (Berlin and Stuttgart, 1901), 432–3; quoted in Steinbeck, *Romantische und nationale Symphonik*, 167. On Raff's 'middle way', see Wolfram Steinbeck, 'Nationale

Symphonik und die Neudeutschen: Zu Joachim Raffs Symphonie "An das Vaterland"', in Helmut Loos, ed., *Musikgeschichte zwischen Ost- und Westeuropa* (Sankt Augustin, 1997), 70–3.

69 Ed[uard] H[anslick], 'Musik', *Die Presse* (24 February 1863); repr. in Eduard Hanslick, 'Die Preissymphonien', *Aus dem Concertsaal*, 279–83 (at 282). The work's great length also posed its difficulties: 'Raff's symphony is the longest we know. With his praise of the "heavenly lengths" of Schubert's C major Symphony, Schumann has caused much misfortune, since not all his followers have had the good sense of Schumann himself not to imitate this "heavenly length" when the heavenly long thread of Schubert's melody is not there as well' (ibid., 282–3).

70 Ibid., 282.

71 Ibid. I am grateful to Alan Krueck (personal communication) for informing me of Helene Raff's claim that her father added this programme on the day for the concert; see Helene Raff, *Joachim Raff: Ein Lebensbild* (Regensburg, 1925), 160. Raff provided a rather more detailed programme in the published score.

72 Ed[uard] H[anslick], 'Concerte', *Die Presse* (16 January 1863); repr. in Hanslick, *Aus dem Concertsaal*, 291.

73 Hanslick, 'Die Preissymphonien', 282.

74 Steinbeck, *Romantische und nationale Symphonik*, 170; see also Steinbeck, 'Nationale Symphonik und die Neudeutschen', 73–4.

75 Wehrmeyer, 'Zur historischen Stellung der Symphonien Anton Rubinsteins', 209.

76 Quoted in ibid., 212. When, after a long hiatus, Rubinstein took up the genre again with his Fourth Symphony ('Dramatic', 1874), his model, by contrast, was Beethoven, and in his final two symphonies he approached a Russian nationalist style at last, with nearly all the themes in the Fifth Symphony ('Russian', 1880), for example, exuding the character of folksongs. Ibid., 215–17.

77 Dahlhaus, *Nineteenth-Century Music*, 266–8 (here at 268).

78 Wolfram Steinbeck has claimed that a similar fruitful comparison can be made between the horn melody that opens the slow introduction to Tchaikovsky's Second and the openings of Schubert's 'Great' C major and Mendelssohn's 'Scottish' symphonies. See Wolfram Steinbeck, 'Russische Rezeption deutscher Symphonik: Zu Čajkovskijs *Zweiter Symphonie*', in *Rezeption als Innovation: Untersuchungen zu einem Grundmodell der europäischen Kompositionsgeschichte*, ed. Bernd Sponheuer, Siegfried Oechsle and Helmut Weill (Kassel and Basel, 2001), 357–66. See also the discussion of the striking

similarities between the terse openings of Volkmann's First Symphony and Borodin's Symphony No. 2 in B Minor, in Falke, *Die Symphonie zwischen Schumann und Brahms*, 157–271, Grotjahn, *Die Sinfonie im deutschen Kulturgebiet*, 282–6, Steinbeck, *Romantische und nationale Symphonik*, 173–4, and Klaus Wolfgang Niemöller, 'Zur Symphonik von Robert Volkmann', in Loos, ed., *Musikgeschichte zwischen Ost- und Westeuropa* (Sankt Augustin, 1997), 57–68.

79 Brian Hart, 'The French Symphony After Berlioz: From the Second Empire to the First World War', in Brown, *The European Symphony from ca. 1800 to ca. 1930: Great Britain, Russia and France*, 529–725; also helpful is Ralph P. Locke, 'The French Symphony: David, Gounod, and Bizet to Saint-Saëns, Franck, and Their Followers', in *The Nineteenth-Century Symphony*, ed. D. Kern Holoman (New York, 1997), 163–94.

80 Dahlhaus, *Nineteenth-Century Music*, 284.

81 Richard Taruskin, 'Nationalism', in Grove Music Online. Oxford Music Online, www. oxfordmusiconline.com/subscriber/article/ grove/music/50846 (accessed 31 December 2008). For an excellent discussion, see Michael Strasser, 'The Société Nationale and Its Adversaries: The Musical Politics of *L'Invasion germanique* in the 1870s', *19th-Century Music*, 24/3 (2001), 225–51.

82 Clemens Hellsberg, *Demokratie der Könige: Die Geschichte der Wiener Philharmoniker* (Zurich, Vienna and Mainz, 1992), 205–93.

83 For the best introduction, see Margaret Notley, *Lateness and Brahms: Music and Culture in the Twilight of Viennese Liberalism* (Oxford and New York, 2007), 3–35 ('Brahms as Liberal, Bruckner as Other'). Following Notley (ibid., 16), I borrow these characterisations from Constantin Floros, 'Einfallsapologetik gegen Verherrlichung des Ausarbeitung', in his *Brahms und Bruckner: Studien zur musikalischen Exegetik* (Wiesbaden, 1980), 30–4.

84 Ernest Gellner, *Language and Solitude: Wittgenstein, Malinowski and the Habsburg Dilemma* (Cambridge, 1998), 11.

85 For a convenient tabular presentation of this dichotomy, see Margaret Notley, 'Bruckner and Viennese Wagnerism', in *Bruckner Studies*, ed. Timothy L. Jackson and Paul Hawkshaw (Cambridge, 1997), 54–71 (at 62). Notley credits Ernest Hanisch, 'The Political Influence and Appropriation of Wagner', trans. Paul Knight, in Ulrich Müller and Peter Wapnewski, eds., *Wagner Handbook* (Cambridge, Mass., 1992), 191.

86 'Über das Dichten und Komponieren' (July 1879), 'Über das Opern-Dichten und Komponieren im Besonderen' (September 1879), and 'Über die Anwendung der Musik auf das Drama' (November 1879), in Richard Wagner, *Gesammelte Schriften und Dichtungen*, 3rd edn, 10 vols. (Leipzig, 1887–8), vol. X (1888), 137–51, 152–75 and 176–93. For discussion, see David Brodbeck, *Brahms: Symphony No. 1* (Cambridge, 1997), 87–90, from which I take the translations from 'On the Application of Music to Drama' that are quoted below. Brahms's First, a watershed work if there ever was one, is nowhere to be seen in Dahlhaus's history, perhaps because its deep engagement with symphonies by Schubert and Schumann, as well as those by Beethoven, works against the circumpolar model, or because it cannot easily be reconciled with the dialectical approach implied by the notion of a 'second age of the symphony'.

87 On the trope of Brahms as Jew in anti-liberal Viennese music criticism around 1890, see Notley, *Lateness and Brahms*, 32–4.

88 For Dahlhaus's discussion of the nature of appropriately symphonic themes, see *Beethoven*, 76–80.

89 As Notley has shown, later critics (she cites Paul Marsop and Paul Bekker) worked out more thoroughgoing critiques of the Romantic symphony along the same lines (*Lateness and Brahms*, 144–68).

90 Notley, *Lateness and Brahms*, 162–6.

91 Theodor Helm, 'Musikbrief aus Wien', *Musikalisches Wochenblatt*, 16 (1885), 97–8.

92 Ed[uard] H[anslick], 'Concerte', *Neue freie Presse* (4 December 1884).

93 Letter to Fritz Simrock of 8 November 1884, in *Johannes Brahms Briefwechsel*, nineteen volumes to date, consisting of sixteen original volumes (rev. edns, Berlin, 1921–2; repr. edn, Tutzing, 1974) and a *Neue Folge* consisting of three volumes to date (Tutzing, 1991–), vol. XI, 79–80.

94 On Bruckner's support among Viennese Wagnerians, see Andrea Harrandt, 'Students and Friends as "Prophets" and "Promoters": The Reception of Bruckner's Works in the *Wiener Akademische Wagner-Verein*', in *Perspectives on Anton Bruckner*, ed. Crawford Howie, Paul Hawkshaw and Timothy Jackson (Aldershot, 2001), 317–27, Harrandt, 'Bruckner in Vienna', in John Williamson, ed., *The Cambridge Companion to Bruckner* (Cambridge, 2004), 26–37, and Notley, 'Bruckner and Viennese Wagnerism'.

95 Thomas Leibnitz, 'Anton Bruckner and "German Music": Josef Schalk and the Establishment of Bruckner as a National Composer', in *Perspectives on Anton Bruckner*,

328–40, at 336. On Brahms in this context, see Notley, *Lateness and Brahms*, 21–5.

96 Leibnitz, 'Anton Bruckner and "German Music"', 336.

97 *Deutsche Zeitung* (23 March 1886) (quoted in Harrandt, 'Bruckner in Vienna', 33).

98 For translations of a number of reviews, see Crawford Howie, *Anton Bruckner: A Documentary Biography*, 2 vols. (Lewiston, 2002), vol. II, 504–16.

99 Dahlhaus, *Nineteenth-Century Music*, 271.

100 Notley, *Lateness and Brahms*, 27–35.

101 Steinbeck (*Romantische und national Symphonik*, 172–3) claims that the composer did not designate the work as a symphony, but in fact the first edition (1876) carries the title *Ländliche Hochzeit. Symphonie in 5 Sätzen für grosses Orchester*, Op. 26. Goldmark later recalled that Brahms was especially well-disposed towards this work and was indignant that anyone would think that it should not be called a symphony simply because its first movement was written in theme-and-variations form rather than sonata form; see Karl Goldmark, *Notes from the Life of a Viennese Composer*, trans. Alice Goldmark Brandeis (New York, 1927), 161–2.

102 sp. [Ludwig Speidel], 'Konzerte', *Fremden-Blatt* (2 March 1888), from which the quotations in the next two paragraphs are also taken. Speidel had first made mention of Goldmark's 'doubly oriental' heritage – and in an entirely negative way – in his review of *The Queen of Sheba* ('Hofoperntheater', *Fremden-Blatt* [12 March 1875]); although the *Deutsche Zeitung* eventually embraced anti-Semitism that did not take place until the later 1890s.

103 Although Speidel has occasionally been identified by modern scholars as a Jew – see, for example, Robert S. Wistrich, *The Jews of Vienna in the Age of Franz Joseph* (Oxford, 1989), 436 and Notley, *Lateness and Brahms*, 34 – he was not and was never identified as such by Vienna's anti-Semites. Like Hanslick, however, he was a traditional German liberal nationalist, who, as Steven Beller has suggested, was especially devoted to the project of complete Jewish assimilation see Steven Beller, *Vienna and The Jews, 1867–1938: A Cultural History* (Cambridge, 1989), 133–4.

104 On Goldmark's identification with the German cultural project, see Goldmark, *Notes from the Life of a Viennese Composer*, 150–1; on the satisfaction he took in Speidel's review of the symphony, see ibid., 157–8.

105 David Brodbeck, 'Dvořák's Reception in Liberal Vienna: Language Ordinances, National Property, and the Rhetoric of Deutschtum', *Journal of the American Musicological Society*, 60 (2007), 71–131.

106 Notice, for example, the subtle difference in emphasis between Hanslick's and Helm's evaluation of Dvořák's Seventh Symphony, heard in the Philharmonic Concerts on 16 January 1887. While Hanslick indicates that 'Dvořák shows himself to be a man who, trained in the study of our German masters, stands on his own feet (Ed[uard] H[anslick], 'Concerte', *Neue freie Presse* [25 January 1887]), Helm took note of the 'Slavic-national complexion that Dvořák liked so much to introduce into the classical sonata and symphonic form' (Theodor Helm, 'Concerte', *Deutsche Zeitung* [21 January 1887]). For more on Hanslick and Helm in this context, see Brodbeck, 'Dvořák's Reception in Liberal Vienna', 100–4 and 110–18.

107 Ed[uard[H[anslick], 'Concerte', *Neue freie Presse* (6 January 1891); repr. in Eduard Hanslick, *Aus dem Tagebuche eines Musikers* (Berlin, 1892), 335–41. Theodor Helm, 'Musikbrief aus Wien', *Musikalisches Wochenblatt*, 22 (22 January 1891), 47.

108 C[amillo] H[orn], 'Wie man "Kritiken" macht', *Ostdeutsche Rundschau*, 18 January 1891.

109 Camillo Horn, *Deutsches Volkblatt* (20 December 1892), quoted in Notley, 'Bruckner and Viennese Wagnerism', 70. Anonymous, *Ostdeutsche Rundschau* (25 December 1892); quoted in Benjamin M. Korstvedt, *Bruckner: Symphony No. 8* (Cambridge, 2000), 6 (where authorship is attributed to Joseph Stolzing). In pan-German circles, the Archangel Michael served as the personification of the German–Austrian people.

110 On the intrigue surrounding this development, see Henry-Louis de la Grange, *Gustav Mahler*, vol. II: *Vienna: The Years of Challenge (1897–1904)* (Oxford and New York, 1995), 116–21, and Hellsberg, *Demokratie der Könige*, 290–1.

111 *Deutsche Zeitung* (27 September 1898), 7; trans. in K. M. Knittel, '"Polemik im Concertsaal": Mahler, Beethoven, and the Viennese Critics', *19th-Century Music*, 29 (2006), 289–317 (at 289). See also E. Th., 'Das jüdische Regime an der Wiener Oper', *Deutsche Zeitung* (4 November 1898).

112 Leon Botstein, 'Gustav Mahler's Vienna', in Donald Mitchell and Andrew Nicholson, eds., *The Mahler Companion* (Oxford, 1999), 8. For a thoughtful overview of this period in the city's musical history, see Margaret Notley, 'Musical Culture in Vienna at the Turn of the Twentieth Century', in Bryan R. Simms, ed., *Schoenberg, Berg, and Webern: A Companion*

to the Second Viennese School (Westport, 1999), 37–71.

113 On Mahler's frequently strained relationship with the orchestra's membership, see Hellsberg, *Demokratie der Könige*, 295–319.

114 For discussion and a sampling of Viennese reviews, see de la Grange, *Vienna: The Years of Challenge*, 148–55, 307–13, 471–6, *Gustav Mahler*, vol. III: *Vienna: Triumph and Disillusion (1904–1907)* (Oxford and New York, 1999), 66–76, 272–9 and 533–43, and *Gustav Mahler*, vol. IV: *A New Life Cut Short (1907–1911)* (New York and Oxford, 2008), 511–24. Also useful is 'Mahler's German-Language Critics', ed. and trans. Karen Painter and Bettina Varwig, in Karen Painter, ed., *Mahler and His World* (Princeton, 2002), 267–378.

115 Weber, *The Great Transformation of Musical Taste*, 306.

116 Notley, 'Musical Culture in Vienna at the Turn of the Twentieth Century', 42–50; Sandra McColl, 'Max Kalbeck and Gustav Mahler', *19th-Century Music*, 20/2 (1996), 167–84.

117 Consider the handling of the *Gesellen* theme that forms the basis of the opening movement of the First Symphony or, more generally, the thematic technique seen in the first movement of the Fourth Symphony. On the sceptical attitude along these lines that Mahler himself eventually adopted concerning Bruckner's accomplishment as a symphonist, see de la Grange, *Vienna: The Years of Challenge*, 332–3.

118 e.h. [Eduard Hanslick], 'Zweites Philharmonisches Concert', *Neue freie Presse* (20 November 1900), trans. in Painter and Varwig, 'Mahler's German-language Critics', 289–90.

119 de la Grange, *Vienna: Triumph and Disillusion*, 607–16.

120 Alma Mahler, *Gustav Mahler: Memories and Letters*, 3rd edn, ed. Donald Mitchell, trans. Basil Creighton (Seattle, 1975), 112.

121 Dahlhaus, *Die Musik des 19. Jahrhunderts*, 284 and 211.

122 Ibid., 284.

5 The symphony since Mahler: national and international trends

DAVID FANNING

Priorities and principles

In 1918, the influential German critic Paul Bekker summed up symphonic composition since Beethoven as the fragmentation of the latter's legacy into various national and regional traditions and its reintegration by Gustav Mahler.[1] Nearly a century further on, any comparable summary of the welter of symphonies since Mahler would be hopelessly reductive. For one thing, it would have to have a dual starting-point, placing Sibelius alongside Mahler to represent the state of the art in 1911 (the year of Mahler's death and of the darkest and most radical of Sibelius's seven numbered symphonies, No. 4). Then it would have to recognise that national traditions of the kind Bekker identified in the nineteenth century have become ever harder to distinguish, thanks to the globalisation of communications, travel and information exchange, and to the spread of symphonic composition to almost all corners of the planet, leaving only Africa and parts of Asia untouched. Finally, unless something extraordinary has been going on beneath the musicological and critical radar, it would have to acknowledge that no symphonist active in the twenty-first century so far commands anything like the stature of a Mahler or a Sibelius. Even the stand-out composers and works chosen for consideration below may seem an odd choice in a hundred years' time (or less!), when reputations have been weighed, sifted and rebalanced.

Nonetheless, Bekker's study is not such a bad place to start. In the course of a mere sixty pages, based on public lectures, he put his finger on the humanist idealism that links Beethoven and Mahler and that has been one of the running threads in symphonic composition up to the present day (the course of this thread has been addressed in Chapter 1). This ethical and social dimension – what Bekker called the symphony's *gemeinschaftsbildende Kraft* (literally 'community-building power'), using a term that goes back through Mahler himself to Wagner, and a concept that was established in Beethoven reception as early as the 1830s[2] – was something that would be taken up with special enthusiasm in Soviet Russia, where Bekker's book was published in translation in 1926. In that country, especially after the Bolshevik Revolution of 1917, all the arts were, broadly speaking, validated according to their potential contribution to the project of forming a new society. It was accordingly there that the symphony retained – in adapted and increasingly distorted forms, but still to a greater degree than anywhere else – the high-mindedness and social ambition that all but fizzled out in Austria and Germany with the death of Mahler.

Related and overlapping imperatives operate in all other geographical branches of twentieth-century symphonism. They have to do with mapping the expressive range of the post-Beethovenian symphony onto large existential issues, often by means of grand-scale dualisms such as good/evil, life/death, light/dark, movement/stasis, mental/physical, old/new. These concepts are all more or less covered by the Russian translation of *gemeinschaftsbildend*, the even more tongue-defying *obobshchestv-lyayushchiy*, which is usually translated back into English as 'generalising', but which actually carries the entirely positive sense of embodying archetypal significance or taking something to a higher plane. It describes symphonic 'content', but content at the opposite extreme from anecdote or pictorialism. In the USSR the term, together with its breadth of connotation, was established by Boris Asafyev in a number of key articles in the 1920s as well as in his translation of Bekker's essay. It was adopted thereafter by virtually all Soviet commentators expounding their own ongoing symphonic tradition. It served to validate the symphony across a broad stylistic, technical and even ideological spectrum. So long as the composer's application was high-minded, the adjective could be used to encompass and affirm, at one extreme, programmatic symphony-cantatas overtly aligned with the Bolshevik project (such as Shostakovich's Second and Third) and at another the purely instrumental, post-Tchaikovskian, essentially apolitical symphony as cultivated by Nikolay Myaskovsky and many of his pupils.

Understood in this broad sense, the community-forming aspect of the symphony is a core belief at least as central to Mahler's symphonies as his more oft-repeated aphorisms, such as, 'To me "symphony" means constructing a world with all the technical means at one's disposal' (summer 1895, while working on the Third Symphony)[3] and, in reported conversation with Sibelius, 'Symphony must be like the world. It must embrace everything' (1907; this conversation is variously considered in chapters 9, 12 and 13 below).[4] If we take a step further and relate the community-forming dimension to the notion of positive and negative poles, we acquire a useful tool for discussing the relative status of individual symphonies and symphonists after Mahler – be it assigned by their contemporaries or afterwards. Those symphonies in which one or other pole is only weakly defined are unlikely to find more than local and ephemeral resonance, since the lack of strong dualisms in effect precludes engagement with existential issues and hence the ability to speak to large audiences. Debates over unjustified neglect (such as might be conducted over the likes of Havergal Brian, Edmund Rubbra or Andrzej Panufnik; Franz Schmidt, Karl Amadeus Hartmann or Hans Werner Henze; Roy Harris, Walter Piston or William Schuman; Myaskovsky, Gavriil Popov or Mieczysław Weinberg, and so on) cannot get very far without taking this aspirational aspect into account, at least as much as style, structure and craftsmanship.

Given the availability through recordings of several thousand symphonies composed since the death of Mahler, it is hardly surprising that few attempts have been made to justify or contradict notions of canonic status; not outside the Soviet Union, at least, where the centralised structures of reward virtually dictated that kind of discourse. Nevertheless, at least one prominent commentator has put his head above the parapet and flagged up a set of principles. Sixty years after Bekker, Robert Simpson – whose own symphonies have a strong claim to higher status than they currently enjoy – listed 'those elements of music a composer must master if he is to write a true symphony'. He proposed: 'the fusion of diverse elements into an organic whole ... the continuous control of pace ... reserves of strength ... such as to suggest size ... the dynamic treatment of tonality ... [and the quality of being] active in all possible ways'.[5] The conspicuous omission here is the ethical dimension identified by Bekker and stressed over and over by Soviet Russian commentators. For precisely this reason, while Simpson's criteria may be helpful in identifying aberrant kinds of symphonies (such as Stravinsky's, which Simpson was determined to marginalise), they only provide blunt tools for critical evaluation.

Simpson looked on Mahler with distaste for what he diagnosed as chronic self-indulgence. His criteria for the 'true symphony' implicitly drew on the counter-examples of Sibelius and Nielsen (his writings about their symphonies do in fact touch on ethos, even if his symphonic desiderata do not). These two near-contemporaries of Mahler continued to write symphonies for fifteen years after the Austrian's death, grappling with the problem of symphonic composition in the post-First World War era in a way that other distinguished figures of their generation such as Elgar, Glazunov, Rachmaninoff and Richard Strauss for one reason or another chose not to. Between them, Sibelius and Nielsen spearheaded a distinct brand of Nordic symphonism with markedly alternative priorities to those of their Austro-German forebears. Those priorities proved attractive to many, especially in Britain and the USA, the other principal centres of twentieth-century symphonic composition, though by the time of Nielsen's international breakthrough in the 1950s, twenty years after his death, it was too late for his idiosyncratic brand of empathy and adventure to be as influential as Sibelius's elementalism had been throughout the 1930s and 40s. Broadly speaking, the Nordic alternative represented a different kind of interface with the 'world' from Mahler's. Its overriding priority was motion rather than emotion, expressed in the image of 'current', which both Sibelius and Nielsen explicitly related to natural phenomena. Like Mahler, they too could trace their priorities back to Beethoven. Indeed, when Sibelius, in the famous exchange already quoted from Mahler's side, expressed his view of the essence of symphony as 'severity of style and the profound logic that create[s] an inner connection between the motifs',[6] he was simply highlighting another dimension inherited from Beethoven, placing the emphasis on means rather than ends. For many years Sibelius lacked a critical advocate as eloquent as Bekker had been for Mahler – someone who might have pointed out that Sibelian 'profound logic' was in practice by no means an end in itself, and still less a means of embodying some kind of Nordic racial suprematism, as an influential strand of American reception had it in the first half of the century.[7] Rather it was the technical manifestation of an elemental outlook on Nature, allied to a stoical humanism and expressed in a paradoxical stylistic fusion of opposed kinds of musical pace, as represented by Beethoven and Wagner. It was Simpson himself who identified that crucial duality in Sibelius's most conspicuously stoical work, the Fourth Symphony.[8]

Clearly Sibelius's and Mahler's concerns as symphonists were by no means as mutually exclusive as their famous conversation might suggest. Sibelius's connection with Nature was as fundamental and passionate as Mahler's, and the motivic interconnections in Mahler's symphonies are as far-reaching as those in Sibelius's. But their articulation of distinct priorities and emphases still defines a polarity that remains useful to any broad historical survey. It also helps to explain why some major composers with very different outlooks – such as Debussy, Schoenberg, Janáček, Bartók and almost everyone associated with the 1950s serial avant-garde – made little or no contribution to the symphony. The general hostility of these composers towards the genre on grounds of its supposed outdatedness masked a simple absence of temperamental affinity. In a century the middle years of which were overshadowed by dictatorships and world war, socio-ethical concerns and the symphonic genre were if anything more relevant to one another, not less. And this is precisely where Mahler, with his unprecedented gift for musical angst and irony, became such a powerful enabling force for the likes of Shostakovich and Schnittke. For them the imagery of conflict, suffering, doubt and compassion – all so close to the surface in Mahler – could be appropriated with a particularly good conscience, since artists in the Soviet Union were officially mandated to comment in those areas. At the same time the quintessentially Mahlerian trope of irony gave them a voice with which to speak to the 'non-official' audience in their homeland. On the other hand, in an age where conceptions of travel and motion, and of cosmos and ecology, evolved just as dramatically as conflict and the capacity for self-destruction, the attractions of the Sibelian outlook to later composers are equally obvious. In this case, admittedly, the archetypal power generally lies deeper beneath the surface, and major symphonists as heterogeneous as Ralph Vaughan Williams, Robert Simpson, Peter Maxwell Davies and Per Nørgård have on the whole tapped into it at the level of large-scale process rather than surface image or style.

So far as the problematic concept of national traditions in twentieth-century symphonism is concerned, it has left traces at least in the sense that Sibelius was taken up with enthusiasm principally in the UK and the USA, while being regarded with widespread incomprehension (at least among critics) in France and Germany. In the latter countries, contributions to the symphony shrank dramatically, in direct proportion both to suspicion of the symphonic ethos and to the turn to alternative aesthetic priorities – such as epicureanism, entertainment, scepticism, alienation and fetishistic games with timbre. In addition, symphonic composition in France had to contend with its inherited association with political conservatism, for which active participants in the tradition such as D'Indy were as much responsible as any commentator.[9] This is one reason why Debussy eschewed the genre, declaring in 1900 that 'the proof of the futility of the symphony has been established since Beethoven'.[10] Blame for premature obituaries of the symphony cannot be laid at the door of critics alone.

Mega-symphonies and anti-symphonies

Bekker offered no comment on the state of symphonic composition in 1918, no diagnosis of or prescription for what in retrospect looks unmistakably like a crisis, and no prognostications of the kind that were much in vogue at this time of competing newly defined –isms. Neither Sibelius nor Nielsen appeared on his intellectual horizons. Indeed they barely did for any Germanic commentator at the time. And had Bekker taken soundings of the Austro-Germanic tradition at almost any point from then until his death in 1937, he could hardly have avoided the conclusion that Mahler proved to be as much a disabling force for symphonists there as he was an enabling one elsewhere. From Bekker's point of view it would have come as a nasty shock to observe that Strauss's 'Alpine' Symphony (1915) – a work as pictorial, self-confident and affirmative as Mahler is philosophical, angst-ridden and doubt-laden – would be the last symphony from that tradition to retain a place in the standard concert repertory.

Not that others in Austria and Germany did not attempt to don the Mahlerian mantle.[11] Arnold Schoenberg for one regarded Mahler as a messianic figure, and his obituary essay is a thinly veiled manifesto, designed to portray himself in the same light as his hero.[12] Having concluded his essay with the battle-cry 'we must fight on, since the Tenth has not yet been revealed to us' (not knowing at that time how much of Mahler's Tenth had actually been composed), Schoenberg set about putting actions to his words. Between 1912 and 1915 he sketched out a symphony that clearly measured itself against the example of Mahler's Eighth, including as it did, at various points in its evolution, vocal settings of Richard Dehmel, Rabindranath Tagore and the Old Testament books of Isaiah and Jeremiah, to be performed by colossal forces.[13] He abandoned the project with only some elements co-opted into his *Jakobsleiter* oratorio – itself incomplete and un-orchestrated – to show for his pains. Evidently the horizons of the 'world' Mahler had sought to encompass symphonically had now become impossibly broad. In fact Schoenberg's desk drawers were littered with unfinished symphonies, the only one of which he returned to was the rebarbative Second Chamber Symphony, begun in 1906, sporadically revisited in the 1910s and finally completed in 1939.

Also emblematic of the crisis was the failure of Schoenberg's pupil Berg to get beyond forty-one bars of the 30- to 45-minute single-movement symphony he planned at roughly the same time as Schoenberg was wrestling with his intractable magnum opus.[14] Those bars are cut from the same cloth as Schoenberg's Orchestral Pieces, Op. 16 (1909), and although this tortured language was perfectly adapted to the expression of alienation, Berg evidently found it impractical to expand to symphonic proportions – not helped by the presence of the overpowering superego of Schoenberg himself. Berg's symphonic impulses deflected instead into the Three Orchestral Pieces of 1913–14, whose title captures their avoidance of the symphonic genre's implicit demand to add up to more than the sum of its parts, in terms of conveying an overarching message or ethos. Those impulses also informed the second act of his opera *Wozzeck* (1914–21), whose five scenes are a simulacrum of a Mahlerian symphony – acknowledged in Berg's programme notes and lectures on the work – albeit largely as a passive container for a drama that is played out by theatrical means.

Equally held in Schoenbergian thrall was Anton Webern, who in 1928 entitled a two-movement chamber work 'Symphony' (a planned third movement was to be summary, but was abandoned on grounds of tautology with the first). Here again the generic term is applied to what is no more than another passive container, this time for the exploration of abstract polyphony and variation principles by chamber forces, on what was for him admittedly a relatively large canvas. Webern's back was resolutely turned on the symphonic ethos of the post-Beethovenian or post-Mahlerian kinds.

Insofar as the Austro-German symphony survived at all, it was largely within the more modest terms of reference of Hindemith. Hindemith's musical language, derived from Bach by way of Reger and Strauss, was well adapted to the expression of urbanity and cynicism but made for a poor fit with the traditional ethical aspirations of the symphony, which in any case his self-proclaimed emphasis on craftsmanship resisted on principle. Of his five works entitled 'symphony', two are derived from his operas and two are primarily *Gebrauchsmusik* (music for performers' recreation rather than for listeners' edification). His *Mathis der Maler* Symphony (1933–4) is a noble and stirring work, but very much a suite travelling on upgrade, barely distinguishable in generic terms from the 'Symphonic Suite' from Berg's *Lulu* and not angled towards symphonic wholeness even to the limited extent of Prokofiev's opera-derived Third Symphony. In fact, Hindemith's only full-on engagement with the genre was his punchy Symphony in E flat of 1940. The general influence of his pungent linear counterpoint and energetic rhythms on symphonists worldwide was certainly huge, but apart from *Mathis der Mahler* his own symphonies have fallen into a disuse that currently shows no sign of reversing.

As much in the news as Hindemith in the early 1920s, the young Ernst Krenek produced three highly talented symphonies in rapid succession, all of which attempt a continuation of the Mahlerian tone but in the accents of post-Regerian linear counterpoint. The result is a curious sense of disempowerment and despondency that is itself emblematic of the German symphonic crisis. Krenek's two subsequent symphonies from the late 1940s have an unapologetic, gutsy energy but insufficient range of further qualities to earn repertoire status. Such qualities are arguably to be found in Alexander Zemlinsky's exuberantly neo-Romantic *Lyric Symphony* (1922–3) and Kurt Weill's acidic Second (1933–4), the latter written on the cusp of its composer's move from Nazi Germany and lent some degree of symphonic tension by that fraught context. It was, however, not until Karl Amadeus Hartmann's eight numbered symphonies, composed between 1936 and 1962, that Germany again produced a symphonist of something close to international standing, thanks to his creatively potent brews of expressionist and neo-classical ingredients. Yet for all their sterling qualities, these are hardly works that can be ranked for imagination and boldness alongside the contemporary symphonies of Vaughan Williams, Copland, Shostakovich or Prokofiev. Similarly, in the next generation, Hans Werner Henze's ten symphonies (1947–2000), which developed from modest neo-classical beginnings to increasingly expressionist richness and high-flown political and philosophical manifestos, lack the sharp focus of contemporary examples by Michael Tippett, Robert Simpson, Valentin Silvestrov, Giya Kancheli and others to be considered below. Even the three symphonies from the 1970s by Wolfgang Rihm, surely the finest German composer of orchestral and chamber music over the past forty years, are far from the most successful of his works.[15]

The symphonic crisis following the First World War was by no means exclusively an Austro-German phenomenon. So far as utopianism and the aspirations of the 'community-forming' symphony are concerned, it found expression in the United States with the work of the maverick Charles Ives. He managed to bring off the near-impossible in his magnificently sprawling Fourth Symphony (1909–16), which confronts vision and reality in layered textures as prescient aesthetically of Schnittke's First Symphony (1968–72) as they are technically comparable to Stravinsky's *The Rite of Spring*. But Ives bit off more than even he could chew with his 'Universe Symphony', sketched between *c.* 1911 and his death in 1954. Here he set out, in full awareness that it could never be more than an aspiration, 'to cast eternal history, the physical universe of all humanity past, present and future, physical and spiritual, to cast them [in] a "universe of tones"'.[16]

Even more obviously doomed to failure was the project known as *Mysterium* that Aleksandr Skryabin was working on in pre-Revolutionary Russia during the twelve years leading up to his untimely death in 1915. With an envisaged performance that would 'involve all people as votaries in a ritual enacting the miracle of terrestrial and cosmic transformation', this was the *augmentatio ad absurdum* of community-forming art.[17] One part of its reconstruction, undertaken by Aleksandr Nemtin from 1970 to 1996, was entitled 'Universe'. Skryabin had already long since abandoned the term 'symphony' in favour of 'poem' (the Third Symphony of 1904, also known as *The Divine Poem*, is pivotal), and his hubristic conception embraced opera, oratorio and symphony in the unique higher form of Mystery. But he did repeatedly talk of his necessarily unfinished magnum opus in terms of symphonies of colours, costumes, gauzes and the like.[18]

It seems that projects of such explicitly cosmic scope needed an additional focal point if completion was going to be a realistic possibility. Vaughan Williams's *A Sea Symphony* (1909), to poems of Walt Whitman, is a fine demonstration of precisely that. Intermittently as inspiring, but far less convincingly sustained, are the symphonic colossi of Charles Tournemire (No. 7, *Les Danses de la Vie* of 1918–22, tracing the history of mankind from primitive pre-history to the future), Havergal Brian (No. 1, 'Gothic', 1919–27 – in its combination of a *Faust*-inspired instrumental movement and a choral setting of the Te Deum, very obviously another would-be successor to Mahler's Eighth), Olivier Messiaen (*Turangalîla*, 1945, a celebration of cosmic-divine love, expanded from its initially planned four movements into ten) and Henri Sauguet (No. 2, *Symphonie allégorique* or 'The Seasons', 1949, conceived as an oratorio–ballet–symphony). The French examples come at the far end of a specific national tradition of 'message symphonies' with polemical import, an outgrowth of Beethovenian ethical symphonism that has only recently received its scholarly due.[19]

Expressions of the symphonic crisis are to be found equally at the opposite extreme from such mega-symphonies, in works that in various ways turned away from high-flown existential ambitions. In post-Great War central Europe, not only was the institutional infrastructure that had supported symphonic composition now under severe strain, but its underlying cultural assumptions and self-confidence had largely drained away too. Symptomatic of a wave of anti-symphonic disgust are the two-minute *Symphonia germanica* (1919) by the Bohemian-born Erwin Schulhoff (a vicious send-up of the German national anthem) and other Dada-associated phenomena such as Russian émigré Jef Golisheff's *Anti-Symphony: Musical-Circular Guillotine* (1919), whose title refers to the implement designed to saw off the rusted-over ears of the concert-goer. Milder anti-authoritarian manifestations characteristic of the post-war age also help to define symphonism through its negative image. These include Prokofiev's *Classical Symphony* (1917), designed, according to the composer, to 'tease the geese' rather than saw off their ears. This ever-popular work completely ignores the positive polarities of social/national/cosmic affirmation and substitutes playful insouciance and balletic physicality; at the same time, the virtual lack of a negative pole other than that same insouciance places it outside the symphonic mainstream. It would take Prokofiev another twenty-five years to overcome his suspicion of the 'long' symphony, already expressed in his early correspondence with his lifelong friend and specialist in protracted symphonic gloom, Myaskovsky. In June 1908, at work on a pre-first symphony and contemplating the 120 score-pages of Myaskovsky's First, Prokofiev responded:

> Your *longueurs*, as you put it, and the 120 pages, make me very wretched. For what can be worse than a long symphony? To me, the ideal symphony is one that runs for 20, maximum 30, minutes and I'm trying to make mine as compressed as possible. Anything that seems in the least bit pompous I'm crossing out with a pencil, in the most ruthless fashion.[20]

Prokofiev did not have the grace to apologise when three months later his own apprentice-piece symphony weighed in at 131 pages.

At almost exactly the same time as Prokofiev's 'Classical', Stravinsky, then domiciled in Paris but partaking in the broadly based cultural project known as 'Russia abroad', took an even more drastic swerve away from the academicised silver-age Russian symphony he had grown up with (and of which he had produced a talented but routine and derivative example as a student in 1905–7 with his Symphony in E flat). This swerve produced his *Symphonies of Wind Instruments* of 1920, an assembly of folk-archaic and religious materials cut-and-pasted into an episodic design that flew in the face of almost every definition of symphonism before or since (except, possibly, at a bizarre tangent, its community-forming power).[21] This was in effect yet another anti-symphony characteristic of the escapism of the time. Its collage-style discontinuities would be hugely influential on resolute symphonic abstainers later in the century, such as Harrison Birtwistle, and so far as actual symphonies are concerned it supplied at least one vital ingredient for the idiosyncratic and maximalised responses of Messiaen's *Turangalîla* and Tippett's Fourth (1976–7).

Nordic and transatlantic renewals

For symphonists looking to get out from under the Austro-German-centred crisis, national distinctiveness remained a tempting option, but by no means a straightforward one. In the United States, it awaited composers who could respond to Dvořák's call to American music to 'strike roots deeply in its own soil' and develop an indigenous concert music based on its own folk heritage.[22] The search for the 'Great American Symphony' that followed was for something less bizarrely individualistic than, yet as open and democratic as, the visionary Ives (whose work remained little known prior to his posthumous rediscovery and whose influence on the symphony in America was negligible until the 1960s), and at the same time for something as well-crafted as, yet less stultifyingly academic than, the nineteenth-century examples of the likes of John Knowles Paine, George F. Bristow, George Templeton Strong and George Chadwick. Conductor Serge Koussevitzky played a sizeable part in commissioning and performing works to that end during his tenure at the Boston Symphony Orchestra from 1924 to 1949. And Nadia Boulanger's school in Paris had a catalytic role in nurturing the technique and neo-classical outlook of numerous Americans who pursued the elusive goal, whether they resisted her influence (as in the case of Roy Harris, who hit something very close to the bull's-eye with his post-Sibelian Third Symphony in 1938) or embraced it (as did Aaron Copland, whose impressive Third Symphony of 1946 creaked under the burden of striving to be an adequate victory symphony).[23] Other musically more developed nations such as Poland, which, like the United States, neverthless lacked a vigorous nineteenth-century symphonic tradition, had shown signs of evolving one from nationalistic roots, as in Ignaz Paderewski's *Polonia* (1903–7) and Mieczysław Karłowicz's *Rebirth* (1907). But an alternative career and early death, respectively, prevented those individuals from developing as symphonists, while the more richly talented Karol Szymanowski adopted the tag of symphony mainly as an intensifier of other genres (tone poem, cantata, piano concerto in his Second, Third and Fourth Symphonies, respectively).

The boldest and most direct confrontations with the central-European symphonic malaise came from the North. Carl Nielsen, who had an ongoing project to renew Danish national song, nevertheless had to recognise during the Great War (in which his country was neutral) that 'nationalism, formerly the object of such pride, has become a kind of spiritual syphilis'.[24] Like Schulhoff, he experienced the need to enshrine that disillusionment in a kind of anti-symphonism, but in his case that led not to escapism or cynicism but to an enhancement of the negative dramatic pole, which in turn demanded to be balanced by enhanced positives. Allied to a strong creative will and to trust in intuition rather than inherited schemes, this produced a uniquely energetic sense of renewal, prophetic of later developments in the Soviet Union. Yet it was only decades after Nielsen's death that his music gained a receptive audience outside the Nordic region, and even then few in France or Germany could find the wavelength.

Nielsen and Sibelius had remarkably little contact with one other, and their mutual respect only burgeoned into outright influence in a minor way from Nielsen's point of view and not at all from Sibelius's. Nevertheless the coincidental parallels in their symphonic careers are illuminating. Each produced a symphonic masterwork in 1911 that would prove pivotal in their output. For Nielsen it was his Third Symphony, the *Sinfonia espansiva*, whose title encapsulates the outward-looking energy that makes this one of the most invigorating symphonies since Beethoven and Brahms (who are among its main stylistic progenitors). For Sibelius it was his untitled Fourth, examined in detail by

Daniel Grimley in Chapter 12, whose resolutely stoical outlook is symbolised in its blankly staring *mezzo-forte* ending, after the possibility of a Tchaikovsky *Romeo and Juliet*-style lyrical consummation has been glimpsed but rejected. At the heart of Sibelius's profoundly discomfiting symphonic drama is a fusion of Wagnerian, Brucknerian and Tchaikovskian elements. 'Anti-modern' it may be, in the composer's words, but only in the sense of turning its back on luxuriance, self-indulgence and exhibitionism.

The follow-ups to these symphonies were each composed while war was raging in Europe. Engaging with that experience at anything deeper than a surface level entailed the most intense creative struggles of Nielsen's and Sibelius's symphonic careers. Those struggles are reflected both in the music itself and in various documented layers of the creative process, but the result in each case – Nielsen's Fourth and Sibelius's Fifth – is a reaffirmation of the Beethovenian *per ardua ad astra* archetype. Such is the risk level along the way, and the willpower exerted in order to achieve reaffirmation, that each work has gained a firm foothold in the permanent repertoire, and together they confirm a fundamental shift in the symphony's geographical centre of activity.

In Nielsen's Fourth Symphony, the title *The Inextinguishable* is a neuter noun: that which is inextinguishable, i.e. the Life Force. Here the honest-to-goodness exhilaration of the *Sinfonia espansiva* is confronted with far more explicit negativity than ever before in Nielsen's output, memorably externalised in the Finale by two sets of timpani pitted both against each other and in tandem against the rest of the orchestra. The outcome is a blazing reassertion of a lyrical theme in Sibelian thirds whose adaptability has marked it out along the way for Darwinian survival. Sibelius's Fifth, untitled as are all his numbered symphonies, overcomes directionless lethargy and works its way round to a pantheistic celebration of tonality and the perfect cadence.[25] As in Sibelius's Second Symphony, the trajectory is towards hymn-like breakthrough, but this is no longer a hymn swelled with nationalist pride, still less with religious faith, but rather one that conveys euphoria through the coordination of layers of motion. That euphoria is redoubled by the presence of associative meaning, since the layers in question comprise runic chant and symbols of Nature both in its immediate manifestation (the famous horn theme inspired by a flock of swans) and in its underlying rock-like permanence (the augmentation of that same theme in the bass register).

Both Nielsen's and Sibelius's symphonies work with the inherited assumptions of large-scale symphonic form, but not within them. Ever since his First Symphony (1891–2), Nielsen had taken a pragmatic approach to tonal layout, allowing movements or works to end elsewhere than their starting-points. This phenomenon has been labelled 'progressive tonality'. But more important than any calculated directional strategy involved is the sense of adventure and openness to experience that motivates it. Mahler, too, was prepared to end in a different key from where he had begun (as he did in symphonies nos. 2, 4, 5, 7 and 9, as Chapter 10 investigates below), and there too the idea is evidently to give primacy to the psychological journey over the imperative to return home. In Nielsen's case, the journey is as intensely experienced within movements as between them, and the effect is arguably more immediate than with Mahler, thanks to greater concentration and focus, arising from more transparent textures and more classical time-scales. For Sibelius, even if he fashioned the drama of the Fifth Symphony out of resistance to and ultimate affirmation of a goal tonality, the return home remained an unchallenged given. But the large-scale layout of his symphonic movements was by no means so predestined. Only after a painful process of revision did he come up with the Fifth Symphony's masterly elision of first movement and Scherzo, while the design of the Scherzo in itself stakes his claim to being the finest exponent of the large-scale *accelerando* in musical history. Whereas Mahler could not easily sustain an affirmative tone and had to let his material fragment, Sibelius could not easily sustain a mood of fragmentation and felt driven to reaffirm. Different temperaments and world views may lean towards one or the other outlook (it is striking that few conductors have been equally at home with both). But the point is that both Mahler and Sibelius squared up to the polarity of affirmation and fragmentation so symbolic of the modern world, and fashioned mighty symphonic dramas out of it.

Nielsen revisited the existential drama of 'The Inextinguishable' in his Fifth Symphony (1920–2), now with even greater programmatic explicitness matched by even surer structural mastery. 'Bloody trenches music' was the response of one of his friends to the mayhem of the first movement, where the side drum attempts a coup against the rest of the orchestra. But behind the Symphony's conflict-torn surfaces, the fundamental dualism was something more abstract, noted by Nielsen in his draft score as 'dark, resting forces; awoken forces' and in an interview as 'resting forces in contrast to active ones'.[26] For Sibelius, the balance shifted back in favour of darkness in the comparatively rarefied world of his Sixth Symphony (1923), a remarkable instance of four supposedly fast(-ish) movements that nevertheless leave a fundamental impression of inwardness and self-denial, as if predicting the composer's ultimate retreat into creative silence. In the mid-1920s, when new kinds of cultural polarity offered themselves – shallow, hedonistic positives and deep, suppressed negatives – Nielsen and Sibelius pursued their respective strategies of engagement and disengagement. Nielsen struck out on a path of proto-polystylism in his *Sinfonia semplice* (1924–5), whose surfaces are riven by protest, panic, wistfulness and satire. In the process he drew – entirely coincidentally – similar implications from the spirit of the age as the teenage Shostakovich was doing while composing his First Symphony at exactly the same time. Meanwhile, Sibelius was tapping ever deeper into elemental forces of Nature and tying the symphonic threads more tightly than ever before in his single-movement Seventh (1924). Nielsen's angina and Sibelius's chronic self-doubt saw to it that their contributions to the symphony each finished before the second quarter of the century.

With the conclusion of those two symphonic careers came, in effect, the end of the generation of symphonists that had grown up alongside the later symphonies of Brahms, Bruckner, Tchaikovsky and Dvořák. The adaptability from which Nielsen and Sibelius both drew strength, and which in turn lent force to their renewal of the symphony as a genre, came partly from their openness of attitude, but also from other funda-mental qualities. For Nielsen, these were empathy and an expanding world-view, which steered him around the temptations of megalomaniac utopian subjectivity and of brittle, cynical objectivity – the chief cause and aftershock, respectively, of the general symphonic crisis. With Sibelius, it was an ability to suggest more than he stated – something none of his many followers managed to emulate successfully. For Nielsen, the symph-ony was the vehicle for adventures into the unknown, in which the range of new experience was not merely welcomed but also actively processed, with nothing discarded in terms of style, and with reach and grasp advancing synergetically. His symphonic career can be roughly concep-tualised as an ever-widening wedge-shape. For Sibelius it was more a matter of digging ever deeper towards a core of truth, discarding inessen-tials, spurning comfort, human presence and ultimately the vehicle of symphonic composition altogether. For Nielsen the symphony was a manifestation of the human mind's capacity for growth; for Sibelius it was the capacity for penetration.

It was the exhilaration of Nielsen's and Sibelius's symphonic journeys, and the sense of their inner necessity and immunity from fashion state-ment, that gave impulse to their careers in the post-Great War era. This was a time when the Western world's self-confidence was being rebuilt in material terms but was still groping for new spiritual, cultural and aes-thetic bases. It was also a time when near-contemporaries such as Elgar, Glazunov, Rachmaninoff, Reinhold Glière and Josef Suk – all of whom had composed superb symphonies in the Mahlerian age – put their symphonic careers on hold or abandoned them altogether. Nielsen and Sibelius stand head and shoulders above their symphonic contemporaries because they not only asked fundamental questions of the symphony and its idealist conceptions but also proposed hard-won solutions that neither leant on the crutches of delusion nor represented a lowering of sights. In effect they built in, and dealt with, the negativity that German symphonists in the wake of Mahler found disabling. Ultimately, the symbolism of their symphonies reflects precisely the kind of inclusiveness and self-reliance that Ives was preaching in America but could not match with symphonic know-how. The natural, if unwitting, heir to Nielsen's humanism-under-threat would be Shostakovich. The heirs to Sibelius, in many cases fully conscious of their debt, were many and varied, including Arnold Bax, William Walton and Vaughan Williams in Britain, Howard Hanson and Roy Harris in America, later Aulis Sallinen in Finland, and later still Peter Maxwell Davies – testimony in itself to the archetypal power of his symphonic explorations of motion.

Around Nielsen and Sibelius in the post-war era a host of more minor symphonists were cultivating various brands of escapism, iconoclasm and avoidance strategies – exemplified in the so-called Celtic twilight of Bax, Rutland Boughton and Granville Bantock, in the hedonistic nostalgia of Zemlinsky's 'Lyric' Symphony and Szymanowski's Third ('Song of the Night', 1914–16) and in the edgy Parisian *style mécanique* of Prokofiev's Second (1924–5). Such symphonies were capable of producing stunning effects, and they stand far above dozens of their contemporaries. The pre-war cult of ecstasy and euphoria lives on in them, as it did in the more embattled arenas favoured by Sibelius and Nielsen. In the Nordic cases, however, ecstasy was earned through struggle, and euphoria arose from coordinated motion, which they derived from the world around them; those are the qualities that have probably helped them secure repertoire status. In the ten-year period after their last symphonies it is hard to detect achievements on a comparable level. While the musical world waited in vain for Sibelius's Eighth – whose manuscript he eventually immolated – unease was growing that the very capacity of the symphony to produce durable goods was disappearing and that Sibelius's much-lauded model for renewal might after all not prove viable. It was against this background that a startling re-engagement with symphonic ideals would emerge in the 1930s.

Competitions, commissions and discussions

In 1927 the Columbia Broadcasting Company announced a competition for the best completion of Schubert's 'Unfinished' B minor Symphony, with a view to the following year's centenary of the composer's death. The parameters were soon widened, to include any new symphony in the Schubertian lyrical spirit. Regional juries were appointed, to which at least 500 works were submitted for preliminary assessment. Final deliberations seem to have been between Czesław Marek's *Sinfonia*, Franz Schmidt's Third, and the eventual winner, Kurt Atterberg's Sixth. Interviewed after his award of $10,000, the Swede claimed not to have taken the competition too seriously (the piece is indeed feeble), and in the resulting mini-scandal his prize-winning work became known as the 'Dollar' Symphony.

The significant thing about the Schubert competition is not so much that it produced no outstanding works, though it could be argued that among the also-rans Havergal Brian's *Gothic* (whose first movement only was submitted) was a good deal more worthy of an award than any of the actual finalists. Rather it was the perceived need for a new lyrical symphony at all. This perception evidently reflected a widespread dissatisfaction – well before the decade was out – with the iconoclasm of the 'Roaring Twenties', whose symphonic representatives include Aaron Copland's *Organ Symphony*, George Antheil's *Jazz Symphony*, Prokofiev's Second and even Nielsen's *Sinfonia semplice* (in which, however, iconoclasm is objectified as the negative pole). Over the next few years a spirit of re-engagement filtered into the symphonic tradition, given social impetus by new challenges: the rise of fascist dictatorships in Europe, the Wall Street Crash of October 1929 and the subsequent economic Depression. The partial re-bourgeoisification of the Soviet Union under Stalin played its part, too, as did emigration from France and Germany to the United States, where the institution of the symphony concert was younger and more vital – albeit in largely conservative ways – than in Central Europe. Re-engagement with the symphony can be traced in the work of composers as diverse as Prokofiev, who was trumpeting the slogan 'New Simplicity' well before his Fourth Symphony actually embodied it in 1930, Hindemith, Copland (already in his Second Symphony of 1932–3), Shostakovich and Walton. And it has parallels in the work of those who continued to shun the symphony, such as Schoenberg and Bartók.

If the Columbia Schubert competition produced no lasting additions to the symphonic repertoire, Serge Koussevitzky had better fortune in 1930 when he commissioned new symphonic works for the fiftieth anniversary of his orchestra, the Boston Symphony. Apart from such estimable pieces as Ravel's Piano Concerto for Left Hand, Gershwin's Second Rhapsody and Copland's Symphonic Ode, Koussevitzky was rewarded with at least two symphonies that still cling to the edges of repertoire status (Roussel's Third and Prokofiev's Fourth), two that have since faded but would have outclassed anything in the Columbia competition (Honegger's First and

Howard Hanson's Second) and one that stands as a major landmark: Stravinsky's *Symphony of Psalms*. Other American orchestras soon followed Koussevitzky's lead in commissioning new symphonic work, with broadcasting stations and eventually even universities not far behind.

At one level, Stravinsky's readoption of the generic title of symphony is no more than a response to the Koussevitzky commission. A recent returnee to the Russian Orthodox communion, he wanted to compose three psalm settings, and it happened that their trajectory from supplication to thanks to praise and epilogue, together with their contrasts of tempo and mood, mimicked the external features of a symphony. In the context of Stravinsky's drastic re-imagining of the genre ten years earlier in the *Symphonies of Wind Instruments*, the *Symphony of Psalms* pointed back towards the symphonic tradition. Ten years further on, he would produce a still closer simulacrum of the classical symphony, though still keeping his distance from its ethical dimensions. His Symphony in C (1938–40) betrays nothing of his fraught personal circumstances at the time, nor of the looming global conflict. It plays at being 'in C', just as it plays at adopting the good manners of symphonic motion. Again the piece was composed for America, where Stravinsky had recently settled. By contrast, his *Symphony in Three Movements* (1942–5) took a step in the direction of the ethical concerns of traditional symphonism, at least if Stravinsky's own remarks concerning the Finale's images of goose-stepping soldiers and Hiroshima are to be trusted (his comments on his own music are almost compulsively misleading). In structural terms, however, the generic relationship is if anything looser than before, since the three pieces only came together as a symphony thanks to a commission from the New York Philharmonic for such a work, as the title partially acknowledges.

Stravinsky's flirtations with symphonism are prophetic in a number of ways. Taken as a whole, they anticipate a phenomenon of the 1960s and 70s, when composers such as Penderecki, Berio, Schnittke and Maxwell Davies who had previously shunned the genre hit the headlines by returning to the symphony, on their own modernist or postmodernist terms. The *Symphony of Psalms* stands as godfather to the new wave of spiritual symphonism and of the fusion of ancient and modern styles that characterised another phase of genre renewal in the second half of the century. And the Symphony in C and *Symphony in Three Movements* are joint role-models for the opportunistic brand of minimalism represented by John Adams (who referenced them blatantly in his quasi-symphony, *Harmonielehre*, of 1985) and by numerous other Americans at the turn of the twenty-first century. There is no need to look that far ahead to detect the influence of the *Symphony of Psalms*. Messiaen may not have needed its example in order to compose his *Turangalîla Symphony* in 1945 – whose techniques arise rather from *The Rite of Spring* and the *Symphonies of Wind Instruments*. But already in 1940 Britten's *Sinfonia da requiem*, in 1943 Hanson's Fourth Symphony, 'Requiem', and in 1945 Honegger's *Symphonie liturgique* were mapping movements from the mass onto those of the traditional symphony, as Schnittke would do in his Second Symphony of 1979–80.

In the end it was neither competitions nor commissions, nor even apostasy from anti-symphonic modernism, that produced the definitive renewal of the 1930s, though all of those were part of the enabling ethos. The renewal happened not in the Nordic regions, where Sibelius and Nielsen had been such vital forces during the previous three decades, nor in France, for all that Nadia Boulanger's harmony class at the American Conservatory at Fontainebleau from 1921 was nurturing it. The decisive breakthroughs, scarcely foreseeable before 1930, came rather in the United States, England and above all in the Soviet Union.

Not resting on his laurels after his serendipitous commissioning in 1930, Koussevitzky kept up his exhortations to American symphonists to produce 'a great symphony from the West'. Roy Harris's First in 1933 was an early near-miss. But the breakthrough piece was his Third (1937), which managed to fuse the open-spaces frontier mentality of the American dream with single-movement symphonic momentum inherited from Sibelius.[27] Harris's Third certainly captured the American imagination far more immediately than did Rachmaninoff's (1936), though the latter has stood the test of time rather better, making a powerful case for the viability of the nostalgic symphony in the modern world (as do the Fourth and Fifth symphonies of Arnold Bax, 1931 and 1931–2). Rachmaninoff's return to the symphony after nearly thirty years has a remarkable near-parallel in the Third Symphony that Elgar left incomplete on his death in 1934 – an emblematic year for the English symphony.

To what extent individual artistic maturity or national/global contexts fostered the symphony's renewal in the mid-1930s remains an open question. Certainly an element of weariness with the brittle cynicism of the Roaring Twenties must have played its part, along with the gathering clouds of new dictatorships and potential conflict. But the violent streak unexpectedly revealed by Vaughan Williams in his Fourth Symphony (1931–4) – something like César Franck imagined through the prism of Hindemith – can be traced independently of the *zeitgeist* back to the Satanic music for his 'masque for dancing' *Job* (1928), which supplied almost as many impulses for his equally fine Fifth and Sixth Symphonies (1938–43 and 1944–7). Walton's First (1931–5) is evidently an attempt to marry the symphonic idiom of Sibelius with the Elgarian ceremonial tradition (which makes for a creaky finale after three strikingly brilliant movements). Edmund Rubbra's First (1935–7) stands not so very far behind them as a creative achievement, and it is animated by an attempt to reconcile symphonic momentum with centuries-old polyphony,[28] just as Tippett's First (1944–5) is a fusion of Beethovenian fugue, Purcellian ground bass and Hindemithian harmony. Even the arch-Romantic Arnold Bax, after his highly Sibelian Fifth (1932), produced a remarkably tough and spare Sixth (1934), regarded by his champions with some justification as his symphonic pinnacle. The cluster of tough-minded English symphonies around 1934 seems to bear out Constant Lambert's contention – in his polemical book *Music Ho!* published that year – to the effect that Sibelius was a far more productive influence than Schoenberg.[29] And while Britten's *Simple Symphony*, also assembled in 1934, is a playful anti-symphonic romp in the manner of Prokofiev's 'Classical', it shares the same quality as most of its fellow-countrymen of facing away both from the folksong tradition (which had been memorably reconciled with symphonism in Vaughan Williams's Third, 'Pastoral', of 1921) and from the prospects of a new cataclysm in central Europe.

In fact, none of these attempted or actual renewals were as fraught in their background circumstances, yet as profoundly consequential, as their contemporaries in the Soviet Union: above all Shostakovich's Fourth and Fifth Symphonies (1934–6, 1937). Here there is no question that the socio-political context is germane, and both works square up to it. Indeed the ferment from which Shostakovich's twin symphonic peaks arose is unique in the extent to which it determined the environment in which composers worked; unique, too, in the degree of documentation and the heat of argument generated. The three-day 'Discussion on Soviet Symphonism' hosted at the Soviet Composers' Union in February 1935 came at the far end of a decade of Soviet debate about the genre. Among the strands of those arguments were: how and whether the legacies of Beethoven, Mahler and the pre-Revolutionary Russian symphony might be co-opted to the cause of the new society, as Pauline Fairclough elaborates in Chapter 16; whether a new topicality based on approved socialist themes could be reconciled with those legacies; and whether new hybrid genres might more productively embrace the disparate interests of the proletariat and the intelligentsia. Those debates were all given a new impulse from 1932 thanks to the new-born concept of Socialist Realism, first applied in the field of literature. Its undeclared purpose was to unite the power-driven agendas of the Party with the ethical traditions of Russian culture. But its mendaciously prescribed 'truthful, historically concrete representation of reality in its revolutionary development', hard enough for writers to adopt, was impossibly nebulous for composers.

Shostakovich, who had plenty to say at the 1935 'Discussion' about the successes and failures of the Soviet symphony, had already announced his work on a 'symphonic credo', namely his Fourth. Debates continue as to how this white-hot masterpiece lives up to or subverts Socialist-Realist expectations. Less debatably, its own undeclared articles of faith may be read from its virtuosic welding together of the everyday and the transcendent, pushing the Mahlerian understanding of the 'world' to regions where utopia and dystopia are hard to separate and where credo and anathema are pronounced with equal vehemence. The fine line Shostakovich treads between utopia and dystopia, euphoria and terror, is one reason why his Fourth Symphony feels like the most exciting and authentic symphonic document of its decade. Composition of the Finale was interrupted in January and February 1936 by the notorious dual denunciations in *Pravda* of his recent operatic and balletic output. There he was informed in no uncertain terms that his recent creative path could not serve as a model either for him or for any of his composer colleagues. Whether or not he considered that the Fourth Symphony might actually help the cause of his rehabilitation could be argued either way. He was certainly not to know that the purges of the Party carried out in 1936 would escalate into full-scale civic Terror in the following year. Although he completed the Fourth Symphony and put it into rehearsal, he had to bow to *force majeure* and withdraw it just before the scheduled premiere, which had to wait another twenty-five years. In an astonishing act of self-reinvention, Shostakovich came up with his Fifth Symphony in 1937. Here the narrowed field of stylistic vision, compared to the Fourth, was richly compensated for by a more disciplined language and structure, trading a degree of vivid representation for gains in reflective philosophical wisdom. In its expressive depths and humanity, the Fifth Symphony offered a safety valve for a population at the height of Stalin's Great Terror, when the more explicit languages of words and images had become too dangerous for candid communication. The symphony was not unintelligently glossed – by author Aleksey Tolstoy, using a standard cliché of Socialist-Realist literary criticism – as 'the Growth of a Personality', a formulation that strikes much the same balance between official acceptability and humanist values as the music itself. As a feat of artistic manoeuvring – both within the panoply of Soviet symphonic styles represented by Shostakovich's most talented Soviet contemporaries (Gavriil Popov, Nikolay Myaskovsky, Vladimir Shcherbachov, Vissarion Shebalin and hosts of others) and within the vacillating agendas of Socialist Realism – the Fifth was an achievement no less staggering than the Fourth. Even in countries that had little or no knowledge of such manoeuvrings, it registered as epoch-making, though approval was far from universal. Stravinsky and Bartók were almost as scornful of Shostakovich's apparent stylistic backsliding as *Pravda* had been of his previous apparent progressivism. Controversies apart, Shostakovich's Fifth soon established itself as the first example of a truly 'community-forming' symphony since Mahler.

In its aspirational *per ardua ad astra* trajectory, unabashedly exploiting the new democratic idiom of film music alongside that of traditional symphonism, Shostakovich's Fifth had managed to hit on a musical formula for Socialist Realism that none of the doctrine's proponents could clearly define or envisage. At a stroke he also brought about what many at the February 1935 'Discussion' had wishfully and prematurely declared: the passing of the symphonic torch from a decadent West to the bolshevised Soviet Union. He would consolidate that achievement four years after the fifth, when his Seventh Symphony, the 'Leningrad', produced another archetypal example of the symphony's community-forming power, enshrining the cruelty of war, resistance and hope in a hugely morale-boosting work, three quarters of it composed in the besieged city itself. The 'Leningrad' became the object of an unprecedented media frenzy – above all in the USA[30] – and together with the Fifth it became a touchstone for critical–aesthetic debates in the West. Hardly a single symphonist anywhere in the world after 1942 could continue to compose symphonies without having Shostakovich's Fifth and Seventh at some level in their consciousness, whether or not they shared similar aspirations. Meanwhile his Sixth Symphony (1939) showed that he could deploy similar theatrical and cinematographic elements to other, more personal and more elusive ends.

The number of symphonists who also wrote film scores, and indeed the number of film composers who wrote symphonies, is legion. Not only Shostakovich but also Honegger, Britten, Walton, Copland, Vaughan Williams and Prokofiev head the former category, with Miklós Rózsa, Bernard Hermann, Franz Waxman and Erich Wolfgang Korngold making worthy contributions in the latter. Along with the imagery of film, the ambivalent tone of voice in Shostakovich's Fifth gave a new lease of life to musical pathos, which might have been thought forever superseded by the sobriety of neo-classicism. Within the symphonic tradition, Shostakovich had learned that tone from Mahler, but his instincts had also been sharpened by the examples of Stravinsky and Hindemith. Even Prokofiev, whose early aversion to symphonic pathos ran deep, proved to be not immune to the power of ambivalence. This is plain from the final pages of his two greatest symphonies – the wartime Fifth (1944) and the post-war Sixth (1945–7). Even his outwardly modest Seventh (1952) ends – at least in its original version – in a wistful retrospection that questions rather than asserts. Having edged his way back to the traditional symphony via a Third Symphony (1928) derived from his lurid opera *The Fiery Angel* and a Fourth (1929–30) based on his far more sober ballet, *The Prodigal Son*, the fact that Prokofiev eventually accomplished so complete a return to the 'long' symphony is remarkable enough in itself. But without the example of Shostakovich, that return would surely not have happened, or at least not with a fraction of the artistic potency it did – though this is a point Prokofiev would have hated to acknowledge. The quality of Shostakovichian ambivalence emerges all the more strikingly when 'victory' symphonies such as Shostakovich's Ninth of 1945 and Prokofiev's Sixth are compared with others where it is absent. Within the Soviet tradition, Aram Khachaturian's gloriously kitschy Third of 1947, also titled Symphony-Poem, is a good example, with its coruscating organ obbligato and fifteen extra trumpets. Elsewhere Copland's extremely blatant Third of 1944–6 can be entered into evidence, with its grafting of his 1942 *Fanfare for the Common Man* into the Finale (even allowing for the fact that the fanfare itself was written more with the oppressed working classes in mind than anything to do with the American Dream or the War effort). Among other symphonies of the mid-1940s, only Vaughan Williams's vehement and desolate Sixth (1944–7) has the stature of Prokofiev's and Shostakovich's finest, and only Messiaen's *Turangalîla* (1946–8), with its very different agenda, holds a comparably firm place in the repertoire.

Conflictlessness and cold war

Neither Beethoven nor Mahler had to contemplate barbarism on the scale of the two world wars, the atrocities of the Nazi death camps and the Gulag, or the cataclysm of the atom bomb. In the post-war era these enormities were visually accessible as never before, with the exception of the Gulag, where memoir-based literature was the prime source, and a time-delayed one at that, thanks to the survival of Stalin's dictatorship until his death in March 1953. Symphonists in these years who clung to Mahlerian ideals, or who might have been otherwise inclined towards creative acts of commemoration, had only a shaky legacy to build on, especially in the Soviet Union. There Shostakovich's Eighth (1943), written in the midst of war but looking beyond it, and Prokofiev's Sixth, written after the war but looking back on its horrors, might have pointed the way. But both works were banned in the aftermath of the 'anti-formalism' campaign that hit Soviet composers in 1948. That campaign, spearheaded by Stalin's henchman Andrey Zhdanov and hence known as Zhdanovshchina (the Zhdanov business), urged composers to re-engage with music for the 'people', not least by returning to ethnic sources, rather than add to the mountain of supposedly elitist symphonies, quartets and sonatas.[31] The ban itself was short-lived, but the works affected (also including Khachaturian's Third Symphony) remained too hot for Soviet promoters and practitioners to handle, which in turn delayed their potential export to the West. Shostakovich read the omens accurately and held off from symphonic composition until the death of Stalin in 1953, when he produced his Tenth. Even this masterpiece had to undergo a three-day peer review in the Union of Composers before being approved for continued public consumption. Since then, however, Shostakovich's Tenth has become widely regarded as his symphonic masterpiece, thanks to its integration of immanence and transcendence at a higher level than the Fourth Symphony, to its harnessing of Beethovenian economy to Bachian counterpoint, to its sheer force of musical personality and not least to its unimpeachable orchestral technique.

Shostakovich's Tenth is in many ways a summary of the achievements of mid-twentieth-century ethical symphonism, and not only in the USSR. Yet it was also to prove an end-point. Though numerous Soviet symphonists responded to its challenge, as they would again in the 1960s following the delayed premiere of Shostakovich's Fourth in December 1961, he himself turned to other branches of the genre – principally to the programmatic-epic (in symphonies nos. 11 and 12) and to the cantata/song-cycle hybrid (in symphonies nos. 13 and 14). Vaughan Williams in England did similarly after his central symphonic triptych, with his film-score-based *Sinfonia Antartica* (No. 7), his elliptical Eighth and his stoical Ninth. Even after the post-Stalin Thaw had given way to a prolonged 'Stagnation' from the mid 1960s, the channels of information exchange that had been tentatively established with the West remained more or less open, ensuring that the Soviet symphony would be less insulated from the rest of the world than before, which also meant more susceptible to Western hang-ups. Gradually the heroic-epic symphony in its pure form became even less viable than it otherwise would have been, though there were still numerous attempts to fashion hybrids with concepts permeating from the West.

Even in the late-Stalin era, from 1948–53, there are some parallels to be drawn between East and West. Soviet symphonists, cowed in the aftermath of the Zhdanovshchina, had to put high ambitions on hold, and the resulting more or less compulsory mildness of tone became known – and increasingly deprecated – by the term coined for that kind of literature: 'conflictlessness'. In the West, too, in the aftermath of the Second World War and genocide, and with the perceived nuclear threat in the headlines, the reaction was to look inwards or backwards, disavowing music's potential community-forming power altogether and proceeding as though only a retreat from humanism into material objectivity or mysticism was artistically responsible. The projects of the 1950s Western avant-garde were seemingly diametrically opposed to Soviet Socialist Realism in stylistic terms, since they were for the most part recklessly adventurist, experimental and hostile to all such received genres as symphony, rather than, as in the USSR, guardedly pusillanimous, conservative and wedded to the past. But the two traditions were at one in their disengagement from social issues. An unwitting pawn in the Cold War, the Western avant-garde was sustained by a network of pundits and politicians who saw its revivified modernism as a potential bulwark against the no-less doctrinaire world view of a newly militant Eastern bloc. And when the CIA's covert financial sustenance collapsed in the 1970s, thanks to economic strictures consequent on the Middle Eastern oil crisis, so too did much of the avant-garde's delusional mythology, along with its hostility to the symphony.

Western symphonists were also in the mood for detoxification. Hence the phenomenon of the 'Cheltenham Symphony' in England, named after the Festival supported by a well-intentioned Arts Council. From the late-1940s through to the 1960s, the Cheltenham Festival commissioned dozens of well-constructed, workmanlike but musically dilute neo-classical symphonies, almost all with worthy aims but narrow horizons, from the likes of Lennox Berkeley, Peter Racine Fricker, Alun Hoddinott, Alan Rawsthorne, William Wordsworth and William Alwyn. Meanwhile in America, institutions such as the Juilliard School and the better-endowed of the universities and orchestras provided havens not only for the experimentalist avant-garde but also for redoubtable symphonists such as Peter Mennin, Paul Creston and William Schuman. Their works were generally speaking as hermetically sealed against the contamination of the outside world as those of the avant-garde, and therefore proved equally ephemeral. Symphonies far superior to theirs were composed in the 1950s by mavericks and independents such as the Dane Vagn Holmboe (No. 8 *Sinfonia boreale*, 1951) and the Englishmen Robert Simpson (No. 2, 1955–6) and Malcolm Arnold (nos. 2 and 3, 1953 and 1957), all of whom found ways to make the Nordic priority of elemental animation feel like part of an ethos of reconstruction. Even a symphony as fine as Tippett's Second (1956–7) – possibly the only one from the 1950s worthy of mention in the same breath as Shostakovich's Tenth (as Mieczysław Weinberg's Fifth of 1962 definitely is) – operates at a highly abstract level of post-Vivaldian-cum-Stravinskyian energeticism. That a composer already as deeply engaged as Tippett with existential and contemporary political issues should only feel able to incorporate them into symphonies after the seismic shifts of the 1960s, is indicative. It would take those shifts, and the painful confrontations they entailed, to re-establish symphonic composition on something like its former level of prestige.

Anti-anti-symphonies, apostates and apostles

The defining event in the symphonic/anti-symphonic battlegrounds of the 1960s was the *Sinfonia* of 1968–9 by Luciano Berio (another focal work of Chapter 12). This deliberately pluralistic rag-bag of a piece is admittedly as much a prisoner of its fashion-conscious decade as the fashions it seeks to comment on. It stands as a culmination of years of symphonic confrontation with phenomena supposedly antithetical to the genre: twelve-note constructivism; stylistic mixtures; chamber and other idiosyncratic forces and layouts; concerto elements; incorporation of vocal/choral forces; aleatoricism (chance elements) and sonorism (extended instrumental techniques and noise effects); religious contemplation and political engagement. (One of the few elements of this kind that did not spark many symphonists was the newish field of electronics, though it did produce at least one superb example in Roberto Gerhard's Symphony No. 3, *Collages*, of 1960.) The results were often appealingly weird and wacky, occasionally wonderful, and in many cases explicable as anti-authoritarian responses to a decade that witnessed the brink of global nuclear conflict (the Cuban missile crisis of October 1962), race riots, the Vietnam War and military conflict in the Middle East.

Among the more headline-grabbing symphonies in the 1960s and early 1970s, the weakest (such as Arvo Pärt's First and Second, or Hans Werner Henze's Sixth) wore one or more of those anti-symphonic elements as embarrassing fashion statements, rather as middle-aged hippies adopted alternative lifestyles. The finest, by contrast, built them in to their symphonies as new negative poles, to be wrestled with in the service of existential conflict on a new plane. Examples of such accentuation of the negative are Shostakovich's Fourteenth (1969), whose contrasting tonal and twelve-note ideas support a dualism of physicality and death, and his Fifteenth (1971), where quotation and self-quotation participate in a drama of memory and creativity. Similarly, in Tippett's Third (1970–2), blues and quotation from Beethoven's Ninth combine to symbolise a questioning of the brotherhood of man. Aesthetic success or failure apart, such renewed receptivity to the notion – and indeed the problems - of community-forming symphonism was furthered by the rediscovery of Mahler following his centenary in 1960 and around the same time of Ives as the godfather to avant-garde experimentalism of a non-doctrinaire, inclusive kind, not to mention the global phenomenon of The Beatles. In their very different ways each of these offered models of transcendental messages conveyed through a fusion of musical vernacular and rarefied experiment.

Socio-economic parallels between the transition from the Roaring 1920s to the 1930s and that from the Swinging 1960s to the 1970s offer a useful means of orientation. In each case, an economic crisis issued a wake-up call to Western societies (felt intensely after 1973 when the OPEC nations suddenly increased the price of oil) and permissive hedonism gave way to more sober outlooks. In terms of the symphony, practice had already been evolving less by expansion and growth than through encounters with new negatives. As the examples of Shostakovich and Tippett suggest, these encounters found a place in a replay of traditional symphonic dramas but now at a higher level – involving contrasts not just between themes and movements but between styles and aesthetics or belief systems. Even Robert Simpson, having published his desiderata for 'true' symphonism in 1967, just at the time when symphonists were deriving new energy from most of the qualities he was excluding, was himself in the middle of a symphonic sabbatical. From this he would return with a vengeance in the 1970s with a succession of imposing works, each of which showed, from the perspective of one who had never dabbled in modernism, how such 'unsymphonic' elements as twelve-note aggregations and atonal stasis could be incorporated as new negative poles. Such negativity, Simpson the composer realised, can create friction and demand to be dealt with, rather than merely presented as neutral material. Simpson's mature symphonies were therefore, in effect, anti-anti-symphonies, and their extensive paraphrases of Beethoven (in No. 4, 1972) or quotations of Bruckner (in No. 9, 1986) appear virtually as manifestos for the enduring eloquence of the symphony in the late twentieth century. But not only that; for Simpson's concentration on substance and inner drive unmasks whole swathes of audience-friendly symphonism – especially in the USA – as feeble-minded by comparison. Conspicuous exceptions to that generalisation are the three symphonies of Christopher Rouse (1986, 1994 and 2011), Elliott Carter's *Symphony of Three Orchestras* (1976) and, even more so, his *Symphonia*, completed in 1996. At the same time, however, Simpson's avoidance of cultural-political topicality, and his resolutely unflashy scoring, have militated against his symphonies' finding a permanent place in a market-driven orchestral repertoire. His power-packed Fifth (1972), was the nearest to a break-through piece.

Appearing a year after Simpson had published his desiderata for 'true symphonism', Berio's *Sinfonia* could hardly have been more subversive of them. It was to be far from the last such act of subversion in the symphonic tradition, even though for Berio it remained a one-off. There was to be no bolder statement of a new negative pole than in Schnittke's First Symphony (1969–72), which he at one stage considered actually dubbing 'anti-symphony'. This was bold by virtue of the fact that the taboos it broke were far more real in the USSR than any operating in the West (which also means, paradoxically, that transgression *per se* was far easier to achieve). Schnittke's First took the confrontation of symphony with its opposites to unheard-of levels, not so much constructing dramas from new positive–negative polarities in a spirit of renewal, as systematically snuffing out all positives until just the faintest hint of redemption dawns in the Finale, with a conglomeration of diatonic chants in resistance to the marauding *Dies irae*. That such willingness to question the essence of the symphony was not a local phenomenon is further confirmed by Tippett's Third Symphony, in which the anxieties of the twentieth century and of the symphony itself are symbolised by the brushing aside of Beethoven's 'Ode to Joy' from the Choral Symphony in favour of a queasy blues. This is the other side of the coin from Simpson's Fourth Symphony (1970–2), which fashions its Scherzo as a paraphrase of the Scherzo from the same Beethoven symphony, but here as an unequivocal statement of faith in the continuing viability of Beethovenian energy.

In principle, Tippett's symphonic trajectory was a continuation of the Stravinskyan project to re-engage with the genre at the same time as redefining its potential – a paradoxical affirmation out of scepticism. By contrast, Schnittke's First, like Berio's *Sinfonia* (which Schnittke knew and analysed) is as much a manifesto as a work of art – from the opposite party platform to Simpson's. Whereas Berio adheres to minimal standards of taste and craft, Schnittke deliberately (or perhaps inadvertently) serves up a mess instead of music, daring commentators to fling up their hands in outrage (which they duly did). In fact there is rather more craft in Schnittke's work than meets the ear. And because of the strength of their scepticism, neither Schnittke's nor Tippett's work is quite the act of apostasy it might seem to be (in the sense of going against the avant-garde's determination to stigmatise the symphony as a dead form). But they certainly prepared the ground for that phenomenon later in the 1970s, when composers such as Penderecki and Maxwell Davies, who had been avant-garde iconoclasts through the 1950s and 1960s, startled the musical world by rediscovering points of contact with symphonic tradition, via Mahler and Sibelius, respectively. Admittedly neither composer is likely to be remembered for his symphonies, which lack the focus and dramatic edge of their most distinctive work. Penderecki's symphonies have been increasingly vitiated by neo-Romantic posturing and

Maxwell Davies' by obsessive-compulsive note-spinning. In neither case is the negative pole dramatised anywhere near as effectively as by Schnittke or Tippett.

The crucible of communicative post-war musical modernism was Poland, where the surface attractions of the avant-garde combusted with the audience-friendly rhetoric of the East. Here, after the first flurries of excitement had died down, most composers willingly ditched the modernist baggage for the sake of re-engagement with the symphony. What they retained from that flirtation, at least for a while, were the elements of chance and sonorism (indebted to Cage and Bartók, respectively), which were later to be replaced by spiritual subject matter and moody contemplation. Witold Lutosławski forged an uneasy compromise with his Second Symphony (1968), styling his two movements as 'Hesitant' and 'Direct' in a way that recalls Sibelius and Nielsen in principle though not in practice (the same ploy features far more potently in the first movement of Tippett's Third, as 'Arrest' and 'Movement').[32] But Lutosławski hit something much closer to the bull's-eye in 1983 with his Third Symphony. Meanwhile Henryk Górecki took a more drastic path from the violence of his Second Symphony ('Copernican', 1972) to the consoling beauty of his Third ('Symphony of Sorrowful Songs', 1976). The latter made little impact on its initial appearance but gained a cult following in 1992, following astute marketing of a CD markedly inferior to the Polish recording that had long been in circulation without attracting much media attention. In one of the most fascinating case-studies of musical appropriation, Górecki's Third then became a soundtrack for documentaries about the Holocaust, which had been no part of the composer's intentions.[33]

The New Spirituality, generally expressed in pacific neo-tonal or neo-modal idioms, was the one ingredient implied in the expansions of 1960s symphonism that Berio had not enshrined in his *Sinfonia* and that Schnittke had barely hinted at in his First Symphony. It would flourish through the 1970s and beyond. Of course, symphonies with more-or-less overt spiritual programmes had been composed periodically through the twentieth century and before, sometimes even with the label 'sacra' attached (beginning with Holmboe's Fourth in 1941, and with Andrzej Panufnik's Third of 1963 as the salient example). The strikingly new project was to marry that impulse with a fresh consideration of folk sources (itself a long-established escape route from modernist-materialist impasses) and increasingly with aspects of ecumenicism and new-age contemplation as well. These dimensions were the flip side to the militant Islamic fundamentalism that fulminated after the Arab–Israeli conflict of 1967 and that came to the surface with the deposing of the Shah of Iran

and the establishment of theocratic rule there in 1979. The rising materialism of the 1980s in the West, with powerful right-of-centre governments
in the UK and USA setting the agenda for revived capitalism and a
precipitous collapse of the socialist alternative, seem to have prompted
an urge among symphonists to redress the balance, with a renewed
emphasis on spiritual values. It is important to recognise that the concomitant rehabilitation of tonality had nothing necessarily to do with
affirmatory aesthetics or right-wing politics but could equally betoken
apostasy from a discredited and dysfunctional avant-garde.

All these trends can be traced quite clearly in the work of four composers who worked in the satellite republics of the Soviet Union and were
thus to some extent immune from the worst effects of centralised control.
The weakest representatives are the three early symphonies of the
Estonian Arvo Pärt, which are a parade of attempts to drag the Soviet
symphony into the world of modern -isms – from serialism and sonorism,
through polystylism and symbolic quotation, to archaism, stopping at the
threshold of the full-blown spiritualism that coincided with his abandon-
ment of the symphony from the 1970s (his Fourth Symphony had its
premiere in Los Angeles in January 2009 and proved a very damp squib).
Far more potent are the seven symphonies of the Georgian Giya Kancheli,
whose starting-point was the encounter with Shostakovich's rehabilitated
Fourth, but which soon moved into polarised regions of contemplation
and explosion, indebted to Stravinsky, Shostakovich and the spirit of
Georgian folk music. Kancheli's symphonies nos. 3 to 6 (1973–81) are
single-movement structures of twenty-five to thirty-five minutes at least
(when taken at the uncompromisingly slow tempi on which Kancheli
insists). All offer fine examples of controlled accumulation and release of
tension. In his eight symphonies (1969–89) the Armenian Avet Terteryan
retained more of the trappings of Polish-style sonorism than did Kancheli,
and at the same time placed folk elements closer to the surface of his music
in the shape of actual folk instruments, making for a remarkable fusion of
militancy and meditation. Finally the Ukrainian Valentin Silvestrov, also
with eight numbered symphonies so far to his name, plus several symphonic upgrades from concertante works, began with flirtations with a
poeticised Webernian pointillism. At the apex of his output is his masterly
Fifth Symphony (1980–2), the finest symphonic embodiment of his self-
declared act of 'disarmament', wherein hypnotic memories of Mahler and
earlier Romantics evoke a beauty that is craved but no longer graspable.
All these works in their various ways show symphonists disengaging from
the world, at a time when the West was facing up to the consequences of
new economic realities and when Ronald Reagan in the USA and Margaret
Thatcher in the UK had sat down heavily on the anti-socialist end of

the political see-saw. Those realities eventually forced the Soviet Union into its reformist period of glasnost and perestroika under Mikhail Gorbachev from 1985, leading ineluctably to the collapse of communism and of the Union itself in 1991.

By comparison with the best work of these four composers, the blend of modernism and spirituality in the 1980s symphonies of the bigger names in post-Shostakovich Russia – principally Edison Denisov, Schnittke and Sofiya Gubaidulina – seems speculative and schematic, largely because of their heavy reliance on symbolism, evidently seeking to compensate for under-developed compositional strategies and insufficient aural filtering. The one symphony of Schnittke's that fully lives up to his reputation is in fact his first to eschew spiritual symbolism altogether, namely the Concerto grosso No. 4/Symphony No. 5 of 1988, a virtuoso genre-fusion that moves from post-Stravinskian concerto grosso to post-Mahlerian symphony, displaying a magnificent gift for dystopian frenzy throughout. The only other symphonies from the last decade or so of the Soviet era that can be ranged alongside Kancheli, Terteryan, Silvestrov and Schnittke's Fifth for communicative intensity are those of the maverick Galina Ustvolskaya, beginning with her Second of 1979 ('True, Eternal Bliss') and ending with the Fifth of 1991 ('Amen'), whose agonised spirituality is conveyed with extreme intransigence and hard-hitting intensity, indebted to Bartók and Stravinsky.

Politics and popular music

Outside the Soviet Union there have been any number of symphonies written with overtly spiritual content, but few that can match Kancheli, Terteryan, Silvestrov and Ustvolskaya for a sense of inner necessity or control over large time-spans. The Scot James MacMillan, directly influenced by Ustvolskaya's work, arguably did so in his First and Third Symphonies ('Vigil', 1997; 'Silence', 2002). MacMillan, a composer with a high profile for his political as well as religious views, has tended to channel the former in the direction of opera and the latter in the direction of symphony. Others have sought a fusion, producing symphonies with comparably grand ambitions but far less creative potency. From China, Tan Dun's 'Symphony 1997: *Heaven, Earth, Mankind*' and his *2000 Today: A World Symphony for the Millennium* are cases in point, their compendious programmes being in inverse proportion to their musical interest. These and other symphonies from the East, such as those by the Japanese Takashi Yoshimatsu, have in their favour a sensibility unencumbered by Western assumptions of taste and technical competence. But their immediately gratifying surfaces and politically correct programmes offer little substance to chew on. Meanwhile symphonies have been written about conflicts in Vietnam, the Balkans and Iraq, about the bringing down of the Berlin Wall and about the terrorist attacks of 11 September 2001. But none of these has generated more than local or ephemeral interest. Meanwhile, those who have dared to broach such topics as power politics, fundamentalist religion, terrorism and climate change – the preoccupations that drove disease, post-communism and civil rights off the front pages in the first decade of the twenty-first century – have generally done so in genres other than symphony, such as opera and oratorio. Yet given the pluralism of postmodern attitudes to style, there would seem to be no reason in principle why fine symphonies should not emerge with such agendas, if only the music and the message can be made to serve one another.

The only other major new trend to have emerged in the symphony since 1990 is a reconsideration of possible interfaces with popular music. Coming from the direction of the high-art composer, John Adams's Chamber Symphony of 1992 achieved an unlikely but effective fusion between Schoenbergian atonality – which occasionally surfaces very usefully as a negative pole in his otherwise relentlessly affirmatory style – and popular cartoons, notably Roadrunner (Adams's 'Son of Chamber Symphony', premiered in 2009, is similarly urbane and hyper-active). Far less interesting is Michael Daugherty's attempt to upgrade the Superman story to symphonic status ('Metropolis' Symphony, 1988–93). Among his eight numbered symphonies to date, Philip Glass's First ('Low', 1992) and Fourth ('Heroes', 1996), paraphrasing albums by David Bowie and Brian Eno, are by no means the most turgid. But from the pop/rock end, perhaps the most interesting phenomenon is New York-based guitarist Glenn Branca, who has produced a series of ambitiously titled symphonies (the latest to the time of writing being No. 13, 'Hallucination City' for 100 guitars, premiered in 2006, No. 14, 'The Harmonic Series', premiered in 2008 and No. 15 'Running through the World like an Open Razor', premiered in 2010). These have won some recognition and if nothing else have a feel of needing their large-scale dimensions in order to convey matters of depth and urgency, avoiding the instant gratification of most of their art-symphony compatriots.

Instead of prognostication

Writing as the centenary of Mahler's death approaches, it is as hard, and as pointless, to make predictions as it would have been for Paul Bekker in 1911. Symphonies are still commissioned, or written in response to non-specific commissions, by such bastions as the London Proms, among the most prominent from that source in the past quarter-century being the Dane Poul Ruders's

Himmelhochjauchzend, zum Tode betrübt (1989) and three from England: Robin Holloway's First (1998–9), which seeks to chart the musical course of the twentieth century; John Casken's First ('Broken Consort', 2004), in which a concertante gypsy ensemble defines the topic of cultural difference; and David Matthews's finely argued Sixth (2007). But symphonies have long since ceased to be solicited by competitions, which nowadays tend to specify the medium (usually small) but not the genre. And they are unlikely to feature as topics for composers' symposia any time soon. The demand for large orchestral works has become more focussed on symphonic poems (in effect if not name) and concertos, which a number of star soloists are happy to support, while the popularity of concertos for orchestra fuels suspicions that for better or worse composers remain daunted by the notion of the symphony (no bad thing, it might be thought). Meanwhile the infrastructure that supported more than 250 years of symphonic composition has shown unmistakable signs of fragility. Pundits both Eastern and Western have been observing – if not lamenting – the shift of the symphony concert to the status of lifestyle accessory driven by the imperatives of marketing, rather than of quasi-religious observance.

As for composers with established reputations as symphonists, of the generation of the 1920s and 1930s still creatively active in the twenty-first century, Henze completed his Tenth in 2000, and only ill health seems to have prevented a continuation of the cycle; Kancheli put a full stop to his symphonic output with No. 7 ('Epilogue', 1986), though he has continued to compose long orchestral pieces that could carry the generic title without embarrassment. Like him, Per Nørgård seemed to have closed the book with his millennial Sixth ('At the End of the Day') only to reopen it with an impressive Seventh in 2006. Fans of the mystical aura of the 'Ninth Symphony' may note the significant number of composers seemingly stalled at its threshold. Maxwell Davies put a comma to his symphonic output with his Eighth ('Antarctic') in 2000, returning only in 2012 with his Ninth, dedicated to Queen Elizabeth II in her diamond jubilee year; Einojuhani Rautavaara reached his Eighth ('The Journey') in 1999, Penderecki his ('Songs of the Past') in 2005 and Silvestrov his in 2007. Schnittke was working on his Ninth up to his death in 1998; but if its reconstruction by Alexander Raskatov is anything like an accurate deciphering of its almost illegible manuscript, it has to be reckoned no more coherent than Schnittke's previous three symphonies.

Finland continues to produce a plethora of high-grade symphonies, thanks to public and political assent to the value of subsidy for the arts (the same applies to opera), and thanks to the creative vigour of individualists such as, above all, Kalevi Aho, whose Fifteenth Symphony was first heard in Manchester in March 2011. Certainly, anyone who can take on and make such a magnificent job of a commission for a symphony to be performed on the slopes of a hillside in Lapland, with musicians up to 300 metres away from the conductor (No. 12, *Luosto*, 2002–3), cannot be accused of lack of symphonic ambition. Aho's Ninth (1994) has a fair claim to being the finest of his numerous post-Mahlerian concertante symphonies (the solo instrument here being trombone, doubling on sackbut). In the year that symphony was composed, Richard Taruskin, introducing an appreciative essay on Vagn Holmboe, produced one of his most apposite sound-bites: 'In the twentieth century the symphony moved to the suburbs.'[34] That remains true today, when Finland, Britain and the USA continue to provide the breeding-ground for fine symphonies. However, in a less well-judged postscript from 2008 Taruskin opined that with Holmboe's death in 1996 the world had lost its 'greatest living traditional symphonist' and that 'there is no one living now to whom such an epithet could be meaningfully applied'.[35] By virtue of openness of outlook and virtuosity of technique, Aho's ongoing symphonic output makes a clear riposte to that claim.

Jeremiads concerning the death of the symphony, or of classical music altogether, have been sprinkled around ever since the 1830s, and they generally look stupid almost as soon as they are made. It would be comforting to respond – as Mahler reportedly did in conversation with Brahms about the death of music – that the urge to compose symphonies and to listen to them is as unstoppable as the flow of water to the sea. If the flow appears to stagnate from time to time, then climate change will inevitably intervene and cut new channels. From the perspective of 1918 it would have been next to impossible for Paul Bekker to foresee the flowering of the symphony in Russia, Britain and the United States in the following decades. Nearly a century on, the seeds of the next symphonic renewal may be just as hard to discern. But so long as the ambition to enshrine the human condition in sound remains intact, they will surely continue to germinate.

Notes

1 Paul Bekker, *Die Sinfonie von Beethoven bis Mahler* (Berlin, 1918), esp. 20, 32, 58–61.

2 See, for example, Gottfried Wilhelm Fink, 'Über die Symphonie', *Allgemeine Musikalische Zeitung*, 37 (1835), cols. 505–11, 521–4, 557–63.

3 Natalie Bauer-Lechner, *Recollections of Gustav Mahler* (London 1980, orig. Leipzig, 1923), 40.

4 See Karl Ekman, *Jean Sibelius: His Life and Personality* (New York, 1946), 191.

5 Robert Simpson, ed., *The Symphony* (Harmondsworth, 1967), vol. II, 13–14.

6 Ekman, *Jean Sibelius*, 191.

7 See Glenda Dawn Goss, *Jean Sibelius and Olin Downes: Music, Friendship, Criticism* (Boston, 1995).

8 Robert Simpson, *Sibelius and Nielsen: A Centenary Essay* (London, 1965), 21.

9 See Brian Hart, 'The French Symphony after Berlioz', in A. Peter Brown, *The Symphonic Repertoire*, vol. III, Part B: *The European Symphony from ca. 1800 to ca. 1930: Great Britain, Russia, and France* (Bloomington, 2008), 527–755, here at 657.

10 Claude Debussy, 'Monsieur Croche the Dilettante-Hater', in *Three Classics in the Aesthetics of Music* (New York, 1962), 17.

11 For the most wide-ranging study of the Austro-German symphony in the inter-war period, see Manuel Gervink, *Die Symphonie in Deutschland und Österreich in der Zeit*

zwischen den beiden Weltkriegen (Regensburg, 1984).

12 'Gustav Mahler', in *Style and Idea* (London, 1975), 449–72; and see commentary in Peter Franklin, *The Idea of Music* (London, 1985), 77–90.

13 See Josef Rufer, *The Works of Arnold Schoenberg* (London, 1962), 115–18, and Jan Maegaard, *Studien zur Entwicklung des dodekaphonen Satzes bei Arnold Schönberg* (Copenhagen, 1972), vol. I, 80–5 and 'Notenbeilage', 93.

14 Published in facsimile and transcription as Alban Berg, *Symphonie-Fragmente* (Vienna, 1984).

15 But see the composer's penetrating introductory texts in Ulrich Mosch, ed., *Wolfgang Rihm: ausgesprochen* (Mainz, 1997).

16 Larry Austin, CD booklet note to Centaur CRC2201 (1994), 3.

17 See Simon Morrison, 'Skryabin and the Impossible', *Journal of the American Musicological Society*, 51 (1998), 283–330, here at 284.

18 See Leonid Sabaneyev, *Erinnerungen an Alexander Skrjabin* (Berlin, 2005), 136 and 263.

19 Hart, 'The French Symphony after Berlioz', 656.

20 Dmitry Kabalevsky, ed., *S.S. Prokof'ev i N. Ya. Myaskovsky: perepiska* [*Prokofiev and Myaskovsky: Correspondence*] (Moscow, 1977), 52.

21 For a definition of symphonic as the opposite of episodic, see Schoenberg, *Style and Idea*, 462. For a speculative comment on the community-forming aspect of the *Symphonies of Wind Instruments*, see Richard Taruskin, *Defining Russia Musically* (Princeton, 1997), 400–5.

22 Cited in Michael Beckerman, 'The Real Value of Yellow Journalism', *Musical Quarterly*, 77 (1993), 749–68, at 749.

23 See Richard Taruskin, *The Oxford History of Western Music*, vol. IV: *The Early Twentieth*

Century (Oxford, 2005), 637–73, and vol. V: *The Late Twentieth Century* (Oxford, 2009), 3–6.

24 Irmelin Eggert Møller and Torben Meyer, eds., *Carl Nielsens Breve* [Nielsen's Letters] (Copenhagen, 1954), 144.

25 See James Hepokoski, *Sibelius: Symphony No. 5* (Cambridge, 1993), esp. 58–60.

26 See David Fanning, *Nielsen: Symphony No. 5* (Cambridge, 1997), 97.

27 See Taruskin, *Oxford History of Western Music*, vol. IV, *The Early Twentieth Century*, 637–73.

28 See Leo Black, *Edmund Rubbra: Symphonist* (Woodbridge, 2008), 41–55.

29 Constant Lambert, *Music Ho!: A Study of Music in Decline* (London, 1934). For a stimulating overview of the British symphony in the 1930s and 40s, see Guido Heldt, 'Erste Symphonien – Britten, Walton und Tippett', in Wolfgang Osthoff and Giselher Schubert, eds., *Symphonik 1930–1950: Gattungsgeschichte und analytische Beiträge* (Mainz, 2003), 84–108. For more comprehensive coverage see Jürgen Schaarwächter, *Die britische Sinfonie 1914–1945* (Cologne, 1995).

30 See Christopher Gibbs, '"The Phenomenon of the Seventh": A Documentary Essay on Shostakovich's "War" Symphony', in Laurel Fay, ed., *Shostakovich and his World* (Princeton, 2004), 59–113.

31 See Alexander Werth, *Musical Uproar in Moscow* (London, 1949).

32 For more on this and other dualisms in Tippett's Third, see Ian Kemp, *Tippett: The Composer and his Music* (London, 1984), 436–56.

33 See Luke Howard, 'Motherhood, *Billboard*, and the Holocaust: Perceptions and Receptions of Górecki's Symphony No. 3', *Musical Quarterly*, 82 (1998), 131–59.

34 'A Survivor from the Teutonic Train Wreck', in Taruskin, *The Danger of Music and Other Anti-Utopian Essays* (Berkeley, 2009), 43.

35 Ibid., 45.

PART II

Studies in symphonic analysis

6 Six great early symphonists

MICHAEL SPITZER

Imagine if a scholar of Renaissance art picked out Leonardo, Raphael and Michelangelo, and ignored Botticelli, Titian, Tintoretto, Veronese, Correggio, Bellini, Giorgione, Mantegna, Donatello, Fra Angelico and countless other Italian masters (not to mention those of France, Germany, Spain, the Low Countries and England). Unthinkable as that would be, it is strange that musical scholars of the classical style are generally comfortable with the notion of a 'big three' of mature artists (Haydn, Mozart, Beethoven) crowning a pyramid of *Kleinmeister*. Yet Jan LaRue's inventory of the eighteenth-century symphony lists 13,000 works by dozens of fine composers.[1] My present purpose is to sketch the evolution of the symphony by focussing on six of these composers, whom, without any apology, I term *great*: Giovanni Battista Sammartini; Johann Stamitz; Johann Christoph Bach; Carl Philip Emanuel Bach; Joseph Martin Kraus; and Luigi Boccherini. Each had a distinctive artistic personality, invented an aspect of the symphony and left behind a wealth of music which can be enjoyed on its own terms.

The watchword 'evolution', on the other hand, would seem to commit us to a story of style culminating in the symphonies of Haydn, Mozart and Beethoven. Whereas Charles Rosen taught us that 'the concept of style creates a mode of understanding, allowing us to place an individual work within an interpretive system',[2] David Schulenberg is right to aver that 'the assignment to a style might be an *impediment* to the understanding of a repertory'.[3] Evolutionary stories are both necessary and problematic. Two unavoidable ones for the early symphony are 'periodicity' and 'cyclicity'. The story of periodicity underpins Eugene Wolf's monograph on the symphonies of Stamitz, arguably the most sophisticated – and unaccountably neglected – study of this repertory.[4] Chapter 8 ('Structure at the Phrase Level: An Evolutionary Theory') presents Wolf's central hypothesis that 'the chronological development of Stamitz's style brought with it an increase in modular breadth, evolving from the small-scale motivic organization characteristic of the Baroque to the broader phrase and period structure of the Classic period'.[5] Wolf fleshes out the familiar narrative that the classical style evolved in multiples of two-bar phrases (two, four, eight, sixteen), a periodicity which is then commuted from phrase to structural level to embrace the binary opposition of first and second groups, the symmetry of exact recapitulation and ultimately the four movements of the cycle epitomised by Mozart's last three symphonies. And yet history did not necessarily march lock-step in Mozart's direction, as we shall see. There is nothing at all inevitable about the triumph of the symmetrical recapitulation or the four-movement symphony. The same is true of the 'cyclic' symphony epitomised by Haydn's Symphony No. 45 in F-sharp minor, the 'Farewell'.[6] Binding the four (or three) movements of the cycle into a unified expression of a compositional plan is a compelling ideal; Haydn's achievement resonates with that of Beethoven and many later composers. Yet I will show that in this respect the 'Farewell' is really a footnote to a larger story stretching, in the first instance, from Sammartini in the 1730s to Boccherini in the 1780s. Thus it is important not to confuse periodic symmetry and cyclic unity with stylistic coherence *per se*. Coherence is possible in manifold forms befitting the attributes of different musical materials in successive historical periods. Conversely, the symmetry of late Mozart, like the unity of middle-period Haydn, is just as much an expression of a unique artistic personality as the ostensible 'irregularity' of the so-called *Kleinmeister*.

The symphony originates, like so much European music, in the dialogue across the Italian Alps. Pursuing this dialogue through several stages of the early symphony, I will look at Stamitz's reception of Sammartini and the stylistic polarity of J. S. Bach's second-oldest and youngest sons. Of the myriad symphonists who reached their maturity in the 1780s, I have chosen Kraus and Boccherini through reasons of artistic quality and because they exemplify the regional dispersion of the genre, in this case to Sweden and Spain. Paradoxically, it was Viennese symphonists such as Monn, Holzbauer and Wagenseil who were peripheral to the development of the genre, notwithstanding their take-up of the four-movement model after the Austrian partita or parthia.[7] Mozart learnt much on his travels.

Early Sammartini, late Stamitz

Sammartini

World-embracing yet formally autonomous, the peculiarly hybrid genre of the symphony was born from a marriage of the Italian operatic overture and the baroque ripieno concerto. But the detail of the marriage contract was complex, as attested by the nineteen early string symphonies Sammartini composed for the Milanese *accademie* (private concerts sponsored by nobility) in the 1730s and early 1740s. Sammartini's 'concert symphonies' – a genre singled out in Scheibe's famous report as being more artful and freely imaginative than either 'dramatic' or 'church' symphonies[8] – owe less to the overture than to the concerto and trio sonata. The overture's influence grew later, with Stamitz at Mannheim. Notwithstanding the conflict of terminology, whereby the rubric 'symphony' was used interchangeably with 'overture', 'concertino' and 'trio sonata', it is instructive to consider Sammartini's overture to his first opera *Memet* alongside the two symphonies he cannibalised for the introductions to acts II and III, nos. 43 and 76.[9] All three movements of the *Memet* overture are substantial, whereas the *Sinfonie avvanti l'opera* by Vinci, Leo and Pergolesi tended to be dominated by their opening movement. The *Memet* overture owes its cyclic balance and characteristic rhythmic drive to the concerto. At the same time, this drive is counteracted by the binary sonata form of all three movements – a conflict which animates Sammartini's later symphonies and drove their stylistic evolution. In these respects, as well as in its three-part texture (independent parts for basso and viola, with violins I and II generally playing in unison), the overture is perfectly in line with symphonies nos. 43 and 76. Haydn notoriously called Sammartini 'un umbroglione' (to Carpani) and 'ein Schmierer' (to Griesinger),[10] yet the cyclicity of his 'Farewell' Symphony is implicit within the architecture of these works. In both their first movements, lack of cadential articulation – what Hepokoski and Darcy call a 'medial caesura' – means that the music sweeps towards the exposition's closing theme.[11] But this ostensible fault actually serves the interest of the cycle, since Sammartini's finales are habitually articulated by regular and sharply defined cadences. They thus afford both goal and closure on a global level. And this is why so many of Sammartini's finales are in a 3/4 or 3/8 dance metre, anticipating the much-misunderstood Tempo di Minuetto finale genre of later symphonies. Historically, cyclic organisation is inherent in the common practice in baroque concertos of ending the first movement on a dominant half-close so as to lead to a transitional slow movement (overture first movements also ended on the dominant). Sammartini consummated this tendency in two cyclic gems of his early period, symphonies nos. 37 and 73.

The first movement of No. 37 in F major implies sonata form but shifts all the signposts, resulting in music of extraordinary continuity. An otherwise clear medial caesura on V at bar 19, including a beat's rest, is followed by a ritornello of the opening theme in G minor. A secondary transition leads to a closing theme in the dominant minor which spills without a break (no double bars or repeat signs) into an eleven-bar development. After a cadence on VI (a feature much-used by Haydn), the recapitulation compresses the exposition's thirty-seven bars to just twenty-one. A half-close on V then tips the movement into an Andante in

Example 6.1a Sammartini, Symphony No. 37, I, bars 66–9.

Example 6.1b Sammartini, Symphony No. 37, III, bars 1–4.

Example 6.2 Sammartini, Symphony No. 73, I, bars 42–7.

the same key. The Minuetto Allegro Finale begins with repeated descents from $\hat{5}$, taking up and fulfilling the contour of the first movement's closing theme and thus affording the work's first satisfying cadential closure (Examples 6.1a and b). The 3/8 Adagio appendix to the 'Farewell''s Finale works in similar fashion to resolve Haydn's own cycle.[12] The development of No. 73/i in A major contains a 33-bar tonic-minor parenthesis which is a miniature sonata form in itself (Example 6.2). Set off texturally from the frame like a trio section (the violins subdivide and the bass drops out, as in many of Sammartini's second groups), the section is a cantabile oasis remarkably like the D major 'trio' within the 'Farewell''s first-movement development. Sammartini's trio is integrated thematically into the cycle: its lyrical material anticipates both the A minor Largo and the second part of the Finale, so that it is meaningful to speak of a thematic 'narrative' cutting across all three movements.

Contrasting a cadentially articulated and periodic finale with a more irregular first movement was Sammartini's initial mode of unifying his symphonic cycles. Nevertheless, cyclic unity was increasingly traded off against the conventionalisation of sonata form in the first movements. This is the chief reason why such unity is more apparent in Sammartini's earlier works. As second subjects were rendered more distinct, they also took on many forms: repeated fragmentary ideas (nos. 15, 26, 72, 73, 75), or a melody characterised by a contrast of mood and style and a dynamic

Example **6.3a** Sammartini, Symphony No. 38, I, bars 27–32.

Example **6.3b** Sammartini, Symphony No. 38, I, bars 63–7.

shift to *piano* (nos. 26, 36, 38 and 41). Structurally, the second group may stabilise an irregular first theme through its sequential harmonic rhythm (nos. 43 and 44) or with a pedal point (No. 39). At the same time, cyclic unity is recuperated by making finales more monothematic; in the Allegro assai of No. 44, the first subject returns in the dominant, and thematic contrast happens within groups rather than between them.

As a rule, Sammartini's recapitulations start with a shortened version of the first group; indeed, the entire recapitulation tends to be abbreviated. Moreover, the material itself is often radically rearranged, a technique Bathia Churgin calls 'thematic interversion'.[13] For instance, in the first movement of No. 38 in F major, the positions of the T and S themes are swapped and their actual detail transformed.[14] Both versions of S involve harmonic sequences, but the F–B♭–C–F sequence at bars 64–67 is much smoother than the unmediated triadic shifts (D–E–F–G) at bars 28–31 (Examples 6.3a and b).

Many of Sammartini's apparent solecisms, *pace* Rosen's insensitive critique, are strategic;[15] they are deliberate infelicities to be resolved in the recapitulation. This processive attitude to form was taken up by Haydn, whose recapitulations also 'knead out' recalcitrant material in his expositions – what Hepokoski terms 'refractory-material-to-be-worked-with'.[16] Was Haydn, then, less than truthful in his comments to Griesinger and Carpani? The question is in any case immaterial, since in the years separating the two composers, Sammartini's influence would have been transmitted through innumerable, indirect, pathways. So too with Mozart. He met Sammartini during the first two of his four visits to Milan (January–March 1770; October 1770–January 1771), but there is no record of Mozart actually having heard Sammartini's symphonies. The influence – be it direct or indirect – is attested, rather, by Mozart's Italianate symphonies themselves, such as K 74, 81, 84 and 95.

Stamitz

Insofar as the symphonies of Johann Stamitz (1717–57) sound more 'symphonic' than Sammartini's, they reveal the capabilities of his virtuoso orchestra at the electoral court of Mannheim.[17] They also reflect the increasing impact of the Italian overture; operas by Jommelli and Galuppi were staples at Mannheim, and Stamitz became even more Italianate after his year-long stay in Paris from 1754, where the 'querelle des bouffons' was raging. Aspects of this symphonic sound include massive texture, slow harmonic pace married to rhythmic drive, string tremolos and drum basses, dynamic variety and textural and timbral contrast due, in part, to the recruitment of pairs of oboes, flutes and horns both soloistically and within an independent wind section. Also important is the drastic simplification of the harmonic palette to the basic triads, so that root-position tonics and dominants resonate with pristine beauty, and the disposition of this sound-mass in symmetrical blocks of eight- and sixteen-bar phrases. All of this is evident in the opening of Stamitz's *Sinfonia* Op. 4, No. 6 in E flat, one of his nine 'late', post-Paris, symphonies (Example 6.4).

Stamitz's most famous Italian borrowing – ironic, because it became the quintessential trade-mark of the Mannheim sound – was the orchestral crescendo, or 'roller' (*Walzen*), exemplified at bar 9 of the tonic group. The 'roller' was not just a dynamic swell but a package of features involving a rising melodic line, tremolo, harmonic acceleration and cumulative addition of instruments. Sonically sensational, it was used in opera for programmatic effect; for example, in the aria 'Veggio il ciel turbato' from Act I, Scene 13 of Jommelli's *Merope* (1741), the crescendo portrays the surging sea. Stamitz rationalised the crescendos' formal function. Thus the nine late symphonies adopt a 'three-crescendo model'.[18] Stamitz places a crescendo in the second phrase of the primary groups, at the start of the development and at the end of the recapitulation. Strikingly, this scheme can even be independent of the original thematic material, suggesting that it was the orchestral sound itself that was 'thematic' for Stamitz and his listeners, assuming the clear organisational role of three sonic pillars. This fact is even more impressive when we consider that

Example 6.4 Stamitz, *Sinfonia* Op. 4, No. 6, I, bars 1–18.

accelerating phrase rhythm alone – epitomised by the logic of the
Schoenbergian sentence – came to supersede the role of the crescendo.
Crescendos are common at the start of Mozart's early symphonies and are
phased out on the path to the 'Jupiter''s opening sentence (the sheer
absence of a *Walzen* here is the 'Jupiter''s most vivid historical marker).
The shift from sound to phrase-rhythm – from *Walzen* to sentence – is
not necessarily a qualitative evolution; in some respects, the former is
more authentically 'orchestral'.

In addition to energising the symphony's sound-world, the overture also promoted greater formal continuity. As in a typical Jommelli or Galuppi overture, a late Stamitz symphony elides the articulating divide between the exposition and development (his early symphonic first movements are binary, with repeats); in any case, the increased length of the movements obviated the need for repetition. Strikingly, full recapitulations are more common in Stamitz's early- and middle-period symphonies, whereas late recapitulations jettison the primary group. The extreme freedom of Stamitz's recapitulations is directly inspired by Sammartini's 'interversion' technique, extended by Stamitz to a kaleidoscopic extreme which anticipates the fluid permutations of Mozart's piano concertos.[19] In Stamitz as in Mozart, the thematic material flows beguilingly in between the bars of the periodic cage, creating a kind of 'double perspective'. This effect is epitomised by Stamitz's second groups. From one standpoint, Stamitz's second groups are consistently more repetitive and periodic than Sammartini's (from the 1742 *Eumene* onwards, the second group of every Jommelli overture is organised as 4+4 bars), and they are increasingly differentiated using solo oboe or flute textures. From another standpoint, the caesura between transition and second group (normally so clear in Sammartini) is often abrogated, relegating S to the status of an interruption of T, resumed when T powers on into the development. The eight-bar second subject (carried by oboes I and II) in Op. 4, No. 6 emerges seamlessly out of the transition and quickly sinks back into an orchestral tutti.

Where Stamitz does depart from the overture is in favouring a four-movement cycle. Of the twenty-nine middle symphonies, eighteen have four movements; all the late works insert a minuet and trio in third position. Hugo Riemann believed that it was Stamitz who put in place the foundations of the great German four-movement symphony.[20] One such foundation was the concept of a slow movement as an enclave of subjectivity. The Adagio tempo of Op. 4, No. 6's second movement is characteristically German, differing from Sammartini's prototypical Andantes. Whereas Sammartini's slow movements rarely escape the continuity of baroque *Fortspinnung* technique, Stamitz's mosaic idiom proceeds as a chain of short-breathed motivic fragments. Individually, the motives encapsulate deep emotions; as a group, they unfold a terse drama. The operatic drama initiated by the ferocious unison gesture in bars 1–2 (Example 6.5a) leads, at the end of the exposition, to the sort of textural magic recognised by all Mozart lovers: a deceptively simple ostinato exchange of motives between violins I and II, underpinned by a pedal, creating a sublime stand-still. Stamitz invented this effect (Example 6.5b).

Stamitz also established the 'Germanic' version of the symphonic minuet *as a concise internal dance movement with regular four-bar groupings*, in contrast to the broader 'Italian' minuet (or Tempo di Minuetto)

Example 6.5a Stamitz, *Sinfonia* Op. 4, No. 6, II, bars 1–5.

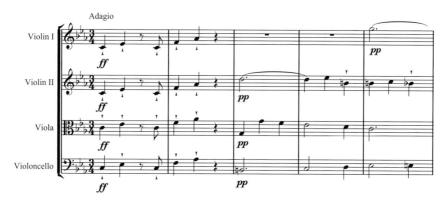

Example 6.5b Stamitz, *Sinfonia* Op. 4, No. 6, II, bars 21–3.

finale.[21] Also typical in Op. 4, No. 6 is the Prestissimo Finale in duple meter. Its peculiar blend of ritornello and 'reverse recapitulation' technique keeps the pace moving: P returns initially in B flat (bar 79), followed by a tonic reprise of S (bar 106) and only at the end of the movement by a recapitulation of P in E flat. The Finale is a show-piece of orchestral virtuosity. *Pace* Riemann, second-generation Mannheim symphonists such as Cannabich reverted to the three-movement overture model. Which model affords a more unified cycle, three movements or four? The debate would continue into the 1780s.

The two streams (*Bäche*)

Johann Christian Bach

After making his reputation as a composer of Italian opera in Milan as a colleague of Sammartini during 1754–62, Johann Christian Bach (1735–82) settled in London in 1762, visiting Mannheim in 1772. A plausible, if counter-intuitive, argument has been made that the Austro-German classical style was the product of the British Enlightenment.[22] Assimilating London's cosmopolitan classicism, Bach invented many of the symphonic lineaments to which Mozart would cleave, following the eight-year-old composer's visit to the city in April 1764 and his exposure to the six symphonies Op. 3 (published 1765). What Mozart's Symphony in D, K 19, emulates from Bach's Op. 3, No. 1 in the same key is a precisely calibrated procession of structural functions attuned to the rhetorical 'beginning–middle–end' model.[23] Bach's and Mozart's first movements both open with Mannheim-like triadic flourishes designed to summon attention and circumscribe tonal space. Sequential transitions lead to lyrical second subjects for reduced forces and dynamics on a dominant pedal (Mozart's theme is an exact parody of Bach's). The second groups of both movements are completed by a succession of four discrete themes expressing varying degrees of closure, the series unfolding a dramatic arc learned from opera seria. Both expositions then proceed directly into a development with no double bars. Each development begins with an ostensibly new idea which subtly pulls together previous threads (a technique perfected by Sammartini), before slipping into the circle of fifths. Both recapitulations elide the first subject, like late Stamitz. Yet Bach's form is poised and harmonious whereas Mozart's bursts with jarring contrasts (such as the horrible *forte* A♯ which ignites the development at bar 46). Bach is the 'classical' artist; growth would confirm Mozart as the 'sentimental' one, according to Schiller's dichotomy. The distinction needs to be stressed, given the propensity to think of Mozart as 'filling' Bach's perfect if 'empty' vessels with 'spirit'.

Bach's second set of symphonies, the Op. 6 of 1770, develop in polarised directions. On the one hand, the perfection is rendered more concise: opening gambits are encapsulated; the plurality of second groups is extended to similarly heterogeneous first groups; and the long sequential transitions are abbreviated into brutally efficient modulatory gestures. On the other hand, Bach's poise toys with stasis, compounded as much by the blossoming of his lyrical gift as by an over-articulation of formal junctures. Epitomising the latter is a tendency to cadence at the end of the retransition – a cardinal sin singled out by Rosen for special reproof, since it cuts the development off from the reprise.[24] Thus the development of No. 3 in E flat settles gently to a repeated cadence in B flat at bars 72–6, and the recapitulation enters like a da capo or ritornello. But Rosen is quite wrong: what this example demonstrates is the persisting vitality of Sammartini's tri-ritornello model, indebted to the concerto (Ritornello 1: I–V; Ritornello 2: V–vi or iii; Ritornello 3: I–I), which separates out the three sections of Bach's sonata form into graceful Doric columns.

Concision and lyricism culminate in the *summa* of Bach's art, the three of the six Op. 18 'Grand Overtures' written for double orchestras (1774–7). Bach used the term 'overture' interchangeably with 'sinfonia'; indeed, some of the Op. 18 set were originally operatic overtures, showing that the two three-movement genres had now converged. Bach's double orchestra, supplying his music with extra resources of sonic richness and concertante dialogue, also allows him to draw in the third genre of concerto. The synergy between tutti and soli in Op. 18 is much suppler than in Haydn's own experiments with concertante symphonies.[25] No. 3 in D major – the finest of the set – was originally the overture to *Endimione*, and it demonstrates the overpowering sensuality of Bach's textures. Concision is epitomised in the gravity-defying brevity of the Allegro's seventeen–bar first group, which supports an expansive exposition of 66 bars. The exposition's 'transition space' has been filled up with stable periodic melodies; the first one (bars 18–25) is remarkable because it sits on the new tonic pedal (A), rather than the more conventionally unstable V of V (E). (The 'real' second subject, at bar 51, is quite different.) The premature A major theme works perfectly well in Bach's *sui-generis* structure, although it can't fully be accounted for by modern sonata-form theories.

The melodic genius of the central Andante, in ABA song form, equals Mozart's, complete with surprising chromatic colourings. Both thematic groups in section A sit in the tonic G major, and Bach keeps things moving with a sure-footed harmonic acceleration from a leisurely opening melody (Example 6.6a) to the much faster contrasting idea at bar 22 (Example 6.6b). The artistry lies in the exquisite care by which this new melody both arrests and follows through the deceptively static flurry of quavers at bars 16–21 (canonically exchanged scales), a passage which works equally well above its alternate tonic and dominant pedals. Only Mozart could emulate this paradoxical blend of motion and standstill.

Carl Philipp Emanuel Bach

What Johann Christian learnt from his older brother during his apprenticeship in Berlin in 1750 resurfaces most openly in the dark rhetoric of slow movements such as the Andante of Op. 6, No. 6 in G minor.[26] This is a metaphor for the subterranean quality of Emanuel Bach's own symphonies, whose essentially private, chamber-music-like character was buried by the dominant public style celebrated even by north Germans such as J. A. P. Schulz. Schulz's 1774 article on the symphony in Sulzer's *Allgemeine Theorie der Schönen Künste* reports that the genre 'is excellently suited for the expression of the grand, the festive, and the noble . . . to summon up all the splendour of instrumental music'.[27] This public style is evinced by Johann Gottlieb Graun's (1702–71) one hundred concert symphonies, which

Example 6.6a J. C. Bach, Symphony Op. 18, No. 3, II, bars 1–4.

Example 6.6b J. C. Bach, Symphony Op. 18, No. 3, II, bars 16–25.

established the genre in Berlin. But on the other hand, some of Schulz's prescriptions fit Bach's mannerism like a glove: 'great and bold ideas, free handling of composition, seeming disorder in the melody and harmony, strongly marked rhythms of different kinds … sudden transitions and digressions from one key to another, which are all the more startling the weaker the connection'. The question, then, is whether a symphony is still a symphony when 'seeming disorder' is not played out against a framework of public communication – 'the grand, the festive, and the noble'.

The question devolves to the idiosyncratic way Emanuel Bach's eighteen symphonies (eight for Berlin in 1741 and 1755–62; ten for Hamburg after 1767) treat classical form, particularly the 'beginning–middle–end' rhetorical model perfected by Johann Christian. Sonata form is present in the first movement of Bach's Symphony in C major, W 182/3, the third of a set of six four-part string symphonies composed in Hamburg in 1773. Yet it is masked by a quasi-postmodern cross-current of baroque and proto-Romantic styles. The surface form is modelled on Tartini's concerto-grosso practice: a tutti ritornello recurs in the dominant at the end of the second group, and in the tonic at the close of the movement, but conspicuously *not* at the structural return of the tonic. The refrains, plus the intervening soloistic passage work, completely detract from the sonata infrastructure. Conversely, the surface is pitted with rhetorical expressive effects associated with the fantasy genre, as in the dramatic A flat interruption at bar 6 of the first movement (Example 6.7a). Fantasy also inspires Bach's cyclic ambitions: he unites all three movements as subsections of a single process. It is at this level that something very sophisticated happens. The run-on slow movement – typically a bridge in a Tartini concerto – is prompted by the interrupted cadence at the sixth bar of the ritornello, the chromatic shock now raised from an A♭ to a B♭ so as to bring back the B–A–C–H motive (Example 6.7b).

Bach confirms the potential for a slow movement to become a prolongation of a cadenza; the Adagio is also a forensic through-composed excursus on ideas from the first movement – a kind of global development section. The chief idea is nothing less than the B–A–C–H (B♭–A–C–B♮) motive – an inconsequential bass pattern in the Allegro's transition (bars 16–19) now promoted to head position in the Adagio.[28] The Adagio builds up to a dramatic face-off between the motive, *fortissimo*, in the bass, and *empfindsam* violin appoggiaturas, *piano* (Example 6.8a), discharging into an Allegretto

Example 6.7a C. P. E. Bach, Symphony in C, W 182 No. 3, I, bars 1–6.

Allegro assai

Example 6.7b C. P. E. Bach, Symphony in C, W 182 No. 3, I, bars 124–8; II, bar 1.

B   A   C   H

Example 6.8a C. P. E. Bach, Symphony in C, W 182 No. 3, II, bars 17–20.

Example 6.8b C. P. E. Bach, Symphony in C, W 182 No. 3, III, bars 1–3.

Example 6.9 C. P. E. Bach, Symphony in C, W 182 No. 3, III, bars 47–51.

rounded binary dance Finale, which transmutes the B–A–C–H motive into a charming *galant* melody (Example 6.8b).

In one sense a literal exorcism of Emanuel Bach's father, the effect also points to his true successor. For as a cyclic 'story' of an abstract interval pattern, the symphony is a model for Beethoven's *Grosse Fuge*: note the eventual domestication of Beethoven's subject into a dance tune in the fugue's Allegro molto Finale. This abstraction – appealing much later to a Beethoven, if not to Bach's immediate contemporaries – is epitomised by the Finale's formal concentration, whose density is out of kilter with the *galant* materials. This is music for *Kenner* rather than *Liebhaber*, demanding a sharpness of attention suited to the intimate performance spaces of chamber music rather than to 'symphonies' proper. The most exquisite detail comes at bar 47 (Example 6.9). 'False reprise' would be a misnomer for the tonic recapitulation which interrupts an E minor cadence at bar 47 (and corrected by the 'true' reprise of bar 61): Bach intends an effect not of plausibility but of shock. The frailty and insularity of this two-bar reprise, hedged on either side by darkness, is broadly suggestive of how Bach's symphonic oeuvre as a whole is overwhelmed by an enormous subjectivity.

The Swedish Mozart and Haydn's wife

Joseph Martin Kraus

> What a loss is this man's death! I own a symphony by him, which I keep in memory of one of the greatest geniuses I have ever known … Too bad about that man, just like Mozart! They both were so young [when they died]. Joseph Haydn.[29]

The culture industry and the cult of genius have conspired to keep many first-rate classical composers in obscurity. Listeners who are lucky enough to come across the music of Joseph Martin Kraus (1756–92), perhaps courtesy of Naxos's pioneering series of *The 18th-Century Symphony*, may be shocked by just how good he is. Born in Miltenberg-am-Main, and educated at Mannheim, Kraus published a treatise *Etwas von und über Musik* as a contribution to a *Sturm-und-Drang* literary circle called the Göttinger Hainbund, joined the court of Gustavus III of Sweden in 1778, eventually becoming Kapellmästare, interrupted his service with a Grand Tour of the European musical capitals (1782–7), during which he met Gluck, Haydn and Mozart, died of tuberculosis in 1792, and left us with twelve surviving symphonies. The symphony singled out by Haydn is the C minor (1783), VB 142, the greatest in that key before Beethoven's, and deserving of Haydn's praise. Yet the epitaph 'the Swedish Mozart' which clung to Kraus, due to the two composers' nearly exact contemporaneity, is inaccurate. More akin to an 'anti-Mozart', Kraus extrapolated different symphonic tendencies compounded variously from Haydn's *Sturm-und-Drang* works of the 1770s, C. P. E. Bach's fantastical idiom, Stamitz's formal models and most of all Gluck's rhetorical directness, whose rawness Kraus disciplined in ways which evoke the sound-world of Beethoven's heroic style.[30]

The Symphony in C minor is doubly interesting because it reworks in Vienna elements of the Symphony in C-sharp minor VB 140, written in Sweden a year earlier in 1782, so allowing us to encapsulate matters of 'stylistic maturity and regional influence'.[31] The slow introduction to VB 140 develops out of the opening phrase of Gluck's *Iphigénie en Aulide*; VB 142 spins Gluck's material far further (Example 6.10a) and conceives dark orchestral sonorities which would never have been heard before (Example 6.10b). VB 142 loses the earlier symphony's minuet (following other late-Mannheim composers such as Cannabich) and entirely

Example 6.10a Kraus, Symphony in C minor, VB 142, I, bars 1–4.

Example 6.10b Kraus, Symphony in C minor, VB 142, I, bars 24–8.

recomposes the outer movements in a deeply satisfying cyclic design. The essence of Kraus's design is that, in the tradition of Sammartini, Stamitz and Emanuel Bach, the form of the finale functions as a cyclic resolution.

Like early Stamitz, the first movement of the C-sharp minor Symphony is bipartite with repeats, the recapitulation of P being delayed until the end. VB 142, conversely, follows late Stamitz in abrogating the articulation between exposition and development and restoring a tonic recapitulation. Another late Stamitz procedure much in evidence in Kraus even before 1782 is to eclipse S with the transition. In the Symphony in C major VB 138 (1781), a strategically trite secondary theme is thrown aside when a fragment of T (bars 33–4) returns and explodes (bars 63–73). This 'outbreak' principle – suggesting a composer bursting through received forms – is taken to another level in VB 142. The most substantial passage in the exposition is the sixty-two-bar-long transition (bars 56–117), bookended by theatrically emphatic caesuras. Whereas the fifty-five-bar-long primary group is equally weighted, the second group in E flat occupies a mere twenty-nine bars (bars 118–45): as in Stamitz, it is an 'oasis' between T and the development.[32] The recapitulation recasts the form radically, eliminating T entirely, thereby cutting the exposition's material from 145 bars to 57. The form is not just foreshortened but rationalised: in terms of modern sonata theory, a 'tri-modular block' (an exposition with two structural caesuras) is normalised – the elision of T notwithstanding – into a recapitulation with a single caesura between P and S.[33] This 'normalisation' is echoed at a global level by the traditional and concise sonata form of the Finale, including its double bars and repeats. The foreshortening gesture is recursive at three levels – exposition; first movement; cycle – projecting the *Sturm-und-Drang* telos in a uniquely intricate structure.

Tri-modular blocks were common in other Viennese symphonies by Wagenseil and Dittersdorf,[34] but were taken up in orchestral music by Haydn and Mozart much later than by Kraus, who learnt the device 'at source' from Mannheim.[35] The C minor Symphony's extraordinarily expansive transition is reminiscent of that in the first movement of Mozart's Piano Concerto in C minor, K 491 (1786), which we know, through studies of the autograph, was interpolated into the exposition at a later stage. Perhaps after hearing VB 142? Did the anti-Mozart influence Wolfgang Amadeus?

Luigi Boccherini

Renewed interest in the chamber music of Boccherini (1743–1805) should lead to his re-evaluation as a symphonist of equal stature to middle-period Haydn (1775–92; between the *Sturm und Drang* and 'London' symphonies).[36] Despite artistic isolation at Arenas and Madrid, Boccherini corresponded with the Esterhaz-bound Haydn, and the two composers were coupled to the former's detriment; the nineteenth-century violinist Giuseppe Puppo christened him 'Haydn's wife', due to the perceived effeminacy of his charming style. Yet their affinity was reciprocal in a deeper way. A born architect and musical logician, Haydn only learned to compose melodies in the 'operatic' symphonies of the late 1770s;[37] a melodic genius from the outset, Boccherini sorted out his formal problems with the Op. 21 symphonies of 1775. The masterworks from the 1780s – particularly the symphonies opp. 35 and 37 – give the lie to the standard epithet, gleaned from the chamber music, that Boccherini was a master of rococo and static 'detail' rather than 'broad effect'.[38] It is the *broadness* of their style, in fact, which suggests comparison with later symphonic masters of repetition and block contrast, such as Schubert and Bruckner, together with a captivating sensuousness and almost luminescent colour. It is extraordinary, then, that this progressive aspect is extrapolated from Sammartini – whom Boccherini met in Milan in 1765.[39] It brings this 'evolutionary' story full circle.

Example 6.11a Boccherini, Symphony in E flat, Op. 35, No. 2, II, bars 39–44.

Example 6.11b Boccherini, Symphony in E flat, Op. 35, No. 2, III, bars 1–5.

Boccherini and Sammartini share many characteristics: a sensitivity for orchestral string textures, often focussing on first and second violins either in octaves or in double counterpoint; a fidelity to the concerto strand of the symphonic fabric, evinced in Boccherini by an effortless accommodation of concertante dialogue; broad major/minor contrasts (see Sammartini's symphonies nos. 7, 14 and 65); and perhaps most of all, a liking for cyclic unity. Of all *galant* or classical symphonists, Boccherini is by far the most preoccupied with patent thematic relationships between movements. A theme or even an entire section or movement may recur (e.g. the opening slow introduction returns before the Finale in Op. 12, No. 4). A particularly sophisticated case is the Andante of Op. 35, No. 2 in E flat, where a new theme, which usurps the expected reprise of the opening C minor first subject (Example 6.11a), returns a few bars later (Example 6.11b) as the first subject of the Finale (many of Beethoven's finales would also be intimated in the middle movements).

Cyclic recurrences throughout Symphony No. 23 in D minor, Op. 37, No. 3 (1787) are particularly extensive and audible, because they correlate with the D minor/major alternation across the work: elements of the four-bar introduction return in the *minore* sections of the Minuetto, Andante amoroso and Finale.

Op. 37, No. 3, one of the high-points of Boccherini's maturity, co-opts major/minor opposition in a patchwork of contrasts, encapsulated in the four-bar phrasing for which he is often denigrated. Yet it is precisely the Symphony's periodicity which makes the non-mediated juxtaposition of textural and tonal blocks so effective, and the overall form so compellingly efficient. The *pianissimo* four-bar D minor introduction (Example 6.12a) is succeeded with a *fortissimo* outburst of D major figuration (Example 6.12b). Four bars later, the D minor material returns, succeeded after four more bars by an equally unmediated block of F major. Although the Symphony is topped, tailed and punctuated by episodes in D minor, it is not really 'in' D

Example **6.12a** Boccherini, Symphony in D minor, Op. 37, No. 3, I, bars 1–4.

Example **6.12b** Boccherini, Symphony in D minor, Op. 37, No. 3, I, bars 5–6.

minor; rather, the quality of the mode is rendered thematic in itself. Equally thematic is the delicious textural effect at bar 5 (the violin octaves, which Boccherini made his own, actually originate in mid-century orchestral Viennese idiom).[40] Paradoxically, this outburst captures our attention while never returning again in the movement (like so many opening gambits by Stamitz and Domenico Scarlatti); the recapitulation pivots on the return not of the D major theme but of the F major block from bar 13, ingeniously reinterpreting the harmonic non sequitur within the primary group (the shift from the chord of A to F) as a Sammartini retransition (Example 6.13). That is, Sammartini's convention of ending his developments on V of VI is utterly transmuted here, allowing Boccherini to get away with a breathtaking reprise

Example 6.13 Boccherini, Symphony in D minor, Op. 37, No. 3, I, bars 63–4.

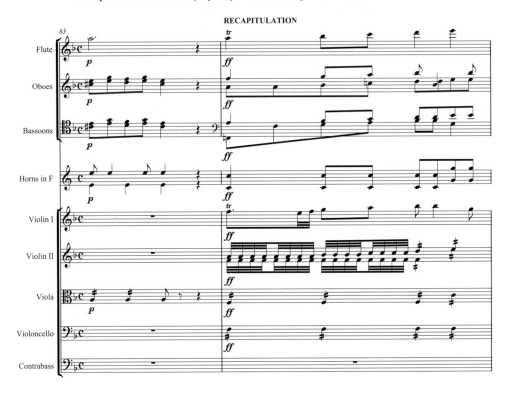

in F, the mediant key. The orchestra is used to project keys as fields of colour; the technique points to the nineteenth century, but its roots are in the Italian *galant*. Without succumbing to Emanuel Bach's hermetic intellectualism, Boccherini applies formal experiments more associated with chamber music to the popular symphonic style – something even the Haydn of the Op. 76 string quartets never managed to achieve.

Boccherini's Op. 7 in C (1769) is a *Symphonie concertante* spotlighting two violins and a cello as soloists. Op. 10, No. 4 (1771) is essentially a guitar concerto, and the Op. 12 symphonies of 1771 were termed *Concerti a grande orchestra*. Even a late symphony such as Op. 37, No. 4 in A is designated *Sinfonia a più istromenti* on the autograph. Where a concerto rubric is not indicated, as in Op. 37, No. 3, concertante obbligato writing is flexibly incorporated within episodes such as the second subject group (as in the two solo violas and solo bassoon of bars 26–31).

In the right hands, a concertante symphony was as viable as a 'regular' symphony. Nothing about the evolution of the early symphony was inevitable. Written from the standpoint of Haydn, Mozart and Beethoven, the story of the symphony suggests that the concerto was entirely digested. The view from Madrid, Stockholm, Hamburg, London, Mannheim and Milan is quite different, however, indicating that this evolutionary story could have moved – and indeed *did* move – in a number of alternative directions.

Notes

1 Jan LaRue, *A Catalogue of 18th-Century Symphonies*, vol. I: *Thematic Identifier* (Bloomington, 1988).

2 Charles Rosen, *The Classical Style* (London, 1972), 19.

3 David Schulenberg, *The Instrumental Music of Carl Philipp Emanuel Bach* (Ann Arbor, 1984), 2.

4 Eugene K. Wolf, *The Symphonies of Johann Stamitz: A Study in the Formation of the Classic Style* (The Hague, 1981).

5 Ibid., 110.

6 James Webster, *Haydn's 'Farewell' Symphony and the Idea of Classical Style: Through-Composition and Cyclic Integration in His Instrumental Music* (Cambridge, 1991).

7 For an opposing view, see Jens Peter Larsen, 'Zur Vorgeschichte der Symphonik der Wiener Klassic', *Studien zur Musikwissenschaft*, 43 (1994), 64–143.

8 Johann Adolf Scheibe, *Critischer Musikus* (Hamburg, 1737–40): 'Sie mit einer grössern Freyheit, was so wohl die Erfindung, als die Schreibart, betrifft, ausgearbeitet werden können' (15 December 1739), 622.

9 All these works are included in Bathia Churgin, ed., *The Symphonies of G. B. Sammartini*, vol. I: *The Early Symphonies* (Cambridge, Mass., 1968).

10 Cited in Bathia Churgin, 'The Symphonies of G. B. Sammartini', 2 vols., (Ph.D. diss., Harvard University, 1963), 10. The following discussion is indebted to Churgin's pioneering study.

11 James Hepokoski and Warren Darcy, *Elements of Sonata Theory: Norms, Types, and Deformations in the Late-Eighteenth-Century Sonata* (New York and Oxford, 2006). Sammartini and Stamitz show that the authors' cast-iron law that '*if there is no medial caesura, there is no secondary theme*' (p. 52) is quite simply wrong on historical grounds.

12 See Webster, *Haydn's 'Farewell' Symphony and the Idea of Classical Style*, 104–10.

13 Churgin, 'The Symphonies of G. B. Sammartini', 220.

14 Henceforth: P = primary theme; S = secondary theme; T = transition.

15 See Charles Rosen, *Sonata Forms* (New York, 1988), 140–3. The brusque voice-leading in Symphony No. 6, bars 6–9, which Rosen finds 'unbelievably ugly' (p. 141), nevertheless comports with the unusual brevity (10 bars) of the first group.

16 James Hepokoski, 'Beyond the Sonata Principle', *Journal of the American Musicological Society*, 55 (2002), 91–154, this quotation 128.

17 Other members of the Stamitz School include F. X. Richter (1709–89), Anton Fils (1733–60), Christian Cannabich (1731–91), Carl Joseph Toeschi (1731–88), Franz Beck (1734–1809), as well as Stamitz's two sons, Carl (1745–1801) and Anton (1750–1809).

18 See Wolf, *The Symphonies of Johann Stamitz*, 299.

19 Ibid., 106.

20 Hugo Riemann, *Denkmäler der Tonkunst in Bayern*, vol. VII/2 (1906), 'Einleitung', i.

21 See Robert Jonas Sondheimer, *Die Theorie der Sinfonie und die Beurteilung einzelner Sinfoniekomponisten bei den Musikschriftstellen des 18. Jahrhunderts* (Leipzig, 1925), 36–7.

22 See Anselm Gerhard, *London und der Klassizismus in der Musik: De Idee der 'absoluten Musik' und Muzio Clementis Klavierwerke* (Stuttgart, 2002).

23 See V. Kofi Agawu, *Playing with Signs: A Semiotic Interpretation of Classic Music* (Princeton, 1991), 52.

24 According to Rosen, 'One could compile a large anthology from 1770 on of ways to avoid a cadence [on vi] at the end of the development' (*Sonata Forms*, 270). But in J. C. Bach's hands, that wasn't the point.

25 See for instance Haydn's *Sinfonia concertante* in B flat, Op. 84, Hob. I/105.

26 Reflecting the popularity of minor-mode symphonies in the 1770s (by Vanhal, Ordonez, as well as Mozart's first G minor symphony, K 183 [1773]), Op. 6, No. 6 is also a salutary reminder that the so-called '*Sturm-und-Drang*' manner was as much a continuation of Sammartini's style (e.g. his Symphony No. 9 in C minor) as the invention of north-German intellectuals.

27 Bathia Churgin, 'The Symphony as Described by J. A. P. Schulz (1774): A Commentary and Translation', *Current Musicology*, 29 (1980), 7–16, this quotation 11.

28 Bach uses the motive throughout his career, as in the Piano Trio in A minor, W 90/1,

bars 63–6, and the Flute Concerto in D minor, H 426, bars 75–8. See Schulenberg, *The Instrumental Music of Carl Philipp Emanuel Bach*, 41–2.

29 Cited in A. Peter Brown, 'Stylistic Maturity and Regional Influence: Joseph Martin Kraus' Symphonies in C-sharp minor (Stockholm, 1782) and C minor (Vienna, 1783)', in Eugene K. Wolf and Edward H. Roesner, eds., *Studies in Musical Sources and Style: Essays in Honor of Jan LaRue* (Madison, 1990), 381–418.

30 The exception – Kraus's paraphrase of a march from *Idomeneo* as part of his *Riksdagsmusik* (VB 154) – is revealing, since the opera is Mozart's most Gluckian work. See Bertil H. van Boer, *Dramatic Cohesion in the Music of Joseph Martin Kraus* (Lewiston, 1989), 329.

31 See A. Peter Brown 'Stylistic Maturity'.

32 Brown's analysis in 'Stylistic Maturity' is misconceived; without reason, he calculates S as sixty-four bars rather than twenty-nine (p. 393).

33 For 'tri-modular blocks', see Hepokoski and Darcy, *Elements of Sonata Theory*, 170–7.

34 Ibid., 171.

35 Wolf, *The Symphonies of Johann Stamitz*, 151, 199 and 272.

36 For a study of the chamber music, see Elisabeth Le Guin, *Boccherini's Body: An Essay in Carnal Musicology* (Berkeley, 2006).

37 James Webster, 'When Did Haydn Begin to Write Beautiful Melodies?', in Jens Peter Larsen, Howard Serwer and James Webster, eds., *Haydn Studies* (New York, 1981), 358.

38 Christian Speck and Stanley Sadie, 'Boccherini', in Stanley Sadie, ed., *The New Grove Dictionary of Music and Musicians*, 2nd edn (London, 2001), 749–64.

39 See Bathia Churgin, 'Sammartini and Boccherini: Continuity and Change in the Italian Instrumental Tradition of the Classic Period', *Chigiana*, 43 (1993), 171–91.

40 Daniel Heartz, *Music in European Capitals: The Galant Style, 1720–1780* (New York, 2003), 981–2.

7 Harmonies and effects: Haydn and Mozart in parallel

SIMON P. KEEFE

'Haydn is called by the courtesy of historians, the father of the symphony', remarked English critic Edward Holmes in 1837, but Mozart is 'the first inventor of the modern grand symphony'.[1] Whether Holmes knew it or not, Haydn's and Mozart's symphonies had already been compared for at least fifty years, in spite of fundamental differences in the two composers' symphonic careers (for instance in the numbers of works, circumstances of composition and venues for premieres). Inevitably, comparisons evolved over time, Mozart initially tending not to fare too well. 'If we pause only to consider [Mozart's] symphonies', wrote the *Teutschlands Annalen des Jahres 1794*, 'for all their fire, for all their pomp and brilliance they yet lack that sense of unity, that clarity and directness of presentation, which we rightly admire in Jos. Haydn's symphonies.'[2] More pointedly, in the London-based *Morning Chronicle* (1789): 'The Overture [that is, symphony] by Mozart, owed its success rather to the excellence of the band, than the merit of the composition. Sterne was an original writer; – Haydn is an original musician. It may be said of the imitators of the latter, as of the former, they catch a few oddities, as dashes – sudden pauses – and occasional prolixity, but scarcely a particle of feeling or sentiment.'[3] Later, with the Haydn–Mozart–Beethoven triumvirate established in critical discourse, Haydn the symphonist began to suffer slightly, perceived as a kind of warm-up act – albeit an extremely good one – for his successors. Foreshadowing a hierarchy to which Holmes evidently subscribed, the *Quarterly Musical Magazine and Review* (1826) explained that Haydn gave the symphony 'form and substance, and ordained the laws by which it should move, adorning it at the same by fine taste, perspicuity of design, and beautiful melody', but that Mozart 'added to the fine creations by richness, warmth and variety' and Beethoven 'endowed it with sublimity of description and power'.[4] Irrespective of orientation, comparisons exemplify our need – apparently infusing musicological DNA – to bring Haydn and Mozart under the same critical lens.

Eagerness to generate links between Haydn and Mozart in order to validate the superiority of their music over that of their contemporaries and immediate predecessors was already apparent at the turn of the nineteenth century. Friedrich Rochlitz, in factually tainted anecdotes about Mozart published in the *Allgemeine musikalische Zeitung* (1798–1801), embroidered stories about Haydn defending *Don Giovanni* against detractors and about Mozart passionately advocating Haydn's symphonies, explaining that 'great men [have] always given great men their due'; Johann Karl Friedrich Triest, in the same journal (1801), set up Haydn as the greatest instrumental composer and Mozart as the greatest musical dramatist in the 'third period' of the eighteenth century, a period he even subtitled 'from J. Haydn and W. A. Mozart to the End of the Last Century'; Thomas Holcroft reported, as routine, debates about the relative statuses of these 'men of uncommon genius' (1798); and Franz Xaver Niemetschek, one of Mozart's earliest biographers (1798), showcased Haydn's and Mozart's mutual admiration, dedicating his volume on 'immortal Mozart' 'with deepest homage to Joseph Haydn . . . father of the noble art of music and favourite of the Muses'.[5] But one of the earliest – perhaps the very earliest – protracted comparisons of Haydn's and Mozart's music, Ignaz Arnold's 'Wolfgang Amadeus Mozart und Joseph Haydn. Nachträge zu ihren Biographien und ästhetischer Darstellung ihrer Werke. Versuch einer Parallele [Postscript to their Biographies and Aesthetic Description of their Works. Attempts at a Parallel]' published in 1810 in the wake of Haydn's death, provides the most promising stimulus for a reconsideration of the relationship between their works.[6] Arnold, already the author of a landmark volume in early Mozart reception, *Mozarts Geist: Seine kurze Biographie und äesthetische Darstellung seiner Werke* (Erfurt, 1803), initially appears to nail his colours to the mast, stating that 'Mozart is indisputably the greatest musical genius of his and all eras' and – in line with the prevailing view – that 'Haydn paved the way that Mozart travelled to immortality.'[7] After a lengthy biographical excursion on Haydn (taken from Georg August Griesinger's account), though, he provides a much more nuanced assessment of the relationship, one in which Haydn and Mozart emerge as equals – two sides of the same coin, a 'holy unity in the most individual diversity'. Both were original geniuses, having positive effects on their surroundings, synthesising stylistic qualities from various quarters and striving successfully to achieve aesthetic beauty; both were 'equally great, strong and forceful' in harmonic terms, Mozart looking 'to clothe his melodies with the force of the harmonies' and Haydn to conceal 'his profound harmonies in the roses and mirthful thread of his melodies'.[8] While 'Haydn's genius looked for breadth', Mozart's sought 'height and depth'.[9] Arnold then considered balanced overall qualities: 'Haydn leads us out of ourselves. Mozart lowers us deeper into ourselves and lifts us above ourselves. That is why Haydn always paints more objective views, and Mozart subjective feelings' (as examples, Arnold cites *The Creation* and *The Seasons* for Haydn and *The Magic Flute*, *La clemenza di Tito* and the Requiem for Mozart).[10] E. T. A. Hoffmann distinguished in likeminded fashion between Haydn and Mozart in his famous review of Beethoven's Fifth Symphony (1810), albeit in more openly poetic terms: while Haydn's works 'are dominated by a feeling of childlike optimism', his symphonies leading us 'through endless, green forest-glades, through a motley throng of happy people', Mozart's take us 'deep into the realm of spirits … We hear the gentle voices of love and melancholy, the nocturnal spirit-world dissolves into a purple shimmer, and with inexpressible yearning we follow the flying figures kindly beckoning us from the clouds to join their eternal dance of the spheres' (Hoffmann cites Symphony No. 39 in E flat, K 543, as an example).[11] All told for Arnold, 'both geniuses stand there equally forceful, equally charming'.[12]

Arnold identified two totemic figures achieving sometimes similar, sometimes different goals, always attentive to force and beauty in their music and ever successful at communicating with their respective audiences. In attempting to re-evaluate the relationship between Haydn's and Mozart's symphonies, we are best served by revisiting writings from the last decades of the eighteenth century and the first decade of the nineteenth, alongside Arnold's account. This period includes not only the greatest works by the two composers, but also Mozart's meteoric posthumous rise in popularity in the 1790s and 1800s and Haydn's equally dramatic establishment as Europe's most famous living musician, a status attributable in no small part to his international symphonic successes in Paris and London. In the spirit of Arnold, I shall look first at Haydn's and Mozart's 'Paris' symphonies, reversing his assessment of the two composers' impact on their musical environments by considering how the environments may have had an impact on them, especially their orchestration. I shall then turn to Mozart's Viennese symphonies from the 1780s and Haydn's 'London' symphonies from the 1790s in an attempt to determine how the most powerful and poignant harmonic effects are achieved.

Mozart's 'Paris' Symphony, K 297 and Haydn's 'Paris' Symphonies, nos. 82–7

The locations for which Haydn and Mozart wrote symphonies were quite different – Haydn's predominantly for Esterházy and only later for Paris and London, and Mozart's for Salzburg, Vienna and other cities to which he travelled around Europe.[13] The Paris symphonies thus offer an ideal viewpoint from which to survey the effect that a particular musical city at a particular time had on symphonies composed by the two men. To be sure, Mozart's and Haydn's circumstances were dissimilar when they wrote their symphonies – Mozart, not particularly well known in Paris in 1778 (at least for his adult musical activities), composed his single work for the Concert spirituel while resident in the city, whereas Haydn, already established as a leading figure on the Parisian scene by the mid 1780s, wrote six works for the *Concert de la Loge Olympique* (1785–6) while still based at home.[14] But both composers, faced with a Parisian audience with whom they were fundamentally unfamiliar, would have had to pay especially close attention to the stylistic and aesthetic resonances of their works in an attempt to guarantee success.

Mozart's letters to his father about his new symphony describe several ways in which he accommodated the Parisian musical public's taste for orchestral effects. He claimed to have been 'careful not to neglect *le premier coup d'archet* – and that is quite sufficient for the "asses" in the audience'; he repeated towards the end of the first movement a passage from the middle that he 'felt sure' would please, hearing it greeted with a 'tremendous burst of applause' on the first occasion and with 'shouts of "Da capo"' on the second; and he played with audience expectations at the beginning of the Finale by moving from *piano* to *forte* eight bars later rather than commencing immediately with the anticipated tutti, such that the audience 'as I expected, said "hush" at the soft beginning, and when they heard the forte, began at once to clap their hands'.[15] Effects aimed at the musical masses, however, represent only half of the equation; for Mozart was apparently just as concerned with the kind of refined orchestral effects that surfaced in Parisian aesthetic discourse in the third quarter of the eighteenth century.[16] The diversity of wind effects recommended in treatises – from simple sustained notes and texturally prized combinations of clarinets, bassoons and horns, to carefully placed, not overused thematic-obbligato writing – is reflected in the first movement in particular; each pair of wind instruments (flutes, oboes, clarinets, bassoons, horns and trumpets) is used independently from and combined with other pairs, reaching a high point in the recapitulation's secondary theme section (see bars 206–27). Here, all six play sustained notes independent of string lines, featuring a different distribution of instruments each time, in addition to the clarinets–bassoons then horns–oboes offering obbligato two-bar extensions to the theme in thirds. Thus, Mozart immerses himself in French orchestration culture, reflecting and feeding into both the fascination for wind timbre among aestheticians and the desire for immediate sonic gratification among the musical public at large. And, judging by his report of the concert at which the work was premiered, he scored a direct hit.[17]

Haydn's 'Paris' Symphonies, nos. 82–7, were praised in the *Mercure de France* (1788) for being 'always sure in their effect'; unlike other composers, Haydn did not 'mechanically pile up effect on effect, without connection and without taste'.[18] Similar to Mozart's K 297 in relation to his earlier works in the genre, Haydn's 'Paris' Symphonies were the grandest he had conceived thus far. As for Mozart, the large orchestral forces at Haydn's disposal allowed not only for big tutti effects on a scale not yet witnessed in his symphonies, but also for a greater degree of textural intimacy on account of the variety of instrumental combinations that could be exploited.

Haydn's extraordinary success in Paris – his symphonies comprised 85 per cent of those performed at the Concert spirituel between 1788 and 1790[19] – can be attributed to a number of musical characteristics in nos. 82–7, including simple and beautiful melodies, humour and general splendour;[20] his attitude to orchestration contributed to the happy state of affairs too. For Haydn, like Mozart, accommodates the general listener – replicating Mozart's *piano* (light scoring) to *forte* (tutti) effect from the Finale of K 297 in the Finale of his own D major Symphony, No. 86, for example – as well as the connoisseur of sophisticated aesthetic taste. He covers the gamut of effects for winds in their capacity as agents texturally independent of string parts, from ornate obbligato writing (the slow movements of nos. 83, 85 and 87 and trios of nos. 82, 85 and 87) to colour-orientated sustained notes; his first movements also exploit wind sonorities in as meticulous and measured a fashion as Mozart's corresponding movement of K 297. In No. 85 in B flat, *La Reine*, Haydn intensifies his employment of independent wind instruments as the movement progresses. Sustained notes in the slow introduction lead to brief oboe–horn echoes in the first theme and a solo oboe presentation of the secondary theme (which is a repeat of the first theme in line with Haydn's monothematic practice); in the development section, Haydn ups the ante with eighteen bars of sustained winds (flute, oboes, bassoons) that accompany the strings' near-quotation of the 'Farewell' Symphony, with an eight-bar dialogue between oboes and violins, and with emphatic tutti-wind crotchets towards the end; in the recapitulation, as if responding to wind prominence in the development, Haydn introduces the wind right at the start of the first theme in both long-note (horn) and echo (oboe) capacities, the moment of formal arrival thus coinciding with the coming together of the winds' two principal roles as independent agents in this movement (held notes and thematic presentation).[21] No. 86 in D charts a similar course, providing more independent wind writing in the development section (oboe and flute thematic fragments at the beginning; tutti wind in the last sixteen bars) than in the exposition, and new independent roles for the bassoon and oboe and the bassoon and flute in the recapitulation's primary and secondary themes respectively. Like Mozart in K 297, so Haydn in the secondary themes of his first movements (except No. 87) also makes a point of promoting independent wind participation, even if only in modest fashion. Overall, then, sounds and sonorities constitute important points of communication between

Haydn and his audience, just as they feature significantly in French aesthetic discourse. As Ernst Ludwig Gerber remarked about Haydn's symphonies in 1790, before the 'London' symphonies had been written: 'Everything speaks when he sets his orchestra in motion. Every subsidiary part, an insignificant accompaniment in the works of other composers, often with him becomes a crucial principal part.'[22]

Mozart's and Haydn's attention to the kind of orchestral effects discussed by French aestheticians demonstrates the synergy of compositional environment and compositional style that is so central to understanding not just their symphonies but all other late eighteenth-century symphonic repertories as well. Mozart's symphonies may have had only equivocal success at the Concert spirituel between 1777 and 1790,[23] but Haydn's utter domination of the orchestral scene in the same period shows how receptivity to listener expectation and subsequent shaping of listener expectation – the positive impact on surroundings mentioned by Arnold – went hand in hand. And the grandeur and intimacy of the 'Paris' symphonies ensured that they became pivotal works in the musical careers of both men, helping to shape ensuing stylistic practices and expectations in Haydn's 'London' symphonies, where listener intelligibility was paramount, and in Mozart's Viennese piano concertos and symphonies, where the sonorous use of orchestral wind instruments in solo and accompanimental roles reached its peak in his instrumental repertory.[24]

Mozart's Viennese symphonies and Haydn's 'London' symphonies

Arnold was only one of numerous late eighteenth- and early nineteenth-century writers to draw attention to Mozart's and Haydn's harmonic and tonal powers. Critical assessments, including those of the London symphonies, were entirely positive where Haydn was concerned. He was praised for his 'exquisitly [*sic*] modulated' Symphony No. 94 ('Surprise'), for being 'wholy unrivaled [*sic*]' in harmony and modulation in a review of his Symphony No. 102, for 'continual strokes of genius, both in air and harmony' in the Symphony No. 103 ('Drum Roll') and, more generally, for handling flexibly even old-fashioned harmonic devices, for introducing 'new modulations, and new harmonies, without crudity or affectation' and (alongside Mozart) for introducing new practices, such as pedal points in upper registers for the purposes of intense expression.[25] Indeed, the skilled cultivation of novelty and unexpectedness – in harmony and other areas – was central to delineating creative genius according to late eighteenth-century German reviewers of instrumental music, and to Haydn's status as creative genius *par excellence*.[26] In contrast, the early reception of Mozart's harmonic and tonal procedures was mixed. He received high praise for 'bold' harmonies and 'overwhelming ... enchanting harmonies' in *Le nozze di Figaro* (1789, 1790), for well-judged modulations *inter alia* that 'touch our hearts and our sentiments' (1789), for 'heavenly harmonies [that] so often moved and filled our hearts with tender feelings' (1791) and for 'very excellent beauties' in modulation (1792).[27] But he also elicited criticism for the 'Haydn' quartets that are 'too highly seasoned' (1787), for such profound, intimate knowledge of harmony that his works in general become difficult for the 'unpractised ear' (*ungeübten Ohre*) (1790) and for 'frequent modulations ... [and] many enharmonic progressions ... [that] have no effect in the orchestra' in *Die Entführung aus dem Serail* 'partly because the intonation is never pure enough either on the singers' or the players' part ... and partly because the resolutions alternate too quickly with the discords, so that only a practised ear can follow the course of the harmony' (1788).[28] Complex harmonic and tonal procedures are not the only features of Mozart's music that sometimes rendered it problematic for contemporaries, but are self-evidently contributing factors.

Underscoring differences in Haydn and Mozart reception is the impression that effects – including harmonic effects – are a fundamental locus for listener *orientation* in Haydn's music, but on occasion a locus for listener *disorientation* in Mozart's music. The effect-laden Allegretto of Haydn's Symphony No. 100 ('Military'), for example, provides a firm hermeneutic anchor for the *Morning Chronicle* (1794):

> It is the advancing to battle; and the march of men, the sounding of the charge, the thundering of the onset, the clash of arms, the groans of the wounded, and what may well be called the hellish roar of war increase to a climax of horrid sublimity! which, if others can conceive, he alone can execute; at least he alone hitherto has effected these wonders.[29]

Indeed, the *locus classicus* of sublimity in Haydn's music, the arrival of light ('Und es ward Licht') in 'Chaos' from *The Creation*, is as forceful a moment of orientation and stabilisation as imaginable, not only resolving the nebulous C minor to C major – 'from paradoxical disorder to triumphant order' – but also reverberating well beyond its immediate confines into the rest of Part I.[30] In Mozart's *Entführung*, in contrast, minor-key arias 'because of their numerous chromatic passages, are difficult to perform for the singer, difficult to grasp for the hearer, and are altogether somewhat disquieting. Such strange harmonies betray the great master, but ... are not suitable for the theatre' (1788).[31] Similarly, the perceived lack of coherence that results from Mozart '[forgetting] the flow of passion in laboriously hunting after new thoughts' (1798) and from his 'explosions of a strong violence' (1800) also implies disorientation.[32]

It is likely that the ever self-aware Mozart suspected that audacious harmonic and tonal twists in his late symphonies would challenge some of his listeners; since he never aspired (understandably) to a lack of popularity and repudiated 'violent' modulations that 'drag you . . . by the scruff of the neck' as well as 'passion, whether violent or not . . . expressed to the point of disgust',[33] we might surmise that any perceived disorientation (whether positively or negatively parsed) represents disorientation intentionally conveyed. At any rate, the potentially disorientating quality of distant-key modulations was recognised as early as 1782 by Johann Samuel Petri: 'abrupt transitions' could be carried out in such a way 'that the listener himself does not know how he happened to be brought so very quickly into a totally foreign key'.[34]

One of Mozart's most celebrated passages of harmonic daring is the secondary development of the second movement of the Symphony No. 39 in E flat, K 543 (bars 91–108: see Example 7.1). It begins in the distant key of B minor, which, although achieved through the enharmonic interpretation of the Cb accompanying the shift to A-flat minor (i), is nonetheless startling, perhaps because it occurs a tritone away from the more 'civilised' key of F minor that initiates the corresponding section in the exposition, perhaps because it intensifies certain features of the earlier passage (wind minims from the first not second bar of the passage; registral highpoint of the movement in the flute; double-stopped second violins), or perhaps because it comes across as an abrasive realisation of the intimation of the minor mode a few bars earlier.[35] But this is only the beginning. In bars 100 and 101 the F♯ and Db harmonies (the former a tritone away again from the starting point of B minor) feel completely out of place, but as VI and IV of the tonic Ab are in the 'right' harmonic orbit for this juncture of the movement. If these chords feel strange, and the B minor starting point does too, is it any wonder that we experience disorientation? Surely we are *meant* to feel this way. Hearing a myriad of harmonic associations and references – B minor as an exploitation of the Cb contained in the preceding A flat minor; F♯ as a reminder of the F minor from the original transition – and hearing the entire passage as a dramatic realisation of the full expressive potential of the original transition material, only tells part of the story. For the passage ultimately inhabits a different expressive world from the rest of the movement – its harmonic disorientation is experienced nowhere else – and thus exists in a kind of self-contained expressive bubble.[36] In interpreting it simultaneously as intimately connected to the discourse of the movement and detached from it too, we begin to see how Arnold's interpretation of the effect of Mozart's music on the listener ('[he] lowers us deeper into ourselves and lifts us above ourselves') might also apply to effects

Example 7.1 Mozart, Symphony No. 39, II, bars 91–108.

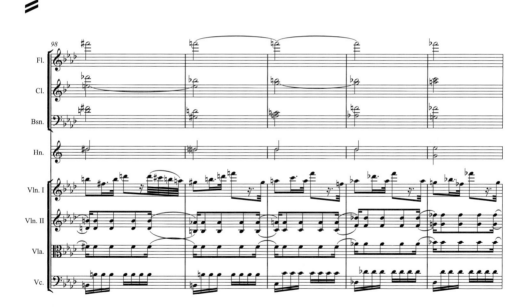

associated with Mozart's manipulation of harmonic materials in a specific movement.

The majority of the development section from the Andante of Mozart's Symphony No. 41 in C ('Jupiter'), K 551, occupies a similar position to the secondary development of K 543/ii in relation to its movement as a whole (see bars 47–55: Example 7.2). Mozart expands the material from the

Example 7.1 (cont.)

transition, prefacing and following the passage with the same harmony, V/ d, and setting the passage off from surrounding material with four texturally sparse bars beforehand (two at the end of the exposition and two at the start of the development) and two bars of harmonic water-treading afterwards (V/d, bars 56–7). The entire harmonic 'business' of the development (V/d–F) is then carried out in just two bars, leading directly into the recapitulation (bars 58–60). Bars 47–55 fulfil an expressive rather than a functional harmonic purpose: whether or not we agree that 'with each fresh ascent the suspensions seem more sharply pointed, creating ever greater yearning',[37] we hear impassioned intensity first and foremost. The passage stands *inside* the movement – building on the harmonic purple patch from the exposition – but *outside* it too, neatly delineated and expressively transcendent.

The famous openings to the development sections of K 543/iv and K 550/iv, though briefer than the passages discussed in K 543/ii and K 551/ii, again inhabit expressive territory that thrives as much on incongruity as congruity in relation to surrounding material. To be sure, the G^7 statement of the head motive in K 543/iv points ahead to a harmonically daring development (A-flat major and E major/minor follow straight away), but it stands apart too, wrenching us from the comfort of the dominant, B♭, and fulfilling no clear-cut harmonic function in appearing immediately before a statement in A flat. And the opening of the even more tonally audacious development section in K 550/iv is a bolt from the blue, implied

Example 7.2 Mozart, Symphony No. 41, II, bars 45–56.

diminished harmonies and uncertain harmonic direction conspiring to confuse. (Even late twentieth-century writers express shock, H. C. Robbins Landon citing it as an example of 'the desperate near-lunacy with which Mozart's music sometimes grimly flirts' and Peter Gülke labelling it

Example 7.2 (cont.)

'nearly atonal' ['*fast atonal*'].)[38] Such moments draw attention to themselves, as much (probably more) for how they differ from surrounding material than for how they contribute to harmonic strategies over protracted periods.[39]

Turning to Haydn's most powerful and poignant harmonic effects in the 'London' symphonies, we can begin to appreciate how the two composers sometimes achieve different effects. In the A^1 reprise section of the Andante from No. 104 in D ('London'), Haydn interpolates a colourful passage (bars 105–17); reinterpreting the D♯ from the A section (bars 23–4) enharmonically as E♭, Haydn continues chromatically to F (the third in D-flat harmony), retaining D-flat major harmony for five bars culminating in a pause (bars 109–13: see Example 7.3). He lands gently on this harmony – approaching it from the orbit of the tonic, G, namely iv (105–6) and ♭II^6 (107–8) – just as he lands gently on C major for the pause in bar 25 in the A section. If we are disorientated at D-flat major harmony representing our temporary point of arrival, we are disorientated only gradually. The next four bars (114–17), while highlighting the point of furthest tonal remove from the tonic G (C-sharp minor), also orientate the listener: the preceding chromatic bass ascent (B♮–D♭, bars 103–13) reverses as a chromatic descent (C♯–A♯, bars 114–17), signalling the

Example 7.3 Haydn, Symphony No. 104, II, bars 103–19.

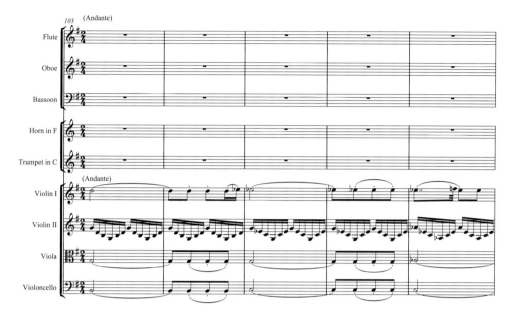

Example 7.3 (cont.)

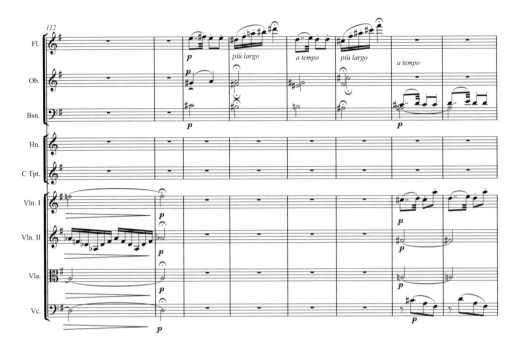

start of a return to the tonic at the precise moment we are furthest from it; and slow tempo and gesture (*più largo* and pauses) as well as harmonies (C sharp and F sharp) forge connections respectively with the slow introduction and development sections of the first movement.[40] Thus Haydn, eschewing Mozart's abrupt, attention-grabbing harmonic shifts, encourages his listener to experience connections and congruity, rather than a potentially disorientating mix of incongruity and congruity, even at a moment of genuine harmonic audacity.

Elsewhere in the 'London' symphonies, too, Haydn pursues the kind of 'breadth' – interpreted here as a forceful harmonic process stretched out over a protracted period and orientating the listening experience – that for Arnold distinguishes his music from Mozart's. The two most ostensibly surprising and dramatic moments in the first movement of Haydn's Symphony No. 100 in G ('Military') are harmonic effects – the onset of the development section in B flat, after a two-bar general pause, and the *forte/fortissimo* tutti shunt to ♭VI in the recapitulation. Both moments are integral components of the movement's narrative, Haydn continually playing with hiatuses and pauses, and exploiting ♭VI harmonies. The portentous end of the slow introduction preceding the main theme (repeated *fortissimo* quavers in the full orchestra, followed by a tutti *fortissimo* semibreve pause) leads to written-out hiatuses before two further thematic presentations in the exposition – tutti crotchets and tied flute semibreves in advance of the main theme in the dominant (see bars 72–4); and two bars of accompanimental figuration by itself before the secondary theme (see bars 93–4) – as well as the clearest hiatus of all at the opening of the development. And ♭VI, which first surfaces as augmented-sixth harmony towards the end of the slow introduction (bar 18), appears at the start of the development (B flat, as ♭VI/D) and in augmented-sixth form at climactic, *forte/fortissimo* junctures later in the section (bars 139, 152 and 162–4). The compressed recapitulation, eradicating the hiatuses of the exposition among other things, explodes in ♭VI, E flat (bar 239), fully exploiting the power that the harmony has accrued during the movement. Neither is its power confined to the first movement: the full orchestra bursts out, *fortissimo*, in A flat (♭VI) towards the end of the second movement (bar 161), and then again, *forte*, in the closing stages of the Finale (bars 245ff.).[41]

Haydn's moments of harmonic disorientation and destabilisation inevitably function as important catalysts for coherent harmonic discourse; rather than inviting us to focus on disorientation itself as Mozart sometimes does, Haydn encourages us to understand it first and foremost as part of an on-going process.[42] His ostentatious slow introduction to No. 99 in E flat is derailed by a C-flat pause (bar 10), and further destabilised by solid preparation for a key (C) that will not materialise; indeed, the V/E flat, final-bar appendage to the introduction in preparation for the tonic at the opening of the exposition feels incongruous and out of place, at least in relation to the music that precedes it. Both unruly elements fuel further discourse: recalcitrant C♭s appear in the exposition's transition (bar 35, marked *sf*), shortly before B♮s inflect the music to C minor *en route* to the dominant; C major initiates the development section, after a stop–start opening in which pauses and harmonic orbit (C) invoke the uncertainties of the slow introduction, but is now part of a smooth, rather than an abrupt and disquieting, modulatory process; and C♭s feature in imitative figures at the end of the development that help re-establish V/E flat, in Neapolitan-sixth harmony (bar 165) that reconfirms the tonic E flat at the end of the secondary theme in the recapitulation, and then as unobtrusive contributors to diminished harmony (bars 174–5), thus illustrating C flat's assimilation as a harmonically congruous and cooperative element of the discourse.[43] In the slow introduction of No. 102 in B flat, too, a harmonically disorientating gesture – an exact repeat of bar 1's unison B♭ five bars later in bar 6, where it disturbs forward momentum, in effect beginning the Symphony again with a second tonality-defining call-to-attention – resurfaces on various occasions in the first and third movements, the incongruous 'pillars' being eventually assimilated as congruous elements of the discourse.[44]

Of course, Mozart's and Haydn's most powerful harmonic utterances in the Viennese and 'London' symphonies sometimes convey similar effects. In the recapitulation of the Finale of Mozart's Symphony No. 38 in D, K 504 ('Prague'), for example, we are likely to admire the force with which the big tutti chords from the development reappear (as iv^6, $\natural III^7$, $\flat VI$; bars 228–32, 236–40, 244–5), orientating us to the tonic, rather than marvel at how the climactic chords themselves may temporarily disorientate. But differences in Mozart's and Haydn's harmonic effects remain tangible on many occasions, and are testimony to the incisively individualistic modus operandi of each composer. In spite of the seriousness with which Mozart essays his harmonic course in his most audacious passages, the self-conscious dimension to his daring manipulations – he intends us surely to reflect upon the ease with which he can disrupt a particular movement only to bring it effortlessly back into line – may strike a chord not only with Haydn's highly cultivated harmonic disorientations and reorientations but also with Haydn's self-conscious attention to the compositional mechanisms of his own creation, as exhibited in his much-touted wit and humour.[45] If in fact a parallel can be drawn here too, the pervasive image of Mozart and Haydn as two sides of the same coin again comes to mind. In our musical and historical imaginations the symphonic achievements of the two men are – and are likely to remain – inextricably intertwined.

Notes

1 *The Atlas*, 591 (10 September 1837), 586.

2 As given in Otto Erich Deutsch, *Mozart: A Documentary Biography*, trans. Eric Blom, Peter Branscombe and Jeremy Noble (3rd edn, London, 1990), 472–3.

3 Quoted in Simon McVeigh, *Concert Life in London from Mozart to Haydn* (Cambridge, 1993), 128.

4 *The Quarterly Musical Magazine and Review*, 8 (1826), 234. The same magazine three years earlier had offered a different take on the relationship among the three composers, but one that still downplayed Haydn's significance: 'The symphonies of Haydn may perhaps be occasionally more distinguished by his felicitous use of particular instruments, for his simplicity and playfulness, and Beethoven's as more powerful, more romantic and original, but considering all the attributes that are required to form the beau ideal or an actual model of composition in this

species, those of Mozart approach the nearest to perfection', *The Quarterly Musical Magazine and Review*, 5 (1823), 233–6; review of *Mozart's Six Grand Symphonies, arranged for the Piano Forte, with Accompaniments*.

5 See Maynard Solomon, 'The Rochlitz Anecdotes: Issues of Authenticity in Early Mozart Biography', in Cliff Eisen, ed., *Mozart Studies* (Oxford, 1991), 1–59, esp. 14–16 (anecdotes dating from 1798); Triest, 'Remarks on the Development of the Art of Music in Germany in the Eighteenth Century', trans. Susan Gillespie, in Elaine Sisman, ed., *Haydn and His World* (Princeton, 1997), 321–94, esp. 357–74; H. C. Robbins Landon, *Haydn: Chronicle and Works. Haydn in England, 1791–1795* (London, 1976), 273; Niemetschek, *Lebensbeschreibung des k. k. Kapellmeisters Wolfgang Amadeus Mozart* (Prague, 1798), trans. Helen Mautner as *Life of Mozart* (London, 1956), 10, 30–1, 33–4, 59–61 and 68–9. For a discussion of Niemetschek's subtle

adjustments to the second edition of his biography – eliminating the dedication to Haydn among other changes – as redolent of the superiority of Mozart over all who had come before (Haydn included), see Simon P. Keefe, 'Across the Divide: Currents of Musical Thought in Europe, c. 1790–1810', in Keefe, ed., *The Cambridge History of Eighteenth-Century Music* (Cambridge, 2009), 663–87, at 668–9.

6 In Arnold, *Gallerie der berühmtesten Tonkünstler des achtzehnten und neunzehnten Jahrhunderts. Ihre kurzen Biografieen, karakterisirende Anekdoten und ästhetische Darstellung ihrer Werke*, vol. I (Erfurt, 1810), 1–118. For brief comparisons from three years earlier in the context of a study of German music in general, see G. L. P. Sievers, 'Charakteristik der deutschen Musik', *Allgemeine musikalische Zeitung*, 9 (1806–7), cols. 699–700.

7 Arnold, *Gallerie*, 3 and 79: 'Mozart ist unstreitig das größte musikalische Genie seines und aller Zeitalter'; 'Er [Haydn] bahnte den Weg, auf dem Mozart zur Unsterblichkeit einging'.

8 Ibid., 13 ('eine heilige Einheit in der individuellsten Mannigfaltigkeit'), 114–15 and 116 ('beide [sind] in der Harmonie gleich groß, gleich stark und kräftig', and 'Mozart sucht seine Melodien mit der Kraft der Harmonien zu bekleiden. Haydn versteckt seine tiefen Harmonien unter Rosen und Mirthengewinde seiner Melodien.').

9 Ibid., 117: 'Haydns Genius sucht die Breite, Mozarts Höhe und Tiefe.'

10 Ibid.: 'Haydn führt uns aus uns heraus. Mozart versenkt uns tiefer in uns selbst und hebt uns über uns. Daher malt Haydn auch immer mehr objektive Anschauungen, und Mozart die subjektiven Gefühle.'

11 *Allgemeine musikalische Zeitung*, 12 (1809–10), col. 632; as given in David Charlton, ed., *E. T. A. Hoffmann's Musical Writings: 'Kreisleriana', 'The Poet and the Composer', Music Criticism*, trans. Martyn Clarke (Cambridge, 1989), 237–8.

12 Arnold, *Gallerie*, 117 ('beide Genien stehen gleich kraftvoll, gleich anmuthig da').

13 No single Haydn symphony is known to have been composed for Vienna exclusively; see A. Peter Brown, *The Symphonic Repertoire*, vol. II: *The First Golden Age of the Symphony: Haydn, Mozart, Beethoven, and Schubert* (Bloomington, 2002), 2. Mozart might have written his final three symphonies with a potential trip to London in mind, although other possibilities include planned subscription concerts in Vienna and the

composer's desire to sell or publish an 'opus' of three symphonies; see Neal Zaslaw, *Mozart's Symphonies: Context, Performance Practice, Reception* (Oxford, 1989), 421–2.

14 Haydn's symphonies nos 90–2 (1788–89) were also commissioned for the *Concert de la Loge Olympique* in Paris.

15 See Emily Anderson, ed. and trans., *The Letters of Mozart and His Family*, 3rd rev. edn, ed. Stanley Sadie and Fiona Smart (New York, 1985), 553 (12 June 1778) and 558 (3 July 1778). Mozart also wrote a second middle movement for the work to accommodate the wishes of Joseph Le Gros, director of the Concert spirituel, while acknowledging that the original movement was 'a great favourite with me and all connoisseurs'. Anderson, *Letters*, 565 (9 July 1778).

16 See Simon P. Keefe, 'The Aesthetics of Wind Writing in Mozart's "Paris" Symphony, K 297', *Mozart-Jahrbuch* 2006, 329–44. The remainder of the paragraph is drawn from the findings of this article.

17 Anderson, *Letters*, 557–8 (3 July 1778).

18 Given in Bernard Harrison, *Haydn: The 'Paris' Symphonies* (Cambridge, 1998), 22.

19 Ibid., 21.

20 See Harrison's musical discussion in ibid., 45–99.

21 The oboe's presentations of the secondary theme begin with two-bar sustained notes, thus also integrating the two roles.

22 Gerber, *Historisch-biographisches Lexicon der Tonkünstler* 2 vols.(Leipzig, 1790, 1792), vol. I, col. 610: 'Alles spricht, wenn er sein Orchester in Bewegung setzt. Jede, sonst blos unbedeutende Füllstimme in den Werken anderer Komponisten, wird oft bei ihm zur entscheidenden Hauptparthie.'

23 See Keefe, 'Aesthetics of Wind Writing', 342.

24 On listener intelligibility in Haydn's Paris and London symphonies, see David P. Schroeder, *Haydn and the Enlightenment: The Late Symphonies and Their Audience* (Oxford, 1990), 75–198; and, in condensed form, Schroeder, 'Orchestral Music: Symphonies and Concertos', in Caryl Clark, ed., *The Cambridge Companion to Haydn* (Cambridge, 2007), 95–111, at 107–111. On wind roles in Mozart's piano concertos and *inter alia* Mozart's Viennese symphonies, see Simon P. Keefe, *Mozart's Piano Concertos: Dramatic Dialogue in the Age of Enlightenment* (Woodbridge and Rochester, NY, 2001); Keefe, *Mozart's Viennese Instrumental Music: A Study of Stylistic Re-Invention* (Woodbridge and Rochester, 2007), 43–62 and 137–64; and Keefe,

'"Greatest Effects with the Least Effort":
Strategies of Wind Writing in Mozart's
Viennese Piano Concertos', in Keefe, ed.,
Mozart Studies (Cambridge, 2007), 25–42.
25 See Landon, *Haydn in England*, 49, 287 and
295; Gerber, *Historisch-biographisches Lexikon
der Tonkünstler*, vol. I, col. 610;
Charles Burney, in Chambers's *Cyclopaedia*, as
given in Zaslaw, *Mozart's Symphonies*, 511;
Allgemeine musikalische Zeitung, 1 (1798–9),
col. 153.
26 Mary Sue Morrow, *German Music
Criticism in the Late Eighteenth Century:
Aesthetic Issues in Instrumental Music*
(Cambridge, 1997), 99–133, esp. 123.
27 Deutsch, *Documentary Biography*, 345, 372
and 355; Cliff Eisen, *New Mozart Documents: A
Supplement to O. E. Deutsch's Documentary
Biography* (London, 1991), 123 and 124.
28 Deutsch, *Documentary Biography*, 290;
Gerber, *Historisch-biographisches Lexikon der
Tonkünstler*, vol. I, col. 979; Deutsch,
Documentary Biography, 328.
29 Given in Landon, *Haydn in England*, 247.
30 See James Webster, 'The Sublime and the
Pastoral in *The Creation* and *The Seasons*', in
Clark, ed., *The Cambridge Companion to
Haydn*, 154–5.
31 Deutsch, *Documentary Biography*, 328.
32 Thomas Holcroft quoted by Landon in
Haydn in England, 273; *Allgemeine
musikalische Zeitung* (November 1800), given
in Landon, *Haydn: Chronicle and Works.
Haydn: the Late Years, 1801–1809* (London,
1977), 408.
33 Anderson, *Letters*, 378 (20 November
1777) and 769 (26 September 1781).
34 Petri, *Anleitung zur praktischen Musik*, rev.
edn (Leipzig, 1782), 281; as given in Annette
Richards, *The Free Fantasia and the Musical
Picturesque* (Cambridge, 2002), 41.
35 For an extended analysis of this movement
see Eric Wen, 'A Tritone Key Relationship in
the Bridge Sections of the Slow Movement of
Mozart's 39th Symphony', *Music Analysis*, 5/1
(1986), 59–84.
36 Leo Treitler, in his narrative reading of K
543/ii, calls the passage an 'emotional roller
coaster', and the music from bar 90 onwards
'unpredictable and psychologically
complex . . . very operatic'. See 'Mozart and the
Idea of Absolute Music', in *Music and the
Historical Imagination* (Cambridge, Mass.,
1989), 176–215, at 211.
37 Elaine Sisman, *Mozart: The 'Jupiter'
Symphony* (Cambridge, 1993), 58.
38 Landon, *Haydn: Chronicle and Works.
Haydn at Eszterháza, 1766–1790* (London,

1978), 609; Gülke, *'Triumph der neuen
Tonkunst': Mozarts späte Sinfonien und ihr
Umfeld* (Kassel and Stuttgart, 1998), 251.
39 On parallels between the K 550/iv passage and
a passage from the corresponding juncture of the
first movement of Mozart's final piano concerto, K
595 in B flat, see Keefe, *Mozart's Viennese
Instrumental Music*, 77–8. Strong contrasts –
including harmonic contrasts – become an
increasingly common characteristic of Mozart's
late chamber and orchestral works, featuring in his
processes of stylistic reinvention; see Keefe,
Mozart's Viennese Instrumental Music, 105–33
and 167–200.
40 The slow introduction to No. 104 is marked
Adagio and delineated by two pauses at the
beginning and one at the end; the development
section moves through C-sharp minor and F-
sharp minor (bars 145–54) *en route* to E minor
(bar 155).
41 The Finale of No. 100, like the first
movement, also incorporates written-out
musical hiatuses, with harmonic ramifications.
For example, the final eight bars of the main
theme are preceded by a woodwind pattern
that ends with a hiatus one beat earlier than we
expect (lacking the final crotchet in bar 40 that
appears in the corresponding segment in the
violins in bar 38); pause bars and harmonic
stasis delay the arrival of the secondary theme
(see bars 77–85); and the development section
begins in stop–start fashion (bars 117–28),
replete with ostentatious timpani solo and
reaffirmation of the dominant. On issues of
through-composition and cyclic integration in
general in Haydn's symphonies, see James
Webster, *Haydn's 'Farewell' Symphony and the
Idea of Classical Style: Through-Composition
and Cyclic Integration in His Instrumental
Music* (Cambridge, 1991).
42 For a lengthy discussion of Haydn's
destabilisation effects – harmonic and
otherwise – see Webster, *'Farewell' Symphony*,
127–55.
43 Webster provides an extended analysis of
the first movement of No. 99, explaining how it
'employs remote keys and sonorities so
pervasively that they become the primary
source of cyclic integration' in ibid., 320–9
(quotation from 320).
44 This process in No. 102 is documented in
Simon P. Keefe, 'Dialogue and Drama: Haydn's
Symphony No. 102', *Music Research Forum*,
11/1 (1996), 1–21.
45 See, in particular, Gretchen A. Wheelock,
*Haydn's Ingenious Jesting with Art: Contexts of
Musical Wit and Humor* (New York, 1992); Mark
Evan Bonds, 'Haydn, Laurence Sterne and the

Origins of Musical Irony', *Journal of the American Musicological Society*, 44 (1991), 57–91. Such a parallel does not mean to imply that the kind of effects discussed above in Haydn's London symphonies are necessarily devoid of humour. Indeed, manifestations of 'obsessive repetition' in the first movement of No. 100, akin to the aforementioned written-out hiatus effects, have a humorous dimension; see Wheelock, *Haydn's Ingenious Jesting with Art*, 178–82.

8 Beethoven: structural principles and narrative strategies

MARK ANSON-CARTWRIGHT

Critical accounts of Beethoven's symphonies have generally focussed on innovative aspects, on the various ways in which Beethoven transforms – and transcends – eighteenth-century models. Joseph Kerman once observed that five of Beethoven's symphonies – the Third, Fifth, Sixth, Seventh and Ninth – embody a new 'symphonic ideal' characterised by 'forcefulness, expanded range and evident radical intent'.[1] More recently, Scott Burnham has explored the long critical reception history of a related, if more narrowly defined, ideal: the 'heroic style' of Beethoven's two most popular symphonies, the Third and the Fifth. (The compositional reception of Beethoven's symphonies – a topic not examined by Burnham – is treated in Chapter 14 of the present volume.) According to Burnham, this style has, for nearly two centuries, 'epitomised musical vitality, becoming a paradigm of Western compositional logic'.[2] But, as Burnham duly acknowledges, the heroic style 'is only one of the stories Beethoven tells'.[3]

The features associated with the 'symphonic ideal' and the 'heroic style' – formal expansion, goal-directed structures, thematic relations between movements, the 'struggle-to-victory' narrative archetype – are unquestionably important and have loomed large in the literature. But they have often overshadowed other structural principles and narrative strategies that are no less pertinent to our experience and understanding of these works. For this reason, this chapter explores the following five aspects of the symphonies, without placing any special emphasis on the familiar ideals and paradigms: formal articulation; rhythm and temporality; ambiguity; chromatic gambits; and finales.

Formal articulation

We may distinguish two broad types of formal articulation in Beethoven's symphonies: one centripetal, based on recurrence; the other centrifugal, based on surprise or contrast. Whereas centripetal articulation tends to facilitate the recognition of formal boundaries, centrifugal articulation is usually disorienting, forcing the listener to reassess prior assumptions about past or future events.

In most of the symphonies, a fairly simple recurring link runs like a narrative thread through the first movement, articulating large sections of the form. All except the Fifth and the Ninth symphonies contain such a link between the exposition's final cadence and the repeat of the exposition. (The Ninth Symphony is the only one in which the exposition is not repeated, though the opening of the development briefly gives the illusion that a repetition is underway.) In the First, Second and Fourth symphonies, the link also occurs at the end of the slow introduction, creating an additional layer of formal resonance.

In the First Symphony, Beethoven articulates the border between the introduction and the Allegro by means of a slowly arpeggiated V^7 chord and a rapid, descending scalar pattern from G to C. The arpeggio idea returns – sometimes varied in rhythm, sometimes without the scalar pattern, but always scored for winds – prior to each main section (or the repeat thereof). When it appears for the third time, at the second ending of the exposition, it leads not to C, as on previous occasions, but to C♯, supporting an A-major $\frac{6}{3}$ chord. This harmonic detour is an elementary example of 'centrifugal articulation' – a not uncommon procedure at the start of developments in works of the Classical period.[4]

At the end of the development, the arpeggio signal quietly unfolds between two *fortissimo* tutti passages: a prolongation of E major harmony (functioning as V/vi, or III♯ at the middleground), and the reprise of the main theme (compare the start of the Allegro, marked *piano* and lightly scored for strings).[5] The descending G–C scale-fragment at the upbeat to the recapitulation not only echoes the upbeat to bar 13, but also seems to 'solve' the problem posed by its inversion, A to E, stated four times in bars 163–70. The familiar arpeggio motive returns for the fifth and final time just before the start of the coda, transposed down a fifth, ushering in the subdominant in bar 263. This echoes the harmonic motion at the start of the movement, albeit in different thematic clothing, and without the former ambiguity, since V^7/IV now *follows* tonic harmony, rather than entering out of nowhere, as in bar 1. In any case, the harmonic association between these passages sets the stage for a more obvious echo of the introduction in bars 271–6, where the bass line of bars 8–11 (F–G–G♯–A–F–G) returns.

In a similar yet more varied manner, recurring motives articulate form in the first movements of the Second and Third symphonies. The Second Symphony contains two such motives, both in the shape of a descending scale: a rapid descent through a twelfth leading to the start of both exposition and recapitulation; a more broadly paced scalar descent through a seventh preparing the repeat of the exposition as well as the start of the development and coda. In the Third Symphony, the associations between formal boundaries are subtler. The opening hammerstrokes of bars 1–2, for instance, return at the end of both the exposition (bars 144–7) and recapitulation (bars 547–50), except that new attacks fill the space between the downbeats, and the two-bar idea is extended to four bars. The third A♭–C♭ also recurs at key points: first, as a melodic interval over bass B♭ in bar 150, providing a harmonic link to the repeat of the exposition; then, in the retransition (bars 382ff.) as a very quiet tremolo over the dominant, but now presented as a harmonic third. This framing device is seldom noted in analytical commentaries that, not surprisingly, focus on the most striking aspect of the retransition: the famous horn call four bars before the recapitulation, where tonic and dominant coincide.[6]

In a conventional sonata form, the A♭–C♭ idea of bar 150 would return at the end of the recapitulation, transposed down a fifth, leading to the key of the subdominant at the start of the coda, just as in the previous two symphonies. But rather than follow this convention, Beethoven simply reiterates the principal theme on plain tonic harmony, letting the music soften to *pianissimo*. He then shatters the calm of bars 555–6 with a *forte* statement of the principal motive first in D flat, then in C major. The irony here is that D♭ does not assume its conventional guise – the seventh of V^7/IV – but enters, without preparation, as a foreground tonic (D♭ also relates to the C♯ famously introduced in bar 7). This passage is an unusually early example of 'tonic assertion', a chromatic technique more characteristic of late nineteenth-century music.[7]

Whereas centripetal articulation clarifies the formal narrative through motivic recurrence or association, centrifugal articulation disrupts – or at least complicates – the narrative in unexpected ways. The A major $\frac{6}{4}$ chord at the start of the development of the First Symphony, noted above, is a fairly conventional instance of such articulation: it is exactly the kind of harmonic 'jolt' listeners had increasingly come to expect at the start of a development section. A more complex example of remote harmonic juxtaposition occurs in the exposition of the first movement of the Seventh Symphony. In bars 134–41, shortly after the first strong cadence in the second key, E major, there is a dramatic shift from E major to C major harmony (I–♭VI). The jarring effect of this passage arises not simply from the remote harmonic relation, but from conflicting thematic and harmonic implications. The grand descending C major arpeggio and the halting effect of rhythmic 'liquidation' (as Schoenberg would put it) strongly suggest a post-cadential or closing function. But the unstable, hovering quality of this remote harmony cannot support that function. The conflict is resolved in the ensuing bars by a gradual motion back to the local tonic E supporting a climactic high G♯ in the top line (bar 152), followed by two iterations of an 'expanded cadential progression' incorporating the descending arpeggio figure. Genuine post-cadential material is presented in bars 164–71.[8]

Unlike the passages just described, which are fairly easily understood once their larger formal contexts become clear, some instances of centrifugal articulation almost defy analysis. I have in mind such passages as the loud fanfare in E flat during the Adagio of the Ninth Symphony (bars 121–3 and again at 131–3), which Maynard Solomon describes as 'vainly striving to break a mood of deep contemplation'.[9] What is centrifugal about the fanfare is not its tonal content – clearly foreshadowed by the earlier tonicisation of E♭ in bars 83ff. and (ultimately) by the marked occurrences of E♭ in the first movement (bar 24 *et passim*) – but rather its rhetoric. Being a military topic within a 'contemplative' movement, the fanfare is a kind of unwelcome guest, appearing out of nowhere and vanishing after its second entrance. It is also, perhaps, a harbinger of the much less pompous – and, indeed, comical – Turkish march that intrudes upon the Finale and is set, ironically, in the same key as the solemn Adagio. Centrifugal articulation of this kind is by no means rare in Beethoven. It is but one of several means by which he creates ambiguity, a central aspect of the music of Beethoven's middle and late periods.

Ambiguity

According to Carl Dahlhaus, around 1802 – the year in which Beethoven began work on the *Eroica* Symphony and also announced his intention to enter upon a 'new path' – there emerges 'a musical thinking that is directed towards radical processuality of form'. In several works of this period, the 'traditional theme' is replaced by a 'thematic configuration' and 'formal ambiguity' emerges as a central compositional strategy.[10] In the first movement of the *Eroica*, for example, bars 3–6 do not simply contain a 'theme'. Rather, the arpeggio motive has a provisional quality, whose meaning can be determined, according to Dahlhaus, only in relation to subsequent statements of that motive, along with its chromatic continuation. The 'static' arpeggio motive is followed in bars 6–7 by a chromatic descent, E♭–D–C♯. In later statements, however, the chromatic continuation *ascends*: E♭–E♮–F in bars 18–19; then B♭–B♮–C in bars 40–1. The main point is that this 'thematic configuration' does not reside in any single presentation of the arpeggio motive and the chromatic continuation, but rather 'is absorbed into the process for which it provides the substance'.[11]

The first movements of the *Eroica* and the Fifth Symphony – notwithstanding their shared 'heroic' traits – exhibit remarkably different formal tendencies. The former is expansive, thematically abundant and continuous; the latter, concise, motivically taut and articulated by rhetorical pauses. The *Eroica*'s unbroken continuity has given rise to much debate concerning the 'true' beginning of the second group: most analysts locate it at bar 83, but some have proposed either bar 45 or 57.[12] No such ambiguity arises at this point in the Fifth Symphony; the second group begins without a doubt at bar 60, the entry of the famous horn call.

Although ambiguity can occur at almost any formal stage, it is most evident at or near the beginning of Beethoven's symphonic movements. A relatively modest example is the famous dominant seventh chord at the start of the First Symphony (which actually predates the 'new path' by a couple of years). Much more complex is the unprecedented – and frequently discussed – dramatic effect of the opening of the Ninth Symphony. Admittedly, any ambiguity surrounding the function of bars 1–16 (as introduction or first theme presentation) soon dissolves; but that does not render the ambiguity trivial. It is precisely the challenge of predicting the movement's formal trajectory on a first hearing that makes this opening so engaging. Similarly, and as Richard Cohn has identified, Beethoven invites the listener at the start of the Scherzo to weigh competing metric interpretations of the first eight bars: do they scan as 2+3+3 or 2+2+2+2?[13]

One of the most frequently cited examples of tonal ambiguity is the opening of the Fifth Symphony (bars 1–5), which could imply either E flat major or C minor. What analysts seldom acknowledge is the importance of this ambiguity at the repeat of the exposition. When the opening idea is heard immediately *following* the E flat major cadence that concludes the exposition, it seems for a moment as if E♭ is still the tonic, even though C (once again) turns out to be the 'real' tonic. The intimate tonal bond between the end of the exposition and the start of the repeat, along with the brevity of the exposition, makes this repeat sound more urgent, perhaps even more formally necessary, than that of most expositions. The sense of urgency has partly to with the fact that the material in the opening five bars is only stated once during the first group. In the *Eroica*, by contrast, the presence of three tonic statements of the opening arpeggio idea within the first group poses a certain risk of redundancy when the exposition is repeated. It was perhaps for this reason – in addition to the sheer length of the movement – that Beethoven originally chose not to include the repeat (although he ultimately decided to include it after trial performances in 1805).

Chromatic gambits

In several of Beethoven's symphonic movements, a telling chromatic note or harmony enters at an early stage and recurs in various guises over the course of the movement. The C♯ in bar 7 of the first movement of the *Eroica* is perhaps the best-known example. The ramifications of that note include its enharmonic potential to function as D♭ – a potential that is realised in the recapitulation's deft modulation to F major, which Donald Tovey admired for its effect of 'strange exaltation' – a rare instance in which II does not function as V/V.[14] Other consequences of the C♯ arise from its 'subthematic' function (to borrow Dahlhaus's term) as part of a chromatic scale-fragment (E♭–D–C♯), as opposed to its recurrence or reinterpretation *qua* C♯/D♭. In the development, a 5–6 semitonal motion over the bass, deployed sequentially, gives rise to modulations from C minor to C-sharp minor to D minor (bars 178–86). At the start of the coda (as noted earlier), Beethoven does not modulate by semitonal inflection, but simply juxtaposes the 'keys' of E flat and D flat. Such placement of the least predictable and most exaggerated manifestation of an opening chromatic idea towards a movement's end is typically Beethovenian.

The enharmonic D♭/C♯ also plays a conspicuous narrative role in the Finale of the Eighth Symphony, where it occurs three times in the same thematic guise: an abrupt semitone shift, C–C♯, with C♯ accented dynamically and durationally (see bars 17, 178 and 372). In addition to this thematic guise, there is a 'subthematic' aspect to consider, specifically the use of ascending semitones at various pitch levels to articulate important formal junctures. The first of these is the G–A♭ shift in bars 47–8, which launches the second group on ♭VI of C major. The recapitulation of this material down a fifth in bars 223–4 strengthens its association with the original C–C♯ jolt. But it is the third occurrence – or set of occurrences – of this jolt, in bars 372–9, that is the most telling. Beethoven reinterprets C♯ as the dominant of F-sharp minor, in which key the opening theme is stated in bars 380–7. The music then seems to become caught in a loop in bars 386–91, where a two-bar pattern occurs in triple succession. Almost imperceptibly, the music slips back to F major in bar 391, by means of the enharmonic reinterpretation of E♯ as F in the bass, and, in the top part, the unaltered common note A, the third of both F major and F-sharp minor. This subtle shift, or slip, down a semitone is the *dénouement* – both literally and figuratively – of the earlier rising semitone; the main drama of the movement is essentially over. Although some wayward chromatic harmonies briefly 'shock' the listener in bars 432–7 (I♭⁷ in place of I, reinterpreted as an augmented sixth going to VII, followed by vii and V⁷), they do not belong to the main action, but rather form an ironic commentary upon the earlier conflicts. From bar 438, the movement concludes – purged, as it were, of its chromatic neuroses – with sixty-five bars of pure, trouble-free diatonicism.

The chromatic pitch G♭ runs like a red thread through all four movements of the Fourth Symphony. Though it does not pervade any single movement to the same extent as, for instance, the C♯ in the first movement of the *Eroica*, G♭ is sufficiently marked for attention to qualify as an important unifying idea for the entire Symphony. In the first movement, G♭ plays a major role in the slow introduction and near the end of the development. Its importance is made clear by its early entrance in bar 2, its return in bar 5 (the longest sustained note yet) and its prolongation in bars 17–24 as F♯, locally V of B minor. It resolves to G in bar 25, part of a rising chromatic line that reaches B♭ in bar 42, the fourth bar of the Allegro vivace. When G♭ returns in the development, it is notated (again) as F♯ (bars 281–301) and, once again, assumes the local function of a dominant. But the notation here is for convenience only, since the 'dominant seventh' prolonged in these bars functions on a deeper level as a German sixth, a function that is unveiled by the flat spelling of the harmony in bars 302–4, and its resolution to a B♭ $^6_4$ chord in bar 305. This $^6_4$ anticipates the tonic of the recapitulation, rather than behaving as a conventional cadential $^6_4$ (this irregular usage is 'corrected', so to speak, in bars 447–51). By making the putative F♯ discharge its true function as G♭, Beethoven solves a major problem posed by the introduction: the fact that the G♭ of bar 17 does not fall back to F (as in bar 6), but instead resolves (eventually) up to G.[15]

In the E flat second movement, G♭ plays a major role, but does not emerge prominently until the central section, starting at bar 50 and leading to the tonicised G-flat major chord of bar 60. The D♭ dominant seventh preparing this goal is the locus of an eloquent dialogue between the violins – a unique passage in this movement. Soon after G♭ is tonicised, it gently falls to F, the fifth of the dominant harmony, in bar 62, and recurs as a passing note in bar 63. The second movement does not explore the enharmonic of G♭. Neither, apparently, does the third movement (whose pervasive use of G♭ need not be catalogued here), unless one includes the rising chromatic line from F to B♭ in bars 175–9, the link between the Trio and the return of the Scherzo (Allegro vivace; the term 'scherzo' does not appear in the score). In the Finale, G flat returns again at key moments in the form – the retransition (bars 165–82) and coda (bars 290–5 and, more emphatically, bars 316–17) – but not as a major character. It plays a supporting role in this light comedy where no single feature claims the kind of attention that G flat does in the first movement. The Fourth Symphony conforms to the eighteenth-century symphonic tradition of the *lieto fine*, insofar as the Finale is shorter and less weighty than the first movement.

Rhythm and temporality

In much of Beethoven's music in general, and in several symphonic movements in particular, rhythm takes centre stage. This is most evident in movements where short, distinctive patterns are repeated for relatively long stretches of time: in the scherzos; in the first movements of the Fifth, Sixth and Seventh symphonies (especially in the development section of the Sixth); and in the second movement of the Seventh Symphony. Another aspect of rhythm to consider is the pacing of musical events, manifested in such phenomena as tempo, harmonic rhythm and hypermetre. While listeners usually measure pace (consciously or unconsciously) in relation to an internal 'clock', some effects of pacing may seem more 'absolute' than others. Thus, the harmonic rhythm of most of the development of the Sixth Symphony sounds 'slow' in an almost absolute sense, as opposed to the Presto at the end of the third movement of that Symphony, which sounds 'fast' relative to the previous tempo. (The abruptness of this change of tempo is also significant.)

I shall explore the narrative role of surface rhythms in three movements: the first movements of the Fifth and the Sixth symphonies; and the Allegretto of the Seventh Symphony. In these movements, a temporal narrative emerges from the dialectic between constancy and change, or between repetition and variation, on both the rhythmic surface and at deeper levels, where hypermetric conflicts sometimes arise. The effect of repetition or constancy with respect to one parameter – striking though it may be – is virtually always complemented or nuanced by simultaneous changes within another parameter, such as dynamics or instrumentation, or by subsequent changes with respect to the initially constant parameter. I shall conclude with an account of metric ambiguity and conflict at deeper levels in the third movement of the Sixth Symphony.

Analyses of the first movement of the Fifth Symphony have rightly drawn attention to metrical ambiguities and conflicts at levels beyond the notated bar.[16] But rhythmic features of the foreground are equally important, especially the varied deployment of the initial four-note motive, with its distinct three-quaver anacrusis. For Heinrich Schenker, the opening two gestures (bars 1–5) and the horn call (bars 59–63) are not only similar in contour and length, but also scan the same way: as a four-bar group preceded by a one-bar anacrusis.[17] Notwithstanding their similarities, the two thematic 'announcements' differ rhythmically in one important respect: the horn call does not repeat the anacrusis figure. Thus, instead of two short gestures, as in bars 1–5, the horn presents a single, longer gesture marked by a succession of three long notes unaccompanied by quavers.

Much of the movement's drama hinges on oppositions between passages pervaded by quavers and passages in which quavers either occur less often, as in the beginning of the second group, or drop out for an extended period, as in the central part of the development. This dramatic process starts in bars 6–21, where overlapping statements of the motive, arranged in groups of three, three and five, produce an effect of acceleration in bars 14–18. The quavers drop out suddenly in bars 19–21, bringing the orchestra to an abrupt halt. The process of acceleration resumes in the transition, and is extended so that the halting effect of the chords spaced two bars apart in bars 56–8 is even more pronounced than those spaced one bar apart in bars 19–21. In the larger context of these changes in surface rhythm, the horn call harks back not only to bars 1–5, but also to bars 18–21.[18] As the second group continues, the four-note motive recurs, but at a palpably slower rate than in the first group: at first, every four bars (bars 65–83), then every two bars (bars 84–93). Meanwhile, the music grows in dynamic intensity to *fortissimo* on the melodic peak, a sustained high B♭ in bar 94, the initial note of the closing theme.

In the first part of the development, Beethoven sustains rhythmic drive through unrelenting quavers, leading (yet again) to a rhythmic halt, or rather a series of halts, in bars 170–9, followed by the horn call, now played by the violins in G minor. What is new here is not the horn call as such, but the counterpointing of its long fourth note with a syncopated descending arpeggio in the low strings – the first strong foreground syncopation in the movement. Several rhythmic factors contribute to the suspense surrounding bars 196–227: the prolonged absence of quavers (longer than at any other time in the movement); the 'liquidation' of the horn call's three long notes, first to pairs of notes or chords (bars 196–209), then to individual chords (bars 210–26); and the hypermetric shift (or reinterpretation) located, according to Schenker, in bar 209.[19]

An echo of bars 168–79 at the start of the coda sets the stage for yet another return of the horn call, in bar 398. That motive now matches, for the first time, the pitches of bars 1–5, thus resolving a fundamental motivic conflict in the movement. But the sense of resolution is complicated by the intrusion of a new countermelody in quaver rhythm, extending to bar 422. What is striking about the quaver patterns is that they begin on downbeats, rather than upbeats (though bar 400 is hypermetrically weak). (Note that such downbeat-orientated patterns of quavers already occur in the closing theme; but there the patterns are comparatively short-lived.) This long string of quavers and the even longer passage in crotchet rhythm that follows in bars 423–69 succeed in keeping the anacrusis figure at bay – but only provisionally. Rhythmically speaking, the movement thus ends in a state of tension that is not fully resolved until the Finale.

The first movement of the Sixth Symphony is largely contemplative in mood, almost devoid of the kind of conflict that pervades the corresponding movement of the Fifth Symphony. In numerous passages, repetition gives rises to a certain quality of stasis that might suggest the timelessness or fixity of the natural order, of nature objectified (*natura naturata*). Yet, for all its repetitiveness, this movement is more properly heard as an evocation of *natura naturans* – the nature of vitality and growth.[20] To expand a little on Beethoven's own remark, the Symphony is not so much a painting (*Malerey*) of nature as an expression of the feelings (*Empfindungen*) arising from our metaphorical identification with nature. In bars 16–25, for example, the tenfold repetition of the same figure sounds alive and nuanced, not mechanical. The passage has an arc-like dynamic shape, growing in intensity to *forte* at bar 20 (articulated by the entry of the bassoon) and then gradually subsiding to *pianissimo* at bar 25. Moreover, the repeated figure introduces the first chromatic note in the movement, a passing B♮, which endows the music with an urge to continue upward, as indeed it does, sequentially, in bars 26–8.

The movement abounds with arc- or wave-like dynamic and/or melodic patterns ranging in length from one to forty bars. The largest of these waves occur in two parallel passages during the first half of the development: the first moves from B-flat major to D major harmony (bars 151–90); the second from G major to E major harmony (bars 197–236). (A linking passage on G follows in bars 191–6.) Each wave gradually builds to its dynamic peak after the durational midpoint (bars 175 and 221, respectively) and is soon followed by a drastic reduction in texture and dynamics. Movement in each passage is projected more through changes in dynamics and texture than by the harmonic shifts, which have a brightening or intensifying effect, but are not strongly goal-directed. Similarly, the loud tutti passage prolonging the dominant at the start of the retransition (bars 263–75) does not 'lead' strongly to the tonic, but instead gives way to the subdominant, with a concomitant diminuendo and (again) a reduction in texture.[21]

The overall rhythmic, melodic and dynamic quality of this movement is thus neither static – despite some elements of stasis – nor propulsive, like that of the Fifth Symphony's opening movement, but rather undulating. Beyond the ebb and flow at local and intermediate levels, one may also observe a global narrative or progression that is not wave-like. The chief point of interest in this narrative is the use of triplets, which make their first modest appearance in the transition (bars 53–64, in every fourth bar). Within the exposition, they occur independently of duple rhythms only once, in bars 111–15, and they continue to play a rather subordinate role in the development. During the opening bars of the recapitulation (bars 289–311), new triplet figuration appears in the first violins (then in the lower strings from bar 304) as a countermelody to the decidedly understated main theme, which migrates from second violins to the winds and back. Here, for the most extended duration thus far, triplets and duplets sound together as equals. In the coda, triplets occur in two places: bars

428–67 (by far the longest passage in which they are unchallenged by duplets); and in the clarinet melody of bars 479–91. Although duplets do have the final say, the narrative played out here in the rhythmic foreground could hardly be called a 'contest' between opposing forces. On the contrary, the shift towards a more balanced distribution of duple and triple subdivisions in the recapitulation and coda has a conciliatory effect, and this enhances the sense of closure at the end of the movement.

It is instructive to compare this movement with another famously repetitive movement, the Allegretto from the Seventh Symphony. As many critics have noted, all the movements of this Symphony are dominated by rhythm; but none is as obsessive or insistent in its use of a single pattern (♩♫♩♩). While every movement contains rhythmic patterns that strongly suggest the metres of ancient Greek poetry, the metre of the Allegretto is the least ambiguous, namely, adonic metre.[22] The movement has a strongly processional character that suggests the noble and serious ethos of epic poetry, if not a specific ancient ritual.

The variation form of this movement unfolds in an additive manner not unlike that found in the opening movement of the Sixth Symphony: the two-bar ostinato provides the constant background against which changes are perceived. Each variation introduces a new instrument carrying the original viola tune in successively higher registers: the second violin, the first violin and, lastly, the winds. The accompanying rhythms become progressively more animated, attaining a peak of complexity in the two-against-three patterning during the tutti of bars 75–98, which coincides with the completion of a process of instrumental expansion. Triplet rhythms persist during the central A major section (bars 102–49). At the return to A minor in bar 150, Beethoven resumes the process of incremental rhythmic subdivision in each variation, called *gradatio* by eighteenth-century theorists, through the addition of semiquavers in the accompanying strings. In the fugato that follows – which unavoidably recalls the fugato in Beethoven's other great processional symphonic movement, the Funeral March of the *Eroica* – the countersubject consists entirely of semiquavers. But whereas the *Eroica*'s fugato builds in intensity to an apotheosis or catastrophe, this one complements the earlier variations without transcending them: it intensifies the narrative without reaching the breaking point. Although the Allegretto contains dynamic peaks and valleys suggestive of life's vicissitudes, it never strays far from the poised ethos of the adonic meter that is its centre of gravity.

The opening eight-bar phrase of the third movement of the Sixth Symphony (a scherzo in all but name) involves conspicuous repetition of a single bar, the implications of which are dramatically played out at subsequent stages of the movement. The motive occupying bar 3 recurs not only in bar 4, where it completes a four-bar group, but also in bar 5, where one would expect a new four-bar group to begin. Two things confirm this expectation: the on-beat grace note and the entrance of the cellos. But there is something irregular about bar 5, and especially its downbeat A. Had bars 5–8 been simply a transposition of bars 1–4 down a fifth, then bar 5 would have started on B♭, rather than A. This hypothesis is borne out in bars 33–40, where the four-bar idea of bars 1–4 is presented sequentially, first on D harmony, then down a fifth. Here, the motivic patterning clarifies rather than conceals the four-bar groups. But at the return of the opening phrase (from bar 53 on, scored tutti and marked *fortissimo*, as opposed to *pianissimo*), the irregular repetition returns with a vengeance, since the motive of bar 3 recurs in four, rather than three, consecutive bars. (Moreover, the downbeats are marked *sf*, and there is no grace note articulating the fifth bar.) The result is a six-bar group (bars 53–8) that can be heard at first as an expansion of bars 1–4 (4+2), but then, in the light of the regular four-bar groups that follow, as 2+4.

Finales

Every finale is marked, aside from any inherently striking qualities, by virtue of its position within a multi-movement cycle. For this reason alone, listeners leaving the concert hall after a performance often take away a stronger impression of the finale than of prior movements. In at least one case – the Ninth Symphony – the power and scale of the Finale is so great that it would be unimaginable to place another work *after* it on the same programme. (This point does not apply to another palpably 'end-accented' work, the Fifth Symphony, which was first performed in the *middle* of the famous benefit concert of 22 December 1808; for the conclusion of that concert, Beethoven composed the Choral Fantasy, Op. 80.)

In at least four symphonies – the Third, Fifth, Seventh and Ninth – the finale is strongly marked or weighted (a possible fifth candidate, the Sixth Symphony, will be considered presently). Such emphasis arises both from striking events within each finale and, often crucially, from events leading up to it. Thus, the Fifth Symphony's Finale stands out not just because of its inherent jubilance – proclaiming C major in contrast to the dark, strained C minor mood of the first and third movements – but also because it follows directly what is perhaps the most suspenseful transition in symphonic history. The transition and the haunting reminiscence of the Scherzo in the development are essential to the Finale's dramatic effect.

Similarly, the Sixth Symphony's Finale is set up by another gripping transition: the fourth movement ('Storm'), which, in Charles Rosen's view, is not a truly independent movement, but an expanded introduction to the Finale.[23] Whereas the tension of the Fifth Symphony's transition resolves all at once at the start of the Finale, the accumulated tension of the 'Storm' resolves gradually, partly within that 'movement', but not fully until bar 9 of the fifth movement ('Shepherd's Song'), where G (a suspended ninth over F) resolves *upwards* to A. One could even reverse the relation between the two movements and hear the fifth movement – devoid of strife, but full of rejoicing – as a grand coda to the 'Storm'. The Sixth Symphony may thus be said to contain a marked or weighted finale only if, following Rosen's lead, we hear the fourth and fifth movements as a single, undivided entity. (This argument cannot be applied to the Fifth Symphony, since the Scherzo – unlike the 'Storm' – *can* be heard as an independent movement.)

The finales that demand interpretation most strongly are those that break most radically with tradition: those of the *Eroica* and the Ninth Symphony. Both movements have inspired numerous analytical solutions or hypotheses. Peter Schleuning has argued that the *Eroica*'s Finale is its focal point, the goal towards which the other movements are directed.[24] In Burnham's view, one motivation for this interpretation may be 'the ease with which such programs are generated for works like the Fifth and Ninth symphonies'.[25] Elaine Sisman, in her thorough, historically informed analysis, describes the movement as a set of 'alternating variations', a formal procedure that Beethoven also 'adopted for all of his slow symphonic variation movements'.[26] Yet neither Sisman nor anyone else, to my knowledge, has adequately interpreted the striking G minor flourish that opens the movement and returns (modified) near the conclusion. Schenker's reading of the opening eleven bars as a prolongation of V^7 of E flat is correct as far as the middleground is concerned. But because of his overriding concern with middleground structure, Schenker erroneously concludes that the harmony in the opening three bars 'has nothing to do with the key of G minor', thereby disavowing any connection between these bars and the tonicised G minor harmony in bars 420–30, not to mention the return of the opening gesture at bar 431.[27] Bars 1–11 pose a tonally open 'problem' to which the variations provide only a partial solution. The modified return in bars 431–5, which Sisman situates within the coda and about which Schenker makes no comment, is not a mere epilogue, but rather the *dénouement* of both the movement and the Symphony.

Unique and fascinating as the *Eroica*'s Finale is with respect to form, its analytical challenges seem modest compared to those posed by the

Finale of the Ninth Symphony. Despite the appeal of the 'Ode to Joy' melody and the direct message of the text, analysts have failed to grasp the movement's formal logic – the most frequently invoked criterion of artistic excellence (one critic even admits that this movement 'defeat[s] analysis').[28] Notwithstanding its clear allusions to familiar genres (opera, symphony, concerto), formal procedures (variation, rondo, sonata, fugue) and musical topics (recitative, learned style, hymn, march), the Finale is simply without precedent. According to James Webster, this movement demands a 'multivalent' analytical approach that is not constrained by rigid formal and generic categories.[29] He describes it as 'through-composed', continually in search of a goal that is 'not merely the Ode to Joy as such, not merely the triumph of D major over D minor', but 'a new musical state of being' that 'does not arrive until the end'.[30] A central feature of the movement is repeated deferral of closure – a hallmark of 'through-composition'. Webster concurs with Maynard Solomon's idea that the programme for this Finale is 'the search for Elysium', a quest that is not completed until the chorus's final cadence on the word 'Götterfunken!' (bar 920).[31]

An important, if seldom noted, aspect of the Finale is the relation between the solo baritone – the first singer to be heard – and the chorus (including both the large group and the smaller ensemble of soloists). The baritone's first utterance, a recitative-like setting of Beethoven's own words, expresses an unnamed individual's desire to hear other, more joyful, tones than those of the preceding three movements. This is not merely a confession ('O Freunde, nicht diese Töne'), but also a call to action ('sondern lasst uns angenehmere anstimmen, und freudenvol-lere'). He himself sings the opening eight lines of Schiller's 'An die Freude', to which the chorus responds with the corresponding part of the second stanza (lines 13–20). (Lines 9–12, beginning with 'Seid umschlungen, Millionen!', are not sung until much later.) This leader–follower relationship between the baritone and the chorus recurs in the Alla marcia section, where the tenor is cast as a hero inviting his brothers to join him on the path to victory. Indeed, the instrumental fugato that immediately follows the tenor's final words seems to portray the battle that he and his brothers expect to win. The fugato's harmonic goal is B major, which yields to B minor, then to a cadential $\frac{6}{4}$ in D major preparing the onset of the first *choral* statement of the opening stanza of the 'Ode to Joy'. This moment of recapitulation enacts a shift of dramatic emphasis from the soloist to the chorus. In the concluding sections of the Finale, no individual is truly set apart from the group; rather, all the voices represent the ideal, collective 'voice' of humanity united in and by joy.

Conclusion

Of the five aspects considered in this chapter, the one that is most basic to our experience of Beethoven's symphonies is temporality. As with any narrative or journey, we experience a symphony in time before we are able to look back on or 'objectify' it. While analysts generally favour a retrospective mode of listening (or understanding) over a prospective or phenomenological one, Beethoven's symphonies invite, and even compel, listeners to adopt the latter mode. Indeed, few other symphonies have demanded so much imagination, engagement and repeated study from listeners and performers. The narratives embodied in these symphonies all have an ending, but the journey of musical and critical discovery afforded by them – like all genuine learning – is infinite.

Notes

1 Joseph Kerman and Alan Tyson, *The New Grove Beethoven* (New York, 1983), 107.
2 Scott Burnham, *Beethoven Hero* (Princeton, 1995), xiii.
3 Ibid., 153.
4 James Webster describes a type of centrifugal articulation as 'remote harmonic juxtaposition', involving the juxtaposition of the dominant of one key with the tonic of another; see *Haydn's 'Farewell Symphony' and the Idea of Classical Style: Through-Composition and Cyclic Integration in His Instrumental Music* (Cambridge, 1991), 134.
5 Beethoven often dramatically emphasises the return through dynamics and instrumentation. The Menuetto is similar to the Allegro of the first movement in this respect: strings only at the opening, marked *piano*; tutti at the return, *forte*, quickly rising to *fortissimo*.
6 A valuable consideration of this passage and its reception history appears in Burnham, *Beethoven Hero*, 13–17.
7 See Daniel Harrison, *Harmonic Function in Chromatic Music: A Renewed Dualist Theory and Its Precedents* (Chicago, 1994), 76.
8 William E. Caplin coined the term 'expanded cadential progression'. Of particular interest to the present discussion are Caplin's detailed analyses of the subordinate groups in the first movements of the First, Third and Ninth symphonies, presented in 'Structural Expansion in Beethoven's Symphonic Forms', in *Beethoven's Compositional Process*, ed. William Kinderman (Lincoln, 1991), 27–54. James Hepokoski and Warren Darcy describe bars 134–64 as a 'deformationally expanded' restatement of bars 130–4; see their *Elements of Sonata Theory: Norms, Types, and*

Deformations in the Late-Eighteenth-Century Sonata (New York and Oxford, 2006), 61.
9 Maynard Solomon, *Beethoven Essays* (Cambridge, Mass. and London, 1988), 6.
10 Carl Dahlhaus, *Ludwig van Beethoven: Approaches to His Music* (Oxford, 1991), 172 and 176.
11 Ibid., 175.
12 See William Horne, 'The Hidden Trellis: Where Does the Second Group Begin in the First Movement of Beethoven's *Eroica* Symphony?' *Beethoven Forum*, 13/2 (2006), 95–147.
13 See Richard L. Cohn, 'The Dramatization of Hypermetric Conflicts in the Scherzo of Beethoven's Ninth Symphony', *19th-Century Music*, 15/3 (1992), 197.
14 Donald Francis Tovey, 'Tonality in Schubert', in *The Main Stream of Music and Other Essays* (New York, 1959), 153.
15 For further remarks on the enharmonic G♭/F♯, see Reinhold Schlötterer '4. Symphonie, Op. 60', in *Beethoven: Interpretationen seiner Werke*, vol. I, ed. Albrecht Riethmüller, Carl Dahlhaus and Alexander Ringer (Laaber, 1994), 439–55.
16 See Heinrich Schenker, 'Beethoven: Fifth Symphony', in *Der Tonwille*, vol. I: issues 1–5 (1921–3), ed. William Drabkin, trans. Ian Bent et al. (Oxford, 2004), 25–33; Andrew Imbrie, '"Extra Measures" and Metrical Ambiguity in Beethoven', in *Beethoven Studies*, ed. Alan Tyson (New York, 1973), 45–66; and Justin London, *Hearing in Time: Psychological Aspects of Musical Meter* (New York and Oxford, 2004), chapter 6.
17 Heinrich Schenker, 'Beethoven: Fifth Symphony', 25. Andrew Imbrie cites

Schenker's analysis and proposes an alternative reading in '"Extra Measures"', 57.

18 The latter association is tonal as well as rhythmic: the articulation of tonic and dominant in bars 19 and 21 is echoed in bars 60 and 62.

19 Schenker, 'Beethoven: Fifth Symphony', 32. Imbrie ('"Extra Measures"', 63) locates the shift within bars 179–81.

20 See Northrop Frye, *Words with Power* (San Diego, 1990), 190.

21 The dominant is regained at bar 282, but is sustained as a chord for only one bar. The remainder of the retransition consists of a melodic link in the first violin, bars 283–8.

22 Although Solomon characterises the five-note pattern as a combination of a dactyl and a spondee, it makes more sense to regard it as an indivisible unit. See Maynard Solomon, *Late Beethoven* (Berkeley and Los Angeles, 2003), chapter 6.

23 Charles Rosen, *The Classical Style: Haydn, Mozart, and Beethoven*, rev. edn (New York, 1997), 402.

24 Peter Schleuning, 'Beethoven in alter Deutung: Der "neue Weg" mit der "Sinfonia eroica"', *Archiv für Musikwissenschaft*, 44 (1987), 165–94.

25 Burnham, *Beethoven Hero*, 4.

26 Elaine R. Sisman, *Haydn and the Classical Variation* (Cambridge, Mass. and London, 1993), 158 and 254–62.

27 Heinrich Schenker, *The Masterwork in Music*, vol. III, ed. William Drabkin, trans. Ian Bent, Alfred Clayton and Derrick Puffett (Cambridge, 1997), 53 (originally published in 1930).

28 See Michael Spitzer, *Music as Philosophy: Adorno and Beethoven's Late Style* (Bloomington and Indianapolis, 2006), 183.

29 James Webster, 'The Form of the Finale of Beethoven's Ninth Symphony', *Beethoven Forum*, 1 (1992), 25–62. Concerning the 'multivalent approach', see 27–8.

30 Ibid., 44–5.

31 Ibid., 61. See also Solomon, *Beethoven Essays*, 14.

9 Cyclical thematic processes in the nineteenth-century symphony

JULIAN HORTON

Introduction

Several authors in this volume cite the famous (if uncorroborated) conversation between Sibelius and Mahler, in which Sibelius valued the symphony for 'the profound logic that created an inner connection' between its component ideas, and Mahler responded that 'a symphony must be like the world. It must embrace everything'.[1] Appealing as these comments are as indicators of the two composers' aesthetics, they also have value because they apostrophise neatly the twin aspirations of thematic rigour and monumentality that constituted dominant nineteenth-century symphonic imperatives. Although it would be quite wrong to construe this as a simple dichotomy – even the most expansive symphonies aspire to thematic coherence, and modest works are no more likely to emphasise overarching motivic processes – the challenge of expressing both high communal ideals and comprehensible thematicism, which gained currency as a central inheritance of the Beethovenian symphonic achievement, has at the very least to be regarded as a productive tension.

As the century progressed, the thematic element of this equation came increasingly to be construed cyclically, as a technique that had to encompass the cycle of movements as well as a work's component forms. In thematic terms, the Beethovenian imperative of originality necessitated a search for ways to imbue whole works with a higher-level material integrity, which depended on strategies ranging from isolated but marked quotations to extensive cross-movement processes of variation and derivation and the wholesale revisiting of passages.[2] Such processes are also often the lynchpin of a symphony's extra-musical meaning. The technical features of 'absolute' music – those aspects that seem autonomous of meaning and function – are simultaneously the basis of its programmatic aspirations, reflecting the characteristically Romantic conviction that music's claim to aesthetic superiority lay in its ability to capture essential meanings in the play of tones itself, apart from any dependence on text.[3]

Widespread though the association of Beethoven with cyclical technique is, however, his status as its progenitor is far from self-evident. In the first place, various commentators have noted integrative techniques in earlier music: James Webster's extensive study of cyclic integration in Haydn's 'Farewell' Symphony is a substantial case in point, and Mary Sue Morrow and Michael Spitzer note similar eighteenth-century strategies in chapters 3 and 6 above.[4] Moreover, overt thematic relationships extending across, as well as within, movements are comparatively rare in Beethoven's symphonies (subcutaneous relationships are of course manifold). The two most well-known examples – the Fifth and Ninth symphonies – hardly match the adventurous cyclical techniques employed by Mendelssohn and Schumann, or even the referential use of the *idée fixe* in Berlioz's *Symphonie fantastique*. And the *Eroica*, as the third claimant in this respect, is even more tenuous: such overt cyclicity as can be detected in the work turns on the plausibility of allowing the famous dissonant C♯ in the first movement's main theme to act as a 'pitch-class motive' resurfacing at later points in the Symphony, for example in the Scherzo's coda (this and other structural principles in Beethoven's symphonies are considered by Mark Anson-Cartwright in Chapter 8).

The thematic links commonly detected in the Fifth Symphony are, furthermore, far from unequivocal. Leaving aside the reprise of Scherzo material preceding the Finale's recapitulation, which functions more as a wholesale sectional transplantation than as an integrated transformation of a thematic idea, claims of thematic 'unity' depend above all upon the provenance of the rhythmic cell, which comprises the first movement's famous 'fate' motive, and is understood to recur in the main themes of the Scherzo and Finale. These are hardly definitive connections: the rhythmic shift from upbeat to downbeat between first-movement and Scherzo forms of the motive is especially problematic for any claim of unambiguous derivation. At best (and accepting the indisputable connection between third and fourth movements), the inter-movement links have to be regarded as implications available to the receptive ear, rather than as analytically unassailable facts.

Cross-referencing in the Ninth Symphony is, in contrast, unmistakable, because inter-movement recall is a matter of near-literal quotation: the main themes of the first three movements pass by parenthetically in the Finale's introduction, intercut with the recitative-like material of the celli and basses, which anticipates the baritone's entry with the words 'O Freunde, nicht diese Töne!'. Quotation is, however, no guarantee of large-scale coherence. On the contrary, the piecemeal quality of the references here secures the recall of prior movements at the expense of large-scale integration: the quotations are disconnected fragments, which are forced apart by the vocal aspirations of the lower strings. And when the baritone later pointedly rebuffs the return of the *Schrekensfanfare* in preparation for the vocal version of the 'Ode to Joy' theme, the fragmentary character of

Beethoven's prior-movement synopsis gains fresh significance. The Finale's ambition, it turns out, is not to synthesise the material of the whole work in a summative instrumental conclusion, but to reject that idea in favour of a design that subsumes the instrumental symphony as a whole into a final realisation of the music's emergent vocality (chapters 2, 8 and 14 all broach this matter).[5] The point of Beethoven's cross-referencing is, in other words, fragmentation, not synthesis.

It is in this light that another plausible inter-movement relationship might be understood: the adumbration of the 'Ode' theme in the first movement's second subject, explained in Example 9.1. As commentators have observed, this anticipation has tonal as well as thematic significance, because the secondary key it establishes (B-flat major) prefigures that of the slow movement, and of the Turkish march setting the words 'Froh, wie seine Sonnen fliegen durch des Himmels prächt'gen Plan' in the Finale.[6] Viewed from the position of the Finale's first vocal stanza, however, this connection looks less like an instance of integration, and more like a prophecy of the instrumental movements' provisionality. In the first movement's lyrical second theme is contained the seeds of the purely instrumental Finale's demise.

This chapter explores the post-Beethovenian legacy of cyclical thinking, focussing on its treatment by six composers: Berlioz, Schumann, Liszt, Tchaikovsky, Bruckner and Mahler. I restrict consideration to overt thematic recurrence and transformation; whilst not denying the presence of concealed thematic, harmonic or tonal features reinforcing cyclical coherence, my aim is to scrutinise only unequivocal surface relationships, as the most analytically and historically tractable evidence of the technique. And since purely musical elements in all of these works support programmatic or narrative ambitions, I also pay attention to their extra-musical connotations, which range from the transparently intentional (Berlioz's *Symphonie fantastique*) to the strongly implied (Bruckner's Fifth Symphony).

Example 9.1 Beethoven, Symphony No. 9, I, subordinate theme and IV, 'Freude' theme.

The 'Romantic generation': Berlioz, Schumann and Liszt

The techniques of thematic integration exhibited in the first generation of post-Beethovenian symphonies can be understood not as responses to an incipient property of Beethoven's symphonies themselves, but as realisations of a dual ideal of musical autonomy and metaphysical significance, which sought evidential verification in Beethoven's examples. The symphonies of Berlioz, Schumann and Liszt are exemplary: all three composers overlaid their movement cycles with overt and variously developmental thematic processes, supporting more-or-less explicit programmatic agendas, to an extent far exceeding anything that Beethoven attempted in the symphonic domain.[7]

The notion of programmatic cyclicity is most blatant in Berlioz's usage. The *Symphonie fantastique* instantiates the notion of the *idée fixe*, which, as Berlioz's first programme for the work identified, functions as 'a musical thought, whose character ... [the artist] finds similar to the one he attributes to his beloved'.[8] This acts as a kind of narrative anchor, which orientates the movement-by-movement scene changes in relation to the protagonist's mental projection of the beloved.[9] Example 9.2 compares the variants of the *idée fixe* as they occur in the five movements.

Example 9.2 Berlioz, *Symphonie fantastique*, variants of the *idée fixe*.

Berlioz here marries cyclical and extra-musical elements in a way that has long-lasting influence. Most importantly, the prime form of the *idée fixe* is also the first theme of the first movement's sonata form. The heroic subjectivity that is often imputed to Beethoven's main themes is thereby made explicit, because the theme's human agency is nominated in the programme. And because the *idée fixe* does not represent simply the artist himself, but rather the idealised object of his affections, Berlioz pulls off the trick of embodying in a single idea both the artist as narrative protagonist and also a relationship between characters (artist and beloved), which allows him to foster the illusion of an unfolding plot.

As this notion develops across the piece, it exemplifies with exceptional clarity the Romantic perception that it is precisely instrumental music's autonomy that allows it to capture essential meanings without direct textual assistance. Thus the inter-movement changes of topic that compel variation of the *idée fixe* (waltz, pastoral, march, gigue) at once facilitate the progression of symphonic movement types (two dances frame an adagio and precede a rondo finale), whilst also providing the circumstances for the changes of scene and character that convey the extramusical narrative. The difference between the central character and the beloved as an object of perception is underscored from the second movement onwards, because from this point Berlioz detaches the *idée fixe* from main-theme functionality: in the second movement and Adagio, it appears in the contrasting middle section; in the March as a fleeting expansion of the final structural cadence; and in the Finale as an episode in the multipart introduction. Altogether, although the treatment of the *idée fixe* is neither as transformationally extensive as Liszt's practice, nor as developmentally exhaustive as the cyclical techniques of many later-century practitioners, its capacity to sustain topical variety furnishes a strikingly clear model for the integration of cyclical and programmatic agendas.

In *Harold en Italie*, Berlioz takes the notion of the symphonic subject as narrative protagonist a stage further, by embodying him in a *concertante* instrument (the solo viola): as a result, the protagonist is not only a theme, but also a soloist who has physical presence. The critical inter-movement thematic links are appraised in Example 9.3. The first clear cross-reference is the recurrence of the introduction's 'Harold' theme as the soloist's response to the pilgrims' 'canto' in the slow movement (beginning Fig. 23). Berlioz uses the same device in the Serenade, folding the viola's 'Harold' theme into the movement's central Allegretto. Both movements exploit a comparable effect: as Berlioz himself put it, the theme is 'superimposed onto the other orchestral voices ... without interrupting their development', reflecting Harold's character as a 'melancholy dreamer' who is 'present during the action but does not

Example 9.3 Berlioz, *Harold en Italie*, variants of the 'Harold' theme.

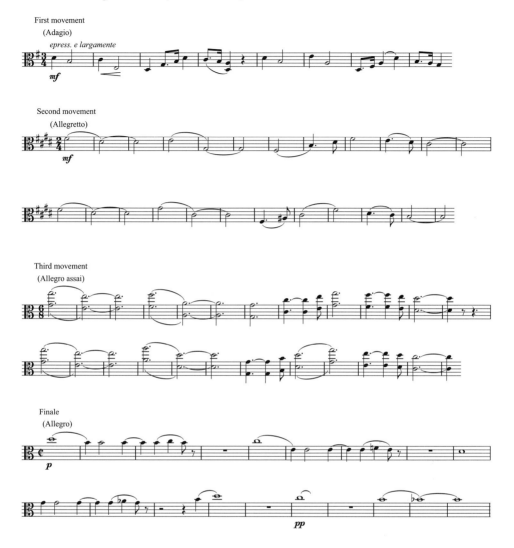

participate in it'.[10] In this respect, the 'Harold' theme is the direct
antithesis of the *Symphonie fantastique*'s *idée fixe*: as the protagonist's
projection of the beloved, the latter is changed by its topical and expressive
circumstances; the former, however, is the protagonist himself, and
(at least before the Finale) remains largely invariant in the midst of topical
change.

Perhaps the most controversial aspect of *Harold en Italie* is the direct
invocation of Beethoven's Ninth in the succession of prior-movement
quotations beginning the Finale, the 'Orgy of the Brigands'. Like
Beethoven, Berlioz begins his Finale with an intercutting between new
and old material: the introduction, first-movement main theme, Pilgrims'

March and Serenade are all rejected in turn; finally, the 'Harold' theme appears, now as a genuine variant rather than a straight quotation. This is, however, quickly dissolved through a kind of textural liquidation, and the brigands' music asserts itself definitively as the start of the sonata action six bars after Fig. 40. The movement yields one final cross-reference: ten bars after Fig. 55, the pilgrims' canto reappears played by an off-stage string trio, which the soloist turns into a quartet by entering eleven bars later. This material again dissipates, and the brigands assert themselves for the rest of the Symphony.

As Mark Evan Bonds has explained, the effect here is diametrically opposed to that achieved by Beethoven. There is no narrative of transcendence; instead, both Harold himself, and the solo instrument that represents him, disappear.[11] At the end, Harold is affiliated with the pilgrims, and so with something approximating the work's moral compass; but this identification counts for nothing, and the last word is given to the surrounding bacchanale. In a sense, *Harold en Italie* and the *Symphonie fantastique* converge in their use of cyclical techniques to invert rather than confirm the Beethovenian struggle–victory symphonic argument. Different though the technique is in each case, their common ground is a shared concept of the narrative goal as a negation of 'utopian semiosis', to use Michael Spitzer's apt term, either in the diabolical afterlife of the 'Witches' Sabbath' or the moral vacuum of the 'Brigands' Orgy'.[12]

Schumann's debt to Berlioz is not only musically implicit, but also textually explicit, because, as David Brodbeck has addressed in Chapter 4, Schumann famously reviewed the *Symphonie fantastique* in the *Neue Zeitschrift für Musik*.[13] In many ways, Schumann's symphonic project can be understood as an attempt to synthesise three lines of symphonic influence: Beethoven's goal-orientated dynamic; Berlioz's conjunction of thematic process and programmatic (literary) narrative; and (as Brodbeck stresses) a lyric monumentality taken from Schubert's 'Great' C major Symphony, the first performance of which Schumann was in part responsible for in 1839.[14]

All of Schumann's four symphonies and the *Overture, Scherzo and Finale* (in many respects a symphony *manqué*) exhibit inter-movement thematic relationships. The technique is most weakly represented in the Symphony No. 1, in which Schumann is primarily concerned to supply conjunctive links between adjacent movements rather than overarching thematic processes. The motto theme with which the first movement's introduction begins – which, as John Daverio explains, was originally conceived as a setting of the final lines of a poem by Adolph Böttger ('O wende, wende deinen Lauf / Im Tale blüt der Frühling auf: 'Oh desist, desist from your present course / Spring blossoms in the valley') – adumbrates

Example 9.4 Schumann, Symphony No. 1, I and II, motto theme.

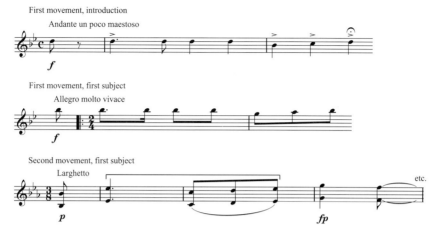

Example 9.5 Schumann, Symphony No. 1, II, bars 112–17 and III, bars 1–5.

the first themes of both the first and second movements, as Example 9.4 reveals.[15] The reappearance of the motto's contour in the slow movement's theme, however, acts more as a memorial trace than a stage in a cyclical process. Conversely, the prefiguring of the Scherzo's theme at the end of the Larghetto, which as Example 9.5 shows is at once the slow movement's coda and the transition into the third movement, functions as an adumbration analogous to the relationship between the first movement's introduction and its exposition. Schumann's ruse here is to reconceive this device as an inter-movement rather than intra-movement strategy.

Anticipations of the Scherzo are worked into the slow movement at other points. Example 9.6 for instance reveals that, whereas the end of the Larghetto adumbrates the Scherzo's head motive, the slow movement's first episode (beginning bar 25) presages its continuation, thereby giving the impression that the Scherzo pieces together material that the slow movement presents disparately.

Example 9.6 Schumann, Symphony No. 1, II, bars 25–6 and III, bars 5–8.

Example 9.7 Schumann, Symphony No. 2, I, bars 1–4.

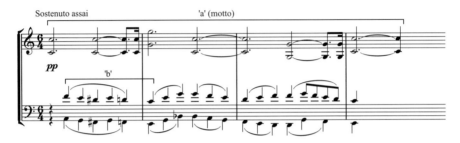

Such connections, however, dissipate in advance of the Finale, which is thematically self-contained. The highly provisional ending of the Scherzo, which comprises a syncopated, fragmentary liquidation of the material of Trio 1, consequently serves to underscore the dissipation of the tentative cyclical attitude with which the first three movements are associated.

The technique of supplying a motto theme in the first movement's introduction, which subsequently generates a web of relationships, is taken up and greatly expanded in the Symphony No. 2. The introduction begins with a composite of two significant ideas, identified in Example 9.7: the motto carried by the brass, labelled 'a'; and the chromatic string counterpoint, labelled 'b'.[16] These two motives relate to the first movement's sonata form in different ways. The motto does not generate the first theme, but rather recurs summatively in the coda (bars 339–46); and motive 'b' reappears, in inversion, as part of the second-theme group (from bar 276). In other respects, Schumann greatly expands the adumbrative model developed in the Symphony No. 1. The motivic fragments presented in bars 25–33, which cede to the motto in bars 34–6, supply the basis of the first theme and the transition in the exposition. The relationship between motto and first-movement sonata is as a result more complex than the straightforward adumbrative process evident in the Symphony No. 1. In effect, the motto is detached from the sonata action, serving as a structural marker, but the adumbrative function of the introduction is preserved through the inclusion of significant additional material.

The Scherzo yields two motivic traces of the first movement. Its main subject is a variant of the figure introduced at bar 341 in the first movement's coda; and the motto theme recurs in the Scherzo's climactic final cadence, bars 384–90. The Adagio, in contrast, anticipates the Finale, which constitutes the Symphony's cyclical centre of gravity. The Finale's form is famously problematic. Table 9.1 attempts clarification, and additionally explains the formal positioning of material from earlier in the Symphony. The first intimation of cyclical thinking emerges with the second theme (bar 63), which comprises a major-key variant of the Adagio's main theme. This material is revisited in inversion in the central episode of the development (bar 191), joined by its prime form in imitation in the cellos and basses from bar 213, an event marked by the entry of the first movement's motto over a punctuating authentic cadence (bars 207–10). The subsequent dissolution of this material leads at bar 280 to the movement's most problematic event: Schumann introduces a new chorale theme, quoting Beethoven's *An die ferne Geliebte*, which thereafter engulfs the sense, thus far attained, that the Finale is a sonata rondo. In effect, the rondo design is liquidated by bar 279, and replaced with an expanded chorale prelude.[17]

Yet although this seems to open up a rift in the design, the topical shift that accompanies it has the long-range effect of enabling the Symphony's most spectacular cyclical coup. Following the impressive 35-bar standing on V in bars 359–93, the chorale stabilises in the tonic major from bar 394, initiating a tonally closed presentation phrase sealed by a perfect cadence in bars 445–51. Schumann then grafts the chorale-like material of the first movement's introduction (beginning bar 15) on as a continuation phrase, shifting to a 3/2 metre in *l'istesso tempo* to accommodate its distinct metrical character. At bar 475, we see that this is the contrasting middle of a ternary form: *An die ferne Geliebte* reappears as an A reprise, punctuated throughout with assertions of the motto theme, leading to a decisive perfect cadence in bars 488–92, after which the coda begins. By rejecting the rondo form and replacing it with a chorale prelude, Schumann establishes a topical environment that is conducive to the wholesale restoration of first-movement material, framed as a closed form which, because it draws on a Beethovenian lied, houses a 'humanised' (or perhaps secularised) sacred topic.

Superficially, the Symphony No. 3 seems less densely constructed than No. 2. Schumann's strategy here is to divide the cyclical thematic action into two threads, which unite at the Symphony's close. The first concerns the harmonic properties of the first movement's main theme, rather than its developmental potential. As Example 9.8a reveals, in its exposition form, the theme displays a tendency to pull towards the dominant, which the rest of the first-theme group does not satisfactorily redress.

Table 9.1 *Schumann, Symphony No. 2, IV, form and distribution of themes*

Bars:	1	63	191	280	359	394	452	475	492
Form:	Sonata rondo								
Large-scale function:	Refrain	Episode	Refrain ⇒ Development	⇒ Chorale prelude	(Sonata retransition?)	Chorale prelude (ternary)			Coda
Inter-thematic function:	A	TR B RT1 A¹	Part 1 Part 2		RT (Standing on V)	(A)	Contrasting middle	(A¹)	
Cyclical Themes:		Adagio	Adagio rectus and inversus+motto	*An die ferne Geliebte*	*An die ferne Geliebte* A introduction	*An die ferne Geliebte*	First-movement introduction continuation+motto	*An die ferne Geliebte*	

Example 9.8a Schumann, Symphony No. 3, I, bars 1–5.

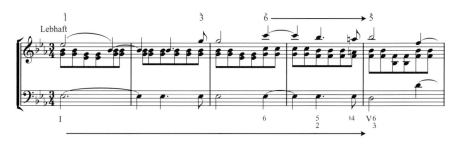

Example 9.8b Schumann, Symphony No. 3, I, bars 411–16.

Example 9.8c Schumann, Symphony No. 3, V, bars 394–9.

The critical agent of this attraction is the theme's $\hat{6}$–$\hat{5}$ figure, which associates with a motion onto V$^6_3$ that is never properly counteracted. The recapitulation, quoted in Example 9.8b, exacerbates this, because it begins over a rhetorically marked $^6_4$ chord (this strategy is taken up again in Chapter 10). Thereafter, the underlying V finds no resolution within the first-theme group, a characteristic that shifts the recapitulation's harmonic centre of gravity towards the second group's closing perfect cadence (bars 515–27). In an extraordinary stroke of large-scale planning, Schumann effectively suspends this issue until the progression preparing the Finale's coda (bars 394–8), where, as Example 9.8c shows, the

Example 9.9a Schumann, Symphony No. 3, II, bars 16–18.

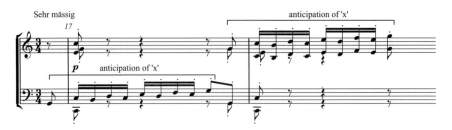

Example 9.9b Schumann, Symphony No. 3, IV, bars 1–8.

Example 9.9c Schumann, Symphony No. 3, V, bars 97–9.

first-movement main theme is recalled triumphantly and made to function as the elaborative material of the Symphony's culminating tonic cadence. Again, the $\hat{6}$–$\hat{5}$ figure is crucial here; whereas in the first movement it acts as a destabilising feature, here it collaborates with the cadential voice leading, as part of the decisive $\hat{6}$–$\hat{5}$–$\hat{1}$ soprano line. In this way, a cyclical thread left hanging by the first movement is picked up as a decisive, framing structural event.

This gesture is additionally important because it forms the terminus of the work's second thematic thread, which centres on the principal subject of the fourth movement, itself a quotation of the E-flat Prelude from Book I of Bach's *Well-tempered Clavier*, marked 'x' in Example 9.9a. Examples 9.9a–c show that this theme is adumbrated in the second movement as a first-theme continuation (beginning bar 17), finds two variants in the fourth movement (prime form and diminution) and resurfaces in the

Example 9.9d Schumann, Symphony No. 3, V, bars 271–9.

Finale as the substance of its transitions and development, subsequently combined with the movement's first theme, in diminution, in the development. This line of thematic action culminates in the standing on V that supplies the transition to the coda in bars 271–398 (Example 9.9d), above which Schumann stacks up 'x' in stretto in bars 271–9. The motive's final appearance coincides with the pre-dominant approach to the crucial cadence in bars 394–8, and comprises two augmented versions of its central segment, as Example 9.9d explains. After this, 'x' is superseded seamlessly by the first-movement main-theme variant; the exhaustion of a thematic process spanning three movements clears the ground for the return and resolution of the first movement's problematic main subject.[18]

Schumann's most extensive experiment with cyclic integration appears in the Symphony No. 4 (his second by order of genesis, but last in order of publication, having been revised in 1851). The recurrence and variation of themes between movements in this work is linked to a radical formal strategy, through which movements are made continuous by elision and co-dependent by formal truncation. Thus each movement references a common fund of ideas, which expands across the work. Simultaneously, the four movements are all in some respect formally incomplete: the first movement comprises a compact sonata form with slow introduction, in which the end of the development bypasses the recapitulation and proceeds directly to the coda; the ternary slow movement abbreviates its A^1 section; the Scherzo sets up the expectation of an $A–B–A^1–B^1–A^2$ design, which is discontinued towards the end of B^1; and the Finale is conjoined with the Scherzo by means of a slow transition, and then truncated through the omission of the first-theme reprise.

The reduction of each movement's formal independence is compensated by a network of thematic transformations, which supplies the impression that formal threads left incomplete within movements are fulfilled between them. The important material is summarised in Example 9.10; its disposition across the work is appraised in Table 9.2. The progress of the material is as follows: the principal idea of the slow introduction, marked 'a', recurs as a subsidiary idea in the A section of the slow movement. The first movement's main theme ('b'), which is also its subordinate theme, forms a counterpoint to the main theme of the Finale. The Finale's first theme is, moreover, a variant of the new 'breakthrough' idea introduced from bar 121 of the first movement ('c'). This theme also forms the basis of the Scherzo's principal subject, presented in combination with motive 'a' from the introduction, which is inverted and played imitatively between the violins and lower strings. And the Trio is a wholesale recomposition of the slow movement's B section, itself a variant of 'a'.

The density of cross-referencing in Symphony No. 4, coupled with its high degree of strategic formal loosening, reflects a notion of symphonism that is quite different from that embodied in the First, Second and Third symphonies, a distinctiveness underscored by Schumann's original intention to call the work a symphonic fantasy.[19] Whereas in the other symphonies cyclical methods tighten the multi-movement design, in the Fourth Symphony they compensate for its collapse, a technique that brings Schumann to the edge of 'two-dimensional form', the merging of form and cycle that Steven Vande Moortele explores in Chapter 11.

Whether we accept Dahlhaus's association of Liszt with the so-called mid-century 'dead time' of the symphony or not (and David Brodbeck's chapter in this volume gives us good grounds for being suspicious of Dahlhaus's model), the modernism of Liszt's contribution to the field is hard to contest. This is founded on two technical innovations: 'two-dimensional' form; and cyclical transformation. These two strategies are intimately related: the coherence of Liszt's forms in his symphonic poems is secured by the method of integrating the diverse characters of the implicit movement types as transformations of a small repertoire of themes.

Example 9.10 Schumann, Symphony No. 4, cyclical relationships.

Table 9.2 *Schumann, Symphony No. 4, movement scheme, forms and thematic relationships*

Movement: 1

Form: Sonata (recapitulation omitted)

Bars:	1	29	86	337
Large-scale function:	Introduction	Exposition	Development	Coda
Theme:	'a', 'a1'	'b'	'b' + 'c'	'b'

Movement: 2

Form: Ternary (reprise incomplete)

Bars:	1	26²	43
Large-scale function:	A	Contrasting middle	A¹ (incomplete)
Theme:	'a', 'a1'	'a1.1'	–

Movement: 3

Form: Scherzo and trio (Trio 2 incomplete)

Bars:	1	65	113	177
Large-scale function:	Scherzo (rounded binary)	Trio (rounded binary)	Scherzo (reprise)	Trio¹ (incomplete reprise)
Theme:	'c' + 'a1'	'a1.1'	'b' + 'c'	'a1.1'

Movement: 4

Form: Sonata (recapitulation incomplete)

Bars:	1	17	78	127	168
Large-scale function:	Introduction	Exposition	Development	Recapitulation (second theme and closing section only)	Coda
Theme:	'c', 'b'	'b' + 'c' (first theme and transition)		–	–

The relationship between form and cyclical transformation, however, has to be rethought when we turn to Liszt's multi-movement works retaining the designation 'symphony', not least because they have distinct generic ancestry: the symphonic poems draw on the early-century tradition of the concert overture, notably as practised by Beethoven, Mendelssohn and Schumann; *Eine Faust-Symphonie* and the *Dante* Symphony are characteristic symphonies in the line of Beethoven's *Pastoral* and numerous mid-century examples by Spohr, Raff, Rubinstein, Gade and others. The technique has the same extra-musical function in both cases (a poetic or literary idea is served by a theme's potential for taking on different identities) but antithetical structural functions (in the symphonic poems, thematic transformation supports the impression of multiple movements in a single-movement form; in *Eine Faust-Symphonie*, transformation supports the impression of a single overarching design in a multi-movement scheme).

Eine Faust-Symphonie is by far Liszt's most substantial essay in this technique. As numerous commentators have observed, its various cyclical relationships dramatise four basic extra-musical elements: the personality of Faust himself (in the first movement); Mephistopheles as a 'negative' image of this personality (in the Finale); Faust's relationship with Gretchen (in the slow movement); and Faust's love for Gretchen as the means of his redemption (in the Finale's vocal coda, the famous *Chorus mysticus*).[20] The disposition of themes, a conspectus of which is offered in Example 9.11, reflects this. The three main subjects of the first movement's exposition embody three personality facets – tragic, amorous and heroic – which are viciously parodied in the Finale at analogous formal locations. Around this scheme, Liszt also works the 'alchemical' theme with which the Symphony begins, the whole-tone and hexatonic ambiguities of which invoke Faust's scientific ambitions. This is also given a sardonic twist in the Finale's introduction: the quest for knowledge is mocked as hubristic and egomaniacal.

Faust's dialogue with Gretchen centres on the slow movement's contrasting middle section, which from four bars after Letter J develops an urgent, recitative-like variant of the first movement's second theme. This cements the dual perspective engendered in the relationship between first and second movements: Gretchen is viewed from Faust's perspective; and Faust from Gretchen's perspective. In the Finale, Liszt finds his crucial arbiter of resolution in an inversion of the idea guiding the Finale of Schumann's Symphony No. 2. Whereas Schumann fulfils his work's dramatic aspirations through the transformation of an instrumental image of the 'distant beloved' into a kind of wordless secular chorale, Liszt reveals the drama's redemptive message at the end by setting the crucial words

Example 9.11 Liszt, *Eine Faust-Symphonie*, cyclical relationships.

Example 9.11 (cont.)

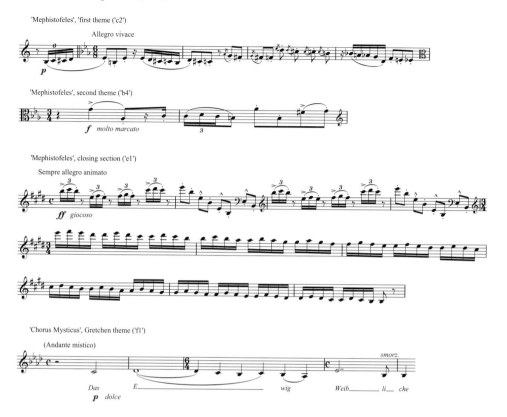

'das ewig Weibliche zieht uns hinan' ('the eternal feminine leads us beyond') to Gretchen's main theme (at Letter B). Both finales instantiate the problem of following Beethoven's Ninth, but offer opposed solutions: Schumann summons Beethoven directly (*An die ferne Geliebte*), but sublimates the overt vocality of the Ninth's Finale into an instrumental finale that can do comparable extra-musical work in a wordless context; Liszt brings two Beethovenian precedents – the 'Pastoral' and the Ninth – into direct contact, by writing a characteristic symphony, which concludes with a redemptive vocal apotheosis.

Austria and Russia: Bruckner and Tchaikovsky

The ideological battles fought over the symphony in the wake of the Lisztian symphonic poem and Wagnerian music drama are keenly reflected in debates about thematic technique. Wagner's critique of Brahms's symphonies pivoted on their thematic aspects: when Wagner likened their material to particles of 'chopped straw', which had been removed from their proper chamber-musical home and given inappropriate symphonic housing, he reinforced critically the conviction that symphonism reliant on Beethovenian thematicism was moribund.[21] At the same time, Brahmsian partisans elevated precisely these properties as vital guarantors of coherence. Max Kalbeck's complaint that Bruckner's Symphony No. 7, a work that became something of a *cause célèbre* of post-Wagnerian symphonism, evinced the composer's 'absolute inability … to think and act according to the laws of musical logic' invoked a benchmark of thematicism, in relation to which Bruckner was perceived to fall some way short.[22] The dispute between the 'Kuchkists' and the conservatoire-based 'Germanic' conservatives in Russia mobilised similar tensions.[23] The 'Mighty Handful' marshalled concepts of national authenticity as justification for breaking with teutonic norms, whilst at the same time relying on those norms as inescapable markers of generic identity. In the territory of the symphony, these controversies fostered works by Balakirev and Borodin on the one hand, and by Anton Rubinstein and Tchaikovsky on the other, all of which wrestle with the problem of how to maintain large-scale symphonic integrity whilst finding a constructive alternative to the Brahmsian method of cellular development.[24]

The symphonies of Bruckner and Tchaikovsky offer an instructive pairing in this regard, not only because they seem, at face value, to exemplify thematic strategies on the 'inside' and 'outside' of the Austro-German tradition, but also because both have, in their own ways, found themselves on the wrong side of attempts to establish what is normative for post-Beethovenian symphonism. As a result, whilst Tchaikovsky could be construed as a symphonist on the margins of a tradition centred on Austria and Germany, Bruckner has been regarded as an outsider in his own cultural context, an Austrian symphonist who shuns Austro-German classic–romantic orthodoxy.

These perceptions are concisely enunciated in Carl Dahlhaus's commentary on the two composers, which deploys the comparison as a point of entry into the issues surrounding the 'second age' of the symphony:

> The difficulties that beset large-scale instrumental music under the premises of 'late romanticism' are to be discovered not so much in Bruckner, who seems to have been born to monumentality and then transplanted into the alien and unsympathetic world of the nineteenth century, as in Tchaikovsky, whose irresistable rise as a symphonist should not obscure the fact that he was primarily a composer of operas and ballets.[25]

For Dahlhaus, Tchaikovsky's theatrical proclivities constrained his symphonic ambitions. In the Symphony No. 4, this is manifest in the relationship between the first movement's main theme and the 'fate' motto with which the introduction begins. Singling out the latter's appearance at the development's climax, Dahlhaus argues that the movement is flawed because both motto and main subject are incompatible with their formal roles: the motto is 'not amenable to development', but is nevertheless made to serve that function; and the first subject's lyric character renders it 'hardly suitable ... for establishing a symphonic movement spanning hundreds of measures'. In sum, 'the grand style fundamental to the genre has been split into a monumentality that remains a decorative façade unsupported by the internal form of the movement, and an internal form that is lyrical in character and can be dramatized only by applying a thick layer of pathos'.[26] The root of the problem is the mistaken belief that a lyrical melody can underpin a monumental symphonism that is Beethovenian in aspiration.[27]

Bruckner's otherness resides not in the vocality of his style, but in the relationship between pitch and rhythm as motivic parameters. As Dahlhaus explains:

> Musical logic, the 'developing variation' of musical ideas ... rested on a premise considered so self-evident as to be beneath mention: that the central parameter of art music is its 'diastematic', or pitch, structure ... Bruckner's symphonic style, however ... is primarily rhythmic rather than diastematic, and thus seems to stand the usual hierarchy of tonal properties on its head.[28]

In the Sixth Symphony, Dahlhaus locates the foundations of the first movement's themes in their rhythmic character; the diversity of thematic variants arises not from a systematic manipulation of interval content, but from the free alteration of pitch and interval around an invariant rhythmic pattern. In contrast to the apparent superficiality of Tchaikovsky's monumental idiom, Bruckner's technique rested for Dahlhaus on the integration of a 'block' formal architecture through 'a system of approximate correspondences', which 'enables monumentality to appear as grand style'.[29]

Both these readings can be challenged. Leaving aside the covert prejudice which caused Dahlhaus to withold credibility from almost every non-German symphony he investigated (Franck's Symphony in D minor and Saint-Saëns's 'Organ' Symphony are also deemed to 'fail', in the latter case for reasons that are strikingly similar to those discovered in Tchaikovsky), Dahlhaus is remiss in considering the precedents for Tchaikovsky's style and the details of both composers' thematic strategies. Tchaikovsky's Symphony No. 4 exhibits manifold debts to earlier works in the Austro-German lineage, especially Schumann's symphonies (and ultimately Schubert, as Chapter 4 identifies): the first movement of the Symphony No. 4 in particular gives the impression of a wholesale misreading of

Example 9.12 Tchaikovsky, Symphony No. 4, I, bars 1–6.

the first movement of Schumann's Symphony No. 2. And Bruckner's focus on rhythm as a binding agent in the Symphony No. 6 has plentiful antecedents in the Beethovenian mainstream: in the first movement of Beethoven's Symphony No. 5, for example, the foundations of motivic coherence are as much rhythmic as they are intervallic, as any attempt to analyse the first theme and transition will quickly establish, and as Mark Anson-Cartwright has clarified above.

In general, Tchaikovsky's Fourth and Fifth symphonies can be grouped together not on chronological grounds (they are separated by some ten years), but because they share a preoccupation with cyclical thematicism, which is more developed than any connections that might be unearthed in symphonies nos. 1–3 or 6. Symphony No. 5 is the more ambitious of the two, pursuing the implications of the first movement's introductory material across its four movements. Symphony No. 4 applies the same idea in a more restricted sense, working the introductory motto into the fabric of the first movement's sonata form and reprising it climactically in the Finale. Both symphonies, moreover, make their cyclical materials do similar programmatic work, since in both cases Tchaikovsky associated his introductory motto with the agency of fate.[30]

Symphony No. 4's design is indebted to Schumann's first two symphonies in two key respects. In the first place, Tchaikovsky honours both of these precedents in presenting significant material (the 'fate' motive 'x' shown in Example 9.12) in advance of the main body of the first movement's sonata design, which is then extensively worked into it, thanks to the motive's interjections at the end of the exposition and recapitulation (bars 193 and 355 respectively), its substantial presence in the development and reliance on its second half as the basis of the coda (beginning in augmentation at bar 366).

Moreover, like Schumann's Symphony No. 2, Tchaikovsky's No. 4 explores the idea that a thread of developmental activity from the first movement should meld, in its Finale, with one initiated in the inner movements, although the process is rather more involved in Schumann's case. Specifically, Tchaikovsky's second, third and fourth movements are related by virtue of a common thematic incipit, which as Example 9.13 makes clear is in all cases a descending tetrachord, marked 'y'.

Example 9.13 Tchaikovsky, Symphony No. 4, II, III and IV, thematic connections.

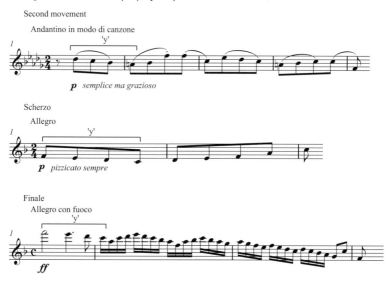

The relationship between 'x' and 'y' is, however, successive rather than integrative: if 'y' links movements as a common *Hauptmotiv*, then 'x' recurs as a 'breakthrough' event at bar 199 of the Finale, which impedes progress towards the coda through wholesale recall of the first movement's introduction. No attempt is made to synthesise these threads: instead, the first-movement reprise functions as a moment of retrospection – a memory of fate's negative associations – which drains away in advance of the Symphony's festive conclusion.

In the Symphony No. 5, the authority of the motto theme (labelled 'x' in Example 9.14) seems, initially, to be more restricted, since after the slow introduction, its influence is suspended for the entirety of the first movement. Thereafter, however, its incursions are regular, and its involvement in the Finale especially is more substantial and more synthetically minded than in the Symphony No. 4. In the slow movement, 'x''s function is disruptive, derailing the progress of the music's ternary form at two junctures, quoted in Example 9.14: first, in bars 99–107, where it frustrates any smooth retransition to the A^1 section, placing that burden on the pre-thematic material of the reprise (bars 108–110); second, in bars 158–69, where it intervenes between the movement's final structural dominant and the coda, which sits entirely above a tonic pedal.

The second intervention is more assertively dissonant than the first: bar 99 brushes aside a four-bar standing on V of C-sharp minor with a diminished third chord, which is then reinterpreted as V^4_2 in the movement's tonic (D major); bar 158 disturbs A^1's final perfect cadence with $\sharp vii^{dim.7}/V$, from which progression to I is salvaged by the assertion of iv^6 in bar 164.

Example 9.14a–e Tchaikovsky, Symphony No. 5, cyclical use of motto theme.

First movement, introduction

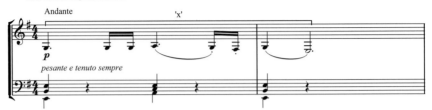

Slow movement, climax of B section

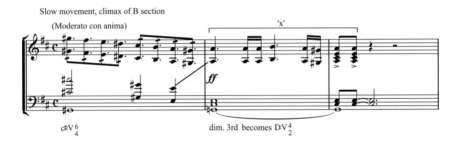

Slow movement, intervention of 'x' before coda

Third movement, coda

Example 9.14 (cont.)

Finale, introduction

The slow movement's success in holding back the influence of the 'fate' motto yields expressive dividends thereafter. In the third movement, 'x' makes only one appearance, in the coda, where it emerges in a quiet, post-cadential waltz variant (beginning bar 241; see Example 9.14d). And by the time of the Finale, the motto's function has effectively been reversed: rather than disturbing the form's progress, it offers a major-mode, intro-ductory antidote to the tempestuous main theme (Example 9.14e quotes its introduction form). As well as supplying the substance of the introduc-tion and the triumphant (but by some accounts shallow) martial coda, 'x' makes two critical and formally analogous appearances in the movement's interior.[31] In the exposition's closing section, it is instrumental in the (ultimately problematic) attempt to secure C major as the closing key (bars 172–201). In the recapitulation, this event is offset by an arduous liquidation of 'x' over V of E minor beginning at bar 426, which eventually emerges onto the half close prefacing the coda.

For Tchaikovsky, cyclical relationships have fairly specific extra-musical connotations, which are held in common between the two works in which he applies them most extensively; indeed, the use of such devices in these symphonies suggests a close affiliation in Tchaikovsky's mind between cyclical thematicism and symphonic engage-ment with the struggle between fate and the heroic subject. For Bruckner, cyclical technique is somewhat more expressively variegated. It is a per-sisting, but by no means progressively evolving, strategy from the Symphony No. 2 (1872, revised 1877) onwards, being prominent in the Third, Fourth and Seventh symphonies, and most substantially repre-sented in the Fifth and Eighth symphonies (the Ninth, being unfinished at the time of the composer's death, remains to an extent a moot point in this regard, given that the Finale's ultimate design remains a matter of speculation).[32]

Bruckner's most comprehensive cyclical exercise is undoubtedly the Symphony No. 5. On the largest scale, Bruckner conceives a symmetrical movement scheme, underscored by tonality, outlined in Figure 9.1.

Figure 9.1 Bruckner, Symphony No. 5, pairing of inner and outer movements by theme and key

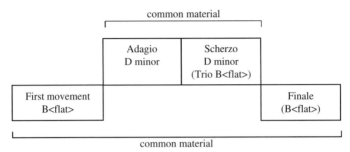

Example 9.15 Bruckner, Symphony No. 5, mvts I and IV, first themes.

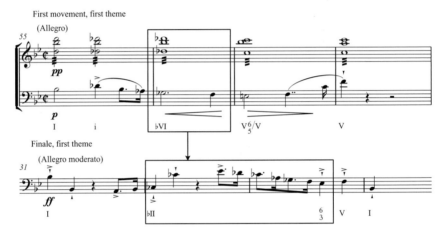

In addition to their shared tonality, the outer movements are related by three means. The most explicit devices are the literal recall of the first movement's introduction as the introduction to the Finale, which generates the impression that both movements proceed as contrasted responses to the same starting point, and the brief, parenthetical allusion to the first movement's main theme in bars 13–22 , which is part of a chain of prior-movement quotations directly referencing the Finale of Beethoven's Ninth Symphony. In addition, the Finale's principal subject shares harmonic properties with that of the first movement; specifically, its ♭II inflection mirrors the ♭VI tendency of the first-movement theme (see Example 9.15). Lastly, the first movement's main theme is reprised in the recapitulation's expanded third-theme group, initially at bar 462; indeed, this part of the form is enlarged specifically to accommodate further developmental activity centred on the theme's recovery.

The harmonic similarity of the outer-movement main themes underpins a more direct connection, which cements their relationship: in bars

Example 9.16 Bruckner, Symphony No. 5, IV, bars 522–5.

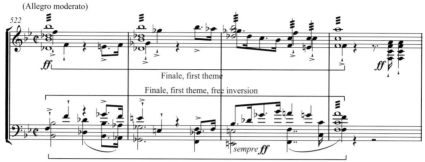

522–5, the two themes are combined, prefigured by the combination of their head motives from bar 518, shown in Example 9.16. This event draws the themes into an overarching harmonic process, since their chromatic inflections have a critical impact on both movements' tonal schemes. It also provides a cyclical rationale for the Finale's form, which is a complex mixture of sonata and double fugue. The first-theme group is a martial fugue; the development comprises two fugues, the first on the important chorale theme introduced at the end of the exposition (bar 175, fugue commencing bar 223), the second combining this theme with the first subject (from bar 270). Although the chorale is never directly combined with the first movement's main theme, the fact that the chorale combines with the Finale main theme sets up a threefold thematic relationship that binds the outer movements, through the sharing of harmonic properties.[33]

Bruckner's long-range strategies here address a broader metaphysical agenda than Tchaikovsky's confrontation between fate and human agency. In the Symphony No. 5 more directly than in any other of his symphonies, Bruckner dramatises the struggle between the secular and the sacred, embodied in a system of topical contrasts, which are indivisible from the work's thematic action. As their martial themes convey, the protagonist of the outer movements is a heroic, secular individual in the Beethovenian sense, a shared agency that the Finale reinforces by contrapuntal combination. The Finale's double fugue seeks reconciliation of this subject with a sacred topic, embodied in the chorale theme; the exhaustive working out of the contrapuntal possibilities of these two themes in the development signifies an effort to reconcile their opposed topics. The chorale's magisterial entry as the climax of the coda in bar 583 performs two key functions in this respect. As a generic device, it turns the coda into a chorale prelude, thereby subsuming prior thematic–topical conflicts into a form that gives the sacred material centre stage. As a tonal event, it initiates a final composing out of the chromatic inflections that characterise first- and last-movement main themes: both first and second

Example 9.17a Bruckner, Symphony No. 5, II, bars 5–8.

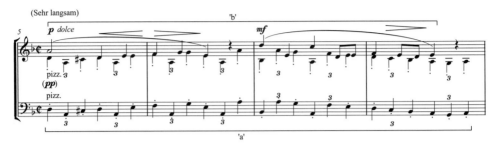

Example 9.17b Bruckner, Symphony No. 5, III, bars 1–8 and 23–30.

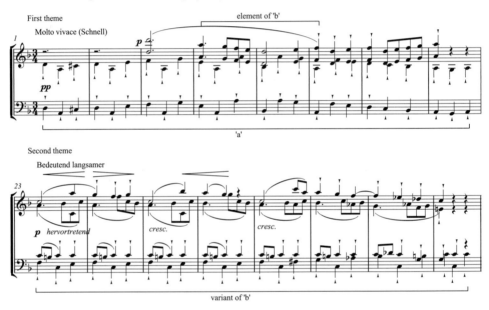

strains begin on flat-side chromatic regions (C flat and G flat) and work their way towards the tonic and its close relations, eventually emerging into the decisive tonic perfect cadence in bars 610–14. The residues of the first-movement theme persisting in the aftermath of this event and forming the substance of the Symphony's final gesture are notably diatonic, as if the reconciliation of the work's thematic, topical and tonal conflicts in its culmi-nating assertion of faith has at last purged the material of its secular uncertainties.

While the outer movements play out their monumental thematic, contrapuntal and tonal drama in the tonic, the Adagio and Scherzo unfold internal relationships grounded in D minor, which interrupt the process that surrounds them. Examples 9.17a and b clarify the relationship.

The string accompaniment with which the Adagio begins, marked 'a', forms a near-ubiquitous feature of the Scherzo. Example 9.17b shows one of its many subtle uses: the Ländler comprising the subordinate theme, beginning at bar 23, is built on a decelerated variant of 'a' transferred into the bass, which persists for the entirety of this material's presentation. And as Example 9.17a shows, the Scherzo's main theme, which is counter-pointed against 'a', is a variant of the oboe theme with which the Adagio begins. The heroic cyclical drama played out by the outer movements is thereby offset by an interior drama grounded in an attempt to transform the Adagio's mournful processional into a more dynamic alternation of dance styles.

Fin-de-siècle: Mahler

In all the works considered thus far, cyclical devices act in the interests of large-scale coherence: that is, they respond to the problem of how to apply thematic techniques as a means of binding disparate movements, whilst invariably conveying an extra-musical message. Yet although Mahler absorbed these precedents thoroughly, he also applied them in ways that sometimes seem to critique the ideal of integration they serve. Whilst all of his nine completed symphonies operate some kind of inter-movement thematicism, it frequently contributes to a kind of collage effect, which questions the notion of inter-movement unification even as it references its guiding method.

Brief comparison of the First and Second symphonies, and a post-script on the Symphony No. 9, serve to introduce Mahler's complex, eliptical approach to cyclical technique. As is well known, the First and Second symphonies form a pair, insomuch as Mahler imagined the latter as narrating the death and resurrection of the heroic subject embodied in the former.[34] The ideal of transcendent integration is most closely emulated in the Symphony No. 1, in which Mahler exploits three crucial inter-movement connections: the primordial music of the Symphony's introduction (Example 9.18a) is transformed as the work's triumphant goal; the main theme of the Finale is a wholesale minor-mode recomposition of the first movement's development material (Example 9.18b); and the 'breakthrough' music of the first movement's climax returns in the Finale, initially in the development and conclusively in the coda (Example 9.18c shows the breakthrough and its return before the Finale's coda).[35]

These three devices are closely related: the second and third are in effect enabling precursors of the first. The introduction's primal descending-fourth

Example 9.18a Mahler, Symphony No. 1, I, bars 7–9 and IV, bars 652–6.

Example 9.18b Mahler, Symphony No. 1, I and IV, thematic relationships.

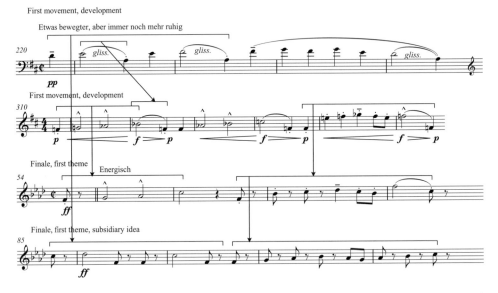

motive recurs in the Finale as a triumphant continuation of the reprised 'breakthrough' event, which is additionally changed through the inclusion of a major version of the Finale's main theme at the breakthrough's apex. As a result, two ideas, which are separate in the first movement (the introduction

Example 9.18c Mahler, Symphony No. 1, I, bars 312–58 and IV, bars 588–632.

theme and the breakthrough) are knitted together. The prematurity of the first version of this event, in the Finale's development (from bar 370), is signalled by means of an abrupt harmonic shift from C to D, which sunders the breakthrough from its continuation; in the coda (from bar 631), by contrast, all of the material is grounded in the global tonic D major. The transformation of the first movement's nature music and its conjunction with the Finale's theme is rich in extra-musical significance. The conversion of an idea initially associated with a nature that is anterior to the first movement's thematic subject into one that ensues from a major-key variant of the Finale's pathetic main theme installs nature as the redeeming agent of the Symphony's heroic subject.

Mahler also employs the wholesale reprise of passages in the Symphony No. 2, but their function here is more elusive. There are two clear instances. The Scherzo's climactic event (bars 465–81) is retrieved as the opening gesture of the Finale, thereby parenthesising the vocal fourth movement; and aspects of this music also recur in the climax preceding the Finale's depiction of the last trumpet (bars 402–17). Dovetailed with this is a larger retrieval: the tumultuous martial music leading into the first movement's retransition gradually emerges out of the Finale's central episode (first movement, bars 282–94; Finale, bars 301–23). Such recurrences mark their formal locations as dramatically disruptive and therefore expressively significant; but they do not project thematic continuities of the sort explored by Schumann and Bruckner.

Otherwise, thematic connections between the outer movements rely principally on a shared preoccupation with chant-like music, and especially with variants of the *Dies irae*, which first surfaces in the first movement's development section at bar 270 (a selection of relationships is given in examples 9.19a, b and c).

Example 9.19a Mahler, Symphony No. 2, I, bars 270–7.

Example 9.19b Mahler, Symphony No. 2, V, bars 62–73.

Example 9.19c Mahler, Symphony No. 2, V, bars 210–11, 216–17, 220–1, 230–3 and 472–4.

Example 9.20 Mahler, Symphony No. 2, IV, bars 22–30.

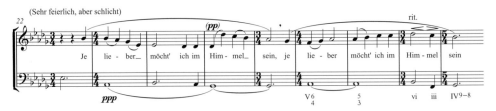

The *Dies irae* is significant, because in the Finale it makes a critical transition from an idea that is incidental to the structural discourse to one that is formally central. The form of the Finale evades simple description. It is probably best regarded as *sui generis*, comprising four large parts (bars 1–42, 43–193, 194–471 and 472–764), the first constituting the introduction, the last the multi-part *Schlußchor*. Parts one, two and four also have a sectional, tableaux-like design; part three initially resembles a sonata form, but this impression disintegrates as the music proceeds. From bar 62, Mahler engineers a thematic conjunction that has central programmatic significance. The *Dies irae* initiates a phrase, which a minor-key adumbration of the *Schlußchor*'s 'Aufersteh'n' theme concludes (from bar 70). In the *Schlußchor*, the latter takes centre stage, whilst the former is jettisoned. The hermeneutic implication is clear: the progress of the material embodies the Symphony's expressive trajectory, from death and judgement to resurrection.

Even more hermeneutically suggestive are the relationships between the Finale and the fourth movement, a setting of 'Urlicht' ('Primal Light') from *Des Knaben Wunderhorn*. The crucial material here is the music first introduced to set the words 'Je lieber möcht' ich im Himmel sein' ('I would rather be in heaven') in bars 22–30, which supplies the last vocal phrase in the movement's A section (Example 9.20). Critically, Mahler illustrates that this is an as yet unfulfilled aspiration by leaving the singer's phrase cadentially unresolved over IV^{9-8}, it being left to the the oboist to supply perfect-cadential closure. The same material serves simultaneously as the climax of the middle section and as an elided, truncated reprise from bar 58, now given added expressive weight through the addition of a pungent ♭VI chord in bar 60. Here, moreover, Mahler allows the vocalist to carry the phrase through to its cadential conclusion, thus underlining the fact that the material now sets the more assured lines 'Der liebe Gott wird mir ein Lichtchen geben / Wird leuchten mir bis das ewig, selig Leben' ('Dear God will give me a little light / Will light my way to eternal, blessed life').[36]

Mahler retrieves this music at an important juncture (bars 655–72) in the Finale's *Schlußchor* on the text of Klopstock's *Auferstehung*, to which

Mahler added his own additional stanzas. Here, he sets his own words 'Mit Flügeln die ich mir errugen / In heißem Liebestreben / Werd' ich entschweben zum Licht / Zu dein kein Aug' gedrungen' ('With wings I have acquired / Shall I soar / In love's ardent striving / To the light to which no eye has penetrated'),[37] in so doing revealing a key strategic motivation behind the extension of Klopstock's poem. In 'Urlicht', both instances of this music set aspirations towards resurrection in eternity, the second more certain in its conviction than the first. In extending Klopstock's text, Mahler in effect uses it as a platform for recovering and fulfilling 'Urlicht''s metaphysical ambition: Klopstock's assertion that 'you will rise again' ('Aufersteh'n, ja aufersteh'n wirst du') is related by Mahler's text to 'Urlicht''s light that will lead 'to eternal, blessed life'.

Although strategically related, these three cyclical threads are not integrated. The first is a quasi-cinematic gesture embodying the rhetoric of crisis, which jolts the music out of its local continuity at strategic formal locations. The second has tangible programmatic significance: a chant signifying the day of judgement is conjoined with a theme connoting resurrection. And the third conveys the agency of that resurrection (the light that leads to eternity). There is, however, no grand synthesis in the manner of Bruckner's Fifth Symphony. Rather, Mahler embeds strands of cyclical discourse within a symphonic context that values expressive fecundity as much as rigorous thematicism. Mahler's symphonic 'world' is a master-genre that can absorb diverse generic and expressive sources (in this case symphony, lied and cantata), in which context thematic cross-referencing principally guarantees narrative orientation rather than any sense of overarching unity.

In the Symphony No. 9, the Scherzo, Rondo burlesque and Adagio are related by two principal means: first, by variation of the descending melodic line and harmonic progression which appears initially in the Scherzo's first waltz episode (bar 90, with the characteristic motion towards ♮VI from bar 96), reprised as a complete hexatonic progression from bar 261, and which references Beethoven's *Lebewohl* Sonata, Op. 81a (Example 9.21, marked 'a');[38] and second, through retention in the Adagio of the turn motive first introduced in bar 320 of the Rondo burlesque (Example 9.21, marked 'b').

There are several ways of understanding these connections. One solution is to regard the Adagio's refrain as uniting previously disparate material. By this reading, the movement begins with a synthetic event: the *Lebewohl* motive, labelled 'a', constitutes its head motive; the turn, labelled 'b', is a subsidiary idea, which consistently saturates the texture in both prime form and augmentation. This interpretation is reinforced by topical considerations. Motive 'a' supports a topical trajectory, in which material portrayed as

Example 9.21 Mahler, Symphony No. 9, thematic relationships between mvts II, III and IV.

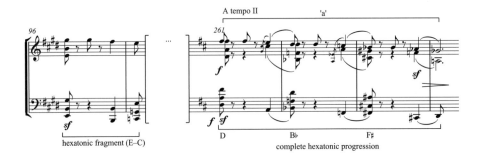

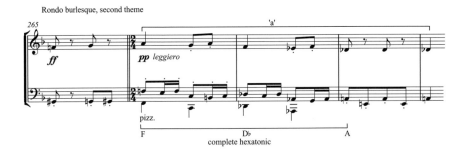

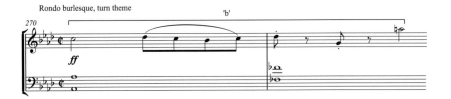

a waltz in the Scherzo becomes a polka in the Burlesque (second theme, bar 266) and finally a hymn in the Adagio: an idea given a secular identity earlier in the work thereby reveals its spiritual core in the last movement. An alternative reading would see the Adagio's refrain not as a thematic prime

Example 9.21 (cont.)

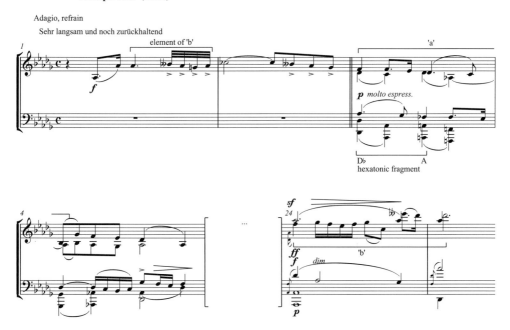

form, towards which the earlier cyclical threads have been working, but rather as a final presentation of ideas that will gradually lose their syntactic cohesion as the movement progresses. In these terms, the two material threads are continuities, initiated earlier in the Symphony, which run through the Adagio's theme and on to its final bars.

The subsequent processes acting on this music have to be contextualised within the Adagio's design, which can be construed as a loose five-part rondo with coda, in which the refrain becomes successively more elaborate, and as a result more texturally and harmonically diffuse. Mahler exploits the rondo form not as a means of grounding the main theme through recursion, but as a vehicle for the successive questioning of its structural integrity. In A^1 (beginning bar 49), the refrain is elaborated with increasingly dense chromatic counterpoint which threatens to obscure its syntactic outline, yielding from bar 73 to a cadential phrase and codetta, which draws out the act of local closure to a point of virtual stasis. A^2, located as the Adagio's major climax (bar 127), begins with even more densely worked textural elaboration in which the turn figure is counterpointed in diminished form against 'a', but this successively thins out as the coda approaches. And the coda itself dwells on 'b', elements of the movement's incipit, and the refrain's continuation material presented for the first time from bar 13, simultaneously fragmenting and decelerating until, by the end, only the turn remains.

Narratives of farewell are pervasive in the discourse on this music, as on the work as a whole.[39] As Vera Micznik has shown, such readings are not unproblematic, especially if they are read as autobiographical.[40] Yet it is hard to ignore the cultural baggage attending this Symphony, and its expressive implications for the material process with which the work concludes. The gradual disappearing from view that Mahler engineers has a fourfold implication. In the context of the Adagio, it supplies a protracted, attenuated liquidation of the movement's primary material. In the context of the Symphony, this is also a dissolution of the cyclical impulse, because the endlessly drawn-out thematic fragmentation invokes a material thread tracking back to the Scherzo. As Mahler's last completed symphony, this dissolution also signifies the exhaustion of the impulse motivating his entire symphonic project (although the extensive materials for Symphony No. 10 complicate this perception). And on the largest scale, it constitutes nothing less than an aural symbol of a symphonic tradition, and the idealism it embodied, fading into history: the ardent utopianism of the Beethovenian symphony, galvanised by the realisation that autonomous musical relationships can convey poetic, literary or metaphysical aspirations, finds its point of ultimate repose. The cultural 'slipping away' ('*das Gleitende*') that Hugo von Hoffmansthal diagnosed in the years preceding the First World War is nowhere more poignantly expressed.[41]

Notes

1 This conversation has been reported numerous times. For an early example, see Karl Ekman, *Jean Sibelius: His Life and Personality*, trans. Edward Birse (New York, 1938), 191; for recent commentary, see Richard Taruskin, *The Oxford History of Western Music*, vol. III: *Music in the Nineteenth Century* (New York and Oxford, 2005), 822.

2 On this matter, see for instance Mark Evan Bonds, *After Beethoven: Imperatives of Originality in the Symphony* (Cambridge, Mass., 1996), esp. 21.

3 For a cogent appraisal of the dialectical relationship between the absolute and the programmatic, see Berthold Hoeckner, *Programming the Absolute: Nineteenth-Century German Music and the Hermeneutics of the Moment* (Princeton, 2002), 1–4.

4 See James Webster, *Haydn's 'Farewell' Symphony and the Idea of Classical Style: Through-Composition and Cyclic Integration in His Instrumental Music* (Cambridge, 1991), esp. chapter 6.

5 The literature on what this means is of course substantial. For recent commentary on this passage and its reception, see for instance

Nicholas Cook, *Beethoven: Symphony No. 9* (Cambridge, 1993), 86–90, David Benjamin Levy, *Beethoven: The Ninth Symphony* (New Haven, 2003), 103, and Stephen Hinton, 'Not "Which" Tones? The Crux of Beethoven's Ninth', *19th-Century Music*, 22/1 (1998), 61–77. The idea that the baritone's words reject the notion of an instrumental finale is expressed succinctly by Lewis Lockwood: 'The baritone, as if stepping outside the picture frame, in effect addresses the other singers, soloist and chorus, and beckons them to join in what now must be not just a symphonic finale but a specifically vocal celebration of joy and brotherhood. He rejects . . . the whole idea of the orchestral exposition of the main theme.' See *Beethoven: The Music and the Life* (New York, 2003), 434–5. Levy, by contrast, insists that the baritone rejects only the returning *Schreckensfanfare* drawn from the Finale's opening.

6 On the tonal relationship between the first movement's subordinate theme and the Adagio, see for example Lockwood, *Beethoven: The Music and the Life*, 431.

7 Cyclical devices are more strongly employed by Beethoven in other genres. The late 'Galitzin' Quartets are a good example, on which subject see Daniel Chua, *The 'Galitzin' Quartets of Beethoven* (Princeton, 1995).

8 Berlioz's two programmes are reproduced in Edward T. Cone, ed., *Berlioz: Fantastic Symphony* (New York and London, 1971), 22–5 and 30–5. The idea that the music's formal scheme should embody metaphorically the 'mental processes of the symphony's beleaguered protagonist' is taken up by Stephen Rodgers; see *Form, Program, and Metaphor in the Music of Berlioz* (Cambridge, 2009), 85–106, this quotation 90.

9 The material integrity of the *Symphonie* has been addressed seminally and in some detail by Edward T. Cone; see 'Schumann Amplified: An Analysis', in Cone, ed., *Berlioz: Fantastic Symphony*, 249–79. More recent analyses include Julian Rushton, *The Music of Berlioz* (New York and Oxford, 2001), 251–66 and Rodgers, *Form, Program, and Metaphor in the Music of Berlioz*.

10 See *The Memoirs of Hector Berlioz*, trans. and ed. David Cairns (New York, 1975), 224–5, Hector Berlioz, *Correspondence générale*, ed. Pierre Citron (Paris, 1983), 184; and also Mark Evan Bonds, 'Sinfonia Anti-Eroica: Berlioz's *Harold en Italie* and the Anxiety of Beethoven's Influence', *Journal of Musicology*, 10/4 (1992), 417–63, at 421. This essay formed the basis for Bonds, *After Beethoven*, chapter 2.

11 See Bonds, 'Sinfonia Anti-Eroica', 440–3 and 448–9. Bonds later on invokes Harold Bloom's concept of misreading in this respect, viewing *Harold* as a 'tessera' or 'antithetical completion' of Beethoven's Ninth. See ibid., 454.

12 See *Music as Philosophy: Adorno and Beethoven's Late Style* (Bloomington, 2006), 209.

13 See Robert Schumann, 'A Symphony by Berlioz', *Neue Zeitschrift für Musik* (3 and 31 July, 4, 7, 11 and 14 August 1835), trans. Edward T. Cone in *Berlioz: Fantastic Symphony*, 220–48.

14 On Schumann's discovery of the 'Great' C major Symphony in the possession of Schubert's brother Ferdinand and its subsequent performance at the Leipzig Gewandhaus under Mendelssohn, see John Daverio, *Robert Schumann: Herald of a 'New Poetic Age'* (Princeton, 1997), 173–4.

15 On this matter, see Daverio, *Robert Schumann*, 231–2.

16 The Symphony No. 2 is of course also rich in allusion and quotation. As various commentators have pointed out, the motto theme quotes Haydn's 'London' Symphony,

No. 104, and there are allusions to Beethoven and Schubert (the 'Great' C major Symphony) throughout. Schumann's reference to the sixth song of Beethoven's *An die ferne Geliebte* in the Finale, which he quotes in numerous other works (most famously the *Fantasie* Op. 17), will be dealt with below. On these matters, see for example Anthony Newcomb, 'Once More between Absolute and Program Music: Schumann's Second Symphony', *19th-Century Music*, 7/3 (1984), 233–50; Daverio, *Robert Schumann*, 317–22.

17 Newcomb sees the movement as a rondo *lieto fine*, which transforms into a sonata form through the agency of the development. See 'Once More between Absolute and Program Music', 245–6.

18 For a consideration of motivic coherence in this coda, see Linda Correll Roesner, 'Schumann', in D. Kern Holoman, ed., *The Nineteenth-Century Symphony* (New York, 1997), 43–77.

19 On the first version of the Symphony No. 4, see Daverio, *Robert Schumann*, 237–41.

20 For an influential view of the form of the first movement and its thematic content, see Richard Kaplan, 'Sonata Form in the Orchestral Works of Liszt: The Revolutionary Reconsidered', *19th-Century Music*, 8/2 (1984), 142–52, and esp. 146–9.

21 Wagner expressed trenchant views on contemporary symphonism, and implicitly that of Brahms; for this quotation, see 'Über die Anwendung der Musik auf das Drama [1879]', in *Gesammelte Schriften und Dichtungen*, 3rd edn (Leipzig, 1887), 183 and also Chapter 4 of the present volume. On Wagner's concept of the symphonic, see John Deathridge, *Wagner Beyond Good and Evil* (Berkeley, 2008), chapter 15.

22 See Max Kalbeck, review of Bruckner's Symphony No. 7, *Die Presse* (3 April 1886), trans. in Crawford Howie, *Anton Bruckner: A Documentary Biography*, vol. II: *Trial, Tribulation and Triumph in Vienna* (Lampeter, 2002), 510.

23 On this dispute, see Richard Taruskin, *Defining Russia Musically* (Princeton, 1997), chapter 8, esp. 123–44.

24 On this issue, see Richard Taruskin, *The Oxford History of Western Music*, vol. III: *Music in the Nineteenth Century*, 786–801.

25 See Carl Dahlhaus, *Die Musik des 19. Jahrhunderts* (Laaber, 1980), trans. J. Bradford Robinson as *Nineteenth-Century Music* (Berkeley and Los Angeles, 1989), 266.

26 Ibid.

27 It should, however, be noted that Dahlhaus writes approvingly of a similar division of

labour in Schubert's 'Unfinished' Symphony; see *Nineteenth-Century Music*, 153–4.

28 Ibid., 272.

29 Ibid.

30 On the programmes of the two symphonies, see David Brown, *Tchaikovsky: The Crisis Years 1874–1878* (London, 1982), 163–7 and *Tchaikovsky: The Final Years 1885–1893* (London, 1991), 148–9.

31 Brown, for instance, comments that 'whereas the Second Symphony's finale had succeeded splendidly, this one ends in failure, for the pompous parading of the Fate materials requires modest musical ideas to strain after an expressive significance beyond their strength'. See *Tchaikovsky: The Final Years 1885–1893*, 155.

32 The extant materials for the Finale of the Ninth are extensive, comprising over 200 folios ranging from advanced orchestral drafts to fragmentary sketches. See *Anton Bruckner. IX. Symphonie D-moll. Finale. Faksimile-Ausgabe*, ed. John A. Phillips (Vienna, 1996). For an overview of the issues surrounding the sources for the Finale of the Ninth, see John A. Phillips and Benjamin-Gunnar Cohrs, 'Einführung in die erhaltenen Quellen zum Finale', in Heinz-Klaus Metzger and Rainer Riehn, eds., *Musik-Konzepte 120-2: Bruckners Neunte im Fegerfeuer der Rezeption* (Munich, 2003), 11–49.

33 On counterpoint in the Finale of the Symphony No. 5, see Julian Horton, 'The Symphonic Fugal Finale from Mozart to Bruckner', *Dutch Journal of Music Theory*, 11/3 (2006), 230–48 and 'Counterpoint and Form in the Finale of Bruckner's Fifth Symphony', *The Bruckner Journal*, 15/2 (2011), 19–28. On the tonal implications of the material, see Horton, *Bruckner's Symphonies: Analysis, Reception and Cultural Politics* (Cambridge, 2004), 130–5.

34 The programmatic connection between the First and Second symphonies is explained by Mahler in a letter to Max Marschalk, dated 26 March 1896: 'I called the first movement "Todtenfeier". It may interest you to know that it is the hero of my D major Symphony who is being borne to his grave, and whose life I reflect, from a higher vantage point, in a clear mirror.' Mahler concludes: 'What it comes to, then, is that my Second Symphony grows directly out of the First.' See *Selected Letters of Gustav Mahler*, ed. Knud Martner, trans. Eithne Wilkins, Ernst Kaiser and Bill Hopkins (London, 1979), 180, translation modified. See also Edward E. Reilly, '*Todtenfeier* and the Second Symphony', in Donald Mitchell and Andrew Nicholson, eds., *The Mahler*

Companion (New York and Oxford, 1999), 84–125, esp. 123–4, and Stephen E. Hefling, 'Mahler's "Todtenfeier" and the Problem of Program Music', *19th-Century Music*, 12 (1988), 27–53. Mahler's programme for the Symphony No. 1 is reproduced in Peter Franklin, *The Life of Mahler* (Cambridge, 1997), 89–90; its formal narrative has been related to that of Jean Paul's novel *Titan* in Robert Samuels, 'Narrative Form and Mahler's Musical Thinking', *Nineteenth-Century Music Review*, 8 (2011), 237–54, at 239–46.

35 On the 'breakthrough' idea see James Hepokoski, *Sibelius: Symphony No. 5* (Cambridge, 1993), 6. Hepokoski adopts the term from Theodor Adorno, *Mahler: A Musical Physiognomy*, trans. Edmund Jephcott (Chicago, 1992), 41, where Adorno advances it as one of three 'essential genres in [Mahler's] idea of form . . . breakthrough (*Durchbruch*), suspension (*Suspension*), and fulfilment (*Erfüllung*)'. Adorno associates breakthrough specifically with the First and Fifth symphonies.

36 For a commentary on the meaning of 'Urlicht', see for example Peter Revers, 'Song and Song-Symphony (I). *Des Knaben Wunderhorn* and the Second, Third and Fourth Symphonies: Music of Heaven and Earth', in Jeremy Barham, ed., *The Cambridge Companion to Mahler* (Cambridge, 2007), 89–107 and esp. 90–2, and Morten Solvik, 'The Literary and Philosophical Worlds of Gustav Mahler', in ibid., 21–34, esp. 31.

37 Klopstock's poem furnishes only the first two stanzas of the text; Mahler's text takes over with the line 'O glaube, mein Herz, o glaube', corresponding to bar 560 of the Finale.

38 The inter-movement uses of the harmonic progression underpinning this are addressed in Christopher Lewis, *Tonal Coherence in Mahler's Ninth Symphony* (Ann Arbor, 1984), 103–5. Vera Micznik has characterised the first appearance of the progression in the waltz episode of the Scherzo as a distorted variant of a baroque ostinato bass; see 'Mahler and the "Power of Genre"', *Journal of Musicology*, 12/2 (1994), 117–51, esp. 134–5.

39 Early commentators explaining the Symphony No. 9 as Mahler's 'farewell to life' include Richard Specht, Paul Stefan, Alban Berg and Paul Bekker. See Richard Specht, *Gustav Mahler* (Berlin, 1913), 355–69, Paul Stefan, *Gustav Mahler: A Study of His Personality and Work*, trans. T. E. Clarke (New York, 1913), for example 142–3, Alban Berg, *Briefe an seine Frau* (Munich, 1965), 238, and Paul Bekker, *Gustav Mahlers Symphonien* (Tutzing, 1969), 339–40. For a recent example, see Jörg Rothkamm, trans. Jeremy Barham,

'The Last Works', in *The Cambridge Companion to Mahler*, 143–61, esp. 145–6.

40 See Vera Micznik, 'The Farewell Story of Mahler's Ninth Symphony', *19th-Century Music*, 20/2 (1996), 144–66.

41 '[Das] Wesen unserer Epoch ist Vieldeutigkeit und Unbestimmtheit. Sie kann nur auf Gleitendem ausruhen und ist sich bewußt, das es Gleitendes ist, wo andere Generationen an das Feste glaubten'; see 'Der Dichter und diese Zeit', in Hugo von Hoffmansthal, *Gesamelte Werke in zehn Einzelbänden. Reden und Aufsätze*, vol. I (Frankfurt am Main, 1979), 54.

10 Tonal strategies in the nineteenth-century symphony

JULIAN HORTON

Introduction

In addition to its vital importance for the social and aesthetic development of art music after the Enlightenment, the symphony is also pivotal for the evolution of tonality. As the most prestigious instrumental genre of the nineteenth century, it embodies on the largest scale changes in the way tonal relations underpin instrumental forms. To trace the development of symphonism from the late eighteenth century to the fragmentation of common practice at the start of the twentieth century is in a sense to observe in microcosm the history of tonality in its common-practice phases.

Understanding this history requires engagement with a variety of theoretical, technological and historical issues. To the extent that the exploration of chromatic tonal relationships undertaken by composers in the first half of the nineteenth century shadowed an emerging consciousness of tonality as a musical system, it reflects a striking shift of theoretical attitude. Where eighteenth-century theory mingled notions of mode, key and harmonic schema with concepts of topic and melodic rhetoric, nineteenth-century theorists, from Alexandre Choron's seminal coinage in 1810 onwards, were increasingly concerned with the system of tonality itself.[1] In parallel, symphonists also responded to major advances in instrumental technology and temperament, which are intimately related to the expansion of tonal means gathering momentum by the mid-nineteenth century. In particular, the rise to dominance of equal temperament and the dissemination of instrumental modifications accommodating this change underlies the increasing confidence with which composers constructed forms around remote tonal relationships.[2]

For a complex of reasons, however, the symphony absorbs these changes relatively slowly: chromatic tonal schemes discovered abundantly in sonatas and quartets of the 1820s and 30s are not for the most part reproduced in contemporaneous symphonies. This, in part, is a matter of organology. The gamut of chromatic keys is less easily explored in an orchestral context, thanks in particular to the restricted modulatory capacity of the French horn and the trumpet, which only eased with the widespread adoption of valve mechanisms.[3] Generic identity is also a contributory factor. Chamber genres were private, domestic media, and therefore offered a relatively safe environment for tonal experimentation. The symphony was by contrast the public genre *par excellence*, and as such carried a weight of communicative expectation that perhaps constrained tonal innovation.

Caution also needs to be exercised in explaining developments in symphonic tonal planning within commonly disseminated conceptions of influence for the nineteenth-century symphony. In particular, the expansion of tonal means is not congruent with the influence of an all-encompassing Beethoven paradigm; it is not at all clear that Carl Dahlhaus's notion of 'circumpolarity', which suggests that nineteenth-century symphonists maintained a debt to Beethoven regardless of their chronological distance from him, extends to Beethoven's use of tonal strategy.[4] In truth, examples of unorthodox strategies are relatively rare in Beethoven's symphonies. Of his nine first movements, for example, only two contain strikingly post-classical expositional tonal schemes: Symphony No. 8/i presents its second theme initially in VI before correcting to V; Symphony No. 9/i contains a second theme in VI. Citation of Schubert as a precedent is even more problematic: by the mid-century, only the 'Great' C major Symphony was widely known, having been belatedly performed in 1839; the 'Unfinished' remained obscure until 1865, when it received its first performance under Johann Herbeck; and although all written before 1820, the symphonies nos. 1–6 were not published until 1884–5. Rather, approaches to tonal planning have to accommodate a degree of generic fluidity: expansions of the tonal system travel between genres, in a way that expressive, formal or thematic devices do not. And here the tracking of transmission and influence becomes problematic at best.

The question of influence raises broader historical problems. Although the narrative of a progressive absorption of chromaticism into established symphonic forms is appealing, it is misleading not least because it invokes the spectre of Schoenberg's notion of tonal collapse. Leaving aside heated debates about the necessity of atonality, it is worth noting that the history of symphonic tonality in the nineteenth century is not necessarily the history of the simple replacement of diatonic relationships with chromaticism. Recognisably classical strategies persist even into the early twentieth century, so that it is perhaps more precise to write on the one hand of an expansion of tonal means that substitutes for classical practices, and on the other hand of the maintenance of diatonic relationships, as possibilities within an enlarged gamut of structural options.

The analyst of these phenomena additionally confronts several ongoing theoretical debates. The structural use of chromatic tonal relationships raises the basic question of whether keys lying beyond the diatonic cycle of relations – or even keys within that cycle, which are not tonic-defining in the manner of the dominant or subdominant – can still perform analogous structural functions. Charles Rosen, evaluating Schumann's use of a tritone key relationship in the Finale of his Piano Sonata Op. 11, emphatically denies such equivalence:

> since (at least before Schoenberg) in no sense can tonalities a tritone apart take on the functions of a tonic and dominant even in rudimentary fashion, this tritone relationship can be heard only in . . . short-range modulations. One can hardly speak of the polarization so vital to the eighteenth-century sonata forms.[5]

In Rosen's terms, one cannot substitute a more distant relation for V in a sonata form and preserve any kind of productive structural tension: we hear a type of tonal 'distance', but not a form-defining relationship. Orthodox Schenkerian approaches tend to amplify this view. The grounding of the *Ursatz* in the model of the perfect authentic cadence necessarily precludes deep-structural participation of chromatic and diatonic tertiary and other relations as anything more than a means of prolonging I or V. In other words, a closing expositional tonicisation of ♭III in a major-key sonata form does not replace the expected V at the background; it simply functions as a chromatic displacement of that dominant, which now occurs at a later point in the structure. Schenkerians unwilling to admit to the possibility of a non-diatonic deep structure are unlikely to concede that chromatic keys can function as dominant substitutes.[6]

Other approaches of fundamentally different theoretical persuasion still either directly or obliquely reinforce this distinction. Robert Bailey's work, designed initially to account for Wagner's tonal habits, has been taken up by various commentators.[7] The idea that nineteenth-century music elaborates a kind of 'second practice' is basic to this attitude: Bailey's concepts of 'expressive tonality' (the pairing of keys a semitone apart), 'directional' tonality (the practice of beginning in one key and ending in another) and the 'double-tonic complex' (continuous motion between two potential tonics) have been brought together under the general observation that nineteenth-century music properly embodies two tonal practices rather than one: a diatonic practice persisting from the eighteenth century, which is monotonal (it is governed by one controlling tonic); and a second practice, which favours the pairing of (sometimes chromatically related) tonalities. In these terms, those aspects of nineteenth-century music retaining classical cadential frameworks comprise its tonal 'structure', whilst tertiary and other relations stand outside this as its tonal 'plot'.[8]

These issues have more recently been taken up by theorists adopting neo-Riemannian attitudes or the theory of transformational networks.[9] Richard Cohn, for instance, has insisted on a basic difference between the asymmetrical properties of diatonic and fifth-based relationships and the kinds of symmetrical tertiary triadic cycles that become widespread in nineteenth-century music. Cohn posits a kind of 'tonal disunity', arising from the coexistence within a single practice of the triad's two 'natures': its diatonic tonal nature; and a kind of 'triadic post-tonality', formed most commonly from successive major- and minor-third cycles.[10] By this argument, we have to regard symmetrical key relationships as standing outside a tonal system founded on principles of cadence and prolongation. When Schubert modulates to F-sharp minor *en route* from B flat to F in the exposition of the first movement of his Piano Sonata D 960 (to pick an example to which Cohn has paid close attention), he exploits the triad's dual nature, enclosing a post-tonal vocabulary of tertiary relationships (the B flat–F sharp motion) within a diatonic practice founded on fifth relationships (the overall I–V motion).[11] Cohn invokes Dahlhaus's notion of a late tonal practice that 'anticipates' free atonality in order to contextualise such practices historically.[12]

Mindful of these considerations, this chapter offers an account of the evolution of symphonic tonal practice from Beethoven to Mahler, focussing on two central features: *intra-movement* strategies, that is tonal strategies informing individual movements; and *inter-movement* strategies, that is strategies unfolding across the cycle of movements. My approach reflects the view that nineteenth-century tonality comprises one expanded system, in which symmetrical and asymmetrical, diatonic and chromatic key relationships can be freely combined or substituted. This has two major ramifications. It implies, first of all, that a diatonic cadence is not the only possible guarantor of tonic identity. We have, in other words, the interplay of classical tonality with what David Kopp calls 'common-tone tonality'; that is, a tonality in which key can be projected through conventional cadential models, or via chromatic relationships in which triads are related by the retention of one or more pivotal pitches, or even (elaborating on Kopp) by parsimonious voice leading towards a tonic.[13] Chromatic thirds are the first such relationships to become standardised in nineteenth-century practice; by the later century, a wide range of chromatic relationships is in play.

Second, the interaction of harmony and tonality in such a context needs to be reconsidered. Movements often embellish an unremarkably diatonic key scheme with chromatic foreground digressions; conversely, chromatic key schemes are sometimes elaborated by an entirely conventional diatonic foreground. Such discrepancies impact upon analytical method. A Schenkerian *Ursatz* remains a workable model for a movement that maintains deep-structural diatonicism, because foreground chroma-ticism can be understood as prolonging a conventional cadential bass motion. But a movement, the tonal scheme of which comprises successive major-third relationships, turns Schenker's fundamental structures into regional elaborations, and so undermines their basic premise. In such a context, we can only maintain the diatonic background by insisting that authentic cadences in the tonic take precedence over large spans of music that reinforce chromatic relationships.

In pursuing these practices, I will pay close attention to the interaction of tonal plot, understood as broadly encompassing the distribution of keys within a piece, bass progression, or the motion and character of the plot's supporting bass, and form. Rethinking of the interaction of these elements constitutes a defining characteristic of nineteenth-century music. It departs most strikingly from classical precedent in situations where tonal plot and bass progression are misaligned: the music may move into the orbit of a given tonality before it is categorically established by bass motion. The relationship between plot, bass and form is throughout represented by bass diagrams, underpinned by Roman-numeral analyses, and overlaid with formal segmentations, which use the following termi-nology: A is main theme; B is subordinate theme; TR is transition; C is closing theme/section; an integer suffix signifies a new section within a broader function (B1, B2); a superscript integer suffix indicates a reprise or repeat (A, A^1). The way in which plot and bass progression interact within the primary thematic material of a movement I will term a form's tonal *premise*; the comparable formulation in subordinate material I will term its *counter-premise*. In a sonata form, the premise is generally synonymous with the first theme, and the counter-premise with the second theme and closing group. In situations where the second theme and closing groups tonicise distinct keys (the so-called 'three-key exposition'), we have what I will term a *double counter-premise*. In sectional or recursive forms (parti-cularly ternary forms or rondos), there is normally an association of primary section and premise, and of subsidiary sections with one or more counter-premises. For the present purposes, we can define the relationship of premises as the specific way in which the plot comes to be formulated.

Intra-movement tonal strategies

Tonal plot

In classical symphonies, tonal plots display an overwhelming degree of diatonic consistency. In the major-key symphonies of Haydn and Mozart, the subordinate theme in a sonata-form exposition, or the first episode in a rondo, overwhelmingly favours V, invariably corrected to I in the recapitulation (for sonata forms) or final episode (for rondos). In comparable minor-key movements, III is predominant, with occasional turns to the dominant minor, corrected to the tonic major or minor under recapitulation. The central episode of a rondo will generally tonicise either IV or vi. Slow movements pursuing ternary designs often deploy the parallel mode (minor or major), the dominant, subdominant or relative minor for the contrasting middle; the minuet da capo will normally frame a trio exploiting the same range of keys.

Many of these habits persist into the nineteenth century. To take sonata-form expositional second-theme keys from across the century as exemplary: expositions modulating directly from I to V can be found in the first movements of Mendelssohn's Symphony No. 4, Dvořák's No. 2, Balakirev's No. 1, Mahler's nos. 1 and 4 and Glazunov's nos. 1 and 7. They also appear in the slow movements of Brahms's symphonies nos. 2 and 4, and in the finales of Schubert's 'Great' C major, Mendelssohn's Symphony No. 5, Schumann's No. 2, Brahms's No. 2, Dvořák's No. 6 and Saint-Saëns's No. 1. Expositional modulations from i to III occur in the first movements of Mendelssohn's Symphony No. 1, Schumann's No. 4, Tchaikovsky's nos. 2 and 6 and Brahms's nos. 1 and 4, and in the finales of Mendelssohn's No. 1 and Dvořák's No. 9.

The most straightforward way in which nineteenth-century plots innovate beyond such schemes is by simple substitution of a more remote key relationship. Submediant second themes in minor-key sonata expositions have well-known Beethovenian and Schubertian precedents. The first movement of Schubert's Symphony No. 4 in C minor (1816), for instance, contains an expositional i–VI plot. Schubert's recapitulatory response is markedly unorthodox. It begins with a dominant reprise of the first theme at bar 177; maintenance of this fifth transposition leads to a return of the second theme in E flat at bar 214. Schubert does not 'correct' the non-tonic reprise until the start of the closing section: the latter stages of the second group modulate, and the closing-section material commences in C major at bar 244. He deployed a similar technique, albeit with a less radical recapitulation, in the first movement of the 'Unfinished' Symphony (1822). The expositional first theme closes with a perfect cadence in B minor, after which the second theme begins, following a four-bar pivot, in G. In the recapitulation, the first group modulates, cadencing in F-sharp minor. The dominant transposition then persists for the second theme, which enters in D major, and only shifts towards B after a modulating sequence and caesura in bars 273–81. The same expositional strategy is also adopted by Beethoven in the first movement of the Symphony No. 9 (1823), although the recapitulation is more direct, switching from D minor to D major for the second theme in the aftermath of the tumultuous first-theme return, before reverting to D minor in the closing section. Schubert sometimes carried his preference for lowered VI relationships into his slow movements: the 'Great' C major's Andante con moto, for example, pits an A minor refrain against an F major episode that is later reprised in the tonic major.

Lowered VI substitutions remained popular throughout the century in major- and minor-key movements. For Dvořák, this strategy evidently held an association with D minor, perhaps in response to Beethoven's example: the first-movement expositions of symphonies nos. 4 (1874) and 7 (1885) both contain B-flat second groups. Brahms deployed the same manoeuvre more sparingly. A clear example appears in the third movement of Symphony No. 3, which comprises a ternary design in which a C minor A section and its reprise frames an A-flat B section. The submediant is still commonplace at the turn of the century. Mahler's Symphony No. 6 (1904) employs it as the second-group key in the first movement's exposition and the initial key of the first Trio in the Scherzo (both in F major).

By the later century, the full gamut of tertiary relationships was in regular use. A clear example of simple minor-third substitution can be found in the third movement of Brahms's Symphony No. 1, in which an A-flat major intermezzo frames a B major trio. In the first movement of his Symphony No. 3 of 1883, the exposition essentially unfurls a I–III scheme, but this is complicated by the fact that both tonalities are modally mixed: the F major first theme has strong connotations of F minor; the A major second theme succumbs to A minor in the closing section. Like Schubert in the 'Unfinished' Symphony, so Brahms also resolves this modulation back towards the tonic in the recapitulation by inserting an additional fifth relationship: the second theme recurs in D major, before being pulled abruptly towards F in bar 155 via a brief caesura (the location of which is suggestively similar to Schubert's). Yet F is not sustained, and the recapitulation closes in D minor, so that it is left to the coda to confirm F as tonic.

More complex situations arise when different ways of dividing the octave are combined, most commonly in the so-called 'three-key scheme' or double counter-premise. In the earlier nineteenth century, such plots often embed tertiary or semitonal relationships within a fifth-based framework. The first movement of Schubert's 'Great' C major Symphony, for instance, contains a three-key exposition, in which a subsidiary theme in E minor is interposed between a C major main theme and an extended G major closing section, creating a tertiary bass arpeggiation outlining the tonic triad, as Example 10.1 explains.

Example 10.1 Schubert, Symphony No. 9, I, bass diagram.

Introduction				Exposition						Development
				A+TR		B			C	
9	24	29	48	61	78	134	174	196	240	254

I e:V i V C:V I V A♭:I C:V I V I e:V i G:V I ♭VI5 ♭6 5 V6 5 I A♭:I V6
                                                              3 4 3 4 3   3

[PAC]

		Recapitulation						Coda		
		A+TR		B				C		
306		316 344	356	440	460	492	514	546	558	570	650

I e:V6 i c:V6 i A♭:I C♭:VI V I V i a:V i C:V I ♭VI5 ♭6 5 V6 5 I V6 5 I
       3   3   3 4 3 4 3   4——3

[PAC]   [PAC]   [PAC]

In the recapitulation, E minor is corrected to C minor and then to A minor, after which the expositional second group is transposed so as to produce C major at the closing section. In one sense, the E minor theme acts as a third divider between I and V within the exposition, which is itself resolved by fifth transposition in the recapitulation as the music moves towards I. Schubert complicates this scheme, however, by according at least middleground significance to A flat, which appears as a chromatic digression within the closing section and is strongly asserted as the framing tonality of the development. As a result, E minor also participates in the symmetrical major-third division of the octave around C, as Example 10.1 shows, and so has a kind of structural double identity. Strikingly, the movement's slow introduction adumbrates the tertiary plan, its two main departures from C major comprising E major and A flat respectively.

The extent and diversity of such tonal plots in later symphonic forms is attested by comparative analysis of two first movements from near-contemporaneous but geographically disparate works: Tchaikovsky's Symphony No. 4 of 1877–8 and Franck's Symphony in D minor of 1886–8. In each case, the i–III trajectory common to classical minor-key forms is taken either as the starting point or framework for the projection of a network of minor-third relationships. The distribution of these relationships within the movements is, however, quite distinct, indicating the sheer flexibility the sonata idea demonstrates in accommodating the later century's expansion of tonal means.

In both movements, the minor-third cycle is facilitated by modal mixture. As Example 10.2 explains, Tchaikovsky presents his first group as a wide-ranging but ultimately tonally closed unit, linked to the second group by a transition suggesting a modulation to III. This is undercut by

Example 10.2 Tchaikovsky, Symphony No. 4, I, bass diagram.

modal mixture when the second theme enters at bar 116 (anacrusis bar 115) in A-flat minor. The expected i–III trajectory is then shifted so that it is orientated around A♭: the second group vacillates between A-flat minor and its enharmonic relative B major, which is secured with the triumphant entry of the closing section at bar 161. The exposition is in this way framed by a tritone, achieved by the pivotal switch from major to minor modes over $\hat{3}$. The recapitulation begins with a non-tonic reprise of the first theme over a $^6_4$ chord in D minor at bar 284 (anacrusis bar 283), which then persists as the initial key of the second group. The bulk of the exposition's second group and closing-section complex now returns transposed, which means that it will ultimately lead to the tonic major. In short, the progression, which in the exposition moved from A-flat minor to B major, now facilitates motion towards F. Thus the recapitulation does not secure the tonic by banishing all alternatives, but by positing it as the goal rather than the starting point of a progression. After this, the coda consolidates F minor. Overlaid onto all of this is a more weakly projected major-third cycle stemming from the tonic: A minor is inserted into the first-theme group at bar 70; and D-flat major preoccupies the first part of the coda (from bar 365) as a large-scale neighbour note to V.

As Edward Aldwell and Carl Schachter have briefly noted, and as Example 10.2 explains, the result of all of this is the complete arpeggiation of a cycle of minor thirds, the mid-point of which is reached by the end of the exposition.[14] By these means, Tchaikovsky in effect balances classical and post-classical tendencies. Primary and secondary themes are exposed in different keys and reprised in the same key, as they would be in a classical sonata form. But because the exposition is underpinned by a cycle rather than an opposition of two keys, Tchaikovsky can bring these themes back in the same non-tonic key (D minor) and still conclude the movement logically in the global tonic (F minor).

Franck, in contrast, employs a standard i–III relationship (D minor–F major) between his expositional first and second groups, but engineers the modulation by repeating his entire slow introduction and first group in F minor, producing a double first-theme premise, the latter part of which tonicises the parallel minor of the second theme's key (F major). One result of this is that the traditional relationship of first group and transition is undermined: the modulation away from the tonic is secured through non-tonic re-presentation of the first theme, leaving only modal parallelism as the agent of contrast with the second group. The recapitulation enacts a series of counter-measures. First, the *fortissimo* reprise of the introduction with which it begins at bar 331 moves quickly from D minor to B minor, so that the exposition's i–iii progression is balanced symmetrically by i–♮vi. More remarkably, a non-tonic reprise of the Allegro first theme ensues from bar 349 in E-flat minor, correcting to D major for the second theme via G minor and a series of sequential extensions of first-group material. This has two consequences: first, the introduction loses its framing function and signals the start of the recapitulation; second, and partly as a result, the subsequent first-group material is significantly less tonally stable than its exposition counterpart, and it is left to the second group and coda to re-establish the tonic (the movement is summarised in Example 10.3).

The preoccupation with third relationships is extended in the second and third movements. The Allegretto's famous conflation of slow movement and scherzo (whereby the latter appears as a middle-section

Example 10.3 Franck, Symphony, I, bass diagram.

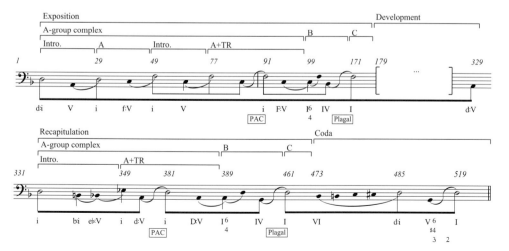

variation of the former's main theme, with which it is then combined at the reprise) is also an exploration of chromatic third relationships, since the scherzo begins in G minor, whereas the movement's key is B-flat minor. The D major Finale elaborates, in turn, on the first-movement recapitulation's motion to B minor, initiating its second theme at bar 72 in B major, and following this at bar 125 with a reprise of the slow movement's main theme in B minor, the result being an idiosyncratic three-theme exposition. The downward motion through the minor-third cycle is continued in the development section, the climax of which (bars 175–202) forcefully establishes A-flat major. The cycle is, however, not completed. F♯ plays no role: the first themes of the Finale and second movement are recapitulated in D major and D minor respectively (bars 268 and 300), and the movement closes, after a retrospective glance towards first-movement material, in the tonic major.

Bass progression and formal function

In classical forms, the tonal plot and the material that articulates it are very often coordinated with cadential bass motion. In nineteenth-century music, bass progression, formal function and plot are by contrast frequently misaligned. An emphatic example can be found in the recapitulation of the first movement of Schumann's Symphony No. 3 (1850), beginning at bar 411 and reproduced in Example 10.4.

Schumann's first theme is reprised over a ⁶₄ chord, resolving the first-inversion German augmented sixth in bars 409–10. This has two immediate consequences. First, the theme's tonic return is not a point of arrival for the bass, which rather remains active across the formal boundary between development and recapitulation. Second, the stability of the tonic is questioned: the ⁶₄ sounds like a suspension over the dominant, which resolves on the first beat of bar 415. In fact, the tonic receives no cadential

Example 10.4 Schumann, Symphony No. 3, I, bars 409–15.

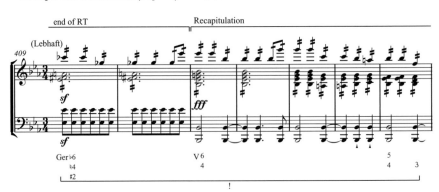

confirmation in the bass for the entirety of the first-group reprise. V is prolonged until bar 430, where it moves upwards towards vi, initiating a passing modulation to V of that key.

The result is that the often discrete formal functions of development and recapitulation are here elided, because the latter is not distinguished by tonic arrival in the bass progression. Recapitulatory elisions over a $\frac{6}{4}$ chord are widespread in nineteenth-century symphonies. A beautiful example occurs in the first movement of Mendelssohn's Symphony No. 4, where a retransitional emphasis on vi is chromatically sidestepped in two bars, and the first theme returns as part of a $V\frac{6}{4}$–$V\frac{5}{3}$ progression in bars 341–4. In the later century, the sense of the $\frac{6}{4}$ as an elaboration of V is replaced by the bolder assertion of the tonic in its second inversion. Examples include the first movements of Tchaikovsky's Symphony No. 1 and Dvořák's Symphony No. 5, which both approach a tonic $\frac{6}{4}$ from a retransitional augmented sixth, and of Tchaikovsky's Symphony No. 5, which approaches the tonic $\frac{6}{4}$ from a diminished third. More striking still is the first movement of Tchaikovsky's Symphony No. 4, the recapitulation of which as we have seen begins with a forceful statement of the first theme over a sustained $\frac{6}{4}$ in the remote key of D minor.

More harmonically audacious recapitulatory elisions can be found at the turn of the century. In the first movement of Mahler's Symphony No. 6, the recapitulation begins at Fig. 28 in the parallel major, reached via a retransitional chromatic ascent (Example 10.5). A major is, however, quickly destabilised by two jarring harmonic devices: the bass turns towards F, which becomes an upper neighbour to the climactic A minor $\frac{6}{4}$ chord at Fig. 29, which forms the true goal of the progression initiated in the retransition. In a strategy owing something to the example of Schumann's Symphony No. 3, the bass E then persists for another thirteen bars, finally resolving to A at Fig. 30.

The maintenance of an active bass progression across a formal boundary is not restricted to recapitulations; the presentation of a second theme over an unstable chord inversion or oblique progression is also common. Example 10.6 shows a lovely instance of transition/second-theme elision in the exposition of the first movement of Mendelssohn's Symphony No. 2 (1840). The transition finds its way conventionally to V/V, reinforced by a nine-bar standing on V in bars 78–82. The initial tonal goal of the second theme is, however, ♭VII, confirmed at the end of the theme's first phrase by an authentic cadence. Instead of resolving the transition's dominant preparation to its tonic (V), Mendelssohn turns the bass C into the root of an augmented triad neighbouring D♭, which then moves by step through ii$\frac{6}{5}$/♭VII onto V/♭VII; it is this dominant that is resolved with the cadence in bars 89–90. A flat does not, however, persist as the secondary key;

Example 10.5 Mahler, Symphony No. 6, I, bars 291–7.

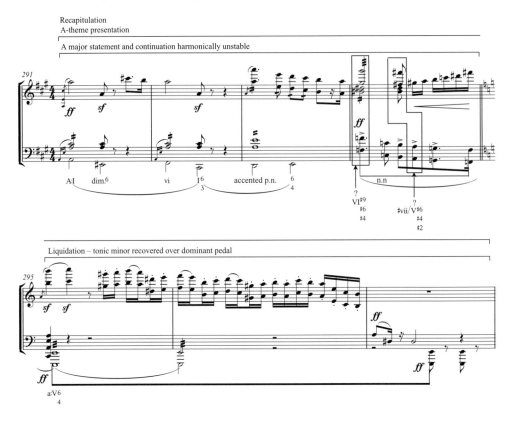

instead, Mendelssohn supplies a cadential extension in bars 90–4, which shifts towards F minor, and the second theme is then restated, via a change of mode, in F major, moving towards an authentic cadence closing in that key in bars 105–6, after which the closing section ensues. Properly speaking, the bass C established in the transition is not resolved until the end of the second theme, remaining active beneath the intervening harmonic digression and retrieved in bar 105.

The double-tonic complex

In the later nineteenth century, the presence of an increasingly chromatic harmonic foreground complicates the idea that an initial theme or section will unambiguously prolong one key. As a result, the association of the parts of a form with a single tonal premise is weakened or else breaks down altogether. Rather, it becomes more accurate to write of the presentation of a harmonic field, defined by a progression that alludes, either by cadence or implication, to multiple, often chromatically related tonics within a single theme group or section, without necessarily confirming any of them. This situation is analogous to the 'double-tonic complex'

Example 10.6 Mendelssohn, Symphony No. 2, I, bars 81–106.

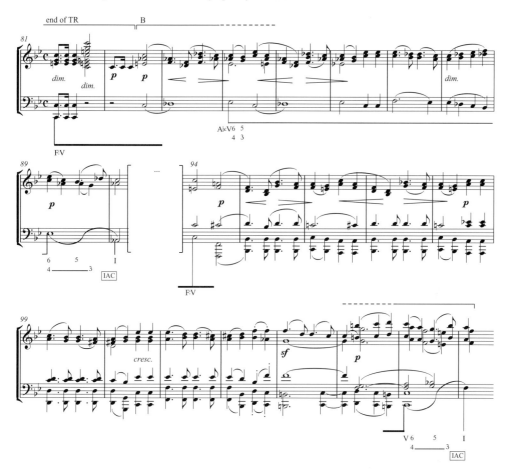

theorised by Bailey as the basis of the 'Einleitung' of Wagner's *Tristan*, in which the music gives up the prolongation of a discrete tonic and shifts continuously between implied third-related keys.[15]

Many subsequent composers grappled with the problem of how to incorporate the idiom of *Tristan* – which populated an open, dramatic form – into the closed structures of the symphony. In the Finale of his Symphony No. 7 (1883), Bruckner composed a first theme, which begins unambiguously with an arpeggiation of the tonic E major (a reference to the first theme of the first movement), but then veers by ascending semitonal voice-leading or SLIDE transformation towards an authentic cadence in A-flat major at its conclusion (see Example 10.7). The triadic major-third progression A flat–E minor in bars 9 and 10 leads to a consequent phrase beginning in V of E, which again modulates by chromatic voice leading, this time reaching a cadence in B-flat major. The ensuing transition finds its way to V of F minor by bar 34, but this preparation is not taken up by the second theme, which begins in A-flat

Example 10.7 Bruckner, Symphony No. 7, IV, bars 1–9.

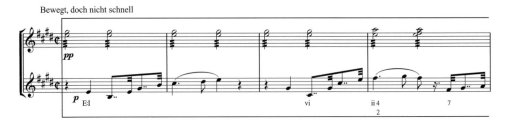

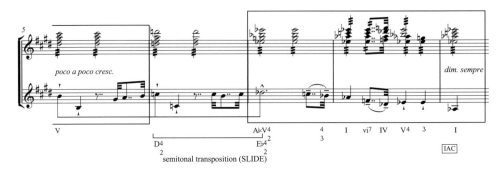

Example 10.8 Bruckner, Symphony No. 7, IV, bars 312–15.

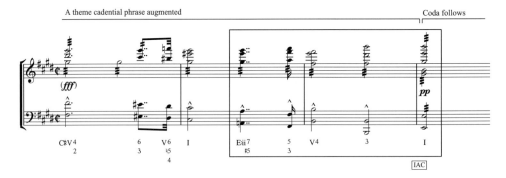

major. The first-theme group is essentially classical in its design – a sentential period is succeeded by a sequential transition tending towards motivic fragmentation – but its harmonic structure departs fundamentally from the classical paradigm, both in its detail and in its general distance from the idea that a first theme should articulate a single tonic key. Rather, Bruckner composes a theme that establishes I and V as starting points, but confirms ♭IV and ♭V by cadence. The tonal strategy of the movement as a whole is not so much about making non-tonic material (the expositional second theme) prolong the tonic in the recapitulation, but rather involves seeking a variant of the first theme that cadences as well as starts in E, achieved finally in the augmentation of the theme's cadence in bars 313–15 leading into the coda, as appraised in Example 10.8.[16]

Example 10.9 Elgar, Symphony No. 1, I, bars 50–8.

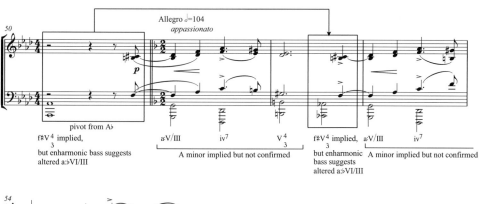

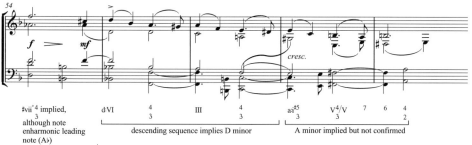

In these circumstances, we might write of *progression as premise*: the theme does not establish a prolonged key, but a progression, in which the eventual tonic is articulated at salient moments.

The main theme in the first movement of Elgar's Symphony No. 1 (1908), reproduced in Example 10.9, is even harder to subsume within a single tonal premise. Arguments about the theme's tonality – chiefly whether it expresses D minor or A minor – persist. Both readings have merit.[17] On the one hand, the principal motive is poised around V of A minor, a region to which the first phrase returns at its end. On the other hand, the key signature implies D minor, and this is reinforced when the first theme is repeated in transposition from performance Fig. 8. The implication of D is undoubtedly of greater significance for the Symphony as a whole, since it constitutes the Adagio's tonic and referential key for the first theme in the Finale.

Yet perhaps the assignment of an unequivocal tonic misses the point, which is the theme's tonal mobility. At the level of tonal plot, its function is not to project a single tonic, but rather to embed the implication of structurally important keys within a chromatic progression, which allocates gestural salience to other harmonic events, including the implication of G flat three bars before Fig. 7. As Example 10.9 displays, the theme's presentation phrase in bars 51–8 moves between implications of A and D minor that are fulfilled neither by cadence nor prolongation. This instability is connected to the theme's non-tonic status even within the first movement, which begins with a markedly diatonic introduction in A-flat major, in which key both the first movement and Finale conclude. The uncomfortable harmonic pivot from the introduction's final bar takes an A-flat tonic bass, temporarily reinterprets it as V$^4_3$ of F sharp over an enharmonic bass, and then quickly forces this to function as a neighbouring chord to V/III in A minor at the start of the Allegro. The ambiguity of this sonority is never satisfactorily dispelled. It functions rather as signifier of the tension between the framing stability of A flat and the harmonic turmoil characterising the principal agent of the first movement's sonata action.

Progressive tonality

The concept of 'progressive' or 'directional' tonality generally refers to the habit of beginning a movement or work in one key and ending it in another.[18] The critical shift between eighteenth- and nineteenth-century practice in this respect resides in the application of progressive schemes in the context of closed instrumental forms. The idea that an act of an opera or part of an oratorio might begin and end in different keys is a commonplace for baroque and classical composers; but the use of the same strategy in an instrumental cycle is highly unusual.

Again, the symphony lagged behind other instrumental cycles in this respect. Despite their accommodation in chamber genres as early as the Finale of Mendelssohn's String Quartet Op. 12 (1829), and their much-scrutinised application in Chopin's single-movement forms of the 1830s and 40s, progressive tonal schemes within a symphonic movement remain relatively rare before 1850.[19] An early example can be found in the third movement of Louis Spohr's Symphony No. 4 (1832), which consists of a D major march yielding, in its coda, to a chorale prelude in B flat subtitled 'Ambrosian Hymn of Praise'. Spohr later employed a descending minor-third plot in the Finale of his Symphony No. 9 in B minor (1849–50), which begins in D major, but shifts to B major at its conclusion. The same scheme is adopted by Liszt in the second movement of his *Dante* Symphony (1855–6): the entry into purgatory is initiated by a sustained $^6_4$ chord of D major; the Magnificat signifying the entry into paradise is grounded in B major.

Four notable examples from the later century occur in the finales of Dvořák's Symphony No. 5 (1875) and (more famously) Mahler's symphonies nos. 1 and 4, and in the first movement of Mahler's Symphony No. 3 (1893–6). Dvořák's Finale traces an overall trajectory from A minor to F, the global key of the Symphony (see Example 10.10: the initial tonality is beamed above the stave, goal tonality below it, a notation also adopted in examples 10.11 and 10.12).

Example 10.10 Dvořák, Symphony No. 5, IV, bass diagram.

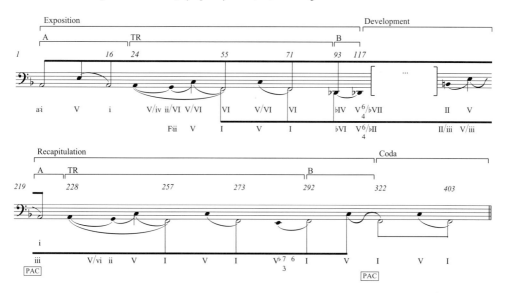

F major is not, however, completely evaded in the movement's initial material; rather, a first-theme group emphasising A minor concludes with a climactic *fortissimo* passage in F major (bars 55–81[1]), which dies away over an F pedal (bars 81–92). Against this, Dvořák sets a tonally mobile second group, which begins in D-flat major, but settles over a ⁶₄ chord of G by bar 117. In the recapitulation, the first theme maintains its expositional trajectory with some regional deviations, commencing in A minor at bar 219 and modulating to F major by bar 273. Dvořák then simply stays in F for his second-theme reprise, beginning at bar 292, and stabilises this key through the addition of a substantial second-group codetta in bars 322–61, which forms the starting point for the coda.

Mahler's examples are more clearly delineated. The Finale of Symphony No. 1 is summarised in Example 10.11. In effect, Mahler here composes a sonata form in F minor, in which a two-key exposition (first theme in F minor; second in D-flat major) is answered by a reversed recapitulation (second theme in F major; first theme in F minor), yielding to a coda that reasserts the first movement's D major tonic.[20] The result is a two-level strategy, as the Example explains: F minor functions as the tonic at the level of the sonata form; D major obtains at the level of the movement cycle. This means that, at least as far as tonality is concerned, the sonata-form body of the Finale itself has two functions – as a single-movement form and as the finale of a cycle – whereas the coda has only one, furnishing the cycle's tonal close. At the same time, D major is anticipated by the 'breakthrough' moment in the development (Fig. 33) addressed in Chapter 9, which starts off in C and

Example 10.11 Mahler, Symphony No. 1, IV, bass diagram.

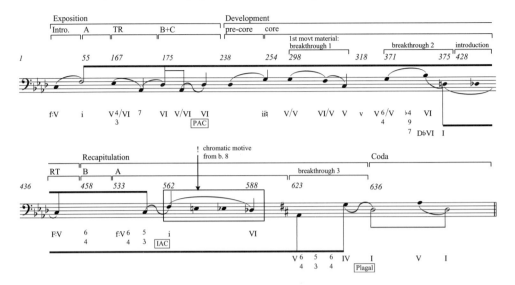

Example 10.12 Mahler, Symphony No. 3, I, bass diagram.

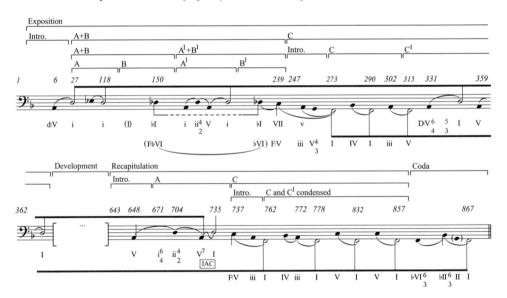

then diverts abruptly to D four bars later. The same material forms the substance of the coda, here, however, presented entirely in D. In this way, Mahler plants a disjunctive tonal event inside the sonata form, which recurs, tonally unified, to complete the Symphony.

The first movement of Symphony No. 3, summarised in Example 10.12, is altogether more complex, reflecting the vast structural expansion that Mahler undertakes (six movements in total, two vocal movements inserted between the Rondo and concluding Adagio and a first movement lasting nearly half an hour). The exposition comprises what James Hepokoski might call a large 'double rotation' of the first and second groups, prefaced by a thematic introduction, and rounded off with a long martial closing group.[21] In the initial rotation, the first group is grounded in D minor and the second shifts between B flat and D before finally asserting D flat at bar 150. In the second rotation, the first group is again a closed unit in D minor, and the second begins as it had in the first rotation, but cedes to the closing section, which sets off in C major at bar 247, consolidates F with the return of the introduction material at bar 273, but turns from Fig. 27 towards D major, in which key the exposition concludes at bar 362, before reverting to D minor for the start of the development.

The recapitulation compresses the exposition's double design into a single span, whilst retaining core features of its tonal scheme. The first theme is again a tonally closed unit in D minor, and the martial closing section returns categorically in F from bar 762; the second group is, however, excised, excepting the incorporation of thematic elements into the march. At base, Mahler replaces the tonal dialectic of the classical sonata with a problem of bifocal orientation. The movement's sustaining tension is between an exposition that surrounds F with D, and a recapitulation that construes F as the goal tonic.

Inter-movement tonal strategies and the cycle of movements

Key schemes governing whole symphonies generally respond to the same expansion of tonal means conditioning tonal strategies within movements. Three issues are of paramount importance: the choice of keys for inner movements; their relationship to the outer movements; the overall trajectory thus created. Again, the crucial factor here is the encroachment of chromatic key relations. Tonicisations of V, IV or vi give way to more remote relations, very often organised so as to reveal clear large-scale strategies, which sometimes reflect more localised key schemes.

Whereas an exhaustive summary of intra-movement tonal plots is hardly feasible here, an overview of inter-movement schemes is more practical. Table 10.1 therefore appraises the key schemes of 163 symphonies by 34 composers, written between 1800 (Beethoven's No. 1) and 1911 (Elgar's No. 2), arranged by chronology of the composer's birth. The list is designed to be representative rather than comprehensive; symphonies by Lachner, Kalliwoda, Burgmüller, Volkmann and others are omitted for this reason, rather than out of any critical bias. Whether or not a composer is represented

Table 10.1 *Cyclical tonal schemes of 163 symphonies composed between 1800 and 1911*

Composer	Symphony	Key	Movement 1	Movement 2	Movement 3	Movement 4	Movement 5	Movement 6
Clementi (1752–1832)	1	C	C	F (slow movement)	C (minuet)	C	–	–
	2	D	D	G (slow movement)	D (minuet) – G (trio)	D	–	–
	3 'Great National'	G	G	C (slow movement)	G (minuet) – C (trio)	G	–	–
	4	D	D	G (slow movement)	d (minuet) – D (trio)	D	–	–
Beethoven (1770–1827)	1	C	C	F (slow movement)	C (minuet)	C	–	–
	2	D	D	A (slow movement)	D (scherzo)	D	–	–
	3 'Eroica'	E flat	E flat	c (slow movement)	E flat (scherzo)	E flat	–	–
	4	B flat	B flat	E flat (slow movement)	B flat (scherzo)	B flat	–	–
	5	c	c	A flat (slow movement)	c (scherzo) – C (trio)	C	–	–
	6 'Pastoral'	F	F	B flat (slow movement)	F (scherzo)	f	F	–
	7	A	A	a (slow movement)	F (scherzo) – D (trio)	A	–	–
	8	F	F	B flat (slow movement)	F (minuet)	F	–	–
	9 'Choral'	d	d	d (scherzo)	B flat (slow movement)	D	–	–
Ries (1784–1838)	1	D	D	a (slow movement)	d (minuet)	D	–	–
	2	c	c	A flat (slow movement)	c (minuet)	c	–	–
	3	E flat	E flat	A flat (slow movement)	E flat (minuet)	E flat	–	–
	4	F	f–F	C (slow movement)	F (scherzo) – D flat (trio)	F	–	–
	5	d	d	B flat (slow movement)	d (scherzo) – G (trio)	d	–	–
	6	D	D	b (minuet) – B (trio)	G (slow movement)	D	–	–
	7	a	a	D (slow movement)	a (scherzo)	a	–	–
	8	E flat	E flat	B flat (slow movement)	E flat (scherzo) – a flat (trio)	E flat	–	–

Onslow (1784–1853)	1	A	A	f sharp (slow movement)	A (minuet) – F (trio)	A	–	–
	2	d	d	F (slow movement)	d (minuet)	D	–	–
Spohr (1784–1859)	1	E flat	E flat	A flat (slow movement)	E flat (scherzo)	E flat	–	–
	2	d	d	B flat (slow movement)	d (scherzo)	D	–	–
	3	c	c	F (slow movement)	c (scherzo)	C	–	–
	4 'Die Weihe der Töne'	F	f–F	B flat (slow movement)	D – B flat (march–chorale prelude)	F (funeral march)	–	–
	5	c	C – c	A flat (slow movement)	C (scherzo) – trio (D flat)	c	–	–
	6 'Historische Symphonie'	G	G	E flat (slow movement)	g (scherzo)	G	–	–
	7 'Irdisches und Göttliches in Menschenleben'	C	C	f (slow movement)	c (finale) – C (adagio)	–	–	–
	8	G	g – G	c (slow movement)	g (scherzo) – E flat (trio)	G	–	–
	9 'Die Jahreszeiten'	b	b	G (scherzo)	B (slow movement)	D – B	–	–
Czerny (1791–1857)	1	c	c	A flat (slow movement)	c (scherzo)	C	–	–
	2	D	D	G (slow movement)	D (scherzo)	D	–	–
	5	E flat	E flat	A flat (slow movement)	E flat (scherzo)	E flat	–	–
	6	g	g	E flat (slow movement)	g (scherzo)	G	–	–
Berwald (1796–1868)	Symphonie capricieuse	D	D	A (slow movement)	D	–	–	–
	Symphonie sérieuse	g	g – G	F	g	G – g	–	–
	Symphonie singulière	C	C	G (slow movement-scherzo hybrid)	c – C	–	–	–
	Symphonie naïve	E flat	E flat	D (slow movement)	B flat (scherzo) – E flat (trio)	E flat	–	–

Table 10.1 (*cont.*)

Composer	Symphony	Key	Movement 1	Movement 2	Movement 3	Movement 4	Movement 5	Movement 6
Schubert (1797–1828)	1	D	D	G (slow movement)	D (minuet)	D	–	–
	2	B flat	B flat	E flat (slow movement)	c (minuet) – E flat (trio)	B flat	–	–
	3	D	D	G (slow movement)	D (minuet)	D	–	–
	4	c	c	A flat (slow movement)	E flat (minuet)	c	–	–
	5	B flat	B flat	E flat (slow movement)	g (minuet)	B flat	–	–
	6	C	C	F (slow movement)	C (scherzo)	C	–	–
	7 (8) 'Unfinished'	b	b	E flat (slow movement)	b (scherzo fragment)	–	–	–
	8 (9)	C	C	a (slow movement)	C (scherzo)	g (march)	C	–
Berlioz (1803–69)	Symphonie fantastique	C	c–C	A (waltz)	F (slow movement)	g (march)	C	–
	Harold en Italie	G	G	E (slow movement)	C (serenade)	g–G	–	–
	Roméo et Juliette	b/B?	b–a (introduction)	F	A (slow movement)	F (scherzo)	e–B (mvts 5, 6, 7)	–
	Grande symphonie funèbre et triomphale	–	f (Marche funèbre)	G? (Oraison funèbre)	B flat (Apothéose)	–	–	–
Mendelssohn (1809–47)	1	c	c	E flat (slow movement)	c (minuet)	c	–	–
	2 'Lobgesang'	B flat	B flat	g (gondola song?)	D (slow movement)	B flat (choral cantata)	–	–
	3 'Scottish'	a	a	F (scherzo)	A (slow movement)	a–A	–	–
	4 'Italian'	A	A	d (slow movement)	A (minuet)	a	–	–
	5 'Reformation'	d	d	B flat (minuet)	g (slow movement)	D	–	–
Schumann (1810–56)	1 'Spring'	B flat	B flat	E flat (slow movement)	d (scherzo)	B flat	–	–
	2	C	C	C (scherzo)	c (slow movement)	C	–	–
	3 'Rhenish'	E flat	E flat	C (Ländler)	A flat (slow movement)	e flat	E flat	–

Composer	Work							
	4	d	d	a (slow movement)	d (scherzo) – B flat (trio)	D	–	–
Liszt (1811–86)	Eine Faust-Symphonie	c	c	A flat (slow movement)	c–C	–	–	–
	'Dante' Symphony	–	d	D–B		–	–	–
Wagner (1813–83)	Symphony	C	C	a (slow movement)	C (scherzo)	C	–	–
Bennett (1816–75)	4	A	A	f sharp (minuet) G (trio)	D (slow movement)	A	–	–
	5	g	g	g (scherzo)	B flat (slow movement)	G	–	–
Gade (1817–90)	Op. 43 (no number)	g	g	B flat (minuet)	D (slow movement)	G	–	–
	1 'Paa Sjølunds fagre Sletter'	c	c	C (scherzo)	F (slow movement)	C	–	–
	2	E	E	a (slow movement)	A (scherzo)	E	–	–
	3	a	a	A (andante)	f sharp (scherzo?)	A	–	–
	4	B flat	B flat	E flat (andante)	g (scherzo)	B flat	–	–
	5	d	d	F sharp (slow movement)	B flat (scherzo)	D	–	–
	6	g	g	D (slow movement)	B flat (minuet?)	G	–	–
	7	F	F	d (slow movement)	B flat (scherzo)	F	–	–
	8	b	b	b (scherzo)	E	b–B	–	–
Raff (1822–82)	1 'An das Vaterland'	D	D	d (scherzo)	B flat (slow movement)	G	d–D	–
	2	C	C	E flat (slow movement)	g (scherzo)	C	–	–
	3 'Im Walde'	F	F	A flat (slow movement)	d (scherzo)	F	–	–
	4	g	g	E flat (scherzo)	c (andante)	g–G	–	–
	5 'Lenore'	E	E	A flat (slow movement)	C (march)	e–E	–	–
	6	d	d	B flat (scherzo)	d (funeral march)	D	–	–
	7 'In den Alpen'	B flat	B flat	g (intermezzo)	C (slow movement)	B flat	–	–
	8 'Frühlingsklänge'	A	A	a (scherzo)	C (slow movement)	A	–	–
	9 'Im Sommer'	e	e	F (scherzo) – D/d (trios)	C (slow movement)	E	–	–

Table 10.1 (*cont.*)

Composer	Symphony	Key	Movement 1	Movement 2	Movement 3	Movement 4	Movement 5	Movement 6
	10 'Zur Herbstzeit'	f	f	a (scherzo) – F (trio)	c sharp (slow movement)	F	–	–
Franck (1822–90)	11 'Der Winter'	a	a	a (scherzo)	F (slow movement)	A	–	–
	Symphony	d	d	b flat (slow movement/scherzo hybrid)	D	–	–	–
Lalo (1823–92)	Symphonie espagnole	d	d	G (scherzo)	a (intermezzo)	d (slow movement)	D	–
	Symphony	g	g	E–e (scherzo)	B flat (slow movement)	G	–	–
Bruckner (1824–96)	'Study' Symphony	f	f	E flat (slow movement)	c (scherzo)	f	–	–
	'0'	d	d	B flat (slow movement)	d (scherzo)	d–D	–	–
	1	c	c	A flat (slow movement)	g (scherzo)	c–C	–	–
	2	c	c	A flat (slow movement)	c (scherzo)	c–C	–	–
	3	d	d	E flat (slow movement)	d (scherzo)	d–D	–	–
	4 'Romantic'	E flat	E flat	c (slow movement)	B flat (scherzo)	e flat–E flat	–	–
	5	B flat	B flat	d (slow movement)	d (scherzo)	B flat	–	–
	6	A	A	F (slow movement)	a (scherzo)	a–A	–	–
	7	E	E	c sharp (slow movement)	a (scherzo)	E	–	–
	8	c	c	c (scherzo)	D flat (slow movement)	c–C	–	–
	9	d	d	d (scherzo)	E (slow movement)	(d)	–	–
Rubinstein (1829–94)	1	F	F	F (scherzo) – B flat (trio)	c (slow movement)	F	–	–
	2 'Ocean'	C	C	e (slow movement)	G (scherzo)	c–C	–	–

Composer	No.	Key	1st mvt	2nd mvt	3rd mvt	4th mvt		
	3	A	A	a (slow movement)	F (scherzo) – C (trio)	A	–	–
	4 'Dramatique'	d	d	d (scherzo) – D (trio)	F (slow movement)	d–D	–	–
	5	G	G	B flat (scherzo) – b flat (trio)	E flat (slow movement)	G	–	–
Borodin (1833–87)	1	E flat	E flat	E flat	D	E flat	–	–
	2	b	b	F (scherzo)	D flat (slow movement)	B	–	–
	3	A	A	–	–	–	–	–
Brahms (1833–97)	1	c	c	E (slow movement)	A flat (intermezzo)	c–C	–	–
	2	D	D	B (slow movement)	G (minuet/ scherzo)	D	–	–
	3	F	F	C (slow movement)	c (intermezzo)	f–F	–	–
	4	e	e	E (slow movement)	C (scherzo)	e	–	–
Saint-Saëns (1835–1921)	1	E flat	E flat	G (scherzo)	E (slow movement)	E flat	–	–
	2	a	a	E (slow movement)	a (scherzo) – A (trio)	A	–	–
	3 'Organ'	c	c	D flat (slow movement)	c (scherzo)	C	–	–
Balakirev (1836–1910)	1	C	C	a (scherzo)	D flat (slow movement)	C	–	–
	2	d	d	b (scherzo)	a (scherzo)	d	–	–
Bizet (1838–75)	Symphony	C	C	a (slow movement)	b (scherzo)	C	–	–
Bruch (1838–1920)	1	E flat	E flat	g (scherzo)	e flat (slow movement)	E flat	–	–
	2	f	f	c (slow movement)	F	–	–	–
	3	E	E	G (slow movement)	E	E	–	–
Dvořák (1841–1904)	1	c	c	A flat (slow movement)	C (scherzo)	C	–	–
	2	B flat	B flat	G (slow movement)	c (scherzo)	B flat	–	–
	3	E flat	E flat	c sharp	E flat	–	–	–
	4	d	d	B flat	d	d	–	–
	5	F	F	A	D	a–F	–	–
	6	D	D	B flat	d	D	–	–
	7	d	d	F	d	d	–	–
	8	G	G	c/C	g	G	–	–
	9 'New World'	e	e	D flat	e	e	–	–

Table 10.1 (*cont.*)

Composer	Symphony	Key	Movement 1	Movement 2	Movement 3	Movement 4	Movement 5	Movement 6
Tchaikovsky (1840–93)	1 'Winter Daydreams'	g	g	E flat (slow movement)	c (scherzo)	G	–	–
	2 'Little Russian'	c	c	E flat (slow movement)	c (scherzo)	C	–	–
	3 'Polish'	D	D	B flat (alla tedesca)	d (slow movement)	b (scherzo)	D	–
	4	f	f	b flat	F	F	–	–
	'Manfred' Symphony	b	b	b	G	b–B	–	–
	5	e	e	D	A	e–E	–	–
Grieg (1843–1907)	6 'Pathétique'	b	b	D (scherzo)	G (finale-type)	b (adagio)	–	–
	Symphony	c	c	A flat (slow movement)	c (intermezzo)	c	–	–
Rimsky-Korsakov (1844–1908)	1	e	e	C (slow movement)	e (scherzo)	E	–	–
	2 'Antar'	–	f sharp	c sharp	B	D flat	–	–
	3	C	C–c	E flat (scherzo) – B (trio)	E (slow movement)	C	–	–
Stanford (1852–1924)	3 'Irish'	f	f	D	B flat	f–F	–	–
	4	F	F	a (intermezzo) – A flat (trio)	d (slow movement)	F	–	–
	7	D	D	B flat (menuet) – b flat (trio)	F–V/D	D	–	–
Elgar (1857–1934)	1	A flat	A flat	f sharp (scherzo)	D (slow movement)	d–A flat	–	–
	2	E flat	E flat	c	C (scherzo)	E flat	–	–
Mahler (1860–1911)	1 'Titan'	D	D	A (scherzo)	d (slow movement)	f–D	–	–
	2 'Resurrection'	–	c	A flat (slow movement)	c (scherzo)	D flat	(c)– E flat	–
	3	D	d–F	A (scherzo?)	c–C	D	F	D (slow movement)
	4	–	G	c–C	G	G–E	–	–

5	–	c sharp	a	D (scherzo)	F (slow movement)	D	–
6 'Tragic'	a	a	a (scherzo)	E flat (slow mvt)	a	–	–
7	–	e	c (slow movement 1)	d (scherzo)	F (slow movement 2)	C	–
8	E flat	E flat	e flat – E flat	–	–	–	–
9	–	D	C (scherzo)	a	D flat (slow movement)	–	–
Glazunov (1865–1936)							
1	E	E	C (scherzo)	e (slow movement)	E	–	–
2	f sharp	f sharp	D (slow movement)	b (scherzo)	f sharp –F sharp	–	–
3	D	D	F (scherzo) – A (trio)	C sharp (slow movement)	D	–	–
4	e flat	e flat	B flat (scherzo) – D flat (trio)	E flat (Finale)	–	–	–
5	B flat	B flat	g (scherzo)	E flat (slow movement)	B flat	–	–
6	c	c	G (slow movement)	E flat (intermezzo)	C	–	–
7	F	F	d (slow movement)	B flat (scherzo)	F	–	–
8	E flat	E flat	e flat (slow movement)	C (scherzo)	E flat	–	–

by their total symphonic output has varied with availability: Glazunov, for instance, is represented in full; Stanford only by symphonies nos. 3, 4 and 7. (Clementi's total symphonic oeuvre remains a matter of speculation; the four symphonies currently published with numerical designations are given here.)[22] Keys are assigned letter names rather than Roman numerals, to avoid designating an overall tonic in situations where a symphony begins and ends in different keys. Major keys are shown with capital letters; minor keys with lower-case letters. The order of the inner movements (scherzo/minuet and slow movement) is clarified on a case-by-case basis. In situations where the trio of a dance movement comprises a self-contained section expressing a notable modulation, its key is shown.

The Table makes clear the extent to which the development of key schemes tracks the chromaticisation of tonality. Beethoven's key choices remain largely conservative. Symphonies nos. 1, 4 and 8 have subdominant slow movements, while No. 2 favours the dominant, and submediant slow movements are preferred in both minor-key symphonies. Two major-key symphonies have minor-key slow movements: the *Eroica* shifts to the relative minor; No. 7 moves to the parallel minor. Only one other instance of modal parallelism occurs, namely the 'Storm' movement of the 'Pastoral' Symphony. Moreover only one Symphony (No. 7) has a non-tonic scherzo, in the relatively remote key of the lowered submediant, although this remoteness is ameliorated by the preceding A minor slow movement and the tonicisation of D major in the Trio.

Despite his more adventurous intra-movement strategies, Schubert's cyclical key schemes also remain closely within the orbit of the tonic. Symphonies nos. 1–3, 5 and 6 all have subdominant slow movements, and the 'Unfinished' responds to its B minor first movement with a subdominant-major slow movement. Symphonies nos. 2 and 5 contain a practice that occurs in none of Beethoven's symphonies, which is that they both introduce minor-key minuets into major-key symphonies. Schubert, however, remains within the cycle of related keys in both cases: the Minuet of No. 5 tonicises the relative minor and of No. 2 the supertonic.

Contemporaries of Beethoven and Schubert are sometimes more audacious. Clementi's Symphony No. 4 goes a step beyond Schubert, in that its Minuet is cast in the tonic minor; the same strategy is developed by Ferdinand Ries, for instance in the modal mixture between outer movements (D major) and Minuet (d minor) in his Symphony No. 1 (1809), or the Minuet and Trio of No. 6 (1822), which tonicises the relative minor (B minor) and then shifts to its parallel major for the Trio, creating a chromatic third relationship with the global tonic D. Ries's precise contemporary Spohr, who composed ten symphonies between 1811 and 1857, nine of which appear in Table 10.1, is more innovative again, experimenting both with progressive schemes within movements (as we have already seen), modal mixture (for instance between tonic and subdominant major and minor in the Symphony No. 8), and chromatic relations (the D-flat major of the Trio in No. 5, which is a semitone above the key of the Scherzo). Franz Berwald's four contributions, written between 1842 and 1845, are at least in this respect more conservative. His most notable experiment occurs in the *Symphonie sérieuse*, the slow movement of which tonicises the lowered leading note.

Mendelssohn and Schumann are only marginally more ambitious than Schubert. The A minor–F major relationship between first movement and Scherzo in Mendelssohn's Symphony No. 3 mimics the same progression in the inner movements of Beethoven's Symphony No. 7, but the submediant Scherzo of No. 5 and the mediant-major slow movement of No. 2 have no Beethovenian or Schubertian precedents. Symphony No. 4 contains possibly Mendelssohn's most unusual scheme. The minor-key Finale departs from Viennese-classical practice: minor-key classical symphonies frequently shift to the tonic major in their finales, but the opposite trajectory has scant precedent (Haydn's Symphony No. 70 constitutes one precursor). Mendelssohn paves the way for the tonic-minor Finale through the choice of iv as the key of the slow movement. The result is a dovetailed modal mixture on the largest scale, in which first movement and Minuet sustain I, whilst slow movement and Finale emphasise iv and i. Schumann is generally more cautious. His most striking decisions are the employment of VI as the key of Symphony No. 3's second movement and the choice of the mediant minor for No. 1's Scherzo. At the same time, No. 2 is the first symphony in the list to remain entirely in the global tonic, albeit shifting from major to minor in the slow movement.

Berlioz and Liszt are both more consistently experimental. The scheme of the *Symphonie fantastique* explores VI, IV and v; *Harold en Italie* similarly tonicises VI in its slow movement; and *Roméo et Juliette* is framed by B, but the love scene tonicises A and the 'Queen Mab' Scherzo F, although the sense of an orthodox symphonic design and global tonic is clouded by dramatic elements. The *Grande symphonie funèbre et triomphale* (1840) is the first example in the Table of a progressive key scheme across an entire symphony (F–B flat), followed by Liszt's *Dante* Symphony (1855–6), in which the 'Inferno' movement occupies a modally inflected D minor, which the entry into paradise exchanges for B major. These strategies are obviously mitigated by circumstantial factors in Berlioz's case (the work's occasional function) and by Liszt's programmatic inclination: classical forms are submerged at best, and the movement plans pay only lip service to generic movement types. Liszt's *Eine Faust-Symphonie* owes more to the classical model; its key scheme is concomitantly less radical.

Symphonies written between 1850 and 1900 generally evince the burgeoning expansion of tonal means. By the mid-century, a clear preference for third-based schemes was emergent. Gade's Symphony No. 5 (1852) is organised around the ascending major-third cycle d–F sharp–B flat–D. Joachim Raff's Symphony No. 5 (1872) adopts a comparable strategy: outer movements in E major and minor frame an A-flat slow movement and a C major march. Raff revisited this idea in his Symphony No. 10, *Zur Herbstzeit*, the third work in his symphonic tetralogy 'The Seasons' (1877–83). Here, the overall trajectory is from F minor to F major, but this is balanced by an A minor Scherzo and a C-sharp minor slow movement. In Symphony No. 8 (*Frühlingsklänge*) he turned instead to minor-third relations, contrasing the global tonic A with a slow movement in C major. Brahms positioned symmetrical major-third relations either side of the tonic in his Symphony No. 1 (1862–76), and in No. 4 (1885) extended the tendency for minor-key symphonies to tonicise VI in their slow movements to the Scherzo as well, creating a large submediant interior framed by the tonic minor. In Symphony No. 3 (1883), he experimented instead with modal mixture, framing an internal mixture on the dominant (C–c) within an encompassing mixture on the tonic (F–f). Bruckner was at least as ambitious after 1872. The Adagio of Symphony No. 3 (1873, revised 1877 and 1889) tonicises ♭II, the first such relation in Table 10.1 after the Scherzo of Spohr's Symphony No. 5. Bruckner revived this practice fourteen years later in the Adagio of Symphony No. 8 (1887, revised 1890), a manoeuvre reflecting the harmonic detail of the work's opening theme. Brahms's strategy of pairing inner and outer movements in his symphonies nos. 3 and 4 is prefigured in Bruckner's No. 5, where the tonic outer movements frame interior movements in the mediant minor. Dvořák's schemes are on the whole less exploratory, with two marked exceptions: Symphony No. 3 (1873) contains a slow movement in ♯vi; No. 9's slow movement (1893) tonicises ♭VII.

Russian symphonists could be equally adventurous. Borodin, Balakirev and Rimsky-Korsakov all experimented with semitonal pairings: Borodin's Symphony No. 1 (1867) pits a D major slow movement against an overall E-flat tonality; Balakirev's Symphony No. 1, begun in 1864 and revised between 1893 and 1897, adopts the same idea in the context of C major; and Rimsky-Korsakov's Symphony No. 3 (1866–73, revised 1886) pairs a ♭III Scherzo with a slow movement in III. All three composers also employed third relations in interesting configurations. Most remarkable is Balakirev's Symphony No. 2, completed in 1908, which arranges minor thirds either side of the tonic D minor in the inner movements, such that a tritone obtains between the Scherzo and slow movement (b–F). Balakirev's strategy is anticipated in part in Borodin's Symphony No. 2 (1876), which applies the b–F tritone between first movement and Scherzo, although Borodin does not pursue the symmetry of Balakirev's design, instead supplying a slow movement in D flat. The schemes of Tchaikovsky and Glazunov are, in comparison, relatively tame. Tchaikovsky does not venture beyond the submediant (in the slow movement of No. 1, the 'Alla tedesca' of No. 3 and the third movement of No. 6) and the lowered leading note (in the Waltz of No. 5); Glazunov's most daring scheme appears in his Symphony No. 3 (1890), where an F major Scherzo and C-sharp minor slow movement contrast the prevailing D major tonality.

Balakirev's use of the tritone signals a point of maximum remove from the fifth-based schemes of the high-classical symphony, which later symphonists also investigated. Prominent in this respect are Mahler's Symphony No. 6 and Elgar's No. 1, both of which centre the tritone opposition on the slow movement. Mahler embeds an E-flat major Andante within a global A minor. In the Symphony's first version, this movement was located third, establishing a direct link between its E-flat ending and the Finale's opening, which begins in C minor and pivots back to A minor in bar 9. The tritone is more starkly exposed in the final printed edition, which reversed the order of the inner movements, thus isolating E flat between the A major ending of the first movement and the A minor of the Scherzo (the early ordering is given in Table 10.1). In Elgar's Symphony No. 1, the A♭ tonic of the first movement and Finale is, as we have already seen, contested by an inclination towards D, which is fulfilled by the Adagio's tonicisation of D major. Elgar's structure is more complex than Mahler's: Mahler's global tonic is grimly maintained in the first movement, Scherzo and Finale; Elgar's tonic is in question until the very end, and its distance from D major is mediated by the Scherzo, which tonicises F-sharp minor.

At the same time, Mahler also standardises the progressive tonal scheme, a practice that other composers generally restricted to overtly programmatic works (Rimsky-Korsakov's *Antar*, for instance, which begins in f sharp and ends in D flat). Five of Mahler's nine symphonies begin and end in different keys. Symphony No. 2 has the most conservative scheme, exchanging its severe initial C minor for E-flat major at the work's conclusion. Later on, he favours two strategies. Symphonies nos. 4 and 7 employ third relationships. Symphony No. 4 begins its Finale in the first movement's tonic of G major, only consolidating the movement's concluding E major in the final section. Symphony No. 7, in contrast, never returns to the first movement's E minor, and C major is boisterously asserted from the outset in the Finale, despite foreground interjections from E major. Mahler's second strategy is the semitonal scheme, which has two contrasting applications: Symphony No. 5 journeys from C-sharp minor to D; No. 9 travels in the opposite direction, depressing the first movement's D major to D flat in the closing Adagio. As

Christopher Lewis noted, these schemes have much in common with the notion of 'expressive tonality' that Robert Bailey describes in Wagner's *Ring* cycle: the semitonal pairing of keys, where ascent has positive and descent negative connotations.[23]

It is worth stressing that the two dimensions addressed in this chapter are not always correlated: exploration of chromatic inter-movement schemes in a symphony is not necessarily a reflection of intra-movement chromatic strategies. Thus the minor-third cycle in the first movement of Tchaikovsky's Symphony No. 4 sits within an essentially conventional movement-cycle scheme, which proceeds from i to I via iv. In contrast, the major-third cycle underpinning the movement succession in Brahms's Symphony No. 1 does not reflect its application within the movements: the exposition in the first movement favours a i–III–iii plot, which remains within the tonic minor or major in the recapitulation; the slow movement contrasts I and vi; as already noted, the third movement contrasts I and ♮II (A flat and B major); and the Finale's exposition follows the three-key plan I–V–iii, which is modified to I–i in the recapitulation before the coda reasserts the tonic major. On other occasions, a much closer affiliation between intra-movement tonal plot and inter-movement tonal scheme is evident. The B-flat tonality of the Adagio of Beethoven's Symphony No. 9 surely reflects the choice of that key for the second group in the first movement's exposition. Several commentators have noted the influence of the semitonal structures embedded in the opening theme of the first movement of Bruckner's Symphony No. 8 on the overall scheme, especially the ♭II–i relationship between the Adagio and its surrounding movements (I have addressed this issue briefly in Chapter 1).[24] And Mahler's progressive schemes frequently prefigure their conclusive tonalities in earlier contexts. The serene E major ending of Symphony No. 4 is pre-empted by that key's startling, unprepared intervention before the coda of the slow movement (Fig. 12), where it interrupts the apparently stable G major tonic. More substantially, the framing D major tonality of Symphony No. 5's second part (movements 3–5) is presaged in the A minor second movement, where it intervenes as a characteristically Mahlerian 'breakthrough' between figs. 27 and 30.

Conclusions

The practices explored here connect with many of the broader formal, historical and aesthetic matters addressed elsewhere in the *Companion*. The use of chromatic relationships both within and between movements often serves expressive ends, which are bound up with manifold literary, poetic and philosophical aspirations, and closely dependent on the importing of idioms between genres. In the later century especially, symphonists had to negotiate not only Beethoven's legacy, but also Wagner's; and this meant acknowledging both Wagner's cultural-political agendas and his tonal practice, especially as developed in *Tristan*. This inevitably entailed cross-generic fertilisation: tonal practices evolving in music drama were put to work in the symphony.[25]

Ambiguity is invariably the critical pivot between tonal means and expressive ends. The displacement of the dominant, competition between non-tonic structural keys, the dislocation of bass progression and formal function, and the elaboration of double-tonic and progressive schemes all generate structural ambiguity of a kind that was alien to the classical symphony. This constituted a central technical means for conveying the narrative and philosophical ideals outlined in Chapter 1: the so-called 'struggle–victory plot' embodied in Beethoven's Symphony No. 5 and the utopian aspiration that goes with it is facilitated by the maintenance of structural ambiguity.

Notwithstanding important studies of isolated works or the habits of individual composers, however, research into both nineteenth-century symphonic tonal strategy and its extra-musical connotations remains in many respects in its infancy. In some ways, developments in musical scholarship are propitious for a change in this situation. The ideas propounded by Robert Bailey in the 1970s and 80s have been applied productively in a symphonic context (notably by Christopher Lewis in relation to Mahler); the marriage of this work with the neo-Riemannian and transformational theories evolving since the early 1990s, which have invariably taken nineteenth-century practice as their point of orientation, bodes well for symphonic analysis. Although analyses of whole instrumental movements from this perspective are as yet relatively rare (Cohn's study of Schubert's D 960 is an honourable exception), it nevertheless offers the possibility of large-scale assessment of symphonic tonality from a fresh theoretical point of view.[26]

In other respects, circumstances are not so conducive. The methodological conditions prevailing in the aftermath of the musicological disputes of the 1990s, particularly the critique of 'formalist' analysis and concomitant attempts to marry musicology with post-structuralist philosophy and critical theory, have produced a situation that broadly favours the study of texted music and especially opera. As a result, whilst the social and aesthetic contexts of the nineteenth-century symphony have received thorough attention, analytical study has comparably languished. It is hoped that this chapter makes plain the scope of the work that remains to be done in this field, both in terms of the sheer range of the repertoire that awaits investigation and the diversity of practices it exhibits.

Notes

1 Choron uses the term to define the arrangement of dominant and subdominant about the tonic in the practice of his time; see Alexandre Choron, 'Sommaire de l'histoire de la musique', in Choron and François Fayolle, *Dictionaire historique des musiciens, artistes et amateurs, morts ou vivants*, vol. I (Paris, 1810–11), xxvii–xxix, trans. by J. Sainsbury as 'Summary of the History of Music', in *Dictionary of Music from the Earliest Ages to the Present Time* (London, 1825). On this subject, see also Brian Hyer, 'Tonality', in Thomas Christensen, ed., *The Cambridge History of Western Music Theory* (Cambridge, 2002), 726–52 and Bryan Simms, 'Choron, Fétis and the Theory of Tonality', *Journal of Music Theory*, 19/1 (1975), 112–38.

2 For a concise summary of the development of instrumental technologies after 1800, see Karl Geiringer, *Instruments in the History of Western Music* (London, 1978), 201–73. For a study of nineteenth-century tonality positing a direct link between the adoption of equal temperament and the increased use of chromatic key relationships, see Gregory Proctor, 'The Technical Basis of Nineteenth-century Chromatic Tonality' (Ph.D. diss., Princeton University, 1978).

3 Blühmel and Stölzel first patented the valve mechanism for the French horn in 1818; the valve trumpet became common in orchestras from the mid-nineteenth century onwards. See Geiringer, *Instruments in the History of Western Music*, 241–3 and 251.

4 See Carl Dahlhaus, *Nineteenth-Century Music*, trans. J. Bradford Robinson (Berkeley, 1989), 152–60.

5 Charles Rosen, *Sonata Forms* (New York and London, 1980), 309–10.

6 In *Der freie Satz*, for instance, Schenker explained such chromatic third relations in terms of middleground mixture. See *Free Composition*, vol. I, trans. Ernst Oster (New York, 1979), 40–1.

7 Robert Bailey, 'The Structure of the *Ring* and Its Evolution', *19th-Century Music*, 1 (1977), 48–61, and 'An Analytical Study of the Sketches and Drafts', in Bailey, ed., *Wagner: Prelude and Transfiguration from* Tristan und Isolde (New York, 1985), 113–48, and see also Christopher Lewis, *Tonal Coherence in Mahler's Ninth Symphony* (Ann Arbor, 1984), William Kinderman and Harald Krebs, eds., *The Second Practice of Nineteenth-Century Tonality* (Lincoln, 1996), and more recently

Matthew Bribitzer-Stull, 'The End of *Die Feen* and Wagner's Beginnings: Multiple Approaches to an Early Example of Double-Tonic Complex, Associative Theme and Wagnerian Form', *Music Analysis*, 25/3 (2006), 315–40.

8 On the plot/structure distinction, see Lewis, *Tonal Coherence in Mahler's Ninth Symphony*, 3.

9 This literature originates with the work of David Lewin, especially *Generalised Musical Intervals and Transformations* (repr. New York and Oxford, 2007), and favours broadly algebraic or geometric perspectives, drawing on Hugo Riemann's concept of the *Tonnetz*, for example as elaborated in 'Ideen zu einer "Lehre von den Tonvorstellungen"', *Jahrbuch der Bibliothek Peters* (1914–15), 1–26. Important contributions include: Richard Cohn, 'Maximally Smooth Cycles, Hexatonic Systems and the Analysis of Late-Romantic Triadic Progressions', *Music Analysis*, 15 (1996), 9–40, 'Neo-Riemannian Operations, Parsimonious Trichords and Their *Tonnetz* Representations', *Journal of Music Theory*, 42/1 (1997), 1–66, 'Introduction to Neo-Riemannian Theory: A Survey and a Historical Perspective', *Journal of Music Theory*, 42/2 (1998), 167–79, 'As Wonderful as Star Clusters: Instruments for Gazing at Tonality in Schubert', *19th-Century Music*, 22/3 (1999), 213–32, and *Audacious Euphony: Chromaticism and the Triad's Second Nature* (New York and Oxford, 2012); Brian Hyer, 'Re-imag(in)ing Riemann', *Journal of Music Theory*, 39 (1995), 101–38; David Kopp, *Chromatic Transformations in Nineteenth-Century Music* (Cambridge 2002); Steven Rings, *Tonality and Transformation* (New York and Oxford, 2011); Dmitri Tymoczko, *The Geometry of Music: Harmony and Counterpoint in the Extended Common Practice* (New York and Oxford, 2011).

10 See Cohn, 'Introduction to Neo-Riemannian Theory', 167–9.

11 Cohn, 'As Wonderful as Star Clusters'.

12 See Cohn, 'Maximally Smooth Cycles, Hexatonic Systems and the Analysis of Late-Romantic Triadic Progressions', 9 and 34. Cohn refers to Dahlhaus, 'Wagner, Richard', in Stanley Sadie, ed., *The New Grove Dictionary of Music and Musicians*, vol. XX (London, 1980), 123.

13 See Kopp, *Chromatic Transformations in Nineteenth-Century Music*, esp. 1–17.

14 See Edward Aldwell and Carl Schachter, *Harmony and Voice Leading* (Belmont, 2003), 612.

15 Bailey defines the double-tonic idea as 'the pairing together of two tonalities . . . in such a way that either triad can serve as the local representative of the tonic complex. Within that complex, however, one of the two elements is at any moment in the primary position while the other remains subordinate to it.' See 'An Analytical Study of the Sketches and Drafts', 121–2.

16 On Bruckner's harmonic idiom, see for example Kevin Swinden, 'Bruckner and Harmony', in John Williamson, ed., *The Cambridge Companion to Bruckner* (Cambridge, 2004), 205–28.

17 For a recent account of this matter, see J. P. E. Harper-Scott, 'A Nice Sub-Acid Feeling: Schenker, Heidegger and Elgar's First Symphony', *Music Analysis*, 24/3 (2005), 349–82.

18 The term 'progressive tonality' was first coined in Dika Newlin, *Bruckner, Mahler, Schoenberg* (New York, 1947).

19 On Chopin's progressive tonality, see Harald Krebs, 'Alternatives to Monotonality in Early 19th-Century Music', *Journal of Music Theory*, 25/1 (1981), 1–16 and Jim Samson, 'Chopin's Alternatives to Monotonality: A Historical Perspective', in Kinderman and Krebs, eds., *The Second Practice of Nineteenth-century Tonality* (Lincoln, 1996), 34–44.

20 For a contrasted reading of this movement, which views the second-theme reprise as a retransition, see Seth Monahan, 'Success and Failure in Mahler's Sonata Recapitulations', *Music Theory Spectrum*, 33/1 (2011), 37–58, esp. 46–8.

21 The concept of rotation is seminally broached in James Hepokoski, *Sibelius: Symphony No. 5* (Cambridge, 1993), 23–6. It is theorised extensively with respect to the classical sonata in Hepokoski and Warren Darcy, *Elements of Sonata Form: Norms, Types, and Deformations in the Late-Eighteenth-Century Sonata* (New York and Oxford, 2006), 611–14, where the following definition is offered: 'Rotational structures are those that extend through musical space by recycling one or more times . . . a referential thematic pattern established as an ordered succession at the piece's outset' (p. 611). For a critique of this idea, see Paul Wingfield, 'Beyond "Norms and Deformations": Towards a Theory of Sonata Form as Reception History', *Music Analysis*, 27/1 (2008), 137–77. For a recent analysis of the first movement from the perspective of sonata theory, see William Marvin, 'Mahler's Third Symphony and the Dismantling of Sonata Form', in Gordon Sly, ed., *Keys to the Drama: Nine Perspectives on Sonata Form* (Aldershot, 2009), 53–72. Again, Monahan reads this movement differently, regarding the D minor march as an introduction and the music from bar 247 as initiating an embedded continuous exposition in F major, which is retrieved with the recapitulation of the march from bar 737. See 'Success and Failure in Mahler's Sonata Recapitulations', 48–50.

22 Clementi's late symphonies survive only as fragments, which have been reconstructed by Alfredo Casella (nos. 3 and 4) and Pietro Spada (nos. 1 and 2). On this matter, see for instance Clive Bennett, 'Clementi as Symphonist', *Musical Times*, 120/1633 (1979), 207 and 209–10.

23 See Bailey, 'The Structure of the *Ring* and Its Evolution', 51 and see also Lewis, *Tonal Coherence in Mahler's Ninth Symphony*.

24 On the large-scale implications of the harmonic orientation of the first movement's main theme in Bruckner's Symphony No. 8, see William E. Benjamin, 'Tonal Dualism in Bruckner's Eighth Symphony', in Kinderman and Krebs, eds., *The Second Practice of Nineteenth-century Tonality*, 237–58 and also Julian Horton, *Bruckner's Symphonies: Analysis, Reception and Cultural Politics* (Cambridge, 2004), 135–43.

25 The early twentieth-century discourse on Bruckner was particularly heavily invested in this issue, even to the extent of regarding his symphonies as the ultimate synthesis of Bachian counterpoint, Beethovenian form and Wagnerian harmony. See for example August Halm, *Von zwei Kulturen der Musik* (Stuttgart, 1947) and *Die Symphonie Anton Bruckners* (Munich, 1923), and most famously Ernst Kurth, *Bruckner*, 2 vols. (Berlin, 1925).

26 For a substantial engagement with the problems of applying recent harmonic theory to the late nineteenth-century symphonic repertoire, see Miguel J. Ramirez, 'Analytic Approaches to the Music of Anton Bruckner: Chromatic Third Relations in Selected Late Compositions' (Ph.D. diss., University of Chicago, 2009).

11 'Two-dimensional' symphonic forms: Schoenberg's Chamber Symphony, before, and after

STEVEN VANDE MOORTELE

The century following the death of Beethoven was an era of extreme formal experimentation in the field of symphonic music. A major and constant concern for many composers was the integration of the separate movements of a multi-movement design by presenting them as an intrinsic whole rather than as a relatively random collection. This concern manifests itself in many ways, the most far-reaching of which doubtless is the phenomenon that I call 'two-dimensional sonata form': the combination of the three or four movements of a sonata form within an overarching single-movement sonata cycle. This chapter explores the use of this pattern of formal organisation in symphonic music of the nineteenth and twentieth centuries. In order to appreciate the significance of two-dimensional sonata form, it is necessary to review some of the other strategies composers have used to integrate the different movements of a multi-movement cycle. The most common of these can be grouped into three categories.

A first group involves thematic connections between otherwise separate and essentially self-contained movements. Examples are numerous and range from the relatively modest restatement of themes from all previous movements in the Finale of Beethoven's Ninth Symphony (1822–4), to the systematic but largely subcutaneous motivic connections between movements in César Franck's 'cyclic' Symphony in D minor (1886–8), and to Antonín Dvořák's rather less subtle deployment of the cyclic principle in his Ninth Symphony (1893). In a second group of works, individual movements remain somehow incomplete, thus requiring the presence of other movements. Anton Bruckner's Eighth Symphony (1890 version) offers a spectacular example. Although the first movement appears outwardly closed, its recapitulation remains unsatisfactory. Only at the end of the Finale's coda does the first movement's main theme (along with themes from all subsequent movements) appear in the aspired tonic major. Thus solving a problem that had persisted since the first movement, the coda transcends its local function, becoming the coda not just of the Finale, but of the entire symphony. A third category, finally, comprises works in which pauses or boundaries between movements become minimised or blurred, as in Felix Mendelssohn's 'Scottish' Symphony (1842) or Camille Saint-Saëns's Third Symphony (1886). Refashioning the end of the penultimate movement as a lead-in to the finale (as in Beethoven's Fifth Symphony, 1807–8) remained an especially popular strategy at least as late as Jean Sibelius's or Alexander Skrjabin's second symphonies (both 1901–2).

Further examples of all three categories abound, and as several of those cited above could illustrate, any combination of these different strategies is possible – Robert Schumann's Fourth Symphony (1841/51, already considered in Chapter 9) is an extreme example. Yet however strong the ties are between different movements and however smooth the transition from one movement to another, at the most fundamental level of formal organisation, the traditional plan of the multi-movement sonata cycle remains firmly in place in all of these symphonies.

Two-dimensional sonata form takes the inverse approach: combining the movements of a sonata cycle within one overarching sonata form, it creates the impression of a fundamentally single-movement composition. This strategy is deployed in several large-scale instrumental works by Franz Liszt, Richard Strauss and the young Arnold Schoenberg amongst others.

That two-dimensional forms hold a special place in the history of symphonic music in the late nineteenth and early twentieth centuries has long been acknowledged, especially by Germanic writers. In an important essay on Schoenberg's Chamber Symphony Op. 9 (1906), Reinhold Brinkmann suggests that the ambition to integrate a multi-movement pattern into a single-movement form is typically symphonic. For Brinkmann, the Chamber Symphony is crucial in this respect: not only does it draw the consequences from 'the problem of symphonic form in the nineteenth century'; it de facto solves it. In its formal organisation, Brinkmann writes, 'the Chamber Symphony is an endpoint'.[1]

To be sure, two-dimensional sonata forms continued to be written after 1906. Yet as we will see, Schoenberg's Chamber Symphony does mark a shift in the role they play in the history of symphonic music. For this reason, the present chapter starts with a somewhat detailed consideration of this composition, introducing a theoretical model of two-dimensional sonata form and illustrating a number of opportunities and problems associated with it. The second half of the chapter offers a *tour d'horizon* of two-dimensional symphonic forms composed before and after Schoenberg's Chamber Symphony.

Schoenberg's Chamber Symphony

Two-dimensional sonata form can be conceptualised as the loose projection of a single-movement sonata form and a multi-movement sonata cycle onto each other.[2] The result is a form that unfolds in two dimensions: the dimension of the (multi-movement) sonata cycle and that of the (single-movement) overarching sonata form. Theoretically speaking, it is possible that all sections of the sonata form and all movements of the sonata cycle neatly coincide. This is the model underlying the concept of 'double-function form' that William Newman coined in 1969 to describe Liszt's Piano Sonata in B minor.[3] In compositional reality, this situation never occurs: not all sections of the sonata form necessarily stand in a one-to-one relationship with movements of the sonata cycle. A movement may coincide seamlessly with a section of the sonata form, but it may also overlap with only part of a section, or with parts of several consecutive sections. Often, entire movements stand between two different sections of the sonata form, thus fulfilling a function in only one of the two dimensions. Following Carl Dahlhaus's coinage, the situation in which formal units of the sonata form and the sonata cycle coincide may be called 'identification'; that in which a movement of the cycle stands between units of the form, 'interpolation'.[4] The opposite of an interpolated movement is an 'exocyclic' unit: a unit that belongs exclusively to the overarching sonata form and plays no role in the sonata cycle.

Interior movements and finales can be either interpolated or identified. For first movements, interpolation is not an option: either the overarching sonata form simultaneously functions as the first movement of the sonata cycle (which has, as it were, soaked up the ensuing movements of the cycle), or there are indications of a more-or-less autonomous sonata-form first movement in the opening portions of the overarching sonata form. Only in the latter case is the first movement of the sonata cycle identified with the initial sections of the overarching form.

As shown in Table 11.1, applying this model to Schoenberg's Chamber Symphony reveals that the first movement of the sonata cycle is identified with the exposition and the beginning of the development (more specifically, the false exposition repeat) of the overarching sonata form, and that the Finale is identified with both the final portion of the recapitulation and the coda of the overarching sonata form. The Scherzo, by contrast, is interpolated, standing between rather than coinciding with different units of the development. The slow movement begins as an interpolated movement, but evolves into a unit that is identified with part of the development.

Table 11.1 *Schoenberg, Chamber Symphony Op. 9*

Overarching sonata form		Sonata cycle	
INTRODUCTION (bars 1–4)			
EXPOSITION (bars 5–135)		**FIRST MOVEMENT (?) (bars 5–141)**	
motto (bars 5–9)			
main theme (bars 10–67)	E – f – E		
transition (bars 68–83)			
subordinate theme group (bars 84–126)	A		
closing group + retransition (bars 127–35)			
DEVELOPMENT (beginning)			
false exposition repeat (bars 136–41)			
transition to Scherzo (bars 142–59)			
		SCHERZO (bars 160–279)	
DEVELOPMENT (core) (bars 280–377)			
		SLOW MOVEMENT (bars 378–434)	
		A (bars 378–414)	
DEVELOPMENT			
resumption (bars 415–34)		B (bars 415–34)	
retransition (bars 435–47)			
RECAPITULATION			
subordinate theme group (bars 448–72)	E		
		FINALE (bars 473–593)	
motto (bars 473–6)		introduction (bars 473–6)	
main theme (bars 477–96)	E	main theme (bars 477–96)	E
CODA (bars 497–593)		transition (bars 497–508)	
		subordinate theme (bars 509–15)	B
		development (bars 516–75)	
		recapitulation (bars 576–93)	E

Even from this superficial overview, it becomes clear why Brinkmann claims that the Chamber Symphony – or, by extension, two-dimensional sonata form in general – solves 'the problem of symphonic form in the nineteenth century'. It is difficult to conceive of a way to integrate the separate movements of a sonata cycle more strongly than by incorporating them in an overarching single-movement form. From this point of view, two-dimensional sonata form really *is* the endpoint of the tendency towards cyclic integration in symphonic music of the nineteenth century.

But there is more to the issue than this. Two-dimensional sonata form does not merely address the integration of the multi-movement sonata cycle; it can also be understood in the context of that other central issue in the *Problemgeschichte* of nineteenth-century sonata-style composition, namely the so-called recapitulation problem. As has often been observed, many composers from the generation of Schumann and Mendelssohn onwards experienced the close analogy between exposition and recapitulation that is essential to eighteenth- and early nineteenth-century sonata form as deeply problematic. Once the onset of the recapitulation had been attained, the rest of the form could, at least in principle, unwind almost mechanically.[5] If two-dimensional sonata form can be said to occupy a crucial position in the history of large-scale instrumental form in the later nineteenth and early twentieth centuries, then this is to a large extent because it engages with both central preoccupations of nineteenth-century form: cyclic integration *and* the recapitulation problem.

Indeed, what is especially fascinating about two-dimensional sonata form is that it deals with one preoccupation through the other. More specifically, the presence of a finale whose beginning coincides with or follows the onset of the recapitulation radically changes the form's internal dynamics. If the finale of the sonata cycle appears identified with the recapitulation of the overarching sonata form, then this adds to the latter's weight as a formal unit. The recapitulation not only acquires a double necessity – in the cycle and in the form – but also an increased independence from the exposition. If, by contrast, the finale is identified mainly with the coda or interpolated between the recapitulation and the coda, then the apex of the form shifts from the recapitulation to the finale or the coda.

In his Chamber Symphony, Schoenberg chooses the latter strategy. Most commentators have opted to let the recapitulation begin with the return of the transition from the exposition in bar 435. Given the absence of both a thematic and a tonal return, however, it is more plausible to hear bars 435–47 not as the beginning of the recapitulation, but as the end of the development; more specifically, as a retransition. This idea is particularly attractive given that the return of a transition as a retransition is not uncommon in sonata forms since the eighteenth century, especially when the order of themes in the recapitulation is inverted. This is exactly what happens in the Chamber Symphony: the recapitulation begins in bar 448 with the subordinate theme group in the tonic, which then leads to the recapitulation of the main theme group (bar 477) in the same way as it led to the closing group in the exposition.

The inversion of the thematic order in the recapitulation has far-reaching consequences. Obviously, it individualises the overall design of the recapitulation from that of the exposition. But it also postpones the most emphatic moment of return, the 'double' return of the main theme in the tonic. A crucial element in this strategy is that, as in the exposition, the recapitulation of the main theme is preceded by a motto. Throughout the composition, this motto functions as a formal marker, returning at almost all major junctions in the form. Its return here seems to suggest, therefore, that the reprise of the main theme is not merely the beginning of a new segment of the recapitulation, but also the beginning of something on a larger scale. Bars 474–593 can be interpreted as a full-fledged finale, with an exposition comprising a main theme, a transition and a subordinate theme, a development (mainly based on subordinate-theme material) and a truncated recapitulation. By multiplying the number of recapitulatory gestures (the return of the subordinate theme in the tonic, the double return of main theme and tonic and the recapitulation of the Finale), Schoenberg sustains the momentum much longer than would have been the case had the recapitulation paralleled the exposition. The presence of a finale that is partly independent of the overarching sonata form's recapitulation not only enables the last of these recapitulatory gestures – which appears, naturally, very late in the piece – but in fact requires it.

All this is not to claim that the integration of a sonata cycle into a single-movement sonata form is not itself deeply problematic. On the contrary, this integration engenders a very strong tension between both dimensions that becomes particularly palpable when a movement of the sonata cycle is identified with units of the overarching sonata form. When they coincide, form and cycle often have very different requirements that are not always easily reconciled. This becomes eminently clear in bars 5–147 of the Chamber Symphony, to the extent that one might debate whether they have a double function at all. Doesn't the first movement rather coincide with the entire overarching sonata form, which has absorbed the three following movements? There can be little doubt that on the most fundamental level, bars 5–147 constitute the exposition and false exposition repeat of the overarching sonata form. Yet it is tempting to read some of the striking features of this exposition as motivated by the simultaneous presence of the first movement of the cycle. Bars 10–57, for instance, which comprise the first and contrasting middle parts of a ternary main theme, may be heard simultaneously as the main theme, subordinate theme and closing group of a smaller-scale exposition in its own right. And the false exposition repeat in bars 136–47 can surely be understood as the abridged first-movement recapitulation (which must remain incomplete in order to avoid premature closure, thus preventing the continuation of the overarching form). But what about bars 58–135? In the overarching sonata form, they constitute the reprise of the opening part of the main theme (concluded by an emphatic cadence), the transition, the subordinate theme and the closing group. Yet all of these functions are incompatible with the development function that the same music has to fulfil in the first movement. The problem is obvious: one and the same group of formal units cannot possibly have the structure of both an exposition-cum-false-repeat and a complete sonata form; and since bars 5–135 clearly have the structure of a sonata-form exposition (a specific succession of formal functions combined with a specific cadential plan), the articulation of the sonata cycle's first movement necessarily remains limited to a mere suggestion of some of its surface characteristics.

Difficulties of balance between both dimensions may also arise with interpolated movements. Here, the risk exists that the presence of an interpolation may seem unmotivated from the point of view of the overarching sonata form and that it may be difficult for the overarching form to resume afterwards. The ways in which composers have integrated interpolated movements into the overarching sonata are among the most analytically interesting aspects of two-dimensional sonata forms. In Schoenberg's Chamber Symphony, the two interpolated movements are integrated into the overarching sonata form in very different ways.

The Scherzo is integrated by thematic means into the development (of the overarching sonata form) that follows it. In bars 335–54, the second phrase from the Scherzo theme (originally in bars 163–4) is developed alongside material from the exposition of the overarching sonata form and even assimilated to the latter's main theme. Integration of the slow movement is rather achieved by formal means. When the overarching sonata form resumes in bar 415, the slow movement is left formally open; this incompleteness is compensated for later in the overarching sonata form. Bars 415–34 initially seem to be the middle section of the slow movement. Instead of leading to the expected recapitulation of the first section, however, they are followed by the return of the transition from the exposition, which belongs to the overarching sonata form. Retrospectively, bars 415–34 can be reinterpreted as a double-functional unit that is both the middle of the slow movement and the resumption of the overarching sonata form's development. Identifying the final unit of an incomplete interpolated movement with the resumption of the overarching sonata form is a very subtle way to shift back from one dimension to the other. Only when no slow-movement recapitulation follows the middle section does it become clear that we have left the dimension of the cycle. The openness of the slow movement is redressed in the coda of the overarching sonata form. Bars 509–15 constitute an almost literal return of bars 382–6 from the slow movement's exposition; these bars can be understood as a postponed slow-movement recapitulation.

Before

Compositions that combine form and cycle as systematically as Schoenberg's Chamber Symphony are relatively rare; and even within this limited group of works, the idea is treated with considerable flexibility, allowing for very different individual solutions. Nonetheless, the issue of how to incorporate a multi-movement pattern into a single-movement design was addressed with some frequency by composers from the 1850s onwards, often in their most progressive large-scale instrumental music.

Few of these compositions, however, are symphonies. When Liszt experimented with two-dimensional form in the 1850s, he did so in the genres of the piano sonata (his 1853 Sonata in B minor has acquired the status of a textbook example), the piano concerto and the symphonic poem. In his *Faust* and *Dante* symphonies, by contrast, he firmly holds to a multi-movement layout. From Liszt, the interest in two-dimensional form spread all over Europe, leaving traces not only in piano sonatas by several of his pupils, but also in such diverse works as Bedřich Smetana's symphonic poems – both the early *Wallensteins Lager* (1859) and *Šarka* (from *Má Vlast*, 1875) spring to mind – Saint-Saëns's Cello Concerto in A minor Op. 33 (1872), several of Strauss's tone poems and Schoenberg's *Pelleas und Melisande* (1903). Yet when composers of the same generations titled a composition 'symphony', that predicate seems to have implied an essential separation of movements.

This is especially striking in the light of Brinkmann's assertion that the problem solved in Schoenberg's Chamber Symphony is a specifically symphonic one. It seems paradoxical that the most inherently symphonic innovation in instrumental music of the second half of the nineteenth century took place outside the genre of the symphony. At the same time, it is not a coincidence that Liszt's interest in incorporating a multi-movement pattern in a single-movement form arose at the highpoint of what Dahlhaus and others have called the 'tote Zeit der Symphonie': the dead era of the symphony (although mindful of David Brodbeck's challenge to this model in Chapter 4). As Dahlhaus remarks, one of the concomitant phenomena of the mid-century crisis of the symphony was what one could call the 'symphonisation' of other genres: while the symphony's own viability as a genre was questioned, typically symphonic characteristics – such as the monumental scale, the multi-movement plan and the ambition to integrate the movements that constitute this plan – migrated to other genres.[6] Thus one might speak not only of the symphonic poem, but also of the symphonic sonata, the symphonic concerto, and later, in Schoenberg and Zemlinsky, even the symphonic quartet.

Several of Liszt's symphonic poems attest to this 'symphonising' tendency. Whether *Ce qu'on entend sur la montagne* (1847–56) combines its relatively obvious overarching sonata form with the 'allegro first movement, the slow movement, and the finale' that Dahlhaus discerned in it remains open to debate.[7] But works such as *Tasso* (1847–54), *Les Préludes* (1849–55) and *Die Ideale* (1856–7) clearly integrate a sonata cycle into an overarching sonata form, thus

Table 11.2 *Liszt*, Les Préludes

Overarching sonata form		Sonata cycle
INTRODUCTION (bars 1–34)		[FIRST MOVEMENT]
EXPOSITION (bars 35–108)		
main theme (bars 35–46)	C	
transition (bars 47–69)		
subordinate theme (bars 70–104)	E	
transition (bars 105–8)		
DEVELOPMENT (bars 109–99)		
opening (core-like) (bars 109–30)		
elaboration of basic motive (bars 131–59)		
new theme (bars 160–81)	a	
elaboration of transition material (bars 182–99)		
		INTERIOR MOVEMENT (bars 200–343)
RECAPITULATION (bars 296–404)		
subordinate theme (bars 296–343)	C	
transition (bars 344–404)		FINALE (bars 344–404)
CODA (bars 405–19)		
main theme recapitulation	C	

transcending a simple single-movement design. In *Les Préludes*, for example, a relatively unadventurous sonata-form plan (slow introduction in bars 1–34, exposition in bars 35–108, development in bars 109–99; see Table 11.2) is interrupted in bar 199 by an interior movement that fuses characteristics of a scherzo and a slow movement. The presence of this movement considerably alters the further course of the form. Not only does it merge seamlessly with the transformed tonic return of the subordinate theme with which the (inverted) recapitulation opens in bar 296, but from bar 344 onwards, what initially appears to be a transformation of the transition from the exposition is expanded in such a way that it alludes to the finale of a sonata cycle. The thematic material from the transition (bars 346–55) has undergone a march-like transformation and is played in a faster tempo than in the exposition. Moreover, it is followed by a new thematic idea that is sequenced and fragmented (bars 356–69) and leads to yet another transformation of subordinate-theme material in bars 370–7. Given that bars 378–404 are a transposed recapitulation of bars 344–69, the entire unit starting in bar 344 can be regarded as a relatively self-contained (but tonally open-ended) miniature finale in ternary form. Only then, in the last bars, does the recapitulation of the main theme enter. It is not difficult to see how the form of *Les Préludes* addresses concerns similar to those in Schoenberg's Chamber Symphony. The inverted recapitulation and the Finale serve the same purpose in both compositions: minimising the analogy between the exposition and recapitulation and thus sustaining the momentum until the very end of the form.

One reason why similar experiments do not occur in the genre of the symphony proper might be that the younger genre of the symphonic poem came with a licence for far-reaching formal innovation unavailable in the more venerable symphony. Another probable reason is that the use of two-dimensional sonata form symphonised the essentially single-movement genre of the symphonic poem, whereas imposing an overarching sonata form on a symphony proper would have resulted in a reduction of its symphonic character. It seems unlikely that two-dimensional form would have been practicable at the grandest symphonic scale, especially after 1850. It would appear that in the genre of the symphony proper, the combination of more conservative generic conventions and the aesthetic of monumentality trumped the tendency towards integration, so that the techniques described at the beginning of this chapter might very well have been the maximum attainable cyclic integration.

Not surprisingly, then, two-dimensional form enters the genre of the symphony proper through the back door: in Strauss's *Sinfonia domestica* (1902–3), a symphony in name, but fundamentally still a tone poem. The *Domestica* is not Strauss's first work to combine single- and multi-movement plans. Both *Don Juan* and *Ein Heldenleben* are two-dimensional sonata forms, and *Macbeth* and *Tod und Verklärung* also contain obvious references to the interior movements of a sonata cycle, even though neither shows any trace of the outer movements. In calling his new piece a symphony, Strauss may have been drawing conclusions from the inflated proportions of his tone poems from the mid 1890s onwards. In the *Domestica*, the multi-movement pattern is present in an unusually direct way: a 'Scherzo', 'Adagio' and 'Finale' are all explicitly labelled in the score. In addition, it has often been observed that the sections before the Scherzo and the Finale 'relate to each other, at least initially, as if they are exposition and recapitulation'.[8]

The form of the *Domestica* is, however, of considerable ingenuity and few of the labels Strauss gives can be taken at face value (see Table 11.3). In the dimension of the cycle, for instance, it is misleading to assume that one movement necessarily ends only when the next one begins. From bar 392 onwards, long before the label 'Adagio' appears in the score, scherzando characteristics give way to a heterogeneous succession of units, none of which seems to allow for an interpretation as part of the Scherzo. Some of them are developmental; others, such as the *Wiegenlied* in bars 517–46 or the unit in bars 559–88, are suggestive of a slow movement. Being tonally closed in G minor and concluding with their proper coda, both units are even more reminiscent of a self-contained slow movement than the unit labelled 'Adagio' (which also has its own coda, but begins in E major and ends in E-flat major).

Table 11.3 *Strauss,* Sinfonia domestica

Overarching sonata form		Sonata cycle	
EXPOSITION (bars 1–392)		**FIRST MOVEMENT (bars 1–152)**	
main theme (bars 1–152)	F	main theme	F
		subordinate theme	B
		Recapitulation	F
subordinate theme (bars 153–361)			
incipient version (bars 153–216)	d		
		SCHERZO (bars 217–337)	
full version (bars 338–61)	D		
closing group + transition (bars 362–92)			
DEVELOPMENT (bars 393–598)			
		SLOW MOVEMENT (bars 599–694)	
DEVELOPMENT (bars 695–823)			
RECAPITULATION (bars 824–1358)		**FINALE (bars 824–1358)**	
CODA (bars 1359–1505)			

The music preceding the Scherzo initially seems to be neither a full-fledged exposition nor an actual (sonata-form) first movement. Not without reason, it has often been described as an introduction that merely presents the composition's main thematic material (labelled as 'themes 1, 2 and 3' in the score). Yet as Walter Werbeck has proposed, the exposition of the over-arching sonata form may in fact extend as far as bar 392. In this reading, the Scherzo becomes an interpolated movement that is strongly integrated and, indeed, functionalised within the overarching sonata form's subordinate-theme group. It transforms the initial, hesitant statement of the third theme in D minor into the grand D major restatement in bars 338–61 and projects its surface characteristics onto what begins as a closing group but soon becomes a transition to the development (bars 362–92).

In the dimension of the overarching sonata form, bars 1–152 (theme 1, theme 2 and the varied return of theme 1, ending with a perfect authentic cadence in the tonic) constitute a ternary form that functions as a main-theme group balancing the lengthy subordinate-theme group. That the middle of the main-theme group bears the label 'theme 2' may be explained by its function in the first movement of the sonata cycle. For it may not be too much of a stretch to claim that the juxtaposition of two starkly contrasting themes, the superficially developmental characteristics of the later portions of part B and the stereotypical retransition preceding the return of part A suggest something of a small-scale sonata-form first movement. In the context of the piece as a whole – that is to say, being followed by three further immediately recognisable movements of a sonata cycle – they certainly *can* be heard as such.

Strauss's thematic labels in the large 'Finale' are equally misleading. It is not difficult to see how this unit can be heard as both a finale and a recapitulation: its formal course and stylistic register differ from the exposition, but at the same time it recapitulates all of its themes (in a more-or-less transformed shape, but in the original key). This recapitulation is, however, less straightforward than it may initially seem. Theme 1 of the double fugue is not a transformation of theme 1 in the exposition, but of theme 3 in the key of theme 1 (or at least its head; the rest is new). Only much later does motivic material from the exposition's theme 1 start to make itself heard.

After

While Strauss, Liszt and the composers between them use two-dimensional sonata form to symphonise the tone poem (or other genres), Schoenberg does exactly the opposite. In his Chamber Symphony, two-dimensional sonata form is what enables the highly un-symphonic compression of the multi-movement plan, a compression that parallels the piece's reduced instrumentation. If the Chamber Symphony can be said to solve the problem of symphonic form, its cost is a significant loss in monumentality and, thus, symphonicity. Therefore, its form is not so much (or not only) an endpoint in the sense of a culmination of nineteenth-century symphonic form, but rather (or also) a reaction against the genre's excesses.

After Schoenberg's Chamber Symphony, two-dimensional sonata form ceased to be the vehicle of the musical avant-garde it had been since the 1850s. In the decades following 1906, its use often constitutes a deliberately conservative gesture. In the few pieces in which it is used otherwise, formal organisation becomes increasingly free, moving away from both sonata form and sonata cycle. Franz Schreker's Chamber Symphony of 1917, for instance, has less in common with Schoenberg's eponymous Op. 9 than its title suggests, treating the combination of multi- and single-movement plans in a considerably less rigorous way. It consists of a lengthy introduction and a sonata form, within which the interior movements of a sonata cycle have been interpolated. More specifically, the (relatively brief) development of the overarching sonata form is preceded by a slow movement and followed by a scherzo. Surprisingly, the slow movement reappears in its entirety between the recapitulation and the coda of the overarching form. Traces of a first movement and a finale, moreover, are lacking.

A similar tendency towards looser large-scale formal organisation can be observed in the First Symphony, Op. 7 (1921) by Ernst Krenek (a student of Schreker). In spite of the proliferation of contrasting sections – some clearly reminiscent of movements from a sonata cycle or sections from a sonata form, others less so – Krenek's Symphony retains a strong sense of overarching formal design, especially through the recapitulation of the opening section right before the coda. The overarching form, however, is not a sonata form, nor can the multi-movement pattern be considered a sonata cycle.[9]

Starkly contrasting with Schreker's and Krenek's handling of two-dimensional form is the Fourth Symphony (1932–3) of the Viennese composer Franz Schmidt. Schmidt's conception of two-dimensional sonata form is significantly more traditional. The first movement of the sonata cycle is identified with the exposition and development of the overarching sonata form (the development simultaneously functions as a recapitulation). The slow movement and the Scherzo are interpolated between the development and the recapitulation, which can be heard as a finale only because of the conspicuous presence of the preceding three movements of a sonata cycle. Schmidt's Symphony is remarkable for its symmetrical design. The middle section of the central slow movement begins with a melody that modulates from G minor to C-sharp minor and is thereupon repeated, now beginning in C-sharp minor and, consequentially, modulating back to G minor. From this middle section, symmetry expands over the entire Symphony. It comprises the introductory trumpet solo, the exposition, the development and the opening section of the slow movement on one side, and the reprise of the slow movement, the interpolated Scherzo, the recapitulation and the concluding trumpet solo on the other. The tritone relationship at the heart of this symmetrical plan is reflected at several other formal levels, such as the tonal organisation of the exposition (main-theme group in C, subordinate-theme group in F sharp) and the recapitulation (main-theme group in F, subordinate-theme group in B).

An important single-movement symphony that stands somewhat apart from the Germanic tradition is Jean Sibelius's Seventh Symphony (1924). This work's most striking characteristic is that its overarching form is slow and that, as a consequence, the different movements do not amount to an orthodox sonata cycle. In addition, neither in the overarching form nor in any of the movements of the sonata cycle does Sibelius make use of standard *Formenlehre* forms. After a slow introduction (bars 1–22), what follows seems to be an exposition that culminates in the statement of the grand trombone theme in C major in bar 60. This theme, along with its two later appearances, first in C minor (bars 222–41), then back in C major (bars 476–507), structures the overarching form. The three statements of the trombone theme provide a framework within which the other sections and interpolated movements appear in an arch-like design (see Table 11.4). The first statement is followed by a development and a scherzo-like interpolated movement, the second statement by another interpolated movement and a unit that forms a pendant to the first development. After the trombone theme's climactic last statement,

Table 11.4 *Sibelius, Symphony No. 7*

Introduction (bars 1–22)	Exposition ⇒ (bars 23–59)	Trombone theme + continuation C major (bars 60–92)	Development (bars 93–155)	Interpolation (bars 156–207)	Dominant preparation (bars 208–21)	Trombone theme + continuation C minor (bars 222–41)	Interpolation (bars 242–408)	[bars 409–48]	Dominant preparation (bars 449–75)	Trombone theme + continuation C major (bars 476–507)	Coda (bars 508–25)

Table 11.5 *Samuel Barber, Symphony No. 1*

Overarching sonata form		Sonata cycle	
EXPOSITION (bars 1–75)		[FIRST MOVEMENT]	
Theme 1 (bars 1–27)	e		
Theme 2 (bars 28–60)	b		
Theme 3 (bars 61–76)	b		
DEVELOPMENT (bars 77–136)			
RECAPITULATION (bars 137–599)		SCHERZO (bars 137–437)	
Theme 1 (bars 137–437)		A (bars 137–229)	B flat
		B (bars 230–94)	
		A' (bars 295–340)	b
		coda (bars 341–437)	
Theme 2 (bars 438–518)		SLOW MOVEMENT (438–518)	
		A (bars 438–65)	F sharp
		B (bars 466–85)	
		A' (bars 486–518)	F
Theme 3 (bars 519–99)		FINALE (bars 519–99)	E
CODA (bars 600–20)			

the Symphony concludes with a coda that recalls the introduction. Boundaries between different sections in Sibelius's Seventh are often remarkably fluid, so that reading a symphonic pattern into it may seem tendentious. It is, however, a reading that the composer himself purposely seemed to invite. After the work had been premiered as 'Fantasia sinfonica', Sibelius not only decided to rename it to 'Symphony No. 7', but also added the (conspicuously German) subtitle 'In einem Satze'.

An echo of Sibelius's Seventh resounds in Samuel Barber's First Symphony (1936), which is similarly subtitled 'In One Movement'. Although there are strong indications that Barber's Symphony was intended as a response to Sibelius's, his single-movement design remains significantly closer to Central-European models. As shown in Table 11.5, it begins with a three-theme exposition. The development that follows gives way not to a recapitulation, but to the three further movements of a sonata cycle: a Scherzo, a slow movement and a Finale. Both interior movements are ternary forms, and their main thematic material is derived from the exposition's main and subordinate themes respectively. At the same time, both movements conspicuously avoid tonal closure, bringing a recapitulation in a key a half step away from their expositions. Each of the interior movements culminates in a grand restatement of the motto-like opening of the main theme. The Finale is a passacaglia on a bass derived from the opening of the main theme that appears thirteen times in total. In the initial variations, thematic material appearing over the bass is either new or else derived from the exposition's third theme (now transposed to the tonic).

The way in which Barber integrates form and cycle is unique: all movements from the Scherzo onwards are identified with the recapitulation of the overarching sonata form. A thematic recapitulation is thus spread out over the three movements in the sense that thematic material from the exposition reappears in the original order as the main thematic content of each movement. From the Finale onwards, this relatively abstract recapitulatory layer is combined with the increasing prominence of the main theme's head motive at pitch, first as a bass for the passacaglia, then, especially from variation eight onwards, saturating the entire texture. At the climax of the Finale (variations eleven and twelve), the head of the main theme is contrapuntally combined with theme three from the exposition.

Barber's First Symphony might very well be the last important two-dimensional sonata form in the orchestral repertoire. In it, this extraordinary principle of formal organization comes full circle. Its function for Barber is the same as for any composer of the Germanic musical avant-garde of the late nineteenth and early twentieth centuries: it guarantees a maximal degree of cyclic integration between the different movements of his Symphony. More than any other composition discussed in this chapter, however, Barber's Symphony attests to two-dimensional sonata form's inherent symphonicity. This may seem surprising, given Barber's chronological and geographical distance from the heyday of two-dimensional sonata form several decades earlier and on another continent. It is, however, exactly because he was working in so different a context that Barber could, as it were, quote two-dimensional sonata form as a token of the nineteenth-century symphonic style that he was trying to emulate. In doing so, he succeeded in what for composers of the generations of Liszt, Strauss and Schoenberg seemed impossible: to write a symphony in two-dimensional sonata form that is truly symphonic.

Notes

1 'Die Kammersinfonie zieht Konsequenzen aus dem sinfonischen Formproblem des 19. Jahrhunderts wie es Schönberg aus seinem Traditionsverständnis heraus begriff, und erklärte es durch sich für erledigt . . . [A]nders also als in den übrigen Schichten der Komposition [harmony, thematic organisation, polyphony, instrumentation] ist hier die Kammersinfonie ein Endpunkt.' See Reinhold Brinkmann, 'Die gepreßte Sinfonie. Zum geschichtlichen Gehalt von Schönbergs Opus 9', in Otto Kolleritsch, ed., *Gustav Mahler. Sinfonie und Wirklichkeit, Studien zur Wertungsforschung*, 9 (Graz, 1977), 133–56 , this quotation 142.

2 For a fuller introduction to the theory of two-dimensional sonata form as well as an analytical discussion of a number of individual works, the reader is referred to the author's *Two-Dimensional Sonata Form: Form and Cycle in Single-Movement Instrumental Works by Liszt, Strauss, Schoenberg, and Zemlinsky* (Leuven, 2009).

3 William S. Newman, *The Sonata since Beethoven* (Chapel Hill, 1969), 134 and 375–7. Newman writes that Liszt's Sonata in B minor 'is not a simple "sonata form" but a double-function form, because its several components also serve as the (unseparated) movements of the complete cycle' (p. 134).

4 Carl Dahlhaus, 'Liszt, Schönberg und die große Form. Das Prinzip der Einsätzigkeit in der Mehrsätzigkeit', *Die Musikforschung*, 41 (1988), 202–13.

5 Needless to say, this doesn't always happen. But modifications to the

course of the recapitulation in sonata forms from the eighteenth and early nineteenth centuries, too, can be understood as attempts to avoid an extreme parallelism with the exposition.

6 Dahlhaus, 'Liszts Idee des Symphonischen', in *Klassische und romantische Musikästhetik* (Laaber, 1988), 392–401.

7 Dahlhaus, 'Liszts Bergsymphonie und die Idee der Symphonischen Dichtung', in Dagmar Droysen, ed., *Jahrbuch des Staatlichen Instituts für Musikforschung*

Preußischer Kulturbesitz 1975 (Berlin, 1976), 96–130, this quotation 99.

8 Walter Werbeck, 'Richard Strauss's Tone Poems', in Mark-Daniel Schmid, ed., *The Richard Strauss Companion* (Westport, 2003), 103–44, this quotation 132.

9 Other notable single-movement German symphonies from the 1920s include Kurt Weill's First Symphony (1921), Max Butting's Chamber Symphony Op. 25 (1923) and the Symphony by Paul Dessau (1926).

12 *Symphony/antiphony*: formal strategies in the twentieth-century symphony

DANIEL M. GRIMLEY

To a greater extent than almost any other musical genre, symphonies are concerned explicitly with the musical representation of time and space. A simple etymology of the word points towards this preoccupation – the idea of 'sounding together' implies both the projection of sounds in/through space and the simultaneity of their presentation. Beyond a work's linear unfolding through time in performance, it is this sense of bringing things together which helps to shape and colour the symphony's particular structural and expressive tensions. Yet the single defining feature of the twentieth-century symphony is the extent to which these categories of time and space have become increasingly contested and contingent. This sense of the symphony's provisional status is partly an issue of ideology – the symphony is anything but a neutral genre, and it carries into the twentieth century perhaps the greatest ideological baggage of any large-scale musical form. Associations of heroic masculine endeavour, musical tautness and abstraction, and the myth of the 'profound logic' which Sibelius supposedly promulgated in his apocryphal conversation with Mahler have remained stubbornly pervasive a century later,[1] even though such models of symphonic expression and design have been the subject, for many critics and composers, of intense resistance and critique. For some, the twentieth-century symphony has simply *run out* of time and space – as an outmoded and historically anachronistic art form, the unwanted vestige of a hierarchic and bourgeois concert culture, as an unaffordable luxury in an age of economic hardship, or as a musical institution whose nineteenth-century associations of community, unity and synthesis can seem unrealistically idealistic and unattainable.[2] For others, the symphony has served as a means for cultural-political expansion – a powerful history can be traced of the musical geography of the twentieth-century symphony, which locates the genre at the heart of wider debates correlating notions of time and space with freedom of expression and self-determination.[3] Simply 'sounding together' has not always been an easy or politically straightforward task, and the idea of community that the symphony has often seemed to elevate can swiftly become more exclusive than inclusive. In that sense, as Theodor W. Adorno perceived, the symphony potentially projects forwards its own sense of negative teleology, of a forceful gathering together that is as much concerned with the negation of time and space – and the implied collapse of a liberal enlightenment world view – as with the democratic celebration of diversity and brotherhood.[4]

But this shifting sense of symphonic time and space also underlines a broader philosophical shift in which music has played a component part. In his rich and provocative history of early twentieth-century modernism, *The Culture of Time and Space, 1880–1918*, Stephen Kern dwells on the impact that technological innovations in mass media and communication had upon the understanding and perception of passing time and spatial relationships.[5] Such essentially scientific projects had enormous implications for the performance and dissemination of music. It would be impossible, for instance, to conceive of a history of the twentieth-century symphony that did not at least acknowledge the fundamental importance of radio, or gramophone recording, for the development of the genre,[6] and a significant later strand for the elaboration of symphonic music can be traced through the Hollywood film score. Yet perhaps the true significance of these developments, as Kern notes, lies in the way in which they changed the nature of time and space themselves. After the advent of radio broadcasting, time and space were no longer understood as fixed, discrete entities – as transcendental Kantian categories that lay beyond the boundaries of individual or collective intervention – but rather emerged as more complex, fluid domains. Henri Bergson, for instance, wrote in his seminal text *Matter and Memory* (1896) about the permeability of memory and perception, and argued that the experience of time was properly a process of active (but unconscious) recollection that collapsed past, present and future into a single, multi-layered flux, an idea that appealed to novelists such as Marcel Proust and James Joyce, whose work abandoned linear narrative structure in favour of a more fractured, fragmentary and self-reflective commentary. The twentieth-century symphony often becomes novelistic – or cinematic – in precisely that sense. The collective utterance whose unity and linear authority is upheld as the apotheosis of the nineteenth-century work is here replaced by a multi-vocality, a large-scale expressive and structural counterpoint of different temporalities and musical spaces, the diversity of which becomes, for Adorno's Mahler, a mirror of the modern world.

The title of this chapter, borrowed from one of the works discussed below, refers to this modernist twentieth-century symphonic context. 'Symphony/antiphony' is a deliberately provocative starting point. It can be read as an antagonistic opposition, as a form of dialogue (question and answer), or as an unstable synergy of multiple voices or musical characters. It supports the idea that the twentieth-century symphony is somehow in terminal decline (a belief that was arguably more prevalent at the start of the century than at its conclusion), and illuminates the way in which, paradoxically, the symphony has continued to regenerate itself through resistance and artistic renewal. But it also provides an insight into the formal strategies that these works adopt, particularly the way in which they negotiate shifting definitions of symphonic space and time. Though the survey is necessarily narrow and omits important streams of symphonic composition purely for reasons of economy, it examines a number of paradigmatic approaches to the problems of rearticulating symphonic time and space. For Sibelius, for example, time and space are emergent properties. His works evoke the feeling of an immeasurably distant past, out of which music seemingly evolves in a constant process of transformation and growth. The primary structural tension in Sibelius's symphonies is created by the disjunction between this growth and the music's strongly goal-directed tendency, which often involves the attainment of a definitive moment of harmonic arrival as an end-in-itself or vanishing point. For Stravinsky, in contrast, time and space in the *Symphony of Psalms* are frozen in a ritualistic theatre that, as Richard Taruskin has noted, points both to Stravinsky's inherited 'Russian traditions' and to the modernist Parisian ideas of objectivity, alienation and distance with which the composer later sought to associate himself.[7] Luciano Berio's *Sinfonia* is similarly ritualistic, but his music arguably comes closest to the Bergsonian model of perception as a complex melding of past, present and future in a single flux or stream of consciousness. It is no coincidence that James Joyce and Samuel Beckett are amongst Berio's literary points of correspondence. Elliott Carter's *Symphony of Three Orchestras* is a powerfully intense evocation of a new musical world – both literally and figuratively, its gestures are motivated by the sense of an American soundscape, one which positively seeks to move away from European legacies and traditions, even while, characteristically, the work reveals its own inner fears and anxieties. The spiralling musical fantasies of Carter's work inspire thoughts of obliteration as much as liberation or escape. The concluding work, Danish composer Pelle Gudmundsen-Holmgreen's *Symphony, Antiphony*, is a forceful deconstruction of the genre, a knowing and allusive game with the shattered fragments and shards of the symphonic tradition refracted through a late twentieth-century critical lens. It offers no summative vision – as the title suggests, the work stubbornly insists that there are two sides to every symphonic story. But, at the very least, Gudmundsen-Holmgreen's work is a powerful testimony to the continued creative energy of the genre, and a vivid affirmation of the symphony as progressive and cutting-edge.

Sibelius: Symphony No. 4

Each of the works considered below challenges the temptation to regard the symphony as a conservative or retrospective form. This is especially true of Sibelius's Fourth Symphony (1909–11). Commentators widely agree that the work is the most 'difficult' and outwardly modernist of Sibelius's symphonies. The Fourth is traditionally seen as a stylistic turning point, away from the expansive late-Romantic panorama of the first two symphonies and the crisp *Junge Klassizität* of the Third, towards a more austere, modernist mode of utterance. But the work also readily reveals Sibelius's concern with fundamental elements of symphonic thought and design: particularly with notions of monumentality (here expressed in remarkably telegrammatic form); development (energetically foregrounded throughout and often privileged over explicit thematic statement or exposition); and the tension between the idea of the symphony as a large-scale public statement and as an inward personal confession. The first movement (Tempo molto moderato, quasi adagio) is exemplary in its concern with the implications of modal mixture for the articulation of large-scale structure. The formal outline of the movement has prompted considerable scholarly debate. Elliott Antokoletz, for example, identifies a 'Sonata Allegro' design, aspects of which correspond with the thematic elements of a rounded binary structure (Fig. 12.1).[8]

As Antolkoletz readily acknowledges, a number of anomalies immediately arise, which challenge this 'Sonata Allegro' reading. The proportions of the individual sections in the plan are highly asymmetrical – there is a strong sense of telescoping towards the final paragraph, so that the feeling of balanced symmetry characteristic of normative rounded binary forms is replaced by an urgent sense of goal direction, only to dissipate and atomise in the very final bars. Furthermore, the recapitulation at bar 87 is highly irregular. Even by early twentieth-century standards of formal syntax, the sense of return is extremely attenuated, and the re-entry of previous material is carefully dovetailed so that the precise moment of reprise is almost impossible to determine. Even the identification of first and second subject

Figure 12.1 Sibelius, Symphony No. 4, I, formal reading (after Antokoletz, 'The Musical Language of the Fourth Symphony')

Exposition, bars 1–53
       Theme 1, bars 1–31
          (Transition, bars 24–9)
       Theme 2, bars 31–40
       Coda, bars 41–53
Development, bars 54–88
Recapitulation, bars 87–114
       Coda, bars 97–114

groups in Antokoletz's chart becomes problematic – the first part of the exposition, for example, is characterised by a rich tapestry of overlapping motivic fragments, none of which emerge sufficiently prominently to gain the status of a thematic sentence in the Schoenbergian sense. And finally, the tonality remains highly unstable throughout – the only genuine sense of harmonic arrival is achieved in the two coda sections, at bars 41 and 97, which provide the strongest point of formal return in the whole movement. In contrast, the opening of the exposition and development are tonally ambiguous – sustained examples of what Schoenberg termed wandering (or 'vagrant') harmony where the music barely suggests any fixed point of tonal orientation. An alternative formal reading of the first movement has therefore been suggested by commentators such as Tim Howell and Veijo Murtomäki,[9] which breaks the music down into two parallel strophes: the first in bars 1–53, ending with a large-scale cadence on F♯; and the second in bars 54–114, closing with a cadence on A. This simpler binary model hears both strophes as goal-directed, progressing from a state of harmonic and textural instability towards provisional moments of cadential articulation, which in turn become the primary points of structural focus.

Local details support this interpretation of the movement's design. The opening gesture is a gloomy textural and harmonic birth. Sibelius's evocative low scoring (cellos, basses, bassoons) creates a dark sonic foundation, resonant with upper harmonic partials, from which the full orchestral timbre slowly emerges and brightens. The first four bars articulate the movement's principal motivic idea ((1̂-2̂-3̂-♯4̂), (0 2 4 6) or pitch class set [4–21]), a harmonically ambiguous device that suggests both C Lydian (with emphasis on the sharpened fourth degree of the scale, F♯) and the first four notes of the whole-tone scale (collection I) (see Example 12.1).

This process of textural and timbral growth is strengthened by the entry of the solo cello (as bardic orator, perhaps?) in bar 6, harmonically suggesting an unstable A melodic minor/dorian collection – the slow, oscillating bass ostinato is now heard as ♯6̂-5̂, effectively underpinning the cello cantilena with a dominant pedal. The gradual entry of the full

Example 12.1 Sibelius, Symphony No. 4, I, bars 1–4.

Example 12.2 Sibelius, Symphony No. 4, I, bars 7–21.

string group, in a sonorous 'chorus' effect, begins to fill out this modal A minor collection, but the viola's D♭ in bar 17 is a 'blue' note, and triggers a local octatonic/E-flat minor inflection that begins to cloud the music's earlier A orientation. The descending steps in the bass in bars 24–5 finally suggest that the movement is beginning to approach its first point of cadential arrival – on C Lydian, resolving the ambiguity of the opening motto. At the last second, however, the gesture is undermined by the chromatic intrusion of C♯, an enharmonic transformation of the viola's D♭ from bar 17. This pitch now acts as a decisive harmonic pivot, turning the music's tonal allegiance away from A (see Example 12.2).

The entry of the brass chorale in bars 29–39 reinforces this shift of harmonic allegiance with a new timbral colour, dynamic contour and rhythmic profile. The initial (0 2 4 6) motive returns in transposed form: [A-B-D♯-C♯], bars 31–2, and the cadence on F♯, with its strong plagal colouring, is an obvious tonicisation of this pitch from the opening page. The coda, bars 41–53, is an echo or afterglow of this moment of harmonic arrival. Even here, however, the music's radiant F-sharp major is clouded by the presence of the sharpened fourth degree (B♯), an enharmonic reference to the C♮ pole of the opening bars.

The insistence of this tritone opposition (C♮-F♯) initiates and underpins the development. The passage begins with complete textual and thematic liquidation, music reduced to spare single lines, motivic fragments and harmonic obscurity in an extreme reinterpretation of classical developmental technique. From this sense of a blank musical void, the movement begins to replay the process of growth from the opening paragraph. The return of the solo cello at bar 57 is a pointed reference to its earlier bardic role in bar 6. The tonal organisation of the passage, soon picked up by the upper strings, is a complex mix of octatonic and whole-tone collections: the music becomes increasingly whole-tone as it approaches its registral ceiling around bar 70. Although this whole-tone bias clouds any sense of tonal centricity, it does succeed in recalling the principal motive in its original form – initially as part of the dusky string figuration in bar 72, and then, in augmentation, in the flute and clarinet. The return of the principal motive marks the start of a gradual process of textual accumulation, reinforced by attempts to assert A as a definitive tonal goal (for example, the timpani entry in bar 77). This sense of imminent tonal arrival is motivated primarily by a rising chromatic bass movement – from the F♯ in bar 76 (a reference, of course, to the end of the exposition space), through G♮ in bar 82 and A♭ in bar 85. The final attainment of A♮ in the bass coincides with the restatement (for the first time) of the principal motive at its original pitch level (C-D-F♯-E; see Example 12.3).

The key difference from the opening, however, is that on this occasion the motive has been harmonically contextualised so that it now establishes A unequivocally as the movement's tonal destination. With this task achieved, the return of the brass chorale in bar 96 serves as a solemn benediction, a hymn-like affirmation of A major's tonic status. But even here, elements of instability remain. As the music fades into silence, the intrusion of C♮s in bar 110 recalls earlier moments of chromatic

Example 12.3 Sibelius, Symphony No. 4, I, bars 95–6.

Example 12.4 Sibelius, Symphony No. 4, II, opening.

interruption (ironically, C♮ was precisely the note withheld at a previous point of disjunction in bar 27). The movement briefly unfolds a whole-tone collection once again (bars 110–11; [C♮-D-E-F♯-B♭]), before pointedly resolving the B♭s down to A♮. Yet closure is once again evaded: the following movement begins by reinterpreting the whole-tone set of the preceding bars as a chromatically altered V^7/F, and the solo oboe takes up the first movement's closing a♮^{2}, transforming a closing cadential gesture into the start of a new melodic curve (see Example 12.4).

The first movement of Sibelius's Fourth adumbrates a number of formal strategies and concerns that preoccupy much of his later music. The first is the thorough reconfiguring of received *Formenlehre* categories: though the movement suggests elements of a rounded binary form or two-part structure, it is in no sense a normative 'sonata allegro'. Second, the Tempo molto moderato exemplifies the characteristically Sibelian process of what James Hepokoski calls the 'interrelationship and fusion of movements':[10] the elision of the final bars means that the Scherzo becomes a giant pendant to the first movement, amplifying, elaborating and subsequently condensing its tonal drama. Third, the movement's manipulation of time and space becomes paradigmatic for later symphonic designs. As

Edward Laufer has suggested in his Schenkerian reading, the Tempo molto moderato is a symbolic journey, 'a struggle to victory, from darkness to light, from nothingness to life, or from turmoil to serenity (somehow all the same poetic idea)';[11] yet it is also a mythic transformation, from the ambiguity of the opening page to the crystallisation of the closing bars. The music articulates its own process of coming-into-being, the sounding manifestation of a creative will through a painful process of musical birth that unfolds a bleak new symphonic soundscape.

Stravinsky: *Symphony of Psalms*

As James Hepokoski has compellingly demonstrated, similar issues of growth, fusion and teleology motivate the formal design of Sibelius's Fifth Symphony (1914–15; rev. 1916 and 1919). Here, the opening bars of the first movement articulate a 'misfired' cadence in E flat, whose chromatic slippage generates the more complex modulatory scheme of the music that follows. Much of the remainder of the Symphony is dedicated to reassembling the intervallic and functional harmonic components of this initial cadential gambit, crystallising, as Hepokoski shows, in the swinging bell-like 'swan hymn' in the Finale. The stratified polymetric structure of the swan hymn texture is remarkable: the music unfolds in several different temporal and registral layers through elaboration of the opening gesture's cadential fourths and fifths (see Example 12.5).

A remarkably similar texture unfolds in the final pages of Stravinsky's *Symphony of Psalms* (1928–30). Stravinsky had already radically recalibrated the idea of symphonic structure (after an early student exercise, the

Example 12.5 Sibelius, Symphony No. 5, IV, 'swan hymn'.

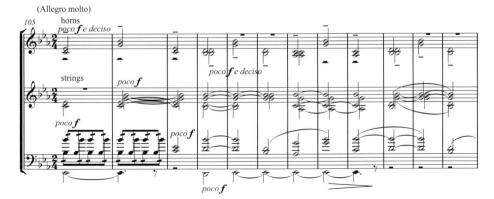

Symphony in E flat), in his *Symphonies of Wind Instruments* (1918–20). Aspects of the *Symphonies of Wind Instruments* superficially resemble the musical language of the opening movement of Sibelius's Fourth: the tendency to break the ensemble down into craggy instrumental groups; a fondness for bell-like attacks in the woodwind and brass; and the block-like design of the work. Yet the two works are strikingly different in more obvious ways. The *Symphonies of Wind Instruments* resists any sense of organic growth or evolution in favour of what Alexander Rehding has termed its 'logic of discontinuity': the abrupt juxtaposition of contrasting statements of musical material that do not appear to evolve or transform, but simply rotate through rhythmic or pitch cycles mechanically even as they converge on C as tonal centre in the final pages.[12] The *Symphony of Psalms* obviously builds on the earlier precedent of the *Symphonies of Wind Instruments* in its preference for sharp juxtapositions, block form and rapt, ritualistic circularity. In part, these qualities are demanded by the work's text, taken from Psalms 38 (verses 13 and 14), 39 (verses 2, 3 and 4) and 150 (complete): the *Symphony* is correspondingly divided into three movements, arranged in an ascending hierarchical order. The first movement is an invocation, a prayer of supplication ('Exaudi orationem meam, Domine': 'Hear my prayer, O Lord'); the second movement is a giant double fugue, an intercession for forgiveness and salvation that results in a 'new song' ('Et immisit in os meum canticum novum': 'And he hath put a new song into our mouth'); the third movement is a hymn of praise ('Laudate Dominum': 'Praise the Lord'), whose closing pages intone the 'new song' born in the second movement. The *Symphony* is thus a glowing affirmation of faith, conceived on a monumental, public scale. It embraces aspects of its earlier nineteenth-century inheritance (the symphony as a large-scale vehicle for the celebration of community) and also attempts to ground the genre in an earlier tradition (music as the shared ritualistic expression of public and private religious belief).[13]

These tensions, between different ideas of symphonic time and space, are reflected in aspects of the music's formal strategy. Much has been written, notably by Pieter van den Toorn, of the first movement's inter-action between different modal collections: predominantly octatonic, but also diatonic (E♭ and C as a binary 'tonic pair'), Gregorian (E Phrygian), and chromatic.[14] The basic opposition of modal materials is adumbrated in the opening bars. The famous 'Psalms' chord, with its characteristic registral scoring (E minor with doubled third (G), and no fifth degree), serves a punctuating role throughout, abruptly closing and initiating phrases as though resetting the clock, yet also prefiguring the movement's final cadence (on G) and establishing the pattern of third relations which predominates throughout. The first appearance of the chord is followed immediately by two arpeggiated dominant seventh chords ($B\flat^7$ and G^7) drawn from octatonic collection 1, whose diatonic chords of resolution (E flat and C respectively) anticipate the tonal frames of the second movement and Finale. For Wilfrid Mellers, these two tonal centres are more important for their associative symbolic character than for their structural function: 'the key of E♭ – whose humanistic associations extend from the compassion of Bach and Mozart to the heroism and power of Beethoven – emerges as Man's key, while C, the 'white note' key in the major and E♭'s relative in the minor, becomes God's key'; the first movement's (Phrygian) E minor, in contrast, becomes the 'key of prayer and intercession'.[15] Such readings are of course problematic – not least for the ways they threaten to assimilate Stravinsky within an Austro-German humanist tradition to which he was only tangentially related. Yet it is interesting to speculate on the presence of similar key associations in other twentieth-century symphonies: the C major of Sibelius's Seventh (1924), for example, is no less concerned with notions of the divine (D major often serves a similar purpose for Vaughan Williams, whereas D major means something very different at the end of Shostakovich's Fifth Symphony). And the appearance of diatonic writing in twentieth-century symphonic music more widely often assumes a similarly symbolic role: keys evoked more for their expressive affect than any attempt to reinvoke anachronistic notions of diatonic functionality.

The opening bars of the first movement of the *Symphony of Psalms* are also paradigmatic in their rhythmic and metrical organisation. The vertical, punctuating syntactic character of the 'Psalms' chord is spliced with the circular additive tendencies of the following bars: the division of the octatonic arpeggiation into sub-blocks of 1+2, 1+1 in bars 2–3. The effect of such cross-cutting is to create a basic tension between different forms of metrical structure: the strong vertical downbeat of the 'Psalms' chord; and the assymetrical, non-periodic grouping of the arpeggiations. Rather than being synthesised into an organic unity (the illusion of a single, linear vector), rhythmic time is broken into its basic dimensions. Similar processes of rhythmic organisation operate elsewhere in the movement. For instance, the augmentation at Fig. 4 (semiquavers becoming quavers) is reversed at Fig. 6. But the complex layering of metrical streams at Fig. 5 (3/2 in the chorus and bassoons versus 8+10+12/4 in the upper woodwind) gives way to a more static improvisatory feel at Fig. 6 (groups of 8+12+24 semiquavers in the oboe). The local climax of this sequence is the neo-Handelian passage at Fig. 9, whose *Zadok*-like combination of ostinato patterns in simultaneous semiquaver and quaver figuration generates a sense of intense surface activity while remaining metrically static and statuesque. The return of this passage at Fig. 12 (at the words 'Remitte mihi', 'Spare me'), presages the movement's short coda and the collision between octatonic and phrygian collections which results in the music's diatonic cadential descent towards G.

The Finale relies upon similar tensions and cross-cuttings, though on a larger and more expansive scale. By comparison with the first movement of Sibelius's Fourth Symphony, the basic formal structure of the Finale is easy to read: a rounded binary main section based on C (labelled simply Tempo minim=80, dominated by its motto-like quaver figure, which Stravinsky associated with the repeated phrase 'Laudate Dominum' and later, misleadingly, claimed was one of the earliest ideas for the work),[16] followed by an extended postlude (for which Mellers invoked Henry Vaughan's 'chime and symphony of nature')[17] in E flat, framed by an introduction and coda that grounds the whole movement in C. The third-based structure of Mellers's tonal pairing is evident throughout: the introduction, for example, superimposes the two centres (the 'Alleluia' before Fig. 1), and dwells on the false-relation E♮/E♭ repeatedly, the choir intoning their quiet hymn of praise in E flat while the orchestra insists on a bell-like ostinato in C (see Example 12.6).

The effect does not suggest dynamic polarisation so much as the insistent rocking between two complementary halves of the same compound harmonic unit. The closing word, 'Dominum', comes to rest on C,

Example 12.6 Stravinsky, *Symphony of Psalms*, III, introduction. © Copyright 1931 by Hawkes and Son (London) Ltd. Revised version: © Copyright 1948 by Hawkes and Son (London) Ltd. Reproduced by permission of Boosey and Hawkes Music Publishers Ltd.

but the presence of B♭ in the chord before Fig. 3 acts both to destabilise the sense of closure, pushing the music forwards into the start of the faster main section, and also serves as a chromatic residue of the earlier E flat-C major mix. Significantly, in the final cadence at the end of the movement, this element of harmonic doubt is removed.

In her study of pages from the sketches for the Finale, Gretchen Horlacher has shown how Stravinsky began the fast main section of the movement by drafting the stratified ostinato texture at Fig. 3 in full, and then cutting and pasting its component rhythmic layers to disrupt its continuity and create a distinctive metrical counterpoint – the bass riff in 3/4 against the movement's prevailing 4/4 (a pattern prepared, in fact, by the orchestral ostinato at Fig. 2). Much of the tonal drama in the main section is generated not only by modal interaction but also by the play of sharp- versus flat-side harmonic tendencies: the bright, diatonic effect of the C-based music at the start intensified by its shift towards E at Fig. 5, and then clouded by the cadence before Fig. 6 (principally octatonic collection II). E flat reasserts itself, both at the beginning of the middle section (Fig. 13) and at Fig. 22, where the closing hymn of praise begins. This is the passage that resembles the Finale of Sibelius's Fifth Symphony: the swinging fifth steps in the bass and polymetrical layering (the bass riff now in four versus the triple-metre choral parts) create a similar suspension of clock time in favour of an ecstatic sense of stillness and infinitude (see Example 12.7).

For Taruskin, such textures exemplify Stravinsky's tendency towards 'hypostatization': the coexistence of independent rhythmic strata in a state of perpetual permutation and recycling.[18] The two passages also serve parallel structural functions, as goals of their respective symphonic journeys: they represent the moment at which symphonic time and space seemingly dissolve and collapse inwards, for Stravinsky not so much in synchronicity but rather in a more enigmatic simultaneity.

Berio: *Sinfonia*

Although they share a similar cyclic view of the Symphony, Sibelius and Stravinsky offer very different metaphors of musical birth, transformation, death and renewal. For Sibelius, the process of musical birth is tense and agonistic – the music seemingly evolves organically but is constantly threatened by its own tendency towards collapse and disintegration; the final bars of both Fourth and Fifth symphonies offer little sustained sense of resolution, only provisional points of rest. The closing bars of Stravinsky's *Symphony* are more affirmative, perhaps, though they retain

Example 12.7 Stravinsky, *Symphony of Psalms*, hymn of praise, opening. © Copyright 1931 by Hawkes and Son (London) Ltd. Revised version: © Copyright 1948 by Hawkes and Son (London) Ltd. Reproduced by permission of Boosey and Hawkes Music Publishers Ltd.

their sense of ritualistic anonymity and disembodiment: in the closing bars of the *Symphony of Psalms*, the grand nineteenth-century idea of symphonic apotheosis becomes radically hollowed out. The life-cycle of Luciano Berio's *Sinfonia* (1967–8) is similarly ambivalent: the work unfolds a gradual growth process that repeatedly ends in death and dissolution. The *Sinfonia*'s musical and textual material is dominated by recurrent symbolic imagery of water, fire, violence and immersion: the image of a cataclysmic drowning is represented several times throughout the work, both through the process of chromatic saturation that floods the outer movements, and in the explicit reference to the drowning scene from Alban Berg's *Wozzeck* that forms the apex of the central movement. Famously a musical deconstruction of the Scherzo from Mahler's Second Symphony, the third movement casts a critical eye on the idea of resurrection (borrowed from the subtitle of Mahler's work). 'Rebirth' here may refer to the *Sinfonia*'s rich intertextuality – references abound, not only to Mahler, but also to Berlioz, Richard Strauss, Debussy, Stravinsky, Hindemith, Boulez and Stockhausen, alongside scat singing and jazz. But it might also refer to the *Sinfonia*'s satisfyingly tight cyclic structure: the fifth (and final) movement replays (or 'resurrects') the first movement's transformation from vertical chordal sonorities to an energetic linear texture, and the closing bars recapture the first movement's own ending (a gesture that itself looks back to the work's opening). In that sense, the *Sinfonia* is explicitly circular: like James Joyce's high-modernist novel *Finnegans Wake*, a work which forms one of the *Sinfonia*'s central literary reference points, the music's end becomes its beginning. But this also points to one of the structuralist games that Berio plays throughout the piece: the idea that, in spite of the constant reference to music beyond the *Sinfonia*'s boundaries in the third movement, the work's own meaning remains continually deferred, collapsing back on itself in an endless cycle of reflexivity. So the idea of resurrection becomes inherently problematic, robbed of its original transcendental connotations. The *Sinfonia*'s seemingly infinite process of re-creation is intimately allied to its own cycle of self-destruction.

David Osmond-Smith has compellingly analysed the *Sinfonia*'s structure in detail, drawing attention to the design of the five individual movements, and carefully charting the work's progress through the intertextual montage of the third movement and beyond.[19] The first movement, for example, is designed around a simple process of symbolic exchange taken from Claude Lévi-Strauss's structuralist text, *Le cru et le cuit* ('The Raw and the Cooked'). Lévi-Strauss's text concerns two native South American accounts of the origin of fire and water, and the transformation from *eau celeste* (rain, precipitation) to *eau terrestre* (lakes,

Example 12.8 Berio, *Sinfonia*, I, opening.

oceans, rivers). This descent (from sky to earth) is mirrored in the move-ment's trajectory, which shifts from the gentle pulsating oscillation of two closely overlapping 'birth' chords (an eight-note 'stack' intervallically constructed from bass fifth and accumulated thirds, and a more resonant four-note set) towards an explosive linear tapestry of sound, the orgiastic celebration of a 'musique rituelle' (from Fig. I). The text itself is fragmen-ted and broken apart – the movement begins with open vowel sounds, suggesting a mythic pre-linguistic ululation, from which key symbolic words gradually emerge ('feu, eau, sang': 'fire, water, blood') as commen-tary upon the narration of lines from Lévi-Strauss's account. The alter-nation of the two opening chords (see Example 12.8) swiftly tends towards saturation – the complete chromatic set is heard as early as Fig. A, though it emerges more forcefully after Fig. I as the 'musique rituelle' gains momentum – the movement's final word is 'tué' ('killed'), a refer-ence to the violent crime that attends the creation of fire/water in Bororo myth, and a link to the following movement, a memorial to the assassi-nated Martin Luther King.

The second movement is similarly concerned with a process of growth, this time expanding a single melodic line outwards from a basic set (0 2 4 8) through four principal cycles plus an open, incomplete fifth cycle (starting at Fig. E): as Osmond-Smith notes, the melody rapidly begins to suggest two complementary whole-tone collections that generate a more complex harmonic field.[20] The sustaining of selected notes of the melody in the orchestra results in a resonant 'halo' of sound, so that the melody seemingly weaves its own polyphonic structure as it proceeds. The text similarly weaves itself together, from a series of the five open vowel sounds, until it reconstructs King's name: the key moment of coordination is the phrase 'O King' at the beginning of the final cycle at Fig. E. In the final bar, King's name is broken into syllables and distributed between the eight individual singers, dissolved once more so that the movement's growth cycle can begin again.

There is little comparable sense of growth in the third movement: rather, the music whirls around as though in a centrifuge, drawing in and ultimately consuming a range of references to dance movements from the nineteenth- and early twentieth-century orchestral repertoire. In this way, Berio collapses time and space into a single fluid whole: the 'Danse de la terre' from Stravinsky's *Le sacre du printemps* seemingly coexists alongside the 'Scène de bal' from Berlioz's *Symphonie fantastique* and Mahler's Scherzo. As Osmond-Smith observes, the Mahler model is already a synthetic intertextual one, containing references both to the trio from Beethoven's Violin Sonata Op. 96 and the closing bars of 'Das ist ein Flöten und Geigen' from Schumann's *Dichterliebe*. But Berio provides an additional layer of analysis and commentary via his literary text, drawn from Samuel Beckett's *The Unnameable*. Beckett's text provides ample opportunity for parody and self-reflection: the opening lines of the play ('Where now'; 'keep going'; 'nothing more restful than chamber music') at the movement's outset are swiftly echoed by more mocking phrases ('You are nothing but an academic exercise'; 'it seems there are only repeated sounds'; 'no time for chamber music') and negation ('hardly a resurrection', punning on Mahler's work). At times, Beckett's work stimulates new unexpected turns in the movement's course: the sudden interjection of the passage from the slow movement of Beethoven's 'Pastoral' Symphony at Fig. X (appropriately, given *Sinfonia*'s preoccupation with water imagery, the 'Scene by the Brook') is accompanied by the line 'It's late now, he shall never hear again the lowing cattle, the rush of the stream', a sequence that, in Beckett's drama, refers to an abattoir and which triggers one of the movement's most violent moments of submersion at Fig. Z.[21] But the Beckett text also provides an insightful commentary on Mahler's work: the Scherzo's generic status as a macabre 'dance of death' whose uncanny inability seemingly to reinvent and develop itself, as Lóránt Péteri has eloquently argued,[22] ultimately ends in nothingness and collapse. Berio's gloss, in retrospect, offers not simply playful postmodern irony, but a much darker reading of twentieth-century musical history, a nightmarish memory of musical events haunted by the ghosts of past and contemporary violence and conflict.

Carter: *Symphony of Three Orchestras*

A similarly energetic and apocalyptic vision of the century is offered by Elliott Carter's *Symphony of Three Orchestras*, a work composed in 1976 to commission from the New York Philharmonic but which is anything but a straightforward celebration or occasional piece. For both Berio and Carter, the idea of the 'symphony' is seemingly more ancient (savage and ritualistic) than its nineteenth-century heritage implies. Yet Carter's work, like Berio's, is also challengingly modern. One of the most immediate characteristics of the *Symphony of Three Orchestras* is its formidable complexity and density of musical detail – in that sense, the work represents one possible end-point of the process of maximalisation (understood here in terms of raw data rather than length or volume alone) identified by Taruskin as one of the defining qualities of the twentieth-century symphony. The work also perpetuates a more chamber-musical idiom: one of the *Symphony*'s more obviously modernist aspects is the way in which it breaks the ensemble down into smaller, more virtuosic assemblages, so that at times the work displays a markedly *concertante* character. Carter's *Symphony* also plays explicitly with notions of time and space. Unlike Berio's *Sinfonia*, Carter's work is performed without a break – the *Symphony* can be heard as a single, gradually descending musical arc, although its internal structural organisation is characteristically more complex. But the basic division of three separate orchestras implies a spatial broadening of the symphonic domain, as well as an intensification of its multiple temporal possibilities – the three orchestras rarely, if ever, coincide rhythmically, and Carter's polymetrical counterpoint ensures that the music constantly offers a shifting array of different temporal and spatial perspectives.

Yet despite this complexity, the *Symphony of Three Orchestras* is also one of Carter's most poetic and imaginative large-scale works. The work's initial impetus is a poem, entitled 'The Bridge', by the early twentieth-century American modernist Hart Crane. Opening with an aerial portrait of the New York skyline from Brooklyn Bridge, Crane's poem is a hymn to the city and the diverse sounds and machine noise of the metropolis – and simultaneously an anxious urban portrait of the new world. David Schiff has christened the work Carter's 'Great New York Symphony'.[23] Brooklyn Bridge itself offers multiple symbolic images: an architectural landmark, a transport artery, a spatial and temporal span that suggests the journey from one continent to another, a metaphor for the flow of human traffic that drove European emigration in the early twentieth century, a progression from the earthly world towards the divine, and also a nostalgic leave-taking ('As apparitional as sails that cross / Some page of figures to be filed away; / – Till Elevators drop us from our day'). Crane's poem suggests a Homeric odyssey, a journey towards an unknown domain or mythic region that is simultaneously an unexpected home-coming, in which the poet appears as both wanderer and vagrant. And, for Carter, this stylised mythic image of the American hobo at the heart of Crane's work is equally a symbol of the artist as a lone, uncompromising modernist pioneer, whose new musical language (unfolded by the *Symphony*) can be heard as an imaginative projection of their explorative spirit. The opening bars of the *Symphony* respond to this imagery in a particularly vivid and direct way: the swooping bird-calls and descending figuration of the introduction (bars 1–10) suggest the soaring bird's-eye view of the city evoked in Crane's poem. The gradual textural and harmonic in-filling (beginning with a rare triadic sonority in the upper strings that is swiftly 'coloured' by more chromatic elements) suggests the slow emergence of a wide, deep panorama, like a camera panning back in the opening scene of a movie to unveil a broad cinematic landscape.[24] The trumpet solo that follows is a musical portrait of the artist as a free, imaginative presence, the work's most sustained and elaborate melodic statement, expanding outwards intervallically with a liberating sense of rhythmic freedom. The *Symphony* thus opens with a striking sense of structural and expressive poise – a feeling of balance and apparent weightlessness, similar to the breezy syntax of Crane's text, which the remainder of the work anxiously begins to destabilise.

The major part of the *Symphony*, following the introduction, is defined by the interaction of the three orchestral ensembles suggested by the work's title. Carter plots the *Symphony*'s course through two statements of a four-movement cycle, but with different ensembles playing different movements at different times in varying orders (see Fig. 12.2), so that the structure can be understood as a twisting, large-scale structural counterpoint that spirals outwards from the introduction towards the forceful unison chords of the coda (from bar 318).

David Schiff has carefully charted the different characters of the individual movements, listing their contrasting expressive, intervallic and metrical properties and tracing their articulation across the course of the work.[25] As is apparent from Figure 12.2, the interlacing of different movements spread across the three orchestras creates a rapidly changing montage of sound. At times, particular ensemble groups may take precedence (Orchestra II in bars 100–5 and 142–50; Orchestra III in bars 121–7 and 199–207), and elements of the opening trumpet motto can be heard echoed in certain passages spread across the main body of the work (for example, in the rhythmic fluidity of Orchestra I's movement 3, bars 105–21 and 157–92). But Carter maintains, in his notes printed at the head of the study score, that 'the listener, of course, is not meant, on first hearing, to identify the details of this constantly shifting web of sound any more than he is to identify the modulations in *Tristan und Isolde*, but rather to hear and grasp the character of this kaleidoscope of musical themes as they are presented in varying contexts'.[26] For most listeners, even on subsequent hearings, Carter's music will hardly seem thematic, at least in a normative sense. Much more compelling, especially from a symphonic perspective, is the interaction and exchange of different timbral and gestural characters. Three basic modes of expression are articulated in the opening round of movements: Orchestra I's sustained, 'inviolate' string chords (bars 37–46),

Figure 12.2 *Carter, Symphony of Three Orchestras,* form

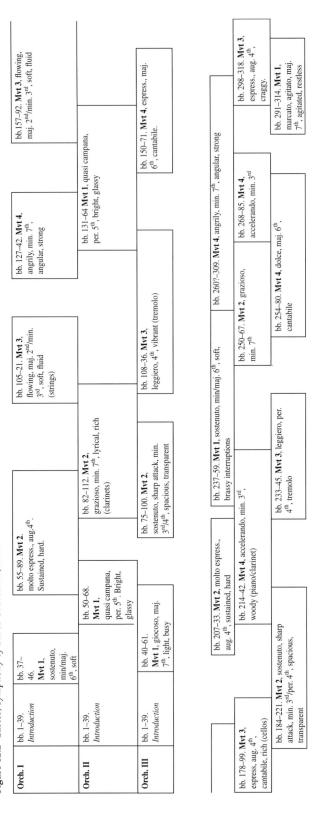

the bright, edgy bell-like timbre of Orchestra II (dominated by perfect fifths, bars 50–68) and the more lively, potentially explosive figuration of Orchestra III's giocoso music (bars 40–61); similarly contrasting modes of gestural behaviour mark each of the subsequent sections. Initially, at least, the pattern of interchange resembles a conversational dialogue. But, as the *Symphony* progresses, the texture becomes increasingly tense and agitated. The return of the giocoso music in Orchestra III at bar 291, for example, is now restless and uneasy, and the second statement of Orchestra I's fourth movement (marked 'angrily') has expanded from merely fifteen bars to almost 50. Rather than working towards resolution or consonance, the level of dissonance rises incrementally as the work progresses, so that the strident series of tutti chords that dramatically sunder the work from bar 318 appear as the end-result of a process of intensification and conflict. The coda is dominated by hollow, repetitive mechanistic ostinati – the polar opposite of the free-flowing, seemingly improvisatory spirit of the trumpet solo that opens the work – and a final cadenza for piano, tuba and double bass, which, as Schiff suggests, completes the 'double dramatic trajectories of the work, from high to low, lyrical to mechanical'.[27] In the context of Crane's poem, it is hard not to hear this ending as a bleak renunciation of individual liberty, a nightmarish vision of the modern city as a crushing weight of machine noise and expressive violence. Schiff summarises the work as 'the most extreme statement of tragic disjunction Carter ever attempted for orchestra'.[28] But Carter's music is characteristically ambiguous, and it is equally possible to enjoy the neat symmetry of the work's closing gesture, the low sounds and resonant timbre in balance with the ethereal luminous sonorities with which the *Symphony* opened.[29] In that way, Carter achieves a compelling sense of structural and expressive poise, and the work completes a circular journey that seemingly brings the listener back to the brink of the opening bars, even as the music plunges into the abyss.

Pelle Gudmundsen-Holmgreen: *Symphony, Antiphony*

Pelle Gudmundsen-Holmgreen's closely contemporary *Symphony, Antiphony*, composed in 1977, is similarly ambivalent, though it plays with radically different musical materials. Born in 1932, Gudmundsen-Holmgreen is a senior representative in Danish music of a tendency described by Poul Nielsen as 'new simplicity' ('ny enkelhed'). 'Simplicity' here refers not to musical meaning or imagination – as is readily apparent, Gudmundsen-Holmgreen's music is anything but simple in that sense. Rather, it refers to a vivid clarity of expression and design, promoted partly in response to the perceived over-intellectualism of the Darmstadt school (principally Boulez and Stockhausen). Implicit also, perhaps, is a characteristically Nordic preoccupation with structure and objectivity – aspects of which Gudmundsen-Holmgreen also shared with members of the New York group including John Cage and (especially) Morton Feldman, composers who otherwise seem remote from any traditional sense of the symphonic. Other formative influences on Gudmundsen-Holmgreen include Samuel Beckett – like Berio, Gudmundsen-Holmgreen was strongly drawn to Beckett's antagonistic, deconstructive approach to received convention, and to the idea of a gestural theatre of the absurd, in which language has been reduced to a series of speech acts whose meaning has been continually deferred or withheld. An important early landmark in Gudmundsen-Holmgreen's work is the Beckett setting *Je ne me tirai jamais. Jamais* (1966), an anti-song cycle whose alternating violence and playfulness responds forcefully to the inherent ambiguity (or multivocality) of Beckett's text. Gudmundsen-Holmgreen's attitude to the symphonic tradition in *Symphony, Antiphony*, is similarly double-edged and destabilising. As Ursula Andkjær Olsen has suggested, 'throughout Gudmundsen-Holmgreen's music speaks a certain productive irony. An irony that has nothing to do with the everyday use of the term, which is closer to sarcasm in its meaning, but an irony that is continually on the move, an instability of meaning, both a yes and a no'.[30] For Andkjær Olsen, Gudmundsen-Holmgreen's music is inhabited by a wild array of speaking voices – not simply individual instruments or instrumental groups, but different kinds of music. The resulting 'sounding together' in *Symphony, Antiphony* is violently unpredictable: a ritualistic theatre that occasionally observes the rules of polite conversational dialogue, but more frequently erupts into 'a kind of mass hysteria or unrestrained anarchy'.[31]

Yet, for all its apparent violence and nihilism, Gudmundsen-Holmgreen's music is richly allusive and tautly designed. The two-part design of *Symphony, Antiphony* is highly asymmetrical: the first part, 'Symphony', which Gudmundsen-Holmgreen maintains can be performed as an independent work, is barely two and a half minutes long, whereas the following 'Antiphony' is almost ten times this length: a massive structural imbalance which the work makes little attempt to redress. 'Symphony' begins by systematically unfolding one of Gudmundsen-Holmgreen's basic musical structures: a chromatic pitch field that expands outwards symmetrically from a single focal pitch (D), divided at the tritone (A♭) until it covers ten of the twelve available chromatic pitch classes (the missing notes are the tritone pair F♮ and B♮; see Example 12.9).

The music simultaneously begins a process of timbral expansion, from the bell-like vibraphone, piano and marimba at the start, through the

Example 12.9 Pelle Gudmundsen-Holmgreen, *Symphony, Antiphony*, opening.

addition of woodwind (playing fragments derived in diminution from the opening pitch structure) and strings (largely playing open strings), and eventually with strident brass fanfares. The entry of the unpitched percussion in bar 23, however, critically destabilises this constructivist process of gradual textural and metrical accumulation, and the 'Symphony' collapses, revealed as an unsustainable fiction, under the weight of a series of crushing blows on the tam tam. Only dying echoes of the opening pitch (D) remain on the lowest string of the double bass, slowly resonating until they fade, exhausted, into complete silence.

One of Gudmundsen-Holmgreen's most striking compositional strategies is the ability to render familiar musical materials suddenly strange and disorientating. The opening of 'Antiphony' is an excellent example of this process: a solo violin plays with a simple three-note motive (D-E-F♯) in varying melodic formations – an idea whose diatonicism sounds all the more shocking after the brutal ending of 'Symphony'. As Andkjær Olsen records, the origin of this device may lie in one of the early technical exercises Gudmundsen-Holmgreen undertook with his first composition teacher, Finn Høffding: the task of finding as many ways as possible of ordering three notes into a melodic sequence.[32] The gesture thus has the quality of a new start, a conscious back-to-basics attempt to rebuild a musical language from scratch after the implosion at the end of the preceding movement. But it also assumes the status of a 'found object' or *objet trouvé*; a pre-existent musical element discovered seemingly by chance and recontextualised within a new stylistic domain. Much of Pelle Gudmundsen-Holmgreen's work is characterised by a similar sense of bricolage, whether referring to actual pieces (such as the Larghetto from Mozart's 'Coronation' Concerto, K 537, in *Plateaux pour Piano et Orchestra*, 2005), or more broadly to musical types, as is the case here. Hence, 'Antiphony' can in one sense be heard as a series of six interlinked variations on material shattered and fractured in the opening 'Symphony'. But in another sense, the 'Antiphony' is generated by the juxtaposition of sharply contrasting blocks of different kinds of music: the violin's innocent diatonic doodling, raucous animal calls in the brass and woodwind, Stravinskian ragtime on the piano, melancholic late-Romantic yearning in the strings and the nostalgic sound of a solo mandolin, playing fragments of what sounds uncannily like the *Song of the Volga River Boatmen*. Each of the six movements in 'Antiphony' highlights one or other of these musical types: in the first, the violin doodles and brass-woodwind animal calls predominate; in the second, the animal calls and mandolin begin to take precedence; the third movement is the shortest, a ragtime cadenza for piano; the fourth is the work's orgiastic climax, a multilayered collision of *Sacre*-like fanfares and ostinati dominated by the heavy brass; the fifth is a complete contrast, a solemn hymnic meditation for piano and flageolet strings; the sixth and final movement is an extended postlude, a Mahlerian paraphrase of swooning cadential string lines and tremolo mandolin that passes into an eerie coda. The final sounds are the wooden saltando rattle of open violin strings and the rasping whirr of unpitched percussion: a dusty musical death.

Gudmundsen-Holmgreen's *Symphony, Antiphony* underlines the contingency of notions of symphonic tradition and inheritance. It collapses familiar conventions of musical time and space, only to reassemble them in a strange and unfamiliar theatre in which collision, superimposition and simultaneity begin to seem consonant even though they never become fully comprehensible in their entirety. Indeed, the work challenges the very idea of such comprehensibility, emphasising the gestural, performative quality of its musical language over and above the question of musical semantics. As Andkjær Olsen suggests, Gudmundsen-Holmgreen's music is figurative (or, rather, connotive), even if it remains unclear precisely what it is supposed to represent. Even as it vividly deconstructs the genre, however, *Symphony, Antiphony* ultimately reinforces the idea of the symphonic as a musical category. It successfully promotes (and problematises) the idea of large-scale musical form, and reaffirms the symphony orchestra as a vehicle for sustained musical communication. In that sense, the work becomes emblematic of a broader trend in twentieth-century symphonic composition. It exemplifies the tendency, demonstrated in different ways by the five works discussed in this chapter, towards fragmentation, alienation and reconstruction: the cyclic process of decay and renewal that becomes a red thread throughout much twentieth-century music, from Sibelius and Stravinsky to Berio and beyond. And, while this process often seems painful, inevitably directed towards its own imminent generic self-destruction, it ensures that the symphony remains an effective mirror of the modern condition. Perhaps, in that way, the twentieth-century symphony remains faithful to its eighteenth-century origins: the subtle merging of public and private space in conversational dialogue, the ritualised 'sounding together' of multiple musical languages, dialects and identities. Never has the need for such dialogue seemed more urgent.

Notes

1 Erik Tawaststjerna, *Sibelius*, trans. Robert Layton, 3 vols. (London, 1986), vol. II, 76–7. The English edition does not list the source, which appears only in Tawaststjerna's Swedish original, rev. Fabian Dahlström and Gitta Henning (Stockholm, 1991), and is from Karl Ekman, *Jean Sibelius: His Life and Personality*, trans. Edward Birse (New York, 1938). As Tomi Mäkelä has recently noted, no documentary evidence for Sibelius's account of the meeting in fact survives, so the authenticity of the conversation is difficult to verify.

2 The case is made by Pierre Boulez at the start of his essay, 'Orchestras, Concert Halls, Repertory, Audiences', in *Orientations*, ed. Jean-Jacques Nattiez, trans. Martin Cooper (London, 1986), 467–70.

3 For some sense of the tensions and contradictions involved, see Richard Taruskin, *The Oxford History of Western Music*, vol. IV: *The Early Twentieth-Century* (New York and Oxford, 2005), esp. chapters 57 ('The Great American Symphony', 637–49) and 59 ('Readings', on Shostakovich's Fifth Symphony, 791–6).

4 Theodor W. Adorno, *Introduction to the Sociology of Music*, trans. E. B. Ashton (New York, 1976), 209–10.

5 Stephen Kern, *The Culture of Time and Space, 1880–1918* (Cambridge Mass., 1983, repr. 2000), 68–70.

6 Arnold Whittall, *Musical Composition in the Twentieth Century* (New York and Oxford, 1999), 10.

7 Richard Taruskin, *Stravinsky and the Russian Traditions: A Biography of the Works through* Mavra (Berkeley, 1996), 1618.

8 Elliott Antokoletz, 'The Musical Language of the Fourth Symphony', in Veijo Murtomäki and Timothy L. Jackson, eds., *Sibelius Studies* (Cambridge, 1997), 296–321, this reference 299–300.

9 Tim Howell, *Jean Sibelius: Progressive Techniques in the Symphonies and Tone Poems* (New York, 1998), 132 and Veijo Murtomäki, *Symphonic Unity: The Development of Formal Thinking in the Symphonies of Sibelius*, trans. Henry Bacon (Helsinki, 1993), 97.

10 James Hepokoski, *Sibelius: Symphony No. 5* (Cambridge, 1993), 29–30.

11 Edward Laufer, 'On the First Movement of Sibelius's Fourth Symphony: A Schenkerian View', in Carl Schachter and Hedi Siegel, eds., *Schenker Studies 2* (Cambridge, 1999), 132–3.

12 The most influential account is Edward T. Cone, 'Stravinsky: The Progress of a Method', *Perspectives of New Music*, 1/1 (1962), 18–26. For a critical review of Cone's analysis and other more recent trends in Stravinsky analysis, see Alexander Rehding, 'Towards a "Logic of Discontinuity" in Stravinsky's *Symphonies of Wind Instruments*: Hasty, Kramer and Straus Reconsidered', *Music Analysis*, 17/1 (1998), 39–65.

13 On Stravinsky's faith and the composition of the *Symphony of Psalms*, see Stephen Walsh, *Stravinsky: A Creative Spring* (New York, 1999), 498–500. See also Taruskin, *Stravinsky and the Russian Traditions*, 1618. Taruskin notes that, 'on 9 April 1926 Stravinsky made confession and took communion for the first time in two decades. From then until the early American years, he would be a devoted son of the Orthodox church.'

14 Pieter van den Toorn, *The Music of Igor Stravinsky* (New Haven, 1983), esp. 344–51. For a critique and response to van den Toorn's work, which argues against the primacy of the octatonic set in Stravinsky's music, see Dmitri Tymoczko, 'Stravinsky and the Octatonic: A Reconsideration', *Music Theory Spectrum*, 24/1 (2002), 68–102.

15 Wilfrid Mellers, '1930: Symphony of Psalms', *Tempo*, New Series, 97 (Stravinsky Memorial Issue, 1971), 19–27, this reference 19.

16 Gretchen Horlacher, 'Running in Place: Sketches and Superimposition in Stravinsky's Music', *Music Theory Spectrum*, 23/2 (2001), 196–216, this reference 200.

17 Mellers, '1930: Symphony of Psalms', 26.

18 Taruskin, *Stravinsky and the Russian Traditions*, 957–65. The term is also discussed by Horlacher.

19 David Osmond-Smith, *Playing on Words: A Guide to Luciano Berio's* Sinfonia (London, 1985).

20 Ibid., 21–6.

21 Ibid., 69–70.

22 Lóránt Péteri, 'The Scherzo of Mahler's Second Symphony: A Study of Genre' (Ph.D. diss., University of Bristol, 2008).

23 David Schiff, 'Carter as Symphonist: Redefining Boundaries', *Musical Times* 139/1865 (1998), 8–13, this reference 10.

24 Ibid.

25 David Schiff, *The Music of Elliott Carter* (London, 1983), 295–301.

26 Elliott Carter, 'A Symphony of Three Orchestras (1976)', reprinted in The Writings of Elliott Carter: An American Composer Looks at Modern Music, ed. Else and Kurt Stone (Bloomington, 1977), 366–7.

27 Schiff, The Music of Elliott Carter, 300.

28 Schiff, 'Carter as Symphonist', 11.

29 It is interesting to compare the quality of this ending with the closing bars of a later millennial symphonic work, Per Nørgård's Sixth Symphony ('At the End of the Day', 1999). Nørgård's work is similarly dark and dominated by extensive use of low registers, but here the music's timbre assumes a rich, burnished quality that suggests saturation rather than obliteration.

30 'Igennem Gudmundsen-Holmgreens musik taler altså en art produktiv ironi. En ironi, der intet har at gøre med den dagligdags brug af ordet, der nærmest sætter dets betydning lige med sarkasme, men en ironi, der hele tiden er på færde, som en betydningsuro, et både ja og nej.' Ursula Andkjær Olsen, 'Hvert med sit Næb': Pelle Gudmundsen-Holmgreens musikalske verden (Copenhagen, 2004), 12.

31 '[E]n art massehysteri, et tøjlesløst anarki'. Ibid., 133.

32 Ibid., 15.

PART III

Performance, reception and genre

13 The symphony and the classical orchestra

RICHARD WILL

Eighteenth-century symphonies are sounding more 'orchestral' than they used to. In the wake of the historical performance movement, ensembles of both period and modern instruments have been attacking the *fortissimi* of Haydn and Mozart (and their many symphony-writing contemporaries) with a gusto once reserved for Beethoven. They have also discovered an unexpectedly rich palette of colours, whether by using period instruments that do not blend so readily as their modern counterparts, or by adjusting balances to reveal unheard combinations – or simply by leaving more space between phrases, a hallmark of historically informed playing that highlights the distinction between one orchestral sound and the next. Inspired by recent discoveries about eighteenth-century orchestras, the new style emphasises just how formidable those ensembles were, as versatile and brilliant in their own ways as their nineteenth- and twentieth-century successors.

The effort to recreate eighteenth-century practices has also illuminated the reciprocity of performance and composition. In performances favouring blend and restraint, as in studies of the symphony privileging form and harmony (as many do), the orchestra comes across as a vehicle for compositional thought rather than a creative resource in its own right. To judge from eighteenth-century reactions, however, listeners were as impressed by orchestras as by the music they played, and symphonies in particular, to paraphrase a dictum of 1774, were understood 'to summon up all the splendour of the orchestra' – as if symphonies were the vehicle for orchestras and not the other way around (this point is variously acknowledged in chapters 3, 6 and 7).[1] The splendour of recent performances offers some corroboration. If symphonies never existed solely to showcase performers, then the newly evident capacities of the eighteenth-century ensemble can certainly be heard to have played a central role in symphonic style. What is more, then as now, effects such as colour, power, resonance and contrast called attention to the musical discipline and organisational infrastructure necessary to foster orchestral virtuosity. Even as orchestras communicated a wealth of symphonic expression, then, symphonies returned the favour. They furnished the script for brilliant performances and celebrated the strength of a remarkable institution.

The orchestral consensus

What we know about eighteenth-century orchestras comes courtesy of a long paper trail: payrolls, concert reviews, travellers' accounts, performance treatises, sheet music and more. They reveal what John Spitzer and Neal Zaslaw dub an 'orchestral consensus' in their definitive *The Birth of the Orchestra*. Encompassing 'what an orchestra was, what instruments it comprised and in what proportions, and how those instruments were organized', it lasted from the 1740s through the early nineteenth century – or, put in terms of the symphony, from about a decade after the genre emerged through to the middle works of Beethoven.[2] Differences between countries, cities and individual orchestras remained significant during this time, inspiring (or being inspired by) distinctive styles of orchestral scoring. Still, enough remained constant that music and musicians could circulate internationally and encounter similar conditions of performance.

At a minimum, every eighteenth-century orchestra could field four-part strings: two violins, viola and a bass line or *basso* covered by cellos and double bass. That force alone, joined by keyboard continuo according to local preference, sufficed for many symphony performances through at least the early 1770s. During those years, numerous works were composed for strings alone in four or even three parts, and the wind parts of many other symphonies were advertised as optional. At the same time, by 1740 most orchestras had winds, initially one or more bassoons, which at first doubled the *basso*; two or more flutes or oboes, sometimes played by the same, 'double-handed' musicians; two or more horns or trumpets, or both; and timpani. Clarinets joined some ensembles as early as the 1750s, but they did not become a standard in symphonies until very late in the century. Much more significant was the eventual creation of independent parts for all the winds. Around the middle of the century, most symphonies employed what were known in sheet music and music catalogues as six-, eight-, or eleven-part scorings. The strings counted as four parts regardless of how many different instruments played the *basso*, and the wind complement could amount to a single pair of oboes, flutes, horns or trumpets (six parts), one pair each of woodwinds and brass (eight parts), or two woodwinds, two horns, two trumpets and timpani (eleven parts). By the 1790s, the standard had grown to fourteen parts or more, the ensemble most typically associated with the modern term 'classical orchestra': four-part strings plus one or two flutes, two oboes, two clarinets (sometimes), one or two bassoons (now playing their own parts rather than doubling the *basso*), two horns, two trumpets and timpani. While expanded and unusual scorings do occur, most symphonies abided by these instrumentations, which in turn matched the most common disposition of orchestras.

Consensus did not extend to the number of players.[3] Depending on finances and needs, performance spaces and taste, orchestras could have as few as ten members and as many as a hundred or more – though few standing orchestras had more than seventy (those assembled for special occasions were often larger). Large or small, most ensembles grew over the course of the century, at least until the 1780s when Spitzer and Zaslaw note a levelling off. On the other hand, during any given period they could differ radically from one another in size. The orchestra of the Concert spirituel in Paris, a leading venue for symphonies from the 1740s to 1790, went from around forty to around sixty members in that time. By contrast, that of Prince Eszterházy had only about fourteen members when Haydn became director in 1761, and about twenty-four when he departed in 1790. Both ensembles got larger, but a Haydn symphony played for Eszterházy by twenty musicians might have been performed in Paris, in the same year, by two or three times that many.

Balance varied as well, though less dramatically. In 1776 Haydn had seven violins, two violas, one cello, one double bass, eight winds and timpani. The high proportion of winds, nearly 50 per cent of the total, was typical for smaller orchestras, while larger ensembles had more strings: at the Concert spirituel in 1774, there were twenty-six violins, four violas, ten cellos and four double basses versus fifteen winds and timpani. Despite that difference, the examples share a strong opposition between treble and bass. The violin sections are large, 35 to 45 per cent of the ensemble, and while the fourteen low strings of the Concert spirituel reflect a French preference for especially strong bass, if one counts bassoons (still largely doubling the *basso* in the 1770s), then the bass constitutes 20 to 30 per cent of both totals. That proportion decreased over time, presumably diminishing somewhat the power of the bass; at the same time, regional variations such as the French enthusiasm for bass also diminished, such that by the early nineteenth century the proportions of balance were largely standardised across Europe.

By that time the instruments themselves had also begun to change, becoming more like their modern counterparts thanks to venting and key systems for the winds and the concave Tourte bow for the strings. For most of the eighteenth century, however, orchestra players stuck with older technologies.[4] Apart from the double bass, which was found in three-, four- and five-string varieties of differing size and resonance, the strings retained a design established in the late seventeenth century and characterised by a flatter profile and lower bridge than the modern instrument. They were strung with gut and played mainly with convex bows. The woodwinds had fingerholes and generally only two or three keys, and the brass remained 'natural' instruments, capable of playing only those notes that belong to the overtone series of the key in which they were pitched.[5] The last point is worth emphasising since it had a formative influence on orchestration. Brass players could change the key of their instrument by inserting extensions into its sounding tube – the longer the extension, the lower the pitch – and a system developed in the 1750s allowed horn players to do so between and eventually within symphony movements. Still, neither horns nor trumpets played much beyond the tonic triad and first five degrees of the scale in symphonies, whose composers mostly avoided the instruments' highest registers, where the overtone series offers more notes. Hence the abilities of the brass shaped the whole symphonic sound, determining when they could be brought to bear and with what kinds of musical material.[6]

Venues and quality

Orchestras played in theatres, churches, a variety of concert rooms and outdoors. The acoustical results would have varied considerably depending on the nature of each space and the size of the ensemble. Spitzer and Zaslaw suggest that the orchestral style of the period was optimised for a dry sound characteristic of theatres and the outdoors, which allowed common effects like abrupt dynamic changes and repeated notes in the strings to be heard clearly. As they point out, however, a new generation of small, hard-surfaced concert rooms increasingly put those same effects into very live spaces that must have made listeners feel like the orchestra was all around them. This more visceral experience gained ground over the course of the century, as orchestras playing in large spaces took on ever more players to achieve comparable immediacy.[7]

Audience behaviour would further have affected orchestral sound, or at least its perception. Used in theatre pieces and church services as well as concerts, symphonies encountered differing degrees of attentiveness. In concerts they served mainly to open or close programmes of instrumental and vocal solos, and descriptions abound of audiences arriving, departing, chatting or playing cards during symphony performances.[8] This does not necessarily mean that the orchestra was ignored; only that its sonorities probably drifted in and out of consciousness, perhaps according to some commonly encountered patterns of orchestration discussed below. Other descriptions, meanwhile, tell of audiences listening closely to symphonies, reacting to specific moments and calling for movements to be encored. Such circumstances presumably favoured the orchestra's capacity for nuance.

A favourite topic of eighteenth-century observers, the quality of orchestral performance turned on many variables, among them money, stability and leadership. The best orchestras resided in the urban capitals and the courts of the German and Austrian nobility, which could muster the considerable resources necessary to underwrite even a small ensemble.[9] In the cities, financing came from ticket sales and, in many cases, core groups of aristocratic sponsors, while in the courts it came from single patrons like Prince Eszterházy. Cities and courts also had the institutions that could keep ensembles together for a season of concerts or longer – sometimes much longer. In the cities, theatres employed musicians for comparatively long seasons and in turn provided most of the players for concert series such as the Concert spirituel (which had much shorter seasons) and for the many individual concerts organised by composers and soloists. The chances were, then, that any given performance in Paris, London, or another major city involved some proportion of musicians who played together regularly. Court orchestras enjoyed still greater stability. The most widely praised ensemble of the century, that of the Elector Palatine in Mannheim, enjoyed such continuity that by the time most of the encomiums appeared in the 1770s, many of its members had decades in service as well as sons and nephews who trained and performed beside them. Together with the skill and longevity of Christian Cannabich, director since 1757, the players' long experience with one another helped to produce a legendarily unified manner of execution.[10]

Leadership had several dimensions.[11] Directors guided the ensemble in performance, typically with the violin from the concertmaster position and sometimes in tandem with a keyboard player. They ran such rehearsals as there were; concerts often had only one, which made the stability of the ensemble and its performance style all the more critical. Directors hired the musicians and they usually composed at least some of the music, another point of particular significance for the symphony. All of the century's most influential composers of symphonies spent time directing orchestras: Giovanni Battista Sammartini in Milan; Cannabich and his predecessor Johann Stamitz in Mannheim; Johann Gottlieb Graun in Berlin; Haydn, Carl Ditters, Antonio Rosetti and others at smaller German and Austrian courts; Johann Christian Bach in London; and François-Joseph Gossec in Paris. Their experience allowed them to capitalise on the existing strengths of specific ensembles and even individual musicians, as well as to develop effective new sounds. More broadly, their insider's knowledge formed the basis for the reciprocity of composition and performance noted above, without which symphony and orchestra alike might have remained colourful accompaniments to other things – their role throughout much of the century. Instead they moved from the background to the foreground of concert life, thanks in no small part to the interaction of musical style and ensemble capability.

Scoring and style

Although symphonies could display an orchestra's abilities through striking effects like the *premier coup d'archet* ('first stroke of the bow', that is, a unison attack in all the strings), the relationship between style and ensemble ran much deeper. From its earliest years, the symphony stood for a modern and essentially comic idiom in which composers changed musical ideas and moods quickly rather than elaborating them at length as in some genres of the first half of the century.[12] The orchestra's capacity for contrast made the changes vivid, an advantage that composers began to exploit already in symphonies for strings alone. Although lacking the colour and volume of winds, these works compensate with an astonishing array of textures, some of them inherited from antecedents of the symphony such as the concerto, trio sonata and dance suite. In four-part writing, the default is often what might be called '2+2': that is, the two violins play in unison, octaves, or close harmony with one another, and the violas and *basso* do the same. Accommodating two-, three- and four-part harmony but only two layers of rhythm, the pattern affords flexibility and clarity and may dominate slow movements and finales, where lyricism and dance set the tone. First movements employ many textures in addition to 2+2, above all 1+1+2 (violin 1 and 2 in imitation or dialogue, viola and *basso* together); 2+1+1 (violins together, viola and *basso* independent); 1+3 (melody in violin 1, remaining parts together); and 1+2+1 (melody in violin 1, inner parts together, independent *basso*). In addition, the viola, *basso*, or both instruments regularly drop out, leaving reduced textures of two or three upper strings. The options can succeed one another with dizzying speed: the first movement of Sammartini's Symphony in C (Jenkins-Churgin 7, *c.* 1730) registers twelve shifts of texture in only 112 bars.[13] Demarcating the arrival of new musical ideas and harmonies, the shifts also create a drama of their own, a comedy of instrumental role switching for which the ideas and harmonies are themselves a vehicle.

Ensemble and style connect further in the so-called *Trommelbass* ('drum bass'), the repeated crotchets or quavers in the *basso* that pervade many symphonies through the 1770s, including those with winds. Accommodating a new emphasis on homophonic, melody-and-accompaniment textures and an associated slowing in the rate of harmonic change, repeated bass notes invested long-held chords with a sense of rhythmic motion. They also highlighted one of the characteristic strengths of the early orchestra, namely its powerful bass: even in a small ensemble, the combination of cellos and basses, frequently doubled by bassoons, continuo and viola, would have given repeated notes a forceful resonance magnified further by the stringed instruments' use of open strings in common keys such as C, G and D. In soft dynamics, the scoring is equally effective, producing an urgently pulsing hum. Frequently criticised as monotonous, the *Trommelbass* was all the same not simply a harmonic crutch but rather another means of conveying orchestral splendour.

Early symphonies with winds show the influence of another symphonic antecedent, the three-movement Italian opera overture or 'sinfonia'. Neapolitan opera in particular cast a long shadow over orchestral technique, beginning in the 1730s with composers such as Giovanni Battista Pergolesi and Leonardo Leo, and continuing through the 1750s with Niccolò Jommelli and Baldassare Galuppi. Pushing contrast and homophonic clarity to new heights, they injected fresh colour through the addition of woodwinds and brass and streamlined the string textures into predominantly 2+2, *Trommelbass*-heavy homophony. They also pioneered widely imitated effects such as fanfare openings taking advantage of the 'natural' range of the brass, quiet passages featuring woodwind solos or the strings alone, and crescendos. The first two actually enjoyed longer lives in the symphony, but the last, generally attributed to Jommelli, came to rival the *premier coup d'archet* as the quintessential symbol of orchestral virtuosity. More than simply an increase in volume, the mid-century crescendo involved a coordinated intensification of melody (which rises), instrumentation (which grows) and rhythm (which subdivides; e.g. crotchets become quavers become semiquavers). All of this happened within four to twelve bars, leaving listeners if not breathless, as one writer claimed, then at least with a vivid impression of the orchestra's entire sonic gamut.[14]

To the extent that sinfonias and concert symphonies can be distinguished (they were frequently marketed together), the latter tend to adapt Neapolitan conventions to a more mercurial and texturally diverse environment.[15] In the 1740s and 50s, both Sammartini and the leading symphonist in Vienna, Georg Christoph Wagenseil, used one or two pairs of winds to double the strings, play brief solos, or support the harmony, either in short punctuating chords or in long tones that sustain behind the strings. They also silenced the winds periodically to expose the contrasting colour of the strings alone. Thus far their works recall Leo or Jommelli, as does the use of slow movements, and the second key areas of fast movements, to feature wind solos or the strings by themselves. Yet the concert symphonies often have more changes of colour than the sinfonias, switching many times between the full ensemble or 'tutti' and various smaller groupings. Despite a predominance of homophony, moreover, the textures frequently grow quite complicated, whether due to counterpoint between the violins (as in many works of Sammartini), or the mixing of strings and winds in different roles. In an elaborate example from the first movement of Wagenseil's Symphony in

G (Kucaba G3), the first violin dialogues with the oboes on the principal melody of the second key area, while the second violin holds a pedal tone with the horn, and violas and *basso* play two distinct accompanimental figures.

Still more elaborate are Johann Stamitz's symphonies, especially the late works of *c*. 1754–7, by which time he was leading an already excellent ensemble at Mannheim and had experienced the orchestras of Paris as well.[16] He was indebted to Jommelli on several counts, including the crescendo, which he used frequently.[17] He also explored new role divisions among the strings, activated the viola and *basso* with scales and melodic figures, and featured the winds – two woodwinds and two horns – with an enthusiasm matched in the 1750s only by other Mannheim composers such as Franz Xaver Richter and Anton Fils. The woodwinds (oboes, flutes or clarinets) always have at least one, and more often two featured episodes in the fast movements, and both woodwinds and horns regularly double the principal melody in the strings, which incorporates plenty of triad- and scale-based material suitable for the brass. In addition, though they frequently sit out the slow movements, the winds dominate the minuet-trio movements found between the slow movement and the finale in all the late works. Indeed, while Stamitz's addition of a fourth movement has been much celebrated as a formal innovation, it was no less consequential for orchestration. Symphonic minuets returned again and again to the brassy, top-heavy sound Stamitz achieved with horn-ready melodies and heavy wind doubling, and likewise innumerable trios served, like his, as oases of pastoral lyricism scored for winds alone or with subdued string accompaniment.

By 1760 the eight-part scoring of strings and two pair of winds, sometimes augmented by trumpets and timpani, had become standard. It would remain so for two decades and even longer among some composers, although performance practice accommodated variations such as the playing of woodwind parts by different instruments in different orchestras and the omission of trumpets and timpani (or their addition to works that lacked them). The parts themselves settled into consistent roles, with the violins presenting most of the melodic ideas, the lower strings playing a lot of *Trommelbass* and other harmonic support, and the winds doubling, sustaining, punctuating and soloing. Equally consistent were contrasts in scoring that lent many symphonies a similar orchestral shape. First and last movements used the full ensemble, slow movements omitted the winds or featured them in solos, and minuets (in four-movement symphonies) performed the same switch in miniature, from tutti scoring in the minuet to strings alone or wind solos in the trio.

Contrast remained a basic principle within movements as well, where the order of colours and textures varied greatly but within common parameters that may have affected audience reception. Most importantly, the opening sections of many first movements incorporated some or all of four common ingredients: 'melodic' tuttis, which were homophonic and used for principal musical ideas; 'concerted' tuttis with counterpoint, motivic action in the *basso* and sustained chords, used for harmonic transitions and cadences; reduced textures for the strings alone or strings with a wind solo, used again for principal ideas; and either a crescendo or quick alternations between tutti and reduced scoring, used for all purposes. Sometimes arranged so consistently as to suggest a kind of orchestrational 'form' (for instance in the Op. 3 symphonies of J. C. Bach), and elsewhere presented in many diverse orders (as in works by Haydn, Gossec, Ditters and other leading figures of the 1760s), these ingredients furnished a precis of orchestral effects likely to be heard later in the symphony. Their appearance near the beginning may further have suited those occasions, mentioned above, in which the finer nuances of style were lost to conversation and other distractions. The opening sequence of scorings primed audiences to perceive the swelling and diminishing of volume, the addition and subtraction of voices and other broad strokes of a performance that now mirrored, now contrasted with the hubbub of social interaction.

Orchestration as variation

Like Stamitz before him, during the 1760s and 1770s Haydn capitalised on his association with a virtuoso court orchestra to create some exceptionally rich orchestrations. The abilities of Eszterházy's players are most evident in the showy pieces Haydn wrote within a few years of becoming their director in 1761, symphonies nos. 6–8, 31 and 72.[18] They include difficult solos for winds and strings along with sounds he would not use again for some years: a wind choir accompanied by pizzicato strings (No. 6); duets in the tenor range for bassoon and cello (nos. 7 and 8); and four soloing horns (nos. 31 and 72). In less extravagant works, the orchestra must still negotiate unusually dense counterpoint – only Mozart and C. P. E. Bach ask for anything comparable – and its wind players must perform solos well beyond the conventional contexts of slow movements, trios and second key areas of fast movements.

The reliability of the musicians undoubtedly encouraged Haydn's signature orchestral technique as well, the use of colour and texture for variation. Theme-and-variation movements offer the most obvious examples, often emphasising orchestral as much as thematic or harmonic development. Two of the early showpieces (nos. 31 and 72) end with finales that review the soloists and orchestral sections in successive variations. Later examples, particularly slow movements from the later 1770s and early 1780s, instead offer systematic, almost textbook-like illustrations of orchestral technique. While alternating between minor- and major-key versions of its theme, for example, the Allegretto of Symphony No. 63 offers the wind section both alone and accompanied; the tutti in dialogue with three-part strings; a grand concluding tutti; and no fewer than four different homophonic string textures, including one in which the flute doubles the melody in the first violins (a favourite sound of Haydn's). Haydn is not always so didactic, but orchestration figures large right through his last, alternating variation set in the second movement of Symphony No. 103, where the strings and winds trade and redecorate both themes.[19]

An aspect of Haydn's broader tendency to develop musical ideas continuously, his use of colour and texture as means of variation also occurs outside actual variation movements. Any thematic repetition is a candidate, whether immediate, as in the parallel phrases of antecedent-consequent pairings, or delayed, as in the reprises and recapitulations of sonata, rondo and minuet forms. The second possibility takes dramatic form in several first movements from the 1760s, where the openings of the recapitulations depart significantly from the movements' opening bars: strings take over what were originally themes for winds, or vice versa (nos. 8, 24, 31 and 72), or the winds interject previously unheard solos and elaborations (nos. 6, 13, 30 and 35). Often encompassing domains beyond orchestration (e.g. nos. 24 and 31 both shift from major to minor), the changes help figure the recapitulation as a new event in a still-unfolding drama.

In the 1770s and 1780s, orchestral variation becomes less dramatic but more pervasive, especially following Haydn's oft-remarked turn towards a more popular style around 1774. During this time his orchestration grows more transparent and consistent, with less counterpoint, more *Trommelbass* and textures of longer duration to match more expansive tunes and forms. The new expansiveness means that melodies are often played twice in succession or divided into antecedent and consequent phrases, in which case the first or antecedent hearing is frequently given to the strings, and the second or consequent to the winds (e.g. nos. 68, 74 or 84). Something similar happens in sonata- and rondo-form reprises, where themes played initially by the strings return doubled by one or more wind instruments – or, if already doubled the first time around, with a different doubling (e.g. nos. 56, 66 and 82). Still another possibility involves themes distributed among multiple instruments, like a swaying minuet tune in the first movement of Symphony No. 76, whose first two bars are played by the horns and flute, the next two by the oboes, and the remaining four by all the winds. Itself an increasingly common way to create contrast within themes, dialogue of this kind practically begs to be varied, and the subtlety of the recombinations belies the apparent simplicity of Haydn's 'popular' manner. By the end of the first movement of No. 76, the wind section has shared the tune in four different ways, each time to a different string accompaniment. Much as in Sammartini's textural changes of several decades before, the switching of instrumental roles becomes a drama all its own.

In the 1770s and 1780s Mozart used colour and texture in comparable ways, though with fewer effects on his recapitulations and reprises. More often he altered immediate thematic repetitions, especially by reconfiguring ever more elaborate dialogues between strings and winds (e.g. K 183 in G minor, K 200 in C, the 'Paris' Symphony K 297 in D, or K 550 in G minor). Variations like these, or like Haydn's of the same period, are common coin among prominent symphonists of the following decades such as Adalbert Gyrowetz, Paul Wranitzky, Anton Eberl, Ignaz Josef Pleyel and Beethoven: witness Beethoven's Symphony No. 1 in C (1800), where all the principal themes of the first movement are rescored in the recapitulation. The new generation did not, however, follow the example of Haydn's own symphonies of the 1790s, in which variation achieves an unparalleled complexity amidst increasingly developmental forms.[20] Whether in variation, rondo, or sonata movements, scarcely a melody returns in the 'London' symphonies without the texture being changed or new instruments adding doubling and countermelodies. In first movements, moreover, where recapitulations routinely depart from the expositions, orchestration takes on quasi-narrative qualities, for example when opening themes are heard twice or more in the course of an exposition, and different scorings raise the question of which version will return later on. The answer typically provides a kind of colouristic 'resolution', as multiple possibilities are combined (nos. 96, 98 and 104), a missing option filled in (No. 100, where a tutti replaces competing string and wind scorings), or other expectations set up and fulfilled. In Symphony No. 102, back-to-back renderings of the opening theme juxtapose a vigorous tutti with a reduced texture featuring solo flute. The second version returns as a 'false recapitulation' midway through the development section, then disappears at the beginning of the real recapitulation. Yet rather than let the flute represent a mistaken alternative or formal disorder, Haydn has it play the theme again just before the final cadence. A colouristic reprise thus settles the last unfinished business of the movement.[21]

New contrasts

The nuance of Haydn's variations, and of colouring generally in the last two decades of the century, was facilitated by modifications to wind scoring. In the 1770s wind instruments began to appear in all slow movements, not just those in which they played solos. In addition, by 1780 many composers had introduced one or two independent bassoon parts as well as multiple upper woodwinds, most commonly one or two flutes with two oboes. With more voices and a more flexible bass than the horns could provide, the wind section became more self-sufficient and appeared more frequently by itself, unsupported by strings. Since the woodwinds alone could now muster harmonies in five or six parts, the section was also more frequently split in two, most commonly in passages where the winds sustained and the brass and timpani punctuated. The separation of the bassoons from the *basso*, finally, together with a rise in independent cello parts and more ambitious writing for the viola, brought an activity to the tenor range that eventually transformed the whole orchestral sound. The tenor instruments became the most versatile in the ensemble, playing solos, furnishing harmonies, doubling melodies at the octave and providing light basses in various reduced textures. While they also united with the double basses to reconstitute the old *basso*, their primary effect was to mitigate the familiar opposition between bass and treble. Already in the 1770s and early 1780s, symphonies by C. P. E. Bach (Wq 183), Gossec (Brook 83–5), Ditters (now von Dittersdorf; see Grave Am1, and the symphonies on Ovid's *Metamorphoses*), Cannabich (nos. 46, 57, 59 and 63) and others showed the effects, their sound growing fuller and more diffuse, and their gradations of colour ever finer.[22]

Mozart was populating his middle ranges even in the early 1770s, writing extensive sustaining parts for the winds and using the inner strings as much to fill in the harmonies – often with double stops, tremolo and arpeggios – as to reinforce the outer parts. He placed particular confidence in the violas, making them equal partners in contrapuntal passages and frequently splitting them into two lines ('*divisi*') that double violin or woodwind pairings an octave below (e.g. K 84, 114, 162 and 200). The last remained a popular device among many composers through the end of the century, and Mozart himself found additional ways to expand the viola's role: the opening of the Symphony in G minor (K 550), with its *divisi* violas murmuring an accompaniment to the violins, is an emblematic example. In the later symphonies as in the piano concertos and operas, Mozart also greatly expanded the responsibilities of the winds. In addition to playing without the strings, they reverse roles with them and accompany melodies that are no longer harmonised within the string section itself – for example, an exchange between bass and treble in the second movement of the

'Jupiter' Symphony (K 551 in C), where strings in bare octaves play against pulsing chords in the bassoons and horns. The winds also acquired enhanced solo roles, especially in melodic dialogues between multiple winds or between winds and strings.[23]

The last innovation is especially significant inasmuch as many other symphonies of the 1780s – Dittersdorf's and Cannabich's, for example, and even Haydn's to an extent – continued to 'feature' the winds, assigning them self-contained and often extended melodies in favourite places (expanded from slow movements, trios and second themes to include variations, rondo episodes and closing themes in sonata forms). Where shorter solos and dialogues occurred, the context tended to be developmental, as when fragments of a theme are sequenced in different keys. Mozart was more likely to build such exchanges into the themes themselves. The Allegro of the 'Prague' Symphony (K 504 in D) opens with a back-and-forth between string antecedent and wind consequent, followed by a repetition of the antecedent with oboe countermelody. At closer range, strings and winds divide the antecedent of the second key area of K 550, with the order of entries reversed on repetition. Closer still, violins, horns and bassoons alternate nearly bar-by-bar in the opening theme of the Symphony in E flat (K 543), constructing a virtual 'tone-colour melody' that later shifts to bass strings, clarinets and flute. No longer only a means for distinguishing parts of a form, or even phrases in a melody, orchestral contrast could now define the very identity of the musical idea.

The force of Mozart's later symphonies opened another dimension of contrast, a familiar but vastly magnified distinction between tutti and reduced scoring. It was inherited, at least in part, from symphonies and orchestras he heard in Mannheim and Paris during 1777–8, which influenced the formal and expressive designs of several of his works.[24] Most striking, passages like the opening of the 'Paris' Symphony reveal a new insistence on the sheer grandeur of the tutti. Three bars of a D major chord, scored for full orchestra and articulated only by minim rhythms, sound all the more massive by comparison to an answering figure for violins alone, and they also postpone any real musical action; the movement gets underway only after the chord and violin figure have been repeated and a contrapuntal development begun. The power of what precedes is due only in part to Mozart's expanded instrumentation (seventeen parts: strings, timpani and six pairs of winds). Appropriately likened to slow introductions, such openings occur also in eight- and eleven-part works written for Mannheim and Paris in the 1770s, whose orchestras must have sounded impressive even without the extra winds (e.g. in Gossec's symphonies in F and C, Brook 83 and 85, or Cannabich's nos. 55 and 57).

After 1780, ever grander tuttis reinforced a long-standing association between symphonies and the sublime. The interwoven textures, chorus-like agglomerations of instruments, and indeed the dynamic and colouristic contrasts of symphonies had already been deemed exalted and awe-inspiring.[25] Now the last of these became epochal in scope. Openings like that of the 'Paris' Symphony became a regular feature of actual slow introductions, sometimes expanded as in Wranitzky's Symphony in D (Op. 36), where a rolling tutti stretches several bars before giving way to an elegant string melody; and sometimes reduced as in many of Haydn's late works, where short bursts of sound alternate with various quiet responses. Other examples engender some of the most memorable fractures in late eighteenth- and early nineteenth-century symphonies. In the first movement of Mozart's 'Jupiter', a tutti blast of C minor answers the trailing off of the strings in the second key area; in the second movement of Haydn's 'Military' Symphony (No. 100), an even bigger blast of A flat (seventeen parts plus triangle, cymbal and bass drum) counters the dwindling to *pianissimo* of the main theme – 'a climax of horrid sublimity', according to one observer.[26] And in the first movement of Beethoven's *Eroica* Symphony (No. 3 in E flat), which adds only a third horn to the standard seventeen-part ensemble, the infamous dissonant tutti of the development section collapses into a familiar if updated reduced texture, woodwind melody accompanied by strings. The narrative weight these moments bear should not obscure their role as orchestral effects, successors to a long line of dramatic contrasts. Once again they broadcast the discipline, breadth and visceral impact that made orchestras famous, and that symphonies absorbed into the very heart of their style.

Notes

1 Johann Georg Sulzer, ed., *Allgemeine Theorie der schönen Künste*, 2nd expanded edn, 4 vols. (Leipzig, 1792–4), s. v. 'Symphonie', 478, trans. in Bathia Churgin, 'The Symphony as Described by J. A. P. Schulz (1774): A Commentary and Translation', *Current Musicology*, 29 (1980), 11. The original reads 'the splendour of instrumental music' but goes on to list specifically orchestral effects appropriate to symphonies. See also Mark Evan Bonds, 'The Symphony as Pindaric Ode', in Elaine Sisman, ed., *Haydn and His World* (Princeton, 1997), 133.

2 John Spitzer and Neal Zaslaw, *The Birth of the Orchestra: History of an Institution, 1650–1815* (Oxford, 2004), 308. Earlier studies include: Adam Carse, *The Orchestra in the XVIIIth Century* (Cambridge, 1940); George B. Stauffer, 'The Modern Orchestra: A

Creation of the Late Eighteenth Century', in Joan Peyser, ed., *The Orchestra: Origins and Transformations* (New York, 1986), 37–68; Michael Broyles, 'Ensemble Music Moves Out of the Private House: Haydn to Beethoven', in Peyser, ed., *The Orchestra: Origins and Transformations*, 97–122; Christoph-Hellmut Mahling and Helmut Rösing, 'Orchester', in Ludwig Finscher, ed., *Die Musik in Geschichte und Gegenwart*, 2nd edn (Kassel, 1994–), Sachteil, vol. VII, cols. 812–52.

3 This paragraph and the following are based on Spitzer and Zaslaw, *The Birth of the Orchestra*, 316–34 as well as appendices A–D, which list sample memberships of eighteenth- and early nineteenth-century orchestras. As the authors emphasise (26–8), documents regarding size and balance must be treated with some caution since standing orchestras

could add extra performers or play at less than full strength, and double-handed players could alter instrumental proportions. See also Dexter Edge, 'Manuscript Parts as Evidence of Orchestral Size in the Eighteenth-Century Viennese Concerto', in Neal Zaslaw, ed., *Mozart's Piano Concertos: Text, Context, Interpretation* (Ann Arbor, 1996), 427–60, and Edge, 'Mozart's Viennese Orchestras', *Early Music*, 20 (1992), 64–88.

4 On instruments see Spitzer and Zaslaw, *The Birth of the Orchestra*, 309–14; Robert Barclay, 'The Development of Musical Instruments: National Trends and Musical Implications', in Colin Lawson, ed., *The Cambridge Companion to the Orchestra* (Cambridge, 2003), 29–36; Barclay, 'Design, Technology and Manufacture before 1800', in Trevor Herbert and John Wallace, eds., *The Cambridge Companion to Brass Instruments* (Cambridge, 1997), 24–37; Ardal Powell, *The Flute* (New Haven, 2002), 107–26; Albert R. Rice, *The Clarinet in the Classical Period* (Oxford and New York, 2003); and Geoffrey Burgess and Bruce Haynes, *The Oboe* (New Haven, 2004), 78–124.

5 For a useful explanation see Arnold Myers, 'How Brass Instruments Work', in Herbert and Wallace, eds., *The Cambridge Companion to Brass Instruments*, 19–23.

6 The most thorough discussion of this issue is Paul R. Bryan, 'The Horn in the Works of Mozart and Haydn: Some Observations and Comparisons', *Haydn Yearbook* (1975), 189–255.

7 Spitzer and Zaslaw, *The Birth of the Orchestra*, 343–69; see also Jürgen Meyer, 'Gedanken zu den originalen Konzertsälen Joseph Haydns', in Thüring Bräm, ed., *Musik und Raum: Eine Sammlung von Beiträgen aus historischer und künstlerischer Sicht zur Bedeutung des Begriffes 'Raum' als Klangträger für die Musik* (Basel, 1986), 27–37; and Stefan Weinzierl, *Beethovens Konzerträume: Raumakustik und symphonische Aufführungspraxis an der Schwelle zum modernen Konzertwesen* (Frankfurt am Main, 2002).

8 On concert programmes and conditions see Mary Sue Morrow, *Concert Life in Haydn's Vienna: Aspects of a Developing Musical and Social Institution* (Stuyvesant, 1989), esp. 141–63; Neal Zaslaw, *Mozart's Symphonies: Context, Performance Practice, Reception* (Oxford, 1989), 517–25; Simon McVeigh, *Concert Life in London from Mozart to Haydn* (Cambridge, 1993), esp. 53–69; William Weber, *The Great Transformation of Musical Taste: Concert Programming from Haydn to Brahms* (Cambridge, 2008), 13–81.

9 For the institutional underpinnings of orchestras and concert series, see especially Spitzer and Zaslaw, *The Birth of the Orchestra*, 137–305; Morrow, *Concert Life in Haydn's Vienna*; McVeigh, *Concert Life in London from Mozart to Haydn*; Jenny Burchell, *Polite or Commercial Concerts?: Concert Management and Orchestral Repertoire in Edinburgh, Bath, Oxford, Manchester, and Newcastle, 1730–1799* (New York, 1996).

10 Eugene K. Wolf, 'The Mannheim Court', in Neal Zaslaw, ed., *The Classical Era: From the 1740s to the End of the 18th Century* (Englewood Cliffs, 1989), 225–33; Wolf, 'On the Composition of the Mannheim Orchestra ca. 1740–1778', *Basler Jahrbuch für historische Musikpraxis*, 17 (1993), 113–38; Christian Schruff, 'Konnte Langweiliges vom Stuhl reißen? Bemerkungen zu Aufführungspraxis und Interpretation der Mannheimer Orchestermusik', in Klaus Hortschansky, ed., *Traditionen – Neuansätze: Für Anna Amalie Abert (1906–1996)* (Tutzing, 1997), 541–54. The membership and training of court orchestras generally is considered in Christoph-Hellmut Mahling, 'The Origin and Social Status of the Court Orchestral Musician in the 18th and Early 19th Century in Germany', trans. Herbert Kaufman and Barbara Reisner, in Walter Salmen, ed., *The Social Status of the Professional Musician from the Middle Ages to the 19th Century* (New York, 1983), 219–64.

11 Spitzer and Zaslaw, *The Birth of the Orchestra*, 384–93; Carse, *The Orchestra in the XVIIIth Century*, 88–109; Robin Stowell, '"Good Execution and Other Necessary Skills": The Role of the Concertmaster in the Late 18th Century', *Early Music*, 16 (1988), 21–33.

12 For recent surveys of stylistic development in the eighteenth-century symphony see the essays by Michael Spitzer, John Irving and Mary Sue Morrow elsewhere in this volume; Richard Will, 'Eighteenth-Century Symphonies: An Unfinished Dialogue', in Simon Keefe, ed., *The Cambridge History of Eighteenth-Century Music* (Cambridge, 2009), 613–47; and Ludwig Finscher, 'Symphonie', in *Die Musik in Geschichte und Gegenwart*, 2nd edn, Sachteil, vol. VIII (1994), cols. 19–56.

13 Authors and numbers following symphony titles refer to thematic catalogues or to the thematic indexes in Barry S. Brook, gen. ed., *The Symphony 1720–1840*, 60 vols. (New York, 1979–86).

14 Johann Friedrich Reichardt, *Briefe eines aufmerksamen Reisenden die Musik betreffend* (Frankfurt am Main, 1774–6), vol. I, 11, trans. with related eighteenth-century comments in

Eugene K. Wolf, *The Symphonies of Johann Stamitz: A Study in the Formation of the Classic Style* (Utrecht, 1981), 235. See also Manfred Hermann Schmidt, 'Typen des Orchestercrescendo im 18. Jahrhundert', in Christine Heyter-Rauland and Christoph-Hellmut Mahling, eds., *Untersuchungen zu Musikbeziehungen zwischen Mannheim, Böhmen und Mähren im späten 18. und frühen 19. Jahrhundert: Symphonie–Kirchenmusik–Melodrama* (Mainz, 1993), 96–132. For representative crescendos see the sinfonia to Jommelli's *Bajazette* in Brook, gen. ed., *The Symphony 1720–1840*, vol. A-1, and the Stamitz symphonies listed in note 16.

15 Will, 'Eighteenth-Century Symphonies: An Unfinished Dialogue', 615–16; Bathia Churgin, *The Symphony 1720–1840*, vol. A-2, xxii–xxiii (Sammartini); John Kucaba, *The Symphony 1720–1840*, vol. B-3, xxv–xxxii (Wagenseil; the works included in this volume show Wagenseil's own differentiation between sinfonia and concert symphony).

16 Stamitz's late works comprise Wolf F3, D3–5, E♭1–2, E♭5a–5b, and E♭6; Wolf, *The Symphonies of Johann Stamitz*, 78.

17 Wolf, *The Symphonies of Johann Stamitz*, 222–6; Helmut Hell, *Die neapolitanische Opernsinfonie in der ersten Hälfte des 18. Jahrhunderts: N. Porpora, L. Vinci, G. B. Pergolesi, L. Leo, N. Jommelli* (Tutzing, 1971), 487–501; Marita P. McClymonds, 'Jomellis Opernsinfonien der 1750er Jahre und ihre Beziehung zum Mannheimer Stil', in Roland Würtz, ed., *Mannheim und Italien: zur Vorgeschichte der Mannheimer: Bericht über das Mannheimer Kolloquium im März 1982* (Mainz, 1984), 97–120.

18 On the Eszterházy orchestra see Sonja Gerlach, 'Haydns Orchestermusiker von 1761 bis 1774', *Haydn-Studien*, 4 (1976), 35–48; H. C. Robbins Landon, *Haydn: Chronicle and Works*, 5 vols. (London, 1976–80), vol. I, 347–57; vol. II, 70–93.

19 On Symphony No. 63 see also Elaine R. Sisman, *Haydn and the Classical Variation* (Cambridge, Mass., 1993), 160–1. Sisman prefers the term 'alternating variation' to the more familiar 'double variation'; ibid., 150–1.

20 Eugene K. Wolf, 'The Recapitulations in Haydn's London Symphonies', *Musical Quarterly*, 52 (1966), 71–89, esp. 81.

21 No. 102 is discussed further in Gesine Schröder, 'Über das "klassische Orchester" und Haydns späte symphonische Instrumentation', in *Musik-Konzepte 41: Haydn* (1985), 79–97, at 86–8.

22 Bryan, 'The Horn in the Works of Mozart and Haydn', *Haydn Yearbook*, 208–9; Sabine Henze-Döhring, 'Orchester und Orchestersatz in Christian Cannabichs Mannheimer Sinfonien', in Ludwig Finscher, Bärbel Pelker, and Jochen Reutter, eds., *Mozart und Mannheim* (Frankfurt am Main, 1994), 257–71.

23 Additional examples can be found in Nathan Broder, 'The Wind Instruments in Mozart's Symphonies', *Musical Quarterly*, 19 (1933), 238–59; Uri Toeplitz, *Die Holzbläser in der Musik Mozarts und ihr Verhältnis zur Tonartwahl* (Baden-Baden, 1978), 13–31.

24 Adam Carse, *The History of Orchestration* (London and New York, 1925), 186–8; Alfred Einstein, *Mozart: His Character, His Work*, trans. Arthur Mendel and Nathan Broder (London, 1945), 225–8; Eugene K. Wolf, 'Mannheimer Symphonik um 1777/1778 und ihr Einfluß auf Mozarts symphonischen Stil', in Finscher et al., eds., *Mozart und Mannheim* (Frankfurt am Main, 1994), 309–30.

25 Bonds, 'The Symphony as Pindaric Ode', 131–53; Will, 'Eighteenth-Century Symphonies: An Unfinished Dialogue', 625–6.

26 *Morning Chronicle* (7 April 1794); quoted in Landon, *Haydn: Chronicle and Works*, vol. III, 247.

14 Beethoven's shadow: the nineteenth century

MARK EVAN BONDS

For aspiring symphonists of the nineteenth century, Beethoven was at once both an inspiration and an obstacle. The responses to his shadow were many and varied, and they changed gradually over the course of time, but from Schubert to Mahler, any composer who engaged with the genre had to come to terms with Beethoven's legacy in one way or another. The first generation that came of age after Beethoven – which is to say, in the 1820s and 30s – included an extraordinary array of composers who took up this challenge: Franz Berwald (1796–1868), Franz Schubert (1797–1828), Hector Berlioz (1803–69), Felix Mendelssohn (1809–47), Robert Schumann (1810–56), Franz Liszt (1811–86) and Richard Wagner (1813–83). Yet with the exception of Berlioz, every one of them struggled with the genre in his youth and then abandoned it for a time before returning to it later in life, often with great ambivalence.

Schumann's early efforts in the genre exemplify the difficulties composers faced in the immediate wake of Beethoven. Like others of his generation, Schumann wanted to prove his artistic mettle by writing a symphony, the most prestigious of all instrumental genres and 'a veritable touchstone for composers and listeners alike', as the critic Adolph Bernhard Marx had noted in 1824.[1] By November 1832, Schumann had managed to complete the first movement of a Symphony in G minor and was even able to hear it performed publicly in his home town of Zwickau. Dissatisfied with what he had heard, he made substantial revisions, acknowledging in the process to a friend that while orchestrating the first movement he had sometimes mistaken 'yellow for blue', and that only through 'many years of study' would he gain 'certainty and mastery' of the art of instrumentation.[2] The young composer nevertheless persevered, added a second movement, and heard both movements performed in the nearby town of Schneeberg on 18 February 1833. Here, however, the still-fragmentary symphony shared the programme with Beethoven's Seventh. No account of the evening survives, but listeners – including the 22-year-old Schumann – could scarcely have avoided making comparisons, even if only in private. After one more performance of the two movements in Leipzig two months later, Schumann abandoned the work entirely and would not return to the genre for another eight years.

Writing a symphony was difficult enough – in addition to a thorough knowledge of orchestration, it required an ability to handle large-scale forms – and sharing a concert programme with Beethoven could only make matters worse, for it made audible to the public what composers themselves had already recognised, that the standards laid down by the older composer in the first three decades of the nineteenth century could not be easily rivalled. Beethoven's nine symphonies would inhibit Schumann and a host of other young composers from competing on this terrain. Yet even after abandoning the genre, Schumann continued to think about it: as editor of the newly founded *Neue Zeitschrift für Musik*, he assigned himself all but a handful of reviews of new symphonies and as late as 1840 was still feeling caught between the demands of originality and the shadow cast by Beethoven:

> It is said so often and to the great irritation of composers that 'coming after Beethoven' they have 'refrained from symphonic plans'. It is true, in part, that aside from a few significant works for orchestra (which were nevertheless of greater interest for the development of their particular composers, and which exercised no decisive influence on the masses or on the progress of the genre), most of the others were only a pale reflection of Beethoven's manner – not to mention those lame, boring symphony-makers who had the ability to imitate adequately the powdered wigs of Haydn and Mozart, but not the heads underneath them.[3]

In his earlier (1835) review of Berlioz's *Symphonie fantastique*, Schumann had named names, identifying a series of composers (other than himself) who had attempted to write symphonies in the wake of Beethoven. He began his list with comments about Ferdinand Ries, 'whose decided individuality could be eclipsed only by a Beethovenian one'; Ludwig Spohr, whose 'gentle speech in the great vaults of the symphony, in which he attempted to speak, did not resonate strongly enough'; and Johann Wenzel Kalliwoda, that 'happy, harmonious being' whose later symphonies proved more technically proficient yet less imaginative than his earlier ones. Schumann concluded his survey by citing only the names of 'younger' composers 'whom we know and value': Ludwig Maurer, Friedrich Schneider, Ignaz Moscheles, Christian Gottlieb Müller, Adolph Friedrich Hesse, Franz Lachner and Felix Mendelssohn, 'whom we intentionally name last'. (Schumann at the time would have known only Mendelssohn's relatively modest Symphony No. 1 and would not have been aware that Mendelssohn had written but withheld from publication two other highly original works, the 'Reformation' and 'Italian' symphonies.) For Schumann, Berlioz's *Symphonie fantastique* was an anomaly, the work of a Frenchman, the exception that proved the rule, and it was almost certainly this work that he had in mind when he later spoke of those significant orchestral compositions that had exercised 'no decisive influence on the masses or on the progress of the genre'.

Neither was Schumann alone in his estimation of the challenge. Already during Beethoven's lifetime critics had perceived the growing reach of his symphonic shadow. The influential critic Amadeus Wendt complained in 1822 that 'the gigantic works of Beethoven appear to have scared off successors in this sphere'.[4] An anonymous reviewer of the premiere of Beethoven's Ninth observed that Beethoven had long since raised the genre to such a height that other composers found it 'difficult to reach even the approaches to this Helicon'.[5] A mere two years after the premiere of the Ninth, the composer and theorist Gottfried Weber identified that work as representing 'an ominous culmination and turning point' in the genre of the symphony.[6] And in his obituary of Beethoven, Friedrich Rochlitz observed that 'for some time now, not one of his competitors has dared even to dispute his supremacy' in instrumental music. 'Strong composers avoid him on this ground; weaker ones subjugate themselves, in that they labour mightily to imitate him.'[7]

In the wake of Beethoven, then, debate centred not on who might step forward as his symphonic successor, but rather whether *anyone* could step forward: the very future of the genre lay in doubt. As identified in Chapter 1, Wagner was neither the first nor the last to proclaim the death of the symphony. This was, however, the first time in the history of music that the future of an entire genre had been called into question not because it was perceived to be old-fashioned, but because the accomplishments in that genre by a single composer were perceived to be unsurpassable.

Beethoven's shadow

I

What had led to this perception? Not everything can be pinned on Beethoven alone. Indeed, the symphony had already established itself as the most demanding and prestigious of all instrumental genres by the end of the eighteenth century, even before Beethoven had ventured into the arena. But in the decades around 1800, a number of broad and fundamental changes on the musical scene had begun to converge in ways that would eventually help endow Beethoven's symphonies with an even greater aura of insuperability:

1. *The growing importance of originality.* Originality had long played an important role in Western music aesthetics, but it took on unprecedented significance in the late eighteenth and early nineteenth centuries, driven in part by the theories of Kant and then later by those of the early Romantics. Beethoven began his career in an age

in which the essential nature of the true artist was perceived to lie in the quality of original genius. Composers were coming to be seen as high priests, mediators between the earthly and the divine, and the public began to take an interest in their lives as individuals, as witnessed by the growing number of biographies of composers that began to appear around this time, including such figures as Mozart (Niemetschek, 1798), J. S. Bach (Forkel, 1802) and Haydn (Griesinger, 1810).

2. *The rise of historical awareness.* It is no coincidence that the first attempts at a comprehensive history of music appeared in the second half of the eighteenth century.[8] By the time Beethoven arrived on the scene in the 1790s, the musical public was beginning to think more and more in terms of historical significance, beyond the circumstances of the here-and-now. The first long-running music journal, the *Allgemeine musikalische Zeitung* of Leipzig, began publication in 1799, and its essays on historical topics appeared alongside appraisals of the latest music, including E. T. A. Hoffmann's celebrated review (1810) of Beethoven's Fifth Symphony. The Hegelian view of history that began to take a (strangle-)hold in German-speaking lands later, in the 1820s, further reinforced the notion of a teleological progression in which Haydn and Mozart paved the way for the all-subsuming phenomenon of Beethoven.

3. *The emergence of the musical canon.* Outside the church, Handel was the first composer whose works enjoyed widespread public favour half a century or more after his death. Poets had laboured under the burden of the past before,[9] but composers had never had much of a past to confront, at least not in the concert hall, for the simple reason that the works of earlier generations had rarely stayed in general circulation. All this began to change in the decades around 1800: the late symphonies of Haydn and Mozart continued to be performed after their composers' deaths, and the public became increasingly conscious of the importance of accurate, authoritative musical texts – hence the posthumous publication of a substantial body of works by Mozart (1798–9) and an attempt to publish a comparable series under Haydn's own supervision (beginning in 1802).

4. *The rise of public culture.* The public concert was scarcely a new phenomenon in the early nineteenth century, but it took on unprecedented importance around this time. Broadening interest in music, the gradual decline of aristocratic patronage and the emerging sense of public culture – manifested in the phenomenon of mass politics and large public gatherings – all helped reinforce the significance of the symphony as a genre. More than any other kind of instrumental music, the symphony gave voice to the drive towards the monumental.

5. *The prestige of the sublime.* By virtue of its size, volume, timbral variety and textural complexity, the symphony was perceived as the sublime musical genre *par excellence*. It accorded perfectly with Edmund Burke's oft-quoted definition of sublime objects as 'vast in their dimensions', as opposed to beautiful ones, which he described as 'comparatively small'. 'Beauty', Burke maintained, should be 'smooth and polished . . . light and delicate', while the great should be 'rugged and negligent . . . solid, and even massive'. Beauty 'should not be obscure', whereas 'the great ought to be dark and even gloomy'. The sublime and the beautiful 'are indeed ideas of a very different nature, one being founded on pain, the other on pleasure'.[10] More than one critic of Burke's time compared the

symphony to the Pindaric ode, not only because of its size and breadth, but also because of its combination of originality and artifice, achievable through the medium of an orchestra consisting of the widest possible variety of instrumental types: strings, winds, brass and percussion. Many critics perceived the symphony as a communal genre, a work that could give voice to the emotions and aspirations of a large body of performers and listeners alike. The symphony, like the Pindaric ode, was considered a sublime genre, capable of arousing a sense of awe and even delightful fear in the spirit of its assembled listeners.[11]

To what degree Beethoven contributed to these changes and to what degree his reputation benefited from them are less important than the fact that already during his own lifetime he was perceived to have raised instrumental music – and the symphony in particular – to unprecedented heights. The generation after Beethoven magnified this perception, for what might be called the 'Age of Carlyle' was inclined to understand history of all kinds as the accomplishments of Great Men: critics found it far more reasonable (and straightforward) to ascribe monumental change to a dominant individual than to amorphous, discontinuous and gradual changes in aesthetics and social practices. Changing conceptions about the role of the listener, the relationship of music to ideas, the nature of art in general and the social function of the symphony all seemed secondary, at the time, to the power of Beethoven's music. And while no responsible historian openly advocates the 'Great Man' school of music history nowadays, its residue remains amply evident. Even Carl Dahlhaus, who was acutely aware of the perils of this approach, argued that 'the new insight that Beethoven *thrust upon the aesthetic consciousness of his age* was that a musical text, like a literary or a philosophical text, harbors a meaning which is made manifest but not entirely subsumed in its acoustic presentation – that a musical creation can exist as an "art work of ideas" transcending its various interpretations'.[12] The image Dahlhaus presents here is one of a composer dragging his generation, seemingly against its will, into a higher state of consciousness about the nature of music, and specifically, about the essential nature of purely instrumental, non-programmatic music. Beethoven's music certainly helped promote this attitude: he was indisputably the leading composer of instrumental music in the early decades of the nineteenth century and repeatedly hailed as such at the time. But it does not follow that his music actually created these changes. The premises for such changes in perception were already firmly in place by 1800, before Beethoven had finished his First Symphony.[13]

II

Still, we must try to separate our perceptions today from those of composers, critics and listeners of the nineteenth century, who for the most part did in fact ascribe to Beethoven an almost mythic power in the history of music, and most particularly in the realm of the symphony. However we may feel about hero-worship nowadays, we cannot ignore the fact that nineteenth-century culture venerated its Great Men, be they from the realm of politics (Napoleon), philosophy (Hegel), or the arts (Goethe). In the post-Napoleonic era, Beethoven emerged as *the* central figure in music, the 'hero' of his art.[14]

Beethoven's nine symphonies, though far fewer in number than Haydn's or Mozart's, stood out all the more by virtue of their variety. In an age that worshipped originality, Beethoven's symphonies, especially from the *Eroica* onwards, were decidedly different from one another. Together, they created what Dahlhaus has aptly termed a 'circumpolar' approach to the genre in that it encompassed a broad spectrum of types, including both long and short (nos. 7 and 8); serious and comic (nos. 5 and 8); heroic and pastoral (nos. 5 and 6); characteristic (nos. 3 and 6); cyclically integrated (No. 5); and even vocal (No. 9). Beethoven also got credit for formal innovations demonstrably not his own: the unexpected return of music from the third movement in the course of the Fifth Symphony's Finale, for example, had a direct forerunner in Haydn's Symphony No. 46 in B major (1772), a work Beethoven may have known from his Bonn years. But Haydn's symphony had been all but forgotten by the nineteenth century, and in the end, public perception trumped actual precedence.

Without question, Beethoven hastened the transformation of the symphonic minuet into a scherzo, a longer, faster and sometimes (as in the case of the Fifth and Ninth) more demonic movement than that found in the typical symphony of the eighteenth century. But it was in his finales that Beethoven posed the greatest challenge to future symphonists. Most spectacularly in the Fifth and Ninth, but also in the Third, Sixth and Seventh, Beethoven explored the various ways in which a finale could function not merely as a last movement but as a culmination of the whole. To underscore this point, the Fifth and Ninth explicitly evoke and reject themes from one or more earlier movements, in effect subsuming and elevating all that has gone before. After Beethoven, the symphony was no longer a series of movements but a closely integrated whole, a drama whose crux occurs only towards the end. Composers responded to this problem of the finale in a variety of ways, as we shall see.

The symphony also came to be seen as something more than a means of entertainment. With or without a verbal programme, descriptive title or evocative movement headings, a symphony was assumed to 'mean' something. In the polemics that erupted in the middle of the nineteenth century over the relative merits of 'absolute' and 'programme' music, everyone wanted to claim the mantle of Beethoven, and both sides pointed to the same works to justify their respective claims. Advocates of absolute music emphasised the technical elements of works like the Fifth Symphony, with its transformation of an opening four-note motive across all four movements. Advocates of programme music, in turn, argued that this same transformation portrayed a series of psychological states, which suggested an implicit story behind the music. Anton Schindler's testimony (1840) that the composer had meant the opening four-note unison motive to represent 'fate pounding at the portal' encouraged listeners to hear the trajectory of the Fifth as a struggle through darkness to light, culminating in the triumph of C major in the Finale. Encouraged by the overtly programmatic elements of the Third and Sixth symphonies, nineteenth-century commentators supplied storylines of varying degrees of detail for the Fourth, Seventh and Eighth symphonies as well. This kind of approach would eventually extend to the symphonic genre as a whole. As the critic Gottfried Wilhelm Fink observed in 1835, a symphony is 'a story, developed within a psychological context, of some particular emotional state of a large body of people', a 'representation of the *Volk* through every instrument drawn into the whole'.[15] Two decades later, the English critic Henry F. Chorley observed in 1854 that a symphony, 'besides being a good symphony, must now express the anguish of the age, or of some age past. There must be story, inner meaning, mystical significance – intellectual tendency.'[16]

Responses to Beethoven

I

Given these perceptions, we can better understand why so many composers of the first post-Beethovenian generation struggled to write symphonies. Berwald suppressed his First Symphony (in A Major) after its unsuccessful premiere in Stockholm in 1820 and would not return to the genre until 1842. Schubert took leave of the symphony in early 1818 after finishing a series of impressive but relatively small-scale works. He returned to the genre briefly in the autumn of 1822 with his Symphony in B minor, D 759, but the work would remain unfinished not so much in spite of its impressive first two movements but because of them: he sketched out a scherzo but could not create a satisfactory finale. In March 1824, Schubert wrote to his friend Leopold Kupelwieser that although he had not composed many new songs recently, he had tried his hand

> at several instrumental works, for I wrote two quartets for violins, viola
> and violoncello, and an octet, and I want to write another quartet; altogether,
> I want to pave my way toward the grand symphony in this manner. The
> latest in Vienna is that Beethoven is to give a concert at which he is to present
> his new Symphony [Op. 125], three movements from the new Mass

[Op. 123], and a new overture [Op. 124]. God willing, I too am resolved to present a similar concert next year.[17]

Schubert's efforts would eventually lead to the 'Great' Symphony in C major, D 944, but this work would remain unknown for all practical purposes until it was discovered by Schumann on a visit to Vienna in early 1839 and conducted by Mendelssohn in Leipzig later that same year. Schumann praised the work for its 'complete independence' from Beethovenian models, wilfully ignoring close parallels between Schubert's second movement and the Allegretto of Beethoven's Seventh Symphony.[18]

Mendelssohn wrote more than a dozen symphonies for string orchestra as a youth and even completed a symphony for full orchestra in 1824 but had second thoughts about it, withholding it from publication for another ten years before issuing it as his Symphony No. 1 in C minor, Op. 11. In the meantime, he completed his 'Reformation' and 'Italian' Symphonies (1830, 1833) but harboured doubts about those works as well: both would remain unpublished at the time of his death.[19] Only by the time he was into his thirties did he gain the confidence to compose symphonies and publish them without substantial delay. He premiered the *Lobgesang* Symphony (No. 2, in B-flat major) in 1840 and saw it into print in 1841, and finished the 'Scottish' Symphony (No. 3, in A minor) in 1841 and had it published two years later. Liszt followed a similar path. He abandoned his unfinished 'Revolutionary' Symphony in 1830 but returned to the genre with great success in the mid-1850s with his *Faust* and *Dante* symphonies. Wagner completed his Symphony in C major in 1832 and started another symphony (in E major) two years later but then abandoned the genre, even as he harboured deeply ambivalent attitudes towards it until the end of his life.

Fully aware that it had become a 'colossal undertaking' to write a symphony in the wake of 'Beethoven's nine masterpieces', as the critic Ignaz Jeitteles observed in 1837, symphonists of the next generation were more inclined to put off tackling the genre until they had developed the requisite skills.[20] Anton Bruckner (1824–96) did not venture into the field until 1863, when he was 38. Johannes Brahms (1833–97) seems to have begun several symphonies during his twenties and thirties but invariably transformed these projects in the direction of other genres such as the piano concerto or the serenade; he did not complete his First Symphony, Op. 68, until the age of 43, and even then only after a protracted struggle. He famously despaired to the conductor Hermann Levi in the early 1870s that he would 'never compose a symphony! You have no idea how it feels to our kind [i.e. composers] when one always hears such a giant marching behind.'[21] The giant, of course, was Beethoven, and Brahms would eventually deal with him in his own distinctive way, as we shall see.

II

Among composers of the first post-Beethovenian generation, Berlioz alone succeeded in establishing himself early on with a series of ambitious and highly original works. Perhaps not coincidentally, Berlioz was the only major symphonist of his time working outside the Germanic-speaking realm. He was also, significantly, the only composer of his generation to confront Beethoven directly from the very start. His *Symphonie fantastique: Épisode de la vie d'un artiste* (1830) is in many respects both a homage and a retort to Beethoven's Third, Fifth, Sixth and Ninth symphonies. The 'hero' of this symphony is an artist who imagines his beloved in the form of a theme Berlioz called the *idée fixe*. Like the short-short-short-LONG motive of Beethoven's Fifth, it resurfaces in every movement, but always in a new guise (the details of this process, and similar techniques in *Harold en Italie*, are addressed in Chapter 9). The happy feelings in the countryside – Berlioz's third-movement 'Scène aux champs' – begins with the obligatory shepherds' calls, but the happiness soon dissolves: one of the two parties disappears towards the end of the movement, and the artist immediately connects this non-response with his own love-life: 'What if she has been unfaithful?' he wonders. What had begun as a serene moment of pastoral repose ends with distant and dissonant thunder on the menacingly soft timpani. In the movement that follows, the 'March to the Scaffold', the thunder is transformed in the artist's mind into the sound of military drums accompanying him to the gallows, where he will be executed for the crime of having killed his beloved. Beethoven's funeral march in honour of a hero has been supplanted by accompanimental music for a convicted criminal. Berlioz called his Finale a 'Dream of a Witches' Sabbath', and here he transforms Beethoven's Elysium into Hades. He presents the *idée fixe* on an E-flat clarinet in a guise he himself called 'trivial and grotesque'. With the intoning of the funereal plainchant *Dies irae* in the low winds (bar 127), he creates a counterpart to the 'Seid umschlungen, Millionen' theme of Beethoven's Ninth. The parallels become more apparent still when Berlioz combines this new theme, first introduced well into the course of the Finale, with the movement's central theme, the 'Witches' Round Dance' (bar 414). In this Finale, the joy of Elysium has been transformed into the joy of Hades.

Berlioz pursued similar strategies in *Harold en Italie*, a 'Symphony in Four Movements with Solo Viola' (1832). Again, the idea of an anti-hero lies at the centre of the work. Loosely based on the character of Byron's epic poem *Childe Harold's Pilgrimage*, this Symphony also presents its central theme across all four movements, though with relatively little change. For all his wanderings through the Italian countryside, our hero (in the guise of the solo viola) changes very little. The second-movement 'Pilgrims' March', like the second movement of Schubert's 'Great' C major Symphony and the second movement of Mendelssohn's 'Italian' Symphony – both unknown to Berlioz at the time – takes the Allegretto of Beethoven's Seventh as its model. The Finale systematically recalls the opening of each of the Symphony's three previous movements, only to reject each one, not in favour of any transcendent theme along the lines of the 'Ode to Joy', but rather to make way for the decidedly unlyrical 'Orgy of the Brigands'. As in the Finale of the *Symphonie fantastique*, the forces of evil win out. Harold – the solo viola – disappears for most of the movement and makes only a feeble reappearance just before the end. Berlioz's second symphony is at once both a homage to and refutation of Beethoven, a classic instance of what the literary critic Harold Bloom has called a 'misreading' of a work by an acknowledged predecessor.[22]

With his 'Dramatic Symphony' *Roméo et Juliette* (1839), Berlioz directly confronted the dichotomy between instrumental and vocal music, moving back and forth between the two throughout this seven-movement work. The Finale owes much to opera, but the key moments of Shakespeare's drama, including the crucial scene at the tomb, are given over entirely to instruments. Whereas Beethoven had held the soloists and chorus in reserve until the very end of the Ninth, Berlioz used voices to introduce the instrumental movements. In 1858, long after the work's premiere, Berlioz explained that 'if there is singing, almost from the beginning, it is to prepare the listener's mind for the dramatic scenes whose feelings and passions are to be expressed by the orchestra'.[23]

When Schumann resumed writing orchestral music in 1841, he did so with such intensity that subsequent writers have dubbed it his 'Year of the Symphony'. In a remarkably short span of time, he completed the first version of his Symphony in D minor (eventually published as No. 4, Op. 120), his First Symphony in B-flat major, Op. 38, and the *Ouverture, Scherzo und Finale*, Op. 52, which lacks only a slow movement to conform to the standard outline of a four-movement symphony. The two full-fledged symphonies align themselves with two different composers: the First Symphony reflects Schumann dealing with Schubert's 'Great' C major Symphony, which Schumann himself had discovered in Vienna a few years before, while the Fourth Symphony represents a direct confrontation with Beethoven. In its original form, the D minor symphony was a work in four movements to be played without a pause, thereby emphasising the none-too-subtle thematic links among its constituent parts. The debt to Beethoven's Fifth is particularly evident in the gradual acceleration and breakthrough from D minor to D major at the join between the third-movement Scherzo and the Finale.

Liszt, who had similarly abandoned an early symphonic project around 1830, found other creative outlets for his orchestral ambitions in the second half of the 1840s, when he began writing a series of concert over-tures, programmatic one-movement works he would later rechristen as 'symphonic poems'. Indeed, the first movement of the unfinished 'Revolutionary' Symphony of 1830 would form the basis of the *Héroïde funèbre* (1849–50; rev. 1854–6). Liszt became the leading composer of orchestral music in what would come to be known as the 'New German School', a movement whose adherents strove for new forms and genres that could synthesise literary and musical arts, with or without a sung text. In this sense, Liszt's initial rejection of the genre of the symphony reflects the power of Beethoven's influence. Yet Liszt would eventually go on to write two multi-movement symphonies, one based on Goethe's *Faust*, the other on Dante's *La divina commedia*, both culminating in passages for chorus and orchestra. These works, together with his symphonic poems, reflect his ambivalent attitude towards the symphony and above all his fascination with the challenges posed by the Ninth Symphony.

The shadow of the Ninth

Because of its unusual vocal Finale, with its integration of so many different forms and styles, Beethoven's Ninth Symphony became an object of protracted attention for critics and composers alike. The critical reception of the Ninth was mixed in the early decades. Even Mendelssohn, the one post-Beethovenian composer who seems to have grasped Beethoven's late style better than any of his contemporaries, harboured ambivalent feelings about the Ninth's Finale. 'The instrumental movements belong to the greatest of all that I know in the world of art', he wrote to his friend the historian Gustav Droysen in 1837. But 'from the point at which the voices enter', Mendelssohn confessed, 'I, too, do not understand the work; that is, I find only isolated elements to be perfect, and when this is the case with such a Master, the fault probably lies with us. Or in the performance.' Schumann felt similarly divided, confiding to his diary in February 1841 that although the first two movements had brought him 'great pleasure', he had 'not yet entirely understood the last two movements, in which I can not yet find the thread'. The noted conductor Hans von Bülow con-demned the Finale for having 'trespassed over music's boundaries' and even omitted it from performances, conducting only the first three movements. And most famously of all, Wagner pointed to the Ninth's Finale as evidence that instrumental music had reached its limits and that even Beethoven, the greatest of all instrumental composers, had been compelled to 'redeem' music from its 'intrinsic element' by introducing a sung text.[24]

Mendelssohn nevertheless openly used the Ninth as a model for his *Lobgesang* (1840), with three instrumental movements followed by a lengthy Finale for orchestra, vocal soloists and chorus. Although warmly greeted at its premiere for Leipzig's festival honouring the four-hundredth anniversary of Gutenberg's printing press, the *Lobgesang* eventually became a whipping boy of sorts, a work that imitated Beethovenian forms all too closely. Without citing it by name, Wagner wrote scornfully of it:

> And why should this or that composer not also write a symphony with chorus? Why should 'The Lord God' not be praised full-throatedly at the end, once He has helped bring about the three preceding instrumental movements as dexterously as possible? . . . As soon as Beethoven had written his last symphony, every musical guild could patch and stuff as much as it liked in its effort to create a man of absolute music. But it was just this and nothing more: a shabby, patched and stuffed bogeyman. No sensate, natural man could come out of such a workshop any longer. After Haydn and Mozart, a Beethoven could and had to appear. The spirit of music necessarily demanded him, and without waiting, there he was. Who would now be to Beethoven that which he was to Haydn and Mozart in the realm of absolute music? The greatest genius would be capable of nothing more here, precisely because the spirit of absolute music no longer has need of him.[25]

Wagner would express no such scorn for two works written a few years later by his close friend and future father-in-law, Franz Liszt, whose *Faust* and *Dante* symphonies both end in brief choruses.

In the end, only a relatively small number of nineteenth-century symphonies would culminate in a vocal finale, as Table 14.1 explains. Far more numerous were those works that end in what might be called an implicitly vocal finale, that is, a movement that evokes the sound of a chorus through purely instrumental means alone (see Table 14.2). The Finale of Brahms's First Symphony (1876) is the best-known instance of such a finale, with multiple 'vocal' themes: the lyrical main melody openly reminiscent of the 'Ode to Joy' (bar 62); an alphorn-like theme that evokes the *ranz des vaches* of alpine shepherds (bar 30); and a chorale-like apotheosis presented by the brass (bar 47). But this is merely one in a long line of symphonic finales that in one way or another suggest the sound of a chorus through instruments alone. Berlioz, Mendelssohn, Gade, Spohr, Raff, Rubinstein, Saint-Saëns and Bruckner had all employed a similar device in at least one earlier symphony, and Mahler would bring the tradition to a spectacular close in the nineteenth century with his First and Third Symphonies.

With the passage of time, Beethoven's shadow began to recede: composers like Berlioz, Mendelssohn, Schumann and Brahms had demonstrated beyond question that the symphony remained a viable genre, an

Table 14.1 *Nineteenth-century symphonies with choral finales*

Date	Work
1824	Ludwig van Beethoven, Symphony No. 9
1839	Hector Berlioz, *Roméo et Juliette* (incorporates voices throughout the entire symphony)
1840	Felix Mendelssohn, *Lobgesang* (premiered as a Symphony, later renamed a 'Symphony-Cantata')
1842	Berlioz, *Symphonie funèbre et triomphale* (originally written 1840; re-arranged, with choral parts added to the finale in 1842)
1856	Franz Liszt, *Eine Symphonie zu Dantes Divina commedia*
1857	Liszt, *Eine Faust-Symphonie* (optional vocal ending added to a work that was largely completed by 1854)
1894	Gustav Mahler, Symphony No. 2

Table 14.2 *Nineteenth-century symphonies with implicitly choral finales*

Date	Work
1808	Ludwig van Beethoven, Symphony No. 6 ('Pastoral'). The Finale, labelled 'Hirtengesang', features an implicitly vocal theme that passes through many instrumental groups; concludes with a four-part, chorale-like setting, *pianissimo*.
1824	Muzio Clementi, 'Great National' Symphony. Uses 'God Save the King' at the end of finale (as well as in the slow movement).
1830	Hector Berlioz, *Symphonie fantastique*. The 'Dream of a Witches' Sabbath' uses the *idée fixe* in call-and-response solo/chorus fashion, followed by the *Dies irae* in low brass.
1830	Felix Mendelssohn, 'Reformation' Symphony. Finale built around variations on the chorale melody of 'Ein' feste Burg ist unser Gott'. The original version had included a flute 'recitative' leading from the slow movement into the Finale.
1832	Ludwig Spohr, Symphony No. 4 (*Die Weihe der Töne*). Third movement incorporates an 'ambrosiansicher Lobegsang', and the Finale consists of variations on the chorale 'Begrabt den Leib in seiner Gruft'.
1842	Mendelssohn, Symphony No. 3 ('Scottish'). Concluding Allegro maestoso evokes the sound of a men's chorus.
1842	Niels Gade, Symphony No. 1. Finale features return of a folksong-like theme (Gade's own) from first movement.
1843	Gade, Symphony No. 2. Finale based on a chorale-like theme.
1851	Anton Rubinstein, Symphony No. 2 ('Ocean'). Chorale-like theme appears at the end of the finale in the work's original four-movement version.
1855	Camille Saint-Saëns, Symphony No. 1. Finale begins with a 'gathering' of instruments into a homorhythmic chorale.
1861	Joachim Raff, Symphony No. 1, Op. 96 (*An das Vaterland*). Incorporates the patriotic song 'Was ist des deutschen Vaterlands?' into both fourth and fifth movements, most spectacularly in the Finale.
1872	Raff, Symphony No. 5 (*Lenore*). Agitated Finale ('Wiedervereinigung im Tode') concludes with a quiet chorale.
1873	Anton Bruckner, Symphony No. 3. Finale transforms minor-mode theme of opening movement into major at end, with brass 'chorale' at very end.
1876	Bruckner, Symphony No. 5. Finale centres on and ends with brass 'chorale'.
1876	Johannes Brahms, Symphony No. 1. Finale incorporates three implicitly vocal themes: the 'Ode to Joy'-like theme, the 'Alphorn' theme and the 'Chorale'.
1886	Saint-Saëns, Symphony No. 3 ('Organ'). Finale culminates in chorale-like theme.
1889	Gustav Mahler, Symphony No. 1. Finale concludes with a theme reminiscent of 'Hallelujah' from Handel's *Messiah* ('And He shall reign for ever and ever').
1896	Mahler, Symphony No. 3. Chorale-like theme throughout the Finale.

attitude that was by no means a given half a century before. These later composers, moreover, had created shadows of their own, so that from the 1840s onwards, layers of influence become all the more difficult to distinguish. The symphonies of Niels Gade (1817–90), for example, bear unmistakable traces of Mendelssohn's approach to the genre in their thematic material, orchestration and formal design. The Symphony in D minor (1888) by César Franck (1822–90), in turn, owes much to Beethoven's Fifth, with its cyclic form and minor-to-major trajectory, yet it could also be argued that Franck's chromaticism, orchestration and intricate web of thematic transformations were shaped even more profoundly by the later music dramas of Wagner.

By the end of the century, the symphonic landscape had changed profoundly. The profusion of individual styles, the growing importance of nationalistic tendencies, the ever-expanding range of harmonic possibilities and the expansion of the orchestra itself all combined to create a broader range of options for symphonists. Composers could also count on more venues in which to present their symphonies, for by 1900 every municipality with aspirations to cultural status either had or wanted to have its own standing orchestra. Even in the New World, an orchestral backwater for most of the nineteenth century, civic orchestras had become a point of special cultural pride. Ensembles that still exist today were established in New York (1842), St Louis (1880), Boston (1881), Chicago (1891), Cincinnati (1894) and Philadelphia (1900).

'A symphony', Mahler is alleged to have declared to Jean Sibelius in 1907, 'must be like the world: it must be all-embracing.'[26] And what was to be embraced, in Mahler's view, included even Beethoven's shadow, so that when in his Second Symphony he reverted to a pattern of tumultuous instrumental movements 'redeemed' by subsequent vocal ones, even the harshest of his contemporary critics did not take him to task for following the model of the Ninth Symphony too closely. Mahler, and other composers after him in the twentieth century, would continue to look to Beethoven as the paradigmatic composer of symphonies, but by 1900, time had healed all – or at least most – anxieties.

Notes

1 Adolph Bernhard Marx, concert review of 13 December 1824, *Berliner Allgemeine musikalische Zeitung*, 1 (29 December 1824), 444. For references to other comments of a similar nature from around this time, see Mark Evan Bonds, *Music as Thought: Listening to the Symphony in the Age of Beethoven* (Princeton, 2006), 118, n. 4.

2 Letter of 17 December 1832 to Friedrich Hofmeister; see Akio Mayeda, *Robert Schumanns Weg zur Symphonie* (Zürich, 1992), 175.

3 *Neue Zeitschrift für Musik*, 12 (10 March 1840), 82.

4 Amadeus Wendt, 'Über den Zustand der Musik in Deutschland. Eine Skizze', *Allgemeine musikalische Zeitung mit besonderer Rücksicht auf den österreichischen Kaiserstaat*, 6 (1822), 762.

5 Anonymous, *Wiener Allgemeine Theater-Zeitung*, 58 (13 May 1824), 230–1, quoted in David Benjamin Levy, 'Early Performances of Beethoven's Ninth Symphony: A Documentary Study of Five Cities' (Ph.D. diss., University of Rochester, 1979), 47.

6 Gottfried Weber, 'Teutschland im ersten Viertel des neuen Jahrhunderts', *Cäcilia*, 4 (1826), 109–10.

7 Friedrich Rochlitz, 'Nekrolog', *Allgemeine musikalische Zeitung*, 29 (28 March 1827), 228.

8 The most notable of these are John Hawkins's *General History of the Science and*

Practice of Music (1776) and Charles Burney's General History of Music (1776–89). Giovanni Battista Martini's Storia della musica (1757–81) and Johann Nicolaus Forkel's Allgemeine Geschichte der Musik (1788–1801) would both remain incomplete and end their coverage with antiquity and the Renaissance, respectively, but are nevertheless products of the same broader impulses.

9 See Walter Jackson Bate, The Burden of the Past and the English Poet (Cambridge, Mass., 1970).

10 Edmund Burke, A Philosophical Inquiry into the Origin of Our Ideas of The Sublime and Beautiful, 2nd edn (London, 1757), Part III, Section XXVII, 'The Sublime and Beautiful Compared'.

11 See Mark Evan Bonds, 'The Symphony as Pindaric Ode', in Elaine Sisman, ed., Haydn and his World (Princeton, 1997), 131–53.

12 Carl Dahlhaus, Nineteenth-Century Music trans. J. Bradford Robinson (Berkeley and Los Angeles, 1989), 10, emphasis mine.

13 See Bonds, Music as Thought, chapters 1 and 2.

14 See Scott Burnham, Beethoven Hero (Princeton, 1995).

15 Gottfried Wilhelm Fink, 'Ueber die Symphonie, als Beitrag zur Geschichte und Aesthetik derselben', Allgemeine musikalische Zeitung, 37 (1835), 559.

16 Henry F. Chorley, Modern German Music: Recollections and Criticisms, 2 vols. (London, 1854), vol. I, 369.

17 Letter to Leopold Kupelwieser, 31st March 1824, in Otto Erich Deutsch, ed., Schubert: Die Dokumente seines Lebens (Kassel, 1964), 235. See also John M. Gingerich, 'Unfinished Considerations: Schubert's "Unfinished" Symphony in the Context of His Beethoven Project', 19th-Century Music, 31 (2007), 99–112.

18 See Mark Evan Bonds, After Beethoven: Imperatives of Originality in the Symphony (Cambridge, Mass., 1996), 115–16.

19 On Mendelssohn's struggles with these works, see Judith Silber, 'Mendelssohn and his "Reformation" Symphony', Journal of the American Musicological Society, 40 (1987), 310–16; John Michael Cooper, '"Aber eben dieser Zweifel": A New Look at Mendelssohn's "Italian" Symphony', 19th-Century Music, 15 (1992), 169–87.

20 Ignaz Jeitteles, 'Symphonie', in Aesthetisches Lexikon, vol. II (Vienna, 1837).

21 Max Kalbeck, Johannes Brahms, 4 vols. (Vienna and Leipzig, 1904–14), vol. I, 171–2.

22 Harold Bloom, The Anxiety of Influence: A Theory of Poetry (New York and Oxford, 1973); Bloom, A Map of Misreading (New York and Oxford, 1975). For more on Harold en Italie as a misreading of Beethoven, see Bonds, After Beethoven, chapter 2.

23 Berlioz, Preface to Roméo et Juliette, trans. in D. Kern Holoman, Berlioz (Cambridge, Mass., 1989), 261.

24 Mendelssohn to Gustav Droysen, 14 December 1837, in Carl Wehmer, ed., Ein tief gegründet Herz. Der Briefwechsel Felix Mendelssohn-Bartholdys mit Johann Gustav Droysen (Heidelberg, 1959), 49; Schumann, Tagebücher: 1836–1854, ed. Gerd Nauhaus (Leipzig, 1987), 147 (entry for 11 February 1841); Hans von Bülow, letter of 17 November 1888 to Siegfried Ochs, Briefe und Schriften, ed. Marie von Bülow, 8 vols. (Leipzig, 1895–1908), vol. VIII, 229.

25 Wagner, Das Kunstwerk der Zukunft (1849), in his Gesammelte Schriften und Dichtungen, 3rd edn, 10 vols. (Leipzig, 1887–8), vol. III, 100–1.

26 Erik Tawaststjerna, Sibelius, trans. Robert Layton, 3 vols. (London, 1976 and 1997), vol. II, 76–7.

15 The symphony as programme music

JOHN WILLIAMSON

On one level, most symphonies are programmatic in some sense, many of these hardly 'musical'. The forces that bear on composers are many and various. Symphonists, most obviously Shostakovich and other Russians, have been subjected to political programmes, but musical politics may play a more subtle role, as in the not implausible suggestion that Vaughan Williams allowed ideas of English musical revival to colour perceptions of his symphonies in ways that may not have been in his mind when he wrote them.[1] That composers have tended to be defensive about associations from outside the sphere of the 'purely musical' since the time of Hanslick is another instance of the force that ideas can have in helping to obfuscate the surprising concreteness that composers' perceptions may sometimes assume. As a result, study of the programme symphony is hardly a matter of establishing tidy categories. The most 'absolute' of works remains open to reinterpretation, which may arise from ancillary information in letters and sketches that are not strictly part of the aesthetic experience bequeathed by the composer. Programmes in symphonies have an awkward habit of attaching themselves in spite of the composer's most studied neutrality in the face of the idea.

Multi-movement symphonies with programmes existed before Liszt wrote his *Faust-Symphonie* and *Symphonie zu Dantes Divina Commedia*. It is arguable that neither work made an epoch. Formally, their three- and two-movement structures sparked no host of imitators (already 'as a rule, narrative or semi-narrative programs like Beethoven's led his contemporaries much further afield from symphonic forms').[2] There were other models for symphonies with voices in Beethoven, Mendelssohn and Berlioz, the significance of which was more to do with their appearance alongside the first symphonic poems so-called, with which Liszt did make history, producing 'the only instrumental genre that can be considered as characteristic for the New German School'.[3] In time, symphonic poem and symphony developed hybrids that created problems of classification and understanding. This was partly because they shared the three qualities that Carl Dahlhaus defined as essential for the emergence of the symphonic poem: preserving the 'classical ideal of the symphony without yielding to a derivative dependence on its traditional formal scheme'; the raising of programme music 'to poetic and philosophical sublimity'; and the union of expression with 'thematic and motivic manipulation'.[4] Nonetheless, the importance of these in altering the nature of the programme symphony should not obscure the fact that other models already existed.

Characteristics and programmes

In the second of her *Lettres d'un Voyageur*, George Sand noted that:

> The first time I heard Beethoven's Pastoral Symphony I was unaware of its true subject-matter and to this enchanting harmony I made up in my head a poem in the manner of Milton. At the very point at which the composer makes the quail and the nightingale sing, I had set the fall of the rebellious angel and his last cry to heaven. When I learnt of my mistake I revised my poem at the second hearing, and it turned out to be in the manner of Gessner, my response being readily attuned to the impression Beethoven had meant to create.[5]

Since Gessner's literary and artistic works are not without pretensions to the sublime, Sand's revised impressions are not entirely purged of Miltonic associations. Nor is it clear that they should be. The history of the programme symphony is only partly about composers' intentions, or indeed about their response to extra-musical stimuli. The search for programmatic points of reference in 'abstract' forms such as the symphony has been a source of entertainment to listeners from the 'Pastoral' onwards, certainly, and even before. One result of this has been to obscure what may legitimately be defined as a 'programme symphony'. The 'Pastoral' helps to formulate one of the difficulties. Beethoven's famous claim that it embodied feeling rather than representation seems to make it a key stage in the evolution of the programme symphony. Yet this has not proved incompatible with viewing it as a 'characteristic symphony' in the baroque manner. F. E. Kirby equated the central concept in the history of the programme symphony, the 'poetic idea', with a 'single emotional character or quality throughout'. He defined 'characteristic' as 'an attribute or set of attributes that distinguishes or characterizes something' and that could involve either uniqueness or typicality, and suggested a repertory based on style and other factors that was the appropriate area for a music of this kind.[6]

The idea of a characteristic symphony has not been without influence. The increasing attention paid to it has led to some rehabilitation of Arnold Schering's views of programmatic traces in composers of the classical era, as when James Webster noted that his 'lack of attention to the distinction between authentic and inauthentic evidence and infelicities in the concrete interpretations' did not prevent his article being 'the best single survey of

Haydn's programmatic symphonies we have'.[7] Webster cites evidence relating to Haydn's portrayal of 'moral characters' or 'characteristics', which seems to go beyond what Kirby had in mind; a later writer on Haydn moves characteristics away from Kirby's style-based examples to 'connotations of emotion, unity, and humanity'.[8] This seems to rehabilitate the programme in Haydn in a manner more akin to Schering's 'poetic idea, programme, or "romanzetto"'; but Webster had already distinguished between 'programmatic or extramusical associations' and symphonies that were ruled by '"characteristic" topoi ... to be understood as associational, rather than as representations of tangible objects', which seems to rework Beethoven's famous formula.[9] And it is clear that Webster views Haydn's 'explicitly characteristic symphonies' as relatively early works devoted to times of the day, weather, the hunt and the sacred.[10]

The question arises as to whether the programme symphony emerged from the characteristic symphony or whether the latter was merely a subset of the former. Webster introduced the notion of a 'strong' programme (as in the case of *Il Distratto*) that depended on the dissemination of a work in association with a specific idea (which could be expanded to embrace a narrative) and thus stood above mere associations or characteristics.[11] That this is a better model for nineteenth-century orchestral music is arguable. But Webster also treats the 'Farewell' Symphony as a programmatic work based on an explicit narrative. There is a leap of faith here that is akin to later enterprises that would be labelled hermeneutic. The famous tale of the elaborately staged withdrawal of the musicians in the Finale is extended to the whole work, and its provenance is assumed to be authentic.[12] That there must inevitably be a doubt about this properly locates the 'Farewell' Symphony in the category claimed by Ludwig Finscher for the uncertain area 'between absolute and programme music', which is where George Sand should probably be located with her pleasant fantasies about Milton and Gessner.[13]

It is possible to note that characteristic and programme symphonies are rightly to be distinguished from one another by degrees of authority in the provenance of ideas or narratives, but that there is constant interchanging of elements between the two areas, reinforced by the open invitation to speculate provided by associations that are usually implicitly extramusical. But this does not resolve the questions of terminology on any firm basis. Even the description 'characteristic symphony' seems a little imposed on music by the musicologists' desire to classify. The most exhaustive study of the characteristic in music between 1750 and 1850 has found only four explicit uses of 'characteristic symphony', among them the 'Pastoral' on the strength of a sketch rather than a title, and Spohr's *Die Weihe der Töne*.[14] The idea of the characteristic is thus as much a tool for interpretation as an explicit genre. And it also helps to distinguish between the 'literary' programme symphony that stems certainly from Liszt and Berlioz, and those works that celebrate nature through the use of topoi; the distinction may be illustrated somewhat later by the contrast between the seasonal symphonies by Raff and his more explicitly literary *Lenore*.

Finally, it is arguable that the nineteenth-century programme symphony operated at least in part by creating its own characteristic topoi to replace more conventional affects, or alternatively marshalled the characteristic into newer contexts by narrative programmes and associations with literature. In support of this may be cited a recent analysis of Mendelssohn's 'Reformation' Symphony by John Toews. He reads the work as programmatic in a double sense: the ambition 'to recreate the essence of Bach's sacred music for a new age'; and 'the elevation of the individual soul into the divine order'.[15] In the first sense, the formal structures are the programmatic content, and the characteristics are the psalm tone, amen and chorale that Mendelssohn cites (quotation is a major theme in studies of programmatic content, as already is evident in Schering's and Webster's tracking of liturgical elements in Haydn's symphonies).[16] The 'Reformation' is therefore 'an historical program symphony' whose generic echoes may be analysed hermeneutically (a more complex version of the explicitly historical symphony that Spohr essayed somewhat later). Bach's music stands for the Reformation that ensured the triumph of the second element. Quotations and generic references became central to, and substitute for the 'characteristic' in the nineteenth-century programme symphony, as 'an essential means of rendering more precise the spoken character of the music'.[17]

Nineteenth-century dilemmas

Beethoven supplied the 'Pastoral' Symphony with something more than mere movement titles. In this respect, arguably he outstripped Berlioz in one of the key works of the emergence of the programme symphony, *Harold en Italie*. The status of Berlioz as a composer of programme symphonies is currently rather uncertain, given that only one of his four symphonies, *Symphonie fantastique*, can be considered programmatic in the strong sense: it was disseminated with a declared extramusical idea elaborated into a narrative. Stephen Rodgers, the latest writer to consider how far Berlioz contributed to the genre, takes a rather broader view of the matter than some of his predecessors.[18] Is *Roméo et Juliette* to be considered dramatic or programmatic, or perhaps a mixture of the two? The question is hardly specific to Berlioz, since there are other works both by contemporaries (for example

Mendelssohn's *Lobgesang*) and by later composers (Mahler's Symphony No. 2 and Sibelius's *Kullervo*) that tell stories partly by instrumental associative means, partly by direct setting of texts. Here the manner in which Berlioz interpreted Beethoven is of interest, since Rodgers points out that Berlioz interpreted Beethoven's Sixth and Ninth symphonies in similar ways, treating the programmatic clues of the one in much the same way as the literary text setting in the other.[19] Regardless of origin, interpretation yielded a 'poetic' narrative. With Berlioz, there is early evidence of Mark Evan Bonds's notion, broached in Chapter 14, of adapting the Ninth Symphony's 'basic strategy to purely instrumental symphonies by imbuing implicitly vocal ideas with a quality of transcendence'.[20] But with Berlioz, a real narrative is often created, whereas modern reading of Beethoven's symphonies tends to concentrate on 'an implied significance that overflows the musical scenario, lending a sense of extramusical narrative to otherwise untranslatable events'.[21] The narrative sense or shape in Beethoven helps to explain why musicologists have manoeuvred 'between absolute and programme music'.

Some commentators in Germany drew quite explicit parallels between Berlioz's achievement in his symphonies and the 'Pastoral': Peter Cornelius saw *Harold en Italie* as the successor to the 'Pastoral' but without Beethoven's inwardness (a topos of New-German Berlioz criticism).[22] But among other commentators on the programme symphony, such as Richard Pohl, who was even more receptive to New-German ideas, it is clear that it was above all the vocal Ninth, not the 'Pastoral', which was the foundation of the modern symphony.[23] That the modern symphony was programmatic was a given, but 'in the higher sense' involving 'a quite specific ring of ideas with a precisely formulated musical content, to ally poetic intentions with the musical content . . .'[24] The specific idea was not necessarily as detailed as a programme book, felt by Pohl to be welcome but not absolutely essential.[25] It is in the face of comments such as these that it becomes apparent that 'programmatic' has come to mean something rather different from the characteristic or the topos.

As the most persistent advocate of programmatic interpretation of the nineteenth-century symphony, Constantin Floros has isolated as the key idea in Liszt the notion of 'Erzählung innerer Vorgänge', elaborated by Liszt as some common factor in nation or epoch whose interest resided more in 'inner events than in the actions of the external world'.[26] The specific turn that the programme symphony took in the nineteenth century was thus in some part an interpretation by writers digesting the lessons of Herder and Hegel; programmes and poetic ideas were reflections of ideals, a notion that jumps out of the pages of Franz Brendel, the chief propagandist of the New German School. When it came to drawing lessons from Berlioz's programme symphonies, he differed in subtle ways from Franz Liszt. One writer has accurately noted that Brendel's starting point was idealism, whereas Liszt was more inclined to invoke nature and its imagined laws.[27] As a result, Brendel gave intellectual credibility to the German tradition that viewed Berlioz as 'more the representation of outer than inner feelings' and hence of a failure to build adequately on the inner psychological *Tonmalerei* represented by Beethoven's Ninth Symphony.[28]

It almost certainly was not Liszt's concern to establish such a picture of Berlioz when he produced his celebrated essay on *Harold*, an essay that is as much about the type of music Liszt wanted to write as the music that Berlioz had written. Thus he compared Berlioz's first two symphonies as poems to Byron, Senancourt and Jean Paul, and specifically related this to psychological depiction.[29] Liszt's aim was 'the poetic programme and the characteristic melody' and something of that was to be found in Berlioz as well as drama; indeed the drama was to be found in symphonic form in Berlioz's *Damnation de Faust* as well as in *Roméo*.[30] Programmes, poetic ideas and the symphonic in Liszt's picture of Berlioz were to some degree independent of genre and also of mere narrative. As Wolfgang Dömling has noted, it was no accident that Liszt chose to write of the symphony by Berlioz that had no direct narrative rather than the *Symphonie fantastique*.[31] Among Liszt's own works, it has been claimed that there are certain instances where 'the program is not the crucial form-determining factor it has long been assumed to be'.[32] This view is based mainly on pieces with allusive titles that hint at Liszt's 'modern' hero of a 'philosophical epoch': *Tasso*, *Prometheus*, *Orpheus* and *Faust*. This group of works is based on 'the numerous and prominent correspondences between these pieces and earlier compositional and theoretical models of sonata construction'.[33] It also continues to treat symphonic poems alongside programme symphonies under the same aesthetic banner; Liszt's highly ambivalent legacy to the writing of programmatic orchestral music. If the traditional picture of the programme symphony in the hands of Berlioz and Liszt involved extensive mixing of genres, then the years that followed Liszt's works produced a plethora of terms and titles that thoroughly confused the concept of how poetic ideas and symphonic music might go together.

Epigoni and hybrids

If we ask what distinguished the programme symphony in the later nineteenth century from the host of other descriptions that owed something to the idea of a symphonic poem, it is possible to answer at the level of generalities:

> The difference between symphony and symphonic poem works itself out less in the intellectual than the formal sphere: the symphonic poem departs persistently from the symphonic plan of order in imitation of the textual or visual model, while the symphony, in spite of all thinkable extramusical 'content', remains committed to this plan of order in its broad outlines.[34]

This distinction relegates the extramusical to the level of the secondary. The definition would do to distinguish symphonic poem from programme symphony, abstract symphony and Finscher's hybrids. But it is at least arguable that it is easier to say what a programme symphony is or might be than to define a symphonic poem. Something of this might be apparent from consideration of that strange area in the composition of symphonic works that stretches from the last symphonic utterances of Liszt and Spohr in the late 1850s to the appearance of Brahms's First Symphony in 1876, a period marked by the evolution of various 'nationalist' symphonists and the earliest works by Bruckner, and by much else that has been described under the term 'forgotten symphonies' (this gap is filled in by David Brodbeck in Chapter 4).[35]

One catalogue of symphonic novelties in the period 1850 to 1875 (Table 15.1) reveals these among numerous other generic titles (some so specific as to be hardly generic).[36] The influence of 'symphonic poetry' is traceable in quite a few of these (even more when descriptive titles augment the generic description), and yet they outnumber the group of explicitly entitled symphonic poems. Although not so noted by Grotjahn, they also stand up well to the number of symphonies whose titles proclaim them to be in some measure programmatic.[37] When we consider this neglected area, it is quite thinkable that Finscher's now celebrated formula be adapted to suggest not merely

Table 15.1 *Rebecca Grotjahn's catalogue of mid-nineteenth-century generic titles*

Symphonie-Fantaisie
Ouverture-Symphonie
Musikalisches Seegemälde in Form einer Symphonie
Sinfonisches Stimmungsbild
Sinfonisches Concertstück
Sinfonie-Kantate
Sinfonische Kantate
Sinfonische Phantasie
Dramatische Phantasie (Sinfonischer Prolog)
Sinfonisches Tongemälde
Sinfonisches Tongedicht
Sinfonische Tonbilder
Sinfonisches Phantasiebild
Sinfonia appassionata
Sinfonische Stücke

the lurking presence of quasi-programmatic content in abstract-seeming symphonies, but also programmatic works whose resemblance to 'absolute music' is close enough to engender confusion, as well as works between symphony and symphonic poem that flirt with the idea of the programmatic but withhold the substance (as in Brahms's tantalisingly entitled *Tragische Ouvertüre*, which has its symphonic counterpart in Draeseke's *Symphonia tragica*).

As an example of the manner in which programmatic elements may infiltrate abstract designs with apparently minimal change to normal working procedures, we can take Friedrich Gernsheim's Symphony No. 3 in C minor, which, the composer noted, had its 'point of departure' in the idea of 'Miriam's Song of Victory' (the composer in his youth had been greatly taken by Handel's *Israel in Egypt*).[38] Yet he denied that it was programme music (perhaps to be expected in a composer reckoned among the followers of Brahms by contemporaries) and insisted that it was a mood picture, thus begging the questions of how far a mood picture incorporated a 'poetic idea', especially since the second movement was acknowledged as a portrait of Miriam herself in distress on a summer night by the banks of the Nile with timbrel. Yet the context of Gernsheim's programmatic comments indicates that this is essentially a work of struggle and triumph on the model of two other symphonies in C minor, and is not to be regarded as more or less programmatic than Beethoven's Fifth or Brahms's First. Nor is it substantially different in style, technique and form from Gernsheim's other symphonies. As one instance we may take a feature of the first movement: the development and reprise are elided, with no real thematic return to the first subject – the reprise is tonal until the entry of the second subject renders it also thematic. This is only slightly more extreme than Gernsheim's practices in his other first movements: to alter the return of the first subject by placing it over a dominant pedal, by inverting its position from treble to bass, or by abbreviating it and altering its continuation. His finales exhibit the same range of tricks with more emphasis perhaps on rescoring than rewriting. The Third Symphony essentially preserves the main features of symphonic form that Gernsheim inherited from Mendelssohn, Schumann and Brahms. Only the presence of a harp (a sign of lurking narrative content) betrays an interesting departure from the composer's normal practice. Of this 'Miriam' Symphony, it is possible to echo Michael Kennedy's summary of Vaughan Williams's *London Symphony*: 'This *is* a programme symphony, but it is also perfectly acceptable as "absolute" music.'[39]

By comparison, a composer like Joachim Raff who had belonged (albeit half-heartedly) to the New German School went rather further in adapting symphonic form to programmatic purposes. This was more marked in works with literary or quasi-literary programmes than in those that recall the characteristic symphony. Thus the symphonies (nos. 8–11) based on the four seasons and the Symphony No. 7, 'In the Alps', all conform to four-movement form and have titles that adhere to content that was typical of such programmes from the Baroque onwards, or reinterpret them in Romantic spirit: 'Spring's Return', 'Man's Hunt', 'First Snow', 'Harvest Laurel', 'By the Hearth', 'In the Inn', 'By the Lake'; and 'Walpurgis Night', 'Ghost Dance', 'The Hunt of the Elves'. The Third Symphony, 'Im Walde', imposes a part structure on the movements in anticipation of Mahler's practice in some symphonies, which reflects a slightly more elaborate programmatic framework, particularly in the Finale, with its evocation of Wotan, Frau Holle and the Wild Hunt. In this it anticipates the much more literary Fifth Symphony, which groups its four movements into three parts: *Liebesglück* (embracing a sonata Allegro and a slow movement); *Trennung* (a military march for a departing hero); and *Wiedervereinigung im Tode*, an Introduction and Ballade based on Gottfried August Bürger's *Lenore*.

This programme includes elements of mood painting such as would have seemed acceptable to Gernsheim. In Bürger's poem, the love idyll is not present; the opening depicts Lenore's beloved far away at the Battle of Prague with Frederick the Great's army. The Symphony's stylised insistence on a happy love affair thus has no direct pictorial stimulus, and results in a sonata structure that is more extensive and tonally more wide-ranging but not substantially different in approach to that of Gernsheim in 'Miriam'. The Andante quasi allegretto is equally plausible as an abstract symphonic argument; in echo perhaps of Liszt's *Faust* Symphony the two movements of Part I privilege E, C and A♭ as tonal centres, but so would Brahms's First Symphony when it appeared a few years later. C is also the key of the march in Part II, in which there are clear signs of an army vanishing into the distance and despairing lamentation in the trio. In this, characteristics and topoi are dominant. In stressing that the Finale is specifically linked to Bürger, Raff thus distinguishes it from the more stylised opening movements and parts, and it is here that a story is most obviously told. Elements of the march return, recalling the examples of Beethoven's Ninth Symphony and Berlioz's *Harold*, the horse's hoof beats sound in percussion, and after some music that can be interpreted loosely as the conversation between Lenore and her ghostly returning soldier, the remainder of the movement is dominated by his horse's galloping figuration (Berlioz's 'Ride to the Abyss' is an obvious model, more so than Liszt's *Mazeppa*), and chorale phrases that reflect both passing funeral cortèges and (after the wild ride has ceased) the dying Lenore's vision of eternity. The riding figuration is a characteristic certainly, and the chorale is one of the nineteenth-century symphony's equivalents of a topos that inhabits programmatic and seemingly abstract works on a regular basis.

Programmes and clues to content thus hang on titles that correspond to Liszt's well-known analogy of the 'thread of Ariadne', the clew that guides the listener through the novel events of the works.[40] Yet musicology has become fairly sophisticated in 'bringing music to speech', and it is arguable that there are plentiful hints in absolute symphonies to suggest a content that is not simply abstract. This remains true of works that followed Weimar or Leipzig. Essentially, music 'between absolute and programme' initially depended on quotations and allusions to provide a content. At times such readings tended towards the excessively concrete: Finscher's attempt to relate Mendelssohn's 'Scottish' Symphony to the European craze for Scott's novels has not found complete favour with commentators.[41] This has not diluted the value of the attempt 'to interpret from their historical context the content of musical works that traditionally had hitherto tended to be reckoned as either absolute or programmatic, and whose trans-musical dimension seems to have been submerged under arbitrary interpretation or vague general concepts'.[42] Initially, such attempts depended on precisely the kind of elements that can be identified in Gernsheim and Raff: chorale, alphorn and quasi-Beethovenian conflict can unlock a content of a kind in Brahms's First Symphony, to which 'quotation' or allusion (the 'Joy' theme) can add a dash of verisimilitude or homage depending on context, though whether this adds up to 'nothing less than the most concrete and most ambitious programme of ideas that was ever to provide the foundation of a symphony between Beethoven and Mahler' is at the very least debatable.[43] It is perhaps more appropriately read as the basis for the kind of 'plot archetypes' that Anthony Newcomb has seen in Schumann and others; the narrative pattern of Beethoven's Fifth, 'suffering leading to healing or redemption', is readable in Brahms and Gernsheim and also, with suitable modifications, in Bruckner.[44] Perhaps this seems meagre as general wisdom outside the context of specific analyses. Nonetheless, Finscher's approach may be seen as the ancestor of the infinitely more subtle reading of Brahms's Second Symphony by Reinhold Brinkmann, perhaps the most valuable study of abstraction yielding content in the literature about the nineteenth-century symphony.[45]

That the generation after Liszt tended to respond in hesitant fashion to programmes in the symphony is also suggested by Tchaikovsky's *Manfred*. That the presence of programmatic elements leads to a looser treatment of traditional form is not especially surprising in Tchaikovsky's case, since his later symphonies, the Fourth and Sixth in particular, tend towards a more episodic separation of subject groups and individual themes that encourages the listener to think programmatically even where precise details are lacking. The resulting weakening of the traditional tensions of sonata form in opening movements proceeds in *Manfred* to the point where it makes less sense to talk about specific forms. Although the opening movement seems to begin with an introduction, a first subject in B minor and a modulating transition, the arrival of the second subject, possibly associated with Astarte, involves changes of key, tempo and metre. The sonata structure then disappears. When the 'first subject' returns, B minor is restored, but not the initial metre or tempo. A Lisztian threnody as combined reprise and coda (as in *Hamlet*) takes over. There is more than one way in which the movement might be assimilated to traditional formal structures, but the modifications operate under extramusical stimulus, as in *Francesca da Rimini*.

Continuity and convergence?

In his history of nineteenth-century music, Carl Dahlhaus claimed that: 'as far as the technical assumptions of the monumental style were concerned, at the stage of compositional evolution around 1900 there was little or no difference between the symphony and the symphonic poem'.[46] He is thinking of the symphony and symphonic poem in the hands of Mahler and Strauss. Although this is far from the clearest formulation in Dahlhaus's book, it is possible to understand his gist from consideration of what he termed *Vermittlung* (mediation) in Liszt between the sonata tradition and the characteristic: the idea of using changes in tone and characteristics to produce formal coherence 'sublates the tradition of the character piece into Liszt's conception of the symphonic'.[47] Characteristics create structural and expressive connections through restatements and transformations rather than defining a dominant tone as previously. This, accordingly, is a key to understanding both movements in symphonies (the first movement of Mahler's Seventh is his illustration of *Weltanschauungsmusik* that in the absence of a specific programme of ideas can be read as 'self-sustaining' and 'formal-logical') and symphonic poems such as those by Strauss.[48]

Here is an acknowledgement that an important reconciliation of ideas was taking place. That Liszt's transformation of the symphonic by programmatic means was an important factor in the genesis of the 'monumental' orchestral style of the early twentieth century recognises on one hand that for all Mahler's insistence that programmes should perish,[49] symphonies might still be 'read' as texts if one knew the signs. On the other hand, the role of Liszt in the evolution of the tone poems of Strauss is acknowledged in anticipation of a prominent argument of recent years. The relationship between Liszt and Strauss has been re-examined with a view to establishing to what extent they shared a common view of the status of the poetic idea in the symphonic. Recent writers have tended to consider the link a strong one: in Walter Werbeck's view, the notion that Liszt wrote poetic music while Strauss wrote witty illustrative programmatic music has ceased to be tenable. The programmes that they chose may have been different in tone and mood, but their approaches were fundamentally similar, albeit with a substantial injection of orchestral polyphony from Wagnerian models in Strauss's case.[50] As chapters 1 and 11 have stressed, it is possible with Strauss to see the convergence between symphony and symphonic poem move to its consummation in single-movement works that now have the dimensions of symphonies, in the *Symphonia domestica* and the *Alpensinfonie*, while with Mahler, the Lisztian 'relativisation' of formal categories enables symphonic movements to employ characteristics as though they were Lisztian poems.[51]

In spite of this, however, the programme symphony and the symphonic poem have remained stubbornly apart. It has become clear that the 'formal-logical' symphony with the associative title (the *Harold* tradition) remained alive and well to the point that commentators have regularly supplied associations that may actually diverge from the starting point of the composer's journey (as the question of the originating idea of Vaughan Williams's *Pastoral Symphony* suggests). The idea that the programme symphony might tend towards a single-movement structure, thus eliding the distinction between it and the symphonic poem, can be traced perhaps in early works by Shostakovich and in Nielsen's Symphony No. 4, but the 'formal-logical' symphony has followed the same path, most famously in Sibelius's Symphony No. 7. His career as a whole followed a curious trajectory leading from a symphony that was at once programmatic, multi-movement and partly choral to a last work that was abstract, single-movement and purely instrumental. As if to indicate that programmatic and absolute still retained certain distinguishing features, the Seventh Symphony was paired at the end of the composer's career with a symphonic poem, *Tapiola*. To complete the picture, sketch studies have revealed that hermeneutic clues relating to Sibelius's sense of nature lurk within his earlier symphonies.[52]

Coda: quotation and characteristics

The importance of quotation as key to content and ideas has been recognised in more than one study. A typical survey of the nineteenth-century symphonic literature has concentrated largely on composers who have contributed to programmatic symphonies and symphonic poems: Mendelssohn and Spohr, Berlioz and Liszt, Mahler and Strauss, with the addition of Saint-Saëns and the debatably programmatic Bruckner. What constitutes quotation is by no means clear, however, since the techniques involved included 'changes of parameters', compositional technique (e.g. fugue to bolster religious sonorities), citation of styles, generic references and thematic combinations.[53] At least a few of these encroach once more on the sphere of characteristics (e.g. *stile-antico* counterpoint in a Haydn symphony). The notion that the symphony could present ideas as in a public oration, as conceived in the eighteenth century, yielded to associations and poetic glimpses afforded by titles, homilies (as Liszt's programmes often appear), appended poems and analogies; the poetic substance of works of art is treated as transmutable from literature to the visual arts to music. As a result, the relationship of 'absolute music' to content became complex. When Gernsheim denied that his associative allusive symphony was programmatic, he anticipated a host of others who rushed on to the bandwagon of absolute music in denial at the evocative power of citation and allusion. But who on hearing the chimes of Big Ben in Vaughan Williams's *London Symphony* can believe that it is only a symphony by a Londoner? And who on discovering the echoes of war in his *Pastoral Symphony* can ever believe in Philip Heseltine's cow staring over a gate?[54] The listener's impressions, like those of George Sand, change under the stimulus of interpretation, authorised and unauthorised, overt in the 'strong' sense, or buried among the fantasies and jottings of composers' private letters and sketches.

Notes

1 Alain Frogley, 'Constructing Englishness in Music: National Character and the Reception of Ralph Vaughan Williams', in Frogley, ed., *Vaughan Williams Studies* (Cambridge, 1996), 1–22, esp. 14–17.

2 Richard Will, *The Characteristic Symphony in the Age of Haydn and Beethoven* (Cambridge, 2002), 171.

3 Christian Martin Schmidt, 'Die Neudeutsche Schule und die symphonische Tradition', in Detlef Altenburg, ed., *Liszt und die Neudeutsche Schule* (Laaber, 2006), 33–8.

4 Carl Dahlhaus, *Nineteenth-Century Music*, trans. J. Bradford Robinson (Berkeley and Los Angeles, 1989), 238.

5 George Sand, *Lettres d'un Voyageur*, ed. Patricia Thomson, trans. Sacha Rabinovitch and Patricia Thomson (Harmondsworth, 1987), 80.

6 F. E. Kirby, 'Beethoven's Pastoral Symphony as a "Sinfonia caracteristica"', *Musical Quarterly*, 56 (1970), 608–12.

7 Arnold Schering, 'Bemerkungen zu J. Haydns Programmsinfonien', *Jahrbuch Peters* (1939), 9–27; James Webster, *Haydn's 'Farewell' Symphony and the Idea of Classical Style: Through-Composition and Cyclic Integration in His Instrumental Music* (Cambridge, 1991), 226.

8 Webster, *Haydn's 'Farewell' Symphony*, 234–5; Will, *The Characteristic Symphony*, 8.

9 Schering, 'Bemerkungen', 11; Webster, *Haydn's 'Farewell' Symphony*, 238.

10 Webster, *Haydn's 'Farewell' Symphony*, 247.

11 Ibid., 113.

12 Ibid., 114.

13 Ludwig Finscher, '"Zwischen absoluter und Programmusik": Zur Interpretation der deutschen romantischen Symphonie', in Christoph-Hellmut Mahling, ed., *Über Symphonien: Beiträge zu einer musikalischen Gattung (Festschrift Walter Wiora zum 70. Geburtstag)* (Tutzing, 1979), 103–15.

14 Jacob de Ruiter, *Der Charakterbegriff in der Musik: Studien zur deutschen Ästhetik der Instrumentalmusik 1740–1850* (Stuttgart, 1989), 94.

15 John Edward Toews, *Becoming Historical: Cultural Reformation and Public Memory in Early Nineteenth-Century Berlin* (Cambridge, 2004), 219–25; see also R. Larry Todd, *Mendelssohn: A Life in Music* (Oxford, 2003), 225–6.

16 Schering, 'Bemerkungen', 24–5; Webster, *Haydn's 'Farewell' Symphony*, 242–4.

17 Paul Thissen, *Zitattechniken in der Symphonik des 19. Jahrhunderts* (Sinzig, 1998), 193; see esp. 29–41 for the 'Reformation' Symphony.

18 Stephen Rodgers, *Form, Program, and Metaphor in the Music of Berlioz* (Cambridge, 2009), 21.

19 Ibid., 22–3.

20 Mark Evan Bonds, *After Beethoven: Imperatives of Originality in the Symphony* (Cambridge, Mass., 1996), 166.

21 Maynard Solomon, 'Beethoven's Ninth Symphony: A Search for Order', *19th-Century Music*, 10 (1986–7), 3–23, esp. 8.

22 Peter Cornelius, *Gesammelte Aufsätze: Gedanken über Musik und Theater, Poesie und bildende Kunst*, ed. Gunter Wagner and James A. Deaville (Mainz, 2004), 243.

23 Richard Pohl, *Franz Liszt: Studien und Erinnerungen* (Leipzig, 1883), 26.

24 Ibid., 230.

25 Ibid., 231.

26 *Musik als Botschaft* (Wiesbaden, 1989), 110; Franz Liszt, *Gesammelte Schriften*, ed. L. Ramann, 6 vols. (Leipzig, 1880–3), vol. IV, 56.

27 Robert Determann, *Begriff und Ästhetik der 'Neudeutschen Schule': Ein Beitrag zur Musikgeschichte des 19. Jahrhundert* (Baden-Baden, 1989), 91.

28 Ibid., 148–9; Franz Brendel, *Geschichte der Musik in Italien, Deutschland und Frankreich: Von den ersten christlichen Zeiten bis auf die Gegenwart*, 3rd edn (Leipzig, 1860), 509 and 513.

29 Franz Liszt, *Gesammelte Schriften*, vol. IV, 98.

30 Ibid., 69 and 98.

31 Wolfgang Dömling, *Franz Liszt und seine Zeit* (Laaber, 1998), 108.

32 Richard Kaplan, 'Sonata Form in the Orchestral Works of Liszt: The Revolutionary Reconsidered', *19th-Century Music*, 8 (1984–5), 152.

33 Ibid.

34 Helmut Rösing, 'Fast wie ein Unwetter: Zur Rezeption von Pastoral- und Alpensinfonie-Gewitter; über verschiedene Darstellungsebenen der musikalischen Informationsübermittlung', in Mahling, ed., *Über Symphonien*, 70.

35 Matthias Wiegandt, *Vergessene Symphonik? Studien zu Joachim Raff, Carl Reinecke und zum Problem der Epigonalität in der Musik* (Sinzig, 1997).

36 Rebecca Grotjahn, *Die Sinfonie im deutschen Kulturgebiet 1850 bis 1875* (Sinzig, 1998), 291–319.

37 Ibid., 321–2.

38 Stephen Luttmann, 'Preface', Friedrich Gernsheim, *Symphony No. 3* (Munich, 2006), iii–iv.

39 Michael Kennedy, *The Works of Ralph Vaughan Williams* (Oxford, 1980), 134.

40 Liszt, *Gesammelte Schriften*, vol. IV, 26–7.

41 Finscher, '"Zwischen absoluter und Programmusik"', 115; Todd, *Mendelssohn*, 434.

42 Finscher, '"Zwischen absoluter und Programmusik"', 115.

43 Ludwig Finscher, 'The Struggle with Tradition: Johannes Brahms', in Ursula von Rauchhaupt, ed., *The Symphony* (London, 1973), 165–74.

44 Anthony Newcomb, 'Once More "Between Absolute and Program Music": Schumann's Second Symphony', *19th-Century Music*, 7 (1983–4), 237.

45 Reinhold Brinkmann, *Late Idyll: The Second Symphony of Johannes Brahms*, trans. Peter Palmer (Cambridge, Mass. and London, 1995).

46 Dahlhaus, *Nineteenth-Century Music*, 364.

47 Carl Dahlhaus, *Klassische und Romantische Musikästhetik* (Laaber, 1988), 398–9.

48 Dahlhaus, *Nineteenth-Century Music*, 364.

49 Ludwig Schiedermair, *Gustav Mahler: Eine biographisch-kritische Würdigung* (Leipzig, 1901), 13; cited and discussed in Constantin Floros, *Gustav Mahler*, vol. I: *Die geistige Welt Gustav Mahlers in systematischer Darstellung* (Wiesbaden, 1977), 20–2.

50 Walter Werbeck, 'Erbe oder Verräter? Richard Strauss und die Symphonische Dichtung von Franz Liszt', in Detlef Altenburg, ed., *Liszt und die Neudeutsche Schule* (Laaber, 2006), 270; a very detailed picture of Strauss's relationship to Liszt is provided by David Larkin, 'Reshaping the Liszt–Wagner legacy: Intertextual Dynamics in Strauss' Tone Poems' (Ph.D. diss., University of Cambridge, 2007), chapter 2.

51 For 'relativization' in Liszt, see Dahlhaus, *Nineteenth-Century Music*, 239.

52 James Hepokoski, *Sibelius: Symphony No. 5* (Cambridge, 1993), 33–41 and 'Rotations, Sketches, and the Sixth Symphony', in Timothy L. Jackson and Veijo Murtomäki, eds., *Sibelius Studies* (Cambridge, 2001), 332–51, esp. 333–5.

53 Thissen, *Zitattechniken*, 179–87.

54 Kennedy, *Works of Ralph Vaughan Williams*, 134 and 155–6.

16 'Symphonies of the free spirit': the Austro-German symphony in early Soviet Russia

PAULINE FAIRCLOUGH

Context and infrastructure

At the time of the October revolution in 1917, Russian musical life was rich and international in outlook.[1] The capital until March 1918, St Petersburg (after 1917 Petrograd, then Leningrad), was well established as a European musical centre, with a flourishing modern music scene. In Switzerland, Stravinsky was still at work on *Les Noces*; in Russia, Prokofiev was just beginning his professional career and the internationally acclaimed star of the Imperial Opera Fyodor Chaliapin was at the height of his international fame when the Bolshevik takeover turned their country upside down. The financial and administrative consequences of the revolution were quickly felt, as previous sources of financial support for musical institutions collapsed, affecting every institution from the Bolshoi and Mariinsky Theatres to the Conservatoires as well as the private finances of Russia's most distinguished musicians and composers. Previously funded by a mixture of Imperial and private sponsorship, in 1918 all institutions became wholly dependent on the State in accordance with the Soviet policy of nationalisation. As early as February 1917, the Petersburg Imperial Orchestra was renamed the State Symphony Orchestra, directed at first by Serge Koussevitzky; under its second conductor Emil Cooper (from 1920), it became the State, then the Leningrad, Philharmonia. By the spring/summer of 1918 there were already several orchestras active in Petrograd, including the demobilised Preobrazhensky orchestra, who gave classical concerts that included two symphonic cycles devoted to Beethoven and to Wagner's music. Other symphonic concerts took place in the Theatre of Music Drama and their programmes consisted of the same mainstream repertoire: Schubert, Mendelssohn, Schumann, Wagner, Rimsky Korsakov, Tchaikovsky and Skryabin. The State Philharmonia ran a series of 'People's Concerts' aimed at the new mass audience: programmes included Mozart's Requiem, Berlioz's *Funeral and Triumphal Symphony*, the Finale of Beethoven's Ninth Symphony, Stravinsky's *Petrushka* and Skryabin's *Prometheus*. In these early years before emigration decimated the ranks of musical talent in Russia, Nikolai Tcherepnin, Albert Coates, Aleksandr Ziloti, Gregor Fitelberg and Serge Koussevitzky were the main conductors at these concerts.[2] In Moscow, theatre orchestras gave the majority of symphonic concerts, headed by the orchestra of the Bolshoi; the Moscow Philharmonia (Mosfil), founded in 1921, was for a time known as Rosfil (the Russian Orchestra of the Soviet Philharmonia), and after 1928 as Sofil (Soviet Orchestra of the Philharmonia). In addition to these pre-revolutionary survivors, one especially important new ensemble was formed: Persimfans, the famous conductorless orchestra, which was founded by Lev Tseitlin in 1922 and survived until 1932.

The body charged with the administration of cultural affairs was Narkompros, the Commissariat for Enlightenment, headed by the liberally inclined Anatoly Lunacharsky (until 1929). But in the traditional informal Russian fashion, various semi-formal 'circles of friends' still met during the 1920s to discuss and share their musical interests, and the most productive of these, at least initially, was the Association for Contemporary Music (ASM) based in Moscow (established in 1923), and its short-lived Leningrad counterpart, the LASM (established in 1926). Their concerns were chiefly the performance of new Western and Soviet music, and their membership was influential enough to sponsor major musical events, symphonic and chamber concerts, and to liaise with the International Society for Contemporary Music in sending Soviet composers to ISCM festivals in Europe. The foremost Soviet musicologist, Boris Asafiev (pseudonym Igor Glebov), coordinated similar events in Leningrad. The other major group was dedicated to furthering the cause of music written by and for the proletariat: the Russian Association of Proletarian Musicians (RAPM). Initially founded in 1923 with a handful of members, RAPM gradually grew in strength and influence to the point where, by 1930, they were easily the dominant force in Soviet musical life. This chapter in Soviet musical history has been well documented, and it is necessary only to note that, with the Central Committee's Resolution of 1932 'On the Reconstruction of Literary and Artistic Organizations', all factionalism in cultural life came to an abrupt halt, to be replaced by creative unions that were directly answerable to the powerful, State-monitored Committee of Arts Affairs.[3]

Despite cultural losses caused by the wave of emigration after 1917, the period 1920 to (approximately) 1937 was an extremely fertile period of cultural exchange between Russia and Western Europe. Visiting foreign conductors included Otto Klemperer and Fritz Stiedry (both until 1937), Oscar Fried (who made his permanent home in Moscow), Bruno Walter, Erich Kleiber, Hermann Abendrot and Heinz Unger; George Szell and Alexander Zemlinsky also visited the Soviet Union. These were musicians deeply steeped in Austro-German tradition and who were largely responsible for the popularity of Mahler in Leningrad in the 1920s and 30s.[4]

Under their direction, Soviet audiences heard an impressive range of Western music, both old and new. A glance at concert programmes from the late 1920s gives a fair idea of typical concert repertoire during these years. In February 1929 Klemperer and the Sofil performed Weill's Suite from *The Threepenny Opera*, Janacek's Sinfonietta, Stravinsky's *Apollon Musagète* and *Petrushka*, Mahler's *Das Lied von der Erde* and Beethoven's Seventh Symphony. An ASM-sponsored concert of May 1928 included Brahms's Fourth Symphony, Respighi's *Pines of Rome* and Strauss's *Don Juan*; their second concert, conducted by V. Savich, featured Liszt's *Les Préludes*, Respighi's *Fountains of Rome* and the Russian premiere of Prokofiev's Suite from *The Steel Step*. Repertoire for workers' concerts was necessarily simpler, consisting of a mixture of songs, chamber works, overtures and symphonies by mostly nineteenth-century Western and Russian composers (Beethoven, Borodin, Liszt, Wagner and Musorgsky featured prominently).

Although the principal aims of the ASM were not specifically didactic, its members were nevertheless involved in the wider project to 'bring music to the masses'. Asafiev was a prolific music writer for the Narkompros popular paper *Zhizn' iskusstva* (*Life of Art*), addressing the issue of how best to introduce the new audiences to what he and others regarded as their shared musical heritage and writing programme notes and brochures for distribution at concerts. It is evident that those in positions of power, like Asafiev, regarded themselves chiefly as facilitators and educators. Although historians tend to divide the 'modern' and 'proletarian' wings very sharply, both sides were driven by educational zeal and shared more common ground than might be assumed. They both believed that the proletariat required guidance on what to listen to; although RAPM was openly opposed to light music in a way that other groups were not, it is clear that for Asafiev, Lunacharsky and other powerful figures in musical life, the emphasis was on education by way of exposure to art music, whether that was to be Mozart, Glinka, Beethoven or even Stravinsky. In short, the whole climate of Soviet musical life in the 1920s and early 30s was directed by a deep-seated patriarchalism in which Western and Russian 'classics' played a central, and fairly uncontroversial, role.[5] The custodians of high art, at least from the non-proletarian side, were not substantially different in background, taste and education than their pre-revolutionary predecessors had been, and only they were able to exert influence over repertoire through inviting foreign conductors and performers, hosting concerts and liaising with the West. Even when RAPM assumed greater power in 1929, their years of triumph were very short-lived, and even then they were not able to exercise significant influence over the mainstream concert life of the Leningrad and Moscow philharmonias. In any case, when it came to orchestral repertoire, their main difference of opinion was not concerning the importance of retaining the Western classical and Romantic legacy (if selectively), but rather on the role of Western modernism in Soviet musical life. In comparison with the bitter disputes over Schoenberg, Hindemith and Stravinsky, the presence of Austro-German classical and Romantic repertoire in Soviet musical life was relatively uncontroversial. Though RAPM are sometimes assumed to have opposed all Western music except for Beethoven, this is a simplification of their position (which was in any case hardly rigidly uniform). An article by Lev Lebedinsky in *Proletarskiy muzïkant* (*Proletarian musician*) in 1929 suggests works by the following composers as suitable for workers' audiences: Schubert, Liszt, Schumann, Wagner, Mozart, Rossini, Bizet, Grieg, Chopin, Haydn, Bach and Verdi.[6] What is more, the scheduling of those works remained stable during the whole period from the revolution to Russia's entry into the Second World War. Although, as will be seen, writers focussed on socio-historical consideration of Western composers, relating them to progressive social trends wherever possible, it is doubtful whether this would have had a significant bearing on actual concert repertoire. The overall picture that emerges when critical and scholarly articles are set alongside concert programmes is one of synergy rather than dictat: the only 'Party line' one could speak of during the 1920s and early-to-mid 1930s is that of mass education. Apart from the huge popularity of more overtly 'revolutionary' figures such as Beethoven, most Western composers slotted in somewhere between passively reflecting social forces and actively resisting capitalism – both equally valid from the point of view of Marxist–Leninist aesthetics.

'The dying culture of the feudal classes': Bach, Mozart and Haydn

Perhaps unexpectedly,[7] one of the staples of Soviet repertoire in the earliest years was Mozart's Requiem.[8] The first People's Concert, in a series promoted by Narkompros targeting specifically proletarian audiences, took place on May Day 1918 in the Winter Palace – a performance of the Requiem as a memorial to the victims of the revolution.[9] As with a number of religious works, including Beethoven's *Missa Solemnis* and even Bach's B Minor Mass, the Requiem's Christian content was considered of less significance than its status as part of the Western classical canon. Musicologists advanced historical arguments as to why such repertoire was appropriate in the new Soviet state. In *Muzïkalnaya nov* (*Musical Virgin Soil*), the journal that from 1924 was the 'Organ of the All-Russian Association of Proletarian Musicians', the proletarian writer Sergey Chemodanov placed Bach, Haydn and Mozart firmly in the context of those artists who belonged to the 'Third Estate' – the title given to those in pre-revolutionary France who were not members of the clergy or the aristocracy. In other words, they were members of the rising eighteenth-century bourgeois class, who overturned medieval feudalism and laid the foundations for republicanism and democracy. Since, Chemodanov argued, 'the whole atmosphere of the pre-revolutionary epoch was saturated with the psychological struggle of two cultures, the obsolete feudal and the rising Third Estate', Bach's music expressed this turning-point in history, while the 'salon elegance' of Haydn and Mozart's music anticipates the victory of the eighteenth-century bourgeoisie 'over the dying culture of the feudal classes'.[10] The 'deep, lucid lyricism' of Bach's Protestant music, 'leading the change from the dark chasms of Catholic gloom' is accompanied by a shift from polyphony to homophony that Chemodanov believes articulates the cult of individualism that saw its full flowering in the sonata forms of Haydn and Mozart: 'Musical monism, which reached its end in Bach's fugues, gave way in the eighteenth century to dualism, which did not only not oppose the individualistic ideology of the third estate, but on the contrary, drew closer to a connection with the interrelation of classes of that time.'[11] In this context, Bach's sacred works represent not an obsolete form of Christian worship but the start of the break from feudal (Catholic) Europe, looking ahead to the Enlightenment and so to Revolution. What was true for Bach was even more so for his successors, and the music of the three titans of the classical style – Mozart, Haydn and Beethoven – is thus interpreted as practically a call to arms: 'It is this very heroism . . . which sustains 18th-century Enlightenment philosophy that serves as the ideology of the third estate, already close to the storm of the French revolution.'[12]

Such overtly political arguments were undoubtedly convenient for the images of composers so accredited with passive revolutionary sympathies. But they did not completely dominate music criticism. Asafiev's articles on Mozart in the popular paper *Zhizn iskusstva* of the following year focus on the composer as a personality and an artist rather than as a vehicle for historical forces. They are also a subtle defence of art for art's sake in the new Soviet context: 'If we feel that art – no abstract concept but a living force produced by great people – is a concrete revelation of this force, then it is impossible to invent a more vital and great, beautiful revelation or expression of this force than the figure of Mozart.'[13] The composer's personal qualities are also asserted: '[Mozart] was not a slave to his own suffering . . . he was not a proud person and his music did not display him as a person, did not postulate or declare his own "I", but [he] created music just to be art, as knowledge of the world through the expression of his own artistic sense in sound.'[14] It would be hard to find a more complete Soviet avowal of the doctrine of art for art's sake than this: once the personality of the composer is placed beyond reproach, their music requires no further justification. From two very different perspectives, then, Soviet readers are urged to accept Bach, Mozart and Haydn as representative of their own time; certainly not as models to be emulated by Soviet composers, but as founders of the classical tradition that was offered to the new Soviet listeners as their own birthright.

Notable by its absence in the journals of the 1920s was any serious discussion of the fact that Mozart and Haydn were dependent on rich aristocratic patrons, and played a full part in court musical life. Boris Shteynpress's 1935 article 'On Mozart's Instrumental Music' confronts this issue at the very same time as repeating essentially the same argument that the classical style was inherently democratic:

> Mozart was obliged to write for the tastes of the ruling class . . . [he] wrote in the epoch of the Enlightenment . . . which arose from the struggle for freedom of bourgeois democrats against the feudal regime and which enveloped the whole area of public life and culture. The distinctive features of this world-view . . . are a deep and steadfast optimism based on a solid faith in the victory of the ennobling force of the human intellect, in progress, in a better future for humanity . . . In place of constrained and abstract religious content . . . and the superficial hedonism of the salon and courtly art, the classical style advanced a new ideo-emotional musical content . . . Haydn gave birth to major images of democracy . . . to mass-ness, the attraction of everyday life, to the spiritual world of "simple people", to a natural expression of human feeling.[15]

Both Mozart and Haydn are seen as compromised figures, unable, for social and financial reasons, to transcend their dependence on aristocratic patronage; and so ultimately, Shteynpress argues, 'the author of the Jupiter Symphony must undoubtedly give way to that of the Eroica and Appassionata'.[16] But it is important to note that there is nothing fundamentally new in Shteynpress's arguments: the Soviet apologia for Western classicism remains the same in the 1930s as it was in the 1920s. Only Asafiev's insistence on the validity of beauty for its own sake finds no echo in the 1930s, which, given the pressurised nature of musical discussions about definable expressive content during that decade, is hardly surprising.

'Every revolution is a grandiose symphony': The Beethoven cult

Beethoven enjoyed a status in the Soviet Union that can only be compared to that of Shakespeare and Pushkin.[17] Since there was enough anecdotal and documentary evidence to paint him as a true revolutionary, he was feted by all sides of the cultural spectrum. Famous incidents such as Beethoven's refusal to stand aside for the Imperial family at Teplitz, his angry rejection of Napoleon after he became Emperor, his flight from Prince Lichnowsky's castle and the letter which followed it ('Prince! What you are, you are by birthright. Of princes there have been and will be thousands. Of Beethovens there is only one')[18] all fed the Soviet image of Beethoven as an artist whose music was directly inspired by the French Revolution and the rhetoric of personal freedom and fraternal equality that surrounded it. Beethoven was not just a fellow-traveller to the Soviets – someone whose ideals were passively sympathetic to the revolution – he was himself claimed as a revolutionary, and as such was an obvious role-model for Soviet composers. For those seeking to render Western classical music appealing and relevant to the proletariat, this romanticised version of Beethoven was invaluable. From Lunacharsky's introductory speeches at workers' concerts to Asafiev's programme notes, to articles in the popular music and arts press, the message was clear: Beethoven was a revolutionary like us, and we are the rightful heirs of his revolutionary message.

Like Lenin and other colleagues in the early Bolshevik administration, Lunacharsky's musical tastes were conservative and his broad aim was social engineering – the cultural education of the proletariat on a vast scale – rather than producing Bolshevik propaganda.[19] In his article 'Great Sisters' of 1926, he reels off a series of assertions typical of this period: 'Not for nothing did Beethoven's music come out of the French revolution; it was saturated with it ... Such a demigod of the musical world as Beethoven ... is able to plunge into the deepest musical poetry which, being expressed in the language of human consciousness, raises mountainous problems, struggles, and victories.'[20] In the centenary year 1927, several music journals devoted whole issues to Beethoven.[21] The Narkompros journal *Muzïka i revoliutsiya* had a special issue in March, headed by Lunacharsky's article 'How Beethoven Lives for Us'; Evgeny Braudo's article 'Beethoven-Citizen' claims that in the *Eroica* 'the musician and social activist is revealed in all his depth and breadth'; 'revolutionary rhythms run through [the *Eroica*] like a red thread; its rhythm is of the electrified crowd rushing to storm the Bastille'.[22]

A more dispassionate note was struck in Boleslav Pshibïshevskiy's article in the RAPM journal *Proletarskiy muzïkant* in 1931. Pshibïshevskiy was the director of the Moscow Conservatoire from 1929, under whom its name temporarily changed to the Feliks Kon Higher Music School. The article was openly mocked and censured in the 1930s;[23] but what is most striking about it now is rather how uncontroversial Pshibïshevskiy's observations actually were. Noting that Beethoven, typically for his time, was 'a revolutionary in

thought but not in deed', he describes the composer's dependence on aristocratic patrons as tragic-comic: 'The point here is not the personal incon-
sistency of Beethoven, but rather the tragedy, though perhaps it would be
better to speak of a tragic-comedy, of the famous petit-bourgeoisie which
allowed itself and its own revolutionary philosopher, Hegel, to be at the same
time the philosopher of the Prussian king, or Beethoven to dedicate the most
revolutionary of all his works, the Ninth Symphony, to that same king,
the reactionary Friedrich Wilhelm III.'[24] Pshibïshevskiy's tone may be less
reverent than that of other writers, but he does go on to assert that Soviet
music needs to synthesise Beethoven's 'dialectic' and Musorgsky's realism to
forge a new proletarian music – hardly an original claim, either in the 1920s
or the 1930s.

As with Mozart and Haydn, the same arguments in support of
Beethoven's revolutionary credentials were voiced in the 1930s as they had
been in the 1920s. After 1932, there might have been a backlash against the
excessive canonisation of Beethoven in the preceding decade, especially as
appropriated by the more militant members of the proletarian wing. But
there was no such reaction; in the absence of any alternative hero, Beethoven
was still the most persuasive revolutionary composer of the past. Pavel Veis's
attack on Pshibïshevsky in 1933 accuses the former Conservatoire director of
'vulgarization and distortion', but nevertheless repeats his central argument:
that Beethoven's music 'undoubtedly belongs to that bourgeois legacy which
has enormous significance for the proletariat'.[25]

Efforts to bring Beethoven's music to the masses continued well into
the 1930s, preserving an important legacy of proletarian activity from
the 1920s. 'Beethoven brigades' were charged with the task of educating
(and entertaining) the Red Army. In 1935, one report of such an
evening at the Theatre Bureau of the Central House of the Red Army
was published in *Sovetskaya muzïka*. One concert included movements
from the Moonlight and Pathètique Sonatas, the first movement of the
Kreutzer Sonata, fragments from *Egmont* and the Scottish songs, inter-
spersed with readings from Beethoven's letters and talks about his life.
Even between acts the audience was not permitted to relax: the brigade
put on readings from Lenin, Goethe, Romain Rolland and Nikolay
Bukharin in the foyer, and held question-and-answer sessions with the
audience. One soldier went straight to the heart of Beethoven's rather
paradoxical position as a revolutionary, asking why he dedicated works
to counts and princes. The reply is predictable: 'He had no choice. It was
a matter of struggle for existence, for pay. But he never humbled himself
before them.'[26]

As Beethoven's close contemporary, Schubert was not afforded anything like the same degree of adulation, but was nevertheless extremely

popular in the 1920s. His centenary year followed Beethoven's in 1928, though it was marked in a far more muted manner. *Muzïka i revoliutsiya*, however, published a special Schubert issue in October that neatly sets out Schubert's rather more ambiguous credentials as a fellow-traveller, much in the same way as Chemodanov had contrived to do with Bach, Haydn and Mozart. Mikhail Pekelis pointed out that Schubert, unlike his direct predecessors, had no links with the aristocracy and wrote his music for amateurs and friends, drawing attention to his use of folk dances and melodies and his new brand of 'lyrical symphonism'.[27] Concert programmes for workers' clubs throughout the 1920s reveal that Schubert songs were regular favourites, whether performed as originally intended, or in special arrangements for folk instruments; a review of such an event in 1928 reports that the overture from *Rosamunde* was played on folk instruments and the F minor *Moment Musical* on balalaika and in a second transcription for mandolin and guitar.[28]

Fellow travellers: Schumann, Berlioz, Liszt, Mendelssohn, Brahms

Of these five composers, Liszt was probably the most popular figure in Russian musical life before the revolution. He had visited Russia in 1842 and 1843 and had close connections both with Vladimir Stasov, Mily Balakirev and the Russian National School and also with Anton Rubinstein, whom he knew and admired as a pianist, composer and conductor. Virtuosic Romantic piano repertoire was a staple of Conservatoire pedagogy and concert life in both Moscow and Petersburg, and this tradition – in which Chopin, Liszt and Schumann featured prominently – continued seamlessly into the Soviet period. During the 1920s, Schumann's orchestral music was not performed with anything like the regularity of Liszt's or Berlioz's but he had his supporters nonetheless. In 1926, Mikhail Ivanov-Boretsky asserted that 'Every bar of Schumann's music is far from formalism … and is saturated with a genuine, deep romanticism understood as the reflection in music of the composer's spiritual life.'[29] As one of the group of artists who marked the transition from classical Enlightenment heroism to a self-absorbed style of individualism and pessimism, Schumann played a role in what Soviet critics perceived as the gradual decline of the Austro-German symphonic tradition and was thus vulnerable to criticism. Ivanov-Boretsky came to his aid again in 1930 with an article on his revolutionary choruses, reproducing the unpublished 1848 song 'To arms!' in his own handwritten manuscript and arguing that only those little acquainted with Schumann's biography would describe him merely as a dreamer who was sunk in his own creative work.[30] A later evaluation of Schumann in 1933 was rather less supportive: Mikhail Cheremukhin grouped Schubert and Schumann together as great realist song composers, citing *Die Schöne Müllerin* and *Dichterliebe* as exemplars, but nonetheless remaining slightly critical of Schumann:

> [Dichterliebe] is already akin to a narcotic hashish: Schumann thinks in fairytale images, is carried away by fairy legends, images from the past. And here we have an interesting contradiction: the more Schumann departs from the realm of the fantastic, the more clearly he strives to 'get away from' relating to genuine reality, the more strongly he summons that reality, not as its master, but as its servant.[31]

Though sitting just outside the scope of this chapter, it is interesting to note that Berlioz – whose revolutionary sympathies were far better documented – fared much better, which perhaps reveals the importance of having an ideologically respectable biography. His *Funeral and Triumphal Symphony* commemorating those who died in the 1830 revolution is obscure in the West today, but was frequently performed in the Soviet 1920s, as was his *Symphonie fantastique*. The first recorded Soviet performance of the *Funeral and Triumphal Symphony* took place on 8 November 1918, at the second of Lunacharsky's 'People's Concerts' in Smolny, Petrograd. Liszt's orchestral works were also regular fixtures in the concert programmes of the 1920s, and, as with Beethoven, there was enough revolutionary lore around him to preserve ideological credibility and his reputation remained stable during the whole Soviet period. In the 1930s he had a powerful supporter in Georgy Khubov, an intelligent and influential music critic. The fact that Liszt's revolutionary interests waned after 1848 was an inescapable part of his biography, which Khubov did not try to ignore; nor did he overlook Liszt's aristocratic connections. In this regard, Khubov's apologia for Liszt recalls earlier defences of Beethoven: '[Liszt] understood early on the pain of moral humiliation of the "artist in the role of a lackey"'; he felt the 'deep dissatisfaction of [his] generation of artists with bourgeois society, [was] conscious of [his] own exceptional creative talent and [his] inability to find a means of concrete application . . . One must understand all this in order to "excuse" his blunders, errors, unhealthy tendencies . . . in order to approach the essence of the internal contradictions of Liszt's creative development.'[32]

Very little mention is made of Mendelssohn in the journals of the 1920s and 30s, but performance data from the Leningrad Philharmonia show that, in Leningrad at least, the most frequently performed work was the Violin Concerto (eighty-four times between 1921 and 1971), with the Third and Fourth symphonies receiving twenty-one and twenty-eight performances respectively.[33] Only the Overture to *A Midsummer Night's Dream* and the Violin Concerto were in Persimfans' repertoire, which suggests that Mendelssohn's music was never strikingly popular, but maintained a steady, uncontroversial presence in Soviet musical life.[34] Where Brahms was concerned, Soviet writers seemed inclined equally to polite uninterest – a common accusation was that of 'academicism' – or genuine enthusiasm. The most notable attempt to situate Brahms in a favourable political context can be found in Ivan Sollertinsky's Leningrad Philharmonic brochures written between 1936 and 1941. As a piece of ideological posturing, Sollertinsky's position is as extreme in its mode of expression as anything penned by a member of RAPM, and it is a reflection of the anti-Western xenophobia of the period that his views were so widely circulated and appreciated:

> Brahms . . . understood that the Liszt–Wagner [mode of] erotic languor and ecstacy, Schopenhaurian, Buddhist or neo-Catholic pessimism, Tristanesque harmony, mystical illumination, dreams of the superman, led straight to modernism and decadence, to the collapse of classical European art culture. This very bacillus of decadence, openly or secretly present in this 'music of the future' represented the greatest danger to Brahms . . . The issue was no less than the future fate of European musical culture: whether it would follow the classical–romantic tradition connected with the great musical past, or to irrepressibly slide along a decadent slope . . . To resist the break-up of European musical culture, to orientate oneself towards the great classical epoch of the past, to embrace strict classical forms, to struggle against the porous, vague, rotten neo-Romantic epigones – such was Brahms's great historical dilemma.[35]

It is unclear whether this kind of writing was actually required in order to facilitate the continuing performance of Brahms's music, or whether Sollertinsky sincerely believed in his own rhetoric, but Brahms's symphonies do seem to have been more frequently played in the 1930s than they had been in the 1920s. There seems to have been no obvious reason for the comparative neglect of Brahms and Mendelssohn in critical literature as well as concert life in the 1920s, other than that neither composer had anything remotely 'revolutionary' in his biography, and so did not make especially attractive topics for Soviet critics eager to demonstrate their ideological and scholarly credentials. Sollertinsky's brochures represent a very different approach from that found in the 1920s: their more aggressively political tone reflects the hardening in cultural attitudes that took place from the mid 1930s on.

One of the most substantial articles in the post-RAPM years to address the wider issue of romanticism in music was that by Lev Kaltat and David Rabinovich, 'Fighting for a Heritage', in the third issue of *Sovetskaya muzïka* in 1933. These former RAPM supporters now offered measured criticism of their former policies, describing RAPM's fixation with

Beethoven and their notions of 'acceptable' repertoire as 'narrow and confined'.[36] More importantly, they go on to describe the German Romantics (Schubert, Schumann, Mendelssohn and Weber) as democratic in their portrayal of the 'petit-bourgeois intellectual . . . the burgher, the craftsman, the peasant' as the heroes of their music. Liszt and Wagner, on the other hand, exemplify the collapse of revolutionary idealism after 1848, where artists could choose one of two paths: that of the proletariat or that of the 'reactionary bourgeois-aristocratic bloc'. The 'third way' represented by Brahms was dogged by 'dead academic forms' and 'expressive epigonism'.[37] No reader of *Muzïka i revoliutsiya* in the 1920s would have found these arguments startling, and their portrayal of the Romantics as democratic also echoes Sollertinsky's arguments on behalf of Mahler and Bruckner, which were published as early as 1929.[38] It is a revealing reminder of how much common ground some former RAPM members and the wider musical community shared after 1932 that by 1938, the same writer, Rabinovich, was bemoaning the lack of Western classical repertoire in the Mosfil 1937–8 season. There were almost no performances of Bach's music, no Handel or Haydn at all, only 'pitiful snatches' of Mozart, one solitary Schubert work (unnamed), no Mendelssohn or Schumann, and only Brahms's Third Symphony and piano concertos were heard.[39] Perhaps in response to this and other criticism they had received, Mosfil announced their 1939–40 season in August 1939, in which Bach's B Minor Mass, Berlioz's *Damnation of Faust*, Mozart's Requiem, Grieg's *Peer Gynt* Suite, Mahler's *Das Lied von der Erde* and Haydn's *The Seasons* were all planned alongside Soviet works. As the 1930s drew to a close, then, these and other canonical works of Western classicism and romanticism still occupied their central role in Soviet musical life.

'The last of the Mohicans': Bruckner, Mahler and Strauss

Of these three late Romantics,[40] Bruckner was by far the least well represented in Soviet programmes. An early performance of his Seventh Symphony (by Fritz Stiedry) in 1926 was apparently coolly received, and in Sollertinsky's list of Mahler and Bruckner performances in the Soviet Union between 1922 and 1942, Bruckner's symphonies were programmed just twenty-three times, as compared with Mahler's forty-six (repeat performances not counted).[41] But Bruckner, like Mahler, had keen supporters. There was a Bruckner and Mahler society that met regularly in Leningrad during the 1920s to perform their symphonies in four-hand arrangements, in which Sollertinsky played an active part.[42] Soviet concert reviews of the 1920s and 30s are intermittently sprinkled with complaints about the dearth of Bruckner performances, and as late as 1935 Aleksandr Ostretsov, reviewing Fried's performance of Bruckner's Seventh Symphony, bemoaned the fact that in Moscow Bruckner's symphonies were still very little known. The substance of his review recalls the historical posturing typical of the 1920s:

> If Mahler's symphonies show us the development of the petit-bourgeois art of Austria ... then Bruckner's art introduces us to the final stage of a romantic idyll – the period of 'peaceful' autumn flowering, already close to extinction. Listening to this music, we feel that the composer was inspired by naïve illusions of burgheresque ideology, with its rapturous attitude to nature and belief in the moral foundation of the patriarchal life of 'good old Vienna', which was itself already crushed by Imperialism.[43]

Sollertinsky was one of the most powerful advocates of Bruckner's music in the 1930s, as he was of Mahler's. But to advocate a favourite composer in this decade required substantial ideological justification: where symphonic repertoire was concerned, every composer needed to be appropriately framed in Soviet rhetoric. In his 1940 brochure for the Leningrad Philharmonia's performance of Bruckner's Seventh Symphony, Sollertinsky argued, much as he had done for Mahler,[44] that Bruckner's music encapsulates the crisis of capitalist social alienation and search for man's true place in the world:

> The fundamental theme of Bruckner's symphonies may be understood as the great internal loneliness of the individual (the Romantic disharmony between the artist and the cruel laws of capitalist reality ...); the overcoming of loneliness in a pantheistic blending of man with nature, with the earth and the cosmos ... of the emotional colour of rural *Landschaft* (though never in the spirit of Strauss's 'Alpine' Symphony); of naïve pastoral song.[45]

With the statement 'Bruckner is the Schubert of the second half of the 19th Century', Sollertinsky sums up his picture of the composer as an artist deeply rooted in folk culture, transplanted to the cruel environment of the capitalist city. However, the fact that Bruckner spent his entire career in the nineteenth century made him a slightly different – even safer – proposition than Mahler, whose last six symphonies and *Das Lied von der Erde* were written in the twentieth century. During the 1920s, some proletarian critics hostile to Western modernism seemed unsure where Mahler belonged – with Schoenberg and Expressionism, or with the late Romantics. In 1922, Evgeny Braudo's article 'On Expressionism in Music' claims that, though Mahler was antipathetic to the Russian listener, he was popular with the German public. This in itself is recognisable in the rhetoric of the time as an insult, which Braudo immediately expands upon: 'It is impossible to ignore the sign of the times in the fact that Mahler holds such sway over the soul of the contemporary West.'[46] In other words, Mahler's popularity was a symptom of the decline of Western culture into decadence; by implied contrast, it was only in the Soviet Union that the more spiritually robust Beethovenian symphonic tradition could be renewed.

The irony is, of course, that Mahler's music swiftly became far more popular in Soviet Russia that it did in some parts of Western Europe, Britain leading the way in its mistrust of what seemed like overblown, over-complex symphonies. Those features of Mahler's music that had always been the most controversial – his juxtapositions of the serious and the banal – registered with Braudo as equally objectionable, complaining of its

> unexpected transitions from . . . gloomy pathos to artificial lightness and gaiety, mannered minor-key fanfares leading to grandiose funeral marches alongside glowing 'rustic' pages in the spirit of Haydn, fairytale craft alongside the most philistine gutter taste. In a word, [it is] a total rejection of that which until now was considered the chief object of a symphonic composition: self-possession, balance and refinement of artistic material . . . We . . . felt . . . a rude sting from this music.[47]

What is striking today about this review is how acute Braudo's experience of Mahler actually was, and how freshly his music sounded to Russian ears. In Leningrad, where Mahler's symphonies were frequently played, critics were more responsive; but in Moscow old prejudices evidently took some time to die (or simply to emigrate). The Moscow ASM critics Viktor Belyayev and Leonid Sabaneyev were both Mahler sceptics; in 1924 Belyayev echoed Braudo's suspicion of Mahler's German popularity, sarcastically dubbing him, together with Strauss, 'the apparent idols of German lands'. It seems curious at first glance that Mahler's music should be more favourably received in the more conservative climate of the 1930s than it was in the 1920s. But as a late Romantic rather than a modernist, Mahler was not a favourite of the Moscow ASM camp; and it is hardly surprising that the proletarian critics did not clamour for performances of symphonies lasting over an hour, and which were completely unplayable by untrained musicians. It was Sollertinsky – a versatile and popular lecturer and scholar in Leningrad and from 1937 to 1944 artistic director of the Leningrad Philharmonic – who did most to popularise Mahler's music in the Soviet Union in the 1930s. Through his programme notes for Philharmonia concerts, public lectures and a monograph devoted to the composer, Sollertinsky propagandised on behalf of Mahler's music, even arguing (albeit rather obliquely) that his symphonies made ideal models for Soviet composers because of their 'democratic' musical language and ambitious expressive scope.

Cheremukhin, the critic who wrote disparagingly of the 'narcotic' effects of Schumann's *Dichterliebe*, was equally at sea when it came to Mahler. In the same article, he links Mahler with Reger and Hindemith as proponents of dry contrapuntalism: 'May this "horizontal unfolding" music be the bearer of valuable realist expression? I don't think so.'[48] Clearly, Sollertinsky had not managed to convince everyone. But it is important to note how few criticisms of Mahler there actually were in the 1920s and 30s; Strauss fared far worse, and yet his music also continued to be performed. As Sollertinsky's writings on Mahler demonstrate, it was relatively easy to paint him as a fellow-traveller, broadly in sympathy with the proletariat. Such anecdotes as Mahler's joining the Vienna May Day parade in 1905 and his Dostoevsky-inspired expression of fraternity ('How can one be happy when a single being on earth still suffers?') were all grist to Sollertinsky's mill in this respect.[49]

The fact that Strauss was still alive and flourishing undoubtedly made him more suspect a figure than Mahler. Critical hostility became even more pronounced after 1933, when Strauss's role as president of the Reichsmusikammer tainted his reputation throughout Europe and America. But even as early as 1923, Sabaneyev (who would soon emigrate to the West) expressed a deeper-seated ambivalence to his music: 'It is easy to relate his creativity to the new Germany and to a militaristic, crassly grandiose striving for pomposity, parade, outer glory. Strauss's creativity is a good barometer of the ... archetypal new German.'[50] Whereas in Beethoven militaristic rhythms reflect the general revolutionary atmosphere, in Strauss they sound like a celebration of victory: 'like some Wagnerian Kaisermarsch'.[51] While not denying Strauss's brilliance, Sabaneyev cautions: 'in the midst of all these attributes ... he has many features of insincerity, pretence ... [and] window-dressing'.[52] Nevertheless, Strauss's tone-poems, in particular *Till Eulenspiegel* and *Don Juan*, were frequently performed throughout the 1920s and it was only after 1933 that criticism of the composer gradually became more pointed and his music less often played.

As the 1930s moved into the period of High Stalinism (approximately 1934–53), there was a shift away from programming Western music and towards celebrating the Russian 'classics', especially Tchaikovsky and Musorgsky. The influx of foreign musicians gradually dried up after 1937, and the signing of the Nazi–Soviet pact in 1939 further damaged relations with the West until the Nazi invasion of the Soviet Union in 1941. Hand in hand with this growing isolationism, though, were more positive developments: after protracted struggles between the Moscow Composers' Union and the Moscow Philharmonia, the 1937–8 season featured festivals both of pre-revolutionary Western and Russian and of new Soviet music.[53] Young, talented Russian conductors like Evgeny Mravinsky and Kirill Kondrashin took the place of their Austro-German predecessors, and the growing establishment of Shostakovich as a major symphonist after the premiere of the Fifth Symphony in 1937, together with the return of Prokofiev in 1936, meant that a strong Soviet tradition at last began to take root in the concert hall. It was, therefore, a combination of positive and negative factors that would see concert repertoire changing in the late 1930s. Once reliant on the personal support of conductors for performances, Soviet composers were empowered by the formations of their Unions in 1932 with the support in publication, radio coverage and concert programming that followed, albeit gradually. While the High-Stalinist period saw Western (and early Soviet) modernism excluded from concert schedules, canonic works of Western classicism and romanticism maintained a relatively stable presence in 1930s Soviet musical life. What began as an inspired project to bring art to the masses thus formed the basis of concert life in the first two decades of the Soviet Union, with Austro-German symphonism at its heart.

Notes

1 The title of the chapter, 'Symphonies of the Free Spirit', is from Igor Glebov, 'Russkaya simfonicheskaya muzïka za 10 let' ['A Decade of Russian Symphonic Music'], *Muzïka i revoliutsiya* [*Music and Revolution*], 11 (1927), 21. I would like to thank David Fanning for his generous loan of materials and Lidia Ader for sending me important articles from Russia. I am extremely grateful to those friends and colleagues who read the draft of this chapter and offered valuable advice and correction: Lidia Ader, Philip Bullock, Marina Frolova-Walker, Levon Hakobian and Simo Mikkonen.
2 Elena Bronfin, *Muzïkalnaya kultura Petrograda pervogo poslereoliutinnogo pyatiletiya 1917–1922* [*The Musical Culture of Petrograd in the First Five Years after the Revolution*] (Leningrad, 1984), 44–8.
3 See principally Amy Nelson, *Music for the Revolution. Musicians and Power in Early Soviet Russia* (Philadelphia, 2004) and Neil Edmunds, *The Soviet Proletarian Music Movement* (Bern, 2000).
4 Oscar Fried had conducted the first performance of Mahler's Fifth Symphony in St Petersburg as early as 1906, to a cool response. See Inna Barsova, 'Mahler in Russia', in Donald Mitchell and Andrew Nicholson, eds., *The Mahler Companion* (New York and Oxford, 1999), 525.
5 It should be noted that the Futurists' famous rejection of past art as advanced in their 1912 manifesto 'A Slap in the Face of Public Taste' found little echo in musical circles. Apart from some early examples of musical 'futurism' in the form of machine-music (most famously in the 'Zavod' ['Factory'] movement of Mosolov's ballet *Stal* [*Steel*]), most of the music written by the early Soviet 'avant-garde' was nothing like as radical as contemporary movements in literary and visual art.
6 Lev Lebedinsky, 'Kontsertnaya rabota v rabochey auditorii' ['Concert Works for Workers' Audiences'], *Proletarsky muzïkant*, 2 (1929), 9.
7 The quotation in the heading is from Sergey Chemodanov, 'Muzïka i teoriya istoricheskogo materializma' ['Music and the Theory of Historical Materialism'], *Muzïkalnaya nov* [*Musical Virgin Soil*], 20 (1923), 16.
8 Regarding symphonic works, Persimfans's repertoire contained only symphonies nos. 40, 41 and another erroneously listed as 'D minor'. This may have been K 385, the 'Haffner' symphony, which is in D major. See S. Ponyatovskiy, *Persimfans – orkestr bez dirizhera* [*Persimfans – the Conductorless Orchestra*] (Moscow, 2003), 188. Of all Mozart's symphonies, nos. 33, 39 and 40 were performed most frequently by the Leningrad Philharmonia, with forty, forty-one and fifty-six performances respectively between 1921 and 1971; but the Requiem was performed eighty-six times in the same period. See Boris Arapov et al., *Leningradskaya gosudarstvennaya ordena trudovogo krasnogo*

znameni filarmonia: stati, vospominania, materiali (Leningrad, 1972), 344.

9 Bronfin, Muzïkalnaya kultura Petrograda, 48.

10 Chemodanov, 'Muzïka i teoriya istoricheskogo materializma', 15–16.

11 Ibid., 16.

12 Ibid.

13 Igor Glebov, 'The Music of Mozart', Zhizn iskusstva [Life of Art] (4 September 1923), 7.

14 Glebov, Zhizn iskusstva (11 September 1923), 10.

15 Boris Shteynpress, 'Ob instrumentalnom tvorchestve Motsarta' ['On Mozart's Instrumental Music'], Sovetskaya muzïka [Soviet Music], 6 (1935), 44–5.

16 Ibid., 58.

17 The quotation in the heading is from Anatoly Lunacharsky, 'Velikie sestrï' ['Great Sisters'], Muzïka i revoliutsitya, 1 (1926), 16.

18 Quoted in H. C. Robbins-Landon, Beethoven (London, 1970), 118.

19 However, Lunacharsky had more adventurous tastes than Lenin; he was a supporter of avant-garde artistic movements in all fields of the arts and, like the modernist ASM, liked Skryabin's music.

20 Lunacharsky, 'Velikie sestrï', 16–17.

21 See the Moscow Conservatoire house journal Muzïkalnoe obrazovanie [Music Education], 2/1–2 (1927) for serious scholarly articles including a facsimile of Sketchbook No. 4, Muzïka i revoliutsitya, 3 (1927) for more political articles, and Sovremennaya muzïka, 21 (1927) for reports of Beethoven-related ASM concerts and lectures.

22 Evgeny Braudo, 'Betkhoven-grazhdanin' ['Beethoven-Citizen'], Muzïka i revoliutsitya, 3 (1927), 22–3.

23 See Pavel Veis, 'O zhurnale "Proletarsky muzïkant' ['About the Journal "Proletarian musician"'], Sovetskaya muzïka, 1 (1933), 135.

24 Boleslav Pshibïshevsky, 'O tvorcheskom metode Betkhovena' [Beethoven's Creative Method'], Proletarsky muzïkant, 5 (1931), 28. Pshibïshevsky here refers to the fact that Friedrich Wilhelm gave Hegel the post of rector at Berlin University in 1830. Beethoven's decision to dedicate his symphony to the Prussian king was financially motivated, since he was extremely poor at the end of his life.

25 Veis, 'O zhurnale "Proletarsky muzïkant"', 135.

26 N. Goncharova, 'Betkhoven v krasnoy armiy' ['Beethoven in the Red Army'], Sovetskaya muzïka, 7–8 (1935), 153.

27 Mikhail Pekelis, 'Frants Schubert', Muzïka i revoliutsiya, 10 (1928), 15.

28 Anon., Muzïka i revoliutsiya, 10 (1928), 41. Schubert's Eighth Symphony was the most popular of the cycle, with the Leningrad Philharmonia playing it 106 times 1921–71, compared with only fifteen performances of the Fifth. Persifmans had only symphonies nos. 8 and 9 in their repertoire. See Arapov et al., Leningradskaya gosudarstvennaya ordena trudovogo krasnogo znameni filarmonia, 359 and Ponyatovskiy, Persimfans, 190.

29 Mikhail Ivanov-Boretsky, 'E. T. A. Gofman' [E. T. A. Hoffmann], Muzïkalnoe obrazovanie, 3–4 (1926), 15.

30 Ivanov-Boretsky, 'Revoliutsionnïe khorï Shumana' ['Schumann's Revolutionary Choruses'] Muzïkalnoe obrazovanie, 2 (1930), 16–19.

31 Cheremukhin, 'K voprosu putyakh sovetskoy muzïki' ['On the Question of the Path for Soviet music'], Sovetskaya muzïka, 5 (1933), 24.

32 Georgy Khubov, 'Frants Liszt', Sovetskaya muzïka, 11 (1936), 24–5.

33 Arapov et al., 'Leningradskaya gosudarstvennaya ordena trudovogo krasnogo znameni filarmonia', 343.

34 Ponyatovskiy, 'Persimfans', 188.

35 Ivan Sollertinsky, 'The Symphonies of Brahms', in Mikhail Druskin, ed., Istoricheskie etyudi [Historical Studies] (Leningrad, 1963), 279–82.

36 Lev Kaltat and David Rabinovich, 'V boyakh za nasleds tvo' ['Fighting for a Heritage'], Sovetskaya muzïka, 3 (1933), 13.

37 Ibid., 22–5.

38 See for example Sollertinsky's 1929 essay 'Problema sovetskogo simfonizma' ['The Problem of Soviet Symphonism'], Zhizn iskusstva, 46 (1929), 1–3.

39 Rabinovich, concert review, Sovetskaya muzïka, 7 (1938), 71. However, it should be borne in mind that some former RAPM members connected with the State music publisher Muzgiz tried to prevent the publication of new Soviet music in the early 1930s, and Rabinovich's complaint may have stemmed from similar hostility to new music as Soviet music was increasingly programmed in the late 1930s. See Simo Mikkonen, 'State Composers and the Red Courtiers: Music, Ideology and Politics in the Soviet 1930s' (Ph.D. diss., University of Jyväskalä, 2007), esp. 134–49.

40 'The last of the Mohicans' was the term used by Valeriyan Bogdanov-Berezovsky in his article 'On the Problem of Soviet Symphonism', Sovetskaya muzïka, 6 (1934), 30.

41 See Lyudmila Mikheyeva, *Pamyati I. I. Sollertinskogo* [*In Memory of I. I. Sollertinsky*] (Leningrad, 1978), 244–6.

42 For a discussion of Sollertinsky's role in introducing Mahler to Shostakovich and of his interpretation of Mahler's music as a model for Soviet composers, see Pauline Fairclough, 'Mahler Reconstructed: Sollertinsky and the Soviet Symphony', *Musical Quarterly*, 85/2 (2001), 367–90.

43 Aleksandr Ostretsov, *Sovetskaya muzïka*, 1 (1935), 73.

44 See Sollertinsky, *Gustav Mahler* (Leningrad, 1932).

45 Sollertinsky, 'Bruckner's Seventh Symphony', in Druskin, ed., *Istoricheskie etyudi* (Leningrad, 1963), 310.

46 Evgeny Braudo, 'Ob ekspressionizme v muzïke' ['On Expressionism in Music'], *Muzïkalnaya letopis* [*Music Chronicle*], 2 (1922), 150.

47 Ibid.

48 Cheremukhin, 'K voprosu o putyakh sovetskoy muzïki', 29.

49 See Henry-Louis de la Grange, *Gustav Mahler*, vol. III: *Vienna: Triumph and Disillusion (1904–1907)* (Oxford and New York, 1999), 165–6.

50 Leonid Sabaneyev, 'Richard Strauss', *K novïm beregam* [*Towards New Shores*], 2 (1923), 36.

51 Ibid., 37.

52 Ibid., 39.

53 See Mikkonen, 'State Composers', 136. Also see Lev Grigoryev and Yakov Platek, *Moskovskaya Gosudarstvennaya Filharmoniya* (Moscow, 1973), 93–111 for details of this shift in emphasis in concert repertoire, and for details of cycles of Wagner, Beethoven, Schumann, Schubert, Mendelssohn, Berlioz and Liszt in the 1937–8 Moscow Philharmonia season.

17 The symphony in Britain: guardianship and renewal

ALAIN FROGLEY

The story of the symphony in Britain, as the reception and embodiment of musical ideology, as a culture of performance and performance institutions, and as a compositional genre cultivated by native composers, can be read as one of the most stirring narratives in music history. A nation widely regarded in the nineteenth century as 'Das Land ohne Musik'[1] (and by logical extension 'Das Land ohne Symphonien', given the centrality of that genre to the dominant Germanic musical culture of the day) in the first half of the twentieth century went from the lowly status of poor dependent of a rich German symphonic tradition, to becoming arguably the most important guardian of that inheritance. It preserved and polished the canonic family heirlooms in performance (including broadcasting and recording), acted as a gatekeeper for which new composers and works should join that canon (for example Sibelius) and contributed treasures to the collection with its own original works.[2] Indeed, by the last quarter of the twentieth century, Britain maintained an almost unique fidelity to the symphony as a living genre, to the extent that, more than in any other leading musical nation, a significant number of its composers of international stature continued to make important contributions to the genre. The conversion – there seems hardly any other word for it – to the cause of former modernist *enfant terrible* Peter Maxwell Davies, the composer of eight symphonies to date, is only the most obvious sign of this phenomenon; the enormous popular success of Anthony Payne's speculative completion of Elgar's Third Symphony (1997) is another.[3] And reviewing the twentieth century, the sheer number of symphonies written in Britain during this period, most notably (for quality, quantity, or both) those by Elgar (two), Vaughan Williams (nine), Bax (seven), Bantock (three), Havergal Brian (an astonishing thirty-two), Walton (two), Rubbra (eleven), Britten (four), Tippett (four), Rawsthorne (three), Alwyn (five), Arnold (nine), Simpson (eleven), George Lloyd (twelve) – the list could go on – is extremely impressive.[4]

Of course, the British fascination with the symphony can be seen to tell a less stirring story: one in which such fidelity reflects in fact precisely the inability of British music to emancipate itself from foreign dominance and nineteenth-century musical values. In this account the symphony represents a continued dependence on Germanic tradition and the cult of absolute music, and an inherent conservatism and resistance to modernism, which in the later 1950s and the 1960s, as the generation of Maxwell Davies and Birtwistle embraced the avant-garde, became a continuing rearguard action against the new.[5] There is certainly some truth to this alternative reading – despite the caution with which we should now approach such potentially simplistic dualities as conservative versus modernist. But the British twentieth-century symphony encompassed an extraordinarily wide range of styles and approaches. The period after 1945 was especially rich, yielding the neo-romanticism of George Lloyd's symphonies, the orchestra and tape collage of Roberto Gerhard's Second (1960), the Caribbean steel-band sounds of Malcolm Arnold's Fourth (1960) and the postmodernist juxtaposition of Beethoven and the blues in Tippett's Third (1972), to take just a few examples. Indeed, the question of genre – of what, beyond a title, really constitutes a symphony in the twentieth century – became as acute in Britain as anywhere else; like their contemporaries elsewhere, some British composers played fast and loose with the term, or hedged their bets with compound titles, or less portentous terms such as 'sinfonietta'. Nevertheless, as we shall see, an influential strand in composition and criticism attempted to define and maintain a more rigorous and in many respects more conservative standard.[6]

Whatever the debate over the actual degree of native distinctiveness in the British symphonic achievement, or its ultimate value, certain questions must be posed. Why and how did Britain maintain this enduring fascination with the symphony? In the compositional realm, what did British composers take from the tradition they inherited, and what new contributions did they bring to it? What impact, if any, did they have outside their own country? Rather than attempting a survey that could only be superficial in a chapter of this length, I will focus here on a few major themes, composers and critical historical junctures: other choices could be made, and different stories told, no doubt. Although reception through performance and criticism will certainly play an important role in this account, my primary focus will be on composition; in a genre which relatively early on established intertextual reference as part of its tradition, composition is at one level the most important and most enduring kind of reception. An emphasis on composition will inevitably place most weight on the period since *c.* 1880, but of course one must begin at the beginning.

International clearing-house

The commercial wealth, relative social openness and cosmopolitanism of eighteenth-century Britain ensured that the emerging genre of the symphony would find a ready market there, at least in London. Indigenous symphonic composition, however, got off to a slow start, and the few native pioneers, such as Thomas Erskine, Earl of Kelly (1732–81), J. A. Fisher (1744–1806) and John Marsh (1752–1828), were overshadowed by émigré colleagues, most notably C. F. Abel and J. C. Bach, and, of course, Haydn, whose twelve symphonies for the impresario Salomon constitute Britain's most enduring, albeit indirect, contribution to the early history of the genre.[7] To this may be added the Royal Philharmonic Society's commission in 1822 of what eventually turned out to be Beethoven's Ninth Symphony.

Beethoven, of course, loomed large across the nineteenth century (and the twentieth, as we shall see), but in many ways more as moral exemplar – gratification-deferring narratives of growth and disciplined triumph over adversity resonated throughout bourgeois Europe and America – than direct musical model. For the latter, British composers were more likely to turn to Haydn, Mozart and Schubert, and later Mendelssohn and Schumann. Although Jurgen Schaarwächter has argued that the leading figures of mid century, Cipriani Potter (1792–1871) and William Sterndale Bennett (1816–75), demonstrated more individuality and independence from German models than has generally been assumed, the nineteenth-century British symphony for the most part rarely strays from continental mores, and relatively conservative ones at that.[8]

This remains largely true even as we approach the twentieth century and the first phase of the so-called English Musical Renaissance. Though the concept requires the careful interrogation that it has recently begun to receive, there was certainly a tremendous upsurge of musical activity during this period, and this affected the symphony as much as any other domain. Most importantly for the symphony, there was a sharp improvement in opportunities for orchestral performance. This was especially marked in London; the capital had for some time lagged well behind the provinces, notably in failing to sustain a stable orchestra to rival an ensemble such as the Hallé in Manchester, and thus failing to fulfil its early promise as a major centre for the nurturing of the genre. The introduction of the Henry Wood Promenade concerts at the Queen's Hall in 1895 confirmed the emergence of orchestral music as a legitimate and established genre in modern British concert life, a status which it had struggled to attain during the course of the nineteenth century, not least against the enduring grip of the oratorio tradition founded by Handel.[9] Although orchestral conditions in London still lagged behind those of most continental centres, it is no doubt hardly coincidental that there was an upsurge in symphonic composition in Britain during this period, at a time when the symphony, as opposed to the symphonic poem and other orchestral genres, was already beginning to wane in its central European heartland. Yet despite this profusion of new works, the symphonies of Charles Stanford (1852–1924) and Hubert Parry (1848–1918), and now lesser-known contemporaries such as Frederic Cowen (1852–1935) and Alexander Mackenzie (1847–1935), remain firmly in the mould of Schumann, Brahms and at times Dvořák. The last of these offered some guidance in the incorporation of nationalistic and folkloristic elements, as featured in Cowen's justly admired 'Scandinavian' Symphony of 1880, or Stanford's 'Irish' Symphony of 1887; as in other countries, such locally or exotically inflected interpretations of an essentially German genre became common during this period. Yet Tchaikovsky and Wagner, who were popular with audiences and became mainstays of the Wood Promenade programmes, had little impact on British orchestral music until Elgar around the turn of the century.[10] It is striking, too, that the most recent German symphonists outside the Brahms camp, Bruckner and Mahler, were largely dismissed in Britain (certainly by critics, who were extremely conservative for the most part), effectively choking off the German symphonic tradition in the mid-1880s with Brahms's last symphonies.[11] Richard Strauss was harder to ignore, but as the acknowledged specialist of the 'inferior' genre of the programmatic symphonic poem, he was treated with considerable suspicion.

Resistance to the more 'progressive' stream of German music was of course part of broader debates about the future of music in general, and in particular the future of absolute music, which nineteenth-century concert life had come so to venerate. This involved, in turn, profound and culturally resonant issues of the proper relationships of intellect, emotion, and sensation and sensuality in music (the colouristic possibilities of the late Romantic orchestra made the latter element especially contentious), and the question of whether the classical symphonic legacy should become primarily a museum of masterworks or a living tradition (evincing a split between custodial performance and creative innovation). As their preferred models suggest, British composers and critics in the last two decades of the nineteenth century favoured a conception of the symphony that emphasised clarity of form, thematic integration, a sense of expressive restraint and control, and a robust diatonicism – all in the service of an idealistic goal of moral improvement.

Not surprisingly, in this great age of empire, racial theorising and growing Anglo-Saxon pre-eminence on the world stage, some saw issues of national and racial character at stake in the history and future of music and the symphony. Hubert Parry, writing on the growth of the symphony in the first edition of Grove's great dictionary, opined that 'the development of pure abstract instrumental music seems almost to have been the monopoly of the German race', and while the programme symphony 'might perhaps be fairly regarded as the Celtic counterpart of the essentially Teutonic form of art', in reality it was 'scarcely even an offshoot of the old symphonic stem'.[12] Given the sense of close Anglo-German racial kinship that still obtained during this period, the inference could be drawn that Anglo-Saxon composers, unlike their French or Italian counterparts, were likewise well-suited to take on the challenges of the genre. The American composer Horatio Parker, professor at Yale and teacher of Charles Ives, whose own works enjoyed considerable success in Britain around the turn of the century, went further, and also saw transnational implications:

> I have great hopes for English music ... The Germans and French have made enormous strides in recent years, but I am not sure that they are in a direction in which [the] Anglo-Saxon need strive to follow. I hope for a powerful school of Anglo-Saxon music in time – less subjective and nerve-racking than that of Continental races, more broad, reserved and self-contained, with a larger respect for that economy of resource which characterizes all true artistry, and I hope that Americans may bear their part in the development of this school.[13]

Though Parker does not mention the symphony specifically (and wrote only one of his own), his extolling of an abstract, reserved and economical musical aesthetic aligns closely with the symphonic approach of most of his British contemporaries. As we shall see, these transatlantic Anglo-Saxon affinities would have implications for mid-twentieth-century symphonic developments.

Not all were so sure, however, that a manly musical Anglo-Saxonism (notions of self-possessed masculinity were central to this racial discourse), based on the more sober strands of German composition, was the right direction for British music. As a new century dawned, more experimental traits began to develop, and a split opened up between the conservatively Teutonic Royal College of Music and the relatively cosmopolitan Royal Academy of Music. The latter was more open to Russian, French, and other non-German music, and to the symphonic poem and programme symphony; RAM products such as Josef Holbrooke and Granville Bantock produced innovative programme symphonies in the first decade of the century, breaking sharply with the prevailing mould. Indeed, questions were beginning to be raised about the creative fruits of the largely RCM-led Renaissance, and in a time of increasing geopolitical competition with Germany, it was disappointing that the works of Parry, Stanford and other luminaries of the movement had failed to make a lasting impact on the continent. When in 1905 Sir Edward Elgar declared that 'English music is white, and *evades everything*', he hit a nerve.[14]

Passing the torch

It was Elgar, in fact, who three years earlier had finally stormed the German citadel, as it were, with the triumphant Düsseldorf performance of *The Dream of Gerontius*, and Richard Strauss's famous encomium to the British composer, hailing him as the 'first English progressivist'[15] – Elgar's remarks therefore carried particular weight. Yet the work in question was an oratorio, by then an English speciality, and there remained a sense that for British music truly to come of age, it had to beat the Germans at their own game, as it were, the symphony (even if most modern German composers, Strauss included, had turned away from it). Elgar duly obliged, with the premiere in Manchester in December 1908 of his Symphony No. 1, which became an extraordinary worldwide success and the first really decisive landmark in the history of the British symphony. A London premiere followed within a few days, and tumultuous public acclaim led to hastily-arranged additional performances; the Symphony was even included in a free concert at the Harrod's department store.[16] It was quickly taken up across the United States; the conductor of the New York premiere, Walter Damrosch, who a few years earlier had urged Elgar to write a symphony (Elgar was 'the only man living who could do it' – a telling indication of how pessimistically some viewed the state of the genre), described the slow movement as the greatest orchestral Adagio since Beethoven.[17] Artur Nikisch, who conducted the Symphony in Leipzig, ranked it with the best of Beethoven and Brahms, and even dubbed it 'the fifth of Brahms';[18] it was warmly received also in Vienna and St Petersburg. Yet Nikisch's remark, though it would have fitted symphonies by Parry or Stanford well enough, seems to miss the mark with Elgar by a wide margin, not least in the dazzling orchestral rhetoric of the work, indebted as much to Wagner, Berlioz and Strauss (and even lighter French composers) as to Brahms. Samuel Langford, reviewing the premiere in the *Manchester Guardian*, surely came closer, in saying that '[Elgar] has refertilised the symphonic form by infusing into it the best ideas that could be gathered from the practice of the writers of symphonic poems' (a genre to which Elgar himself had contributed).[19] Despite its outwardly conservative four-movement plan, recent commentators have viewed the work as an extraordinarily original response to symphonic tradition (not least in the unusual tonal and formal scheme of the first movement, where there is even some disagreement over the key of the main portion of the movement),[20] and as a piece riven by the contradictions of incipient musical modernism. Edwardian audiences were nevertheless struck primarily by a sense of power and mastery, and responded enthusiastically, and with national pride, to the message of 'a massive hope for the future' which was as far as Elgar would go in identifying any programmatic content. In terms of rivalry with Germany, it was surely appropriate, if arrived at largely circumstantially, that the satirical magazine *Punch* should tie the success of the Symphony in with a current scare over British naval vulnerability to a growing German navy.[21]

Yet in the same way that Elgar's climaxes seem to be disintegrating even as they attain their summit (James Hepokoski's astute observation),[22] Elgar's triumph, and with it an established place for British symphonic composition on the international stage, was short-lived (at least for now), as the whole symphonic tradition that he so brilliantly embraced, and the institutional performance culture that sustained it, came under increasing strain.[23] Just a few weeks into 1909 the first performance of Schoenberg's String Quartet No. 2 announced his momentous break with tonality. Elgar's Second Symphony was premiered less than a week after the death of Mahler (who had conducted the First Symphony in New York) in 1911, but failed to capture the public imagination in the same way as its predecessor. The last major landmark of the British symphony to appear before the First World War was a work that seemed more in tune with the swiftly changing social and artistic ethos. Vaughan Williams's *A London Symphony*, premiered in London on 27 March 1914, was immediately acclaimed, although wider success would be delayed until after the War. His first work in the genre, the Whitman-based choral *A Sea Symphony*, had been premiered in 1910; moving beyond its predecessor's generalised spiritual quest, *A London Symphony* offered a more obviously modernist engagement (indebted to another dimension of Whitman) with the metropolis, the nation, and by implication the largest empire in the world. It attempted ambitiously to forge a sense of historical and spatial totality in a vision largely untouched by Elgar's nostalgic autobiography, in the process drawing on popular and folk music, modern French models and even Stravinsky. Vaughan Williams's voice is more obviously communal than personal, in a unique work, which although not as fully realised as Elgar's symphonies, was ultimately more original, and more nationalistically distinctive; indeed, the quiet Epilogue would turn out to be something of an English symphonic trademark.[24] Yet the Epilogue, in taking the doubt and disintegration confronted (more explicitly than in Elgar) throughout the work and dissolving it into mystical oblivion, seems now darkly prophetic of the events that would shortly rock the fundamental assumptions both of Western civilisation and the symphonic tradition itself.

Ashes to ashes

The First World War called into question, and to some decisively repudiated, all optimistic narratives of human progress, and to the more extreme pessimists, notions of traditionally coherent and authentic personal expression across the arts. Given the symphony's close association with such narratives of individual and communal selfhood, it came under particular pressure. Added to that was the growing impact, or at least wider dissemination, of pre-war modernist challenges to tonality and formal continuity – the foundations of the symphony – particularly in the works of Schoenberg and Stravinsky. In continental Europe, through a variety of factors addressed by David Fanning in Chapter 5, the symphony would prove to be to all intents and purposes moribund as a continuous living tradition: only in the Anglo-Saxon world, in Scandinavia and in the Soviet Union, would it find significant new life. In social and political terms, Britain, though certainly plagued by economic problems, was the least affected of any major musical nation by the kind of radical upheavals experienced elsewhere during the inter-war 'long weekend' of the 1920s and 1930s, and so it is perhaps no surprise that symphonic narrative continued to make more sense than in most other places.

Yet even in Britain a clear sense of direction was slow to emerge in the 1920s and even beyond. Numerous symphonies were written, adding new voices and styles to the already significant diversity of the pre-war period, but few seemed more than ad hoc solutions: with some notable exceptions, the symphonies of the inter-war years were a mixed bag, and offered many false dawns. Matters were complicated by broader questions over the cultivation of a distinctively British (or at least English) national musical style: was this a good thing, and if so, what should it, or did it, comprise? For many people the emerging leader of British music was Vaughan Williams; but the contemplative and folksong-inflected pastoral ethos that was the most prominent and influential strand of his music in the early 1920s seemed ill-suited to traditional symphonic dialectic. Indeed, when his third work in the genre, *A Pastoral Symphony*, appeared, it constituted for some almost an anti-symphony.[25] This work also raised a central question for the symphony anywhere in the post-war era (one which had begun to rear its head even in the decade before 1914): to what degree could the genre be separated from the tonal system, and the attendant phrase structures, thematic rhetoric and developmental protocols that had underpinned its evolution? In Vaughan Williams's case this question turned not only on his folksong-derived melodic materials, but also the attenuated cadential drives of his modal harmonic materials, influenced by Debussy and Ravel. In retrospect it has been possible to discern in this work cogent and original musical argument rather than the rambling rumination emphasised in contemporary responses; yet the inconclusive ending, with a wordless soprano suspended in space, as it were, was in certain respects more subversive of established generic precepts than any ending in Mahler or Sibelius: it certainly did not offer an obvious model for symphonic progeny. Vaughan Williams himself would not start sketching another symphony until the end of the decade – the longest symphonic hiatus in his career. The refusal of the other leading composer of the early 1920s, Gustav Holst, to engage in any traditional way with the symphony contributed to the uncertainty.

In the meantime others were trying different paths. For most British composers the major issues of the period were the (very slow) absorption of elements of continental modernism and, given a broad rejection of atonality, how to revivify tonality in the modern age; also at issue was the rise of popular music, especially jazz, and whether this had its place in a symphonic context (the genre had, after all, always included dance elements, and jazz was still viewed primarily in terms of dance). That said, contemporary popular music had little impact on Arnold Bax, who was in many respects the leading British symphonist of the period up to the mid 1930s; he was certainly the most prolific mainstream figure, producing all seven of his symphonies during the inter-war years (Vaughan Williams completed only two between 1918 and 1939). Yet despite in some ways offering an antithesis to Vaughan Williams, favouring a more traditional orchestral rhetoric and lush chromaticism, based in part on pre-1914 Russian models, Bax was seen by many – and continues to be seen, despite efforts at reclamation – to be too prone to rhapsodic construction for a place in the symphonic pantheon.[26] At least in his symphonies of the 1920s; by the 1930s, however, Bax, like many of his contemporaries, was attempting to emulate a more rigorous model – Sibelius, to whom we shall need to turn in more detail shortly.

By this time a number of enormously important developments had taken place in the infrastructure of musical dissemination and appreciation, and while these were enjoyed virtually worldwide and thus are not uniquely British, Britain played a leading role in several key areas. Most important were recording and broadcasting, which opened up vast new audiences for classical music, and new ways of listening – repeatedly, in the case of records, something perhaps of special relevance for the demanding genre of the symphony. Vaughan Williams's *A London Symphony* was the first British symphony to be recorded in its entirety, in 1925, and both the Elgar symphonies would follow several years later, conducted by the composer, as part of his extraordinary and to that point unparalleled investment in the new medium. Of even wider impact was the swift expansion in classical music coverage, including contemporary music, by the young BBC, which received a tremendous boost in 1927 when the Corporation took over the Proms series, with the latter's commitment to providing in most years a complete Beethoven cycle, as well as a good deal of other core symphonic repertory.[27] The kind of broader musical culture yearned for by Elgar in his Peyton lectures was becoming a reality.[28]

It was still rare to hear Mahler or Bruckner in London, despite the efforts of the BBC with more recent music from Central Europe. Sibelius was a quite different matter, however: around 1930 he was coming to be seen not only as the most desirable model for the British symphony, a position he would hold until the 1950s, but also more broadly as the authentic face of musical modernism.[29] It was largely under this influence that a number of British composers would begin to converge and engage with the symphony in a more coherent fashion; or at least in a way that engaged directly with the Beethovenian tradition, rather than more diffuse late-Romantic conceptions of the genre. One of the most influential (if idiosyncratic) books of the period, Constant Lambert's 1934 *Music Ho!*, having extolled the virtues of jazz, and questioned the genuine originality and importance of Stravinsky and Schoenberg, proceeded to enthrone Sibelius as the true musical god of the first quarter of the twentieth century – the heir to Beethoven, and a more genuinely radical and modernist figure than any of his contemporaries.[30] The British Sibelius cult actually had a long history, going back at least to Bantock (to whom the Finn dedicated his Third Symphony), but now became unusually widespread and intense. At a time when Sibelius was generally out of favour in Germany and the rest of continental Europe, such adulation was rivalled (outside Finland) only in the United States.[31] Sibelius seemed to offer a way to reclaim the symphony from Romantic excess, offering formal discipline and clarity without the perceived artificiality and emotional detachment of Franco-Russian neo-classicism. On both sides of the Atlantic it can be argued that as with Parry and Parker at the turn of the century, loose conceptions of race once again played a role, in this case drawing on a perceived kinship between certain Anglo-Saxon traits of temperament and a broader Nordic identity (an affinity commonly identified in contemporary racial theorising). Peter Franklin notes that Sibelius was frequently treated as an honorary Briton in terms of character, not least in a sense of emotional restraint and control.[32] Such affinities became all the more suggestive as Sibelius's long-mooted Eighth Symphony failed to materialise, and it began to appear that the Seventh, premiered in the mid 1920s, might have been his last (as it indeed turned out to be):[33] with no obvious Scandinavian successor in sight, and the symphony apparently dormant in Germany, the idea that the baton of the mainstream symphonic tradition might pass to a British composer or composers, as it had for a fleeting moment with Elgar, seemed increasingly plausible.

Almost right on cue, December 1934 saw the premiere of a symphony that to many appeared to deliver on this promise, and in decidedly Sibelian terms: Walton's First Symphony was received almost as enthusiastically as Elgar's First. Yet it was a year of mixed portents and omens for the British symphony, open to differing oracular interpretations. By coincidence, Elgar's Third was originally scheduled for inclusion in the same BBC Symphony Orchestra season that unveiled the Walton, but the composer died in February, leaving the work only incompletely sketched; Holst, who died a few months later, had also been at work on a symphony, his first attempt at what seems to have been intended as a relatively traditional approach to the genre; Delius also passed away that year, though without ever having shown any inclination towards the symphony. All of this did nothing to dampen the intense anticipation of the Walton, though heightened expectations seem to have affected the composer, who was unable to complete the Finale in time for the premiere. Yet the performance, of the first three movements only, went ahead anyway, a sign of the importance placed on the creation of a work in this exalted genre by Britain's leading composer of the post-war generation. Walton did produce a finale in time for a performance the following November, and the work went from strength to strength, receiving more performances in its first few years than any British symphony since Elgar's First; a recording was rushed out within less than two months of the first performance of the complete version, underlining the importance both of this Symphony and of the relatively new technological medium.[34]

Many were led to hail Walton as the new leader of British music, and the conversion of a former *enfant terrible* to the symphony, and in its ideal guise as the pinnacle of seriousness and 'pure' music, added further weight to the epiphany. Walton's Symphony was widely compared to those of Sibelius (and to some degree Beethoven), yet in retrospect the connections, though obvious, seem mostly superficial, for example the long oboe note with concluding flourish which opens the first movement, or the extensive use of pedal notes in the same (although even these do not function in the same way as Sibelius's). One can argue for some sense of gradual revelation of a long-deferred telos in the first movement, confirmed by almost overwhelmingly massive brass writing, but the course of the Symphony as a whole seems less inevitable, and the Finale has disappointed many; it is notable more for its incorporation of popular music elements, in the jazzy fugue that dominates the movement, than for the rather forced Sibelian grandeur of the closing pages, with their apotheosis of first-movement material. In any case, the Symphony (again echoing Elgar's First), proved to be something of a magnificent dead end. Walton himself would not return to the genre for over twenty-five years, producing in 1960 the fascinating but poorly received Second Symphony (his last, as it turned out).

By the time the complete version of Walton's First appeared, however, another remarkable British work (which Walton thought the greatest symphony since Beethoven)[35] had presented a much more disturbing modern response to the Beethovenian symphonic tradition – one which risked making the Walton, and particularly its triumphal conclusion, sound hollow. Vaughan Williams's explosive Fourth Symphony, premiered in April 1935, challenged audiences and critics not just on account of its violent dissonance and rhythmic disjunctions – which though in such stark contrast to his *A Pastoral Symphony* had in fact been brewing for some time in his more recent scores – but for its full-scale engagement with a Beethovenian legacy of orchestral rhetoric and thematic development that he had avoided in most of his mature music. Most troubling of all, it presents a bleakly parodistic and disturbing encounter with that legacy, twisting formal and gestural elements of Beethoven's Fifth and Ninth symphonies in a way that seems to repudiate the *per aspera ad astra* plot archetype of these works (an archetype audaciously reinvented in Walton's First): rather than contemplatively withdraw from such aspirations, as in his previous symphony, Vaughan Williams now confronted them head on, with a ferocious irony in places that rivals that of Shostakovitch. The work has always been something of an enigma, apparently even to its own composer, and attempts to explain its towering anger in terms of the First World War, the state of contemporary Europe or frustrations in Vaughan Williams's personal life, are inevitably and damagingly reductive (though all probably played a part, the war in particular).[36] They have also distracted attention from the work's more purely musical achievement, which represents perhaps the most ambitious attempt of the period in any country to integrate atonal (or at least antitonal) elements into the traditional thematic and formal procedures of the symphony, partly through the manipulation of tightly constructed melodic cells. The composer's widow claimed that the work sprang from reading a review of a modernist orchestral piece by another composer, and at one level it may be viewed as a barbed commentary on developments in contemporary music.[37]

Vaughan Williams's Fourth owed little, if anything, to Sibelius, but his serene Fifth, begun in 1938 but not completed until 1943, is dedicated to the Finn and bears definite traces of his influence; it joins the later symphonies of Bax, Walton's First and E. J. Moeran's G minor symphony of 1939 as one of the most important monuments to the Sibelius cult in England. Across the Atlantic, too, Sibelius left his mark on a number of notable symphonies, including Samuel Barber's First, already considered in Chapter 11, and Roy Harris's Third; both are in one movement, echoing Sibelius's Seventh, a formal model less obviously influential in Britain. But American composers were also attentive to developments in British music. Vaughan Williams's symphonies, beginning with *A London Symphony* in the 1920s, established a strong presence in America, as did those of Bax, a number of which were premiered there. Vaughan Williams's Fourth was particularly successful in the United States, where its accommodation of certain modernist elements into a symphonic context – though not its explicit violence and parody – would prove influential on American symphonists of the 1940s, including figures such as David Diamond and Peter Mennin, now largely neglected. More broadly, the Second World War cemented the sense of Anglo-Saxon affinity, especially in the idea of fighting an heroic battle for freedom and democracy over totalitarianism; it also brought in as ally, albeit relatively briefly, the other great symphonic nation of the era, Russia (brutal totalitarianism in that country notwithstanding).

Yet the most successful British symphony to emerge from the war years and their immediate aftermath, an international success rivalling that of Elgar's First, was not one of triumphant heroism, but a work widely interpreted as portraying, after glimmers of hope in its first movement, only devastation: Vaughan Williams's Sixth Symphony, begun in 1944 and premiered in 1948, ends in a movement of frozen near-paralysis, apparently drained of all life, that many interpreted as representing a post-nuclear abyss (though resisting all explicit programmatic interpretation, the composer himself referred to it privately as 'the Big Three').[38] His remaining three symphonies, with the partial exception of the Eighth (1956), are broadly pessimistic; heroism is engaged directly in the seventh of the cycle, *Sinfonia Antartica* (1953), based on his music for the 1948 film *Scott of the Antarctic*, but in terms only of endurance and stoicism, while the Ninth (1958) is a profoundly ambivalent work involving a programme centred on Hardy's *Tess of the D'Urbervilles*. Thus concludes what is still surely the most impressive and wide-ranging symphonic cycle to have been composed by a British composer to date.

Wider still and wider

This is to run ahead a little, however. By the late 1940s a new generation of composers, most notably Benjamin Britten and Michael Tippett, had come to the fore.[39] Britten was at this time establishing opera as the core of his life's work, and, always wary of anything redolent of the British musical establishment as represented by Vaughan Williams and his

generation, engaged only obliquely with the mainstream symphonic tradition (even when British perception of that mainstream later came to
include his beloved Mahler).[40] Although Tippett was also critical of some
trends in British inter-war music, he was not as hostile as Britten to the
prevailing climate, and the centrality of Beethoven and the sonata archetype – never congenial for Britten – to his aesthetic seemed to demand
involvement with the symphony. He would eventually produce four
published works that mark important stylistic junctures in his varied
career, and which to some degree epitomise broader concerns of the
time.[41] His Symphony No. 1 (1945) attempts with tremendous energy
(though not complete success) the difficult task, first tackled by Beethoven
in his last period, of combining dualistic sonata conflict with the more
monistic, continuous structures of pre-classical music, as in the variations
on a ground bass that form the work's slow movement. Over a decade later
in his Second Symphony (1957), Tippett tackled a new challenge, that of
incorporating in a symphonic context the dramatic ruptures and discontinuities pioneered by Stravinsky, and which from this point on were to
shape a broader style-shift in Tippett's music. The Third Symphony
(1972) takes this one step further, engaging with directions in post-war
continental music: in the first movement the composer conceptualises a
dualism between musical archetypes that he characterises as 'arrest' and
'movement', a reaction in part to what he saw as the 'motionless' quality
typical of the music of Boulez and other leading figures of the 1950s and
1960s.[42] But in the Finale of the work he also dramatically confronted the
humanistic significance of the symphonic legacy in a post-Auschwitz,
post-Hiroshima world. His own text asks, 'They sang that when she
waved her wings / The Goddess Joy would make us one / And did my
brother die of frost-bite in the camp / And was my sister charred to cinders
in the oven?', and Tippett juxtaposes quotations of the so-called 'horror
fanfare' that launches the Finale of Beethoven's Ninth with powerful
evocations of the blues genre, and with material from earlier in the
Symphony. The Fourth Symphony, which followed six years later, returns
to a familiar archetype of symphonic narrative, in the form of a one-
movement birth-to-death scenario, beginning and ending with the evocation of human breathing.

Tippett's ambitious and humanistic view of the symphony established
him as the natural successor to Vaughan Williams. While most British
symphonists of the post-war era did not on the whole attempt to reach so
far, Tippett's symphonies do reflect certain broader trends, above all the
impetus to bring within the bounds of the genre a wider and wider range
of contrasting materials and styles: to build on its history as a metaphor
for the exploration, even resolution, of psychological and social contrast or

conflict, as a vehicle for trying to make coherent the increasing fragmentation of post-Enlightenment modernity, which was being pushed to new limits after 1945, in Britain as elsewhere. Though this expansion of symphonic range was paralleled to some degree in other countries, most notably the United States, the extent of Britain's commitment to the genre at this time was essentially unique. Indeed, the 1950s and 1960s constituted the most fertile period of any for the British symphony, in terms of the sheer number of new works produced, and the number of talented younger figures entering the scene: Malcolm Arnold, Alan Rawsthorne, Peter Racine Fricker, Richard Rodney Bennett, Robert Simpson, to name only some of the most prominent. Some of the new names, notably Benjamin Frankel, Egon Wellesz, Franz Reizenstein, Roberto Gerhard, and later Andrzej Panufnik, were émigrés escaping from fascist or communist continental regimes, giving a newly literal dimension to the idea of Britain as a refuge for a central European symphonic tradition neglected by, or driven from, its birthplace.

Of course the commitment to the symphony reflected to some degree the relative conservatism of British music, and the full reach of continental modernism as it was developing at this time, especially electronic music, would not really take hold in Britain until the mid 1960s. Not surprisingly, the two leading young British composers who were receptive to continental trends in the 1950s, Peter Maxwell Davies and Harrison Birtwistle, did not turn to the symphony at this point (Birtwistle has never done so). Nevertheless, the range of new materials assimilated into the symphony during this period remains impressive. Although a Hindemithian neo-classicism (already evident in Tippett's First) was the prevailing style for many, there were a number of attempts to assimilate twelve-tone procedures into a symphonic context (and in a more traditional way than Webern), as in the symphonies of Humphrey Searle, and even, idiosyncratically, in Walton's Second; although this at one level challenged the tonal foundations of the genre, twelve-tone techniques lent themselves well to thematic development and transformation, and could even assimilate tonal elements, as Berg had demonstrated soon after the invention of the method. Other currents were also in the air, however, which had to do more with genres and styles than raw musical materials. Mahler had finally started to make a significant impact in Britain,[43] along with Shostakovitch (both already important to Britten, of course, despite his own ambivalence towards the symphony); Malcolm Arnold's inclusion of popular and light musical styles, including brass-band music, in a number of his symphonies, suggests the influence of both composers, and a continuing expansion of social and political terms of reference. Like a number of his contemporaries, including William Alwyn, Arnold was heavily involved in writing film music, and several works from this period, most notably Vaughan Williams's *Sinfonia Antartica*, have strong connections to the cinema.

The fact that Vaughan Williams was still composing symphonies in the 1950s helped maintain a sense of continuity with the pre-war scene, even as Britten rose to take the older man's place as the leading figure in British music. But the early 1960s saw genuine upheaval, precipitated in part by the appointment in 1959 of William Glock as BBC Controller of Music. Glock set out to give more prominent coverage to continental (and American) musical modernism, especially music since 1945, than it had received under the previous regime, and a rift developed between the new modernism and an older conservative British consensus, with contemporary tonal music (which by extension still included most recent symphonies) becoming a polemical issue. Many tonal composers felt marginalised by the new regime; though the real extent to which they were deliberately frozen out remains a matter of debate, the perception was real enough, and caused profound distress in a number of cases. Yet in the case of the symphony even the more modernist, primarily atonal, composers, such as Alexander Goehr and Jonathan Harvey, were still contributing to the genre; as noted already in the case of Tippett's Third, a more conceptual, abstract understanding of symphonic principles could allow for use of materials well beyond the bounds of tonal or even twelve-tone procedures. And at the end of the decade, the extraordinary young prodigy Oliver Knussen made a personal approach to the symphony, complete with complex (though hardly old-fashioned) unification, the centre of his early output, which included three symphonies.

It is true that Knussen and Tippett aside, many of these works tended to be one-off experiments with the symphony. But in any case, as it turned out, the perceived modernist institutional hegemony was not the permanent climate-change that it had seemed at the outset. With regard to the symphony, the single most striking sign of change came in the mid 1970s, when Peter Maxwell Davies embarked on writing a symphony, and acknowledged direct influence from none other than Sibelius. That Davies' language in the work was nevertheless uncompromisingly modernist is less important, perhaps, than the willingness to invoke Sibelius, and the fact that he then went on to write seven more works in this genre, the most recent, *Antarctic Symphony* (2001), commissioned to commemorate Vaughan Williams's own Antarctic film score and symphony of 50 years earlier;[44] indeed Davies' symphonic output as a whole now constitutes one of the most impressive British contributions to the genre. His change of heart was, of course, part of a broader re-evaluation of a narrow conception of modernism that began to gather pace around 1980, and entailed a fracturing of avant-garde hegemony spreading well beyond British music. That said, most of his younger colleagues, including Marc-Anthony Turnage and Thomas Adés, have avoided the symphony, though they have certainly written large-scale orchestral works that can be described as symphonic. James MacMillan is an exception, having composed three symphonies to date; yet even though MacMillan is perhaps the most successful of recent British composers in cultivating a wide audience for complex modern music, his symphonies, like those of Maxwell Davies, cannot be said for the moment to have firmly established themselves in the repertoire. It is a sobering fact for modern British symphonists that none of them has been able to come even close to competing with the runaway success of Anthony Payne's speculative completion of Elgar's Third Symphony, premiered in 1997, an extraordinary phenomenon that highlights the continuing gulf between much contemporary composition and the broader musical public.[45] To this may be added the popularity of recordings of symphonies by Vaughan Williams and Bax, and by once obscure composers such as George Lloyd and William Alwyn: such composers have benefited enormously from the recording boom that began with the advent of the compact disc in the early 1980s. At a time when Scandinavian countries in particular, and Germany to a lesser extent, have been reviving their symphonic output, perhaps Britain is in compositional terms no longer the citadel of a living symphonic tradition that it once was. Yet the appointment of a British conductor, Simon Rattle, to the helm of the Berlin Philharmonic Orchestra in 2002, an event quite unthinkable a century ago, shows just how far Britain's wider relationship with the symphony and its institutions has been transformed since the days of 'Das Land ohne Musik'.

Notes

1 Though the term came to prominence with Oscar Schmitz's book *Das Land ohne Musik: Englische Gesellschaftsprobleme* (Munich, 1904), the idea it embodies was certainly widespread by the mid nineteenth century.

2 Of course the United States and Russia, especially the former, also have some claims to this title. Yet in terms of composition, despite an impressive national symphonic output, no American symphony has yet established itself firmly in the repertoire, even in its country of origin (a partial exception is Copland's Third, but even that maintains only a toehold); in Russia, totalitarian conservative musical policies, Socialist Realism in particular, can be seen to have artificially boosted the genre. Yet parallels can certainly be drawn, in that the

prominence of the symphony in all three countries has been seen to some degree as a product of 'lateness', a process of catching up in musical cultures that struggled to establish an independent profile in art music during the nineteenth century, but eventually came into their own in the twentieth.

3 Except where stated otherwise, all dates are of the first performance.

4 Somewhat surprisingly, the most comprehensive study to date of the British symphony is by a German musicologist: Jürgen Schaarwächter, *Die Britische Sinfonie 1914–1945* (Köln-Rheinkassel, 1994); despite a detailed focus on the period specified in the title, the book also ranges widely across the entire history of the genre in Britain.

Schaarwächter's account is weighted primarily towards the documentary and descriptive. A more critical and analytical approach to the twentieth-century repertoire is offered in the chapters by Peter Evans and Jim Samson, which deal with instrumental music *c.* pre-1960 and post-1960 respectively, in Stephen Banfield, ed., *The Blackwell History of Music in Britain*, vol. VI: *The Twentieth Century* (Oxford, 1995). See also Ralph Hill, *The Symphony* (Harmondsworth, 1949), and the chapters on British composers in Robert Simpson, ed., *The Symphony*, vol. II: *Elgar to the Present Day* (Harmondsworth, 1967).

5 The most forceful – and at times controversial – recent expression of this viewpoint is found in Robert Stradling and Meirion Hughes, *The English Musical Renaissance, 1840–1940: Constructing a National Music*, 2nd edn (Manchester, 2001).

6 The present discussion will for the most part restrict itself to works specifically titled 'symphony'. Perhaps the most precise definition of the rigorous strand in British writing on the symphony, an approach which though not uniquely British received unusually strong advocacy in this country, is set out in the editor's Introductions to the two volumes of the Penguin survey cited in note 4. Robert Simpson, distinguished symphonist, critic, and expert on Beethoven, Bruckner, Nielsen and Sibelius (from whom his values ultimately derive), sets out a number of key attributes, including most crucially 'the fusion of diverse elements into an organic whole', 'the continuous control of pace' and the idea that a 'true symphony . . . is active in all possible ways . . . the composer must never allow any prime element of the music (rhythm, melody, harmony, tonality) to seem to die, so that artificial respiration is necessary' (vol. I, 13–14 and see also Chapter 5 in the present volume). On this basis Simpson excludes works such as Stravinsky's symphonies, which he considers brilliant but essentially balletic and episodic in nature, especially in their treatment of tonality.

7 See Jan LaRue and Eugene K. Wolf, 'Symphony', Section I/12, in Stanley Sadie and John Tyrrell, eds., *The New Grove Dictionary of Music and Musicians* (London, 2001), 825–6.

8 See Jürgen Schaarwächter, 'Cipriani Potter, Georg Alexander Macfarren and Mid-19th-Century British Symphonism', in Wolfgang Schult and Henrik Verkerk, eds., *Deutschland und England: Beiträge zur Musikforschung, Jahrbuch der Bachwochen Dillenburg (2002)* (Munich, 2002), 77–91. Notable also during this period is the emergence of a female British symphonist, Alice Smith (1839–84).

9 See Simon McVeigh and Cyril Ehrlich, 'The Modernisation of London Concert Life Around 1900', in Michael Talbot, ed., *The Business of Music* (Liverpool, 2002), 96–120; also Leanne Langley, 'Agency and Change: Berlioz in Britain (1870–1920)', *Journal of the Royal Musical Association*, 132 (2007), 306–48.

10 It would be beyond the scope of this chapter to consider the social composition of audiences, though the Proms were one example of a wider movement to reach a more variegated range of the population, through lower ticket prices and other aspects of the concert experience. The most famous window onto the social dimensions of Edwardian concert life is chapter 6 of E. M. Forster's novel *Howards End* (1910). A colourful and more extended picture of audience taste and reactions of the time can be found in A. H. Sidgwick, *The Promenade Ticket: A Lay Record of Concert-going* (London, 1914).

11 For an introduction to the history of Mahler reception in Britain see Donald Mitchell, 'The Mahler Renaissance in England: Its Origins and Chronology', in Andrew Nicholson and Donald Mitchell, eds., *The Mahler Companion* (New York and Oxford, 1999), 548–64.

12 'Symphony', in George Grove, ed., *A Dictionary of Music and Musicians*, vol. IV (London, 1889), 38–9.

13 See Isabel Parker Semler, in collaboration with Pierson Underwood, *Horatio Parker: A Memoir for his Grandchildren, Compiled from Letters and Papers* (New York, 1975, repr. of 1942 edn), 110. The date and exact source of this passage are unclear, but from the context it seems likely that it was written in Parker's journal and refers to his 1899 trip to England. For further discussion of Parker's views see Alain Frogley, '"The Old Sweet Anglo-Saxon Spell": Racial Discourses and the American Reception of British Music, 1895–1933', in Julie Brown, ed., *Western Music and Race* (Cambridge, 2007), 244–57, at 251–2.

14 The emphasis is Elgar's. He made these remarks in one of the public lectures he delivered during his relatively brief tenure of the Peyton Chair created for him in 1905 at Birmingham University: see Edward Elgar and Percy M. Young, *A Future for English Music, and Other Lectures* (London, 1968), 49.

15 See Jerrold Northrop Moore, *Edward Elgar: A Creative Life* (Oxford, 1984), 368–9.

16 Moore, *Edward Elgar*, 548–9. Information in this paragraph is drawn primarily from Moore, *Edward Elgar*, 544–50.

17 See Richard Smith, *Elgar in America: Elgar's American Connections between 1895 and 1934* (Rickmansworth, 2005), 117.

18 *Musical Times* (1 June 1909), quoted in Moore, *Edward Elgar*, 548.

19 *Manchester Guardian* (4 December 1908), quoted in Moore, *Edward Elgar*, 547.

20 See J. P. E. Harper-Scott, *Edward Elgar, Modernist* (Cambridge, 2006), chapter 3.

21 Moore, *Edward Elgar*, 549–50.

22 See James Hepokoski, 'Elgar', in D. Kern Holoman, ed., *The Nineteenth-Century Symphony* (New York, 1997), 329.

23 Ibid., 340.

24 Though prefigured in the ending of Elgar's Second Symphony, which itself echoes Brahms's Third, Vaughan Williams's approach again seems more detached and distancing.

25 See, for instance, Constant Lambert, *Music Ho! A Study of Music in Decline* (London, 1934), 150–2; for other reactions to the symphony see Michael Kennedy, *The Works of Ralph Vaughan Williams*, rev. edn (Oxford, 1980), 155–7.

26 The most comprehensive study of Bax is Lewis Foreman, *Bax: A Composer and His Times*, 3rd rev. edn (Woodbridge, 2007). An even more prolific composer to emerge during the 1920s was Havergal Brian (1876–1972), who would go on to write thirty-two symphonies; unlike Bax, however, Brian never achieved broad recognition, and despite inspiring small numbers of devoted advocates over the years and occasional revivals of his work, he remains a marginal figure. His First Symphony, the 'Gothic', composed between 1919 and 1927, is nevertheless notorious for its sheer scale and length, involving five choirs and four offstage brass groups as well as an extremely large orchestra, thirty-seven-part writing for the voices in places, and a performing time of almost two hours.

27 See Jenny R. Doctor, David C. H. Wright and Nicholas Kenyon, eds., *The Proms: A New History* (London, 2007), chapter 3.

28 See Elgar and Young, *A Future for English Music, and Other Lectures*, 211.

29 See Laura Gray, 'Sibelius and England', in Glenda Dawn Goss, ed., *The Sibelius Companion* (Westport, 1996), 281–95; and Peter Franklin, 'Sibelius in Britain', in Daniel M. Grimley, ed., *The Cambridge Companion to Sibelius* (Cambridge, 2004), 182–95.

30 See Lambert, *Music Ho!*, 326–32.

31 See Glenda Dawn Goss, *Jean Sibelius and Olin Downes: Music, Friendship, Criticism* (Boston, 1995).

32 Franklin, 'Sibelius in Britain', 190–5.

33 Nielsen had also written his last symphony by this point, but the Dane was as yet virtually unknown in Britain, a situation that remained largely unchanged until the 1960s.

34 See Stephen Lloyd, *William Walton: Muse of Fire* (Woodbridge, 2001), 140.

35 Ursula Vaughan Williams, *R. V. W.: A Biography of Ralph Vaughan Williams* (London, 1964), 205.

36 See Kennedy, *Works of Ralph Vaughan Williams*, 243–8 on the early reception of the symphony; the personal background is broached in director Tony Palmer's 2007 documentary film *O Thou Transcendent: The Life of Ralph Vaughan Williams*.

37 Ursula Vaughan Williams, *R.V.W*, 190.

38 See Oliver Neighbour, 'The Place of the Eighth among Vaughan Williams' Symphonies', in Alain Frogley, ed., *Vaughan Williams Studies* (Cambridge, 1996), 213–33, at 224; see Kennedy, *Works of Ralph Vaughan Williams*, 300–4 on the early performance history and reception of the Symphony.

39 Another figure from the same generation who, although of lesser stature, was nevertheless a significant symphonist is Edmund Rubbra (1901–86). His eleven symphonies are, however, dominated by contrapuntal continuity rather than sonata dialectic: unlike Tippett, he did not for the most part attempt to combine the two, and his symphonies have generally been regarded as standing outside the mainstream.

40 He produced four works bearing the title, as well as the Sinfonietta Op. 1 of 1932, but all involve some qualifying twist in the title and content: *Simple Symphony* (1933–4); *Sinfonia da Requiem* (1941); *Spring Symphony* (1949); and Symphony for Cello and Orchestra (1963). Only the latter has been viewed as coming close to invoking traditional forms and developmental techniques, although for an alternative view see Arved Ashby, 'Britten as Symphonist', in Mervyn Cooke, ed., *The Cambridge Companion to Britten* (Cambridge, 1999), 217–32.

41 His unpublished Symphony in B flat of 1933 is overtly Sibelian in inspiration, and thus very much of its time: see Ian Kemp, *Tippett: The Composer and His Music* (London, 1984), 79–80.

42 Ibid., 439.

43 Indeed, Britain would become a centre of the Mahler revival, a status reinforced by Deryck Cooke's widely admired completion of the Tenth Symphony (first version 1964) – yet another facet to Britain's role as curator of a now expanded symphonic tradition. Britain

also played an enormously important role in the Nielsen and Sibelius revivals of the 1960s.
44 The work was commissioned jointly by the Royal Antarctic Survey and the Philharmonia Orchestra, and Davies was required to visit Antarctica in the course of composition.

45 See Richard Witts, 'Remastering the Past: "Renewal" in Recent British Music', *Musical Times*, 142 (2001), 7–10, who interprets both the Payne–Elgar work and Davies' *Antarctic Symphony* as signs of retrenchment in British music.

18 The symphony, the modern orchestra and the performing canon

ALAN STREET

On 4 March 2011 a new work, Adam Schoenberg's *American Symphony*, received its world premiere at the Lyric Theatre in Kansas City, USA. Commissioned by the Kansas City Symphony Orchestra, the 25-minute piece is cast in five movements, whose individual titles (including I: 'Fanfare', II: 'White on Blue', IV: 'Prayer' and V: 'Stars, Stripes, and Celebration') collectively evoke the sense of national identity engendered, according to the composer, by the 2008 American presidential election. For Schoenberg (born 1980), its conception shares a sense of healing mission with the 'quintessential American symphony', Copland's Third; paralleling Copland's perceived search for 'beauty and peace' in the immediate aftermath of the Second World War, the *American Symphony* 'is about our collective ability to restore hope within ourselves and our neighbors, both here and around the world'.[1] Particular stylistic homage is paid to Barber and Gershwin in the penultimate movement, which is explicitly dedicated 'to those lost in 9/11, hurricane Katrina, and all victims of violence and war'.[2] Such national and global affinities are in turn accompanied by the desire to incorporate a recognisably contemporary idiom in the guise of electronic dance music, an influence which colours not only the work's Finale, but also its central 'Rondo' movement.

The three initial performances given by the Kansas City Symphony under its music director, Michael Stern (two at their then home base in Missouri and the last on tour in Lawrence, Kansas), marked an important point of transition for the orchestra insofar as its subsequent 2011–12 season would be the first in its new home location, the Kauffman Center for the Performing Arts. Having occupied a series of temporary venues since its formation in 1982 (its predecessor, the Kansas City Philharmonic, was dissolved in 1982 in the year preceding its fiftieth anniversary), the orchestra now benefits from the use of a privately funded *c.* £220 million arts complex comprising a dedicated 1,600-seat concert hall and an 1,800-seat theatre, the latter of which also involves the orchestra in productions staged by the city's Lyric Opera and the Kansas City Ballet. A raft of new commissions, along with an array of internationally established American soloists (Joshua Bell, Yo-Yo Ma, Emmanuel Ax, Joyce DiDonato and others), indicate a wish to project the mood of an extended gala occasion.

But whereas the first half of the current season features symphonies in just two of its seven programmes (namely Shostakovich's Tenth Symphony and Mahler's 'Resurrection' Symphony), the second half is dominated by the genre, with three symphonies combined on a single pre-classical and classical programme (by J. C. Bach and J. M. Kraus preceding Haydn's Symphony No. 101, 'The Clock') and the concluding concert bringing together Hovhaness's Second Symphony, 'Mysterious Mountain', and Beethoven's Ninth Symphony.

The longevity of the symphony as a transatlantic cultural import is further underscored by the 2011–12 programme of the San Francisco Symphony Orchestra, its centenary season. While devoted principally to the home ensemble, the occasion is being further commemorated by invited touring residencies from all six of the major American symphony orchestras (Boston, Chicago, Cleveland, Los Angeles, New York and Philadelphia). No specific symphonic cycle is included, nor does the season feature a new commission explicitly associated with the genre. Nonetheless, the symphonic tradition is represented by a more-or-less complete timeline reaching from Mozart's 'Haffner' Symphony, K 385, through to John Harbison's Fourth Symphony, composed in 2003. Limited canonical intention can perhaps be inferred from the presence of two separate performances of Shostakovich's Sixth Symphony (by the Cleveland Orchestra under Franz Welser-Möst and the San Francisco Symphony Orchestra conducted by Osmo Vänskä). Moreover the launch of a short sequence devoted to 'American Mavericks' incorporating Henry Brant's orchestral transcription of Ives's Piano Sonata No. 2, retitled 'A *Concord* Symphony', arguably assumes as much contextual significance from being paired with Copland's Orchestral Variations, the composer's transcription of his own Piano Variations, as it does from any direct association with Ives's recognised symphonic corpus. As with the Kansas City season, however, an impression of cultural-historical commonality will be provided by a concluding performance of Beethoven's Ninth Symphony – the latter chosen in preference to a work of distinctively American provenance, or even a Mahler symphony that might better reflect the orchestra's recent successes in the field of sound recording.

Players, pieces to play and a place in which to play them; a tradition of creative continuity and innovation presenting the opportunity for civic celebration with the arrival of a suitable landmark anniversary. Articulated so simply, such fundamental considerations as underpin the survival of the symphony as a cultural form might appear all too parochial in scope compared with the boundless dynamism of internet-enabled digital transmission. And yet the multiple pressures bearing down on the modern orchestra – of continuing cultural pertinence, funding and the like – seem set to turn the perpetual anticipation of impending crisis into a concrete reality. Writing in 1986, J. Peter Burkholder was ready to categorise the predominantly retrospective nature of the repertoire according to an impasse conjoining 'The Twentieth Century and the Orchestra as Museum'.[3] In April 2011, the Philadelphia Orchestra board's decision to file for bankruptcy seems to offer tangible proof of aesthetic and economic obsolescence at the highest level of institutional attainment. In large part, the majority vote was made with a view to avoiding the risk of potential liquidation, a move accompanied in May 2011 by the launch of a *c.* £110 million funding campaign. Yet one of the primary causes of the financial shortfall – the orchestra's inability to meet its pension obligations to its players – gives evidence of a performing body potentially divided against itself and thereby at inevitable odds with the civilising precepts that constitute both the means and ends of its most enduring cultural legacy.

Defining the performing canon of the symphony at this particular historical juncture thus appears to be something of a hollow enterprise, at least at face value. Indeed a pragmatic if not altogether pessimistic appraisal might take it to operate predominantly within the niche circuit that circumscribes retirement-age entertainment consumption. True, marketing strategies are required to refresh the presiding logic of a familiar repertoire kept in a state of steady rotation. But in blunt terms, the attendant advertising copy, a few evocative catchwords aside, can be all but summed up in the clichéd competition tie-breaker formula of fifteen words or fewer, namely: Beethoven, Berlioz, Bruckner, Dvořák, Haydn, Mahler, Mendelssohn, Mozart, Rachmaninov, Schubert, Schumann, Shostakovich, Sibelius and Tchaikovsky.

In Burkholder's assessment, the shock of the new instigated by Schoenberg, Stravinsky, Webern, Hindemith, Ives, Messiaen, Henze and others associated with the first and second waves of modernism was always mitigated by an underlying attitude of respect towards the extant repertoire. Far from bespeaking an anxiety of influence, finding a secure position in the works museum entailed negotiating a contradictory set of principles – principally 'lasting value, links to tradition, individuality, and familiarity' – without questioning the overriding ritual pretext of art-for-art's-sake.[4] If Burkholder stops short of equating modernist musical aesthetics with culture-industry means–ends economics, the implications for an analysis of the symphonic performing canon again seem heavily predetermined. While it is beyond the scope of the present chapter to address this issue in forensic detail, I shall at least aim to return to it tangentially. Some more exact positioning of the notion of canon construction is, however, required in the initial instance if the cultural impact of what orchestras have done and continue to do in the name of the symphony is to be better represented.

In Joseph Kerman's well-known definition, a canon is 'an enduring exemplary collection of books, buildings, or paintings authorized in some way for contemplation, admiration, interpretation, and determination of value'.[5] For music, however, the correct term to apply is repertory, since whereas a canon 'is an idea', a repertory is 'a program of action',[6] assembled not by critics, but by performers. Seeking to evaluate the canon debate from a musical perspective at the end of the 1990s, Mark Everist questioned whether any such sharp distinctions could be drawn either in relation to performative cultural praxis as conducted in the non-performing arts, or on behalf of music where professional identities are never so clearly delineated.[7] Dahlhaus's further attempt to arbitrate between 'the canon *chosen* and the canon *chosen from*' also failed to exert sufficient interpretative leverage in Everist's eyes.[8] Rather, the complex matrix of individual and institutional investments required an altogether thicker mode of accounting, a necessity met by Barbara Herrnstein Smith's recognition of the 'contingencies of value'.[9]

Adapting Herrnstein Smith's reflection on the canon – the term 'works' is here substituted for the word 'texts' – thus begins to offer some additional conceptual traction, as follows:

> What is commonly referred to as 'the test of time' . . . is not, as the figure implies, an impersonal and impartial mechanism; for the cultural institutions through which it operates . . . are, of course, all managed by *persons* (who, by definition, are those with cultural power and commonly other forms of power as well); and, since the works that are selected and preserved by 'time' will always tend to be those which 'fit' (and, indeed, have often been *designed* to fit) *their* characteristic needs, interests, resources, and purposes, that testing mechanism has its own built-in partialities accumulated in and thus *intensified by* time.[10]

Furthermore, as William Weber elaborated the theme within the same essay collection, approaches to the musical canon could be insightfully finessed by acknowledging the differing perspectives projected by three modes of musical canon formation variously dependent on scholarly, pedagogical and performance-based activity.[11] While each of these dimensions relies on a variable amalgam of conventions, circumstances and tastes, Weber identifies four key criteria that contribute to a sense of cohesive purpose; namely craft, repertory, criticism and ideology. And while all three facets have historically functioned as a source of authority in the service of taste formation, he suggests, 'performance is ultimately the most significant and critical aspect of musical canon [since] . . . what emerged as the core of canonicity in musical life, beginning in the eighteenth century, was the public rendition of selected works'.[12] This said, simply performing works does not in and of itself establish them as part of a canon. On the contrary, Weber adds, 'the musical culture has to assert that such an authority exists, and define it at least to some degree in systematic fashion'.[13]

With an enhanced picture of canonicity to hand, then, the mapping of any specific genre ought, at least within defined temporal and geographical limits, to be much more feasible. Even so, as Weber observes, repertoire study per se has still to be conducted in either exhaustive depth or breadth. The normative status of nineteenth-century canonic practices can, as Dahlhaus notes, enable the recognition of certain historical junctures at which institutional priorities were adjusted.[14] Thus the Leipzig Gewandhaus's decision to perform Beethoven's *Eroica* Symphony not at the beginning of its concerts given on 29 January and 5 February 1807, but in a position immediately following the intermission, marks a decisive shift in aesthetic appreciation that was repeated in similar fashion up to three times per season over several decades. Moreover, as Weber has argued, if it is possible uncritically to overstate the case for an active pursuit of the idea of absolute music based on actual performance records throughout the nineteenth century in its entirety, still the commitment to instrumental music fostered firstly by the London Philharmonic Society (from 1813) and later by the Vienna Philharmonic (through its subscription concerts beginning in 1860) provides palpable evidence of performing-canon formation in the making. Nevertheless, the prevailing impression, incompletely rendered as it is, does not amount to 'a universally authorized play-list' so much as 'a set of interlocking canons' affected in varying degrees 'by performing resources, institutional characteristics, and social traditions'.[15]

The twentieth-century and predominantly post-Second World War remit of the present chapter is no less bound by the obligation to secure some kind of meaningful orientation on a cultural map that has long since become thoroughly global in scale. One point of departure might begin by fusing Dahlhaus's sense of normativity with Weber's assertion that the ideology of musical canon 'was manipulated to social and political ends from its very start: the classical . . . tradition never had social autonomy'.[16] Totalitarian politics consequently presents a darker lens through which to observe shifting candidacies for canonical primacy. For instance, in Amy Nelson's account of Soviet musical development in the early decades after 1917, the coincidence of the tenth anniversary of the October Revolution with the centenary of Beethoven's death gave renewed celebratory impetus to the promotion of Communist Russia as the composer's 'second motherland'.[17] Identified with the revolution from the first days of Soviet power, Beethoven, as Pauline Fairclough explains in Chapter 16, emblematised a timeless relevance grounded in the unmistakable expression of 'revolutionary passion, courage, and brotherhood'.[18] And the symphonies, in particular the Third, Fifth and Ninth, rendered the universalising message of heroism and freedom accessible to all especially palpable. Hence the Moscow Soviet's conductorless orchestra, Persimfans, made a complete Beethoven cycle the recognised centrepiece of its 1926–7 concert season, with the Fifth Symphony intended as a specific tribute to the events of the October Revolution. Fascist cultural policy in Germany, conversely, while initially wedded to the idea of the symphony as a unifying national force, began to distance itself from the principle of music as an active political medium as early as 1936. As described by Karen Painter, Bruckner rather than Beethoven assumed the role of idealised figurehead, with broadcast performances of his symphonies, at least so far as incomplete records show, achieving parity with those of Beethoven in 1938 – the year in which plans for the Anschluss were assembled prior to their announcement in Linz on 13 March 1938.[19]

Christopher H. Gibbs's exemplary tracing of the individual work biography attaching to Shostakovich's 'Leningrad' Symphony during the period of its American reception, which spanned the summer of 1942 and the succeeding 1942–3 concert season, appears at first glance to offer a compelling case-study for the transition from one geopolitical world order to another.[20] Put simply, the early phase of native media and public interest which led to forty-six complete performances of the work among the five premier American orchestras and the NBC Orchestra in just seven months from July 1942 to January 1943 was followed by a period of studied neglect, such that the work appeared during only sixteen seasons in Boston, Chicago, Cleveland, New York and Philadelphia between 1948 and 2000. A question of cold-war distancing only relieved in the era of Perestroika? Possibly. And yet as John Henry Mueller's early sociological appraisal intimated in 1951, there was plainly a contradiction to note in the fact that a symphony conceived under the rule of Communism should have become caught up in 'the normal capitalistic competition' that existed 'between two national radio chains and the Eastern orchestras'.[21] In short, it may be unjustifiably reductive to suppose that market forces, then as now, were in the paramount position to dictate what passed for canonic authority. After all, the performance of Mahler's 'Resurrection' Symphony given by the New York Philharmonic to mark the tenth anniversary of the terrorist attacks which took place on 11

September 2001 was given free of charge – and as a gesture recalling the same orchestra's performance of the work as a televised tribute on 24 November 1963 following the assassination of John F. Kennedy. Nevertheless, the institution-specific status accorded to individual works or composer cycles at any point on the calendar is perhaps less revealing of the predilections exercised by particular taste communities than of a gradually advancing tendency towards economically sensitive homogenisation that has merely gathered speed post-1945.

The only truly panoramic vantage-point from which to test this assumption would of necessity depend on the assembly of an almost unimaginably encyclopaedic database comprising records not just for live, but also for recorded symphonic performances. Building on the collaborative project begun between herself and her husband in the 1940s, Kate Hevner Mueller's 1973 study of the concert repertoires accumulated by twenty-seven American symphony orchestras in their subscription seasons from 1842–3 to 1969–70 represents an admirable attempt at such an undertaking.[22] In part an updating of John Henry Mueller's 1951 anatomy of orchestral performance patterns, Kate Hevner Mueller's survey bases its analytical aspect on the percentage of programme time accorded first of all to composers as named individuals, and secondarily as representatives of national origins. Additional consideration is also afforded to the part played by conductors in their roles as music directors. Hence with relatively modest variables in play, six putative 'life cycles' are advanced, which purport to show the relative positioning of composers, whether indeterminate, stable, increasing or decreasing, throughout the twentieth century to 1970. The fact that genre specificity is not a priority makes the interpretative element of the survey only partially informative for present purposes. Nonetheless, aside from a few evaluative biases (the 'subtleties and excellencies' of Mozart's symphonies, for example, are contrasted favourably with the 'overlong', critically venerated symphonies of Mahler,[23] even though both are acknowledged as a key contribution to the rising fortunes of their respective creators), a few telling indicators do arise. Already Bruckner's Fourth, Seventh and Ninth symphonies and the non-choral symphonies of Mahler (with the exception of the Ninth) are regarded as repertoire staples. Likewise Shostakovich's Fifth Symphony, together with Prokofiev's First and Fifth symphonies, are effectively recognised as 'standard' repertoire components. The symphonies of Beethoven and Brahms are shown to occupy an unchanging position as central pillars, albeit with Brahms's Third Symphony being the least frequently performed of his four. Some mild surprises are nevertheless apparent: for instance a growing enthusiasm for Mozart's symphonies is attributed to more frequent performances of the

'Haffner', K 395 and the 'Prague', K 504, as well as K 550 and the 'Jupiter', K 551; and twelve Haydn symphonies ranging from No. 12 in E to No. 91 in E flat were in fact given their first American performances only during the 1960s. A greater preference for the Second and Fourth symphonies of Schumann over and against the First and Third is taken in the context of a gradual decline in repertoire presence, while a continuing indeterminacy surrounds Dvořák, despite increasing representation of the Eighth and Ninth symphonies in particular during the 1960s. Performances of Sibelius's Second Symphony and Rachmaninov's Second Symphony oppose an overall curve of growth and decline understood to disclose a completed life cycle within the first seventy years of the twentieth century. Yet American-born and trained composers were not the obvious beneficiaries; only Ives's 'Holidays' Symphony and Barber's First Symphony are specifically identified as repertoire choices apart from Copland's Third.

The printed database which John and Kate Mueller began to assemble and which is reprinted as Part II of the 1973 survey was collated largely by hand from programme booklet records (kept either by the orchestras themselves, or in a more piecemeal way in the collections of major public libraries). Almost four decades later, any similar undertaking finds itself equally handicapped by the lack of extensive digital archiving. Relying as it does on an ad hoc combination of internet resources and published monographs, the present commentary cannot pretend to the same level of pioneering authority embodied in the Muellers' work. Nonetheless, by foregrounding a number of data sketches based on widely available source materials, it is hoped that a more complete impression of the associated prospects and pitfalls for symphonic repertoire interpretation after 1900 can be found. Beginning with a capsule *tour d'horizon* spanning five continents over a four-year period (2010–13), then, a contemporary snapshot can be obtained of professional orchestras working as concert-giving institutions in Argentina (the Buenos Aires Philharmonic during 2012), Australia (the Melbourne Symphony Orchestra in 2011), China (the Shanghai Symphony Orchestra during its 2010–11 season), Egypt (the Cairo Symphony Orchestra during its 2010–11 season), Iceland (the Iceland Symphony Orchestra during its 2011–12 season), Japan (the NHK Symphony Orchestra during its 2011–12 season) and the United Kingdom (the Orchestra of the Age of Enlightenment in 2012–13).[24] At the coarsest level, it is possible to identify a sense of centre and periphery based on frequency of occurrence: thus Beethoven's *Eroica*, Fifth and Ninth symphonies assume a familiar pre-eminence through their appearance in four individual orchestral seasons, yet are in fact eclipsed numerically by Tchaikovsky's Fourth Symphony, which will eventually have been performed in five. More enlightening is the presence of just a single symphony cycle – of Beethoven, in Iceland. The strongest response to the Mahler anniversaries across 2010 and 2011 in fact took place in Shanghai, with performances of the First, Third, Fourth, Fifth and Tenth symphonies (the last in the completion by Rudolf Barshai). Only one new commission bearing the title 'symphony' appears – Stuart Greenbaum's Second, 'Double Planet', premiered in Melbourne. However, the sense of an increasingly cinema-led programming agenda that might be implied by the inclusion of Howard Shore's 'Lord of the Rings' Symphony in Iceland is variously offset by performances of symphonies by Bernstein (No. 1), Casella (No. 2) and Tippett (No. 1) by the NHK orchestra. More significant still, perhaps, is the inclusion of a programme combining Britten's Cello Symphony and Elgar's First Symphony in Buenos Aires. In the light of unresolved tensions surrounding sovereignty of the disputed Falkland Islands, it might at least be tentatively supposed that the symphony still has some form of harmonising cultural role to play.

Founded in 1781 and 1842 respectively, the Leipzig Gewandhaus and New York Philharmonic orchestras possess extended archival records from which to assess the trajectory of the symphony.[25] Tracing a timeline marked out in decade-length intervals beginning with the 1910–11 season gives a fair sense of developing programming philosophies as they arose from the nineteenth-century pattern of mixed, often vocally dominated repertoire selections. In the case of the New York Philharmonic, the first thing likely to catch the statistician's eye is the sheer number of concerts mounted, at least until the 1950–1 season. It is only at this point, indeed, that the applied chronological filter coincides with the familiar framework of three contrasting genre pieces, albeit typically with the longest placed last irrespective of repertoire status. The role of conductors such as Mitropoulos, Monteux, Szell and Bernstein is notable in this context. For their predecessors (including Mahler, Damrosch, Toscanini and Barbirolli), selective historical archaeology exposes a repertoire most strongly dependent on the symphonies of Beethoven, Brahms, Mendelssohn (the Fourth), Schumann and Tchaikovsky. Stanford's Third Symphony (1910–11), Hadley's First Symphony (1920–1), Wagenaar's Third (1940–1) and Thompson's Second (1940–1) all surface by virtue of a single performance through to the beginning of the Second World War and at no time subsequently. Less obviously anticipated patterns discernible after 1945 include the relatively limited programming space allotted to Mahler, Nielsen and Sibelius – all three prominent recording priorities for Leonard Bernstein in his time as music director. Of notable post-war European symphonic composers, just Henze (Ninth Symphony, 2000–1) is represented; by comparison American composers fare only slightly more favourably, with William Schuman's Third and

Ninth symphonies being performed to commemorate his 70th birthday (1980–1), and Bernstein's First, 'Jeremiah', marking his death in 1990 and the succeeding tenth anniversary in 2000.

Programming by the Leipzig Gewandhaus throughout the twentieth century shows a partially divergent bias if the same parameters are applied. With fewer concerts given per season, Beethoven, Bruckner and Tchaikovsky are the most frequently represented, a complete Beethoven cycle being given for the bicentenary celebration of his birth (1970–1) directed by Peter Maag, Erich Bergel, Arvid Jansons, Norman del Mar, Lothar Seyfarth and Herbert Blomdstedt. (The Fourth and Fifth symphonies were performed on 15 December 1970 in a guest performance by Yevgeny Mravinsky and the Leningrad Philharmonic.) Aside from the single performances granted to Draeseke's *Sinfonia tragica* (directed by Arthur Nikisch) and Weingartner's Third Symphony (conducted by the composer) in 1910–11, the specific context established for a prominent symphonic work is interestingly disclosed by the sequence of pieces beginning with W. F. Bach's *Sinfonia* in D minor and progressing through Waelrant, Senfl and Hassler to a performance of Bruckner's Eighth Symphony conducted by Bruno Walter (1930–1). While it would be premature to assume an incipient nationalist impulse, the programme presence of Pfitzner's C major Symphony and Pepping's First Symphony (both 1940–1), succeeded in the post-war era by performances of the Second symphonies of both Khrennikov (1950–1) and Khatchaturian (1960–1) offers some evidence of changing artistic affinities during the years of National-Socialist and Communist control. No stark reorientation becomes apparent if the pre-unification programming of 1980–1 is compared with its counterpart from thirty years later. Instead, a sequence of performances of Mozart's early and late symphonies running throughout 1980–1 is counterbalanced by a complete Mahler cycle presented between 17 and 29 May 2011, the former nonetheless given exclusively by the Gewandhaus Orchestra rather than as part of an international festival opened and closed by the resident ensemble as was the case in 2011.

Orchestral touring continues to function as a significant mode of cultural transmission, albeit without the same aura of calendar-defying odyssey that it may once have possessed. That the New York Philharmonic under Josef Stransky and Henry Hadley undertook a nationwide tour extending to Canada in their 1920–1 season is not immediately remarkable; that it should have lasted for more than two months and included approximately fifty concert venues is. If a rudimentary comparison is made with the Royal Concertgebouw Orchestra's touring programme for 2011–12, then the picture of repertoire not only deriving from the subscription season, but also embedding each orchestra in something like a grand classical and Romantic tradition is hard to miss. Both orchestras might legitimately be perceived as representing global pre-eminence in their respective eras. But the performances of Dvořák's 'New World' and Beethoven's Fifth Symphony that sustained the New York Philharmonic are only marginally different from those of Brahms's Second and Schubert's 'Unfinished' (under Myung-Whun Chung) with which the Concertgebouw will tour to Beijing.

Amateur orchestras, even as they aspire to match the standards of professional performers, are of course less constrained by either tradition or salary-related obligations. Programming ambition is especially apparent in the archive of the Kensington Symphony Orchestra, whose 1991–2 season inclusion of Berlioz's *Romeo et Juliette* and Bruckner's Ninth symphonies is paralleled by Vaughan Williams's Sixth, Walton's Second and Maxwell Davies' Fifth, together with Sibelius's Seventh and Shostakovich's Ninth in their season for 2011–12.[26] Less well placed to take advantage of conservatoire student participation away from the English capital, Nottingham's two amateur orchestras, the Symphony and Philharmonic, are to an extent less adventurous, yet still able to present Shostakovich's Tenth Symphony (the Nottingham Symphony Orchestra in 2011–12) and Mahler's Fifth Symphony (the Nottingham Philharmonic also in 2011–12) in programmes comparable to those current in the professional domain.[27] Acting locally while thinking globally has of course become far more prominent in the wake of social media projects such as the 2008 conception of a YouTube Symphony Orchestra, auditioned through internet-posted video files. Partnered with established professional orchestras around the world, the ensemble has so far intersected with the symphonic genre in two ways: first, in the Google/YouTube commissioning of a new work from Tan Dun, his Internet Symphony No. 1, *Eroica*; and second, through the Scherzo of Brahms's Fourth Symphony and the Finale of Tchaikovsky's Fourth, which were respectively used to open and close the orchestra's initial public concert performance, which took place at Carnegie Hall, New York, on 15 April 2009 under the direction of Michael Tilson Thomas. To date, the artistic returns from this event and its successor, held in Sydney during March 2011, have ostensibly been somewhat modest. Even so, YouTube's claim of 50 million viewings linked to its dedicated channels for the orchestra suggest that the institution's cultural allure is far from exhausted.

The conviction that 'music is an adventure and not just an amenity' was vividly realised by both Edward Clark and William Glock as architects of programme planning for the BBC.[28] Appointed in 1924, Clark, together with his assistant Julian Herbage, oversaw the first decade of music-making by the BBC Symphony Orchestra, which began in 1930. As sedimented history, the sequence of first broadcast performances and world premieres makes fascinating reading – in part for its long-since recognised counterpointing of modernism and traditionalism, but also as a testament to the diversity of symphonic scores being composed during the period. Bliss's 'Colour' Symphony (1932), Vaughan Williams's Fourth Symphony (1935) and the complete version of Walton's First Symphony (1935) are only the most established representatives of a British symphonism encompassing, for example, Granville Bantock (1936), George Lloyd (1935), Edmund Rubbra (1937) and Bernard van Dieren (1936). Webern's Symphony, Op. 21 (1931), Shostakovich's First Symphony (1932), Prokofiev's Third Symphony (1934) and Schmidt's Fourth Symphony (1938) were all given UK premieres during this time, as was William Grant Still's 'Afro-American' Symphony (1936) and the 'Dance' Symphony Copland fashioned in 1930 from his then unpublished ballet, *Grohg* (1935).[29]

Stravinsky's acid verdict on the unthinking practice of 'buying up surplus symphonies as the Government buys up surplus corn' was plainly a caveat that Glock took to heart when compiling his 1963 Music Policy document for the BBC.[30] The desire to continue breaking down the divide between past and present was doubtless part of the same mission to balance enterprise and attractiveness that in 1966 brought an end to the practice of routinely including complete Beethoven and Brahms symphony cycles as part of the annual BBC Promenade Concerts season. By comparison, constructive changes to the nature of scheduling on the then BBC Music Programme implemented in 1965 made possible a complete cycle of all the Haydn symphonies at a time when they were not fully available on LP records. The further desire to plan the BBC Symphony Orchestra's annual Royal Festival Hall concert series as a distinctive sequence of live events was particularly apparent in the fiftieth anniversary season (1980–1): Britten's 'Spring' Symphony, the first symphonies of Gerhard and Tippett and Zemlinsky's *Lyric Symphony* were variously distributed throughout individual programmes in which either a sense of historical derivation or period association could be clearly perceived.[31]

At its base, programme planning is understandably less concerned with posterity than the need to balance the perennial tensions obtaining between artistic purpose and economic viability. For Bramwell Tovey, the music director's contribution is consequently that of a fiscally responsible curator: 'a programmer of music that needs to include traditional, neglected and contemporary repertoire'.[32] Deploring the antipathy towards repertoire renewal historically exhibited by conductors seeking career advance, Leon Botstein has in turn identified 'masterpiece mania', star-driven marketing and internationalist anonymity as further wrong turns in the quest to revivify the sense of a communally based concert life.[33] Just as the orchestra itself can only hope to survive through imaginative collaboration – as 'an ensemble of possibilities' in Pierre Boulez's words[34] – so the music director, Botstein proposes, must display a flair for culturally literate, even cross-institutional thematic planning. Leonard Slatkin's involvement in St Louis is taken as one measure of community-based success. And prior to his departure for Berlin, the eighteen-year association formed between Simon Rattle and the City of Birmingham Symphony Orchestra clearly represented another. In either case, the message is straightforward: that coherent, engaging and non-didactic approaches mark the best prospects if the public taste for classical music is to be successfully revitalised.

Though much has been written about Rattle's time in Birmingham, the presence of the symphony as an aspect of repertoire has not, to the best of my knowledge, been foregrounded. The aspiration to create outstanding musical events shared by Rattle and the orchestra's general manager and latterly chief executive, Ed Smith, was grounded in a readiness to integrate new music inspired primarily by Boulez's preferred strategies for pro-gramming. Given that concert content was partly influenced by record-company interests, the most even-handed evaluation of Rattle's tenure is supplied by records detailing the subscription concert series programmes that were given in Birmingham Town Hall and subsequently Symphony Hall (officially from 15 April 1991).[35] Altogether, only four complete in-season symphony cycles were presented: of Brahms (1987–8), Nielsen (1992–3) and Beethoven (twice: in 1995–6, the orchestra's seventy-fifth anniversary; and in 1997–8, Rattle's final season as music director). Major recording projects such as those involving Mahler and Sibelius were in fact prepared gradually over several seasons. And the most memorable themed concept, *Towards the Millennium*, launched in 1990 as an advancing annual celebration of each individual decade of the twentieth century, was distinctively sutured by the inclusion of the symphony as a living genre for every single stage prior to the 1990s – from Suk's *Asrael* Symphony and Mahler's Seventh Symphony representing the period 1900–10 to Lutosławski's Third Symphony representing the 1980s. Few if any features of the accumulated worklist aside from the complete omission of Tchaikovsky and the presence of just a single Schumann symphony – the Second – seem aberrant. But what does still resonate powerfully is the sheer capacity to reconfigure established expectations with seemingly limitless initiative and an unfailingly sure creative instinct.

To have so long deferred any particular consideration of recording as a determining force in the canonisation of the symphony is perhaps an all-too-readily apparent admission of defeat. Commentators such as Lance W. Brunner and Robert Philip have already formulated authoritative accounts of the early history and performance-practice implications of recorded orchestral performance.[36] Yet still it is instructive to restate that the contemporary omni-availability of orchestral audio-visual material is actually just a century or so old, and that the path-breaking recording of Beethoven's Fifth Symphony made in the autumn of 1911 by the Odeon-Streichorchester and Eduard Künneke in Germany was the corollary of capitalist enterprise seeking to combat the monopoly of celebrity vocal artists enjoyed by American competition. Other familiar marketplace practices offsetting innovation with duplication and increased affordability were also quick to coalesce. Thus the availability of reduced-price releases from Aeolian on their Vocalion label (1923–6) overlapped with the release (by 1925) of complete Beethoven symphony cycles on both Parlophone and Deutsche Grammophon's Polydor label, as well as the latter's landmark recordings, under the direction of Oskar Fried, of Bruckner's Seventh and Mahler's 'Resurrection' symphonies.

Attempting to compete with the extended historical legacy of volume-driven, low-risk standard repertoire saturation, many of today's orchestras have sought to make a virtue of necessity by managing their own media opportunities autonomously. Own-label live concert CD and download releases, already a developing reality in the 1990s, continue to expand to fill the void left by major recording companies either unable or unwilling to commit the required financial resources needed for studio recording. Thus the *LSO Live* series, to take one notable example, now has available five complete symphony cycles (of Beethoven, Brahms, Elgar, Mahler and Sibelius) featuring conductors such as Colin Davis, Valery Gergiev and Bernard Haitink, in two cases (Haitink/Beethoven and Davis/Sibelius) revisiting repertoire they have already recorded as complete cycles at least once before. Audio-visual formatting on DVD continues to appear from the major companies, but also in a more recognisably didactic guise in the San Francisco Symphony Orchestra's *Keeping Score* productions. Here the symphonic genre predominates, with examples from the *Eroica* to Ives's 'Holidays' Symphony and Shostakovich's Fifth Symphony being discussed and illustrated by Michael Tilson Thomas in conjunction with a complete concert performance of each work. And if the sense of occasion associated with live concert attendance seems otherwise beyond reach due to limitations of time and distance, then the Berliner Philharmoniker's web-based Digital Concert Hall is now capable of bridging the divide between event and either cinema or home-theatre listening. Live relays and an extensive archive of video recordings are available subject to subscription access of between 48 hours and a complete calendar year's duration. Selection, at least at the time of writing, is by conductor, composer or soloist, but not by work; the intending public, it would seem, is not taken to seek membership on the pretext of piece specificity or generic preference.

For Ananay Aguilar, the constructed nature of the recorded live event conjured up around amalgamated assumptions of possession, spontaneity and focus remains, for all its artifice, an exemplar of *Werktreue* philosophy.[37] Referring specifically to the *LSO Live* Mahler symphony cycle produced in 2007–8, she asserts that the stated 80/20 division between actual concert material and subsequent recorded patching, while open to question, is still predicated on the pursuit of a settled sonic image, and thus a fidelity to compositional intention. Writing almost seventy years earlier on the concept of the broadcast symphony (and returning appropriately to a text addressed at the very start of this volume), Theodor W. Adorno found no such affirmative thread in the prospect of technology-enabled democratisation.[38] Supposedly targeted at the opportunity for social betterment embodied in the American Midwestern farmer's wife, the symphony variously reduced to atomised chamber proportions, disarticulated into a purely sequential medley and all but electrocuted as a hollow monochrome effigy could only foster a benighted state of false consciousness through the manipulative spectacle of individuals proving themselves, in Adorno's words, 'to be small cultural owners within big ownership culture'.[39]

Listening to Beethoven as if it were Tchaikovsky while at the same time treating the symphony as a piece of domestic furniture would appear to be the irredeemable consequences of the culture industry's ubiquitous presence in Adorno's diagnosis, a thesis which Jürgen Habermas has further traced according to the historical shift from a culture-debating to a culture-consuming public sphere. In Habermas's formulation, serious involvement with culture 'produces facility while the consumption of mass culture leaves no lasting trace'.[40] Charting the same trajectory in respect of the Western classical tradition, Leon Botstein and Edward Rothstein each recognise a concomitant progression in which active participation has been largely supplanted by passive appreciation, performing ability by listener familiarity, and a concept of musical literacy that was once socially and aesthetically formative by a contemporary illiteracy that is attuned almost exclusively to the pursuit of subjective gratification.[41] Canon, if it persists at all, functions either as a nostalgic form of ritual observance, or as a bulwark against the possibility of creative renewal. And yet as Peter Franklin has argued, an alternative diagnosis is possible – one which takes the commonplace of symphonic ambition commodified in the service of the Hollywood soundtrack as the pretext for a reflexively empowered politics of reading.[42] Admittedly this may exist at a minimal remove from the mode of distracted coercion that Adorno so abhorred in mass culture, as Franklin acknowledges.

Nevertheless, the established nineteenth-century disposition to interpret the symphony in imagistic terms alongside the genre's capacity to elicit transgressive – that is, openly emotive – subjective responses in the context of public audition together confirm an associative value system that not only enabled a more fully socialised experience of the medium than was ever permitted by musical absolutism, but also one that subsequently found a compelling grammatical fit in the multimedia genre of the Hollywood narrative film.

Attempting an ethnographic appraisal of the symphony concert's ritual significance in 1987, Christopher Small proposed that the implicit faith in Western bourgeois self-fashioning it predominantly enshrined was increasingly doomed to extinction.[43] A symbol of alienated labour division, he argued, its capacity to evoke a wide range of human experience ultimately embracing the triumph and apotheosis of the human spirit was at the same time defined as much by the lived realities it chose to exclude – for example, the circumstances of deprivation, persecution, racial discrimination and dispossession that typically fall outside the material conditions enjoyed by the developed world's middle classes. That the contemporary fate of symphonic canonicity might be somewhat more equivocal than Small supposed is nonetheless evinced by the differing cultural resonances emanating from two avowedly utopian projects inspired by the Western classical lineage, namely the Venezuelan *El Sistema* programme (begun in 1975) and the Seville-based West-Eastern Divan Orchestra (founded in 1999). The industrial advance that Small associates with symphonic institutions is certainly paralleled by the state exploitation of Venezuelan oil resources that has been used to fund José Antonio Abreu's nationally integrated network of *núcleos*, responsible for delivering free, open-access music instruction. But far from confirming Small's negative impression of Westernised *Wunderkind* conformity, Abreu's express desire to facilitate a democratised plan of social action presently enables approximately 370,000 students, 70–90 per cent of whom are deemed to live in poverty,[44] to participate in a pyramidal concept that leads to palpably enhanced social and professional opportunities.

The concert and recording activity that this has engendered – by the Simón Bolívar Youth Orchestra, and latterly the Teresa Carreño Youth Orchestra and Caracas Youth Symphony Orchestra – is predicated on exposure to music by Beethoven, Chávez, Estévez, Mahler, Orbón, Revueltas, Tchaikovsky and others that is encountered in progressively more complex versions as the participants advance in age. To the extent that recreative rather than creative priorities have so far determined the progress of *El Sistema*, it might be presumed that enabling colonisation is the guiding cultural impulse. And yet the conservatoire-level integration of indigenous musics and jazz is indicative of an eclectic educational strategy that is increasingly being extended to include drama and dance as part of an overarching Venezuelan National University of the Arts. For its part, the West-Eastern Divan Orchestra operates in a context more openly riven by geopolitical discord. As Rachel Beckles Willson relates, however, the model of Jewish, Muslim and Christian cooperation that it is taken to represent comes far closer to an extension of Eurocentric idealised expectation than a symbolic solution to Middle-Eastern ideological conflict imagined and implemented from within.[45] Focussing on performances of Beethoven's Ninth Symphony given by the orchestra in Seville and Madrid during August 2006, Beckles Willson observes a series of competing appropriations caught between Adalusian neglect of local music education at one extreme and a romanticising, orientalist attitude towards the escalating war between the Israeli defence forces and Hezbollah at the other. Beethoven, in short, was viewed as saving the players from themselves, their independent identities being emblematised as representatives of an ongoing Palestinian impasse. And hence it is no small irony in the present context to suppose, along with Beckles Willson, that the orchestra's chosen repertoire might function in 'a totalising, synthetic, teleological and monumental sphere' that at the same time 'tends towards another type of essentialism, namely an unmeasured sense of superiority in its own aesthetic autonomy'.[46]

No convenient coda can be appended to the two examples set by *El Sistema* and the West-Eastern Divan Orchestra other than to register the prevailing evaluative contingencies which overcode the rudimentary co-ordinates of repertoire assimilation and dissemination that together underpin the concept of a performing canon. For Christopher Small, an enlightened transformation of the blind observance encoded in the symphony-based concert, if it could be realised at all, would need to stem from an infinitely more involved and self-aware complex of relations among performers and listeners than had become the norm for the later twentieth century.[47] The extent to which the twenty-first century is capable of answering to this programme is beginning to become a little clearer: but whether it can continue to engender sufficient empathy and enthusiasm to secure a vital future must inevitably remain in the balance.

Notes

1 From the composer's programme note, available at www.adamschoenberg.com/asymphony.html (accessed 14 February 2012).

2 Ibid.

3 J. Peter Burkholder, 'The Twentieth Century and the Orchestra as Museum', in Joan Peyser, ed., *The Orchestra: Origins and Transformations* (Milwaukee, repr. 2006), 409–32.

4 Ibid., 413.

5 Joseph Kerman, 'A Few Canonic Variations', *Critical Inquiry*, 10 (1983), 107.

6 Ibid., 107.

7 Mark Everist, 'Reception Theories, Canonic Discourses, and Musical Value', in Nicholas Cook and Mark Everist, eds., *Rethinking Music* (New York and Oxford, 1999), 378–402.

8 Carl Dahlhaus, *Foundations of Music History*, trans. J. B. Robinson (Cambridge, 1983), 92.

9 Barbara Herrnstein Smith, 'Contingencies of Value', *Critical Inquiry*, 10 (1983), 1–35.

10 Ibid., 29.

11 William Weber, 'The History of Musical Canon', in Nicholas Cook and Mark Everist, eds., *Rethinking Music* (New York and Oxford, 1999), 336–55.

12 Ibid., 340.

13 Ibid., 349.

14 See Dahlhaus, *Foundations of Music History*, 94 and 100. See also William Weber, *The Great Transformation of Musical Taste: Concert Programming from Haydn to Brahms* (Cambridge, 2008), 180–1.

15 Weber, 'The History of Musical Canon', 347.

16 Ibid., 354.

17 Amy Nelson, *Music for the Revolution: Musicians and Power in Early Soviet Russia* (Philadelphia, 2004), 89.

18 Ibid., 188.

19 Karen Painter, *Symphonic Aspirations: German Music and Politics, 1900–1945* (Cambridge, Mass. and London, 2007), 246–7.

20 Christopher H. Gibbs, '"The Phenomenon of the Seventh": A Documentary Essay on Shostakovich's "War" Symphony', in Laurel E. Fay, ed., *Shostakovich and His World* (Princeton and Woodstock, 2004), 59–113.

21 John Henry Mueller, *The American Symphony Orchestra: A Social History of Musical Taste* (London, 1958), 227.

22 Kate Hevner Mueller, *Twenty-Seven Major Symphony Orchestras: A History and Analysis of Their Repertoires Seasons 1842–43 Through 1969–70* (Bloomington, 1973).

23 Ibid., xxvi and xxviii.

24 The information is taken from the following internet sources, all accessed between December 2011 and February 2012: Buenos Aires Philharmonic (www.teatrocolon.org.ar/en/index.php?id=conciertos); Melbourne Symphony Orchestra (www.mso.com.au/cpa/htm/htm_home.asp); Shanghai Symphony Orchestra (www.sh-symphony.com/en/index.asp); Cairo Symphony Orchestra (www.cairo-symphony.com/); Iceland Symphony Orchestra (www.sinfonia.is/); NHK Symphony Orchestra (www.nhkso.or.jp/en/index.html); and the Orchestra of the Age of Enlightenment (www.oae.co.uk/).

25 See Johannes Forner, Andreas Göpfert, Fritz Hennenberg, Brigitte Richter and Ingeborg Singer, *Die Gewandhaus-Konzerte zu Leipzig 1781–1981*, 2 vols. (Leipzig, 1981); and the New York Philharmonic digital archives available at: http://archives.nyphil.org/

(accessed between December 2011 and February 2012).

26 Information available at: www.kso.org.uk (accessed 23 January 2012).

27 Information available at: www.nottinghamsymphony.org.uk/ and www.nottinghamphilharmonic.co.uk/ (both accessed 23 January 2012).

28 William Glock, *Notes in Advance* (Oxford and New York, 1991), 211.

29 See Nicholas Kenyon, *The BBC Symphony Orchestra: The First Fifty Years 1930–80* (London, 1981), 447–61.

30 Stravinsky quoted in Glock, *Notes in Advance*, 117.

31 See Kenyon, *The BBC Symphony Orchestra*, 509–12.

32 Bramwell Tovey, 'The Conductor as Artistic Director', in José Antonio Bowen, ed., *The Cambridge Companion to Conducting* (Cambridge, 2003), 213.

33 Leon Botstein, 'The Future of Conducting', in Bowen, ed., *The Cambridge Companion to Conducting*, 302.

34 Pierre Boulez quoted in Isaac. Stern, ed., *The Evolution of the Symphony Orchestra: History, Problems and Agendas* (London, 1990), 9.

35 Subscription series programmes for the duration of Rattle's CBSO tenure (1980–98) are reproduced in Nicholas Kenyon, *Simon Rattle: From Birmingham to Berlin* (London, 2001).

36 Lance W. Brunner, 'The Orchestra and Recorded Sound', in Peyser, ed., *The Orchestra*, 475–528; Robert Philip, *Performing Music in the Age of Recording* (New Haven and London, 2004).

37 Ananay Aguilar, 'LSO Live: Reassembling Classical Music', artofrecordproduction.com (accessed on 19 July 2011).

38 Theodor W. Adorno, 'The Radio Symphony: An Experiment in Theory', in *Current of Music: Elements of a Radio Theory*, ed. Robert Hullot-Kentor (Cambridge and Malden, 2009), 144–62.

39 Ibid., 157.

40 Jürgen Habermas, *The Structural Transformation of the Public Sphere: An Inquiry into a Category of Bourgeois Society*, trans. Thomas Burger and Frederick Lawrence (Cambridge, Mass., 1991), 166.

41 Leon Botstein, 'Listening through Reading: Musical Literacy and the Concert Audience', *19th-Century Music*, 16 (1992), 129–45; Edward Rothstein, 'The New Amateur Player and Listener', in Peyser, ed., *The Orchestra*, 529–44.

42 Peter Franklin, 'The Boy on the Train, or Bad Symphonies and Good Movies: The Revealing Error of the "Symphonic Score"', in

Daniel Goldmark, Lawrence Kramer and Richard Leppert, eds., *Beyond the Soundtrack: Representing Music in Cinema* (Berkeley, Los Angeles and London, 2007), 13–26.

43 Christopher Small, 'Performance as Ritual: Sketch for an Enquiry into the True Nature of a Symphony Concert', in Avron Levine White, ed., *Lost in Music: Culture, Style and the Musical Event* (London, 1987), 6–32. For a complementary interpretation, see also Bruno Nettl, 'Mozart and the Ethnomusicological Study of Western Culture: An Essay in Four Movements', in Katherine Bergeron and Philip V. Bohlman, eds., *Disciplining Music: Musicology and its Canons* (Chicago and London, 1992), 137–55.

44 Tricia Tunstall, *Changing Lives: Gustavo Dudamel, El Sistema, and the Transformative Power of Music* (New York and London, 2012), 36.

45 Rachel Beckles Willson, 'Whose Utopia? Perspectives on the West-Eastern Divan Orchestra', *Music and Politics*, 3 (2009), 1–21.

46 Ibid., 20.

47 Small, 'Performance as Ritual: Sketch for an Enquiry into the True Nature of a Symphony Concert', 30–1.

Bibliography

Adorno, Theodor W., *Hegel: Three Studies*, trans. Shierry Weber Nicholson
(Cambridge, Mass., 1993).

Introduction to the Sociology of Music, trans. E. B. Ashton (New York, 1976),
209–10.

Mahler: A Musical Physiognomy, trans. Edmund Jephcott (Chicago, 1992)

'The Radio Symphony: An Experiment in Theory', in *Essays on Music*, ed.
Richard Leppert, trans. Susan H. Gillespie (Berkeley and Los Angeles, 2002),
251–70.

Agawu, V. Kofi, *Playing with Signs: A Semiotic Interpretation of Classic Music*
(Princeton, 1991).

Music as Discourse: Semiotic Adventures in Romantic Music (New York and
Oxford, 2009).

Aldwell, Edward and Carl Schachter, *Harmony and Voice Leading*, 3rd edn (Belmont,
2003).

Anderson, Emily, ed., *The Letters of Mozart and His Family*, 3rd rev. edn, ed.
Stanley Sadie and Fiona Smart (New York, 1985).

Antokoletz, Elliott, 'The Musical Language of the Fourth Symphony', in
Veijo Murtomäki and Timothy L. Jackson, eds., *Sibelius Studies*, 296–321.

Arapov, Boris, et al., *Leningradskaya gosudarstvennaya ordena trudovogo krasnogo
znameni filarmonia: stati, vospominania, materiali* (Leningrad, 1972).

Arnold, Ignaz, *Gallerie der berühmtesten Tonkünstler des achtzehnten und neunzehnten Jahrhunderts. Ihre kurzen Biografieen, karakterisirende Anekdoten und
ästhetische Darstellung ihrer Werke*, vol. I (Erfurt, 1810).

Ashby, Arved, 'Britten as Symphonist', in Mervyn Cooke, ed., *The Cambridge
Companion to Britten* (Cambridge, 1999), 217–32.

Bailey, Robert 'An Analytical Study of the Sketches and Drafts', in Bailey, ed., *Wagner:
Prelude and Transfiguration from Tristan und Isolde* (New York, 1985), 113–48.

'The Structure of the Ring and Its Evolution', *19th-Century Music*, 1 (1977), 48–61.

Banfield, Stephen, ed., *The Blackwell History of Music in Britain*, vol. VI: *The
Twentieth Century* (Oxford, 1995).

Barclay, Robert, 'Design, Technology and Manufacture before 1800', in
Trevor Herbert and John Wallace, eds., *The Cambridge Companion to Brass
Instruments* (Cambridge, 1997), 24–37.

'The Development of Musical Instruments: National Trends and Musical
Implications', in Colin Lawson, ed., *The Cambridge Companion to the Orchestra*
(Cambridge, 2003), 22–41.

Barham, Jeremy, ed., *The Cambridge Companion to Mahler* (Cambridge, 2007).

Barsova, Inna, 'Mahler in Russia', in Mitchell and Nicholson, eds., *The Mahler Companion*, 517–30.

Bate, Walter Jackson, *The Burden of the Past and the English Poet* (Cambridge, Mass., 1970).

Bauer-Lechner, Natalie, *Recollections of Gustav Mahler* (London 1980, orig. Leipzig, 1923).

Beckerman, Michael, *Dvořák and His World* (Princeton, 1993).

'The Real Value of Yellow Journalism', *Musical Quarterly*, 77 (1993), 749–68.

Bekker, Paul, *Gustav Mahlers Symphonien* (Tutzing, 1969).

Die Sinfonie von Beethoven bis Mahler (Berlin, 1918).

Beller, Steven, *Vienna and The Jews, 1867–1938: A Cultural History* (Cambridge, 1989).

Benjamin, William, 'Tonal Dualism in Bruckner's Eighth Symphony', in Kinderman and Krebs, eds., *The Second Practice of Nineteenth-Century Tonality*, 237–58.

Bennett, Clive, 'Clementi as Symphonist', *Musical Times*, 120/1633 (1979), 207 and 209–10.

Berg, Alban, *Briefe an seine Frau* (Munich, 1965).

Berlioz, Hector, Preface to *Roméo et Juliette*, trans. in D. Kern Holoman, *Berlioz* (Cambridge, Mass., 1989), 261.

Beveridge, David R., *Rethinking Dvořák: Views from Five Countries* (New York and Oxford, 1996).

Black, Leo, *Edmund Rubbra: Symphonist* (Woodbridge, 2008).

Bloom, Harold, *The Anxiety of Influence: A Theory of Poetry* (New York and Oxford, 1973).

A Map of Misreading (New York and Oxford, 1975).

Boer, Bertil H. van, *Dramatic Cohesion in the Music of Joseph Martin Kraus* (Lewiston, 1989).

'The Symphony on the Periphery', in Morrow and Churgin, eds., *The Eighteenth-Century Symphony*, 687–734.

Bogdanov-Berezovsky, Valeriyan, 'On the Problem of Soviet Symphonism', *Sovetskaya muzïka*, 6 (1934), 30.

Bonds, Mark Evan, *After Beethoven: Imperatives of Originality in the Symphony* (Cambridge, Mass., 1996).

'Haydn, Laurence Sterne and the Origins of Musical Irony', *Journal of the American Musicological Society*, 44 (1991), 57–91.

Music as Thought: Listening to the Symphony in the Age of Beethoven (Princeton, 2006).

'Sinfonia Anti-Eroica: Berlioz's *Harold en Italie* and the Anxiety of Beethoven's Influence', *Journal of Musicology*, 10/4 (1992), 417–63.

'The Symphony as Pindaric Ode', in Elaine Sisman, ed., *Haydn and his World* (Princeton, 1997), 131–53.

Wordless Rhetoric: Musical Form and the Metaphor of the Oration (Cambridge, Mass., 1991).

Botstein, Leon, 'The Future of Conducting', in José Antonio Bowen, ed., *The Cambridge Companion to Conducting* (Cambridge, 2003), 286–304.

'Gustav Mahler's Vienna', in Mitchell and Nicholson, eds., *The Mahler Companion*, 6–37 .

'Listening through Reading: Musical Literacy and the Concert Audience', *19th-Century Music*, 16 (1992), 129–45.

Boulez, Pierre, 'Orchestras, Concert Halls, Repertory, Audiences', in *Orientations*, ed. Jean-Jacques Nattiez, trans. Martin Cooper (London, 1986), 467–70.

Braudo, Evgeny, 'Betkhoven-grazhdanin' ['Beethoven-Citizen'], *Muzïka i revoliutsitya*, 3 (1927), 22–3.

'Ob ekspressionizme v muzïke', *Muzïkalnaya letopis*, 2 (1922), 150.

Brendel, Franz, *Geschichte der Musik in Italien, Deutschland und Frankreich: Von den ersten christlichen Zeiten bis auf die Gegenwart*, 3rd edn (Leipzig, 1860).

Bribitzer-Stull, Matthew, 'The End of *Die Feen* and Wagner's Beginnings: Multiple Approaches to an Early Example of Double-Tonic Complex, Associative Theme and Wagnerian Form', *Music Analysis*, 25/3 (2006), 315–40.

Brinkmann, Reinhold, 'Die gepreßte Sinfonie. Zum geschichtlichen Gehalt von Schönbergs Opus 9', in Otto Kolleritsch, ed., *Gustav Mahler. Sinfonie und Wirklichkeit, Studien zur Wertungsforschung*, 9 (Graz, 1977), 133–5.

Late Idyll: The Second Symphony of Johannes Brahms, trans. Peter Palmer (Cambridge, Mass., 1997).

Brodbeck, David, *Brahms: Symphony No. 1* (Cambridge, 1997).

'Brahms, the Third Symphony, and the New German School', in Walter Frisch and Kevin Karnes, eds., *Brahms and His World*, rev. edn (Princeton, 2009), 95–116.

'Dvořák's Reception in Liberal Vienna: Language Ordinances, National Property, and the Rhetoric of *Deutschtum*', *Journal of the American Musicological Society*, 60 (2007), 71–132.

Broder, Nathan, 'The Wind Instruments in Mozart's Symphonies', *Musical Quarterly*, 19 (1933), 238–59.

Bronfin, Elena, *Muzïkalnaya kultura Petrograda pervogo poslereoliutinnogo pyatiletiya 1917–1922* (Leningrad, 1984).

Brook, Barry S. and Barbara Heyman, gen. eds., *The Symphony, 1720–1840: A Comprehensive Collection of Scores in Sixty Volumes*, 60 vols. (New York, 1979–1986).

Brown, A. Peter, 'Stylistic Maturity and Regional Influence: Joseph Martin Kraus' Symphonies in C-sharp minor (Stockholm, 1782) and C minor (Vienna, 1783)', in Eugene K. Wolf and Edward H. Roesner, eds., *Studies in Musical Sources and Style: Essays in Honor of Jan LaRue* (Madison, 1990), 381–418.

ed., *The Symphonic Repertoire*, vol. II: *The First Golden Age of the Viennese Symphony: Haydn, Mozart, Beethoven, and Schubert* (Bloomington, 2002).

ed., *The Symphonic Repertoire*, vol. III, Part A: *The European Symphony ca. 1800–ca. 1930: Germany and the Nordic Countries* (Bloomington, 2007).

The Symphonic Repertoire, vol. IV: *The Second Golden Age of the Viennese Symphony: Brahms, Bruckner, Dvořák and Selected Contemporaries* (Bloomington, 2003).

Brown, A. Peter and Brian Hart, *The Symphonic Repertoire*, vol. III, Part B: *The European Symphony ca. 1800–ca. 1930: Great Britain, Russia, and France* (Bloomington, 2008).

Brown, David, *Tchaikovsky: The Crisis Years 1874–1878* (London, 1982).
  Tchaikovsky: The Final Years 1885–1893 (London, 1991).

Broyles, Michael, 'Ensemble Music Moves Out of the Private House: Haydn to Beethoven', in Peyser, ed., *The Orchestra*, 97–122.

Brunner, Lance W., 'The Orchestra and Recorded Sound', in Peyser, ed., *The Orchestra*, 475–528.

Bryan, Paul R., 'The Horn in the Works of Mozart and Haydn: Some Observations and Comparisons', *Haydn Yearbook* (1975), 189–255.
  Johann Wanhal, Viennese Symphonist: His Life, and His Musical Environment (Stuyvesant, 1997).

Burchell, Jenny, *Polite or Commercial Concerts?: Concert Management and Orchestral Repertoire in Edinburgh, Bath, Oxford, Manchester, and Newcastle, 1730–1799* (New York, 1996).

Burgess, Geoffrey and Bruce Haynes, *The Oboe* (New Haven, 2004), 78–124.

Burkholder, J. Peter, 'Brahms and Twentieth-Century Music', *19th-Century Music*, 8 (1984/85), 75–83.
  'The Twentieth Century and the Orchestra as Museum', in Peyser, ed., *The Orchestra*, 409–32.

Burnham, Scott, *Beethoven Hero* (Princeton, 1995).
  'Novel Symphonies and Dramatic Overtures', in Perrey, ed., *The Cambridge Companion to Schumann*, 148–72.

Burnham, Scott and Michael Steinberg, *Beethoven and His World* (Princeton, 2000).

Caplin, William E., *Classical Form: A Theory of Formal Functions for the Instrumental Music of Haydn, Mozart, and Beethoven* (New York and Oxford, 1998).
  'Structural Expansion in Beethoven's Symphonic Forms', in Kinderman, ed., *Beethoven's Compositional Process*, 27–54.

Carpani, Giuseppe, *The Lives of Haydn and Mozart*, trans. L. A. C. Bombet, 2nd edn (London, 1818), 107–8.

Carse, Adam, *The History of the Orchestra* (New York and London, 1925).
  The Orchestra in the XVIIIth Century (Cambridge, 1940).

Carter, Elliott, 'A Symphony of Three Orchestras (1976)', reprinted in *The Writings of Elliott Carter: An American Composer Looks at Modern Music*, ed. Else and Kurt Stone (Bloomington, 1977).

Celenza, Anna Harwell, *The Early Works of Niels W. Gade: In Search of the Poetic* (Ashgate, 2001), 169–76.

Chemodanov, Sergey, 'Muzïka i teoriya istoricheskogo materializma', *Muzïkalnaya nov*, 20 (1923), 16.

Cheremukhin, Mikhail, 'K voprosu putyakh sovetskoy muzïki', *Sovetskaya muzïka*, 5 (1933), 24.

Chorley, Henry F., *Modern German Music: Recollections and Criticisms*, 2 vols. (London, 1854), vol. I, 369.

Chua, Daniel, *The 'Galitzin' Quartets of Beethoven* (Princeton, 1995).

Churgin, Bathia, 'Sammartini and Boccherini: Continuity and Change in the Italian Instrumental Tradition of the Classic Period', *Chigiana*, 43 (1993), 171–91.

'The Symphonies of G. B. Sammartini', 2 vols. (Ph.D. diss., Harvard University, 1963).

'The Symphony as Described by J. A. P. Schulz (1774): A Commentary and Translation', *Current Musicology*, 29 (1980), 7–16.

ed., *The Symphonies of G. B. Sammartini,* vol. I: *The Early Symphonies* (Cambridge, Mass., 1968).

Cohn, Richard L., 'As Wonderful as Star Clusters: Instruments for Gazing at Tonality in Schubert', *19th-Century Music*, 22/3 (1999), 213–32.

Audacious Euphony: Chromaticism and the Triad's Second Nature (New York and Oxford, 2012).

'The Dramatization of Hypermetric Conflicts in the Scherzo of Beethoven's Ninth Symphony', *19th-Century Music*, 15/3 (1992), 188–206.

'Introduction to Neo-Riemannian Theory: A Survey and a Historical Perspective', *Journal of Music Theory*, 42/2 (1998), 167–79.

'Maximally Smooth Cycles, Hexatonic Systems and the Analysis of Late-Romantic Triadic Progressions', *Music Analysis*, 15 (1996), 9–40.

'Neo-Riemannian Operations, Parsimonious Trichords and Their *Tonnetz* Representations', *Journal of Music Theory*, 42/1 (1997), 1–66.

Cone, Edward T., ed., *Berlioz: Fantastic Symphony* (New York and London, 1971).

'Stravinsky: The Progress of a Method', *Perspectives of New Music*, 1/1 (1962), 18–26.

Cook, Nicholas, *Beethoven: Symphony No. 9* (Cambridge, 1993).

Cooper, John Michael, '"Aber eben dieser Zweifel": A New Look at Mendelssohn's "Italian" Symphony', *19th-Century Music*, 15 (1992), 169–87.

Mendelssohn's 'Italian' Symphony (New York and Oxford, 2003).

Cornelius, Peter, *Gesammelte Aufsätze: Gedanken über Musik und Theater, Poesie und bildende Kunst*, ed. Gunter Wagner and James A. Deaville (Mainz, 2004).

Dahlhaus, Carl, *Foundations of Music History*, trans. J. B. Robinson (Cambridge, 1983).

Klassische und Romantische Musikästhetik (Laaber, 1988).

'Liszt, Schönberg und die große Form. Das Prinzip der Einsätzigkeit in der Mehrsätzigkeit', *Die Musikforschung*, 41 (1988), 202–13.

'Liszts Bergsymphonie und die Idee der Symphonischen Dichtung', in Dagmar Droysen, ed., *Jahrbuch des Staatlichen Instituts für Musikforschung Preußischer Kulturbesitz 1975* (Berlin, 1976), 96–130.

'Liszts Idee des Symphonischen', in Dahlhaus, *Klassische und romantische Musikästhetik* (Laaber, 1988), 401–12.

Ludwig van Beethoven: Approaches to His Music trans. Mary Whittall (Oxford, 1991).

Die Musik des 19. Jahrhunderts (Laaber, 1980), trans. J. Bradford Robinson as *Nineteenth-Century Music* (Berkeley and Los Angeles, 1989).

'Symphonie und symphonischer Stil um 1850', *Jahrbuch des Staatlichen Instituts für Musikforschung Preußischer Kulturbesitz* 1983/84, ed. Dagmar Droysen-Reber and Günther Wagner (Kassel, 1987), 34–58.

'Wagners Stellung in der Musikgeschichte', trans. by Alfred Clayton as 'Wagner's Place in the History of Music', in *Wagner Handbook*, ed. Ulrich Müller and Peter Wapnewski, trans. and ed. John Deathridge (Cambridge, Mass. and London, 1992), 99–117.

Daverio, John, *Robert Schumann: Herald of a 'New Poetic Age'* (New York and Oxford, 1997).

Deathridge, John, *Wagner beyond Good and Evil* (Berkeley, 2008).

Debussy, Claude, 'Monsieur Croche the Dilettante-Hater', in *Three Classics in the Aesthetics of Music* (New York, 1962), 3–71.

Determann, Robert, *Begriff und Ästhetik der 'Neudeutschen Schule': Ein Beitrag zur Musikgeschichte des 19. Jahrhundert* (Baden-Baden, 1989).

Deutsch, Otto Eric, *Mozart: A Documentary Biography*, trans. Eric Blom, Peter Branscombe and Jeremy Noble, 3rd edn (London, 1990).

Doctor, Jenny R., David C. H. Wright and Nicholas Kenyon, eds., *The Proms: A New History* (London, 2007).

Dömling, Wolfgang, *Franz Liszt und seine Zeit* (Laaber, 1998).

Dörffel, Alfred, *Geschichte der Gewandhausconcerte zu Leipzig*, 2 vols. (Leipzig, 1884).

Edge, Dexter, 'Manuscript Parts as Evidence of Orchestral Size in the Eighteenth-Century Viennese Concerto', in Zaslaw, ed., *Mozart's Piano Concertos*, 427–60.

'Mozart's Viennese Orchestras', *Early Music*, 20 (1992), 64–88.

Edmunds, Neil, *The Soviet Proletarian Music Movement* (Bern, 2000).

Ehlers, Paul, 'Das Regensburger Bruckner Erlebnis', *Zeitschrift für Musik*, 104 (1937), 745–8.

Einstein, Alfred, *Mozart: His Character, His Work*, trans. Arthur Mendel and Nathan Broder (London, 1945).

Eisen, Cliff, ed., *Mozart Studies* (Oxford, 1991).

Ekman, Karl, *Jean Sibelius: His Life and Personality*, trans. Edward Birse (New York, 1938).

Elgar, Edward and Percy M. Young, *A Future for English Music, and Other Lectures* (London, 1968).

Everist, Mark, 'Reception Theories, Canonic Discourses, and Musical Value', in Nicholas Cook and Mark Everist, eds., *Rethinking Music* (New York and Oxford, 1999), 378–402.

Fairclough, Pauline, 'Mahler Reconstructed: Sollertinsky and the Soviet Symphony', *Musical Quarterly*, 85/2 (2001), 367–90.

A Soviet Credo: Shostakovitch's Fourth Symphony (Aldershot, 2006).

Fanning, David, ed., *The Breath of the Symphonist: Shostakovich's Tenth* (London, 1988).

Nielsen: Symphony No. 5 (Cambridge, 1997).

Shostakovich Studies (Cambridge, 1995).

Fay, Laurel E., ed., *Shostakovich and His World* (Princeton and Woodstock, 2004).

Fink, G. W., 'Preissinfonie', *Allgemeine musikalische Zeitung*, 39 (1837), cols. 201–9, 217–22.

'Symphonie oder Sinfonie', in *Encyklopädie der gesammten musikalischen Wissenschaften: oder Universal-Lexicon der Tonkunst*, ed. Gustav Schilling, 6 vols. (Stuttgart, 1838; repr., Hildesheim and New York, 1974), vol. VI, 541–51.

'Ueber die Symphonie, als Beitrag zur Geschichte und Aesthetik derselben', in *Allgemeine musikalische Zeitung*, 37 (1835), cols. 505–11, 521–4, 557–63.

Fink, Robert, 'Beethoven Antihero: Sex, Violence and the Aesthetics of Failure, Or Listening to the Ninth Symphony as Postmodern Sublime', in Andrew Dell'Antonio, ed., *Beyond Structural Listening: Postmodern Modes of Hearing* (Berkeley, 2004), 109–53.

Finscher, Ludwig, 'The Struggle with Tradition: Johannes Brahms', in Ursula von Rauchhaupt, ed., *The Symphony* (London, 1973), 165–74.

'Symphonie', in *Die Musik in Geschichte und Gegenwart*, 2nd edn, Sachteil, vol. VIII (1994), cols. 19–56.

'"Zwischen absoluter und Programmusik": Zur Interpretation der deutschen romantischen Symphonie', in Christoph-Hellmut Mahling, ed., *Über Symphonien: Beiträge zu einer musikalischen Gattung (Festschrift Walter Wiora zum 70. Geburtstag)* (Tutzing, 1979), 103–15.

Finson, Jon, *Robert Schumann and the Study of Orchestral Composition: The Genesis of the First Symphony Op. 38* (Oxford, 1989).

Floros, Constantin, *Brahms und Bruckner: Studien zur musikalischen Exegetik* (Wiesbaden, 1980).

Gustav Mahler, vol. I: *Die geistige Welt Gustav Mahlers in systematischer Darstellung* (Wiesbaden, 1977).

Foreman, Lewis, *Bax: A Composer and His Times*, 3rd rev. edn (Woodbridge, 2007).

Forner, Johannes, Andreas Göpfert, Fritz Hennenberg, Brigitte Richter and Ingeborg Singer, *Die Gewandhaus-Konzerte zu Leipzig 1781–1981*, 2 vols. (Leipzig, 1981).

Forsberg, Suzanne, 'Joseph and Placidus von Camerloher', in Morrow and Churgin, eds., *The Eighteenth-Century Symphony*, 339–52.

Franklin, Peter, 'The Boy on the Train, or Bad Symphonies and Good Movies: The Revealing Error of the "Symphonic Score"', in Daniel Goldmark, Lawrence Kramer and Richard Leppert, eds., *Beyond the Soundtrack: Representing Music in Cinema* (Berkeley, Los Angeles and London, 2007), 13–26.

The Idea of Music (London, 1985).

The Life of Mahler (Cambridge, 1997).

'Sibelius in Britain', in Daniel M. Grimley, ed., *The Cambridge Companion to Sibelius* (Cambridge, 2004), 182–95.

Frisch, Walter, *Brahms and the Principle of Developing Variation* (Berkeley and Los Angeles, 1990).

Brahms: The Four Symphonies (New Haven, 2003).

'"Echt symphonisch": On the Historical Context of Brahms' Symphonies', in *Brahms Studies*, vol. II, ed. David Brodbeck (Lincoln and London, 1998), 114–16.

Frogley, Alain, 'Constructing Englishness in Music: National Character and the Reception of Ralph Vaughan Williams', in Frogley, ed., *Vaughan Williams Studies* (Cambridge, 1996), 1–22.

'"The Old Sweet Anglo-Saxon Spell": Racial Discourses and the American Reception of British Music, 1895–1933', in Julie Brown, ed., *Western Music and Race* (Cambridge, 2007), 244–57.

Vaughan Williams's Ninth Symphony (New York and Oxford, 2001).

ed., *Vaughan Williams Studies* (Cambridge, 1996).

Frye, Northrop, *Words with Power* (San Diego, 1990).

Geiringer, Karl, *Instruments in the History of Western Music* (London, 1978), 201–73.

Gellner, Ernest, *Language and Solitude: Wittgenstein, Malinowski and the Habsburg Dilemma* (Cambridge, 1998).

Gerber, Ernst Ludwig, *Historisch-biographisches Lexicon der Tonkünstler*, 2 vols. (Leipzig, 1790, 1792).

Gerhard, Anselm, *London und der Klassizismus in der Musik: De Idee der 'absoluten Musik' und Muzio Clementis Klavierwerke* (Stuttgart, 2002).

Gerlach, Sonja, 'Haydns Orchestermusiker von 1761 bis 1774', *Haydn-Studien*, 4 (1976), 35–48.

Gervink, Manuel, *Die Symphonie in Deutschland und Österreich in der Zeit zwischen den beiden Weltkriegen* (Regensburg, 1984).

Gibbs, Christopher H., '"The Phenomenon of the Seventh": A Documentary Essay on Shostakovich's "War" Symphony', in Laurel Fay, ed., *Shostakovich and His World*, 59–113.

ed., *The Cambridge Companion to Schubert* (Cambridge, 1997).

Gilliam, Bryan, 'The Annexation of Anton Bruckner: Nazi Revisionism and the Politics of Appropriation', in Hawkshaw and Jackson, eds., *Bruckner Studies* (Cambridge, 1997), 72–90.

Gjerdingen, Robert, 'The Symphony in France', in Morrow and Churgin, eds., *The Eighteenth-Century Symphony*, 551–70.

Glebov, Igor, 'The Music of Mozart', *Zhizn iskusstva* [*Life of Art*] (4 September 1923). 'Russkaya simfonicheskaya muzïka za 10 let', *Muzïka i revoliutsiya*, 11 (1927), 21.

Glock, William, *Notes in Advance* (Oxford and New York, 1991), 211.

Goethe, Johann Wolfgang, *Wilhelm Meisters Wanderjahre,* Book II, in *Sämtliche Werke,* vol. XVII, ed. Karl Richer (Munich, 1985–98).

Goldmark, Karl, *Notes from the Life of a Viennese Composer*, trans. Alice Goldmark Brandeis (New York, 1927).

Goncharova, N., 'Betkhoven v krasnoy armiy', *Sovetskaya muzïka*, 7–8 (1935), 153.

Goss, Glenda Dawn, *Jean Sibelius and Olin Downes: Music, Friendship, Criticism* (Boston, 1995).

ed., *The Sibelius Companion* (Westport, 1996).

Grange, Henry-Louis de la, *Gustav Mahler*, vol. II: *Vienna: The Years of Challenge (1897–1904)* (Oxford and New York, 1995).

Gustav Mahler, vol. III: *Vienna: Triumph and Disillusion (1904–1907)* (Oxford and New York, 1999).

Gustav Mahler, vol. IV: *A New Life Cut Short (1907–1911)* (New York and Oxford, 2008).

Grave, Margaret H., 'Dittersdorf's First-Movement Form as a Measure of his Symphonic Development' (Ph.D. diss., New York University, 1977).

Gray, Laura, 'Sibelius and England', in Glenda Dawn Goss, ed., *The Sibelius Companion* (Westport, 1996), 281–95.

Grimley, Daniel M., ed., *The Cambridge Companion to Sibelius* (Cambridge, 2004).

Grimley, Daniel M., and Julian Rushton, eds., *The Cambridge Companion to Elgar* (Cambridge, 2005).

Grotjahn, Rebecca, *Die Sinfonie im deutschen Kulturgebiet 1850 bis 1875: Ein Beitrag zur Gattungs- und Institutionengeschichte* (Sinzig, 1998).

'Zur Bedeutung der Sinfonie im Musikleben 1850 bis 1875', in Christoph-Hellmut Mahling and Kristina Pfarr, eds., *Aspekte historischer und systematischer Musikforschung* (Mainz, 2002), 49–57.

Gülke, Peter, *'Triumph der neuen Tonkunst': Mozarts späte Sinfonien und ihr Umfeld* (Kassel and Stuttgart, 1998).

Habermas, Jürgen, *The Structural Transformation of the Public Sphere: An Inquiry into a Category of Bourgeois Society*, trans. Thomas Burger and Frederick Lawrence (Cambridge, Mass., 1991).

Halm, August, *Die Symphonie Anton Bruckners* (Munich, 1923).

Von zwei Kulturen der Musik (Stuttgart, 1947).

Hanslick, Eduard, *Aus dem Concertsaal* (Vienna, 1870).

Aus dem Tagebuche eines Musikers (Berlin, 1892).

Harper-Scott, J. P. E., *Edward Elgar: Modernist* (Cambridge, 2009).

'A Nice Sub-Acid Feeling: Schenker, Heidegger and Elgar's First Symphony', *Music Analysis*, 24/3 (2005), 349–82.

'Vaughan Williams's Antic Symphony', in Matthew Riley, ed., *British Music and Modernism 1895–1960* (Aldershot, 2010), 175–96.

Harrandt, Andrea, 'Bruckner in Vienna', in John Williamson, ed., *The Cambridge Companion to Bruckner* (Cambridge, 2004), 26–37.

'Students and Friends as "Prophets" and "Promoters": The Reception of Bruckner's Works in the *Wiener Akademische Wagner-Verein*', in Howie, Hawkshaw and Jackson, eds., *Perspectives on Anton Bruckner* (Aldershot, 2001), 317–27.

Harrison, Bernard, *Haydn: The 'Paris' Symphonies* (Cambridge, 1998).

Harrison, Daniel, *Harmonic Function in Chromatic Music: A Renewed Dualist Theory and Its Precedents* (Chicago, 1994).

Hawkshaw, Paul and Timothy L. Jackson, eds., *Bruckner Studies* (Cambridge, 1997).

Heartz, Daniel, *Haydn, Mozart and the Viennese School 1740–1780* (New York and London, 1995).

Music in European Capitals: The Galant Style, 1720–1780 (New York, 2003).

Hefling, Stephen E., 'Mahler's "Todtenfeier" and the Problem of Program Music', *19th-Century Music*, 12 (1988), 27–53.

Heldt, Guido, 'Erste Symphonien – Britten, Walton und Tippett', in Wolfgang Osthoff and Giselher Schubert, eds., *Symphonik 1930–1950: Gattungsgeschichte und analytische Beiträge* (Mainz, 2003), 84–108.

Hell, Helmut, *Die neapolitanische Opernsinfonie in der ersten Hälfte des 18. Jahrhunderts: N. Porpora, L. Vinci, G. B. Pergolesi, L. Leo, N. Jommelli* (Tutzing, 1971), 487–501.

Hellsberg, Clemens, *Demokratie der Könige: Die Geschichte der Wiener Philharmoniker* (Zurich, Vienna and Mainz, 1992), 205–93.

Henze-Döhring, Sabine, 'Orchester und Orchestersatz in Christian Cannabichs Mannheimer Sinfonien', in Ludwig Finscher, Bärbel Pelker and Jochen Reutter, eds., *Mozart und Mannheim* (Frankfurt-am-Main, 1994), 257–71.

Hepokoski, James, 'Beethoven Reception: The Symphonic Tradition', in Jim Samson, ed., *The Cambridge History of Nineteenth-Century Music* (Cambridge, 2001), 424–59.

'Beyond the Sonata Principle', *Journal of the American Musicological Society*, 55 (2002), 91–154.

'The Dahlhaus Project and Its Extra-Musicological Sources', *19th-Century Music*, 14/3 (1991), 238–9.

'Elgar', in Holoman, ed., *The Nineteenth-Century Symphony*, 327–44.

Sibelius: Symphony No. 5 (Cambridge, 1993).

'Rotations, Sketches, and the Sixth Symphony', in Jackson and Murtomäki, eds., *Sibelius Studies*, 332–51.

Hepokoski, James and Warren Darcy, *Elements of Sonata Theory: Norms, Types, and Deformations in the Late-Eighteenth-Century Sonata* (New York and Oxford, 2006).

Hill, George R., 'The Concert Symphonies of Florian Leopold Gassmann (1729–1774)' (Ph.D. diss., New York University, 1975).

Hill, Ralph, *The Symphony* (Harmondsworth, 1949).

Hinton, Stephen, 'Not "Which" Tones? The Crux of Beethoven's Ninth', *19th-Century Music*, 22/1 (1998), 61–77.

Hoeckner, Berthold, *Programming the Absolute: Nineteenth-Century German Music and the Hermeneutics of the Moment* (Princeton, 2002).

Hoffmann, E. T. A., 'Beethovens Intrumentalmusik', in *Sämtliche Werke* vol. II/1, 55–8, 60–1 and 62–4.

E. T. A. Hoffmann's Musical Writings: 'Kreisleriana', 'The Poet and the Composer', Music Criticism, ed. David Charlton, trans. Martyn Clarke (Cambridge, 1989).

Review of Beethoven's Fifth Symphony, *Allgemeine musikalische Zeitung*, 12 (1809/10), cols. 630–42, 652–69.

'[Review of Beethoven's Fifth Symphony]', trans. Martin Clarke, with David Charlton and Ian Bent, in Ian Bent, ed., *Music Analysis in the Nineteenth Century*, 2 vols. (Cambridge, 1994), vol. II, 141–60.

Hoffmansthal, Hugo von, 'Der Dichter und diese Zeit', in Hugo von Hoffmansthal, *Gesamelte Werke in zehn Einzelbänden. Reden und Aufsätze*, vol. I (Frankfurt am Main, 1979).

Holoman, D. Kern, ed., *The Nineteenth-Century Symphony* (New York, 1997).

Horlacher, Gretchen, 'Running in Place: Sketches and Superimposition in Stravinsky's Music', *Music Theory Spectrum*, 23/2 (2001), 196–216.

Horne, William, 'The Hidden Trellis: Where Does the Second Group Begin in the First Movement of Beethoven's *Eroica* Symphony?', *Beethoven Forum*, 13/2 (2006), 95–147.

Horton, Julian, *Bruckner's Symphonies: Analysis, Reception and Cultural Politics* (Cambridge, 2004).

'Counterpoint and Form in the Finale of Bruckner's Fifth Symphony', *The Bruckner Journal*, 15/2 (2011), 19–28.

'The Symphonic Fugal Finale from Mozart to Bruckner', *Dutch Journal of Music Theory*, 11/3 (2006), 230–48.

Howard, Luke, 'Motherhood, *Billboard*, and the Holocaust: Perceptions and Receptions of Górecki's Symphony No. 3', *Musical Quarterly*, 82 (1998), 131–59.

Howell, Tim, *Jean Sibelius: Progressive Techniques in the Symphonies and Tone Poems* (New York, 1998).

Howie, Crawford, *Anton Bruckner: A Documentary Biography*, 2 vols. (Lewiston, 2002).

Howie, Crawford, Paul Hawkshaw and Timothy Jackson, eds., *Perspectives on Anton Bruckner*, (Aldershot, 2001).

Hyer, Brian, 'Re-imag(in)ing Riemann', *Journal of Music Theory*, 39 (1995), 101–38.
 'Tonality', in Thomas Christensen, ed., *The Cambridge History of Western Music Theory* (Cambridge, 2002), 726–52.

Imbrie, Andrew, '"Extra Measures" and Metrical Ambiguity in Beethoven', in Alan Tyson, ed., *Beethoven Studies* (New York, 1973), 45–66.

Ivanov-Boretsky, Mikhail, 'E. T. A. Gofman', *Muzïkalnoe obrazovanie*, 3–4 (1926), 15.
 'Revoliutsionnïe khorï Shumana', *Muzïkalnoe obrazovanie*, 2 (1930), 16–19.

Jackson, Timothy L., *Tchaikovsky: Symphony No. 6 (Pathétique)* (Cambridge, 1999).

Jackson, Timothy L. and Veijo Murtomäki, eds., *Sibelius Studies* (Cambridge, 2001).

Jeitteles, Ignaz, 'Symphonie', in *Aesthetisches Lexikon*, vol. II (Vienna, 1837), 361–3.

Jenkins, Newell, and Bathia Churgin, *Thematic Catalogue of the Works of Giovanni Battista Sammartini* (Cambridge, Mass., 1976).

Kabalevsky, Dmitry, ed., *S. S. Prokof'ev i N. Ya. Myaskovsky: perepiska* (Moscow, 1977).

Kalbeck, Max, *Johannes Brahms*, 4 vols. (Vienna and Leipzig, 1904–14).

Kaltat, Lev and David Rabinovich, 'V boyakh za nasledstvo', *Sovetskaya muzïka*, 3 (1933), 13.

Kaplan, Richard, 'Sonata Form in the Orchestral Works of Liszt: The Revolutionary Reconsidered', *19th-Century Music*, 8/2 (1984), 142–52.

Keefe, Simon P., 'Across the Divide: Currents of Musical Thought in Europe, *c.* 1790–1810', in Keefe, ed., *The Cambridge History of Eighteenth-Century Music* (Cambridge, 2009).
 'The Aesthetics of Wind Writing in Mozart's "Paris" Symphony, K 297', *Mozart-Jahrbuch 2006*, 329–44.
 'Dialogue and Drama: Haydn's Symphony No. 102', *Music Research Forum*, 11/1 (1996), 1–21.
 '"Greatest Effects with the Least Effort": Strategies of Wind Writing in Mozart's Viennese Piano Concertos', in Keefe, ed., *Mozart Studies* (Cambridge, 2007), 25–42.
 Mozart's Piano Concertos: Dramatic Dialogue in the Age of Enlightenment (Woodbridge and Rochester, NY, 2001).
 Mozart's Viennese Instrumental Music: A Study of Stylistic Re-Invention (Woodbridge and Rochester, 2007).
 ed., *The Cambridge History of Eighteenth-Century Music* (Cambridge, 2009).

Kemp, Ian, *Tippett: The Composer and His Music* (London, 1984).

Kennedy, Michael, *The Works of Ralph Vaughan Williams*, rev. edn (Oxford, 1980).

Kenyon, Nicholas, *The BBC Symphony Orchestra: The First Fifty Years 1930–80* (London, 1981).
  Simon Rattle: From Birmingham to Berlin (London, 2001).
Kerman, Joseph, 'Beethoven's Minority', in Kerman, *Write All These Down: Essays on Music* (Berkeley, 1994), 217–37.
Kerman, Joseph and Alan Tyson, *The New Grove Beethoven* (New York, 1983).
  'A Few Canonic Variations', *Critical Inquiry*, 10 (1983), 107–25.
Kern, Stephen, *The Culture of Time and Space, 1880–1918* (Cambridge Mass., 1983, repr. 2000).
Khubov, Georgy, 'Frants Liszt', *Sovetskaya muzïka*, 11 (1936), 24–5.
Kimball, G. C., 'The Symphonies of Leopold Hofmann (1738–1793)' (Ph.D. diss., Columbia University, 1985).
Kinderman, William, ed., *Beethoven* (Berkeley and Los Angeles, 1995).
  Beethoven's Compositional Process (Lincoln, 1991).
Kinderman, William and Harald Krebs, eds., *The Second Practice of Nineteenth-Century Tonality* (Lincoln, 1996).
Kirby, F. E., 'Beethoven's Pastoral Symphony as a "Sinfonia caracteristica"', *Musical Quarterly*, 56 (1970), 608–12.
  'The Germanic Symphony of the Nineteeth Century: Genre, Form, Instrumentation, Expression', *Journal of Musicological Research*, 14 (1995), 193–221.
Knittel, K. M., '"Polemik im Concertsaal": Mahler, Beethoven, and the Viennese Critics', *19th-Century Music*, 29 (2006), 289–321.
Koch, Heinrich Christoph, *Musikalisches Lexikon* (Frankfurt, 1802, repr. Hildesheim, 1964).
Konrad, Ulrich, 'Der Wiener Kompositionswettbewerb 1835 und Franz Lachners *Sinfonia passionata*: Ein Beitrag zur Geschichte der Sinfonie nach Beethoven', in Franz Krautwurst, ed., *Augsburger Jahrbuch für Musikwissenschaft 1986* (Tutzing, 1986), 209–39.
Kopp, David, *Chromatic Transformations in Nineteenth-Century Music* (Cambridge 2002).
Korstvedt, Benjamin, 'Anton Bruckner in the Third Reich and After: An Essay on Ideology and Bruckner Reception', *Musical Quarterly* 80 (1996), 132–60.
  Bruckner: Symphony No. 8 (Cambridge, 2000).
Krebs, Harald, 'Alternatives to Monotonality in Early 19th-Century Music', *Journal of Music Theory*, 25/1 (1981), 1–16.
Kross, Siegfried and Marie Luise Maintz, eds., *Probleme der symphonischen Tradition im 19. Jahrhundert* (Tutzing, 1990).
Kucaba, John, 'The Symphonies of Georg Christoph Wagenseil' (Ph.D. diss., University of Boston, 1967).
Kurth, Ernst, *Bruckner*, 2 vols. (Berlin, 1925).
Lambert, Constant, *Music Ho!: A Study of Music in Decline* (London, 1934).
Landon, H. C. Robbins, *Beethoven* (London, 1970).
  Haydn: Chronicle and Works, 5 vols. (London, 1976–80).
  Mozart: the Golden Years (London, 1989).

Langley, Leanne, 'Agency and Change: Berlioz in Britain (1870–1920)', *Journal of the Royal Musical Association*, 132 (2007), 306–48.

Larkin, David, 'Reshaping the Liszt-Wagner Legacy: Intertextual Dynamics in Strauss' Tone Poems' (Ph.D. diss., University of Cambridge, 2007).

Larsen, Jens Peter, 'Zur Vorgeschichte der Symphonik der Wiener Klassic', *Studien zur Musikwissenschaft*, 43 (1994), 64–143.

LaRue, Jan, *A Catalogue of 18th-Century Symphonies,* vol. I: *Thematic Identifier* (Bloomington, 1988).

LaRue, Jan, Eugene K. Wolf, Mark Evan Bonds, Stephen Walsh and Charles Wilson, 'Symphony', in Stanley Sadie and John Tyrrell, eds., *The New Grove Dictionary of Music and Musicians* (London, 2001), 812–49.

Laufer, Edward, 'On the First Movement of Sibelius's Fourth Symphony: A Schenkerian View', in Carl Schachter and Hedi Siegel, eds., *Schenker Studies 2* (Cambridge, 1999), 132–3.

Layton, Robert, *A Guide to the Symphony* (New York and Oxford, 1995).

Le Guin, Elisabeth, *Boccherini's Body: An Essay in Carnal Musicology* (Berkeley, 2006).

Lebedinsky, Lev, 'Kontsertnaya rabota v rabochey auditorii', *Proletarsky muzïkant*, 2 (1929), 9.

Levy, David Benjamin, *Beethoven: The Ninth Symphony* (New Haven, 2003).
  'Early Performances of Beethoven's Ninth Symphony: A Documentary Study of Five Cities', (Ph.D. diss., University of Rochester, 1979), 47.

Lewin, David, *Generalised Musical Intervals and Transformations* (repr. New York and Oxford, 2007).

Lewis, Christopher, *Tonal Coherence in Mahler's Ninth Symphony* (Ann Arbor, 1984).

Liszt, Franz, *Gesammelte Schriften*, ed. L. Ramann, 6 vols. (Leipzig, 1880–3).

Lloyd, Stephen, *William Walton: Muse of Fire* (Woodbridge, 2001).

Locke, Ralph P., 'The French Symphony: David, Gounod, and Bizet to Saint-Saëns, Franck, and Their Followers', in Holoman, ed., *The Nineteenth-Century Symphony* (New York, 1997), 163–94.

Lockwood, Lewis, *Beethoven: The Music and the Life* (New York, 2003).

London, Justin, *Hearing in Time: Psychological Aspects of Musical Meter* (New York and Oxford, 2004).

Lunacharsky, Anatoly, 'Velikie sestrï' ['Great Sisters'], *Muzïka i revoliutsitya*, 1 (1926), 16.

Luttmann, Stephen, 'Preface', Friedrich Gernsheim, *Symphony No. 3* (Munich, 2006).

Maegaard, Jan, *Studien zur Entwicklung des dodekaphonen Satzes bei Arnold Schönberg* (Copenhagen, 1972).

Mahler, Alma, *Gustav Mahler: Memories and Letters*, 3rd edn, ed. Donald Mitchell, trans. Basil Creighton (Seattle, 1975).

Mahler, Gustav, *Selected Letters of Gustav Mahler*, ed. Knud Martner, trans. Eithne Wilkins, Ernst Kaiser and Bill Hopkins (London, 1979).

Mahling, Christoph-Hellmut, 'The Origin and Social Status of the Court Orchestral Musician in the 18th and Early 19th Century in Germany', trans. Herbert Kaufman and Barbara Reisner, in Walter Salmen, ed., *The Social Status of the Professional Musician from the Middle Ages to the 19th Century* (New York, 1983), 219–64.

ed., *Über Symphonien: Beiträge zu einer musikalischen Gattung (Festschrift Walter Wiora zum 70. Geburtstag)* (Tutzing, 1979).

Mahling, Christoph-Hellmut and Helmut Rösing, 'Orchester', in Ludwig Finscher, ed., *Die Musik in Geschichte und Gegenwart*, 2nd edn (Kassel, 1994–), Sachteil, vol. VII, cols. 812–52.

Marvin, William, 'Mahler's Third Symphony and the Dismantling of Sonata Form', in Gordon Sly, ed., *Keys to the Drama: Nine Perspectives on Sonata Form* (Aldershot, 2009), 53–72.

Maus, Fred Everett, 'Intersubjectivity and Analysis: Schumann's Essay on the *Fantastic* Symphony', in Ian Bent, ed., *Music Theory in the Age of Romanticism* (Cambridge, 1996), 125–37.

Mayeda, Akio, *Robert Schumanns Weg zur Symphonie* (Zürich, 1992).

McClary, Susan, *Feminine Endings: Music, Gender, and Sexuality* (Minneapolis, 1991).

McClymonds, Marita P., 'Jomellis Opernsinfonien der 1750er Jahre und ihre Beziehung zum Mannheimer Stil', in Roland Würtz, ed., *Mannheim und Italien: zur Vorgeschichte der Mannheimer: Bericht über das Mannheimer Kolloquium im März 1982* (Mainz, 1984), 97–120.

McColl, Sandra, 'Max Kalbeck and Gustav Mahler', *19th-Century Music*, 20/2 (1996), 167–84.

McVeigh, Simon, *Concert Life in London from Mozart to Haydn* (Cambridge, 1993).
  'The Symphony in Britain', in Morrow and Churgin, eds., *The Eighteenth-Century Symphony*, 629–61.

McVeigh, Simon and Cyril Ehrlich, 'The Modernisation of London Concert Life Around 1900', in Michael Talbot, ed., *The Business of Music* (Liverpool, 2002), 96–120.

Mattheson, Johann, *Das neu-eröffnete Orchestre* (Hamburg, 1713; repr. Laaber, 2004).

Mellers, Wilfrid, '1930: Symphony of Psalms', *Tempo*, New Series, 97 (Stravinsky Memorial Issue, 1971), 19–27.

Mercer Taylor, Peter, *The Cambridge Companion to Mendelssohn* (Cambridge, 2004).

Meyer, Leonard B., 'Innovation, Choice, and the History of Music', *Critical Inquiry*, 3 (1983), 517–44.
  Style and Music: Theory, History, and Ideology (Chicago, 1989).

Meyer, Jürgen, 'Gedanken zu den originalen Konzertsälen Joseph Haydns', in Thüring Bräm, ed., *Musik und Raum: Eine Sammlung von Beiträgen aus historischer und künstlerischer Sicht zur Bedeutung des Begriffes 'Raum' als Klangträger für die Musik* (Basel, 1986), 27–37.

Micznik, Vera, 'The Farewell Story of Mahler's Ninth Symphony', *19th-Century Music*, 20/2 (1996), 144–66.
  'Mahler and the "Power of Genre"', *Journal of Musicology*, 12/2 (1994), 117–51.

Miel, M[arie], 'Über Sinfonie, über die Sinfonien Beethovens, und über ihre Aufführung in Paris', *Neue Zeitschrift für Musik*, 1 (1834), 101.

Mikheyeva, Lyudmila, *Pamyati I. I. Sollertinskogo* (Leningrad, 1978).

Mikkonen, Simo, 'State Composers and the Red Courtiers: Music, Ideology and Politics in the Soviet 1930s' (Ph.D. diss., University of Jyväskalä, 2007).

Mitchell, Donald, 'The Mahler Renaissance in England: Its Origins and Chronology', in Nicholson and Mitchell, eds., *The Mahler Companion*, 548–64.

Mitchell, Donald and Andrew Nicholson, eds., *The Mahler Companion* (New York and Oxford, 1999).

Monahan, Seth, 'Success and Failure in Mahler's Sonata Recapitulations', *Music Theory Spectrum*, 33/1 (2011), 37–58.

Morrison, Simon, 'Skryabin and the Impossible', *Journal of the American Musicological Society*, 51 (1998), 283–330.

Moore, Jerrold Northrop, *Edward Elgar: A Creative Life* (Oxford, 1984).

Morrow, Mary Sue, *Concert Life in Haydn's Vienna: Aspects of a Developing Musical and Social Tradition* (Stuyvesant, 1989).

  German Music Criticism in the Late Eighteenth Century: Aesthetic Issues in Instrumental Music (Cambridge, 1997).

Morrow, Mary Sue and Bathia Churgin, eds., *The Symphonic Repertoire,* vol. I: *The Eighteenth-Century Symphony* (Bloomington, 2012).

Mosch, Ulrich, ed., *Wolfgang Rihm: ausgesprochen* (Mainz, 1997).

Mueller, John Henry, *The American Symphony Orchestra: A Social History of Musical Taste* (London, 1958).

Mueller, Kate Hevner, *Twenty-Seven Major Symphony Orchestras: A History and Analysis of Their Repertoires Seasons 1842–43 Through 1969–70* (Bloomington, 1973).

Murtomäki, Veijo, *Symphonic Unity: The Development of Formal Thinking in the Symphonies of Sibelius*, trans. Henry Bacon (Helsinki, 1993).

Musgrave, Michael, *The Music of Brahms* (Oxford, 1994).

  ed., *The Cambridge Companion to Brahms* (Cambridge, 1999).

Myers, Arnold, 'How Brass Instruments Work', in Herbert and Wallace, eds., *The Cambridge Companion to Brass Instruments* (Cambridge, 1997), 19–23.

Neighbour, Oliver, 'The Place of the Eighth among Vaughan Williams' Symphonies', in Alain Frogley, ed., *Vaughan Williams Studies* (Cambridge, 1996), 213–33.

Nelson, Amy, *Music for the Revolution: Musicians and Power in Early Soviet Russia* (Philadelphia, 2004).

Nettl, Bruno, 'Mozart and the Ethnomusicological Study of Western Culture: An Essay in Four Movements', in Katherine Bergeron and Philip V. Bohlman, eds., *Disciplining Music: Musicology and its Canons* (Chicago and London, 1992), 137–55.

Newcomb, Anthony, 'Once More between Absolute and Program Music: Schumann's Second Symphony', *19th-Century Music*, 7/3 (1984), 233–50.

Newlin, Dika, *Bruckner, Mahler, Schoenberg* (New York, 1947).

Newman, William S., *The Sonata since Beethoven* (Chapel Hill, 1969).

Niemetschek, Franz Xaver, *Lebensbeschreibung des k. k. Kapellmeisters Wolfgang Amadeus Mozart* (Prague, 1798), trans. Helen Mautner as *Life of Mozart* (London, 1956).

Niemöller, Klaus Wolfgang, 'Zur Symphonik von Robert Volkmann', in Helmut Loos, ed., *Musikgeschichte zwischen Ost- und Westeuropa* (Sankt Augustin, 1997), 57–68.

Nietzsche, Friedrich, *The Birth of Tragedy and the Case of Wagner*, trans. Walter Kaufmann (New York, 1967).

Notley, Margaret, 'Brahms as Liberal: Genre, Style, and Politics in Late Nineteenth-Century Vienna', *19th-Century Music*, 17 (1993), 107–23.

'Bruckner and Viennese Wagnerism', in Hawkshaw and Jackson, eds., *Bruckner Studies*, 54–71.

Lateness and Brahms: Music and Culture in the Twilight of Viennese Liberalism (New York and Oxford, 2007).

'Musical Culture in Vienna at the Turn of the Twentieth Century', in Bryan R. Simms, ed., *Schoenberg, Berg, and Webern: A Companion to the Second Viennese School* (Westport, 1999), 37–71.

Oechsle, Siegfried, 'Die problemgeschichtliche Vitalität der Symphonie im 19. Jahrhundert', in Mahling and Pfart, eds., *Aspekte historischer und systematischer Musikforschung*, 19–27.

Symphonik nach Beethoven: Studien zu Schubert, Schumann, Mendelssohn und Gade (Kassel, 1992).

Olsen, Ursula Andkjær, '*Hvert med sit Næb*': Pelle Gudmundsen-Holmgreens musikalske verden (Copenhagen, 2004).

Osmond-Smith, David, *Playing on Words: A Guide to Luciano Berio's* Sinfonia (London, 1985).

Painter, Karen, ed., *Mahler and His World* (Princeton, 2002).

Symphonic Aspirations: German Music and Politics, 1900–1945 (Cambridge, Mass., 2007).

Pederson, Sanna, 'On the Task of the Music Historian: The Myth of the Symphony after Beethoven', *Repercussions*, 2 (1993), 5–30.

'A. B. Marx, Berlin Concert Life, and German National Identity', *19th-Century Music*, 18/2 (1993), 87–107.

Pekelis, Mikhail, 'Frants Schubert', *Muzika i revoliutsiya*, 10 (1928), 15.

Perrey, Beate, ed., *The Cambridge Companion to Schumann* (Cambridge, 2007).

Peyser, Joan, ed., The Orchestra: Origins and Transformations (New York, 1986).

Philip, Robert, *Performing Music in the Age of Recording* (New Haven and London, 2004).

Plantinga, Leon, *Schumann as Critic* (New Haven and London, 1967).

Pohl, Richard, *Franz Liszt: Studien und Erinnerungen* (Leipzig, 1883).

Ponyatovskiy, S., *Persimfans – orkestr bez dirizhera* (Moscow, 2003).

Portowitz, Adena, 'J. C. Bach', in Morrow and Churgin, eds., *The Eighteenth-Century Symphony*, 662–83.

Powell, Ardal, *The Flute* (New Haven, 2002).

Proctor, Gregory, 'The Technical Basis of Nineteenth-century Chromatic Tonality' (Ph.D. diss., Princeton University, 1978).

Pshibïshevsky, Boleslav, 'O tvorcheskom metode Betkhovena', *Proletarsky muzïkant*, 5 (1931), 28.

Raff, Helene, *Joachim Raff: Ein Lebensbild* (Regensburg, 1925).

Ramirez, Miguel J., 'Analytic Approaches to the Music of Anton Bruckner: Chromatic Third Relations in Selected Late Compositions' (Ph.D. diss., University of Chicago, 2009).

Rehding, Alexander, 'Towards a "Logic of Discontinuity" in Stravinsky's *Symphonies of Wind Instruments*: Hasty, Kramer and Straus Reconsidered', *Music Analysis*, 17/1 (1998), 39–65.

Rice, Albert R., *The Clarinet in the Classical Period* (Oxford and New York, 2003).

Richards, Annette, *The Free Fantasia and the Musical Picturesque* (Cambridge, 2002).

Riemann, Hugo, 'Ideen zu einer "Lehre von den Tonvorstellungen"', *Jahrbuch der Bibliothek Peters* (1914–15), 1–26.

Rings, Steven, *Tonality and Transformation* (New York and Oxford, 2011).

Rochlitz, Friedrich, 'Nekrolog', *Allgemeine musikalische Zeitung*, 29 (28 March 1827), 228.

Rodgers, Stephen, *Form, Program, and Metaphor in the Music of Berlioz* (Cambridge, 2009).

Roesner, Linda Correll, 'Schumann', in Holoman, ed., *The Nineteenth-Century Symphony*, 43–77.

Rosen, Charles, *The Classical Style* (London, 1972).

   The Romantic Generation (Cambridge, Mass. 1998).

   Sonata Forms (New York, 1988).

Rösing, Helmut, 'Fast wie ein Unwetter: Zur Rezeption von Pastoral- und Alpensinfonie-Gewitter; über verschiedene Darstellungsebenen der musikalischen Informationsübermittlung', in Mahling, ed., *Über Symphonien*, 65–89.

Rothstein, Edward, 'The New Amateur Player and Listener', in Joan Peyser, ed., *The Orchestra* (repr. Milwaukee, 2006), 529–44.

Rudolf, Kenneth E., 'The Symphonies of Georg Mathias Monn (1715–1750)' (Ph.D. diss., University of Washington, 1982).

Rufer, Josef, *The Works of Arnold Schoenberg* (London, 1962).

Ruiter, Jacob de, *Der Charakterbegriff in der Musik: Studien zur deutschen Ästhetik der Instrumentalmusik 1740–1850* (Stuttgart, 1989).

Rushton, Julian, *Berlioz: Roméo et Juliette* (Cambridge, 1994).

   The Music of Berlioz (New York and Oxford, 2001).

Sabaneyev, Leonid, *Erinnerungen an Alexander Skrjabin* (Berlin, 2005).

   'Richard Strauss', *K novïm beregam*, 2 (1923), 36.

Samson, Jim, 'Chopin's Alternatives to Monotonality: A Historical Perspective', in Kinderman and Krebs, eds., *The Second Practice of Nineteenth-century Tonality*, 34–44.

Samuels, Robert, *Mahler's Sixth Symphony: A Study in Musical Semiotics* (Cambridge, 1995).

   'Narrative Form and Mahler's Musical Thinking', *Nineteenth-Century Music Review*, 8 (2011), 237–54.

Sand, George, *Lettres d'un Voyageur*, ed. Patricia Thomson, trans. Sacha Rabinovitch and Patricia Thomson (Harmondsworth, 1987).

Schaarwächter, Jürgen, *Die Britische Sinfonie 1914–1945* (Cologne, 1994).

   'Cipriani Potter, Georg Alexander Macfarren and Mid-19th-Century British Symphonism', in Wolfgang Schult and Henrik Verkerk, eds., *Deutschland und England: Beiträge zur Musikforschung, Jahrbuch der Bachwochen Dillenburg (2002)* (Munich, 2002), 77–91.

Schenker, Heinrich, 'Beethoven: Fifth Symphony', in *Der Tonwille*, vol. I: issues 1–5
(1921–3), ed. William Drabkin, trans. Ian Bent et al (Oxford, 2004), 25–33.
*Beethoven's Ninth Symphony: A Portrayal of Its Musical Content, with Running
Commentary on Performance and Literature as Well* trans. John Rothgeb (New
Haven, 1992).
Schering, Arnold, 'Bemerkungen zu J. Haydns Programmsinfonien', *Jahrbuch Peters*
(1939), 9–27.
Schiedermair, Ludwig, *Gustav Mahler: Eine biographisch-kritische Würdigung*
(Leipzig, 1901).
Schiff, David, 'Carter as Symphonist: Redefining Boundaries', *Musical Times* 139/
1865 (1998), 8–13.
The Music of Elliott Carter (London, 1983).
Schleuning, Peter, 'Beethoven in alter Deutung: Der "neue Weg" mit der "Sinfonia
eroica"', *Archiv für Musikwissenschaft*, 44 (1987), 165–94.
Schlötterer, Reinhold, '4. Symphonie, Op. 60', in Albrecht Riethmüller, Carl Dahlhaus
and Alexander Ringer, eds., *Beethoven: Interpretationen seiner Werke*, vol. I
(Laaber, 1994), 439–55.
Schmalfeldt, Janet, 'Form as the Process of Becoming: The Hegelian Tradition and the
"Tempest" Sonata', *Beethoven Forum*, 4 (1995), 37–71.
*In the Process of Becoming: Analytic and Philosophical Perspectives on Form in Early
Nineteenth-Century Music* (New York and Oxford, 2011).
Schmid, Manfred Hermann, 'Typen des Orchestercrescendo im 18. Jahrhundert',
in Christine Heyter-Rauland and Christoph-Hellmut Mahling, eds.,
*Untersuchungen zu Musikbeziehungen zwischen Mannheim, Böhmen und
Mähren im späten 18. und frühen 19. Jahrhundert: Symphonie – Kirchenmusik –
Melodrama* (Mainz, 1993), 96–132.
Schmidt, Christian Martin, 'Die Neudeutsche Schule und die symphonische
Tradition', in Detlef Altenburg, ed., *Liszt und die Neudeutsche Schule* (Laaber,
2006), 33–8.
Schmitz, Oscar, *Das Land ohne Musik: Englische Gesellschaftsprobleme* (Munich,
1904).
Schoenberg, Arnold, *Style and Idea* (London, 1975).
Schroeder, David P., *Haydn and the Enlightenment: The Late Symphonies and Their
Audience* (Oxford, 1990).
Schröder, Gesine, 'Über das "klassische Orchester" und Haydns späte symphonische
Instrumentation', in *Musik-Konzepte 41: Haydn* (1985), 79–97.
'Orchestral Music: Symphonies and Concertos', in Caryl Clark, ed., *The Cambridge
Companion to Haydn* (Cambridge, 2007), 95–111.
Schruff, Christian, 'Konnte Langweiliges vom Stuhl reißen? Bemerkungen zu
Aufführungspraxis und Interpretation der Mannheimer Orchestermusik', in
Klaus Hortschansky, ed., *Traditionen – Neuansätze: Für Anna Amalie Abert
(1906–1996)* (Tutzing, 1997), 541–54.
Schulenberg, David, *The Instrumental Music of Carl Philipp Emanuel Bach* (Ann
Arbor, 1984).
Schumann, Robert, '[Review of Berlioz: Fantastic Symphony] (1835)', in Ian Bent,
trans. and ed., *Music Analysis in the Nineteenth Century*, vol. II, 161–94.

Tagebücher: 1836–1854, ed. Gerd Nauhaus (Leipzig, 1987).

Schwartz, Judith K., 'François-Joseph Gossec', in Morrow and Churgin, eds., *The Eighteenth-Century Symphony*, 585–626.

Semler, Isabel Parker, in collaboration with Pierson Underwood, *Horatio Parker: A Memoir for his Grandchildren, Compiled from Letters and Papers* (New York, 1975, repr. of 1942 edn).

Shteynpress, Boris, 'Ob instrumentalnom tvorchestve Motsarta', *Sovetskaya muzïka*, 6 (1935), 44–5.

Sidgwick, A. H., *The Promenade Ticket: A Lay Record of Concert-going* (London, 1914).

Sievers, G. L. P., 'Charakteristik der deutschen Musik', *Allgemeine musikalische Zeitung*, 9 (1806–7), cols. 699–700.

Silber, Judith, 'Mendelssohn and his "Reformation" Symphony', *Journal of the American Musicological Society*, 40 (1987), 310–36.

Simms, Bryan, 'Choron, Fétis and the Theory of Tonality', *Journal of Music Theory*, 19/1 (1975), 112–38.

Simpson, Robert, *Carl Nielsen, Symphonist* (London, 1952).

   The Essence of Bruckner (London, 1967).

   Sibelius and Nielsen: A Centenary Essay (London, 1965).

   ed., *The Symphony*, 2 vols. (London, 1966 and 1967).

Sipe, Thomas, *Beethoven: Eroica Symphony* (Cambridge, 1998).

Sisman, Elaine, *Haydn and the Classical Variation* (Cambridge, Mass. and London, 1993).

   Mozart: The 'Jupiter' Symphony (Cambridge, 1993).

   ed., *Haydn and His World* (Princeton, 1997).

Small, Christopher, 'Performance as Ritual: Sketch for an Enquiry into the True Nature of a Symphony Concert', in Avron Levine White, ed., *Lost in Music: Culture, Style and the Musical Event* (London, 1987), 6–32.

Smith, Barbara Herrnstein, 'Contingencies of Value', *Critical Inquiry*, 10 (1983), 1–35.

Smith, Richard, *Elgar in America: Elgar's American Connections between 1895 and 1934* (Rickmansworth, 2005).

Sollertinsky, Ivan, 'Bruckner's Seventh Symphony', in Mikhail Druskin, ed., *Istoricheskie etyudi* (Leningrad, 1963), 310.

   Gustav Mahler (Leningrad, 1932).

   'Problema sovetskogo simfonizma' ['The Problem of Soviet Symphonism'], *Zhizn iskusstva*, 46 (1929), 1–3.

   'The Symphonies of Brahms', in Mikhail Druskin, ed., *Istoricheskie etyudi* (Leningrad, 1963), 279–82.

Solomon, Maynard, *Beethoven Essays* (Cambridge, Mass. and London, 1988).

   'Beethoven's Ninth Symphony: A Search for Order', *19th-Century Music*, 10 (1986–7), 3–23.

   Late Beethoven (Berkeley and Los Angeles, 2003).

   'The Rochlitz Anecdotes: Issues of Authenticity in Early Mozart Biography', in Cliff Eisen, ed., *Mozart Studies*, 1–59.

Solvik, Morten, 'The International Bruckner Society and the NSDAP: A Case Study of Robert Haas and the Critical Edition', *Musical Quarterly*, 83 (1998), 362–82.

Sondheimer, Robert Jonas, *Die Theorie der Sinfonie und die Beurteilung einzelner Sinfoniekomponisten bei den Musikschriftstellen des 18. Jahrhunderts* (Leipzig, 1925).

Specht, Richard, *Gustav Mahler* (Berlin, 1913).

Speck, Christian and Stanley Sadie, 'Boccherini', in Stanley Sadie, ed., *The New Grove Dictionary of Music and Musicians*, 2nd edn (London, 2001), 749–64.

Spitzer, John and Neal Zaslaw, *The Birth of the Orchestra: History of an Institution, 1650–1815* (New York and Oxford, 2004).

Spitzer, Michael, *Music as Philosophy: Adorno and Beethoven's Late Style* (Bloomington, 2006).

Stauffer, George B., 'The Modern Orchestra: A Creation of the Late Eighteenth Century', in Peyser, ed., *The Orchestra*, 37–68.

Steinbeck, Wolfram, 'Franz Lachner und die Symphonie', in Stephan Hörner and Hartmat Schick, eds., *Franz Lachner und seine Brüder: Hofkapellmeister zwischen Schubert und Wagner* (Tutzing, 2006), 133–43.

'Nationale Symphonik und die Neudeutschen: Zu Joachim Raffs Symphonie "An das Vaterland"', in Loos, ed., *Musikgeschichte zwischen Ost- und Westeuropa*, 70–3.

'Russische Rezeption deutscher Symphonik: Zu Čajkovskijs *Zweiter Symphonie*', in *Rezeption als Innovation: Untersuchungen zu einem Grundmodell der europäischen Kompositionsgeschichte*, ed. Bernd Sponheuer, Siegfried Oechsle and Helmut Weill (Kassel and Basel, 2001), 357–66.

Steinbeck, Wolfram and Christoph von Blumröder, *Die Symphonie im 19. and 20. Jahrhundert* (Laaber, 2002).

Steinberg, Michael, *The Symphony: A Listener's Guide* (New York and Oxford, 1995).

Stefan, Paul, *Gustav Mahler: A Study of His Personality and Work*, trans. T. E. Clarke (New York, 1913).

Stern, Isaac, ed., *The Evolution of the Symphony Orchestra: History, Problems and Agendas* (London, 1990).

Stowell, Robin, '"Good Execution and Other Necessary Skills": The Role of the Concertmaster in the Late 18th Century', *Early Music*, 16 (1988), 21–33.

Stradling, Robert and Meirion Hughes, *The English Musical Renaissance, 1840–1940: Constructing a National Music*, 2nd edn (Manchester, 2001).

Strasser, Michael, 'The Société Nationale and Its Adversaries: The Musical Politics of *L'Invasion germanique* in the 1870s', *19th-Century Music*, 24/3 (2001), 225–51.

Sulzer, Johann Georg, ed., *Allgemeine Theorie der schönen Künste*, 2nd expanded edn, 4 vols. (Leipzig, 1792–4).

Swinden, Kevin, 'Bruckner and Harmony', in John Williamson, ed., *The Cambridge Companion to Bruckner* (Cambridge, 2004), 205–28.

Talbot, Michael, *The Finale in Western Instrumental Music* (New York and Oxford, 2001).

Tank, Ulrich, *Studien zur Esterházyschen Hofmusik von etwa 1620 bis 1790* (Regensburg, 1981).

Taruskin, Richard, *Defining Russia Musically* (Princeton, 1997).

   The Oxford History of Western Music, vol. III: *The Nineteenth Century* (New York and Oxford, 2009).

   The Oxford History of Western Music, vol. IV: *The Early Twentieth Century* (New York and Oxford, 2005).

   The Oxford History of Western Music, vol. V: *The Late Twentieth Century* (New York and Oxford, 2009).

   Stravinsky and the Russian Traditions: A Biography of the Works through Mavra (Berkeley and Los Angeles, 1996).

   'A Survivor from the Teutonic Train Wreck', in Taruskin, *The Danger of Music and Other Anti-Utopian Essays* (Berkeley, 2009), 43–5.

Tawaststjerna, Erik, *Sibelius*, trans. Robert Layton, 3 vols. (London, 1976 and 1997).

Thissen, Paul, *Zitattechniken in der Symphonik des 19. Jahrhunderts* (Sinzig, 1998).

Todd, R. Larry, *Mendelssohn: A Life in Music* (Oxford, 2003).

Toeplitz, Uri, *Die Holzbläser in der Musik Mozarts und ihr Verhältnis zur Tonartwahl* (Baden-Baden, 1978), 13–31.

Toews, John Edward, *Becoming Historical: Cultural Reformation and Public Memory in Early Nineteenth-Century Berlin* (Cambridge, 2004).

Tovey, Bramwell, 'The Conductor as Artistic Director', in José Antonio Bowen, ed., *The Cambridge Companion to Conducting* (Cambridge, 2003), 205–19.

Tovey, Donald Francis, *Essays in Musical Analysis*, vol. I: Symphonies (London, 1935).

   Essays in Musical Analysis, vol. II: *Symphonies (II), Variations and Orchestral Polyphony* (London, 1935).

   'Tonality in Schubert', in *The Main Stream of Music and Other Essays* (New York, 1959).

Treitler, Leo, 'Mozart and the Idea of Absolute Music', in Treitler, *Music and the Historical Imagination* (Cambridge, Mass., 1989), 176–215.

Triest, Johann Karl Friedrich, 'Remarks on the Development of the Art of Music in Germany in the Eighteenth Century', trans. Susan Gillespie, in Elaine Sisman, ed., *Haydn and His World* (Princeton, 1997), 321–95.

Tunstall, Tricia, *Changing Lives: Gustavo Dudamel, El Sistema, and the Transformative Power of Music* (New York and London, 2012).

Tymoczko, Dmitri, *The Geometry of Music: Harmony and Counterpoint in the Extended Common Practice* (New York and Oxford, 2011).

   'Stravinsky and the Octatonic: a Reconsideration', *Music Theory Spectrum*, 24/1 (2002), 68–102.

Tyson, Alan, ed., *Beethoven Studies* (New York, 1973).

Vande Moortele, Steven, *Two-Dimensional Sonata Form: Form and Cycle in Single-Movement Instrumental Works by Liszt, Strauss, Schoenberg, and Zemlinsky* (Leuven, 2009).

van den Toorn, Pieter, *The Music of Igor Stravinsky* (New Haven, 1983).

Vaughan Williams, Ursula, *R. V. W.: A Biography of Ralph Vaughan Williams* (London, 1964).

Veis, Pavel, 'O zhurnale "Proletarsky muzïkant' ['About the Journal "Proletarian musician"'], *Sovetskaya muzïka*, 1 (1933), 135.

Vilari Torrens, Josep M., 'The Symphony in Catalonia, *c.* 1760–1808', in Malcolm Boyd and Juan José Bowen, *Music in Spain during the Eighteenth Century* (Cambridge, 1998).

Voss, Egon, *Richard Wagner und die Instrumentalmusik: Wagners symphonische Ehrgeiz* (Wilhelmshaven, 1977).

Wagner, Richard, *Gesammelte Schriften und Dichtungen*, 3rd edn, 10 vols. (Leipzig, 1887–8).

    Richard Wagner's Prose Works, trans. William Ashton Ellis, 8 vols. (London, 1895–9).

Walsh, Stephen, *Stravinsky: A Creative Spring* (New York, 1999).

Weber, Gottfried, 'Teutschland im ersten Viertel des neuen Jahrhunderts', *Cäcilia*, 4 (1826), 109–10.

Weber, William, *The Great Transformation of Musical Taste: Concert Programming from Haydn to Brahms* (Cambridge, 2008).

    'The History of Musical Canon', in Cook and Everist, eds., *Rethinking Music*, 336–55.

Webster, James, 'The Form of the Finale of Beethoven's Ninth Symphony', *Beethoven Forum*, 1 (1992), 25–62.

    Haydn's 'Farewell' Symphony and the Idea of Classical Style: Through-Composition and Cyclic Integration in His Instrumental Music (Cambridge, 1991).

    'When Did Haydn Begin to Write Beautiful Melodies?', in Jens Peter Larsen, Howard Serwet and James Webster, eds., *Haydn Studies* (New York, 1981), 358–88.

Wehrmeyer, Andreas, 'Zur historischen Stellung der Symphonien Anton Rubinsteins', in Mahling and Pfarr, eds., *Aspekte historischer und systematischer Musikforschung*, 209–11.

Weinzierl, Stefan, *Beethovens Konzerträume: Raumakustik und symphonische Aufführungspraxis an der Schwelle zum modernen Konzertwesen* (Frankfurt am Main, 2002).

Wen, Eric, 'A Tritone Key Relationship in the Bridge Sections of the Slow Movement of Mozart's 39th Symphony', *Music Analysis*, 5/1 (1986), 59–84.

Wendt, Amadeus, 'Über den Zustand der Musik in Deutschland. Eine Skizze', *Allgemeine musikalische Zeitung mit besonderer Rücksicht auf den österreichischen Kaiserstaat*, 6 (1822), 762.

Werbeck, Walter, 'Richard Strauss's Tone Poems', in Mark-Daniel Schmid, ed., *The Richard Strauss Companion* (Westport, 2003), 103–44.

Werth, Alexander, *Musical Uproar in Moscow* (London, 1949).

Wheelock, Gretchen A., *Haydn's Ingenious Jesting with Art: Contexts of Musical Wit and Humor* (New York, 1992).

Whittall, Arnold, *Musical Composition in the Twentieth Century* (New York and Oxford, 1999).

Wiegandt, Matthias, *Vergessene Symphonik? Studien zu Joachim Raff, Carl Reinecke und zum Problem der Epigonalität in der Musik* (Sinzig, 1997).

Will, Richard, *The Characteristic Symphony in the Age of Haydn and Beethoven* (Cambridge, 2002).

'Eighteenth-Century Symphonies: An Unfinished Dialogue', in Simon Keefe, ed., *The Cambridge History of Eighteenth-Century Music* (Cambridge, 2009), 613–47.

Williamson, John, ed., *The Cambridge Campanion to Bruckner* (Cambridge, 2004).

Willson, Rachel Beckles, 'Whose Utopia? Perspectives on the West-Eastern Divan Orchestra', *Music and Politics*, 3 (2009), 1–21.

Wingfield, Paul, 'Beyond "Norms and Deformations": Towards a Theory of Sonata Form as Reception History', *Music Analysis*, 27/1 (2008), 137–77.

Wistrich, Robert S., *The Jews of Vienna in the Age of Franz Joseph* (Oxford, 1989).

Witts, Richard, 'Remastering the Past: "Renewal" in Recent British Music', *Musical Times*, 142 (2001), 7–10.

Wolf, Eugene K., 'The Mannheim Court', in Neal Zaslaw, ed., *The Classical Era: From the 1740s to the End of the 18th Century* (Englewood Cliffs, 1989), 225–33.

'Mannheimer Symphonik um 1777/1778 und ihr Einfluß auf Mozarts symphonischen Stil', in Finscher et al., eds., *Mozart und Mannheim*, 309–30.

'On the Composition of the Mannheim Orchestra ca. 1740–1778', *Basler Jahrbuch für historische Musikpraxis*, 17 (1993), 113–38.

'The Recapitulations in Haydn's London Symphonies', *Musical Quarterly*, 52 (1966), 71–89.

The Symphonies of Johann Stamitz: A Study in the Formation of the Classic Style (Utrecht, 1981).

Wollenberg, Susan, and Simon McVeigh, eds., *Concert Life in Eighteenth-Century Britain* (Aldershot, 2004).

Young, D., 'The Symphonies of Karl von Ordonez (1734–1786)' (Ph.D. diss., University of Liverpool, 1980).

Zaslaw, Neal, *Mozart's Symphonies: Context, Performance Practice, Reception* (Oxford, 1989).

ed., *Mozart's Piano Concertos: Text, Context, Interpretation* (Ann Arbor, 1996).

Index

Note: A few compositions receiving very frequent or detailed treatment are indexed under their titles (cross-referenced from the composer); the remainder appear as subheads under the composer's name.

Cambridge Companions to Music